BRITISH WRITERS

BRITISH WRITERS

JAY PARINI

Editor

SUPPLEMENT VIII

Charles Scribner's Sons

an imprint of the Gale Group

New York • Detroit • San Francisco • London • Boston • Woodbridge, CT

Charles Scribner's Sons
an imprint of The Gale Group
27500 Drake Rd.
Farmington Hills, MI 48331-3535

Library of Congress Cataloging-in-Publication Data

British Writers. supplement VIII/Jay Parini, editor in chief.
   p. cm.
  Includes bibliographical references and index.
  ISBN 0-684-80656-8 (hardcover: alk. paper)
   1. English literature—Bio-bibliography. 2. English literature—History and criticism. 3. Authors, English—Biography. I Parini, Jay.

PR85.B688 Suppl.8
820.9—dc21
[B]   2001020992

The paper used in this publication meets the requirements of ANSI/NIS) Z39.48-1992 (Permanance of Paper).

Acknowledgments

Acknowledgment is gratefully made to those publishers and individuals who permitted the use of the following materials in copyright:

SIMON ARMITAGE *Verse,* v. 8, 1991; v. 9, 1992. Reproduced by permission. *Poetry Review,* v. 87, Autumn, 1997 for "Bright Boroughs of Heaven," by Michael Hulse. Reproduced by permission of the author. Armitage, Simon. From *Zoom!* Newcastle Upon Tyne, 1989. Copyright © 1989 by Newcastle Upon Tyne. All rights reserved. Reproduced by permission. Armitage, Simon. From *Kid.* Copyright © 1992. All rights reserved. Reproduced by permission. Armitage, Simon. From *Book of Matches.* 1993. Copyright © 1993. All rights reserved. Reproduced by permission. Armitage, Simon. From *The Dead Sea Poems.* 1995. Copyright © 1995. All rights reserved. Reproduced by permission. Armitage, Simon. From *Killing Time.* 1999. Copyright © 1999. All rights reserved. Reproduced by permission. Armitage, Simon. From *CloudCuckooLand.* 1997. Copyright © 1997. All rights reserved. Reproduced by permission.

ALAN BENNETT *The Observer,* December 9, 2001. Reproduced by permission. *Literary/Film Quarterly,* v. 27, 1999. Reproduced by permission. Hunt, Albert. From *British Television Drama in the 1980's.* Cambridge University Press, 1993. Copyright © 1993 by Cambridge University Press. All rights reserved. Reproduced by permission of the publisher and the author.

WENDY COPE *The Dark Horse,* Winter, 1995–1996. Reproduced by permission. Cope, Wendy. From *Making Cocoa for Kingsley Amis.* Faber and Faber Limited, 1986. Copyright © 1986 by Wendy Cope. All rights reserved. Reproduced by permission. *Poetry Review,* v. 82, Winter, 1992/93 for "Dana Gioia on Wendy Cope," by Dana Gioia. Reproduced by permission of the author. Cope, Wendy. From *The River Girl.* Reproduced by permission.

FRANCES CORNFORD Cornford, Frances. From *On a Calm Shore.* The Cresset Press, 1960. Copyright © 1960 by Frances Cornford. All rights reserved. Reproduced by permission. Cornford, Frances. From *Collected Poems.* The Cresset Press, 1954. Copyright © 1954 by The Cresset Press. All rights reserved. Reproduced by permission. Cornford, John. From *Understanding the Weapon, Understanding the Wound.* Carcanet New Press, 1976. Copyright © 1976 by

Jonathan Galassi. All rights reserved. Reproduced by permission. Pound, Ezra. From *Collected Early Poems of Ezra Pound.* New Direction Books, 1926. Copyright © 1926 by The Trustees of Ezra Pound. All rights reserved. Reproduced by permission. de la Mare, Walter. From *The Complete Poems of Walter de la Mare.* Alfred A. Knopf, Inc., 1970. Copyright © 1970 by The Literary Trustees of Walter de la Mare and the Society of Authors as representatives. All rights reserved. Reproduced by permission.

SARAH KANE Stephenson, Heidi and Natasha Langridge. From *Rage and Reason: Women Playwrights on Playwriting.* Methuen Publishing Limited, 1997. Copyright © 1997 by Methuen Publishing Limited. All rights reserved. Reproduced by permission. Kane, Sarah. From *Skin.* 1997. Copyright © 1997 by Methuen Publishing Limited. All rights reserved. Reproduced by permission.

MICHAEL LONGLEY Longley, Michael. From *The Weather in Japan.* Jonathan Cape, 2000. Copyright © 2000 by Johnathan Cape. All rights reserved. Reproduced in the U.S. by permission of Peter Fraser & Dunlap Group. In the rest of the World by permission of Random House UK Limited. Longley, Michael. From *The Ghost Orchid.* Johnathan Cape, 1995. Copyright © 1995 by Michael Longley. All rights reserved. Reproduced in the U.S. by permission of Peter Fraser & Dunlap Group. In the rest of the World by permission of Random House UK Limited. Longley, Michael. From *Gorse Fires.* Secker & Warburg, 1991. Copyright © 1991 by Michael Longley. All rights reserved. Reproduced by permission. Hughes, Ted. From *Lupercal.* Faber and Faber Limited, 1960. Copyright © 1960 by Ted Hughes. All rights reserved. Copyright renewed copyright © 1988 by Ted Hughes. Reproduced by permission. *The Canadian Journal of Irish Studies,* July 16[1], 1990. Reproduced by permission. Murphy, Mike. From *Reading the Future: Irish Writers in Conversation with Mike Murphy.* Lilliput Press, 2000. Copyright © 2000 by Lilliput Press. All rights reserved. Reproduced by permission. Longley, Michael. From *Causeway.* Arts Council of Northern Ireland, 1971. Copyright © 1971 by Arts Council of Northern Ireland. All rights reserved. Reproduced by permission of the author. Healy, Dermot. From *Force 10 in Mayo.* Mayo County Council, 1991. Copyright

Editorial and Production Staff

Contents

Subjects in Supplement VIII

Introduction

It was Henry David Thoreau who said, in *Walden*, that "books must be read as deliberately and reservedly as they are written." One of the purposes of this ongoing series is to encourage readers to read "deliberately and reservedly," reconsidering major authors and learning about forgotten or unknown authors who have nevertheless contributed important work to the British literary tradition, which reaches back into the medieval period and continues to this moment, a lively and abundant tradition of good writing.

The contributors articles to this volume are all professionals: teachers, scholars, and writers. As anyone glancing through the collection will notice, writers are held to the highest standards of writing and scholarship. Their essays, which focus on the life and work of a particular author, each conclude with a bibliography of work by the author and about the author; these are meant to direct the reading of those should want to pursue a subject further.

In *British Writers, Supplement VIII* we present essays on a wide variety of writers. None of these has yet been discussed in previous volumes in the series, yet all seem worthy of consideration. The range of subjects covered stretches from the literature written in Old Norse, a precursor of modern English, to such contemporary poets and playwrights as Michael Longley, Simon Armitage, Peter Reading, Alan Bennett, and Sarah Kane—all writers who have made a significant impact on the literary scene in the last few decades.

In keeping with previous volumes in the series, we also turn occasionally to major writers from the British Commonwealth (or countries once in some way associated with Britain). One of the most widely studied and discussed writers in the world today is the Kenyon writer Ngũgĩ wa Thiong'o, whose major career in fiction and drama is discussed in detail here. Another important writer discussed here is the Australian poet, Christopher Wallace-Crabbe.

This particular supplement is rich in authors from the past, such as the early Scottish poet William Dunbar and the playwright Robert Greene, Shakespeare's contemporary. More recent writers covered in this collection include George Russell (also called AE), James Macpherson, Mary Elizabeth Braddon, Barbara Comyns, A.E. Coppard, Frances Cornford, and Charles Maturin. These interesting and important writers were, for various reasons, neglected in previous volumes and supplements. We try to make up for that here.

JAY PARINI

Chronology

1272–1307	Reign of Edward I
1276	The prince of North Wales, Llewelyn II, refuses to pay homage to England's Edward I, who invades North Wales and forces Llewelyn to surrender
1282	Llewelyn II leads a second attack against Edward and fails; Wales falls to English rule
1297	William Wallace (Braveheart) leads attacks against British troops in an attempt for Scottish sovereignty
1305	William Wallace is captured, tried, and hanged
1307–1327	Reign of Edward II
ca. 1325	John Wycliffe born
	John Gower born
1327–1377	Reign of Edward III
ca. 1332	William Langland born
1337	Beginning of the Hundred Years' War
ca. 1340	Geoffrey Chaucer born
1346	The Battle of Crécy
1348	The Black Death (further outbreaks in 1361 and 1369)
ca. 1350	Boccaccio's *Decameron*
	Langland's *Piers Plowman*
1351	The Statute of Laborers pegs laborers' wages at rates in effect preceding the plague
1356	The Battle of Poitiers
1360	The Treaty of Brétigny: end of the first phase of the Hundred Years' War
1362	Pleadings in the law courts conducted in English
	Parliaments opened by speeches in English
1369	Chaucer's *The Book of the Duchess*, an elegy to Blanche of Lancaster, wife of John of Gaunt
1369–1377	Victorious French campaigns under du Guesclin
ca. 1370	John Lydgate born
1371	Sir John Mandeville's *Travels*
1372	Chaucer travels to Italy
1372–1382	Wycliffe active in Oxford
1373–1393	William of Wykeham founds Winchester College and New College, Oxford
ca. 1375–1400	*Sir Gawain and the Green Knight*
1376	Death of Edward the Black Prince
1377–1399	Reign of Richard II
ca. 1379	Gower's *Vox clamantis*
ca. 1380	Chaucer's *Troilus and Criseyde*
1381	The Peasants' Revolt
1386	Chaucer's *Canterbury Tales* begun
	Chaucer sits in Parliament
	Gower's *Confessio amantis*
1399–1413	Reign of Henry IV
ca. 1400	Death of William Langland
1400	Death of Geoffrey Chaucer
1408	Death of John Gower
1412–1420	Lydgate's *Troy Book*
1413–1422	Reign of Henry V
1415	The Battle of Agincourt
1420–1422	Lydgate's *Siege of Thebes*
1422–1461	Reign of Henry VI
1431	François Villon born
	Joan of Arc burned at Rouen
1440–1441	Henry VI founds Eton College and King's College, Cambridge
1444	Truce of Tours
1450	Jack Cade's rebellion
ca. 1451	Death of John Lydgate
1453	End of the Hundred Years' War
	The fall of Constantinople
1455–1485	The Wars of the Roses
ca. 1460	Births of **William Dunbar** and John Skelton
1461–1470	Reign of Edward IV

CHRONOLOGY

CHRONOLOGY

1547–1553	Reign of Edward VI
1548–1552	Hall's *Chronicle*
1552	The second Book of Common Prayer
ca. 1552	Edmund Spenser born
1553	Lady Jane Grey proclaimed queen
1553–1558	Reign of Mary I (Mary Tudor)
ca. 1554	Births of Walter Raleigh, Richard Hooker, and John Lyly
1554	Lady Jane Grey executed
	Mary I marries Philip II of Spain
	Bandello's *Novelle*
	Philip Sidney born
ca. 1556	George Peele born
1557	Tottel's *Miscellany*, including the poems of Wyatt and Surrey, published
ca. 1558	Thomas Kyd born
1558	Calais, the last English possession in France, is lost
	Birth of Robert Greene
	Mary I dies
1558–1603	Reign of Elizabeth I
1559	John Knox arrives in Scotland
	Rebellion against the French regent
ca. 1559	George Chapman born
1561	Mary Queen of Scots (Mary Stuart) arrives in Edinburgh
	Thomas Hoby's translation of Castiglione's *The Courtier Gorboduc*, the first English play in blank verse
	Francis Bacon born
1562	Civil war in France
	English expedition sent to support the Huguenots
1562–1568	Sir John Hawkins' voyages to Africa
1564	Births of Christopher Marlowe and William Shakespeare
1565	Mary Queen of Scots marries Lord Darnley
1566	William Painter's *Palace of Pleasure*, a miscellany of prose stories, the source of many dramatists' plots
1567	Darnley murdered at Kirk o'Field
	Mary Queen of Scots marries the earl of Bothwell
1569	Rebellion of the English northern earls suppressed
1570	Roger Ascham's *The Schoolmaster*
1571	Defeat of the Turkish fleet at Lepanto
ca. 1572	Ben Jonson born
1572	St. Bartholomew's Day massacre
	John Donne born
1574	The earl of Leicester's theater company formed
1576	The Theater, the first permanent theater building in London, opened
	The first Blackfriars Theater opened with performances by the Children of St. Paul's
	John Marston born
1576–1578	Martin Frobisher's voyages to Labrador and the northwest
1577–1580	Sir Francis Drake sails around the world
1577	Holinshed's *Chronicles of England, Scotlande, and Irelande*
1579	John Lyly's *Euphues: The Anatomy of Wit*
	Thomas North's translation of *Plutarch's Lives*
1581	The Levant Company founded
	Seneca's *Ten Tragedies* translated
1582	Richard Hakluyt's *Divers Voyages Touching the Discoverie of America*
1584–1585	Sir John Davis' first voyage to Greenland
1585	First English settlement in America, the "Lost Colony" comprising 108 men under Ralph Lane, founded at Roanoke Island, off the coast of North Carolina
1586	Kyd's *Spanish Tragedy*
	Marlowe's *Tamburlaine*
	William Camden's *Britannia*
	The Babington conspiracy against Queen Elizabeth
	Death of Sir Philip Sidney
1587	Mary Queen of Scots executed
	Birth of Virginia Dare, first English child born in America, at Roanoke Island

CHRONOLOGY

CHRONOLOGY

xvii

CHRONOLOGY

CHRONOLOGY

CHRONOLOGY

Acquittal of the seven bishops imprisoned for protesting against the Declaration

William of Orange lands at Torbay, Devon

James II takes refuge in France

Death of John Bunyan

Alexander Pope born

1689–1702 Reign of William III

1689 Parliament formulates the Declaration of Rights

William and Mary accept the Declaration and the crown

The Grand Alliance concluded between the Holy Roman Empire, England, Holland, and Spain

War declared against France

King William's War, 1689–1697 (the first of the French and Indian wars)

Samuel Richardson born

1690 James II lands in Ireland with French support, but is defeated at the battle of the Boyne

John Locke's *Essay Concerning Human Understanding*

1692 Salem witchcraft trials

Death of Sir George Etherege

1694 George Fox's *Journal*

Voltaire (François Marie Arouet) born

Death of Mary II

1695 Congreve's *Love for Love*

Death of Henry Vaughan

1697 War with France ended by the Treaty of Ryswick

Vanbrugh's *The Relapse*

1698 Jeremy Collier's *A Short View of the Immorality and Profaneness of the English Stage*

1699 Fénelon's *Les Aventures de Télémaque*

1700 Congreve's *The Way of the World*

Defoe's *The True-Born Englishman*

Death of John Dryden

James Thomson born

1701 War of the Spanish Succession, 1701–1714 (Queen Anne's War in America, 1702–1713)

Death of Sir Charles Sedley

1702–1714 Reign of Queen Anne

1702 Clarendon's *History of the Rebellion* (1702–1704)

Defoe's *The Shortest Way with the Dissenters*

1703 Defoe is arrested, fined, and pilloried for writing *The Shortest Way*

Death of Samuel Pepys

1704 John Churchill, duke of Marlborough, and Prince Eugene of Savoy defeat the French at Blenheim

Capture of Gibraltar

Swift's *A Tale of a Tub* and *The Battle of the Books*

The Review founded (1704–1713)

1706 Farquhar's *The Recruiting Officer*

Deaths of John Evelyn and Charles Sackville, earl of Dorset

1707 Farquhar's *The Beaux' Stratagem*

Act of Union joining England and Scotland

Death of George Farquhar

Henry Fielding born

1709 The *Tatler* founded (1709–1711)

Nicholas Rowe's edition of Shakespeare

Samuel Johnson born

Marlborough defeats the French at Malplaquet

Charles XII of Sweden defeated at Poltava

1710 South Sea Company founded

First copyright act

1711 Swift's *The Conduct of the Allies*

The *Spectator* founded (1711–1712; 1714)

Marlborough dismissed

David Hume born

1712 Pope's *The Rape of the Lock* (Cantos 1–2)

Jean Jacques Rousseau born

CHRONOLOGY

1713   War with France ended by the Treaty of Utrecht

The *Guardian* founded

Swift becomes dean of St. Patrick's, Dublin

Addison's *Cato*

Laurence Sterne born

1714–1727   Reign of George I

1714   Pope's expended version of *The Rape of the Lock* (Cantos 1–5)

1715   The Jacobite rebellion in Scotland

Pope's translation of Homer's *Iliad* (1715–1720)

Death of Louis XIV

1716   Death of William Wycherley

Thomas Gray born

1717   Pope's *Eloisa to Abelard*

David Garrick born

Horace Walpole born

1718   Quadruple Alliance (Britain, France, the Netherlands, the German Empire) in war against Spain

1719   Defoe's *Robinson Crusoe*

Death of Joseph Addison

1720   Inoculation against smallpox introduced in Boston

War against Spain

The South Sea Bubble

Gilbert White born

Defoe's *Captain Singleton* and *Memoirs of a Cavalier*

1721   Tobias Smollett born

William Collins born

1722   Defoe's *Moll Flanders*, *Journal of the Plague Year*, and *Colonel Jack*

1724   Defoe's *Roxana*

Swift's *The Drapier's Letters*

1725   Pope's translation of Homer's *Odyssey* (1725–1726)

1726   Swift's *Gulliver's Travels*

Voltaire in England (1726–1729)

Death of Sir John Vanbrugh

1727–1760   Reign of George II

1728   Gay's *The Beggar's Opera*

Pope's *The Dunciad* (Books 1–2)

Oliver Goldsmith born

1729   Swift's *A Modest Proposal*

Edmund Burke born

Deaths of William Congreve and Sir Richard Steele

1731   Navigation improved by introduction of the quadrant

Pope's *Moral Essays* (1731–1735)

Death of Daniel Defoe

William Cowper born

1732   Death of John Gay

1733   Pope's *Essay on Man* (1733–1734)

Lewis Theobald's edition of Shakespeare

1734   Voltaire's *Lettres philosophiques*

1736   **James Macpherson born**

1737   Edward Gibbon born

1738   Johnson's *London*

1740   War of the Austrian Succession, 1740–1748 (King George's War in America, 1744–1748)

George Anson begins his circumnavigation of the world (1740–1744)

Frederick the Great becomes king of Prussia (1740–1786)

Richardson's *Pamela* (1740–1741)

James Boswell born

1742   Fielding's *Joseph Andrews*

Edward Young's *Night Thoughts* (1742–1745)

Pope's *The New Dunciad* (Book 4)

1744   Johnson's *Life of Mr. Richard Savage*

Death of Alexander Pope

1745   Second Jacobite rebellion, led by Charles Edward, the Young Pretender

Death of Jonathan Swift

1746   The Young Pretender defeated at Culloden

Collins' *Odes on Several Descriptive and Allegorical Subjects*

1747   Richardson's *Clarissa Harlowe* (1747–1748)

CHRONOLOGY

Franklin's experiments with electricity announced

Voltaire's *Essai sur les moeurs*

1748   War of the Austrian Succession ended by the Peace of Aix-la-Chapelle

Smollett's *Adventures of Roderick Random*

David Hume's *Enquiry Concerning Human Understanding*

Montesquieu's *L'Esprit des lois*

1749   Fielding's *Tom Jones*

Johnson's *The Vanity of Human Wishes*

Bolingbroke's *Idea of a Patriot King*

1750   The *Rambler* founded (1750–1752)

1751   Gray's *Elegy Written in a Country Churchyard*

Fielding's *Amelia*

Smollett's *Adventures of Peregrine Pickle*

Denis Diderot and Jean le Rond d'Alembert begin to publish the *Encyclopédie* (1751–1765)

Richard Brinsley Sheridan born

1752   Frances Burney and Thomas Chatterton born

1753   Richardson's *History of Sir Charles Grandison* (1753–1754)

Smollett's *The Adventures of Ferdinand Count Fathom*

1754   Hume's *History of England* (1754–1762)

Death of Henry Fielding

George Crabbe born

1755   Lisbon destroyed by earthquake

Fielding's *Journal of a Voyage to Lisbon* published posthumously

Johnson's *Dictionary of the English Language*

1756   The Seven Years' War against France, 1756–1763 (the French and Indian War in America, 1755–1760)

William Pitt the elder becomes prime minister

Johnson's proposal for an edition of Shakespeare

1757   Robert Clive wins the battle of Plassey, in India

Gray's "The Progress of Poesy" and "The Bard"

Burke's *Philosophical Enquiry into the Origin of Our Ideas of the Sublime and Beautiful*

Hume's *Natural History of Religion*

William Blake born

1758   The *Idler* founded (1758–1760)

1759   Capture of Quebec by General James Wolfe

Johnson's *History of Rasselas, Prince of Abyssinia*

Voltaire's *Candide*

The British Museum opens

Sterne's *The Life and Opinions of Tristram Shandy* (1759–1767)

Death of William Collins

Mary Wollstonecraft born

Robert Burns born

1760–1820   Reign of George III

1760   James Macpherson's *Fragments of Ancient Poetry Collected in the Highlands of Scotland*

William Beckford born

1761   Jean-Jacques Rousseau's *Julie, ou la nouvelle Héloïse*

Death of Samuel Richardson

1762   Rousseau's *Du Contrat social* and *Émile*

Catherine the Great becomes czarina of Russia (1762–1796)

1763   The Seven Years' War ended by the Peace of Paris

Smart's *A Song to David*

1764   James Hargreaves invents the spinning jenny

1765   Parliament passes the Stamp Act to tax the American colonies

Johnson's edition of Shakespeare

Walpole's *The Castle of Otranto*

Thomas Percy's *Reliques of Ancient English Poetry*

Blackstone's *Commentaries on the Laws of England* (1765–1769)

1766   The Stamp Act repealed

CHRONOLOGY

Swift's *Journal to Stella* first published in a collection of his letters

Goldsmith's *The Vicar of Wakefield*

Smollett's *Travels Through France and Italy*

Lessing's *Laokoon*

Rousseau in England (1766–1767)

1768   Sterne's *A Sentimental Journey Through France and Italy*

The Royal Academy founded by George III

First edition of the *Encyclopaedia Britannica*

Maria Edgeworth born

Death of Laurence Sterne

1769   David Garrick organizes the Shakespeare Jubilee at Stratford-upon-Avon

Sir Joshua Reynolds' *Discourses* (1769–1790)

Richard Arkwright invents the spinning water frame

1770   Boston Massacre

Burke's *Thoughts on the Cause of the Present Discontents*

Oliver Goldsmith's *The Deserted Village*

Death of Thomas Chatterton

William Wordsworth born

1771   Arkwright's first spinning mill founded

Deaths of Thomas Gray and Tobias Smollett

Walter Scott born

1772   Samuel Taylor Coleridge born

1773   Boston Tea Party

Goldsmith's *She Stoops to Conquer*

Johann Wolfgang von Goethe's *Götz von Berlichingen*

1774   The first Continental Congress meets in Philadelphia

Goethe's *Sorrows of Young Werther*

Death of Oliver Goldsmith

Robert Southey born

1775   Burke's speech on American taxation

American War of Independence begins with the battles of Lexington and Concord

Samuel Johnson's *Journey to the Western Islands of Scotland*

Richard Brinsley Sheridan's *The Rivals* and *The Duenna*

Beaumarchais's *Le Barbier de Séville*

James Watt and Matthew Boulton begin building steam engines in England

Births of Jane Austen, Charles Lamb, Walter Savage Landor, and Matthew Lewis

1776   American Declaration of Independence

Edward Gibbon's *Decline and Fall of the Roman Empire* (1776–1788)

Adam Smith's *Inquiry into the Nature & Causes of the Wealth of Nations*

Thomas Paine's *Common Sense*

Death of David Hume

1777   Maurice Morgann's *Essay on the Dramatic Character of Sir John Falstaff*

Sheridan's *The School for Scandal* first performed (published 1780)

General Burgoyne surrenders at Saratoga

1778   The American colonies allied with France

Britain and France at war

Captain James Cook discovers Hawaii

Death of William Pitt, first earl of Chatham

Deaths of Jean Jacques Rousseau and Voltaire

William Hazlitt born

1779   Johnson's *Prefaces to the Works of the English Poets* (1779–1781); reissued in 1781 as *The Lives of the Most Eminent English Poets*

Sheridan's *The Critic*

Samuel Crompton invents the spinning mule

Death of David Garrick

1780   The Gordon Riots in London

Charles Robert Maturin born

CHRONOLOGY

1781   Charles Cornwallis surrenders at Yorktown

Immanuel Kant's *Critique of Pure Reason*

Friedrich von Schiller's *Die Räuber*

1782   William Cowper's "The Journey of John Gilpin" published in the *Public Advertiser*

Choderlos de Laclos's *Les Liaisons dangereuses*

Rousseau's *Confessions* published posthumously

1783   American War of Independence ended by the Definitive Treaty of Peace, signed at Paris

William Blake's *Poetical Sketches*

George Crabbe's *The Village*

William Pitt the younger becomes prime minister

Henri Beyle (Stendhal) born

1784   Beaumarchais's *Le Mariage de Figaro* first performed (published 1785)

Death of Samuel Johnson

1785   Warren Hastings returns to England from India

James Boswell's *The Journey of a Tour of the Hebrides, with Samuel Johnson, LL.D.*

Cowper's *The Task*

Edmund Cartwright invents the power loom

Thomas De Quincey born

Thomas Love Peacock born

1786   William Beckford's *Vathek* published in English (originally written in French in 1782)

Robert Burns's *Poems Chiefly in the Scottish Dialect*

Wolfgang Amadeus Mozart's *The Marriage of Figaro*

Death of Frederick the Great

1787   The Committee for the Abolition of the Slave Trade founded in England

The Constitutional Convention meets at Philadelphia; the Constitution is signed

1788   The trial of Hastings begins on charges of corruption of the government in India

The Estates-General of France summoned

U.S. Constitution is ratified

George Washington elected president of the United States

Giovanni Casanova's *Histoire de ma fuite* (first manuscript of his memoirs)

The *Daily Universal Register* becomes the *Times* (London)

George Gordon, Lord Byron born

1789   The Estates-General meets at Versailles

The National Assembly (Assemblée Nationale) convened

The fall of the Bastille marks the beginning of the French Revolution

The National Assembly draws up the Declaration of Rights of Man and of the Citizen

First U.S. Congress meets in New York

Blake's *Songs of Innocence*

Jeremy Bentham's *Introduction to the Principles of Morals and Legislation* introduces the theory of utilitarianism

Gilbert White's *Natural History of Selborne*

1790   Congress sets permanent capital city site on the Potomac River

First U.S. Census

Burke's *Reflections on the Revolution in France*

Blake's *The Marriage of Heaven and Hell*

Edmund Malone's edition of Shakespeare

Wollstonecraft's *A Vindication of the Rights of Man*

Death of Benjamin Franklin

1791   French royal family's flight from Paris and capture at Varennes; imprisonment in the Tuileries

Bill of Rights is ratified

Paine's *The Rights of Man* (1791–1792)

CHRONOLOGY

Boswell's *The Life of Johnson*

Burns's *Tam o'Shanter*

The *Observer* founded

1792   The Prussians invade France and are repulsed at Valmy September massacres

The National Convention declares royalty abolished in France

Washington reelected president of the United States

New York Stock Exchange opens

Mary Wollstonecraft's *Vindication of the Rights of Woman*

William Bligh's voyage to the South Sea in H.M.S. *Bounty*

Percy Bysshe Shelley born

1793   Trial and execution of Louis XVI and Marie-Antoinette

France declares war against England

The Committee of Public Safety (Comité de Salut Public) established

Eli Whitney devises the cotton gin

William Godwin's *An Enquiry Concerning Political Justice*

Blake's *Visions of the Daughters of Albion and America*

Wordsworth's *An Evening Walk* and *Descriptive Sketches*

1794   Execution of Georges Danton and Maximilien de Robespierre

Paine's *The Age of Reason* (1794–1796)

Blake's *Songs of Experience*

Ann Radcliffe's *The Mysteries of Udolpho*

Death of Edward Gibbon

1795   The government of the Directory established (1795–1799)

Hastings acquitted

Landor's *Poems*

Death of James Boswell

John Keats born

Thomas Carlyle born

1796   Napoleon Bonaparte takes command in Italy

Matthew Lewis' *The Monk*

John Adams elected president of the United States

Death of Robert Burns

1797   The peace of Campo Formio: extinction of the Venetian Republic XYZ Affair

Mutinies in the Royal Navy at Spithead and the Nore

Blake's *Vala, Or the Four Zoas* (first version)

Mary Shelley born

Deaths of Edmund Burke, Mary Wollstonecraft, and Horace Walpole

1798   Napoleon invades Egypt

Horatio Nelson wins the battle of the Nile

Wordsworth's and Coleridge's *Lyrical Ballads*

Landor's *Gebir*

Thomas Malthus' *Essay on the Principle of Population*

1799   Napoleon becomes first consul

Pitt introduces first income tax in Great Britain

Sheridan's *Pizarro*

Honoré de Balzac born

Thomas Hood born

Alexander Pushkin born

1800   Thomas Jefferson elected president of the United States

Alessandro Volta produces electricity from a cell

Library of Congress established

Death of William Cowper

Thomas Babington Macaulay born

1801   First census taken in England

1802   The Treaty of Amiens marks the end of the French Revolutionary War

The *Edinburgh Review* founded

1803   England's war with France renewed

The Louisiana Purchase

Robert Fulton propels a boat by steam power on the Seine

1804   Napoleon crowned emperor of the French

Jefferson reelected president of the United States

Blake's *Milton* (1804–1808) and *Jerusalem*

The Code Napoleon promulgated in France

Beethoven's *Eroica* Symphony

Schiller's *Wilhelm Tell*

Benjamin Disraeli born

1805   Napoleon plans the invasion of England

Battle of Trafalgar

Battle of Austerlitz

Beethoven's *Fidelio* first produced

Scott's *Lay of the Last Minstrel*

1806   Scott's *Marmion*

Death of William Pitt

Death of Charles James Fox

Elizabeth Barrett born

1807   France invades Portugal

Aaron Burr tried for treason and acquitted

Byron's *Hours of Idleness*

Charles and Mary Lamb's *Tales from Shakespeare*

Thomas Moore's *Irish Melodies*

Wordsworth's *Ode on the Intimations of Immortality*

1808   National uprising in Spain against the French invasion

The Peninsular War begins

James Madison elected president of the United States

Covent Garden theater burned down

Goethe's *Faust* (Part 1)

Beethoven's Fifth Symphony completed

Lamb's *Specimens of English Dramatic Poets*

1809   Drury Lane theater burned down and rebuilt

The *Quarterly Review* founded

Byron's *English Bards and Scotch Reviewers*

Byron sails for the Mediterranean

Goya's *Los Desastres de la guerra* (1809–1814)

Alfred Tennyson born

Edward Fitzgerald born

1810   Crabbe's *The Borough*

Scott's *The Lady of the Lake*

Elizabeth Gaskell born

1811–1820   Regency of George IV

1811   Luddite Riots begin

Coleridge's *Lectures on Shakespeare* (1811–1814)

Jane Austen's *Sense and Sensibility*

Shelley's *The Necessity of Atheism*

John Constable's *Dedham Vale*

William Makepeace Thackeray born

1812   Napoleon invades Russia; captures and retreats from Moscow

United States declares war against England

Henry Bell's steamship *Comet* is launched on the Clyde river

Madison reelected president of the United States

Byron's *Childe Harold* (Cantos 1–2)

The Brothers Grimm's *Fairy Tales* (1812–1815)

Hegel's *Science of Logic*

Robert Browning born

Charles Dickens born

1813   Wellington wins the battle of Vitoria and enters France

Jane Austen's *Pride and Prejudice*

Byron's *The Giaour* and *The Bride of Abydos*

Shelley's *Queen Mab*

Southey's *Life of Nelson*

1814   Napoleon abdicates and is exiled to Elba; Bourbon restoration with Louis XVIII

Treaty of Ghent ends the war between Britain and the United States

Jane Austen's *Mansfield Park*

Byron's *The Corsair* and *Lara*

Scott's *Waverley*

CHRONOLOGY

Wordsworth's *The Excursion*

1815 Napoleon returns to France (the Hundred Days); is defeated at Waterloo and exiled to St. Helena

U.S.S. *Fulton*, the first steam warship, built

Scott's *Guy Mannering*

Schlegel's *Lectures on Dramatic Art and Literature* translated

Wordsworth's *The White Doe of Rylstone*

Anthony Trollope born

1816 Byron leaves England permanently

The Elgin Marbles exhibited in the British Museum

James Monroe elected president of the United States

Jane Austen's *Emma*

Byron's *Childe Harold* (Canto 3)

Coleridge's *Christabel, Kubla Khan: A Vision, The Pains of Sleep*

Benjamin Constant's *Adolphe*

Goethe's *Italienische Reise*

Peacock's *Headlong Hall*

Scott's *The Antiquary*

Shelley's *Alastor*

Rossini's *Il Barbiere di Siviglia*

Death of Richard Brinsley Sheridan

Charlotte Brontë born

1817 *Blackwood's Edinburgh* magazine founded

Jane Austen's *Northanger Abbey* and *Persuasion*

Byron's *Manfred*

Coleridge's *Biographia Literaria*

Hazlitt's *The Characters of Shakespeare's Plays* and *The Round Table*

Keats's *Poems*

Peacock's *Melincourt*

David Ricardo's *Principles of Political Economy and Taxation*

Death of Jane Austen

Death of Mme de Staël

Branwell Brontë born

Henry David Thoreau born

1818 Byron's *Childe Harold* (Canto 4), and *Beppo*

Hazlitt's *Lectures on the English Poets*

Keats's *Endymion*

Peacock's *Nightmare Abbey*

Scott's *Rob Roy* and *The Heart of Mid-Lothian*

Mary Shelley's *Frankenstein*

Percy Shelley's *The Revolt of Islam*

Emily Brontë born

Karl Marx born

Ivan Sergeyevich Turgenev born

1819 The *Savannah* becomes the first steamship to cross the Atlantic (in 26 days)

Peterloo massacre in Manchester

Byron's *Don Juan* (1819–1824) and *Mazeppa*

Crabbe's *Tales of the Hall*

Géricault's *Raft of the Medusa*

Hazlitt's *Lectures on the English Comic Writers*

Arthur Schopenhauer's *Die Welt als Wille und Vorstellung (The World as Will and Idea)*

Scott's *The Bride of Lammermoor* and *A Legend of Montrose*

Shelley's *The Cenci*, "The Masque of Anarchy," and "Ode to the West Wind"

Wordsworth's *Peter Bell*

Queen Victoria born

George Eliot born

1820–1830 Reign of George IV

1820 Trial of Queen Caroline

Cato Street Conspiracy suppressed; Arthur Thistlewood hanged

Monroe reelected president of the United States

Missouri Compromise

The *London* magazine founded

Keats's *Lamia, Isabella, The Eve of St. Agnes, and Other Poems*

CHRONOLOGY

Hazlitt's *Lectures Chiefly on the Dramatic Literature of the Age of Elizabeth*

Charles Maturin's *Melmoth the Wanderer*

Scott's *Ivanhoe* and *The Monastery*

Shelley's *Prometheus Unbound*

Anne Brontë born

1821   Greek War of Independence begins

Liberia founded as a colony for freed slaves

Byron's *Cain*, *Marino Faliero*, *The Two Foscari*, and *Sardanapalus*

Hazlitt's *Table Talk* (1821–1822)

Scott's *Kenilworth*

Shelley's *Adonais* and *Epipsychidion*

Death of John Keats

Death of Napoleon

Charles Baudelaire born

Feodor Dostoyevsky born

Gustave Flaubert born

1822   The Massacres of Chios (Greeks rebel against Turkish rule)

Byron's *The Vision of Judgment*

De Quincey's *Confessions of an English Opium-Eater*

Peacock's *Maid Marian*

Scott's *Peveril of the Peak*

Shelley's *Hellas*

Death of Percy Bysshe Shelley

Matthew Arnold born

1823   Monroe Doctrine proclaimed

Byron's *The Age of Bronze* and *The Island*

Lamb's *Essays of Elia*

Scott's *Quentin Durward*

1824   The National Gallery opened in London

John Quincy Adams elected president of the United States

The *Westminster Review* founded

Beethoven's Ninth Symphony first performed

William (Wilkie) Collins born

James Hogg's *The Private Memoirs and Confessions of a Justified Sinner*

Landor's *Imaginary Conversations* (1824–1829)

Scott's *Redgauntlet*

Death of George Gordon, Lord Byron

1825   Inauguration of steam-powered passenger and freight service on the Stockton and Darlington railway Bolivia and Brazil become independent Alessandro Manzoni's *I Promessi Sposi* (1825–1826)

1826   André-Marie Ampère's *Mémoire sur la théorie mathématique des phénomènes électrodynamiques*

James Fenimore Cooper's *The Last of the Mohicans*

Disraeli's *Vivian Grey* (1826–1827)

Scott's *Woodstock*

1827   The battle of Navarino ensures the independence of Greece

Josef Ressel obtains patent for the screw propeller for steamships

Heinrich Heine's *Buch der Lieder*

Death of William Blake

1828   Andrew Jackson elected president of the United States

Henrik Ibsen born

George Meredith born

Dante Gabriel Rossetti born

Leo Tolstoy born

1829   The Catholic Emancipation Act

Robert Peel establishes the metropolitan police force

Greek independence recognized by Turkey

Balzac begins *La Comédie humaine* (1829–1848)

Peacock's *The Misfortunes of Elphin*

J. M. W. Turner's *Ulysses Deriding Polyphemus*

1830–1837   Reign of William IV

1830   Charles X of France abdicates and is succeeded by Louis-Philippe

CHRONOLOGY

The Liverpool-Manchester railway opened

Tennyson's *Poems, Chiefly Lyrical*

Death of William Hazlitt

Christina Rossetti born

1831 Michael Faraday discovers electromagnetic induction

Charles Darwin's voyage on H.M.S. *Beagle* begins (1831–1836)

The Barbizon school of artists' first exhibition

Nat Turner slave revolt crushed in Virginia

Peacock's *Crotchet Castle*

Stendhal's *Le Rouge et le noir*

Edward Trelawny's *The Adventures of a Younger Son*

1832 The first Reform Bill

Samuel Morse invents the telegraph

Jackson reelected president of the United States

Disraeli's *Contarini Fleming*

Goethe's *Faust* (Part 2)

Tennyson's *Poems, Chiefly Lyrical*, including "The Lotus-Eaters" and "The Lady of Shalott"

Death of Johann Wolfgang von Goethe

Death of Sir Walter Scott

Lewis Carroll born

1833 Robert Browning's *Pauline*

John Keble launches the Oxford Movement

American Anti-Slavery Society founded

Lamb's *Last Essays of Elia*

Carlyle's *Sartor Resartus* (1833–1834)

Pushkin's *Eugene Onegin*

Mendelssohn's *Italian Symphony* first performed

1834 Abolition of slavery in the British Empire

Louis Braille's alphabet for the blind

Balzac's *Le Père Goriot*

Nikolai Gogol's *Dead Souls* (Part 1, 1834–1842)

Death of Samuel Taylor Coleridge

Death of Charles Lamb

William Morris born

1835 Hans Christian Andersen's *Fairy Tales* (1st ser.)

Robert Browning's *Paracelsus*

Samuel Butler and **Mary Elizabeth Braddon** are born

Alexis de Tocqueville's *De la Democratie en Amerique* (1835–1840)

1836 Martin Van Buren elected president of the United States

Dickens' *Sketches by Boz* (1836–1837)

Landor's *Pericles and Aspasia*

1837–1901 Reign of Queen Victoria

1837 Carlyle's *The French Revolution*

Dickens' *Oliver Twist* (1837–1838) and *Pickwick Papers*

Disraeli's *Venetia* and *Henrietta Temple*

1838 Chartist movement in England

National Gallery in London opened

Elizabeth Barrett Browning's *The Seraphim and Other Poems*

Dickens' *Nicholas Nickleby* (1838–1839)

1839 Louis Daguerre perfects process for producing an image on a silver-coated copper plate Faraday's *Experimental Researches in Electricity* (1839–1855)

First Chartist riots

Opium War between Great Britain and China

Carlyle's *Chartism*

1840 Canadian Act of Union

Queen Victoria marries Prince Albert

Charles Barry begins construction of the Houses of Parliament (1840–1852)

William Henry Harrison elected president of the United States

Robert Browning's *Sordello*

Thomas Hardy born

CHRONOLOGY

1841 New Zealand proclaimed a British colony

James Clark Ross discovers the Antarctic continent

Punch founded

John Tyler succeeds to the presidency after the death of Harrison

Carlyle's *Heroes and Hero-Worship*

Dickens' *The Old Curiosity Shop*

1842 Chartist riots

Income tax revived in Great Britain

The Mines Act, forbidding work underground by women or by children under the age of ten

Charles Edward Mudie's Lending Library founded in London

Dickens visits America

Robert Browning's *Dramatic Lyrics*

Macaulay's *Lays of Ancient Rome*

Tennyson's *Poems*, including "Morte d'Arthur," "St. Simeon Stylites," and "Ulysses"

Wordsworth's *Poems*

1843 Marc Isambard Brunel's Thames tunnel opened

The Economist founded

Carlyle's *Past and Present*

Dickens' *A Christmas Carol*

John Stuart Mill's *Logic*

Macaulay's *Critical and Historical Essays*

John Ruskin's *Modern Painters* (1843–1860)

1844 Rochdale Society of Equitable Pioneers, one of the first consumers' cooperatives, founded by twenty-eight Lancashire weavers

James K. Polk elected president of the United States

Elizabeth Barrett Browning's *Poems*, including "The Cry of the Children"

Dickens' *Martin Chuzzlewit*

Disraeli's *Coningsby*

Turner's *Rain, Steam and Speed*

Gerard Manley Hopkins born

1845 The great potato famine in Ireland begins (1845–1849)

Disraeli's *Sybil*

1846 Repeal of the Corn Laws

The *Daily News* founded (edited by Dickens the first three weeks)

Standard-gauge railway introduced in Britain

The Brontës' pseudonymous *Poems by Currer, Ellis and Action Bell*

Lear's *Book of Nonsense*

1847 The Ten Hours Factory Act

James Simpson uses chloroform as an anesthetic

Anne Brontë's *Agnes Grey*

Charlotte Brontë's *Jane Eyre*

Emily Brontë's *Wuthering Heights*

Bram Stoker born

Tennyson's *The Princess*

1848 The year of revolutions in France, Germany, Italy, Hungary, Poland

Marx and Engels issue *The Communist Manifesto*

The Chartist Petition

The Pre-Raphaelite Brotherhood founded

Zachary Taylor elected president of the United States

Anne Brontë's *The Tenant of Wildfell Hall*

Dickens' *Dombey and Son*

Elizabeth Gaskell's *Mary Barton*

Macaulay's *History of England* (1848–1861)

Mill's *Principles of Political Economy*

Thackeray's *Vanity Fair*

Death of Emily Brontë

1849 Bedford College for women founded

Arnold's *The Strayed Reveller*

Charlotte Brontë's *Shirley*

Ruskin's *The Seven Lamps of Architecture*

Death of Anne Brontë

1850 The Public Libraries Act

CHRONOLOGY

First submarine telegraph cable laid between Dover and Calais

Millard Fillmore succeeds to the presidency after the death of Taylor

Elizabeth Barrett Browning's *Sonnets from the Portuguese*

Carlyle's *Latter-Day Pamphlets*

Dickens' *Household Words* (1850–1859) and *David Copperfield*

Charles Kingsley's *Alton Locke*

The Pre-Raphaelites publish the *Germ*

Tennyson's *In Memoriam*

Thackeray's *The History of Pendennis*

Wordsworth's *The Prelude* is published posthumously

1851 The Great Exhibition opens at the Crystal Palace in Hyde Park

Louis Napoleon seizes power in France

Gold strike in Victoria incites Australian gold rush

Elizabeth Gaskell's *Cranford* (1851–1853)

Meredith's *Poems*

Ruskin's *The Stones of Venice* (1851–1853)

1852 The Second Empire proclaimed with Napoleon III as emperor

David Livingstone begins to explore the Zambezi (1852–1856)

Franklin Pierce elected president of the United States

Arnold's *Empedocles on Etna*

Thackeray's *The History of Henry Esmond, Esq.*

1853 Crimean War (1853–1856)

Arnold's *Poems*, including "The Scholar Gypsy" and "Sohrab and Rustum"

Charlotte Brontë's *Villette*

Elizabeth Gaskell's *Crawford and Ruth*

1854 Frederick D. Maurice's Working Men's College founded in London with more than 130 pupils

Battle of Balaklava

Dickens' *Hard Times*

James George Frazer born

Theodor Mommsen's *History of Rome* (1854–1856)

Tennyson's "The Charge of the Light Brigade"

Florence Nightingale in the Crimea (1854–1856)

Oscar Wilde born

1855 David Livingstone discovers the Victoria Falls

Robert Browning's *Men and Women*

Elizabeth Gaskell's *North and South*

Olive Schreiner born

Tennyson's *Maud*

Thackeray's *The Newcomes*

Trollope's *The Warden*

Death of Charlotte Brontë

1856 The Treaty of Paris ends the Crimean War

Henry Bessemer's steel process invented

James Buchanan elected president of the United States

H. Rider Haggard born

1857 The Indian Mutiny begins; crushed in 1858

The Matrimonial Causes Act

Charlotte Brontë's *The Professor*

Elizabeth Barrett Browning's *Aurora Leigh*

Dickens' *Little Dorritt*

Elizabeth Gaskell's *The Life of Charlotte Brontë*

Thomas Hughes's *Tom Brown's School Days*

Trollope's *Barchester Towers*

1858 Carlyle's *History of Frederick the Great* (1858–1865)

George Eliot's *Scenes of Clerical Life*

Morris' *The Defense of Guinevere*

Trollope's *Dr. Thorne*

1859 Charles Darwin's *The Origin of Species*

Dickens' *A Tale of Two Cities*

Arthur Conan Doyle born

George Eliot's *Adam Bede*

CHRONOLOGY

Fitzgerald's *The Rubaiyat of Omar Khayyám*

Meredith's *The Ordeal of Richard Feverel*

Mill's *On Liberty*

Samuel Smiles's *Self-Help*

Tennyson's *Idylls of the King*

1860 Abraham Lincoln elected president of the United States

The *Cornhill* magazine founded with Thackeray as editor

James M. Barrie born

William Wilkie Collins' *The Woman in White*

George Eliot's *The Mill on the Floss*

1861 American Civil War begins

Louis Pasteur presents the germ theory of disease

Arnold's *Lectures on Translating Homer*

Dickens' *Great Expectations*

George Eliot's *Silas Marner*

Meredith's *Evan Harrington*

Francis Turner Palgrave's *The Golden Treasury*

Trollope's *Framley Parsonage*

Peacock's *Gryll Grange*

Death of Prince Albert

1862 George Eliot's *Romola*

Meredith's *Modern Love*

Christina Rossetti's *Goblin Market*

Ruskin's *Unto This Last*

Trollope's *Orley Farm*

1863 Thomas Huxley's *Man's Place in Nature*

1864 The Geneva Red Cross Convention signed by twelve nations

Lincoln reelected president of the United States

Robert Browning's *Dramatis Personae*

John Henry Newman's *Apologia pro vita sua*

Tennyson's *Enoch Arden*

Trollope's *The Small House at Allington*

1865 Assassination of Lincoln; Andrew Johnson succeeds to the presidency

Arnold's *Essays in Criticism* (1st ser.)

Carroll's *Alice's Adventures in Wonderland*

Dickens' *Our Mutual Friend*

Meredith's *Rhoda Fleming*

A. C. Swinburne's *Atalanta in Calydon*

1866 First successful transatlantic telegraph cable laid

George Eliot's *Felix Holt, the Radical*

Elizabeth Gaskell's *Wives and Daughters*

Beatrix Potter born

Swinburne's *Poems and Ballads*

1867 The second Reform Bill

Arnold's *New Poems*

Bagehot's *The English Constitution*

Carlyle's *Shooting Niagara*

Marx's *Das Kapital* (vol. 1)

Trollope's *The Last Chronicle of Barset*

George William Russell (AE) born

1868 Gladstone becomes prime minister (1868–1874)

Johnson impeached by House of Representatives; acquitted by Senate

Ulysses S. Grant elected president of the United States

Robert Browning's *The Ring and the Book* (1868–1869)

Collins' *The Moonstone*

1869 The Suez Canal opened

Girton College, Cambridge, founded

Arnold's *Culture and Anarchy*

Mill's *The Subjection of Women*

Trollope's *Phineas Finn*

1870 The Elementary Education Act establishes schools under the aegis of local boards

Dickens' *Edwin Drood*

Disraeli's *Lothair*

Morris' *The Earthly Paradise*

CHRONOLOGY

Dante Gabriel Rossetti's *Poems*

Saki [Hector Hugh Munro] born

1871 Trade unions legalized

Newnham College, Cambridge, founded for women students

Carroll's *Through the Looking Glass*

Darwin's *The Descent of Man*

Meredith's *The Adventures of Harry Richmond*

Swinburne's *Songs Before Sunrise*

1872 Max Beerbohm born

Samuel Butler's *Erewhon*

George Eliot's *Middlemarch*

Grant reelected president of the United States

Hardy's *Under the Greenwood Tree*

1873 Arnold's *Literature and Dogma*

Mill's *Autobiography*

Pater's *Studies in the History of the Renaissance*

Trollope's *The Eustace Diamonds*

1874 Disraeli becomes prime minister

Hardy's *Far from the Madding Crowd*

James Thomson's *The City of Dreadful Night*

1875 Britain buys Suez Canal shares

Trollope's *The Way We Live Now*

T. F. Powys born

1876 F. H. Bradley's *Ethical Studies*

George Eliot's *Daniel Deronda*

Henry James's *Roderick Hudson*

Meredith's *Beauchamp's Career*

Morris' *Sigurd the Volsung*

Trollope's *The Prime Minister*

1877 Rutherford B. Hayes elected president of the United States after Electoral Commission awards him disputed votes

Henry James's *The American*

1878 Electric street lighting introduced in London

Hardy's *The Return of the Native*

Swinburne's *Poems and Ballads* (2d ser.)

Births of **A. E. Coppard** and Edward Thomas

1879 Somerville College and Lady Margaret Hall opened at Oxford for women

The London telephone exchange built

Gladstone's Midlothian campaign (1879–1880)

Browning's *Dramatic Idyls*

Meredith's *The Egoist*

1880 Gladstone's second term as prime minister (1880–1885)

James A. Garfield elected president of the United States

Browning's *Dramatic Idyls Second Series*

Disraeli's *Endymion*

Radclyffe Hall born

Hardy's *The Trumpet-Major*

Lytton Strachey born

1881 Garfield assassinated; Chester A. Arthur succeeds to the presidency

Henry James's *The Portrait of a Lady* and *Washington Square*

D. G. Rossetti's *Ballads and Sonnets*

P. G. Wodehouse born

1882 Triple Alliance formed between German empire, Austrian empire, and Italy

Leslie Stephen begins to edit the *Dictionary of National Biography*

Married Women's Property Act passed in Britain

Britain occupies Egypt and the Sudan

1883 Uprising of the Mahdi: Britain evacuates the Sudan

Royal College of Music opens

T. H. Green's *Ethics*

T. E. Hulme born

Stevenson's *Treasure Island*

1884 The Mahdi captures Omdurman: General Gordon appointed to command the garrison of Khartoum

Grover Cleveland elected president of the United States

CHRONOLOGY

The *Oxford English Dictionary* begins publishing

The Fabian Society founded

Hiram Maxim's recoil-operated machine gun invented

1885 The Mahdi captures Khartoum: General Gordon killed

Haggard's *King Solomon's Mines*

Marx's *Das Kapital* (vol. 2)

Meredith's *Diana of the Crossways*

Pater's *Marius the Epicurean*

1886 The Canadian Pacific Railway completed

Gold discovered in the Transvaal

Births of **Frances Cornford** and Ronald Firbank

Henry James's *The Bostonians* and *The Princess Casamassima*

Stevenson's *The Strange Case of Dr. Jekyll and Mr. Hyde*

1887 Queen Victoria's Golden Jubilee

Rupert Brooke born

Haggard's *Allan Quatermain* and *She*

Hardy's *The Woodlanders*

Edwin Muir born

1888 Benjamin Harrison elected president of the United States

Henry James's *The Aspern Papers*

Kipling's *Plain Tales from the Hills*

T. E. Lawrence born

1889 Yeats's *The Wanderings of Oisin*

Death of Robert Browning

1890 Morris founds the Kelmscott Press

Agatha Christie born

Frazer's *The Golden Bough* (1st ed.)

Henry James's *The Tragic Muse*

Morris' *News From Nowhere*

Jean Rhys born

1891 Gissing's *New Grub Street*

Hardy's *Tess of the d'Urbervilles*

Wilde's *The Picture of Dorian Gray*

1892 Grover Cleveland elected president of the United States

Conan Doyle's *The Adventures of Sherlock Holmes*

Shaw's *Widower's Houses*

J. R. R. Tolkien born

Rebecca West born

Wilde's *Lady Windermere's Fan*

1893 Wilde's *A Woman of No Importance* and *Salomé*

1894 Kipling's *The Jungle Book*

Moore's *Esther Waters*

Marx's *Das Kapital* (vol. 3)

Audrey Beardsley's *The Yellow Book* begins to appear quarterly

Shaw's *Arms and the Man*

1895 Trial and imprisonment of Oscar Wilde

William Ramsay announces discovery of helium

The National Trust founded

Conrad's *Almayer's Folly*

Hardy's *Jude the Obscure*

Wells's *The Time Machine*

Wilde's *The Importance of Being Earnest*

Yeats's *Poems*

1896 William McKinley elected president of the United States

Failure of the Jameson Raid on the Transvaal

Housman's *A Shropshire Lad*

1897 Queen Victoria's Diamond Jubilee

Conrad's *The Nigger of the Narcissus*

Havelock Ellis' *Studies in the Psychology of Sex* begins publication

Henry James's *The Spoils of Poynton* and *What Maisie Knew*

Kipling's *Captains Courageous*

Shaw's *Candida*

Stoker's *Dracula*

Wells's *The Invisible Man*

1898 Kitchener defeats the Mahdist forces at Omdurman: the Sudan reoccupied

Hardy's *Wessex Poems*

Henry James's *The Turn of the Screw*

CHRONOLOGY

C. S. Lewis born

Shaw's *Caesar and Cleopatra* and *You Never Can Tell*

Alec Waugh born

Wells's *The War of the Worlds*

Wilde's *The Ballad of Reading Gaol*

1899   The Boer War begins

Elizabeth Bowen born

Noël Coward born

Elgar's *Enigma Variations*

Kipling's *Stalky and Co.*

1900   McKinley reelected president of the United States

British Labour party founded

Boxer Rebellion in China

Reginald A. Fessenden transmits speech by wireless

First Zeppelin trial flight

Max Planck presents his first paper on the quantum theory

Conrad's *Lord Jim*

Elgar's *The Dream of Gerontius*

Sigmund Freud's *The Interpretation of Dreams*

V. S. Pritchett born

William Butler Yeats's *The Shadowy Waters*

1901–1910   Reign of King Edward VII

1901   William McKinley assassinated; Theodore Roosevelt succeeds to the presidency

First transatlantic wireless telegraph signal transmitted

Chekhov's *Three Sisters*

Freud's *Psychopathology of Everyday Life*

Rudyard Kipling's *Kim*

Thomas Mann's *Buddenbrooks*

Potter's *The Tale of Peter Rabbit*

Shaw's *Captain Brassbound's Conversion*

August Strindberg's *The Dance of Death*

1902   Barrie's *The Admirable Crichton*

Arnold Bennett's *Anna of the Five Towns*

Cézanne's *Le Lac D'Annecy*

Conrad's *Heart of Darkness*

Henry James's *The Wings of the Dove*

William James's *The Varieties of Religious Experience*

Kipling's *Just So Stories*

Maugham's *Mrs. Cradock*

Stevie Smith born

Times Literary Supplement begins publishing

1903   At its London congress the Russian Social Democratic Party divides into Mensheviks, led by Plekhanov, and Bolsheviks, led by Lenin

The treaty of Panama places the Canal Zone in U.S. hands for a nominal rent

Motor cars regulated in Britain to a 20-mile-per-hour limit

The Wright brothers make a successful flight in the United States

Burlington magazine founded

Samuel Butler's *The Way of All Flesh* published posthumously

Cyril Connolly born

George Gissing's *The Private Papers of Henry Ryecroft*

Thomas Hardy's *The Dynasts*

Henry James's *The Ambassadors*

Alan Paton born

Shaw's *Man and Superman*

Synge's *Riders to the Sea* produced in Dublin

Yeats's *In the Seven Woods* and *On Baile's Strand*

1904   Roosevelt elected president of the United States

Russo-Japanese war (1904–1905)

Construction of the Panama Canal begins

The ultraviolet lamp invented

The engineering firm of Rolls Royce founded

Barrie's *Peter Pan* first performed

CHRONOLOGY

Cecil Day Lewis born

Chekhov's *The Cherry Orchard*

Conrad's *Nostromo*

Henry James's *The Golden Bowl*

Kipling's *Traffics and Discoveries*

Georges Rouault's *Head of a Tragic Clown*

G. M. Trevelyan's *England Under the Stuarts*

Puccini's *Madame Butterfly*

First Shaw-Granville Barker season at the Royal Court Theatre

The Abbey Theatre founded in Dublin

1905 Russian sailors on the battleship Potemkin mutiny

After riots and a general strike the czar concedes demands by the Duma for legislative powers, a wider franchise, and civil liberties

Albert Einstein publishes his first theory of relativity

The Austin Motor Company founded

Bennett's *Tales of the Five Towns*

Claude Debussy's *La Mer*

E. M. Forster's *Where Angels Fear to Tread*

Henry Green born

Richard Strauss's *Salome*

H. G. Wells's *Kipps*

Oscar Wilde's *De Profundis*

1906 Liberals win a landslide victory in the British general election

The Trades Disputes Act legitimizes peaceful picketing in Britain

Captain Dreyfus rehabilitated in France

J. J. Thomson begins research on gamma rays

The U.S. Pure Food and Drug Act passed

Churchill's *Lord Randolph Churchill*

William Empson born

Galsworthy's *The Man of Property*

Kipling's *Puck of Pook's Hill*

Shaw's *The Doctor's Dilemma*

Yeats's *Poems* 1899–1905

1907 Exhibition of cubist paintings in Paris

Henry Adams' *The Education of Henry Adams*

Henri Bergson's *Creative Evolution*

Conrad's *The Secret Agent*

Births of **Barbara Comyns**, Daphne du Maurier, and Christopher Fry

Forster's *The Longest Journey*

André Gide's *La Porte étroite*

Shaw's *John Bull's Other Island* and *Major Barbara*

Synge's *The Playboy of the Western World*

Trevelyan's *Garibaldi's Defence of the Roman Republic*

1908 Herbert Asquith becomes prime minister

David Lloyd George becomes chancellor of the exchequer

William Howard Taft elected president of the United States

The Young Turks seize power in Istanbul

Henry Ford's Model T car produced

Bennett's *The Old Wives' Tale*

Pierre Bonnard's *Nude Against the Light*

Georges Braque's *House at L'Estaque*

Chesterton's *The Man Who Was Thursday*

Jacob Epstein's *Figures* erected in London

Forster's *A Room with a View*

Anatole France's *L'Ile des Pingouins*

Henri Matisse's *Bonheur de Vivre*

Elgar's First Symphony

Ford Madox Ford founds the *English Review*

1909 The Young Turks depose Sultan Abdul Hamid

The Anglo-Persian Oil Company formed

Louis Bleriot crosses the English Channel from France by monoplane

CHRONOLOGY

Admiral Robert Peary reaches the North Pole

Freud lectures at Clark University (Worcester, Mass.) on psychoanalysis

Serge Diaghilev's Ballets Russes opens in Paris

Galsworthy's *Strife*

Hardy's *Time's Laughingstocks*

Malcolm Lowry born

Claude Monet's *Water Lilies*

Stephen Spender born

Trevelyan's *Garibaldi and the Thousand*

Wells's *Tono-Bungay* first published (book form, 1909)

1910–1936 Reign of King George V

1910 The Liberals win the British general election

Marie Curie's *Treatise on Radiography*

Arthur Evans excavates Knossos

Edouard Manet and the first post-impressionist exhibition in London

Filippo Marinetti publishes "Manifesto of the Futurist Painters"

Norman Angell's *The Great Illusion*

Bennett's *Clayhanger*

Forster's *Howards End*

Galsworthy's *Justice* and *The Silver Box*

Kipling's *Rewards and Fairies*

Norman MacCaig born

Rimsky-Korsakov's *Le Coq d'or*

Stravinsky's *The Firebird*

Vaughan Williams' *A Sea Symphony*

Wells's *The History of Mr. Polly*

Wells's *The New Machiavelli* first published (in book form, 1911)

1911 Lloyd George introduces National Health Insurance Bill

Suffragette riots in Whitehall

Roald Amundsen reaches the South Pole

Bennett's *The Card*

Chagall's *Self Portrait with Seven Fingers*

Conrad's *Under Western Eyes*

D. H. Lawrence's *The White Peacock*

Katherine Mansfield's *In a German Pension*

Edward Marsh edits *Georgian Poetry*

Moore's *Hail and Farewell* (1911–1914)

Flann O'Brien born

Strauss's *Der Rosenkavalier*

Stravinsky's *Petrouchka*

Trevelyan's *Garibaldi and the Making of Italy*

Wells's *The New Machiavelli*

Mahler's *Das Lied von der Erde*

1912 Woodrow Wilson elected president of the United States

SS *Titanic* sinks on its maiden voyage

Five million Americans go to the movies daily; London has four hundred movie theaters

Second post-impressionist exhibition in London

Bennett's and Edward Knoblock's *Milestones*

Constantin Brancusi's *Maiastra*

Wassily Kandinsky's *Black Lines*

D. H. Lawrence's *The Trespasser*

1913 Second Balkan War begins

Henry Ford pioneers factory assembly technique through conveyor belts

Epstein's *Tomb of Oscar Wilde*

New York Armory Show introduces modern art to the world

Alain Fournier's *Le Grand Meaulnes*

Freud's *Totem and Tabu*

D. H. Lawrence's *Sons and Lovers*

Mann's *Death in Venice*

Proust's *Du Côté de chez Swann* (first volume of *À la recherche du temps perdu*, 1913–1922)

Barbara Pym born

Ravel's *Daphnis and Chloé*

1914 The Panama Canal opens (formal dedication on 12 July 1920)

CHRONOLOGY

Irish Home Rule Bill passed in the House of Commons
Archduke Franz Ferdinand assassinated at Sarajevo
World War I begins

Battles of the Marne, Masurian Lakes, and Falkland Islands
Joyce's *Dubliners*

Norman Nicholson born

Shaw's *Pygmalion* and *Androcles and the Lion*
Yeats's *Responsibilities*

Wyndham Lewis publishes *Blast* magazine and *The Vorticist Manifesto*

1915 The Dardanelles campaign begins

Britain and Germany begin naval and submarine blockades
The *Lusitania* is sunk

Hugo Junkers manufactures the first fighter aircraft
Poison gas used for the first time

First Zeppelin raid in London

Brooke's *1914: Five Sonnets*

Norman Douglas' *Old Calabria*

D. W. Griffith's *The Birth of a Nation*

Gustav Holst's *The Planets*

D. H. Lawrence's *The Rainbow*

Wyndham Lewis's *The Crowd*

Maugham's *Of Human Bondage*

Pablo Picasso's *Harlequin*

Sibelius' Fifth Symphony

1916 Evacuation of Gallipoli and the Dardanelles

Battles of the Somme, Jutland, and Verdun

Britain introduces conscription

The Easter Rebellion in Dublin

Asquith resigns and David Lloyd George becomes prime minister
The Sykes-Picot agreement on the partition of Turkey
First military tanks used

Wilson reelected president president of the United States

Henri Barbusse's *Le Feu*

Griffith's *Intolerance*

Joyce's *Portrait of the Artist as a Young Man*
Jung's *Psychology of the Unconscious*

Moore's *The Brook Kerith*

Edith Sitwell edits *Wheels* (1916–1921)
Wells's *Mr. Britling Sees It Through*

1917 United States enters World War I

Czar Nicholas II abdicates

The Balfour Declaration on a Jewish national home in Palestine
The Bolshevik Revolution

Georges Clemenceau elected prime minister of France
Lenin appointed chief commissar; Trotsky appointed minister of foreign affairs
Conrad's *The Shadow-Line*

Douglas' *South Wind*

Eliot's *Prufrock and Other Observations*

Modigliani's *Nude with Necklace*

Sassoon's *The Old Huntsman*

Prokofiev's *Classical Symphony*

Yeats's *The Wild Swans at Coole*

1918 Wilson puts forward Fourteen Points for World Peace
Central Powers and Russia sign the Treaty of Brest-Litovsk
Execution of Czar Nicholas II and his family
Kaiser Wilhelm II abdicates

The Armistice signed

Women granted the vote at age thirty in Britain
Rupert Brooke's *Collected Poems*

Gerard Manley Hopkins' *Poems*

Joyce's *Exiles*

Lewis's *Tarr*

Sassoon's *Counter-Attack*

Oswald Spengler's *The Decline of the West*

CHRONOLOGY

Strachey's *Eminent Victorians*

Béla Bartók's *Bluebeard's Castle*

Charlie Chaplin's *Shoulder Arms*

1919 The Versailles Peace Treaty signed

J. W. Alcock and A. W. Brown make first transatlantic flight

Ross Smith flies from London to Australia

National Socialist party founded in Germany

Benito Mussolini founds the Fascist party in Italy

Sinn Fein Congress adopts declaration of independence in Dublin

Eamon De Valera elected president of Sinn Fein party

Communist Third International founded

Lady Astor elected first woman Member of Parliament

Prohibition in the United States

John Maynard Keynes's *The Economic Consequences of the Peace*

Eliot's *Poems*

Maugham's *The Moon and Sixpence*

Shaw's *Heartbreak House*

The Bauhaus school of design, building, and crafts founded by Walter Gropius

Amedeo Modigliani's *Self-Portrait*

1920 The League of Nations established

Warren G. Harding elected president of the United States

Senate votes against joining the League and rejects the Treaty of Versailles

The Nineteenth Amendment gives women the right to vote

White Russian forces of Denikin and Kolchak defeated by the Bolsheviks

Karel Čapek's *R.U.R.*

Galsworthy's *In Chancery* and *The Skin Game*

Sinclair Lewis' *Main Street*

Katherine Mansfield's *Bliss*

Matisse's *Odalisques* (1920–1925)

Ezra Pound's *Hugh Selwyn Mauberly*

Paul Valéry's *Le Cimetière Marin*

Yeats's *Michael Robartes and the Dancer*

1921 Britain signs peace with Ireland

First medium-wave radio broadcast in the United States

The British Broadcasting Corporation founded

Braque's *Still Life with Guitar*

Chaplin's *The Kid*

Aldous Huxley's *Crome Yellow*

Paul Klee's *The Fish*

D. H. Lawrence's *Women in Love*

John McTaggart's *The Nature of Existence* (vol. 1)

Moore's *Héloïse and Abélard*

Eugene O'Neill's *The Emperor Jones*

Luigi Pirandello's *Six Characters in Search of an Author*

Shaw's *Back to Methuselah*

Strachey's *Queen Victoria*

George Mackay Brown born

1922 Lloyd George's Coalition government succeeded by Bonar Law's Conservative government

Benito Mussolini marches on Rome and forms a government

William Cosgrave elected president of the Irish Free State

The BBC begins broadcasting in London

Lord Carnarvon and Howard Carter discover Tutankhamen's tomb

The PEN club founded in London

The *Criterion* founded with T. S. Eliot as editor

Kingsley Amis born

Eliot's *The Waste Land*

A. E. Housman's *Last Poems*

Joyce's *Ulysses*

D. H. Lawrence's *Aaron's Rod* and *England, My England*

Sinclair Lewis's *Babbitt*

O'Neill's *Anna Christie*

Pirandello's *Henry IV*

Edith Sitwell's *Façade*

Virginia Woolf's *Jacob's Room*

Yeats's *The Trembling of the Veil*

Donald Davie born

1923 The Union of Soviet Socialist Republics established

French and Belgian troops occupy the Ruhr in consequence of Germany's failure to pay reparations

Mustafa Kemal (Ataturk) proclaims Turkey a republic and is elected president

Warren G. Harding dies; Calvin Coolidge becomes president

Stanley Baldwin succeeds Bonar Law as prime minister

Adolf Hitler's attempted coup in Munich fails

Time magazine begins publishing

E. N. da C. Andrade's *The Structure of the Atom*

Brendan Behan born

Bennett's *Riceyman Steps*

Churchill's *The World Crisis* (1923–1927)

J. E. Flecker's *Hassan* produced

Nadine Gordimer born

Paul Klee's *Magic Theatre*

Lawrence's *Kangaroo*

Rainer Maria Rilke's *Duino Elegies* and *Sonnets to Orpheus*

Sibelius' *Sixth Symphony*

Picasso's *Seated Woman*

William Walton's *Façade*

1924 Ramsay MacDonald forms first Labour government, loses general election, and is succeeded by Stanley Baldwin

Calvin Coolidge elected president of the United States

Noël Coward's *The Vortex*

Forster's *A Passage to India*

Mann's *The Magic Mountain*

Shaw's *St. Joan*

1925 Reza Khan becomes shah of Iran

First surrealist exhibition held in Paris

Alban Berg's *Wozzeck*

Chaplin's *The Gold Rush*

John Dos Passos' *Manhattan Transfer*

Theodore Dreiser's *An American Tragedy*

Sergei Eisenstein's *Battleship Potemkin*

F. Scott Fitzgerald's *The Great Gatsby*

André Gide's *Les Faux Monnayeurs*

Hardy's *Human Shows and Far Phantasies*

Huxley's *Those Barren Leaves*

Kafka's *The Trial*

O'Casey's *Juno and the Paycock*

Virginia Woolf's *Mrs. Dalloway* and *The Common Reader*

Brancusi's *Bird in Space*

Shostakovich's *First Symphony*

Sibelius' *Tapiola*

1926 Ford's *A Man Could Stand Up*

Gide's *Si le grain ne meurt*

Hemingway's *The Sun also Rises*

Kafka's *The Castle*

D. H. Lawrence's *The Plumed Serpent*

T. E. Lawrence's *Seven Pillars of Wisdom* privately circulated

Maugham's *The Casuarina Tree*

O'Casey's *The Plough and the Stars*

Puccini's *Turandot*

1927 General Chiang Kai-shek becomes prime minister in China

Trotsky expelled by the Communist party as a deviationist; Stalin becomes leader of the party and dictator of the Soviet Union

Charles Lindbergh flies from New York to Paris

J. W. Dunne's *An Experiment with Time*

Freud's *Autobiography* translated into English

CHRONOLOGY

Albert Giacometti's *Observing Head*

Ernest Hemingway's *Men Without Women*

Fritz Lang's *Metropolis*

Wyndham Lewis' *Time and Western Man*

F. W. Murnau's *Sunrise*

Proust's *Le Temps retrouvé* posthumously published

Stravinsky's *Oedipus Rex*

Virginia Woolf's *To the Lighthouse*

1928　The Kellogg-Briand Pact, outlawing war and providing for peaceful settlement of disputes, signed in Paris by sixty-two nations, including the Soviet Union

Herbert Hoover elected president of the United States

Women's suffrage granted at age twenty-one in Britain

Alexander Fleming discovers penicillin

Bertolt Brecht and Kurt Weill's *The Three-Penny Opera*

Eisenstein's *October*

Huxley's *Point Counter Point*

Christopher Isherwood's *All the Conspirators*

D. H. Lawrence's *Lady Chatterley's Lover*

Wyndham Lewis' *The Childermass*

Matisse's *Seated Odalisque*

Munch's *Girl on a Sofa*

Shaw's *Intelligent Woman's Guide to Socialism*

Virginia Woolf's *Orlando*

Yeats's *The Tower*

1929　The Labour party wins British general election

Trotsky expelled from the Soviet Union

Museum of Modern Art opens in New York

Collapse of U.S. stock exchange begins world economic crisis

Robert Bridges's *The Testament of Beauty*

William Faulkner's *The Sound and the Fury*

Robert Graves's *Goodbye to All That*

Hemingway's *A Farewell to Arms*

Ernst Junger's *The Storm of Steel*

Hugo von Hoffmansthal's *Poems*

Henry Moore's *Reclining Figure*

J. B. Priestley's *The Good Companions*

Erich Maria Remarque's *All Quiet on the Western Front*

Shaw's *The Applecart*

R. C. Sheriff's *Journey's End*

Edith Sitwell's *Gold Coast Customs*

Thomas Wolfe's *Look Homeward, Angel*

Virginia Woolf's *A Room of One's Own*

Yeats's *The Winding Stair*

Second surrealist manifesto; Salvador Dali joins the surrealists

Epstein's *Night and Day*

Mondrian's *Composition with Yellow Blue*

1930　Allied occupation of the Rhineland ends

Mohandas Gandhi opens civil disobedience campaign in India

The *Daily Worker*, journal of the British Communist party, begins publishing

J. W. Reppe makes artificial fabrics from an acetylene base

John Arden born

Auden's *Poems*

Coward's *Private Lives*

Eliot's *Ash Wednesday*

Wyndham Lewis's *The Apes of God*

Maugham's *Cakes and Ale*

Ezra Pound's *XXX Cantos*

Evelyn Waugh's *Vile Bodies*

1931　The failure of the Credit Anstalt in Austria starts a financial collapse in Central Europe

Britain abandons the gold standard; the pound falls by twenty-five percent

Mutiny in the Royal Navy at Invergordon over pay cuts

Ramsay MacDonald resigns, splits the Cabinet, and is expelled by the Labour party; in the general election the National Government wins by a majority of five hundred seats

The Statute of Westminster defines dominion status

Ninette de Valois founds the Vic-Wells Ballet (eventually the Royal Ballet)

Coward's *Cavalcade*

Dali's The *Persistence of Memory*

John le Carré born

O'Neill's *Mourning Becomes Electra*

Anthony Powell's *Afternoon Men*

Antoine de Saint-Exupéry's *Vol de nuit*

Walton's *Belshazzar's Feast*

Virginia Woolf's *The Waves*

1932   Franklin D. Roosevelt elected president of the United States

Paul von Hindenburg elected president of Germany; Franz von Papen elected chancellor

Sir Oswald Mosley founds British Union of Fascists

The BBC takes over development of television from J. L. Baird's company

Basic English of 850 words designed as a prospective international language

The Folger Library opens in Washington, D.C.

The Shakespeare Memorial Theatre opens in Stratford-upon-Avon

Faulkner's *Light in August*

Huxley's *Brave New World*

F. R. Leavis' *New Bearings in English Poetry*

Boris Pasternak's *Second Birth*

Ravel's *Concerto for Left Hand*

Peter Redgrove born

Rouault's *Christ Mocked by Soldiers*

Waugh's *Black Mischief*

Yeats's *Words for Music Perhaps*

1933   Roosevelt inaugurates the New Deal

Hitler becomes chancellor of Germany

The Reichstag set on fire

Hitler suspends civil liberties and freedom of the press; German trade unions suppressed

George Balanchine and Lincoln Kirstein found the School of American Ballet

Beryl Bainbridge born

Lowry's *Ultramarine*

André Malraux's *La Condition humaine*

Orwell's *Down and Out in Paris and London*

Gertrude Stein's *The Autobiography of Alice B. Toklas*

Anne Stevenson born

1934   The League Disarmament Conference ends in failure

The Soviet Union admitted to the League

Hitler becomes Führer

Civil war in Austria; Engelbert Dollfuss assassinated in attempted Nazi coup

Frédéric Joliot and Irene Joliot-Curie discover artificial (induced) radioactivity

Einstein's *My Philosophy*

Fitzgerald's *Tender Is the Night*

Graves's *I, Claudius* and *Claudius the God*

Toynbee's *A Study of History* begins publication (1934–1954)

Waugh's *A Handful of Dust*

Births of **Alan Bennett** and **Christopher Wallace-Crabbe**

1935   Grigori Zinoviev and other Soviet leaders convicted of treason

Stanley Baldwin becomes prime minister in National Government; National Government wins general election in Britain

Italy invades Abyssinia

Germany repudiates disarmament clauses of Treaty of Versailles

CHRONOLOGY

Germany reintroduces compulsory military service and outlaws the Jews

Robert Watson-Watt builds first practical radar equipment

Karl Jaspers' *Suffering and Existence*

André Brink born

Ivy Compton-Burnett's *A House and Its Head*

Eliot's *Murder in the Cathedral*

Barbara Hepworth's *Three Forms*

George Gershwin's *Porgy and Bess*

Greene's *England Made Me*

Isherwood's *Mr. Norris Changes Trains*

Malraux's *Le Temps du mépris*

Yeats's *Dramatis Personae*

Klee's *Child Consecrated to Suffering*

Benedict Nicholson's *White Relief*

1936   Edward VII accedes to the throne in January; abdicates in December

1936–1952   Reign of George VI

1936   German troops occupy the Rhineland

Ninety-nine percent of German electorate vote for Nazi candidates

The Popular Front wins general election in France; Léon Blum becomes prime minister

Roosevelt reelected president of the United States

The Popular Front wins general election in Spain

Spanish Civil War begins

Italian troops occupy Addis Ababa; Abyssinia annexed by Italy

BBC begins television service from Alexandra Palace

Auden's *Look, Stranger!*

Auden and Isherwood's *The Ascent of F-6*

A. J. Ayer's *Language, Truth and Logic*

Chaplin's *Modern Times*

Greene's *A Gun for Sale*

Huxley's *Eyeless in Gaza*

Keynes's *General Theory of Employment*

F. R. Leavis' *Revaluation*

Mondrian's *Composition in Red and Blue*

Dylan Thomas' *Twenty-five Poems*

Wells's *The Shape of Things to Come* filmed

1937   Trial of Karl Radek and other Soviet leaders

Neville Chamberlain succeeds Stanley Baldwin as prime minister

China and Japan at war

Frank Whittle designs jet engine

Picasso's *Guernica*

Shostakovich's Fifth Symphony

Magritte's *La Reproduction interdite*

Hemingway's *To Have and Have Not*

Malraux's *L'Espoir*

Orwell's *The Road to Wigan Pier*

Priestley's *Time and the Conways*

Virginia Woolf's *The Years*

1938   Trial of Nikolai Bukharin and other Soviet political leaders

Austria occupied by German troops and declared part of the Reich

Hitler states his determination to annex Sudetenland from Czechoslovakia

Britain, France, Germany, and Italy sign the Munich agreement

German troops occupy Sudetenland

Edward Hulton founds *Picture Post*

Cyril Connolly's *Enemies of Promise*

du Maurier's *Rebecca*

Faulkner's *The Unvanquished*

Graham Greene's *Brighton Rock*

Hindemith's *Mathis der Maler*

Jean Renoir's *La Grande Illusion*

Jean-Paul Sartre's *La Nausée*

Yeats's *New Poems*

Anthony Asquith's *Pygmalion* and Walt Disney's *Snow White*

Ngũgĩ wa Thiong'o born

CHRONOLOGY

1939   German troops occupy Bohemia and Moravia; Czechoslovakia incorporated into Third Reich

Madrid surrenders to General Franco; the Spanish Civil War ends

Italy invades Albania

Spain joins Germany, Italy, and Japan in anti-Comintern Pact

Britain and France pledge support to Poland, Romania, and Greece

The Soviet Union proposes defensive alliance with Britain; British military mission visits Moscow

The Soviet Union and Germany sign nonaggression treaty, secretly providing for partition of Poland between them

Germany invades Poland; Britain, France, and Germany at war

The Soviet Union invades Finland

New York World's Fair opens

Eliot's *The Family Reunion*

Births of Seamus Heaney and **Michael Longley**

Isherwood's *Good-bye to Berlin*

Joyce's *Finnegans Wake* (1922–1939)

MacNeice's *Autumn Journal*

Powell's *What's Become of Waring?*

1940   Churchill becomes prime minister

Italy declares war on France, Britain, and Greece

General de Gaulle founds Free French Movement

The Battle of Britain and the bombing of London

Roosevelt reelected president of the United States for third term

Betjeman's *Old Lights for New Chancels*

Angela Carter born

Chaplin's *The Great Dictator*

J. M. Coetzee born

Disney's *Fantasia*

Greene's *The Power and the Glory*

Hemingway's *For Whom the Bell Tolls*

C. P. Snow's *Strangers and Brothers* (retitled *George Passant* in 1970, when entire sequence of ten novels, published 1940–1970, was entitled *Strangers and Brothers*)

1941   German forces occupy Yugoslavia, Greece, and Crete, and invade the Soviet Union

Lend-Lease agreement between the United States and Britain

President Roosevelt and Winston Churchill sign the Atlantic Charter

Japanese forces attack Pearl Harbor; United States declares war on Japan, Germany, Italy; Britain on Japan

Auden's *New Year Letter*

James Burnham's *The Managerial Revolution*

F. Scott Fitzgerald's *The Last Tycoon*

Huxley's *Grey Eminence*

Shostakovich's *Seventh Symphony*

Tippett's *A Child of Our Time*

Orson Welles's *Citizen Kane*

Virginia Woolf's *Between the Acts*

1942   Japanese forces capture Singapore, Hong Kong, Bataan, Manila

German forces capture Tobruk

U.S. fleet defeats the Japanese in the Coral Sea, captures Guadalcanal

Battle of El Alamein

Allied forces land in French North Africa

Atom first split at University of Chicago

William Beveridge's *Social Insurance and Allied Services*

Albert Camus's *L'Étranger*

Joyce Cary's *To Be a Pilgrim*

Edith Sitwell's *Street Songs*

Waugh's *Put Out More Flags*

1943   German forces surrender at Stalingrad

German and Italian forces surrender in North Africa

Italy surrenders to Allies and declares war on Germany

CHRONOLOGY

Cairo conference between Roosevelt, Churchill, Chiang Kai-shek

Teheran conference between Roosevelt, Churchill, Stalin

Eliot's *Four Quartets*

Henry Moore's *Madonna and Child*

Sartre's *Les Mouches*

Vaughan Williams' *Fifth Symphony*

1944   Allied forces land in Normandy and southern France

Allied forces enter Rome

Attempted assassination of Hitler fails

Liberation of Paris

U.S. forces land in Philippines

German offensive in the Ardennes halted

Roosevelt reelected president of the United States for fourth term

Education Act passed in Britain

Pay-as-You-Earn income tax introduced

Beveridge's *Full Employment in a Free Society*

Cary's *The Horse's Mouth*

Huxley's *Time Must Have a Stop*

Maugham's *The Razor's Edge*

Sartre's *Huis Clos*

Edith Sitwell's *Green Song and Other Poems*

Graham Sutherland's *Christ on the Cross*

Trevelyan's *English Social History*

W. G. Sebald born

1945   British and Indian forces open offensive in Burma

Yalta conference between Roosevelt, Churchill, Stalin

Mussolini executed by Italian partisans

Roosevelt dies; Harry S. Truman becomes president

Hitler commits suicide; German forces surrender

The Potsdam Peace Conference

The United Nations Charter ratified in San Francisco

The Labour Party wins British General Election

Atomic bombs dropped on Hiroshima and Nagasaki

Surrender of Japanese forces ends World War II

Trial of Nazi war criminals opens at Nuremberg

All-India Congress demands British withdrawal from India

De Gaulle elected president of French Provisional Government; resigns the next year

Betjeman's *New Bats in Old Belfries*

Britten's *Peter Grimes*

Orwell's *Animal Farm*

Russell's *History of Western Philosophy*

Sartre's *The Age of Reason*

Edith Sitwell's *The Song of the Cold*

Waugh's *Brideshead Revisited*

Births of Wendy Cope and Peter Reading

1946   Bills to nationalize railways, coal mines, and the Bank of England passed in Britain

Nuremberg Trials concluded

United Nations General Assembly meets in New York as its permanent headquarters

The Arab Council inaugurated in Britain

Frederick Ashton's *Symphonic Variations*

Britten's *The Rape of Lucretia*

David Lean's *Great Expectations*

O'Neill's *The Iceman Cometh*

Roberto Rosselini's *Paisà*

Dylan Thomas' *Deaths and Entrances*

1947   President Truman announces program of aid to Greece and Turkey and outlines the "Truman Doctrine"

Independence of India proclaimed; partition between India and Pakistan, and communal strife between Hindus and Moslems follows

General Marshall calls for a European recovery program

First supersonic air flight

Britain's first atomic pile at Harwell comes into operation

Edinburgh festival established

Discovery of the Dead Sea Scrolls in Palestine

Princess Elizabeth marries Philip Mountbatten, duke of Edinburgh

Auden's *Age of Anxiety*

Camus's *La Peste*

Chaplin's *Monsieur Verdoux*

Lowry's *Under the Volcano*

Priestley's *An Inspector Calls*

Edith Sitwell's *The Shadow of Cain*

Waugh's *Scott-King's Modern Europe*

1948 Gandhi assassinated

Czech Communist Party seizes power

Pan-European movement (1948–1958) begins with the formation of the permanent Organization for European Economic Cooperation (OEEC)

Berlin airlift begins as the Soviet Union halts road and rail traffic to the city

British mandate in Palestine ends; Israeli provisional government formed

Yugoslavia expelled from Soviet bloc

Columbia Records introduces the long-playing record

Truman elected of the United States for second term

Greene's *The Heart of the Matter*

Huxley's *Ape and Essence*

Leavis' *The Great Tradition*

Pound's *Cantos*

Priestley's *The Linden Tree*

Waugh's *The Loved One*

1949 North Atlantic Treaty Organization established with headquarters in Brussels

Berlin blockade lifted

German Federal Republic recognized; capital established at Bonn

Konrad Adenauer becomes German chancellor

Mao Tse-tung becomes chairman of the People's Republic of China following Communist victory over the Nationalists

Peter Ackroyd born

Simone de Beauvoir's *The Second Sex*

Cary's *A Fearful Joy*

Arthur Miller's *Death of a Salesman*

Orwell's *Nineteen Eighty-four*

1950 Korean War breaks out

Nobel Prize for literature awarded to Bertrand Russell

R. H. S. Crossman's *The God That Failed*

T. S. Eliot's *The Cocktail Party*

Fry's *Venus Observed*

Doris Lessing's *The Grass Is Singing*

C. S. Lewis' *The Chronicles of Narnia* (1950–1956)

Wyndham Lewis' *Rude Assignment*

George Orwell's *Shooting an Elephant*

Carol Reed's *The Third Man*

Dylan Thomas' *Twenty-six Poems*

A. N. Wilson born

1951 Guy Burgess and Donald Maclean defect from Britain to the Soviet Union

The Conservative party under Winston Churchill wins British general election

The Festival of Britain celebrates both the centenary of the Crystal Palace Exhibition and British postwar recovery

Electric power is produced by atomic energy at Arcon, Idaho

W. H. Auden's *Nones*

Samuel Beckett's *Molloy* and *Malone Dies*

Benjamin Britten's *Billy Budd*

Greene's *The End of the Affair*

Akira Kurosawa's *Rashomon*

Wyndham Lewis' *Rotting Hill*

CHRONOLOGY

Anthony Powell's *A Question of Upbringing* (first volume of *A Dance to the Music of Time*, 1951–1975)

J. D. Salinger's *The Catcher in the Rye*

C. P. Snow's *The Masters*

Igor Stravinsky's *The Rake's Progress*

1952–

Reign of Elizabeth II

At Eniwetok Atoll the United States detonates the first hydrogen bomb

The European Coal and Steel Community comes into being

Radiocarbon dating introduced to archaeology

Michael Ventris deciphers Linear B script

Dwight D. Eisenhower elected president of the United States

Beckett's *Waiting for Godot*

Charles Chaplin's *Limelight*

Ernest Hemingway's *The Old Man and the Sea*

Arthur Koestler's *Arrow in the Blue*

F. R. Leavis' *The Common Pursuit*

Lessing's *Martha Quest* (first volume of *The Children of Violence*, 1952–1965)

C. S. Lewis' *Mere Christianity*

Thomas' *Collected Poems*

Evelyn Waugh's *Men at Arms* (first volume of *Sword of Honour*, 1952–1961)

Angus Wilson's *Hemlock and After*

1953   Constitution for a European political community drafted

Julius and Ethel Rosenberg executed for passing U.S. secrets to the Soviet Union

Cease-fire declared in Korea

Edmund Hillary and his Sherpa guide, Tenzing Norkay, scale Mt. Everest

Nobel Prize for literature awarded to Winston Churchill

General Mohammed Naguib proclaims Egypt a republic

Beckett's *Watt*

Joyce Cary's *Except the Lord*

Robert Graves's *Poems 1953*

1954   First atomic submarine, *Nautilus,* is launched by the United States

Dien Bien Phu captured by the Vietminh

Geneva Conference ends French dominion over Indochina

U.S. Supreme Court declares racial segregation in schools unconstitutional

Nasser becomes president of Egypt

Nobel Prize for literature awarded to Ernest Hemingway

Kingsley Amis' *Lucky Jim*

John Betjeman's *A Few Late Chrysanthemums*

William Golding's *Lord of the Flies*

Christopher Isherwood's *The World in the Evening*

Koestler's *The Invisible Writing*

Iris Murdoch's *Under the Net*

C. P. Snow's *The New Men*

Thomas' *Under Milk Wood* published posthumously

1955   Warsaw Pact signed

West Germany enters NATO as Allied occupation ends

The Conservative party under Anthony Eden wins British general election

Cary's *Not Honour More*

Greene's *The Quiet American*

Philip Larkin's *The Less Deceived*

F. R. Leavis' *D. H. Lawrence, Novelist*

Vladimir Nabokov's *Lolita*

Patrick White's *The Tree of Man*

1956   Nasser's nationalization of the Suez Canal leads to Israeli, British, and French armed intervention

Uprising in Hungary suppressed by Soviet troops

Khrushchev denounces Stalin at Twentieth Communist Party Congress

Eisenhower reelected president of the United States

Anthony Burgess' *Time for a Tiger*

CHRONOLOGY

Golding's *Pincher Martin*

Murdoch's *Flight from the Enchanter*

John Osborne's *Look Back in Anger*

Snow's *Homecomings*

Edmund Wilson's *Anglo-Saxon Attitudes*

1957 The Soviet Union launches the first artificial earth satellite, *Sputnik I*

Eden succeeded by Harold Macmillan

Suez Canal reopened

Eisenhower Doctrine formulated

Parliament receives the Wolfenden Report on Homosexuality and Prostitution

Nobel Prize for literature awarded to Albert Camus

Beckett's *Endgame* and *All That Fall*

Lawrence Durrell's *Justine* (first volume of *The Alexandria Quartet*, 1957–1960)

Ted Hughes's *The Hawk in the Rain*

Murdoch's *The Sandcastle*

V. S. Naipaul's *The Mystic Masseur*

Eugene O'Neill's *Long Day's Journey into Night*

Osborne's *The Entertainer*

Muriel Spark's *The Comforters*

White's *Voss*

1958 European Economic Community established

Khrushchev succeeds Bulganin as Soviet premier

Charles de Gaulle becomes head of France's newly constituted Fifth Republic

The United Arab Republic formed by Egypt and Syria

The United States sends troops into Lebanon

First U.S. satellite, *Explorer 1*, launched

Nobel Prize for literature awarded to Boris Pasternak

Beckett's *Krapp's Last Tape*

John Kenneth Galbraith's *The Affluent Society*

Greene's *Our Man in Havana*

Murdoch's *The Bell*

Pasternak's *Dr. Zhivago*

Snow's *The Conscience of the Rich*

1959 Fidel Castro assumes power in Cuba

St. Lawrence Seaway opens

The European Free Trade Association founded

Alaska and Hawaii become the forty-ninth and fiftieth states

The Conservative party under Harold Macmillan wins British general election

Brendan Behan's *The Hostage*

Golding's *Free Fall*

Graves's *Collected Poems*

Koestler's *The Sleepwalkers*

Harold Pinter's *The Birthday Party*

Snow's *The Two Cultures and the Scientific Revolution*

Spark's *Memento Mori*

1960 South Africa bans the African National Congress and Pan-African Congress

The Congo achieves independence

John F. Kennedy elected president of the United States

The U.S. bathyscaphe *Trieste* descends to 35,800 feet

Publication of the unexpurgated *Lady Chatterley's Lover* permitted by court

Auden's *Hommage to Clio*

Betjeman's *Summoned by Bells*

Pinter's *The Caretaker*

Snow's *The Affair*

David Storey's *This Sporting Life*

1961 South Africa leaves the British Commonwealth

Sierra Leone and Tanganyika achieve independence

The Berlin Wall erected

The New English Bible published

Beckett's *How It Is*

Greene's *A Burnt-Out Case*

CHRONOLOGY

Koestler's *The Lotus and the Robot*

Murdoch's *A Severed Head*

Naipaul's *A House for Mr Biswas*

Osborne's *Luther*

Spark's *The Prime of Miss Jean Brodie*

White's *Riders in the Chariot*

1962 John Glenn becomes first U.S. astronaut to orbit earth

The United States launches the spacecraft *Mariner* to explore Venus

Algeria achieves independence

Cuban missile crisis ends in withdrawal of Soviet missiles from Cuba

Adolf Eichmann executed in Israel for Nazi war crimes

Second Vatican Council convened by Pope John XXIII

Nobel Prize for literature awarded to John Steinbeck

Edward Albee's *Who's Afraid of Virginia Woolf?*

Beckett's *Happy Days*

Anthony Burgess' *A Clockwork Orange* and *The Wanting Seed*

Aldous Huxley's *Island*

Isherwood's *Down There on a Visit*

Lessing's *The Golden Notebook*

Nabokov's *Pale Fire*

Aleksandr Solzhenitsyn's *One Day in the Life of Ivan Denisovich*

1963 Britain, the United States, and the Soviet Union sign a test-ban treaty

Birth of Simon Armitage

Britain refused entry to the European Economic Community

The Soviet Union puts into orbit the first woman astronaut, Valentina Tereshkova

Paul VI becomes pope

President Kennedy assassinated; Lyndon B. Johnson assumes office

Nobel Prize for literature awarded to George Seferis

Britten's *War Requiem*

John Fowles's *The Collector*

Murdoch's *The Unicorn*

Spark's *The Girls of Slender Means*

Storey's *Radcliffe*

John Updike's *The Centaur*

1964 Tonkin Gulf incident leads to retaliatory strikes by U.S. aircraft against North Vietnam

Greece and Turkey contend for control of Cyprus

Britain grants licenses to drill for oil in the North Sea

The Shakespeare Quatercentenary celebrated

Lyndon Johnson elected president of the United States

The Labour party under Harold Wilson wins British general election

Nobel Prize for literature awarded to Jean-Paul Sartre

Saul Bellow's *Herzog*

Burgess' *Nothing Like the Sun*

Golding's *The Spire*

Isherwood's *A Single Man*

Stanley Kubrick's *Dr. Strangelove*

Larkin's *The Whitsun Weddings*

Naipaul's *An Area of Darkness*

Peter Shaffer's *The Royal Hunt of the Sun*

Snow's *Corridors of Power*

1965 The first U.S. combat forces land in Vietnam

The U.S. spacecraft Mariner transmits photographs of Mars

British Petroleum Company finds oil in the North Sea

War breaks out between India and Pakistan

Rhodesia declares its independence

Ontario power failure blacks out the Canadian and U.S. east coasts

Nobel Prize for literature awarded to Mikhail Sholokhov

Robert Lowell's *For the Union Dead*

Norman Mailer's *An American Dream*

Osborne's *Inadmissible Evidence*

CHRONOLOGY

Pinter's *The Homecoming*

Spark's *The Mandelbaum Gate*

1966   The Labour party under Harold Wilson wins British general election

The Archbishop of Canterbury visits Pope Paul VI

Florence, Italy, severely damaged by floods

Paris exhibition celebrates Picasso's eighty-fifth birthday

Fowles's *The Magus*

Greene's *The Comedians*

Osborne's *A Patriot for Me*

Paul Scott's *The Jewel in the Crown* (first volume of *The Raj Quartet*, 1966–1975)

White's *The Solid Mandala*

1967   Thurgood Marshall becomes first black U.S. Supreme Court justice

Six-Day War pits Israel against Egypt and Syria

Biafra's secession from Nigeria leads to civil war

Francis Chichester completes solo circumnavigation of the globe

Dr. Christiaan Barnard performs first heart transplant operation, in South Africa

China explodes its first hydrogen bomb

Golding's *The Pyramid*

Hughes's *Wodwo*

Isherwood's *A Meeting by the River*

Naipaul's *The Mimic Men*

Tom Stoppard's *Rosencrantz and Guildenstern Are Dead*

Orson Welles's *Chimes at Midnight*

Angus Wilson's *No Laughing Matter*

1968   Violent student protests erupt in France and West Germany

Warsaw Pact troops occupy Czechoslovakia

Violence in Northern Ireland causes Britain to send in troops

Tet offensive by Communist forces launched against South Vietnam's cities

Theater censorship ended in Britain

Robert Kennedy and Martin Luther King Jr. assassinated

Richard M. Nixon elected president of the United States

Booker Prize for fiction established

Durrell's *Tunc*

Graves's *Poems 1965–1968*

Osborne's *The Hotel in Amsterdam*

Snow's *The Sleep of Reason*

Solzhenitsyn's *The First Circle* and *Cancer Ward*

Spark's *The Public Image*

1969   Humans set foot on the moon for the first time when astronauts descend to its surface in a landing vehicle from the U.S. spacecraft *Apollo 11*

The Soviet unmanned spacecraft *Venus V* lands on Venus

Capital punishment abolished in Britain

Colonel Muammar Qaddafi seizes power in Libya

Solzhenitsyn expelled from the Soviet Union

Nobel Prize for literature awarded to Samuel Beckett

Carter's *The Magic Toyshop*

Fowles's *The French Lieutenant's Woman*

Storey's *The Contractor*

1970   Civil war in Nigeria ends with Biafra's surrender

U.S. planes bomb Cambodia

The Conservative party under Edward Heath wins British general election

Nobel Prize for literature awarded to Aleksandr Solzhenitsyn

Durrell's *Nunquam*

Hughes's *Crow*

F. R. Leavis and Q. D. Leavis' *Dickens the Novelist*

Snow's *Last Things*

Spark's *The Driver's Seat*

1971   Communist China given Nationalist China's UN seat

CHRONOLOGY

Decimal currency introduced to Britain

Indira Gandhi becomes India's prime minister

Nobel Prize for literature awarded to Heinrich Böll

Bond's *The Pope's Wedding*

Naipaul's *In a Free State*

Pinter's *Old Times*

Spark's *Not to Disturb*

Birth of Sarah Kane

1972   The civil strife of "Bloody Sunday" causes Northern Ireland to come under the direct rule of Westminster

Nixon becomes the first U.S. president to visit Moscow and Beijing

The Watergate break-in precipitates scandal in the United States

Eleven Israeli athletes killed by terrorists at Munich Olympics

Nixon reelected president of the United States

Bond's *Lear*

Snow's *The Malcontents*

Stoppard's *Jumpers*

1973   Britain, Ireland, and Denmark enter European Economic Community

Egypt and Syria attack Israel in the Yom Kippur War

Energy crisis in Britain reduces production to a three-day week

Nobel Prize for literature awarded to Patrick White

Bond's *The Sea*

Greene's *The Honorary Consul*

Lessing's *The Summer Before the Dark*

Murdoch's *The Black Prince*

Shaffer's *Equus*

White's *The Eye of the Storm*

1974   Miners strike in Britain

Greece's military junta overthrown

Emperor Haile Selassie of Ethiopia deposed

President Makarios of Cyprus replaced by military coup

Nixon resigns as U.S. president and is succeeded by Gerald R. Ford

Betjeman's *A Nip in the Air*

Bond's *Bingo*

Durrell's *Monsieur* (first volume of *The Avignon Quintet*, 1974–1985)

Larkin's *The High Windows*

Solzhenitsyn's *The Gulag Archipelago*

Spark's *The Abbess of Crewe*

1975   The U.S. *Apollo* and Soviet *Soyuz* spacecrafts rendezvous in space

The Helsinki Accords on human rights signed

U.S. forces leave Vietnam

King Juan Carlos succeeds Franco as Spain's head of state

Nobel Prize for literature awarded to Eugenio Montale

1976   New U.S. copyright law goes into effect

Israeli commandos free hostages from hijacked plane at Entebbe, Uganda

British and French SST Concordes make first regularly scheduled commercial flights

The United States celebrates its bicentennial

Jimmy Carter elected president of the United States

Byron and Shelley manuscripts discovered in Barclay's Bank, Pall Mall

Hughes's *Seasons' Songs*

Koestler's *The Thirteenth Tribe*

Scott's *Staying On*

Spark's *The Take-over*

White's *A Fringe of Leaves*

1977   Silver jubilee of Queen Elizabeth II celebrated

Egyptian president Anwar el-Sadat visits Israel

"Gang of Four" expelled from Chinese Communist party

First woman ordained in the U.S. Episcopal church

After twenty-nine years in power, Israel's Labour party is defeated by the Likud party

Fowles's *Daniel Martin*

Hughes's *Gaudete*

1978   Treaty between Israel and Egypt negotiated at Camp David

Pope John Paul I dies a month after his coronation and is succeeded by Karol Cardinal Wojtyla, who takes the name John Paul II

Former Italian premier Aldo Moro murdered by left-wing terrorists

Nobel Prize for literature awarded to Isaac Bashevis Singer

Greene's *The Human Factor*

Hughes's *Cave Birds*

Murdoch's *The Sea, The Sea*

1979   The United States and China establish diplomatic relations

Ayatollah Khomeini takes power in Iran and his supporters hold U.S. embassy staff hostage in Teheran

Rhodesia becomes Zimbabwe

Earl Mountbatten assassinated

The Soviet Union invades Afghanistan

The Conservative party under Margaret Thatcher wins British general election

Nobel Prize for literature awarded to Odysseus Elytis

Golding's *Darkness Visible*

Hughes's *Moortown*

Lessing's *Shikasta* (first volume of *Canopus in Argos, Archives*)

Naipaul's *A Bend in the River*

Spark's *Territorial Rights*

White's *The Twyborn Affair*

1980   Iran-Iraq war begins

Strikes in Gdansk give rise to the Solidarity movement

Mt. St. Helen's erupts in Washington State

British steelworkers strike for the first time since 1926

More than fifty nations boycott Moscow Olympics

Ronald Reagan elected president of the United States

Burgess's *Earthly Powers*

Golding's *Rites of Passage*

Shaffer's *Amadeus*

Storey's *A Prodigal Child*

Angus Wilson's *Setting the World on Fire*

1981   Greece admitted to the European Economic Community

Iran hostage crisis ends with release of U.S. embassy staff

Twelve Labour MPs and nine peers found British Social Democratic party

Socialist party under François Mitterand wins French general election

Rupert Murdoch buys *The Times* of London

Turkish gunman wounds Pope John Paul II in assassination attempt

U.S. gunman wounds President Reagan in assassination attempt

President Sadat of Egypt assassinated

Nobel Prize for literature awarded to Elias Canetti

Spark's *Loitering with Intent*

1982   Britain drives Argentina's invasion force out of the Falkland Islands

U.S. space shuttle makes first successful trip

Yuri Andropov becomes general secretary of the Central Committee of the Soviet Communist party

Israel invades Lebanon

First artificial heart implanted at Salt Lake City hospital

Bellow's *The Dean's December*

Greene's *Monsignor Quixote*

1983   South Korean airliner with 269 aboard shot down after straying into Soviet airspace

U.S. forces invade Grenada following left-wing coup

Widespread protests erupt over placement of nuclear missiles in Europe

The £1 coin comes into circulation in Britain

Australia wins the America's Cup

Nobel Prize for literature awarded to William Golding

Hughes's *River*

Murdoch's *The Philosopher's Pupil*

1984   Konstantin Chernenko becomes general secretary of the Central Committee of the Soviet Communist party

Prime Minister Indira Gandhi of India assassinated by Sikh bodyguards

Reagan reelected president of the United States

Toxic gas leak at Bhopal, India, plant kills 2,000

British miners go on strike

Irish Republican Army attempts to kill Prime Minister Thatcher with bomb detonated at a Brighton hotel

World Court holds against U.S. mining of Nicaraguan harbors

Golding's *The Paper Men*

Lessing's *The Diary of Jane Somers*

Spark's *The Only Problem*

1985   United States deploys cruise missiles in Europe

Mikhail Gorbachev becomes general secretary of the Soviet Communist party following death of Konstantin Chernenko

Riots break out in Handsworth district (Birmingham) and Brixton

Republic of Ireland gains consultative role in Northern Ireland

State of emergency is declared in South Africa

Nobel Prize for literature awarded to Claude Simon

A. N. Wilson's *Gentlemen in England*

Lessing's *The Good Terrorist*

Murdoch's *The Good Apprentice*

Fowles's *A Maggot*

1986   U.S. space shuttle *Challenger* explodes

United States attacks Libya

Atomic power plant at Chernobyl destroyed in accident

Corazon Aquino becomes president of the Philippines

Giotto spacecraft encounters Comet Halley

Nobel Prize for literature awarded to Wole Soyinka

Final volume of *Oxford English Dictionary* supplement published

Amis's *The Old Devils*

Ishiguro's *An Artist of the Floating World*

A. N. Wilson's *Love Unknown*

Powell's *The Fisher King*

1987   Gorbachev begins reform of Communist party of the Soviet Union

Stock market collapses

Iran-contra affair reveals that Reagan administration used money from arms sales to Iran to fund Nicaraguan rebels

Palestinian uprising begins in Israeli-occupied territories

Nobel Prize for literature awarded to Joseph Brodsky

Golding's *Close Quarters*

Burgess's *Little Wilson and Big God*

Drabble's *The Radiant Way*

1988   Soviet Union begins withdrawing troops from Afghanistan

Iranian airliner shot down by U.S. Navy over Persian Gulf

War between Iran and Iraq ends

George Bush elected president of the United States

Pan American flight 103 destroyed over Lockerbie, Scotland

Nobel Prize for literature awarded to Naguib Mafouz

Greene's *The Captain and the Enemy*

Amis's *Difficulties with Girls*

Rushdie's *Satanic Verses*

1989   Ayatollah Khomeini pronounces death sentence on Salman Rushdie; Great Britain and Iran sever diplomatic relations

F. W. de Klerk becomes president of South Africa

Chinese government crushes student demonstration in Tiananmen Square

CHRONOLOGY

Communist regimes are weakened or abolished in Poland, Czechoslovakia, Hungary, East Germany, and Romania

Lithuania nullifies its inclusion in Soviet Union

Nobel Prize for literature awarded to José Cela

Second edition of *Oxford English Dictionary* published

Drabble's *A Natural Curiosity*

Murdoch's *The Message to the Planet*

Amis's *London Fields*

Ishiguro's *The Remains of the Day*

1990   Communist monopoly ends in Bulgaria

Riots break out against community charge in England

First women ordained priests in Church of England

Civil war breaks out in Yugoslavia; Croatia and Slovenia declare independence

Bush and Gorbachev sign START agreement to reduce nuclear-weapons arsenals

President Jean-Baptiste Aristide overthrown by military in Haiti

Boris Yeltsin elected president of Russia

Dissolution of the Soviet Union

Nobel Prize for literature awarded to Nadine Gordimer

1992   U.N. Conference on Environment and Development (the "Earth Summit") meets in Rio de Janeiro

Prince and Princess of Wales separate

War in Bosnia-Herzegovina intensifies

Bill Clinton elected president of the United States in three-way race with Bush and independent candidate H. Ross Perot

Nobel Prize for literature awarded to Derek Walcott

1993   Czechoslovakia divides into the Czech Republic and Slovakia; playwright Vaclav Havel elected president of the Czech Republic

Britain ratifies Treaty on European Union (the "Maastricht Treaty")

U.S. troops provide humanitarian aid amid famine in Somalia

United States, Canada, and Mexico sign North American Free Trade Agreement

Nobel Prize for literature awarded to Toni Morrison

1994   Nelson Mandela elected president in South Africa's first post-apartheid election

Jean-Baptiste Aristide restored to presidency of Haiti

Clinton health care reforms rejected by Congress

Civil war in Rwanda

Republicans win control of both houses of Congress for first time in forty years

Prime Minister Albert Reynolds of Ireland meets with Gerry Adams, president of Sinn Fein

Nobel Prize for literature awarded to Kenzaburo Õe

Amis's *You Can't Do Both*

Naipaul's *A Way in the World*

1995   Britain and Irish Republican Army engage in diplomatic talks

Barings Bank forced into bankruptcy as a result of a maverick bond trader's losses

United States restores full diplomatic relations with Vietnam

NATO initiates air strikes in Bosnia

Death of Stephen Spender

Israeli Prime Minister Yitzhak Rabin assassinated

Nobel Prize for literature awarded to Seamus Heaney

1996   IRA breaks cease-fire; Sein Fein representatives barred from Northern Ireland peace talks

Prince and Princess of Wales divorce

Cease-fire agreement in Chechnia; Russian forces begin to withdraw

Boris Yeltsin reelected president of Russia

Bill Clinton reelected president of the United States

CHRONOLOGY

Nobel Prize for literature awarded to Wisława Szymborska

1996   British government destroys around 100,000 cows suspected of infection with Creutzfeldt-Jakob, or "mad cow" disease

1997   Diana, Princess of Wales, dies in an automobile accident

Unveiling of first fully-cloned adult animal, a sheep named Dolly

Booker McConnell Prize for fiction awarded to Arundhati Roy

1998   United States renews bombing of Bagdad, Iraq

Independent legislature and Parliaments return to Scotland and Wales

Ted Hughes, Symbolist poet and husband of Sylvia Plath, dies

Booker McConnell Prize for fiction awarded to Ian McEwan

Nobel Prize for literature awarded to Jose Saramago

1999   King Hussein of Jordan dies

United Nations responds militarily to Serbian President Slobodan Milosevic's escalation of crisis in Kosovo

Booker McConnell Prize for fiction awarded to J. M. Coetzee

Nobel Prize for literature awarded to Günter Grass

2000   Penelope Fitzgerald dies

J. K. Rowling's *Harry Potter and the Goblet of Fire* sells more than 300,000 copies in its first day

Oil blockades by fuel haulers protesting high oil taxes bring much of Britain to a standstill

Slobodan Milosevic loses Serbian general election to Vojislav Kostunica

Death of Scotland's First Minister, Donald Dewar

Nobel Prize for literature awarded to Gao Xingjian

Booker McConnell Prize for fiction awarded to Margaret Atwood

George W. Bush, son of former president George Bush, becomes president of the United States after Supreme Court halts recount of closest election in history

Death of former Canadian Prime Minister Pierre Elliot Trudeau

Human Genome Project researchers announce that they have a complete map of the genetic code of a human chromosome

Vladimir Putin succeeds Boris Yeltsin as president of Russia

British Prime Minister Tony Blair's son Leo is born, making him the first child born to a sitting prime minister in 152 years

2001   In Britain, the House of Lords passes legislation that legalizes the creation of cloned human embryos

British Prime Minister Tony Blair wins second term

Margaret Atwood's *The Blind Assassin* wins Booker McConnell Prize for fiction

Kazuo Ishiguro's *When We Were Orphans*

Trezza Azzopardi's *The Hiding Place*

Terrorists attack World Trade Center and Pentagon with hijacked airplanes, resulting in the collapse of the World Trade Center towers and the deaths of thousands. Passengers of a third hijacked plane thwart their hijackers, resulting in a crash landing in Pennsylvania. The attacks are thought to be organized by Osama bin Laden, the leader of an international terrorist network known as al Qaeda

Ian McEwan's *An Atonement*

Rushdie's *Fury*

Peter Carey's *True History of the Kelly Gang*

Death of Eudora Welty

Death of W. G. Sebald

List of Contributors

SCOTT ASHLEY. Sir James Knott Research Fellow in History at the University of Newcastle. He has just completed a book on images of barbarians in the early Middle Ages and is beginning one on primitivism in Britain and Ireland from 1750 to 1950. **James Macpherson**

SUSAN BALÉE. Writer. Her essays and reviews have appeared in *The Hudson Review, The Weekly Standard, The Women's Review of Books, The Philadelphia Inquirer, Victorian Literature and Culture,* and a variety of other magazines. She is the author of the first biography of Flannery O'Connor (Chelsea House, 1994), and two memoirs of growing up in the South (the first appeared in *Grand Tour* in 1997; the second is forthcoming in *Sunscripts* 2002). Balée teaches creative writing at the Suncoast Writers' Conference and the Philadelphia Writers' Conference. She lives outside Philadelphia. **Mary Elizabeth Braddon**

PAUL BIBIRE. Writer and lecturer. Formerly a lecturer in the School of English, University of St. Andrews, and of the Department of Anglo-Saxon, Norse, and Celtic, University of Cambridge. Since retirement he has been an honorary lecturer at the University of St. Andrews in Scotland in the Department of Medieval History in the School of History. Research includes Old English and Old Norse language and literature; West and North Germanic philology; the historical development of the phonological and morphological systems of Old English and Old Norse from their Indo-European and Germanic origins; Old English dialects; the development of Germanic legend and its representation in early English and Scandinavian poetry; Norse paganism and pagan mythology (sources for its knowledge and modes of its understanding); Icelandic sagas and other prose (in particular formal analysis); Norse court (*skaldic*) poetry. **Old Norse Literature**

FRED BILSON. Lecturer in English, linguistics, and computer studies. Currently works supporting dyslexic students at the University of Glamorgan, Trefforest, South Wales. **Alan Bennett**

SANDIE BYRNE. Fellow in English at Balliol College, Oxford. Her publications include works on eighteenth- and nineteenth-century fiction and twentieth-century poetry. **William Dunbar**

GERRY CAMBRIDGE. Poet and Editor. Edits the Scottish-American poetry magazine, *The Dark Horse*. His own books of verse include *The Shell House* (Scottish Cultural Press, 1995), *'Nothing But Heather!': Scottish Nature in Poems, Photographs and Prose* (Luath Press, 1999), illustrated with his own natural history photographs, and *The Praise of Swans* (Shoestring Press, 2000). Cambridge was the 1997–1999 Brownsbank Fellow, based at Hugh MacDiarmid's former home, Brownsbank Cottage, near Biggar in Scotland. His latest collection is *Madame Fi Fi's Farewell and Other Poems* (Luath Press, 2002). **Wendy Cope**

JULIE HEARN. Writer. Former journalist who, in 1999, received an M.St in women's studies from Oxford University. It is a continuing source of amusement to her that she went from writing a weekly mother and baby column for the national Daily Star to researching witch-hunting and maternal power in early modern England. Her first novel is to be published by Oxford University Press in January 2003. **Barbara Comyns**

BRIAN HENRY. Assistant Professor of English and Director of the Creative Writing Program, University of Georgia. Author of *Astronaut*, a book of poetry published in three countries. Editor of *Verse* and Senior Editor of Verse Press. Poetry critic for the *New York Times Book Review*, *The Kenyon Review*, *Boston Review*, and many other publications. Previous contributor to *British Writers* ("John Keats") and *American Writers* ("Anne Carson," "Richard Ford," "Charles Simic," "David Foster Wallace"). **Simon Armitage**

PHILIP HOBSBAUM. Emeritus Professor of English Literature and Doctor of Letters at the University of Glasgow. Pupil of F. R. Leavis at Downing College, Cambridge; research student with William Empson at the University of Sheffield (from which he received an honorary Doctor of Letters in 2002). Hobsbaum has started several famous creative writing groups whose members have included Peter Redgrove, Seamus Heaney, and Alasdair Gray. Author of seven critical books, including *Metre, Rhythm and Verse Form* (1996); four collections of poems; sixty contributions to reference works; seventy-seven articles, mostly concerned with modern poetry, in academic and literary journals. **Francis Cornford and T. F. Powys**

JUDITH KITCHEN. Writer-in-Residence at the State University of New York, Brockport. She is the author of two collections of personal essays, a study of the work of William Stafford, one book of poetry, and a novel. Winner of the S. Mariella Gable Award from Graywolf Press, she has co-edited two anthologies of nonfiction for W. W. Norton. She divides her time between upstate New York and the Olympic Peninsula. **W. G. Sebald**

MELISSA KNOX. is the author of *Oscar Wilde: A Long and Lovely Suicide* (Yale University Press, 1992), a psychoanalytic biography, and *Oscar Wilde in the 1990s: The Critic as Creator* (Camden House, 2002). She has written on numerous literary figures, among them Anaïs Nin, Dorothy Parker, Paul Monette, and Harold Pinter. She is

writing a book on women over forty who experience pregnancy and childbirth. **Charles Robert Maturin**

J. ROGER KURTZ. Associate Professor of English at the State University of New York, Brockport. A scholar of East African literatures and the author of *Urban Obsessions, Urban Fears: The Postcolonial Kenyan Novel* (1998), he is currently engaged in a study of the life and work of Marjorie Oludhe Macgoye. **Ngũgĩ wa Thiongo**

JOSEPH LENNON. Assistant Professor of English at Manhattan College in New York City. He has published essays, articles, reviews, and poems in *Irish Studies* and literary journals such as *The Recorder* and *The Denver Quarterly* and is included in Nortre Dame's *Anthology of Irish American Poetry*. His essays have been published in numerous collections, including *Ireland and Post-colonial Theory* (Cork UP). Presently he is completing a book entitled *The Oriental and the Celt: Irish Orientalism and Empire* (forthcoming with Syracuse UP). **George Russell (AE)**

PHILIP HAYDN BEUNO FRANCIS PARRY. Professor and writer. Parry is a graduate of the University of Bristol, of the University of Birmingham's Shakespeare Institute, and of the University of St Andrews. He has taught at the last institution since 1976 where he specializes in Shakespeare studies (and has written about cross-dressing, boy actors, and color-blind casting); twentieth-century British and American drama; and in theater history and dramaturgical theory. He has also written and directed plays that have been performed at the Edinburgh Festival Fringe. **Sarah Kane**

ROBERT POTTS. Co-editor of *Poetry Review* magazine and Politics Editor of the *Times Literary Supplement*. He has written about poetry for a number of publications including *British Writers*. **Peter Reading**

JOHN REDMOND. Visiting Assistant Professor at Macalester College, St. Paul, Minnesota. Previously, he taught at Queen Mary and Westfield

College, London, and took his doctorate at St. Hugh's College, Oxford. His first collection of poems, *Thumb's Width*, was published by Carcanet Press, Manchester, in 2001 and nominated for The Guardian First Book Award. He is an assistant editor of *Thumbscrew*. **Michael Longley**

N. S. THOMPSON. Lecturer in English at Christ Church, Oxford. He is the author of *Chaucer, Boccaccio and the Debate of Love* (1997) and articles on medieval and modern literature for a variety of journals, as well as many reviews for the *Times Literary Supplement*. He has translated several works from the Italian and a selection of his poetry was included in *Oxford Poets 2001: An Anthology*. **A. E. Coppard**

ANDREW ZAWACKI. Writer. Coeditor of the international journal *Verse* and a reviewer for *Boston Review*, he is the author of a book of poetry, *By Reason of Breakings* (University of Georgia Press, 2002), and a chapbook, *Masquerade* (Vagabond Press, 2001). A former fellow of the Slovenian Writers' Association, he edited the anthology *Afterwards: Slovenian Writing 1945–1995* (White Pine Press, 1999). He studies in the Committee on Social Thought at the University of Chicago. **Christopher Wallace-Crabbe**

BRITISH WRITERS

SIMON ARMITAGE

(1963–)

Brian Henry

BORN IN HUDDERSFIELD, West Yorkshire, on 26 May 1963, Simon Armitage was raised in Marsden and attended Colne Valley High School, where he was an average student. After high school, he studied geography at Portsmouth Polytechnic (now the University of Portsmouth), then worked with juvenile delinquents for two years before returning to school for a Certificate of Qualification in Social Work at Manchester University, where he wrote a thesis on the psychology of television violence. After receiving his degree, he worked as a probation officer in Manchester for six years before quitting his job to devote himself full-time to writing. That decision has given Armitage the freedom to become, according to the poet-critic David Wheatley, "the most imaginative and prolific poet now writing" in England (p. 55).

Having grown up in Huddersfield, an industrial town north of London, Armitage was not exposed to poetry in a concentrated fashion until he graduated from Portsmouth Polytechnic, enrolled in Peter Sansom's poetry writing workshop, and started reading twentieth-century poetry. Armitage's earliest influences were Ted Hughes, Philip Larkin, Tony Harrison, W. H. Auden, Paul Muldoon, Frank O'Hara, Robert Lowell, John Berryman, and Weldon Kees. He read voraciously, and his poetic sensibility developed with astonishing speed. Within a decade, this young poet from a working-class background became acknowledged as the heir to Auden and Larkin. Formally versatile yet accessible, original yet aware of tradition, and consummately English in its diction and concerns, Armitage's poetry appeals to a broad spectrum of readers. Critics tend to praise Armitage's skill and virtuosity, which they link to Auden, and general readers look to Armitage for his unsentimental examinations of ordinary English life, for which Larkin was famous. Increasingly, critics have celebrated both aspects of Armitage's work, as when William Scammell writes, "one of the pleasures of reading [Armitage] is to enjoy the craftsmanly marriage between streetwise idioms and ancient verse forms." Scammell also argues that Armitage "renders ... arguments between elitism and populism obsolete" (pp. 52–53).

Despite his meteoric rise to poetic fame, Armitage did not immediately find support from the *Times Literary Supplement*, the *London Review of Books*, Faber and Faber, and other arms of the London poetry establishment. Rather, his early poetry was supported by small Yorkshire magazines such as *The Wide Skirt* and *The North,* as well as other non-London-based magazines, such as *Verse* and *Slow Dancer*. He published several small poetry pamphlets and won an Eric Gregory Award before the small press Bloodaxe released his first book, *Zoom!* (1989), which was a Poetry Book Society Choice and a finalist for the Whitbread Prize. Armitage then wrote a "poem film for television," *Xanadu*, which was commissioned by BBC Television, before switching to Faber and Faber, England's most prestigious publisher of poetry. Two books quickly followed: *Kid* (1992), which won the 1992 Forward Prize for Poetry and the 1993 *Sunday Times* Young Writer of the Year Award, and *Book of Matches* (1993). At this time, Armitage served briefly as poetry editor of the English publisher Chatto and Windus and of *The Guardian*. He received a 1994 award from the Lannan Foundation, and left his job as a probation officer and published *The Dead Sea Poems* (1995) the next year. In 1997, Armitage published his longest book to date, *Cloud-CuckooLand*, and his thousand-line millennium poem, *Killing Time*, was released on 24 December 1999. A *Selected Poems* appeared in 2001 as a

Poetry Book Society Choice, consolidating Armitage's prodigious output into a single volume.

In addition to his poetry collections, Armitage has published several books of prose—*Moon Country: Further Reports from Iceland* (1996), a mixed-genre travelogue written with Glyn Maxwell as a sequel to Auden's and Louis MacNeice's *Letters from Iceland*; *All Points North* (1998), a nonfiction book about Yorkshire; and *Little Green Man* (2001), a novel. Commissioned by the West Yorkshire Playhouse, his translation of Euripides' play *Heracles* was published, as *Mister Heracles*, in 2000. But Armitage remains first and foremost a poet. One of the best-selling poets in England, he regularly reads his poems on national radio, has given numerous readings around the world, and, more recently, has taught poetry writing at Manchester Metropolitan University and at the Writers' Workshop at the University of Iowa. He has a daughter, Emmeline, with his second wife, Sue Roberts, a producer at BBC Radio.

From the beginning of his career, Armitage's poems have been marked by wit and vigor, as well as by a colloquial yet well-crafted lyricism. The poet-critic David Kennedy has remarked on "the deliberately casual and colloquial components of Armitage's style," connecting it to his Northern English identity: "Armitage's work can be seen as representative of a poetry and a community of sensibility that have blossomed primarily in the North of England ... and which have come to be closely identified with the large town of Huddersfield and its environs" (p. 87). Armitage discussed this duality in a 1991 interview in *Verse*:

> The place where I live offers the urban and the rural, both at very short notice. The moors behind our house are some of the bleakest and most extreme in the country, but at the same time we are within an hour of about five major cities and a handful of big towns. Perhaps that's why a lot of my poems exist at that uncomfortable linguistic intersection where the back street meets the sheep dip.
>
> (p. 94)

Elsewhere in the interview, Armitage states, "I do have a Northern voice and I try to speak with it" (p. 94), and he also gives his "long and prepared speech which defends to the hilt my use of idiom and catchphrase in relation to idiolectical poetry:"

1. It's my voice: that's how I speak.

2. It allows me to get nearer, or associates me more closely with the speaker in the monologues.

3. Most idioms or catchphrases are images of some type, and whilst I'm not exactly "revitalising" them I am asking them to work a little harder, not just perform their common function, but introduce a second, sometimes literal or sometimes punning element.

4. They contain a good deal of music and rhythm which isn't disharmonious with the way I'm trying to construct poems.

5. ... I don't hold with the view that cliché represents a bias against the truth, in terms of there only being one truth, or poetry owning the franchise on truth.

6. I should very much like to coin an idiom. ... I like to think that ... my own efforts sitting alongside more established turns of phrase do not look out of place.

(p. 97)

This emphasis on speaking with a voice outside the literary elite, associated primarily with London and Oxford, has produced in Armitage a poetry of borders and thresholds in which seemingly opposite states—life and death, light and darkness, violence and socially acceptable behavior—are considered together if not reconciled. More recently, Michael Hulse has identified two poets "inside" Armitage: one "who knows the stories the lads are telling, ... who is defined by curiosity, zest, sociability," and one who is "humbled to a sense of smallness by the abiding power of final things." Hulse explains that "the split isn't apparent in language and technique—both poets speak in the same fast, colloquial idiom"; rather, "the divide is between the light and dark of the mind" (p. 66).

ZOOM!

Armitage's debut, *Zoom!*, immediately established him as the leading poet of his generation:

the book was widely praised by critics and proved a commercial success as well, eventually selling more than 10,000 copies. Critics reviewing *Zoom!* frequently referred to Armitage's reinvigoration of colloquial language, including clichés. Brimming with slang and bustling with energy, many of the poems in *Zoom!* seem poised between popular and high culture, between the pool hall and the university. The poems are sufficiently entertaining for general readers, but adequately literary for critics, a balance often achieved through puns, double meanings, and allusions. "Ivory," for example, consists almost entirely of clichés and slang:

No more malarkey,
　no baloney. No more cuffuffle
　or shenanigans …

No more blab,
　none of that ragtag

and bobtail business,
　or ballyhoo
　or balderdash …

(p. 74)

The poem's final imperative—"from this point forward / it's ninety-nine / and forty-four hundredths / per cent pure" (p. 74)—applies as much to language as to ivory. Hackneyed language becomes the impurity in need of elimination, or at least refreshing.

　Although nearly half of the poems in *Zoom!* are composed in quatrains, the poems in the book are freer, more casual than those in Armitage's later books. *Zoom!* reveals a poet still learning the craft, and thus can be read as Armitage's apprentice work—albeit the work of a highly skilled apprentice. David Wheatley has called the Armitage of *Zoom!* "a man with a story to tell, sometimes funny, sometimes hair-raising" (p. 73). The first poem in the book, "Snow Joke," introduces Armitage's most common poetic characteristics—a masterful handling of vernacular, a propensity toward anecdote, propulsive lyricism, a biting wit, and a dark vision:

Heard the one about the guy from Heaton Mersey?
　Wife at home, lover in Hyde, mistress

in Newton-le-Willows and two pretty girls
　in the top grade at Werneth prep. Well,

he was late and he had a good car so he snubbed
　the police warning-light and tried to finesse
　the last six miles of moorland blizzard,
　and the story goes he was stuck within minutes.

(p. 9)

The reader quickly realizes the poem is not a "joke" after all—"of course, there isn't a punchline" (p. 9)—but the story nevertheless has an ending:

They found him slumped against the steering wheel
　with VOLVO printed backwards in his frozen brow.
　And they fought in the pub over hot toddies
　as to who was to take the most credit.

Him who took the aerial to be a hawthorn twig?
　Him who figured out the contour of his car?
　Or him who said he heard the horn, moaning
　softly like an alarm clock under an eiderdown?

(p. 9)

The narrative strategy here—explaining what happened to the driver through pub talk—shows why Armitage's poetry is regarded so highly. Though accessible, "Snow Joke" is neither predictable nor traditional; the poem contains astonishing psychological, emotional, and technical depth beneath its inviting surface.

　Yet Armitage seems to be a poet often working the surface of things. He seeks honesty in his poems, avoiding obfuscation or social niceties, as when he writes "why write of whispering / when all we ever did that year was shout" (p. 12) in "Why Write of the Sun." This approach produces a medley of unappealing objects, events, and characters in *Zoom!*—a greenhouse "gone to seed" (p. 13), a man who shoots rabbits at night, people falling to their deaths from army helicopters, a house that no one will buy, drug dealers who become addicted to what they sell. Although a number of poems in the book plumb the darker side of humanity, "November" emerges as the most candid and unsettling poem in the volume: "We walk to the ward from the badly parked car / with your grandma taking four short steps to our two. / We have brought her here to die and we know it" (p. 47). Though disturbing, the poem's unflinching examination of how contemporary society manages the elderly, with "their pasty bloodless smiles, / ... their slack breasts, their stunned brains and their baldness" (p. 47), is thoroughly effective because of the commonness of the situation it depicts. The poem's narrator and his friend are so distraught they must "numb [themselves] with alcohol" later: "Inside, we feel the terror of dusk begin. / Outside we watch the evening, failing again, / and we let it happen. We can say nothing" (p. 47). The bleakest of the poems in *Zoom!*, "November," serves to weigh down the youthful buoyancy found elsewhere in the volume.

The dramatic monologues in *Zoom!*—such as "Very Simply Topping Up the Brake Fluid," narrated by an auto mechanic who humanizes the machine-centered activity; "Poem by the Boy Outside the Fire Station," narrated by a would-be arsonist; and "Eyewitness," narrated by a person whose "acuity is not what it used to be" (p. 51)—introduce a form that Armitage develops with distinction throughout his career. One of the book's most humorous monologues, "Ten Pence Story," is narrated by a ten-pence coin:

Out of the melting pot, into the mint;
next news I was loose change for a Leeds pimp,
burning a hole in his skin-tight pocket
till he tipped a busker by the precinct.

...

My lowest ebb was a seven month spell
spent head down in a stagnant wishing well

...

When they fished me out I made a few phone calls,
fed a few meters, hung round the pool halls.

(p. 64)

Despite the poem's humor, "Ten Pence Story" succeeds in engendering sympathy for the coin, which has its own "ambition": "to be flipped in Wembley's centre circle, / to twist, to turn, to hang like a planet, / to touch down on that emerald carpet" (p. 65).

More haunting than the other monologues, "Bylot Island" is written in the form of a science student's diary. The poem situates the student in a difficult environment, a conservation area in the Canadian Arctic, which is made more difficult by the other two people stationed there; one "is an oddity," and the other has asthma and keeps the narrator awake at night with his "wheezing" (p. 34). When the three have eaten all the food and the boat does not arrive on its scheduled day to pick them up, the narrator realizes they have been abandoned:

Sat on the summit all day almost praying for the sight
of the ship coming into the skyline. Nothing.

...

Sometimes when the wind rattles through the awning
we imagine the traces of strong, familiar voices
calling our names. Our names. This is serious.
At night we listen for the sea freezing over.

(p. 35)

Other poems in *Zoom!* demonstrate technical and scientific knowledge, a realm of understanding that frequently emerges in Armitage's later poems. "Getting at Stars," for example, uses text from *The New Book of Knowledge* to construct a verse essay on stars that succeeds in moving through science toward human truth: "Those who travel to the stars and back will find / an added distance in their brothers' eyes. / The speed of light is a treacherous thing" (p. 28).

KID

Armitage's second book, *Kid* (1992), extends the strengths of *Zoom!* and reveals further depths to the poet's imagination and stylistic repertoire. As with *Zoom!*, critics were generous with their praise. David Kennedy claimed that Faber's publication of *Kid* "marks the arrival in the 'mainstream' of one of the freshest and most original new voices of recent years" and "could be said to represent a long overdue foregrounding of a vigorous vernacular type of poetry." Kennedy believes that many of the poems in *Kid* demonstrate "a concern to write a poetry that rejects nothing and a belief in its power to redeem the ordinary" (p. 87).

The poems also develop Armitage's preoccupation with violence. The book's opening poem,

SIMON ARMITAGE

"Gooseberry Season," is a dramatic monologue narrated by a murderer who is also a family man. The poem begins "Which reminds me" (p. 1), highlighting the colloquial style of the poem, which is presented as speech as well as written text. A destitute drifter who stops at the narrator's house for water then stays for several months without paying rent or doing any work, the victim eventually elicits the family's hatred:

One evening he mentioned a recipe

for smooth, seedless gooseberry sorbet
but by then I was tired of him: taking pocket money
from my boy at cards, sucking up to my wife and on
  his last night
sizing up my daughter. He was smoking my pipe
as we stirred his supper.

(p. 1)

The family has reached its breaking point, no longer able to distinguish the boundary between right and wrong: "Where does the hand become the wrist? / Where does the neck become the shoulder?" (p. 1). Pushed "over the razor's edge / between something and nothing" (p. 1), they drown him in the bath and discard his body in a field at "the county boundary" (p. 2). Admitting the unsavory nature of his tale, the narrator says,

This is not general knowledge, except
in gooseberry season, which reminds me, and at the
  table
I have been known to raise an eyebrow, or scoop the
  sorbet
into five equal portions, for the hell of it.
I mention this for a good reason.

(p. 2)

Because there are four people in his family, the fifth portion is intended for the man they murdered. The last line of the poem serves two purposes: it further emphasizes the poem's colloquial quality, and it acts as a veiled threat to the listener.

Many of the figures in *Kid* find themselves "between something and nothing." Few people in these poems are employed, and those with jobs do not keep them for long. A sonnet with such jaunty rhythms it approaches light verse, "Poem"

is a portrait of a man who is both model citizen and flawed human. The first three lines of each quatrain present his qualities, which are then undercut by the last line:

And every week he tipped up half his wage.
And what he didn't spend each week he saved.
And praised his wife for every meal she made.
And once, for laughing, punched her in the face.

(p. 29)

The final couplet offers a tidy resolution: "Here's how they rated him when they looked back: / sometimes he did this, sometimes he did that" (p. 29). Armitage's concern with the whole of humanity, not just the beautiful or salutary aspects, results in a frequently disturbing collection.

Replete with dramatic monologues, *Kid* presents even more unsavory characters than *Zoom!*: the professional pickpocket of "Brassneck," the jilted lover of "Alaska," and the furious young man in the book's title poem, which is a litany directed at Batman by his former sidekick, Robin. The only poem not written in stanzas, "Kid" maintains formal integrity through a consistent pentameter and feminine slant rhymes:

Batman, big shot, when you gave the order
to grow up, then let me loose to wander
leeward, freely through the wild blue yonder
as you liked to say, or ditched me, rather,
in the gutter ... well, I turned the corner.

(p. 37)

Here, Armitage's fondness for slang combines with Robin's famously comic exclamations to produce some new convoluted outbursts: "Holy robin-redbreast-nest-egg-shocker! / Holy roll-me-in-the-clover" (p. 37). Despite its specific cultural references, the poem emerges as a widely applicable coming-of-age story, in which the adolescent male is forced to grow up on his own. The narrator's injured yet defiant tone at the beginning of the poem becomes more confident: "I'm not playing ball boy any longer / ... now I'm taller, harder, stronger, older. / ... now I'm the real boy wonder" (p. 37).

A similarly extravagant relationship to language appears in "The Metaphor Now Standing at

Platform 8," a dramatic monologue in which the train becomes a metaphor and the conductor becomes the poet. Another dramatic monologue, "Judge Chutney's Final Summary," loses itself entirely in metaphor and cliché as the judge attempts to sentence himself:

Members
  of the jury,
  you have surfed

the tidal wave,
  listened
  with patience,

held out
  against the avalanche
  of evidence

and now
  I admit it.
  I am guilty.

                                  (p. 31)

Guilty of following "trains of thought / into overgrown sidings," the judge wants to leave nothing behind "but the truth, plus / all my worldly goods" (pp. 31–32, 34). Language in these poems becomes a worn medium that requires careful attention, otherwise it "is less use than half a scissor" (p. 42).

One of the most remarked-upon aspects of *Kid* is Armitage's series of homages to the American poet Weldon Kees, who reportedly committed suicide in San Francisco in 1955. Armitage uses Kees's Robinson, a persona taken from an Edward Hopper painting, and reinvents him for 1990s England. "Looking for Weldon Kees" introduces the poet and his alter ego:

I'd heard it said by Michael Hofmann
  that *Collected Poems* would blow my head off,
but,
      being out of print
      and a hot potato,
      it might be a hard one
      to get hold of

                                  (p. 13)

The poem relates the circumstances of Kees' disappearance—he stopped his car by the Golden

Gate Bridge, "locked both doors / of his Tudor Ford / and took one small step / off the face of the planet," leaving "no will, no note, ... / not even a whiff of spontaneous combustion" (p. 13). Kees's disappearance is what allows Armitage to encounter Robinson in his imagination. Their relationship is complicated—"since we first shook hands we'd had more ups and downs / than San Francisco" (p. 14)—yet Robinson delivers Kees's *Collected Poems* to Armitage, and Armitage's own explorations of Kees's persona ensue. The parsimonious Robinson is "in two minds" (p. 18) as well as paranoid: "Down on the shore the moon like a torch; / whichever way he walks it finds him, follows him, / will not flinch when he spins round to surprise it" (p. 25). "Robinson's Life Sentence" is to "rise early" to perform the same tasks every day. Acknowledging the tedium of mindless routine, the Robinson poems explore the situation of the isolated individual in an alienating society. "Robinson's Resignation" rejects everything associated with this society:

Because I am done with this thing called work,
  the paper-clips and staples of it all.
  The customers and their huge excuses,
  their incredulous lies and their beautiful
  foul-mouthed daughters. I am swimming with it,
  right up to here with it. And I am bored,
  bored like the man who married a mermaid.

                                  (p. 87)

He ultimately renounces friendship as well as work, and the last line of the poem announces the end to language: "This is my final word. Nothing will follow" (p. 87).

BOOK OF MATCHES

Armitage's third major volume, *Book of Matches,* makes use of his work as a probation officer while exploring the limits and possibilities of language to convey reality. The book is named after the series of thirty poems organized around the concept of telling one's life story with a lit match in hand. The first poem explains the premise behind the series:

My party piece:

SIMON ARMITAGE

I strike, then from the moment when the matchstick
conjures up its light, to when the brightness moves
beyond its means, and dies, I say the story
of my life—

dates and places, torches I carried,
a cast of names and faces, those
who showed me love, or came close,
the changes I made, the lessons I learnt—

then somehow still find time to stall and blush
before I'm bitten by the flame, and burnt.

(p. 3)

Most of these loosely rhyming poems are fourteen lines long, and thus present a contemporary variation on the sonnet sequence; and in their transmutations and explorations of the self, the poems also recall John Berryman's *Dream Songs* as well as more straightforward confessional poetry. The "party piece" itself resembles an act of confession; but with no priest involved, the poet's only hopes for absolution come from himself or the reader. *Book of Matches* then, emerges as a self-portrait of the poet as a young man, complete with childhood vignettes, fears, and life philosophies; but rather than finish his story when a match burns out, he continues lighting matches until the entire book of matches has been used. This strategy serves as an effective, inventive frame for the individual poems and the series itself.

The poet's observations range from the banal—"My mind works / quickly and well these days, / and I like the look of myself of late" (p. 4)—to the humorously morbid—"I've made out a will; I'm leaving myself / to the National Health" (p. 23). Individual poems frequently mimic what a reformed criminal might say to a probation officer or answer on a behavioral questionnaire: "I rate myself as a happy, contented person, / in spite of troubles here and there" (p. 5); "I am able to keep my mind steadily / on one job or plan as long as necessary" (p. 7). Other poems present an intimidating persona—"People talk nonsense and I put them straight" (p. 9)—or seem to parody popular psychology: "it has helped me more than I could measure / to separate life into two divisions, / of things that is, and things that isn't" (p. 5). One of the most memorable poems in the series narrates a childhood wrongdoing:

I am very bothered when I think
of the bad things I have done in my life.
Not least that time in the chemistry lab
when I held a pair of scissors by the blades
and played the handles
in the naked lilac flame of the Bunsen burner;
then called your name, and handed them over.

O the unrivalled stench of branded skin
as you slipped your thumb and middle finger in,
then couldn't shake off the two burning rings.
Marked,
the doctor said, for eternity.

Don't believe me, please, if I say
that was just my butterfingered way, at thirteen,
of asking you if you would marry me.

(p. 13)

The combination of childlike innocence and violence captures the series' balancing act between adolescence and adulthood. Critic Ian Gregson finds in *Book of Matches* "an increasing sobriety ... accompanied by less concern with jaunty, polished surfaces" (p. 72). The poet's "witty and self-conscious facility" has been complicated by "a consistent preoccupation with the self" (p. 77) in the book.

This preoccupation with the self also includes the poet's health. Having been diagnosed with a spinal disease, ankylosing spondylitis, after writing *Kid*, Armitage perhaps naturally turns to his body as subject in *Book of Matches*. The disease fuses the bones in his spine together when he rests, leading him to say "Don't let me sleep" (p. 21). Elsewhere, the pain in his spine transforms from "a spark of light" and a halo to "a noose, / a girdle, then a belt, a Hula-Hoop / of inflammation" (p. 22) that burns him "at the stake" of the spine. In the final poem in *Book of Matches,* the poet seems to be attempting suicide: "Tonight I'm blank, burnt out, parked / in the garage, with the engine running" (p. 32). Yet the matchbook frame for the poems, and the act of writing itself, divert his attention from self-destruction:

I tear the last match from the book,
fetch it hard and once
across the windscreen. In the glass

I'm taken with myself, caught in the act—
conducting light, until the heat licks
up against my thumb and fingertips, unlocks

7

my hand, gives me a start, trips

something in the flashbulb of my heart.

(p. 32)

The poet's reflection in the car's windshield mirrors the self-reflection in the poems, and poetry ultimately serves as a release from the pain of living and remembering.

After such a powerful and substantial group of poems, most individual poems would be unable to carry similar weight. Yet several of the shorter poems in *Book of Matches* rank among Armitage's strongest work. As with his other books, the dramatic monologue figures prominently. In "Hitcher," the narrator, "tired, under the weather," picks up a hitchhiker whose optimism disgusts him, so he hits the hitchhiker six times in the face and, without stopping the car, pushes him out, where he goes "bouncing off the curb, then disappearing down the verge" (p. 46). *Book of Matches* also includes several affecting personal lyric poems. "You" addresses the difficulty of being a writer with a jealous partner, who "comb[s] through" his writing looking for herself and, finding other women instead, calls the poet "a cheat, a bastard, a liar" (p. 42) and destroys the writing. Despite being about a former love, "To His Lost Lover" emerges as more tender:

Now they are no longer
  any trouble to each other

he can turn things over, get down to that list
  of things that never happened, all of the lost

unfinishable business.
  For instance … for instance,

how he never clipped and kept her hair …

(p. 51)

The poem becomes a negative list, a catalogue of actions he never performed and gestures of affection he never made, but now wishes he had.

Book of Matches ends with "Reading the Banns," a sequence of twelve short poems in couplets that explore the preparations for a marriage with both skepticism and kindness. The most touching poem depicts the poet discovering that the "waves of ink / across the writing pad" (p. 60) are the results of his fiancée practicing her new signature. Yet Armitage identifies something of the funeral in the wedding, as when he sees "nine morning suits / all hanging from the picture rail, / all covered, zipped, and tagged" and calls them "body bags" (p. 67). In the end, each poem's brevity and the lack of development in the sequence prohibits it from attaining the strengths that distinguish "Book of Matches," and the book's beginning series remains its central achievement while anticipating the even darker concerns of Armitage's next book.

THE DEAD SEA POEMS

Composed of twenty-four short poems and a 512-line poem in iambic pentameter, "Five Eleven Ninety Nine," *The Dead Sea Poems* continues Armitage's experimentation with presenting a few short poems alongside a longer work. The title poem recalls the Dead Sea Scrolls and re-imagines their discovery through the eyes of their professed author, who is a poet. The dramatic monologue is narrated by a wanderer whose travels are interrupted by the discovery in "cool sand" of "poems written in my own hand" (p. 1). The narrator relates the results of his find comically and colloquially:

Being greatly in need of food and clothing,

and out of pocket, I let the lot go
  for twelve times nothing, but saw them again
  this spring, on public display, out of reach

under infra-red and ultra-sonic,
  apparently worth an absolute packet.

(pp. 1–2)

This revisionist approach to the Dead Sea Scrolls combines the drama of a desert pilgrimage with the capitalist system of supply and demand while raising issues of authorship and ownership. Armitage's real achievement, however, is his humorous, ironic tone, which emerges as both hyperbolic and self-deprecatory. He inflates the role of the poet while demonstrating the poet's naivete and ineptitude in practical matters, and he leaves the narrator "singing the whole of the work / to myself, every page of that innocent, / everyday, effortless verse" (p. 2).

Violence emerges as a link between *The Dead Sea Poems* and Armitage's earlier books. In "From the Middle Distance," the scarecrow narrator asks, "Who set me up, / hammered this stake from the nape of my neck / to my left foot, down through the hips and ribs?" (p. 6). The most controversial and visceral poem in the book, "I Say I Say I Say," begins with two startling questions: "Anyone here had a go at themselves / for a laugh? Anyone opened their wrists / with a blade in the bath?" (p. 9). The juxtaposition of colloquial speech—"had a go," "for a laugh"— and jaunty rhythm with the subject of suicide produces a profoundly disturbing poem, made even more discomfiting by its direct address to the reader:

> Those in the dark
> at the back, listen hard. Those at the front
> in the know, those of us who have, hands up,
> let's show that inch of lacerated skin
> between the forearm and the fist.
>
> (p. 9)

The phrase "in the dark" first reads literally as "in the darkened part of the room," but the phrase "in the know" in the next sentence casts "in the dark" more figuratively: To be "in the dark" in this poem also means to be ignorant of suicide and suicide attempts. Knowledge here becomes a potentially devastating power. Both ironic and earnest, the poem's tone wavers between addressing its subject seriously and parodying the contemporary tendency in poetry to broadcast one's personal problems. Thus, the poem also can be read as a commentary on confessional poetry. Its title contributes to its faux-confessional stance, since "I Say I Say I Say" can be read as a tendency toward incessant speech or personal disclosure—a position that characterizes much confessional poetry.

In its attempt to discard the lies that often follow a suicide attempt—"A likely story: you were lashed by brambles / picking berries" (p. 9)—the poem becomes brutally straightforward: "Let's

tell it / like it is: strong drink, a crimson tidemark / round the tub, ... white towels / washed a dozen times, still pink" (p. 9). The narrator presses for the reader/audience member to "come clean, come good" (p. 9), while forbidding any real emotion at the end of the poem, insisting instead, "repeat with me the punch line 'Just like blood' / when those at the back rush forward to say / how a little love goes a long long long way" (p. 9). This sardonic recommendation—that is, when someone offers the hopeful advice that "a little love goes a long way," reply "just like blood"— further widens the gulf in the poem between those who have tried to commit suicide and those who have not. Confronting suicide so directly while retaining his propensity for double meanings and wit shows Armitage at his darkest and most unsettling.

The title of the book's long poem, "Five Eleven Ninety Nine," refers to 5 November 1999, the last Bonfire Night of the millennium. (Bonfire Night is an English tradition that commemorates Guy Fawkes and the failed Gunpowder Plot of 1605.) Armitage makes deft use of the apocalyptic dimension of both the millennium and the bonfire while positioning the poem between dusk and dawn, darkness and light, cold and heat, bleakness and hope. Thick with sound play—rhyme, internal rhyme, consonance, alliteration, and assonance—and with scintillating repetition, the poem stands as one of Armitage's most resonant narrative poems. It begins almost optimistically:

The makings of the fire to end all fires,
the takings of the year, all kinds of cane
and kindling to begin with, tinder sticks,
the trunk and branches of a silver birch

brought down by lightning, dragged here like a plough
through heavy earth from twenty fields away.
Timber: floorboards oiled and seasoned, planking,
purlins, sleepers, pelmets, casements, railings,

sacks of sweepings, splinters, sawdust, shavings.

(p. 36)

There is a buoyant aspect to this catalogue of items to be burned in the bonfire. Rather than gesture toward destruction, they seem to signify abundance and possibility; everything will be released from its current state into another state, will be transformed by fire in a glorious ceremony. The ritual of collecting and arranging the items also brings the people together in a way that does not occur in their daily lives. The ceremony acquires a religious aspect as people flock to the pile to make their offerings.

Everything imaginable is added to the pyre, including "litter," "flotsam," and "dreck," and the participants painstakingly "stack the fire at the eleventh hour" (p. 38). After such intensive preparation, "someone makes a move, a match gets struck" (p. 40), and the fire slowly comes to life after some hissing, steaming, and smoking. Armitage compares the fire's efforts to catch to the chain of human conversation:

> More smoke
> without fire, then a further space alive
> with light, a chamber deep inside aglow
>
> for good this time, fuelled with the right stuff,
> feeding on something loose for long enough
> to tempt another thing to burn, combust,
> to spread its word, to chatter its own name
>
> through a stook of canes, to start a whisper
> here and there that spreads across the broad base,
> a rumour handed down, passed round and shared.
>
> (p. 40)

Despite the fire, the observers are cold; they "feel / the bite of frost from the nape of the neck / to the heels, a cold current through the spine" (p. 41). This fact acquires an apocalyptic element, which is compounded by the events that follow: a roof collapses, a window "pops from its frame" (p. 42), a girl's boots are "melted to her feet" (p. 42), and people and animals burn themselves. Armitage's addition of folklore to the scene—a blind man arrives and describes the bonfires from the past, "when fires / would singe an eyebrow from a mile away" (p. 43)—further bolsters its biblical and apocalyptic elements. The world around the bonfire indeed seems to be ending:

> buildings swim in the haze of the heat.
> And rockets set out for parks and gardens
> and nose-dive into purple streets. And sparks
> make the most of some moments of stardom.

> And flakes of ash and motes of soot float up,
> cool down, fall out, then go to ground.
>
> …
>
> And eyes
> if they blink are ablaze on the inside.
> Gunpowder battles it out in the sky
> where rockets go on unzipping the night.
>
> (p. 44)

However, the poem ends not in fire but in ice, so it is fitting that "the brightness fades" (p. 46) and the people frantically search for more fuel for the flames, eventually offering everything they can find to the fire. "A people waiting for a word or sign" (p. 48), they realize

> we have given all of what we own
> and what we are, and it has come to this:
> this place, this date, this time, these tens of us,
> all free but shadowless and primitive,
>
> no more than silhouettes or negatives
> or hieroglyphics, stark and shivering.
>
> …
>
> an hour at most before the very last.
>
> (p. 49)

Their only hope, ironically, is to burn a large cross that someone finds in a garage. The strongest of the group carries it, Jesus-like, to the site of the bonfire; and like Jesus he falls on the way, but "stands up straight and walks / beneath a window where his mother waves / and calls his name" (p. 51). He stops to rest, and a woman wipes his face with "a handkerchief trimmed with lace" (p. 51), and he falls two more times before he "rounds the corner on his knees / and finds his feet when he sees the remains / of the light and heat, and raises the cross / to its full height" (p. 51). The cross stays upright where he has set it, "held up by nothing more than air" (p. 51), until someone knocks it over, where it keeps the fire burning for another hour "but not a minute more" (p. 52). The bonfire ends when "blackness follows every burst of flames" (p. 53) despite the group's final attempt to keep the fire lit, by feeding it money, photographs, important documents, and clothing. This desperation results only in their return "to houses that are empty, frozen, stone, / to rooms that are skeletal, stripped, unmade, / uncurtained windows, doorways open wide" (p. 56). Like the world in T. S. Eliot's "The Hollow Men," the bonfire apocalypse ends not with a bang but a whimper.

CLOUDCUCKOOLAND

Armitage's longest and most ambitious volume to date, *CloudCuckooLand* is divided into three sections: "Thin Air," a group of fourteen individual poems; "The Whole of the Sky," eighty-eight poems about constellations; and "Eclipse," a verse play in twelve scenes. The first poem in *CloudCuckooLand*, "A Glory," demonstrates Armitage's recently developed ability to locate the spiritual within the quotidian: "Right here you made an angel of yourself, / free-falling backwards into last night's snow" (p. 3). Although the angel in the first line becomes a snow angel, the resonance and autonomy of the first line inject a celestial note into the poem, which nevertheless remains earthbound. The vulnerability of the snow angel—"cattle would trample roughshod over it, / … somebody's boy might try it on for size" (p. 3)—causes insomnia in the speaker of the poem and compels him to "backtrack / to the place" later that night and "keep watch" (p. 3) over the snow angel, knowing the sun's warmth will erase its presence the next day. The introduction of the idea of mortality at the end of the poem humanizes the snow angel, which, though neither heavenly nor human, still faces annihilation. The subsequent poems in *CloudCuckooLand* explore the celestial/human dichotomy and attempt to illuminate the areas where the mortal and the ethereal overlap, thus finding the spiritual in the quotidian and the earthly in the ethereal.

One of the book's most successful poems, "The Tyre," recounts a childhood incident in which a large tire is released from its stasis by a group of children. After rolling the tire across the moor "down to meadows, fields, onto level ground" (p. 4), they lose control of it, and the tire disappears. The children create a mental list of possible disasters—"a man on a motorbike taken down, /

a phone-box upended, children erased" (p. 5)—but cannot find the tire, or any trace of it, in the village. "Not there or anywhere" (p. 5), the vanished tire is explained by the children through superstition:

> Being more in tune with the feel of things
> than science and facts, we knew that the tyre
> had travelled too fast for its size and mass,
> and broken through some barrier of speed,
>
> …
>
> and at that moment gone beyond itself,
> towards some other sphere, and disappeared.
>
> (p. 5)

Despite his scientific background and knowledge, Armitage here seems less inclined to align himself with "science and facts" and more likely to depend on "the feel of things" for answers. Though written from the vantage point of childhood and with an adult awareness of the imaginative freedom of youth, the poem celebrates the inexplicable, particularly the conjunction of the magical and the mundane.

An ambitious gathering of poems exploring the cosmos and humankind's relationship to the cosmos, "The Whole of the Sky" further develops the overlap of the earthly and the otherworldly. Although critics were less impressed with this series than with *Book of Matches* or "Five Eleven Ninety Nine"—the Irish poet-critic David Wheatley's opinion, that "The Whole of the Sky" suffers from "over-extension and garrulousness" (p. 73), is characteristic of the critical response to the work—"The Whole of the Sky" is Armitage's most extensive series of poems to date and therefore deserves serious critical attention.

The inaugural poem in the group, "The Mariner's Compass," begins modestly—"Living alone, I'm sailing the world / single-handed in a rented house"—but then embraces "the old-fashioned thought / of plotting a course by the stars." The narrator/armchair astronomer must remain solitary, for "under the rules, close contact / with another soul means disqualification" (p. 25). Every poem afterward portrays, in an economical style dominated by quatrains, a brief vignette somehow related to the constellation or astronomical tool of its title. "Hercules," for example, presents the demi-god's twelve labors as domestic chores, none of which are accomplished:

after not having the spine to dig the vegetable patch,
not picking the fruit before the fruit went bad,
after not walking the dog once all day for crying out
  loud
I collapsed, exhausted, on my side of the unmade bed.
                                            (p. 30)

Armitage reimagines the mythological tales behind the constellations, transporting them into the present day for reinterpretation. "Aquarius" offers cultural commentary in its meditation:

We take exception to that chain of hotels
that asks us to think of the dying planet
by skimping on towels and not flushing the toilet.
This is about metered water and laundry bills, isn't it?
                                            (p. 35)

"The Ram" illustrates the effects of industrialism on the natural world, which requires a revision to mythology:

Half-dead, hit by a car, the whole of its form
a jiggle of nerves, like a fish on a lawn.
To help finish it off, he asked me to stand
on its throat …
Then he lifted its head, wheeled it about

            …

till its eyes, on stalks, looked back at its bones.
                                            (p. 64)

Though mythological or celestial in their concerns, the poems do not ignore the quotidian objects that fill people's lives. Ultimately, these poems imply that life on earth is a mirror image of the constellations—"Night-fishing the lake under the southern stars / we could have been fishing the sky" ("The Southern Fish, " p. 84)—and that little has changed since human beings first started gazing into the cosmos and creating narratives. Although celestial, the constellations embody and contain all that lies in human nature. Because "whatever comes at the Earth at the speed of light / will be here upon us, then beyond us, instantly" ("Sagitta, " p. 109), in Armitage's cosmos, things move too quickly for the spiritual to take hold.

It seems ironic, then, that the verse play "Eclipse" does not jettison the spiritual from its field of concerns. In fact, the piece emerges as a statement against the possibility of objectivity, scientific or otherwise. With compelling characters, a formal suppleness that uses traditional rhyme schemes and internal rhymes as well as contemporary idiom, and a sophisticated handling of time, "Eclipse" is a masterful verse play. Originally commissioned by the National Theatre in England for the BT Connections Project for performance by young adults, "Eclipse" occurs before, during, and after a total solar eclipse on 11 August 1999. The play's twelve scenes alternate between dramatic monologues reflecting on the day of the eclipse and dramatic scenes occurring on the day itself.

The cast consists of six teenage friends— Klondike, the oldest of the group and its leader; Tulip, a boyish girl; Polly and Jane, vain twins; Midnight, a boy who went blind at ten from staring at the sun through binoculars; and Glue Boy, who sniffs glue continuously during the play— and Lucy Lime, who is unknown to the other children when she appears. Derived from the Latin word for "light," Lucy's name acquires significance when she, like light, disappears during the eclipse. The first scene of "Eclipse" occurs in the waiting room of a police station, where the six teenagers reestablish their version of the events of the eclipse in order to reaffirm their stories before each is questioned by the police. Klondike reminds a nervous Midnight of the "facts":

The oldies were up on the flat with the van,
we were down in the crags.
They were waiting to gawp at the total eclipse of the
  sun,
we were kids, having fun.
It was August eleventh, nineteen ninety-nine …
The first and last that we saw of [Lucy Lime].
                                            (I, p. 116)

Although they claim to have "nothing to say" and "nothing to hide" (I, p. 117), they feel responsible for Lucy's disappearance and fearful of the consequences. Armitage then deftly moves between the present and the past, alternating scenes between six dramatic monologues narrated by the teenagers during their police interviews (the twins are represented together with one scene, and the barely articulate Glue Boy surprisingly narrates the last two monologues) and five dramatic situations portraying the events on the day of the eclipse.

Midnight protests, "don't ask me / to say what I saw, I'm profoundly blind" (II, p. 118), but he explains to the police how his encounter with Lucy has changed him:

I was different then,
    did a lot of praying, wore a cross, went to church,
    thought I was walking toward the light of the Lord—
    … Lucy put me on the straight
    and narrow. There's no such thing as the soul,
    there's bone and there's marrow.

(II, p. 118)

This strategy—one teenager discussing Lucy's effects on him or her in the monologue, with a dramatization of that meeting in the next scene—carries throughout the rest of "Eclipse," offering both subjective (first-person) and objective (third-person) points of view. When he first meets Lucy, Midnight is walking in a cave with his crucifix held in front of him, and Lucy says, "you can put that thing down, I'm not Dracula's daughter … don't point it at me. It's loaded" (III, p. 123). The double meaning of "loaded" here helps convey Lucy's preternatural maturity—she is aware of the power of words, how different meanings can infiltrate someone's mind, how an object can be meaningless to one person and "loaded" with meaning to another. Lucy tells riddles, knows tricks, and is exceptionally quick-tongued and sharp-witted. Polly and Jane describe her as a "strange looking creature" (III, p. 125), and no one knows what to think of her. She bets the other children that she can "get Midnight to tell a lie," which the others say is impossible because he is "a proper Christian" (III, p. 126). She first convinces Midnight she hears sounds that he does not hear, then tricks him into lying that he, too, hears the sounds—gulls, an airplane, a boy flying a kite. When confronted with his lying by the others, who are angry because they have lost their bet—and some of their most treasured possessions—Midnight throws his crucifix onto the ground and stalks away. Lucy

picks up the crucifix and puts it in her bag, where she also puts the objects she won from the others. Though monetarily insignificant, the items are of great personal value to their owners, and Lucy's taking possession of them represents her taking possession of a piece of each of them.

The subsequent monologues in "Eclipse" describe how Lucy has changed the other children's lives. Before they met her, the twins were superficial:

We were something else before the daylight vanished.
Whatever we touched was touched with varnish.
Whatever we smelt was laced with powder or scent.
Whatever we heard had an earring lending its weight.
Whatever we saw was shadowed and shaded out of
    sight.
Whatever we tasted tasted of mint.
Whatever we spoke had lipstick kissing its lips.

(IV, p. 132)

They were "muddled up, / not thinking straight," but after meeting Lucy, they became "clear" (IV, p. 133). The next scene presents the impetus for this change. While Polly and Jane have left the others to find a mirror in which to primp, the others begin a game of hide and seek, with Lucy as the seeker. The twins return before Lucy has started looking for the others, and the game never begins because they start ridiculing Lucy's appearance. What they consider "pale and pasty" and "plain and hairy," Lucy considers "pure and simple. Basically beautiful" (V, pp. 135–136). She advises the twins to "be yourself, … not somebody else" (V, p. 137) because it is "better to look the way you were meant to be / than done up like a tailor's dummy and a Christmas tree" (V, p. 137). After considering this challenge, the twins go to the shore, where Lucy removes their jewelry and some of their most expensive articles of clothing and puts them in her bag.

The teenagers initially resist the change that Lucy compels within them and resent her intrusiveness. Tulip despises Lucy when she is with her, but later reveals in her police interview that she is no longer a tomboy and is "blossoming" (VI, p. 145) because of Lucy. After Lucy plays a trick on Klondike—throwing water in his face when he expected a kiss—he tells her, "you shouldn't joke [about] … rhymes and religion.

Old things" (VII, p. 147). When Lucy responds with the flippant "I don't believe in all that claptrap" (VII, p. 147), he shows her the contents of his leather bag, which holds "the skin of a poisonous snake" (VII, p. 148) and other charms that he imbues with supernatural powers—"things for dreaming things up" (VII, p. 149). Lucy calls him "an overgrown boy scout" (VII, p. 149), so Klondike performs a ceremony to demonstrate the magical powers of one of the items—an eagle feather—but after he apparently causes a plane to fly overhead, Lucy reveals that he had performed his ceremony not with the feather but with a rubber duck, thus dispelling the illusion he had created and his self-delusion. Tulip then threatens Lucy with a knife, but rather than being afraid, Lucy insults Tulip: "you don't have to look like a man, to be as strong as one. … What will you do when your balls drop, Tulip? Grow a beard?" (VII, p. 151). In order to avoid violence, Klondike encourages them to arm-wrestle to decide who is stronger, but when they are supposed to begin, Lucy grabs the electric fence beside her and the shock knocks Tulip to the ground—Lucy, wearing the rubber boots Tulip had lost in her bet, was insulated from the electricity. Klondike himself threatens Lucy, and appears ready to attack her when the eclipse begins.

Klondike's attraction to the supernatural emerges as a kind of black magic during the eclipse. Per his direction, the children stand in specific positions "in a triangular formation" (VII, p. 154), wear protective glasses, and chant:

Fallen fruit of burning sun
  break the teeth and burn the tongue,

open mouth of the frozen moon
  spit the cherry from the stone.

(VII, p. 155)

Because Glue Boy is not with the others at the beginning of the eclipse, Klondike forces Lucy to join them even though she does not know the chant. When Glue Boy returns, he bumps into Lucy, who removes the glue bag from his head and grabs his hands. Glue Boy begins to hallucinate and narrates what he sees as some of the other children briefly leave the group to retrieve

the objects that Lucy had taken from them—Midnight's crucifix, Tulip's boots, Klondike's cow skull, and the twins' clothing, jewelry, and make-up. Although the products of hallucination, Glue Boy's "dreams" assess the core of each person through metaphor, and he emerges as a poetic interpreter of the other children. His dreams stop when Lucy, distressed that she and Glue Boy are stuck together with glue, starts spinning him around in an attempt to extricate herself from him. She shouts "Let me go!" (XI, p. 167) just as the eclipse reaches complete darkness, and she disappears. Because Lucy represents science and technology—unadorned, demystified reality—she exists in conflict with Midnight's religious views, the twins' blinding self-love, Glue Boy's perpetual hallucinations, and Tulip's and Klondike's delusions and superstitions. However, the supernatural prevails when Lucy disappears.

During his police interview, Glue Boy cannot piece together any bits of information because of his damaged mind, so he speaks in fragments, which he explains to the police apologetically: "I was all of a dither back then, / disconnected, fuse blown in the head, loose ends, / nobody home, fumes on the brain" (X, p. 162). He then offers to recite the "rhyme" the teenagers have composed for Lucy's memorial service. The rhyme reads like an extended, exploded version of what they chanted during the eclipse:

under the bullet hole of the moon
  under the entry wound of the sun
  under the glass eye of the moon
  under the bloody nose of the sun

          …

under the cyanide pill of the moon
  under the screaming mouth of the sun
  under the chocolate coin of the moon
  under the chocolate coin of the sun

(XII, p. 171)

Glue Boy's "testimony" implies how nothing ultimately connects "under the moon" or "under the sun." Language is a scattered and imprecise medium by which to explain a fragmented, shifting world where the sun and moon can trade places.

SIMON ARMITAGE

KILLING TIME

Commissioned by the New Millennium Experience Company, published as a book by Faber, and broadcast as a full-length film on England's Channel 4 on New Year's Day, 2000, *Killing Time* (1999) is Armitage's official millennium poem. Yet the thousand-line poem ultimately carries less weight and proves to be less haunting, or even millennial, than "Five Eleven Ninety Nine" from *The Dead Sea Poems*. The critical reception to *Killing Time* was mixed, though the poem's high public profile insured its popular success.

In *Killing Time* Armitage explores the mass cynicism, materialism, and communication that characterize the world at the end of the millennium. The poem follows the most prominent news stories of 1999—such as the Columbine High School shootings in Colorado, operation Desert Fox, the eclipse—in an attempt to reclaim the media-speak that has debased both language and event. Armitage reproduces and reclaims these news stories, simultaneously using the language of media and attempting to transform that language into poetry. The task is a daunting one, and Armitage's ambivalence prohibits him from expressing either exuberance or sentimentality. As a result, *Killing Time* emerges as his angriest book.

Armitage organizes *Killing Time* around nine main scenes, each of which begins "Meanwhile" and has one or two brief light verses preceding and following it. The book also includes two ballads that act as modern parables. This structure resembles news programs' feature stories padded with sound bites and soft stories. The book's first ballad identifies the contemporary news-hungry person as "a new freak in the ape-house, / some monkey gone wrong" (p. 3). The monkey is mostly machine, barely animal:

loud-speakers for earplugs,
  a microphone tongue,

fibre-optics for body hair,
  a mouse for a hand,
  a fax-machine derrière,
  a joystick gland,

two screens for eyeballs,
  a microchip brain ...

                                        (p. 3)

With "no nerves" and "no heart" (p. 3), the monkey has "a huge appetite," not for food but for news. The monkey, then, becomes both the source of news and the consumer of news, the metaphor aptly conveying contemporary society's relationship to the news it needs.

The most inventive part of *Killing Time* recreates the Columbine High School massacre, replacing guns and bullets with flowers:

> Meanwhile, somewhere in the state of Colorado,
>   armed to the teeth
>   with thousands of flowers,
>   two boys entered the front door of their own high
>   school
>   and for almost four hours
>   gave floral tributes to fellow students and members
>   of staff,
>   beginning with red roses
>   strewn amongst unsuspecting pupils during their
>   lunch hour,
>   followed by posies
>   of peace lilies and wild orchids.
>
>   (p. 22)

Despite the potential for flippancy here, Armitage maintains the metaphor until the flowers themselves seem dangerous. The metaphor takes a political turn when Armitage writes, "the law of the land / dictates that God, guts and gardening made the country / what it is today," replacing the National Rifle Association with "the flower industry" (p. 24). More culturally oriented than political, another section of *Killing Time* raises the issue of the millennium itself, alluding to the incorrect date—31 December 1999—most of the world selected as the turning point, when in fact the millennium ended on 31 December 2000. As people around the globe celebrate, "a million souls are focused on keeping themselves to themselves, / determined to opt out, / not to be moved by a fictional date and a fictional time" (p. 46). Although these people live in "irrelevant valleys / and insignificant vales, / on pointless hills and featureless stretches of heath," they are sufficient in number to convey "a silence so profound it figures on the Richter scale" (p. 46). This moment in *Killing Time*, in which silence is set against massive noise, recalls the 1999 eclipse that established the premise for his verse play in *CloudCuckooLand*. Here the eclipse is fodder for the news, not a dramatic setting, and Armitage writes about it as an actual event, not as a projected scenario:

> Meanwhile, because more people worship the sun these days
> than God, millions flock
> to England's toe-end, to see for themselves the great blaze
> turning a blind eye,
> to stand in the shade of a satellite moon as it casts a shadow of doubt
> over the South West, over modern lives. The spectacle lasts
> no more than a minute
> or two …
>
> (p. 34)

The poem bemoans the contemporary attitude that transforms the eclipse into a "spectacle," not an opportunity for contemplation. Nevertheless, Armitage uses the eclipse to surmise that "each individual truly felt / … a huge sense of time / and space, and subsequently a loneliness bordering on guilt" (p. 37).

Ultimately, Armitage reveals that the "interference jamming the air, / that babble of white noise, / that signal bending and burning the ears / was the radiation of the news" (p. 51). No event, he implies, escapes the "whir" of cameras, the "trill" of mobile phones, or the "hum" of tape recorders, hence the "background drawl" interfering with what the technology is intended to portray—the news (p. 51). The last piece of light verse in *Killing Time* introduces the possibility of no news:

> And finally, last week in a West Yorkshire village nothing happened at all.
> An incident room is being set up at the scene, and security cameras installed.
>
> (p. 52)

Yet, perhaps predictably, the absence of news becomes news, and the book ends on a note simultaneously humorous and cynical. It is this kind of balancing act that characterizes Armitage's best work and promises more similarly skilled performances in the future.

SELECTED BIBLIOGRAPHY

I. POETRY. *Zoom!* (Newcastle Upon Tyne, 1989); *Kid* (London, 1992); *Xanadu: A Poem Film for Television* (Newcastle Upon Tyne, 1992); *Book of Matches* (London, 1993); *The Dead Sea Poems* (London, 1995); *CloudCuckooLand* (London, 1997); *Killing Time* (London, 1999); *Selected Poems* (London, 2001).

II. PROSE. *Moon Country: Further Reports from Iceland*, with Glyn Maxwell (London, 1996); *All Points North* (London, 1998); *Little Green Men* (London, 2001).

III. TRANSLATION. *Mister Heracles: After Euripides* (London, 2000).

IV. ANTHOLOGIES. *The Penguin Book of Poetry from Britain and Ireland Since 1945*, with Robert Crawford (London, 1998); *Short and Sweet: 101 Very Short Poems* (London, 1999).

V. CRITICAL STUDIES. G. Mort, review of *Zoom!*, in *Poetry Review* 80, no. 1 (1990); L. Norfolk, review of *Zoom!*, in *Times Literary Supplement*, 5 January 1990; M. Glover, review of *Zoom!*, in *Agenda* 28, no. 4 (1991); T. Dooley, review of *Kid*, in *Times Literary Supplement*, 3 July 1992; Philip Gross, review of *Kid*, in *Poetry Review* 82, no. 2 (1992); David Kennedy, "Out of Huddersfield," in *Verse* 9, no. 3 (1992); William Cookson, review of *Book of Matches*, in *Agenda* 31, no. 3 (1993); Ian Gregson, "Matchstick Boy," in *Poetry Review* 83, no. 4 (1993); Peter Henry, review of *Kid*, in *Poetry Wales* 28, no. 3 (1993); Robert Potts, review of *Book of Matches*, in *Times Literary Supplement*, 17 December 1993; F. Gibbons, review of *The Dead Sea Poems*, in *Poetry Review* 85, no. 3 (1995); L. MacKinnon, review of *The Dead Sea Poems*, in *Times Literary Supplement*, 13 October 1995; Daniel McGuinness, review of *Book of Matches*, in *Antioch Review* 53, no. 1 (1995); John Hartley Williams, "Immanent Departures," in *New Statesman and Society*, 27 October 1995; Michael Hulse, "Bright Boroughs of Heaven," in *Poetry Review* 87, no. 3 (1997); James Lasdun, review of *CloudCuckooLand*, in *Times Literary Supplement*, 7 November 1997; William Scammell, "Of That and This," in *New Statesman*, 14 November 1997; Robert Potts, review of *Killing Time*, in *Times Literary Supplement*, 24 December 1999; Carol Rumens, "New Take on the Times," in *Poetry Review* 90, no. 1 (2000); Rachel Campbell-Johnston, "Leader of the Lad-Lit Gang," *The Times*, 25 July 2001; Alexis Hartley, "Necessary Wobbles: Simon Armitage and Reader-Author Relations," honors thesis, University of Queensland (2001); Jeremy Noel-Tod, "Profile: Simon Armitage," in *Areté* 4 (2001); Marion Thain, "An 'Uncomfortable Intersection': The Meeting of Contemporary Urban and Rural Environments in the Poetry of Simon Armitage," in *Worldviews* 5 (2001); David Wheatley, "From Lid Lit to Lad Lit," in *Poetry Review* 91, no. 3 (2001); S. Corbett, review of *Selected Poems*, in *Poetry Wales* 37, no. 3 (2002).

VI. INTERVIEWS. With Chris Greenhalgh, in *Bête Noire* 12/13 (1991); with Jane Stabler, in *Verse* 8, no. 1 (1991); with Mike Alexander, in *Sonnet Central*, http://www.sonnets.org/armitage.htm (2002).

ALAN BENNETT

(1934–)

Fred Bilson

ALAN BENNETT WAS born in Leeds, Yorkshire, on 9 May 1934, the second of two sons of Walter Bennett and Lilian Mary Bennett (née Peel). Mr. Bennett was a butcher, working first for the Cooperative Wholesale Society and later having his own shop. He died soon after retiring and moving from Leeds to the village of Clapham, Yorkshire, where Bennett still has a home. His mother died some years later, having suffered from depression.

At the age of eleven, Bennett was admitted to a prestigious local school, and then at seventeen won a place at Cambridge University in another competitive examination. But after two years' military service spent learning Russian, he decided to go to Oxford instead and passed his history degree with first-class honors.

On graduation, Bennett taught medieval history. He seems at this time to have been mildly depressive—by his own report, lacking motivation for the work and not enjoying it. However, Bennett was to escape from this early. He joined three other performers (Jonathan Miller and Peter Cook from Cambridge and Dudley Moore from Oxford) in *Beyond the Fringe,* a satirical revue that gave all of them the opportunity of a career in television, film, and the theater. At the time it seemed valuable in helping to demolish outdated attitudes and outmoded language.

In the early 1960s, Britain was still dominated by old-fashioned, rigid, conservative habits of thought, which enjoyed complete prestige. It was a world where women could be hanged, homosexuals could be imprisoned and black people ritually humiliated in TV comedy programs. Many found this intolerable, and satire was one method of changing public attitudes.

Satire works through parody and pastiche. It carefully imitates the language (the cadences and the vocabulary) used by people in power to mock the attitudes implicit in what they say; to subvert the language is to subvert the power. *Beyond the Fringe* was a show with a series of sketches and monologues of this kind. For example, they attack the British war film so common at this time, in which ruthless senior officers sacrifice younger men. Here Cook is the senior officer and Miller the victim. The team catches the note of schoolboy slang that covers the ruthlessness:

> COOK: I want you to lay down your life, Perkins. We need a futile gesture at this stage … Get up in a crate, Perkins, pop over to Bremen … don't come back. God, I wish I was going with you.
> MILLER: Goodbye, sir— or is it au revoir?
> COOK: No, Perkins
>
> (Bergan, *Beyond the Fringe … and Beyond,* p. 38)

For Bennett, *Beyond the Fringe* was followed by satirical sketch writing on television, especially in the show *On the Margin*, which ran from 9 November 1966 for six half-hour slots.

Bennett gave up teaching in 1962 and has spent the rest of his life as a creative artist. He has homes in London (where he writes), in Yorkshire (where he finds he can't write), and in New York.

In 1969, Bennett first encountered Miss Shepherd, an eccentric and unhygienic lady who lived in a truck (a van in English terms). By 1972 she was living in a shed in his garden and keeping her possessions in a succession of vans parked in the front garden of Bennett's London house. She was to remain there, living in squalor, until her death in 1989. She suffered from paranoid delusions, and her speech had two thumbprints that Bennett uses in his writing. One was a dysphasia that led her to describe, for example, "important matters" as "mattering things;" the other was a habit of qualifying statements with a "probably" at the end, as though she would not commit herself to the truth of anything.

Bennett is unmarried. For some time he was harried by journalists who wished to find out if he was homosexual. He refused to answer, as was his right. However, in an interview with Stephen Schiff published in the *New Yorker* (6 September 1993), he reported that having come to the end of a long relationship with a lady who had been his housekeeper, he was in a relationship with a male friend.

Alexander Games, in *Backing into the Limelight,* gives the most up-to-date account of Bennett's life, professional career, and relationships with the press. Bennett particularly distrusts journalists: "Journalists seldom get it right and . . . don't catch the tone in which [your words] are said, cutting out the qualifications (and I am all qualifications)" (*Telling Tales,* p. 9).

BENNETT'S THEMES

Bennett is not in any sense nostalgic, though this is his reputation. He has written a great deal about the life of his family but looks back at it without sentimentality. "Though my childhood was, I suppose, happy, I do not see it as bathed in . . . golden light. . . . I see it as dull now as I saw it as dull then; safe too and above all ordinary" (*Telling Tales,* p. 10).

As a child in the 1930s and 1940s he learned a code of behavior, a language of response to situations, which was very rigidly enforced. Social changes have now made much of this code irrelevant. Nostalgia would be one response, but he has no desire to return to that straightened society. However, as Joseph O'Mealy says, "he realizes what a privilege it is to have a choice in this matter, and one of his overriding concerns . . . is with those who can't go back because they have never left" (*Critical Introduction,* p. 21).

Bennett writes then about the treatment of those George Oliver in *Getting On* calls the "leftovers" (*Plays One*, p.113)—sad clerks facing redundancy; widows and retired married couples frightened and embarrassed by life. Sometimes his lines acquire almost proverbial status, for example catching the refusal of the old to try new experiences in the phrase "we can't be branching out into yogurt at our ages." He has written particularly about the north of England because this is the England of his childhood, and its speech patterns are his speech patterns.

To Bennett, the writer is a spy, observing and reporting on people without their knowledge, but bound by a duty to be loyal and serve their interests. He has examined this in a series of plays about spies who have betrayed England, and in biographical plays on Kafka, Proust, and Joe Orton. *The Laying on of Hands: Stories* (2001) is much darker. He reported that he found it difficult to write because "I think [the book] is as dark as I could let myself be publicly without being rejected altogether. Writing is a deplorable profession. It makes you into a half person who can feel strongly about something but is always holding something back. We can justly be accused of exploiting people because that is exactly what we do." (Amelia Hill, *The Observer,* 9 December 2001).

BENNETT AS PROFESSIONAL ACTOR AND PLAYWRIGHT

Bennett has appeared as an actor in the West End and on television both in his own plays and in works by Shakespeare, John Osborne, and Ben Travers. In addition, he has been active in recording for audiotape both his own material and English children's classics.

As a playwright and television dramatist he has always been thoroughly professional, delivering his commissions early and being willing to undertake considerable rewrites. As an actor and as a writer, he has a strong sense of the deliverable line and has provided major roles for some leading British actors—John Gielgud, Alec Guinness, Maggie Smith, Thora Hird, and Patricia Routledge, among others—and has often been instrumental in enabling them to develop new directions. His work in *Forty Years On* (1968) is credited with having persuaded Gielgud to branch out into modern comedy, in which the actor built a large reputation late in life.

Writing in 1993, Albert Hunt noted in Bennett's work the importance of gossip, which is structural within the plays and has subversive force. "To say that Bennett's work is built around gossip is not in any way to disparage that work. . . . The people and institutions in our society who are in the business of inventing and upholding what Louis Buñuel called 'official reality' [do not gossip]. Gossip . . . is an antidote to 'official reality' " (p. 24).

Gossip is conspiratorial. The talker includes the listener by appealing to shared values, shared language, and shared experience. Curiously, it can be repetitive—new gossip is always welcome, but the retelling of old anecdotes helps shape our understanding of our experience.

For John Bull, Bennett's *Forty Years On* was the first shot in a necessary campaign to reestablish a viable commercial theater. Using a phrase derived from Bennett's mock sermon "Take a Pew" in *Beyond the Fringe*, Bull divides current English playwrights into the nonpolitical "smooth men" (Bennett, Michael Frayn, Alan Ayckbourn, Peter Nichols, Tom Stoppard, Simon Gray) and the political "hairy men" who are committed to a socialist view of the theater. The smooth men write plays that are neutral in political terms, rather than committed. They locate their plays in rooms (rather than in the street, say, or the workplace) and tend to write in a mode reminiscent of the Theatre of the Absurd or of Samuel Beckett.

The theatrical event is a production rather than a script, so that it is created in the dialog between performance and reception, cast and audience. With the smooth men, the audience is able comfortably to bring what they see into conformity with middle-class expectations. Bull centers on the way in which Gielgud in *Forty Years On* and Kenneth More in *Getting On* contributed to this process. (Bull, pp. 11–12).

Joseph O'Mealy in *Alan Bennett: A Critical Introduction* provides a fuller analysis of Bennett's intellectual status, showing exactly how Bennett has been stimulated by Beckett and Kafka, and also enlarging on his known interest in the work of Erving Goffman, to provide analysis of Bennett's stagecraft in terms of Goffman's analysis of social interactions.

TWO VOICES

Bennett is a master writer of comic prose. To show something of how the effect is achieved, consider the anecdote—perhaps his most famous and certainly one of his favorites—that describes his mother's meeting with one of his father's customers. "A few years later when my dad had sold the shop but we were still living in Leeds, my mother came in one day and said, 'I ran into Mrs. Fletcher down the road. She wasn't with Mr. Fletcher; she was with another feller—tall, elderly, very refined-looking and we passed the time of day.' " Realizing this was T. S. Eliot (Mrs. Fletcher's son-in-law), Bennett tried to explain to his mother who T. S. Eliot was, but "without much success, *The Waste Land* not figuring very largely in Mam's scheme of things." Finally he tells her, "The thing is . . . he won the Nobel Prize." "Well," she said, with that unerring grasp of inessentials which is the prerogative of mothers, "I'm not surprised. It was a beautiful overcoat" (*Writing Home*, pp. ix–x).

Daphne Turner points out the switching between use of the northern voice ("dad," "Mam") and the southern voice ("my mother"). Bennett "puts himself into her camp and respects her scale of values," but through his use of the southern, educated voice in the narration "he controls the syntax rhetorically to produce a climax ('T. S. Eliot') . . . and a comic *litotes* (not figuring very largely)" (pp. 150–151).

Bennett calls "this awkward encounter with Mr. Eliot a parable, a prefiguring of how [I should write] in two different voices, metropolitan ('speaking properly') and provincial ('being yourself')" (*Writing Home*, pp. x–xi). The linguistic subtlety noted here is not unique to Bennett; if it were, he would not have a wide audience. Most of us can manage this kind of code-switching in daily conversation. The "provincial" voice carries the narrative line entirely in language available to Mrs. Bennett; where Mrs. Bennett is silent, the narrative line cannot reach. Did she pass the time of day with T. S. Eliot or only with Mrs. Fletcher?

Bennett can only speculate on what took place: "Mam smiling desperately, as she and Dad always did when they were out of their depth;

nodding a good deal too, so as not to have to speak; and . . . trying to 'speak properly' without 'putting it on' . . . it was class and temperament, not want of education, that held their tongues" (p. x).

The overt comedy in this anecdote comes from the "metropolitan" voice, which is an educated voice. Certainly, you need to know who T. S. Eliot was to appreciate the story, and you need to be able to read the synecdoche in "*The Waste Land* not figuring very largely in Mam's scheme of things"; *The Waste Land* stands here for the whole of Eliot's work or his achievement. But you could also read the synecdoche in the reverse direction; if you did not know previously, you would now guess that one of Eliot's works was called *The Waste Land*.

Additionally, the *litotes* of "not figuring very largely in Mam's scheme of things" is technically well judged. In fact, it did not figure at all. This understatement is a primary feature of English writing in the twentieth century and is part of an ironic distancing of the writer from direct, raw experience.

What puzzles most of us initially is why T. S. Eliot should turn up in Leeds at all. But life handles coincidence better than literature does. Once we know that Mrs. Fletcher had been a customer of Mr. Bennett, the wonder is that the Bennetts did not meet him more often. There is even a trace of resentment on this head in Bennett's account.

FORTY YEARS ON

Bennett's *Beyond the Fringe* is not in print at this writing, and his work in a popular television series *On the Margin* has been junked by the BBC, though many in his original audience still know by heart large parts of the mock sermon "Take a Pew" or the sketch where an Oxford academic sends a telegram to a call girl.

By 1968, Bennett had written his first play, still very much in the mode of satiric revue. Sir John Gielgud agreed to take the leading role (the Headmaster) in the first production of *Forty Years On*, and Bennett has documented Gielgud's participation in the development of the play (*Writing Home*, pp. 243–259).

Forty Years On is a confident work that constantly changes mood and direction. A crowded set represents the hall of Albion House. Albion is, of course, a poetic name for England, and Albion House is a small, mediocre English public school (that is, in American terms, a prep school); the Headmaster is due to retire the day following the action and is to be succeeded by Franklin, one of his housemasters. Franklin is putting on a play, *Speak for England, Arthur,* to be acted by members of the staff and boys. The Headmaster has been persuaded to take part and read some of the speeches impromptu.

One center of interest here is authority; the Headmaster is relinquishing the school and Franklin is taking it on. This is paralleled by their reactions to the play: Franklin attempts to impose order on it while the Headmaster is keen to censor the text as it emerges. The ludicrousness of this effort reflects the ludicrousness of some of the actions of the Lord Chamberlain, who had had the right to censor plays for public performance until 1968, the year of the play's production.

The school is small-scale. The Headmaster admits, "We aren't a rich school, we aren't a powerful school, not any more. We don't set much store by cleverness at Albion House so we don't run away with all the prizes. We used to in the old days . . . but we bequeathed our traditions to other schools, and if now we lead where we follow, it is because of that" (*Plays One*, p. 29).

The dramatic tradition at Albion House is small-scale too, ranging over "that first trailblazing production of *Dear Octopus* and last year's brave stab at *Samson Agonistes*" (p. 29). It is a paradigmatic example of what the British theater had been offering before John Osborne and the new dramatists. On the one hand, the classic play; on the other, the comfortable and shoddy play like Dodie Smith's *Dear Octopus* (1939). This is a sentimental work about the power of the family (the "octopus") over its members—it embraces and smothers, but the play welcomes that embrace.

Like Franklin himself, *Speak for England, Arthur* represents something new on the scene. Not that the Headmaster necessarily approves. "If you're going to take the radical step and throw Dodie Smith out of the window . . . you've got to have something to put in her place" (p. 67). This is, of course, the objection always made to satires like *Beyond the Fringe* and *Forty Years On*. Partly the answer is that you do not—some things are so bad they must just be ended.

Forty Years On has a double structure moving from the school with its masters, boys, matron, and bursar's secretary into the production of *Speak for England, Arthur* and out again.

Speak for England, Arthur owes much to a radio tradition very popular in the 1940s, the scrapbook. In a scrapbook a narrative line would form a spine, telling the history of one year from January to December, and the narrative would be interspersed with items like music, radio comedy shows, sports commentaries, and the like.

The narrative spine of *Speak for England, Arthur* concerns a Conservative MP (member of Parliament), Hugh, and his wife, nicknamed Moggie. "Moggie" in England is the word used for a pet cat of which you are quite fond, but which is no great beauty; she would have been given this nickname in childhood. They take refuge for the duration of the war in one of the rooms set up in the cellars of the luxurious Claridge's Hotel that acted as air-raid shelters. Hugh has been an opponent of Prime Minister Neville Chamberlain's appeasement policy. They are accompanied by Hugh's nanny, Nursie. They move in on 3 September 1939 and are still there on VE Day in 1945. A number of scenes tell their story: the war begins, rationing is introduced, their son Christopher becomes a prisoner of war.

This spine is interspersed with readings from the lectern and acted scenes (mostly pastiche) that move from 1900 to 1945; Bennett calls this the "double cog" of the structure. They come together at the end to make a statement about England today.

The readings and dramatic scenes represent the reading and theatrical taste of the English middle classes of the period (Oscar Wilde, Lewis Carroll, Bloomsbury, T. E. Lawrence, the "snobbery with violence" novelists) but above all memoirs—gossip about the famous. Memoirs of course imply memory, and the limitations of memory are one of the preoccupations of the play—what Bennett calls "the dull distorting effects of time, in phrases which sound right, but aren't. 'Patience is mine. I will delay saith the Lord' [for 'Vengeance is mine. I will repay']" (*Writing Home*, p. 258).

Memory is also selective. As Bennett says, "The Headmaster remembers and reveres the Lost Generation of 1914. . . . Franklin shrugs them off but recalls. . . . the Second World War" (p. 258). Bennett is dealing with history here, and as a historian he is concerned with the origins of historical explanation and the making of historical myth on the basis of selective memory.

The threat of violence in our personal lives mirrors the threat of violence that war brings. In the middle of the first act, Bennett has a technically accomplished incident in which the framing play, the function of which is generally to interrupt the framed play, is itself interrupted. We hear offstage the sound of singing, gradually getting louder in "tipsy hearty voices." Told that Franklin has gone off to stop it, and that it is spontaneous, the Headmaster responds, "Spontaneous? Then it must be stopped at once" (p. 51). The singing has been the chanting of a smutty parody of a psalm, of the sort known in England as a rugby club song. In fact it is the rugby team, and Franklin drags in the team captain, who reports that Albion House has just beaten Stowe 17–6. (Stowe at this time had the reputation of being the most minor of the public schools.) This news almost brings the play to an end. The Headmaster is transformed. But the threat of disruption, even violence, from the drunken young men passes when they leave.

This piece of business is strongly reminiscent of the episode in the film of William Golding's *Lord of the Flies* (1963) in which boys of the choir school enter in procession on the beach; they include some of the most vicious characters in that work. Bennett may also be thinking of the victory of England in the World Cup soccer final of 1966, which unleashed displays of loutish behavior.

The dramatic climax of *Speak for England, Arthur,* which gives the play its title, is the scene, taken from history, in which Prime Minister Chamberlain announces to the House of Commons in October 1938 that he has bought peace with Germany by sacrificing Czechoslovakia. It is when the Labor Party's Arthur Greenwood rises to speak for the opposition that a Conservative MP, disgusted with the betrayal of Munich, calls out, "Speak for England, Arthur."

This action fixed Chamberlain forever as a villain, but as a historian, Bennett is concerned about giving a balanced view. He knows that there are many who would be content to see Chamberlain take on all the guilt of Munich so that it sinks with him. But it will not. At this point, Bennett gives us a mock trial of Chamberlain, like the trial in *Alice in Wonderland.* "This is not a court of justice, it is a court of history," says the judge. Sounding for all the world like a schoolmaster, he goes on: "And in this court we judge solely by appearances. . . . Why are you wearing that ridiculous wing-collar?" (p. 87). *Speak for England, Arthur* is packed with parodies of literary texts—some are affectionate, as of T. E. Lawrence (Lawrence of Arabia); some are hostile, as in the parodies of the "snobbery with violence" school of John Buchan (1875–1940) or "Sapper," the pen-name of H. C. McNeile (1888–1937). Both wrote adventure novels in which typically a heroic middle-class Englishman saves Britain from a conspiracy led by sinister foreigners. The works are strongly xenophobic and anti-Semitic. Both writers were enormously popular and influential in their day; their books were filmed and Buchan was to become Governor-General of Canada.

But above all, the play is full of a love of England, for all the confusion that dealing with it brings. This shows best at the end of each act. At the end of act 1, Bennett writes a monologue supposedly representing a night remembered by one of the Lost Generation who died in World War I. The fictitious speaker and his friends are a group of young men who leave a ball in London on 3 August 1914—the night before war is declared—and motor down to Kent. They are the first generation to know the joy of motoring at high speed, and Bennett catches the uniqueness of this one moment in time. They find Kimber House locked up but make their way in and explore the old house, climbing up to the roof; "there would be other nights and time yet, I thought . . . then, suddenly, just before dawn we heard the nightingales."

This is, of course, England as Eden; 1914 as the Land of Lost Content. Powerful as the myth is, the play shatters the mood instantly. We return to the main action of the play in Albion House. Matron bangs down a crate of milk bottles for the boys and the act ends (p. 65).

The parallel ending of act 2 deals with the present (1968). The principals and the Headmaster, shedding costumes and gowns, recite a litany about the time: "A sergeant's world it is now. . . . The hedges come down from the silent fields. . . . A butterfly is an event. . . . Once we had a romantic and old-fashioned conception of honour, of patriotism, chivalry and duty. . . . But . . . it didn't have much to do with justice, with social justice anyway. And in default of that justice, and in pursuit of it . . . the great words came to be cancelled out" (p 95).

Finally comes a real estate agent's view of England. In the final speech of the play, Bennett has a speech in which one of the characters speaks of England as though it were for sale:

"To let. A valuable site at the cross-roads of the world. At present on offer to European clients. Outlying portions of the estate already disposed of to existing tenants. Of some historical and period interest. Some alterations and improvements necessary" (p. 96).

At the end of the play, the Headmaster hands the school over to Franklin. The boys sing the hymn "All people that on Earth do dwell." The first sung item in the play was a straight rendition of the popular school song "Forty Years On"; the last is a straight rendering of a hymn. In England nowadays, hymns have a social rather than a religious function—they are almost folksongs that mark events in the collective life of the country. Their other use in this play is for the rugby club parodies (not by Bennett, but traditional). Now the forms that have been mocked in parody are being handed back to their everyday use.

Like the Headmaster, Bennett too was moving on. Satire and parody remained among Bennett's skills, but he was now to look for new modes of expression.

GETTING ON AND HABEAS CORPUS

Bennett followed *Forty Years On* with two plays that represent attempts to write within two different genres. *Getting On* (1971) is a realistic drama and *Habeas Corpus* (1973) is a standard farce, rather dated, as Bennett admits, but a favorite both with him and with amateur dramatic companies (*Plays One,* pp. 17–18). These plays presented the author with the problem of characterization and the need to judge how explicitly the development of the characters can be depicted. His views are suggested in an article he wrote in which he refers to Louis Malle's film *Lacombe, Lucien* (1974). In France during the German occupation, Lacombe becomes a member of the *milice,* a French armed police force working with the Germans; he meets a Jewish family and exploits them, eventually helping their daughter escape; in the end he is shot. He has not changed or developed in any way as a result of his experiences. "The stock way to tell such a story would be to see the boy's experience . . . as a moral education . . . but [the film] doesn't. . . . To have quite unobtrusively resisted the tug of conventional story-telling and the lure of resolution seemed to me honest" ("Seeing Stars," p. 16).

Another influence was the work of the sociologist Erving Goffman. In 1980 Bennett reviewed, anecdotally rather than systematically, Goffman's 1981 book *Forms of Talk* (in *Writing Home,* pp. 302–312) and when he made a documentary, *Dinner at Noon* (1988), he based it on an earlier Goffman work, *The Presentation of Self* (1956). The documentary did not entirely work because the conversations among the guests were not interesting enough, and Bennett had to use more voice-over than he originally intended—a salutary warning to those who think writers like Bennett just use things they hear people say on the bus.

Goffman's early field work had been done in a hotel and contrasts the behavior of the staff "out there" in the hotel itself with their behavior "in here" in the kitchen. "Out there" (or in theatrical terms "onstage") requires "impression management" while "in here" ("backstage") allows a greater degree of informality, though rules of social interaction still apply.

O'Mealy provides many analyses of Bennett's work in terms of a more rigorous systemization of Goffman's work. (For *Dinner at Noon* see *Critical Introduction*, p. 20.)

In *Getting On,* George Oliver, a Labor MP, shares his home with Polly, his second wife, and Andy, his seventeen-year-old son by his first marriage. He and Polly have two younger children, whom we do not see.

Polly brings home Geoff Price, a young man of nineteen, who helps with odd jobs around the house. Brian Lowther, a Conservative MP, is George's closest friend. He is a homosexual who must conceal his sexuality but is being blackmailed. Enid Baker, Polly's mother, is an independent lady in her sixties but may be seriously ill. Geoff and Polly have a relationship (unknown to George) as later do Geoff and Brian (unknown at first to both George and Polly). Brian's homosexuality is reported to his constituency party, and they tell him that they will not run him at the next election. Enid says that the doctor has told her she is in good health, but, though neither Polly nor George can be sure she is telling the truth, they do not check. At the end of the play, Geoff goes off to Spain to start a new job, and Brian and Polly both feel bereft and lonely without him. At the same time, Andy rebuffs George and claims the right to privacy and independence of action.

Daphne Turner, pointing out the parallels between this play and Osborne's *Look Back in Anger,* sees Bennett as "us[ing] the larger than life quality of stage writing, the way it addresses a meeting, to characterize George." It is suitable that George is a Labor MP, and that we see him practicing his speeches. Turner likes the long, eloquent speeches that make him entertaining—especially when he compares a chicken farm to a concentration camp (Turner, p. 141).

On the other hand, O'Mealy finds George "a bore . . . since we know he cares nothing about anyone but himself, we soon stop listening." Famously, Kenneth More, who created George onstage, substantially revised the script; for example, he had George promise to ring the doctor to check up on Enid. More wanted to make the play both more comic and more humane. O'Mealy suggests this represents "the veteran performer giving . . . a lesson in how deeply ingrained the impulse towards impression management truly is" (*Critical Introduction*, pp. 9–12).

Much of the action of the play goes on in the gaps left by George's rare silences. We first see Andy alone, for example, in a scene in which he comes into the kitchen, drinks from a bottle of milk he takes from the fridge, replaces the bottle and switches off the light. He is wordless, and his words do not fit into his father's conversations. When later he attempts to discuss whether he should leave school, his father will not hear of it. There is no reference to Andy's needs. The discussion is in abstract terms: education is a good thing. As Andy tries to formulate his ideas, George oppresses them and shows an incoherence that is a direct result of George's coherence, each reinforcing the other.

To Geoff and to many other supposedly inferior people, George is rude and patronizing. He has just returned to London from a visit to his constituency in the North of England to consult with local people about their problems.

He is contemptuous of them, especially of a West Indian woman who claims the people next door are poisoning her cat, so he does nothing about it (pp. 108–109). Geoff says that it must be awful to have been alive during the war and have your earliest memories, you know, sort of seared by it. George seizes on the word to ridicule Geoff. "I was evacuated to Harrogate [a very safe spa town]," replies George, "and that was a bit [pause] searing. Were you [pause] seared at all, Polly?" (p. 107).

Much of the play's action takes place in these silences. When George is rude to Geoff, and asks Polly if she was seared, the stage direction reads, "Polly pointedly ignores him." Eventually Geoff

is able to make a simple declaration that he fancies Polly and her response is an incoherent "Yes, I do. I mean yes" (p. 128). But despite this induced incoherence, those around George retain their autonomy. Geoff leaves for Spain; Andy tells his father that he is not having a sexual relationship but, "When I do start, and I care and you say things like that . . . I shall just go. . . . And sometimes, Dad, keep your mouth shut. That's cool. I commend it to you" (p. 182).

George, then, so much imposes his patterns and his analysis on the situations around him that he cannot see what is going on. It is perhaps only in the last moments of the play that he realizes he can sometimes be wrong. Reading the local paper from his constituency, he finds a story about the West Indian woman whose cats were being poisoned by her neighbors. "I thought she was mad. She wasn't. They were. She's taken them to court and they've been fined" (p. 183). This time it is his language that is simple and slightly non-coherent. In the end, nothing has changed. It is as though, even in this early play, Bennett leaves his characters with their autonomy and resists "the tug of conventional story-telling and the lure of resolution."

WORK FOR TELEVISION

Bennett began to write television drama in the 1970s, and one of the central critical problems concerning those works has been whether this was a "golden age" of television. Critics like Hunt, who believe it was, tend to rate Bennett highly.

The first of his television plays, *A Day Out* (1972), was shot on location in West Yorkshire. In 1911, a group of men gather at a war memorial in Halifax to cycle to Fountains Abbey, a local beauty spot. They are of different social classes, with different politics and different personalities, bound only by the fact that they enjoy cycling together. At Fountains Abbey, they play cricket and eat a packed lunch; one of them has a brutal sexual relationship with a local girl and another attempts a flirtation with an upper-middle-class girl. Two moods prevail. One is the sense of a new world opening up, and the welcome given by the English countryside to these men; the other is the sense of their being what would then be called "pals." In 1914, the "pals" would join the army in groups, and many would die—Bennett's Uncle Clarence, Mrs. Bennett's brother, was one. The film ends with an epilogue set in 1919 in which four survivors gather with their bicycles at another, newer war memorial. Bennett was commemorating the sense that sometimes delight can come unexpectedly. The fact that the film is set in the past does not make it nostalgic.

In *Sunset Across the Bay* (1975) a retired couple, displaced from Leeds by housing clearance, have settled in Morecambe, a seaside holiday town in Lancashire. They face a life of tranquil monotony, interspersed by embarrassment, when, for example, they try an ethnic restaurant (where they fail to branch out into yogurt). During a visit from their son they drive up to the Lake District, where the wife recalls Wordsworth from her schooldays and recites "I wandered lonely as a cloud." But the son goes, and the moment passes. Eventually the husband suffers a stroke in a public toilet, and the wife is too embarrassed to go in and check on why he is so long. She waits until he she can ask a man to do it. By then her husband is dead; his last words, using a euphemism for "urinate," are "I'll just go and shed a tear." The pastoral melancholy of the play is balanced by the dignity that Bennett allows the protagonists, and the feeling that their fate should be of interest to us all.

The remainder of the television plays of this period are collected in *Office Suite* (1981) and *The Writer in Disguise* (1985). Among these, *All Day on the Sands* (1979) deals with the stresses within a family caused by the father's loss of his job and the deterioration of relationships that results; *Afternoon Off* (1978) tells of an Asian waiter humiliated in his quest for a girlfriend; and *Me, I'm Afraid of Virginia Woolf* (1978) tells how a literature teacher in night school, who lives with an oppressive mother and has an oppressive relationship with his girlfriend, ends up beginning a relationship with a male student. This ending typifies the feel of much of Bennett's work; it is nonjudgmental, and Bennett is an almost

unique example of a writer who depicts a homosexual relationship as devoid of ideological content. The playing of "A Wonderful Guy" over the credits is non-ironic; in other works the joy is found in a heterosexual relationship.

Available as both text and videotape, *Talking Heads* (1987), is a highly popular and innovative series of dramatic monologues. In each, we see only a single actor representing a single character, but each character describes encounters with other people whom we do not see. One of the puzzles in the form is judging how far these stories of encounters with others are true, and how far they are fictions by our central character. Bennett wrote the first play as a single drama *A Woman of No Importance* in 1982. Then came a series of six broadcast in 1988 followed by a further six, written over a longer period culminating in *Waiting for the Telegram* in 1998.

Originally a dismissive phrase to describe static television that simply broadcasts talk, rather than true visual images, "talking heads" becomes in Bennett's hands the expression of a highly concentrated, direct and intimate reading of a single human being. Bennett originally suggested the use of a series of mid-shots tracking in to close-up and then tracking out again. In production, a static viewpoint with the camera in a medium to close shot and with the actor minimizing movement turned out to be more compelling, though Bennett is not sure why (*Talking Heads*, pp. 10–11).

The monologue hands over to the character control of the discourse; viewers are never quite sure whether they are being addressed or whether the character is musing, "thinking aloud." The character also has complete autonomy. Viewers may perceive some irony that the character misses, and above all, they should not take the discourse at face value.

Bed Among the Lentils, one of the first series of *Talking Heads*, is the tale of a vicar's wife who hates religion and the church, and despises both her husband and the band of church people that surrounds him. It is not until she collapses in the church that we realize, as she does not at the time, that she is alcoholic. Searching for sources of liquor, she encounters Mr. Ramesh, an Indian storekeeper, with whom she has a joyous affair. He makes her a bed among the lentils in the storeroom, and she trickles her fingers through the lentils. Is this a detail that validates the story or merely an extra in a fanciful scenario? He persuades her that love would be nicer if she were sober, so she joins Alcoholics Anonymous. Her husband believes that he has been responsible for the change. Now accepted everywhere, they have a great future in the church before them.

Joseph O'Mealy catches the significance of location in this play and analyzes it in terms of Goffman. It begins "backstage" with Susan in her kitchen dressed in a housecoat; in this context she is apparently being self-revealing in her story. The play ends "onstage" in the dining room, her hair and clothes immaculate, a model of impression management.

The second series of *Talking Heads* is very much darker in tone and includes *Waiting for the Telegram*. An old lady in a home, where she flirts with her male nurse Francis, remembers with grief the death of her first sweetheart in World War I. She remembers the women in the street waiting for the telegram and the form letter from the king that would tell them they had lost someone in the trenches. She has carried with her the regret of having refused to make love with Edward before he went to war; this in turn reminds her that she will get a telegram from the queen on her hundredth birthday. And as Francis is homosexual, he may face an early death as Edward did. The play is a cool, well-balanced look at the cost of war and falsity in human relationships.

ENJOY

By 1980, Bennett had the reputation of being a writer who celebrated in his television plays a northern England of melancholy pastoralism lightened by wit. *Enjoy* (1980) therefore came as a shock to its audiences, who found it disturbing and did not receive it warmly. Unusually, it was set in the working-class conurbation of Leeds rather than in one of the smaller northern towns.

Wilfred and Connie Craven (Mam and Dad) live in the last remaining house in their street. They are both old—he has lost the feeling in his arm and she is losing her mind. Their daughter, Linda, is a personal secretary and has just gone to Sweden with her boss. There is also one other person, whom Wilfred will not mention—their son, Terry.

A paper is pushed through the door. The local council has allocated them an observer who will come in and make notes but will not speak to them. We are not told what the observer is writing down. She is part of the system by which people's lives are menaced. In this case, the observer is a Ms. Craig, who is in fact a man dressed as a woman. Linda returns, and she is obviously a prostitute. She has not been to Sweden, but to Swindon (a rather dull market town in southern England). She has come to pack because she is going to Saudi Arabia to be married. Left alone in the room, Ms. Craig walks over to the mantelpiece and describes the objects in such a way that we realize this must be Terry.

The second act introduces Anthony, a local lout also with his own observer, who has come to show Dad a pornographic magazine with a photo of Linda in it. It is Ms. Craig who lets him in. Following a quarrel, Anthony strikes Dad, and Dad collapses. Anthony leaves together with his observer, who has not intervened. Mam sends for a neighbor to lay Dad out; while they are washing him, he recovers. However, he is now incontinent and will be hospitalized. Linda is off on another sexual adventure. The house will be re-erected in a theme park where it will be on permanent exhibition. Workmen begin to demolish it. Ms. Craig will be living out in the countryside where Leeds is only "a glow on the horizon"—a phrase from Bennett's childhood used to describe what those who watched cities burning after air raids would see.

The play is firmly in the tradition of the Theatre of the Absurd. Speech is incongruous. Some of Mam and Dad's speech is taken from advertising: "Sweden boasts some fine modern architecture plus a free-wheeling attitude towards personal morality," Dad explains, and then switches codes: "But our Linda's a sensible girl; she won't be bowled over by that" (p. 269). Other sections of the text depend on Mam's dysphasia following her earlier institutionalization.

Motivations are arbitrary. Anthony behaves badly because his bad behavior is what his observer is observing. Linda's sexual couplings are arbitrary. Small occurrences, like the pushing of a paper through the front door, represent major crises; Dad's apparent death is almost incidental to the action. The play ends with the set itself being demolished.

It is a deeply disturbing play. On a sociological level, Bennett forces his audience to realize that they sentimentalize the lives of previous generations, which they see as warm but which were in fact often cold and violent. They would not live this life themselves, but they want someone to be living it now, so that they can visit it—they want a northern theme park with real people in it.

Sexually it is even darker. Men (Dad, Anthony, Linda's chauffeur) are predatory and sexually abusive; only Ms. Craig escapes this by escaping the male orientation. Intrusively, critics have suggested that Ms. Craig is a self-portrait. This is not, of course, a literary judgment, and Bennett rightly resents it. Daphne Turner discusses this at some length (pp. 95–97).

KAFKA'S DICK

Franz Kafka, a German writer who lived in Prague, is now considered a major figure. His friend and literary executor, Max Brod, was also a well known writer—seriously considered at one time for the Nobel Prize—whose reputation today depends on his work promoting Kafka. This 1986 stage play considers the status of being a writer—how a reputation is built up and how the reputation of a writer affects those around him—and should be read in conjunction with the introduction, a cogent essay on Kafka as a writer.

The title is a pun. A dick is a private policeman. Kafka had two—his father, Hermann Kafka, and Brod, who policed the reputation of his work. Both appear in the play along with Kafka himself. A dick is also a penis, and Kafka was, apparently, obsessed by the belief that his was particularly small. Bennett challenges the general belief that if we know some piece of gossip about the writer (for example that Proust wrote in a cork-lined room) we have a clue to the writing. We do not, and Bennett resents the substitution of gossip for intelligent analysis. He questions too the value of biography in explaining the work of writers.

Kafka's Dick opens with a scene in Prague in about 1919. Thinking he is dying, Kafka urges Brod to burn all his writing. Brod agrees readily and pretends to be going out to buy paraffin; Kafka begins to backpedal. Brod tells Kafka about the Nazi book-burnings in 1933. By then Kafka was dead, but Brod was still alive. It is not an anachronism. We cannot keep what we know now out of our judgments about the past; we cannot have a picture of Kafka as an unknown writer with five years left to live.

Keeping up the theme of burning, Brod points out to Kafka that the Nazis cannot burn his work, because Brod would already have done it. If Kafka relents, he might end up as famous as Brod. But Kafka is infuriated when Brod says his most famous short story, *Metamorphosis,* is about a man who turns into a cockroach. "Beetle," Kafka responds furiously. Then, in a marvelous unconscious pun on the phrase "words fail me," he says, "You write one thing, the reader makes it into another. You try to be honest, only words fail you" (*Plays Two,* p. 32).

Kafka goes off to bed; he is reluctant to do so because he dreams the future. The next scene (the dream) is set in the present day and is firmly in the Theatre of the Absurd mode. Sydney is an insurance clerk (like Kafka) and is writing a biographical article on him. Sydney's father is infirm and believes he is about to be institutionalized; he is desperately trying to improve his mind. He goes off with a book he believes is a thriller (it is called *The Trial*). Sydney and his wife, Linda, are in fact expecting the visitor who will arrange for Father to be put away, but conceal this from him. Brod enters, carrying the family tortoise (a shy, retiring animal) which metamorphoses into Franz Kafka. There is some good business where everyone tries to hide the Kafka books from Kafka (who does not know they have not been burned), and Kafka (who is flirting with Linda) tries to hide the food she

ALAN BENNETT

gives him that he cannot eat. The truth comes out when Father brings back *The Trial,* complaining that it is not a detective story.

Linda has summoned the police, and a policeman turns up in the form of Kafka's father, Hermann. By threatening to tell his son's secret, (which is well known to everyone) Hermann persuades Kafka to say he loves him. But after a mock trial of Kafka, Hermann realizes that if he had been a good father, Kafka might never have been a writer. We owe him as much as we owe Brod.

The final scene is set in heaven, where Hermann is God, and everyone else is a celebrity (Linda is Nurse Edith Cavell, the World War I heroine, Father is Bertrand Russell) so that Kafka, there as himself, is there as a celebrity. Kafka reflects, "Heaven is going to be hell" (p. 116).

It is a subtly crafted play, setting Kafka-Hermann and Sydney-Father against one another as Oedipal situations. Additionally, Father is the common reader; desperately trying to keep up, he keeps going off to work things out and comes back only to find the truth has changed.

The play considers a host of questions about writing. How do we evaluate the personal agony of a writer? Is biographical detail relevant? Kafka was never famous in his lifetime. "He knows he's Kafka. He doesn't know he's KAFKA," says Brod (p. 55). Bennett has been famous throughout his creative career. Have audience expectations colored his writing? What is it like to eclipse your own fame, as Brod did, to build someone else's?

SPIES

Bennett wrote a group of three plays about spies, *The Old Country* (1977), *An Englishman Abroad* (television 1983; play 1988), and *A Question of Attribution* (1988). They relate to a group of well-placed, Cambridge-educated British spies who passed secrets to the Soviet Union. Three—Guy Burgess, Donald Maclean, and "Kim" Philby—fled into exile in Russia as they were about to be arrested. Sir Anthony Blunt remained in England and held important posts as an art expert, including keeper of the queen's pictures. He thus both betrayed the queen and protected her from exploitation.

Bennett sees spies as a metaphor for writers. They observe other people, discover their secrets, and report on them. Sometimes they betray them. Occasionally, as a result of that betrayal, they must live in exile, but when they do they take with them the whole of their cultural baggage. In fact, when he wrote *The Old Country* he was reportedly thinking more of W. H. Auden's self-imposed exile in America (*Plays Two,* p. ix).

The Old Country is set in Russia, but Bennett at first conceals that fact. He does not want us to make a priori judgments about his central character, Hilary. He and his wife, Bron, have a comfortable, shabby life out in the country, and they have a visit from another couple, Eric and Olga. Only Olga is not quite English. It is only later when a third couple, Duff and Veronica (Hilary's sister), arrives that we realize that we are in Russia. Duff tells Hilary he might now be able to return to England. By the end of the play this has been arranged, partly with Olga's help. Eric pleads to be allowed back too, but he is not important enough and is not of the right social class. Desperately he reminds Duff that he has been his lover, but even this does no good. He remains trapped in exile by his social class.

It is not only the Russian background of the play that suggests Anton Chekhov. Here too are the interest in trees and plants, the round of visitors, the long, closely knit and allusive conversations, and the sense of nostalgia for the center (Moscow, London) where life is quick and exciting. Above all, there is the presence of the "unnecessary man"—the man who has no function in society for all his culture and charm. Why should England want Hilary back?

The play abounds in irony, but what remains is the impression of a corrupt class supporting its own. Duff tells Hilary, "People died. Some of them first class. And I think you will probably be made to stand in a corner for three or four years. . . . And financially no more problems. Television, the Sundays [newspapers] . . . falling over themselves." The mildness of the prison term suggested is compounded by its description in the childish phrase "stand in a corner" (p. 253).

ALAN BENNETT

An Englishman Abroad (revised from a television play) and *A Question of Attribution* make a double bill in the theater. *An Englishman Abroad* recounts the meeting in Moscow between the actress Coral Brown and Guy Burgess. Despite his treachery, Burgess remains thoroughly English in his tastes and avid for gossip of London, while offering Brown a meal of raw garlic and tomatoes. Shabby, a petty thief, a con man, he persuades Brown to buy him some clothes in London. The play ends with him in his new finery as the "the picture of an upper-class Englishman" singing Gilbert and Sullivan's "For He Is an Englishman." As in the title *Me, I'm Afraid of Virginia Woolf,* the lyric has both the original and a reinterpreted force. Burgess of course "might have been a Roosian" but "remains an Englishman" (p. 299). Yet in what sense is he an Englishman? Is being English just wearing a suit?

A Question of Attribution begins with Sir Anthony Blunt being questioned by the security services. Blunt is investigating a picture by Titian. Originally it had been thought there were portraits of two men in the picture, but further scientific investigation shows there are actually three; one has been concealed by overpainting. In the same way, it had been thought there were only two spies—Burgess and Maclean—but now Blunt's head might be in the frame as well. He might be a third spy.

Blunt encounters HMQ (Her Majesty the Queen) and they discuss attribution—the process by which the history and genuineness of a painting is decided. "Facts not chat" is her motto (p. 345). As Blunt says, "I was talking about Art, I'm not sure she was" (p. 346).

GEORGE III

Bennett's historical play and film (more fully, the 1992 play *The Madness of George III,* first produced 1991, published 1992, and the 1994 film *The Madness of King George*) were written as the result of his interest in the political situation during the king's madness. It paralyzed government, because government was, to an extent that has not been generally realized in Bennett's view, in the hands of a single indi-

vidual. Bennett was also intrigued by medical evidence that the king's madness was the result of a physical illness, porphyria (from the Latin for "purple"), so named because it turns the urine purple—ironically, the color of royalty.

Joseph O'Mealy, discussing the changes that occurred in devising the film script, makes the point that Bennett's decision to excise much of the political detail made for a better product.

> The film version . . . downplays the "groundwork of politics" as it embraces the "domestic melodramas" of generational conflict and marital disruption. . . . By downplaying and simplifying the political and constitutional issues featured in the drama and foregrounding the family in crisis, Bennett also finds himself working in another very American medium, that of the classic American family drama like *Death of a Salesman* and *Long Day's Journey into Night.*
>
> ("Royal Family Values," p. 90)

In fact, the political items turned out to interest the audience largely insofar as they related to current events, as in Prime Minister William Pitt's statement that a project meant he needed "five more years"—a statement echoed in a slogan adopted by supporters of the 1980s prime minister Margaret Thatcher.

The Madness of George III opens with the entrance of the king and his court, who come down the stairs at a "brisk pace set by the king." (The king is given to sudden and violent movement, and his entrances are heralded by a call of "Sharp! Sharp! The King! The King!") At the foot of the stairs, the king is attacked and stabbed by Margaret Nicholson. She is mad and believes the crown has taken her property, but her stabbing is powerless—she has used a table knife. Her madness, lost land, and powerlessness prefigure the depiction of the king in the play.

The dynamism of the king, who holds the power, contrasts with the futility of the opposition and the prince of Wales. The prince displeases his parents. The king claims to know his country—mills, factories, farms. His hobbies are learning and astronomy; the prince's are fashion and furniture.

The king is proud that England is a civilized country—Nicholson will be confined in an institution, whereas in France she would have been tortured to death. He is a despot, though: "When people in parliament go against my wishes, I find it very vexing. Try as I can, it seems to me disloyalty." Pitt says he should not take it personally. "How else am I supposed to take it but personally?" he asks (p. 6).

King George's court is formal, stiff, boring. In contrast, at night between him and the queen there is a warm informality. She is in bed knitting and he greets her: "When we get this far I call it dandy, eh?" (p. 8). But he is in pain with a bilious attack and falls into the hands of his doctors. Their incompetence and his impatience are obvious. A royal tour of Gloucester is proposed, and the king looks forward to its informality. "Live like an ordinary couple. Mr. and Mrs. King. People of fashion" (p. 11). It is while they are away that the first signs of the reappearance of the king's madness are seen—at four o'clock in the morning he bangs on the door of the dean of a cathedral whom he wants to see.

The King's increasing madness causes a breakdown in government since his personal approval is needed for most business to be completed. Prime Minister Pitt is compelled to seek support in Parliament to prevent calls from opposition politicians for a Preince Regent to be appointed. In reviewing Bennett's work, Hunt had talked of the centrailty of gossip in Bennett's writing; the entire crisis gives rise to a politics of gossip.

The treatment eventually adopted for the king, supervised by Dr. Willis, is to restrain him. Faced with the king's tendency to gabble inappropriately at all times and to "talk filth," Willis has the king strapped into a high-backed chair and reduces him to inactivity and silence. The chair is a throne: the sane king on the throne is silenced by convention; the mad king in the chair is silenced through being bound and gagged.

> KING: (Howling) I am the King of England!
> WILLIS: No, sir, you are the patient.
>
> (p. 44)

The first act ends with the playing of the anthem "Zadoc the Priest," written by Handel for the coronation of George II and used ever since for that purpose.

As part of his treatment the king is separated from the queen, and this feeds two distressing delusions. George believes that the queen is sleeping with the prince of Wales, and that he himself is having an affair with Lady Pembroke, one of the queen's attendants. The constitutional crisis leads the prince of Wales to behave maliciously (an unhistorical note that was felt to be dramatically necessary, to Bennett's distress).

The play does not dwell on the madness itself. The incoherent speech, violence, and incontinence are there, but the focus is on the recovery of function. The king had had the habit of saying "What? What?" at the end of sentences to encourage others to speak because he was listening. Previously infuriating, the reemergence of this pattern is the sign that things will be well.

King George has learned from the experience that he can hide his madness and appear sane. At one point, there is a scene between him and the queen, where he taunts her in German: "I want to sleep with Elizabeth [Pembroke] . . . her tits are bigger than yours." Willis, listening to this, knows this is filth, but as the queen cannot bring herself to translate it, he is powerless to restrain the king. It is an interesting historic twist. George I had lost some of the powers of the king because he could only speak German; for George III, the ability to speak German is a secret power.

One of the lyrical moments in the play as the king recovers is to see him and Willis in a group reading Shakespeare's *King Lear*. The king is reading Lear's part and is congratulated. "It's the way I play it," he says, making explicit the element of theater in being king. At the end of the play he dismisses those of his servants who had been closest to him during his madness—a necessary move because the king's needs are absolute. (This is often misread as the shameful act of a shamed man.) Dismissing Willis, he quotes Shakespeare's *Henry IV, Part 2*: "Presume not that I am the thing I was"; this is Prince Henry casting off Falstaff (as if both kings intended to say "I am now king, you some fool I no longer need").

Possibly the king is also suggesting that when he dies, his prince of Wales will reform in the same way as Henry V, and the Happy English Royal Family Show will go on.

THE LADY IN THE VAN

By the time he came to write this 1999 play, Bennett had fully written up his real-life experiences with "Miss Sheppard" (as he called her in the play); they were included in later editions of *Writing Home*. The material was so well known that the process was akin to adaptation.

In creating the play, Bennett introduced a variety of characters—neighbors, a social worker, a lout, Miss Shepherd's brother—to make a lively street scene. He also brought in his Mam to counterbalance Miss Shepherd; his Mam wants to live with him and he will not let her, but he lets Miss Shepherd stay. Miss Shepherd needs hospitalization but refuses it; his Mam has to be hospitalized. Bennett explores openly and without further concealment the anger he felt at the three mad women who imposed themselves on him for twenty years. (The third is Margaret Thatcher.) So great is the anger that he even strikes Miss Shepherd at one point.

Bennett introduces himself as two characters. Alan Bennett in the play is his public self. But there is also Alan Bennett 2, his secret sharer, unseen by anybody else except Miss Shepherd after her death. Alan Bennett 2 is first seen working at his desk—he is Bennett's writer self.

The compression of the events of many years into a few hours creates two structural problems. First, it tends to make the experience funnier. When Miss Shepherd parks her garbage truck outside Alan Bennett's house she asks to borrow a tape measure because "one and a half inches is the ideal gap [between tire and sidewalk]. I came across it in a Catholic magazine under tips on Christian parking" (p. 12). The contrast between the imposition of the parking itself, and the fuss about the gap is, in the hands of a Maggie Smith, hilarious. So it looks as though Miss Shepherd's stay was fun. In fact, Alan Bennett is dealing with someone beyond all reason.

Second, again because of the compression, it looks as though at some point Alan Bennett allows Miss Shepherd to stay, which would have

been a good act, almost saintly. He wants to make the point that it was not like that. Her stay (like Mam's illness) crept up on him in stages through a series of crises—the fact she was a always being harassed by drunks meant he could not work, so he agreed to get her off the road. This was taking the easy way out. Looking after her, like looking after Mam, is an assigned role, not an assumed one.

Above all, Alan Bennett is driven to protest directly to the audience at the end of the play: "Look this is just one path through my life—me and Miss Shepherd. . . . Lots of other stuff happened." "They know that," says Alan Bennett 2.

Alan Bennett is still writing, and has begun to publish short prose fictions, which are perhaps the beginning of a new direction. He is a deeply loved, very clever, funny, tragic writer.

SELECTED BIBLIOGRAPHY

I. PLAYS. *Plays One*, containing *Forty Years On*, 1968, *Getting On*, 1971, *Habeas Corpus*, 1973, and *Enjoy*, 1980 (London and Boston, 1991); *The Wind in the Willows* (London and Boston, 1991); *The Madness of George III* (London and Boston, 1992); *Plays Two*, containing *The Old Country*, 1977, *Kafka's Dick*, 1986, *The Insurance Man*, 1986, *An Englishman Abroad*, 1988, and *A Question of Attribution*, 1988 (London, 1998); *The Lady in the Van* (London, 2000).

II. PROSE FICTION. *Father, Father Burning Bright* (London, 1988); *The Clothes They Stood Up In* (London, 1998; New York, 2001); *The Laying On of Hands: Stories* (New York, 2001).

III. TELEVISION PLAYS AND DOCUMENTARIES. *Office Suite*, containing *Green Forms*, 1978, and *A Visit from Miss Prothero*, 1978 (London and New York, 1981); *Objects of Affection and Other Plays for Television*, containing *A Day Out*, 1972, *Our Winnie*, 1982, *A Woman of No Importance*, 1982, *Rolling Home*, 1982, *Marks*, 1982, *Say Something Happened*, 1982, *Intensive Care*, 1982, and *An Englishman Abroad*, 1983 (London, 1982); *The Writer in Disguise*, containing *Me, I'm Afraid of Virginia Woolf*, 1978, *Afternoon Off*, 1978, and *All Day on the Sands*, 1979 (London, 1985); *Dinner at Noon* (London, 1988); *The Abbey* (London, 1995); *The Complete Talking Heads* (London, 1998).

IV. FILMS. *A Private Function* (Great Britain, 1984); *Prick Up Your Ears* (Great Britain, 1987); *The Madness of King George* (Great Britain, 1994).

V. AUTOBIOGRAPHY. *Telling Tales* (London, 2000).

VI. OTHER WORKS. With Peter Cook, Jonathan Miller, and Dudley Moore, *The Complete Beyond the Fringe*, ed. by Roger Wilmut (London, 1987); *Writing Home* (London, 1994, rev. and exp. to include diary version of *The Lady in the Van,* 1997); "Seeing Stars," in *London Review of Books* (3 January 2002).

VII. BIOGRAPHICAL STUDIES. Ronald Bergan, *Beyond the Fringe . . . and Beyond: A Critical Biography of Alan Bennett, Peter Cook, Jonathan Miller, and Dudley Moore* (London, 1989); Stephen Schiff, "The Poet of Embarrassment," in *New Yorker* (6 September 1993); Alexander Games, *Backing Into the Limelight: The Biography of Alan Bennett* (London, 2001); Amelia Hill, "A Bad Case of Writer's Block Deepens the Dark Mood of Alan Bennett," in *Observer* (9 December 2001).

VIII. CRITICAL STUDIES. Albert Hunt, "Talking Heads, Bed Among the Lentils (Alan Bennett)," in George W. Brandt, ed., *British Television Drama in the 1980s* (Cambridge and New York, 1993); John Bull, *Stage Right* (London and New York, 1994); Daphne Turner, *Alan Bennett: In a Manner of Speaking* (London, 1997); Joseph O'Mealy, "Royal Family Values: The Americanization of Alan Bennett's *The Madness of George III*," in *Literature/Film Quarterly* 27, no 2 (1999), and *Alan Bennett: A Critical Introduction* (New York, 2001).

MARY ELIZABETH BRADDON

(1835–1915)

Susan Balée

MARY ELIZABETH BRADDON, who published nearly ninety books in the course of her life, was not only a prolific Victorian novelist but also one of the most popular. Braddon's greatest success came with two of her first novels, *Lady Audley's Secret* (1862) and *Aurora Floyd* (1863). These best-selling books were categorized as "sensational" fiction, and Braddon is credited, with Wilkie Collins, as a co-creator of this genre of literature. The "sensation novel," as it was known then and now, is characterized by intricate plotting, a pervasive sense of mystery and suspense (there is always at least one dark secret at the core of the story), and an examination of two normally forbidden subjects for the Victorians: sex (in these novels, usually seduction, bigamy, prostitution) and violent crime (usually murder). Also, and perhaps most striking for its first readers, the sensation novel stands out for its unconventional heroines.

The heroines of sensation novels, such as Lady Audley and Aurora Floyd, scorn the limited opportunities available to middle-class women in mid-Victorian Britain because they refuse to be subordinate to men and to accept unconditionally their roles as wives and mothers, or, if unmarried, as ill-paid governesses to other people's families. In the early 1860s, however, these were virtually the only respectable alternatives they had.

As this essay will later discuss both novels in more detail, here it is enough to say that *Lady Audley's Secret* and *Aurora Floyd* first made Mary Elizabeth Braddon famous, and they also made her infamous. Attacked in their own time as immoral, Braddon's novels paved the way for detective fiction by bridging the gap between the sensational murder trials regularly reported in the newspapers and the literary novel. Her work was also closely linked to stage melodrama, and many of her novels were made into plays (not always with her permission). Like the melodrama, sensation novels were a democratic art form because they drew fans from all the classes, including the working classes. Sensation novels and melodramatic plays also resembled each other because both depend primarily on incident, with characters simply acting out the plot. The characters are exaggerated types, villains and heroes, and they express exaggerated emotions such as hatred, fear, illicit love, and jealousy. These emotions and the incident-filled plots work on the "senses" of the audience, shocking and exciting readers and viewers. Mary Elizabeth Braddon understood the appetite of her readers, just as she understood the appetite of theatergoers—after all, she spent nearly seven years as an actress before she turned to novel-writing as a primary occupation.

Although Braddon's career was prolific—she went on writing well into the twentieth century—it is her connection with the sensation novel that makes her an important British writer. Her novels are among the first to point out the duality of Victorians, who publicly lauded the sanctity of marriage and the family, of house, home, and church, even while newspapers reported and court trials revealed the dark underside of bad marriages and unhappy households. The avid readership enjoyed by sensation novels in their time signals a cultural crisis during the 1860s, a time of massive social change reflected, and perhaps even spurred, by novels such as those penned by Mary Elizabeth Braddon.

CHILD OF AN UNHAPPY MARRIAGE

Mary Elizabeth Braddon was born in London on 4 October 1835, the last child of Fanny and Henry Braddon. Henry Braddon had trained as a lawyer, but his career was spent primarily as a dishonest and disreputable businessman. Although father was the black sheep of his otherwise respectable Cornwall family, his youngest daughter remembered him fondly as a handsome and kind father who gave her a sixpence every Sunday. Braddon's novels are populated with impecunious fathers, such as the one in *Eleanor's Victory* (1863), whose daughter frequently echoes Braddon's own sentiments about her progenitor. "Papa was nobody's enemy but his own," she later wrote in her unpublished memoir, *Before the Knowledge of Evil* (p. 29).

When Mary was four years old, Fanny Braddon discovered that her husband was having an affair. Although it was legally impossible for a woman to get a divorce in 1839 on the grounds of her husband's adultery, Fanny nevertheless opted to separate from Henry Braddon, taking her young daughter with her. (Mary's elder sister, Maggie, lived with their grandmother, and her brother, Edward, boarded at a London prep school when Mary was a little girl because their father could not afford to support them.) During these years, Fanny and her daughter moved often, and Fanny, a single mother, struggled to support them both with small sums and gifts from both sides of their family.

Braddon remembered her mother as her "constant companion and confidante" (p. 30), and they remained exceptionally close for the rest of their lives. Fanny Braddon did her best to educate her daughter well, and she was herself a gifted writer and musician. She sent Mary to a day school when she could afford it, and taught her at home when she could not. Thus, before the age of ten, Mary had learned to speak and read French, to play the piano proficiently, and to recite long speeches from Shakespeare. The last skill was one she would soon use to help support her mother and herself. At the age of sixteen, Mary Elizabeth Braddon took the stage name of Mary Seyton and became an actress.

AN ACTRESS OF THE 1850S

In the 1850s, acting was not considered a respectable occupation for women. Actresses were considered immoral for two reasons. First, the fact that they publicly "exposed" themselves linked them to prostitutes, on the grounds that, when playing male roles, they often wore tights and literally revealed parts of themselves to men that would normally be taboo for the eyes of anyone other than a husband. These "breeches parts," as they were called, led to the charge that actresses were sexually emancipated in a way that was deeply frowned upon in Victorian England. Sexuality in women was feared and, as the physician William Acton made clear in his 1857 treatise *The Functions and Disorders of the Reproductive Organs,* good women were asexual women; wives only engaged in the sexual act in order to procreate and realize their dreams of motherhood. (Men, as Acton and other physicians pointed out, had drives too strong to be mastered. Like animals, they could not help themselves, but they were urged to keep masturbation or conjugal activity to a minimum of one to three times a month lest it make them crazy or "impotent" in the workplace.)

The second reason actresses were perceived as immoral stemmed from the very nature of their craft—they were not *sincere,* but *acting.* As Claire Tomalin points out in her book *Invisible Woman,* about the life of Ellen Ternan, the actress who became Charles Dickens' mistress, "To pretend to be what you were not and to make a good job of it made you morally suspect" (p. 16). On the other hand, to be good at the craft of acting could also make a woman financially independent. A single woman who became an actress instead of a governess would never have the latter's respectability, but she could make a much better living: a good actress could earn as much or more than her male counterparts.

As we know from her memoir, Braddon was stagestruck from a very young age. With her mother, she attended plays at the best London theaters with private-box tickets given to them by Fanny Braddon's nephew, John Thadeus Delane, the editor of the London *Times*. When Mary decided to become an actress in 1852, she did so with the full support of her mother, who served as her companion and chaperone throughout her acting career. Having her mother as a chaperone and changing her name from Braddon to Seyton were doubtless two ways that Mary appeased what surely would have been objections from other family members.

Still, the stage was preferable to poverty, and many characters in Braddon's fiction, such as Flora in *A Lost Eden* (1904) and Mary in *Rough Justice* (1898), choose stage careers to avoid genteel penury; moreover, despite their profession, Flora and Mary remain morally virtuous.

Jennifer Carnell, in her 2000 biography of Mary Elizabeth Braddon, has the most to say about the seven years the novelist spent on the boards. As Carnell discovered, Braddon spoke very little about her years on the stage, even later in life, because of the stigma still attached to actresses. Nevertheless, Carnell uncovered playbills and memoirs by other actresses who shared the stage with Mary "Seyton," and it is clear that Braddon had an active career in the provincial stage for several years, though her parts were rarely those of the leading lady. Finally, in 1856, Braddon made her acting debut at the Surrey Theatre in London, and though the plays she starred in were tolerably well received, she did not garner the fame she had hoped for. A leading lady who could make it in London might see her weekly salary quintuple and her financial independence become a certainty. However, if she did not strike the high note of success in the metropolis, she would be forced to return to acting in the provinces, where the pay was far poorer, the work much harder, and the chance of a London performance not likely to come again.

According to Carnell, this is what happened to Braddon. She joined Henry Nye Chart's company in Brighton, where she performed supporting parts for the next three years while honing her writing skills. Frequently Braddon was forced to play either old ladies, such as Gertrude in *Hamlet,* or men, such as the earl of Westmoreland in *Henry IV.* Critics noted that she was too young for the old lady parts and showed a disturbingly unwomanly "inclination to appear in male habiliments" for the male roles. Although Braddon was tall and had a good stage presence, several commentators noted that her voice was weak and that often she came across as "insipid" (pp. 53–61).

By 1859, Braddon must have known she was never going to make it big as an actress and that if she remained on the stage it would be only as a "walking lady" (supporting player) in provincial theaters. Her character Justina, from *A Strange World* (1875), comments on the lives of unsuccessful actresses: "Those I know are like horses in a mill, and go the same round year after year. When I think that I may have to lead that kind of life until I die of old age, I almost feel that I should like to drown myself" (p. 19). Braddon chose a very different option and began to write fiction and poetry in earnest. With the help of three male mentors, she swiftly achieved fame and a successful career that would span several decades.

Despite the shift in her creative focus, however, Braddon never lost her interest in the stage. She wrote several plays and many novels that read like plays (a contemporary critic noted that the only difference between a stage melodrama and a sensation novel was that "one is a drama acted, the other is a drama narrated"). Moreover, Braddon's novels show a breadth of knowledge about both contemporary and classic drama, and many of her characters are professional actors and actresses. Her experiences on the stage served her well as a novelist, as did the attention of three older men who helped to launch her writing career in the late 1850s.

THE THREE MENTORS

Mary Elizabeth Braddon's first literary mentor was the novelist Edward Bulwer Lytton (1803–1873), a baron and a member of parliament who financed his aristocratic lifestyle by writing popular novels. His early novels, such as *Pelham; or, The Adventures of a Gentleman* (1828), dealt with the aristocracy and politics; they were known as "fashionable" novels, and Bulwer Lytton acquired a reputation as both a dandy and a wit. Bulwer Lytton also wrote "Newgate novels," or novels based on the actual lives of murderers and other criminals (the Newgate Calendar listed the prisoners of Newgate Prison, their crimes and punishment). Newgate novels figure among the ancestors of sensation novels, but they are different in that their antiheroes generally repent their crimes or are at least severely punished for them; furthermore, the criminals are all men, and sensation novels often feature female villains.

Eugene Aram (1832) is the best-known of Bulwer Lytton's Newgate novels, but his career spanned much of the century, and he went on to pen best-selling domestic novels (*The Caxtons*, 1849), historical novels (*The Last of the Barons*, 1843), and tales of the occult (*A Strange Story*, 1862). In the course of his career, Bulwer Lytton also wrote poetry and plays and edited a literary magazine. In his time, Edward Bulwer Lytton was a famous and well-respected author, much admired by Charles Dickens and Benjamin Disraeli. Now, unfortunately, most of his books are out of print, and he is known primarily for the writers he influenced—such as Mary Elizabeth Braddon.

Braddon first met him in 1854, probably thanks to her editor uncle, John Delane. She told Bulwer Lytton of her literary ambitions and the famous writer championed them. In an interview in 1888, Braddon recalled that Bulwer Lytton "undertook to correct and criticize my first story [and] was the first author of note to give me any real encouragement" (Hatton, p. 28). Their correspondence lasted for decades, and Braddon listened carefully to her mentor's advice. In fact, much of what we know about Braddon's approach to fiction and what she tried to achieve—in her sensation novels, her penny potboilers for the lowest-level reader, and her mainstream domestic novels—we know because of her correspondence with Bulwer Lytton.

Like many future novelists, however, Braddon first broke into print as a poet. Many of her poems were published in provincial newspapers while she was still acting with the Brighton theater company. The poems were generally topical, focused on current events such as the Indian Mutiny of 1857 (when Indian soldiers turned on their British officers and killed them, after which the British empire reasserted its power by sacking the city of Delhi). Her brother, Edward, served the British government in India, but that was not Braddon's only reason for lauding the destruction of Delhi—hers was a general senti-

ment felt by citizens of England at the time. To be patriotic was to be imperialistic, and it would be many years before the English would question their policies in the countries they had colonized. Hence, one of Braddon's Indian Mutiny poems ends with the British soldiers drinking the queen's health near the stacked corpses of the inhabitants of Delhi that they have just slaughtered: "Whilest their blood steeps the soil which their deeds have defiled / Whilest they lie like slain tigers in ghastly heaps piled" (*Beverley Recorder*, 21 November 1857, p. 4).

One person who noticed her poems was the wealthy Yorkshire squire John Gilby (1821–1884). Gilby had inherited a good income from his father and used it to pursue his sporting interests, primarily racing horses. He went on to own many successful racehorses, and Braddon's knowledge of horses and the track (notable in *Aurora Floyd,* whose reviewers condemned the author's knowledge as "unladylike") at least partially derived from her association with Gilby. Meanwhile, Gilby championed Braddon's writing, paying her a wage so that she could leave the stage and focus on it. Braddon was no doubt glad to have the equivalent of an artist's grant to write, though it is also clear that Gilby's motives were not merely for the advancement of literature.

Charles Reade, another sensation novelist and a friend of Braddon, described Gilby as hopelessly in love with her, attempting to make her famous as a writer so that they would be equal financially and he could ask her to marry him without shame on either side. It is unlikely, however, that Braddon felt a similar emotion for Gilby. Not only was he fourteen years older than she, he was also crippled and choleric. He could ride horses, but he had to walk with the aid of canes (he was paralyzed in both legs). At the racetrack, thanks to his bad temper and his handicap, he was known as "the devil on two sticks."

Jennifer Carnell refers to Gilby as "an impossible taskmaster," and certainly his letters to Braddon telling her what the subjects of her poems should be (Garibaldi and all things Italian), how she should write them, what she should read (Gilby was well educated, with interests that included botany and astronomy), whom she should see, and how she should spend her time sound maddening. Furthermore, Braddon was discovering that she hated writing about Garibaldi and reading lots of history to bolster her verse; she found herself far more drawn to fiction and began sending stories to magazines such as *The Welcome Guest,* edited by John Maxwell (1825–1895).

Maxwell was an Irishman, an orphan from Limerick who had come to London in his late teens and made a success of publishing. Contemporaries described him as a tall man, strikingly handsome with a hearty manner and loud, Irish-accented voice. At the time Braddon met him in April 1860, Maxwell was also the father of seven children, though separated from the wife who had borne them. His wife, Mary Anne, had grown increasingly insane after the birth of her last child, and she was confined to the care of a relative outside of Dublin.

Meanwhile, Gilby, who had at first been delighted at her success with *The Welcome Guest,* soon grew very jealous of its editor. After her first couple of stories appeared there, Braddon focused her energies on fiction instead of poetry. (By the time she was publishing fiction, Braddon, at Gilby's insistence, had changed from her stage name of "Seyton" back to her family name, so all of her future novels and stories would be published under the name M. E. Braddon.) In addition, Braddon began to ignore Gilby's demands that she consult him first about anything she wrote. Instead, she consulted Maxwell.

Gilby, realizing at last that Maxwell was his rival, wrote a final, enraged letter to Braddon on 20 February 1861. This letter is both venomous and pathetic; in it, Gilby accuses his one-time protégée of ingratitude and dishonorable behavior. "You have become such an actress that you cannot speak without acting—I have worked as hard and done as much for you as it was possible for a gentleman to do for a woman in your position. . . . I can only feel a pity for you not unmingled with contempt, and wonder if you have one redeeming trait left in your character" (20 February 1861, in Wolff Collection).

Not surprisingly, Braddon's relationship with Gilby ended with this letter, but her relationship with John Maxwell grew daily stronger. Within a few months she had moved in with him and was pregnant with his child. She bore him five children in the course of their life together and became a mother to the six surviving children by his first wife. Together they survived a scandal when Maxwell's first wife died in 1874, though they were finally able to marry each other.

John Gilby's life did not turn out so happily. He grew ever more cranky and irritable, and his mental stability was completely breached when he lost his fortune in 1884 and had to move from his estate to a smaller house. In May of that year, at the age of sixty-two, he hung himself.

BRADDON AND "THE SENSATIONAL SIXTIES"

Mary Elizabeth Braddon came of age as a fiction writer during a tumultuous era in English history. In addition to the Indian Mutiny of 1857, mentioned above, the British had recent memories of an exceptionally bloody conflict in Crimea (1853–1856). By 1860, English newspapers and journals showed a fear of foreign invasion, most notably from France, where Napoleon's nephew, Louis Napoleon (Napoleon III), sat upon the throne. The lead editorial in the May 1859 issue of the *New Monthly Magazine,* the journal that, at that same time, was running Mrs. Henry Wood's *East Lynne,* another best-selling sensation novel, highlights the national paranoia: "More and more is the conviction forced upon us that Napoleon III is determined on crushing in turn all those powers who combined to overthrow his uncle" (p. 123). Meanwhile, across the Atlantic, John Brown had attacked Harper's Ferry and the American Civil War was heating up.

Fears of what might be happening outside the borders of Great Britain were equaled only by what was happening inside the borders. Women, many of whom had been deprived of mates by the Crimean War and male emigration to the colonies, began to significantly outnumber men in England. By 1860 there were nearly 3 million single (or "surplus") women who would very likely never get married. At the same time, there were virtually no respectable jobs for single, middle-class women other than that of governess.

The plight of these women was frequently written about during the late 1850s and 1860s, and many reforms occurred during these years to give more rights to women.

Meanwhile, all was certainly not well with married women, either. Despite the cultural icon of the "angel in the house"—the wife and mother who serves as the spiritual center of the Victorian household—more women than ever were complaining about the mistreatment of rapacious husbands who, immediately upon marrying them, gained full legal rights to their wives' property, money, and, in the event of a separation, their children. The Matrimonial Causes Act of 1857 provided some relief, insofar as it permitted certain (very wealthy) spouses to get free of each other, but it was hardly an equal opportunity law. Men could sue successfully for divorce by citing their wives' adultery, but women had to prove desertion, cruelty, rape, bestiality, or incest in addition to adultery.

Not until 1870 did the Married Women's Property Act become law, enabling married women to hang on to the fortunes they had possessed before marriage. Significantly, this act became law just as the popularity of the sensation novel was finally beginning to wane. Further, by the 1870s, employment rights for women had also opened up considerably. Universities began to admit women for the first time in the 1860s, and so the first professional women began their careers in the early 1870s.

In the debates about women's employment that raged through the 1850s and 1860s, the main objection to women working was the idea that women would be "unsexed" if they did men's work. Critics such as the writer John Ruskin feared that women who took jobs outside the household would lose their femininity and their central role as the moral "angel" of the home. People who argued for higher education for women and broadened employment opportunities, such as the Victorian feminist Harriet Martineau, observed that single women's greatest obstacle was "the jealousy of men in regard to the industrial independence of women" ("Female Industry," in *The Edinburgh Review*, April 1859, p. 329).

That economics underlay all of these arguments cannot be doubted; that the sensation novel reflected and influenced them is also probable. The sudden appearance of this particular genre of literature in 1859, with its defiant, anti-angel-in-the-house heroines, just at the moment when debates over the status and future roles of women were peaking, seems to indicate that the sensation novel was responding to these issues. When women finally achieved a variety of educational and employment rights in the 1870s, the sensation novel died out as a literary genre. A further fact that bolsters this link is that almost all of the contemporary objections to the sensation novel centered on its portrayal of women. Margaret Oliphant, the most outspoken critic of the sensation novelists—and particularly of M. E. Braddon—published a series of articles in *Blackwood's Magazine* in the 1860s that deplored the novels' depiction of women.

> Writers who have no genius and little talent, make up for it by displaying their acquaintance with the accessories and surroundings of vice, with the means of seduction, and with what they set forth as the secret tendencies of the heart. . . . What is held up to us as the story of the feminine soul as it really exists under its conventional coverings, is a very fleshly and unlovely record.
> (in *Blackwood's* 102, 1867, p. 209)

The heroines of sensation novels, such as Braddon's Lady Audley and Aurora Floyd, do indeed suffer from dangerous passions, passions that they are willing to commit crimes to satisfy. On the other hand, the heroines of sensation novels could hardly outdo the heroines of real-life court reportage. In 1857, Madeleine Smith, the upper-middle-class daughter of a wealthy Scottish architect, was accused of poisoning her lower-class lover so that she could marry a more suitable man. Her case was covered extensively in the newspapers and later linked to the appearance of Lady Audley in 1861.

LADY AUDLEY'S SECRET *AND MURDER MOST FOUL*

Victorians loved a good murder, hence the popularity of the 1830s Newgate novels about convicted criminals and, later, sensation novels of the 1860s. As Richard D. Altick observed in his book about sensational Victorian murder trials, "It was in, or just before, the early Victorian era that homicide first became institutionalized as a popular entertainment, a spectator sport" (p. 10). For much of the nineteenth century, both murder trials and hangings were public events; spectators were welcome and they came in droves. Upper-class spectators often paid exorbitant sums to rent apartments that overlooked the gallows on a hanging day, and women were just as bloodthirsty as men when it came to attending hearings for the accused and hangings for the convicted. Meanwhile, newspapers, realizing what sold copies, began covering murder trials in exhaustive detail. Many of the most shocking trials in the mid-nineteenth century involved women's issues.

For example, in 1836–1837, three pieces of a mutilated corpse were found in different places around London. When put together, the parts added up to Hannah Brown, a widow washerwoman. It turned out that her fiancé, James Greenacre, had murdered Hannah when he found out that she had lied about the amount of property she would be bringing to the marriage. He dismembered her with a saw and then traveled around London disposing of her body parts. In 1849, Maria Manning, a former lady's maid in the household of a duchess, was married to a railway guard but had as an occasional lover an Irishman named Patrick O'Connor. On 9 August 1849, the Mannings invited O'Connor to dinner, killed him, and buried him under the kitchen floor in quicklime. They took his money and went their separate ways but were eventually caught. They made up half an hour before both were hanged for murder.

In 1856, William Palmer, a horse-racing doctor, poisoned several people, including his wife, mother-in-law, an assortment of his children (illegitimate and legitimate), and a man whose horse had beat his in a race. Then, in 1857, the upper-middle-class Madeleine Smith poisoned her erstwhile lover in Scotland. Newspaper reports covered her trial to the last detail and "not within living memory, if ever, had the dock

at Edinburgh . . . been graced by so young, glamorous, and well-born a prisoner" (p. 178). From these factual court cases came both stage plays and fiction. Sensation novels sprang from the soil of true crime and, as Altick notes, "every good new Victorian murder helped legitimize, and prolong the fashion of, sensational plots" (p. 79).

Just as Greenacre, Manning, Smith, and countless other Victorian murderers had killed their victims in recognizable English settings, so did murder in fiction come home to roost. Gothic novels of the 1790s (another antecedent to sensation novels of the 1860s) dealt with murder in remote locales, usually Italy or Germany, and in exotic settings, usually castles, or ruins, but the sensation novel dealt with murder in contemporary English settings—London lodgings, country manors—exactly the places where the real murders, reported in the daily papers, took place. Henry James, in a famous review of Braddon's sensation novels, noted that these "most mysterious of mysteries" were far more frightening than the old Gothic novels because they were the mysteries "which are at our own doors" ("Miss Braddon," *Nation*, 9 November 1865, p. 594).

Thus, *Lady Audley's Secret* begins with a description of Audley Court, "a glorious old place . . . a spot in which Peace seemed to have taken up her abode. . . . A noble place; inside as well as out" (p. 2). However, there seems to be something sinister lurking amid this peacefulness, near a path lined with lime trees, because "it seemed a chosen place for secret meetings or for stolen interviews; a place in which a conspiracy might have been planned or a lover's vow registered with equal safety" (p. 3). Braddon continually plays upon the setting, between what one sees on the surface and what one senses beneath it: "The very repose of the place grew painful from its intensity, and you felt as if a corpse must be lying somewhere within that grey and ivy-covered pile of building—so deathlike was the tranquility of all around" (p. 21).

Taking a page from the sensational murder trial of the seemingly respectable Madeleine Smith, Braddon crafts her heroine in terms of the same contradiction between appearance and reality.

Thus, Lady Audley appears as an "angel in the house," lovely and feminine (blond, blue-eyed, fragile), but beneath that attractive exterior reside the dark passions of a murderess, a woman who is willing to kill her husband in order to retain her place in society.

In brief, the plot of *Lady Audley's Secret* is as follows: Lady Audley, formerly a governess, is raised in status when Sir Michael Audley falls in love with and marries her. Lucy Audley has a secret: she is really Helen Talboys, already married to George Talboys, who went to Australia to seek fortune and did not come back. They have a son that Helen has left with her father, hiding the boy as she has hidden the fact of her first marriage. Her nephew by marriage to Sir Michael, the lazy lawyer Robert Audley, feels there is something odd about his young aunt, but he cannot put his finger on it. In the beginning of the novel, he is also strongly attracted to her, a fact that disturbs him.

Then George Talboys suddenly returns and goes to visit his close boyhood chum Robert Audley. While looking at a portrait of Robert's new aunt (who is out of town at the time), George realizes that his wife is not dead (as he had thought), but bigamously married to another man. He does not tell Robert of this, nor does Robert have a chance to find out before George disappears. As it happens, Lady Audley has pushed her inconvenient first husband down a secluded well on Sir Michael's estate and left him for dead. Soon enough, she is trying to poison her second husband, and, in the meantime, Robert has overcome both his laziness and his attraction to his aunt: he is trying to discover the reason behind the sudden disappearance of his friend.

Robert Audley becomes an amateur detective; as a barrister with a small private income, he is not investigating this case for crass financial reasons but out of his own friendship (formed at Eton) with George. Readers who, for most of the novel, know no more than Robert Audley, follow him as he pieces together the clues that solve the puzzle.

Sensational murder trials, then, not only helped produce sensational novels about murder, but they also highlighted the work of detectives, both those employed by the police and amateur sleuths like Robert Audley. Thus sensation novels paved the way for detective fiction, a genre of literature still enormously popular today.

However, the main revelation of trials like that of Madeleine Smith was the realization that outwardly respectable people—especially middle- and upper-class women—might be concealing shameful inner desires and secret crimes. The newspapers made famous criminals familiar to the reading public, and in the name of truth they were explicit in their reporting of sexual and criminal misconduct, particularly that of women. Unlike some sensation novelists, Braddon did not simply lift her plots straight out of the newspapers' criminal reports and thinly disguise them as fiction, but she was aware of the power of the daily newspapers: "I undoubtedly believe that they give the best picture of the events of the day. They really are, as they profess to be, mirrors reflecting the life and views of the period" (in *Daily Telegraph*, 4 October 1913, p. 9).

BIGAMY *AND* AURORA FLOYD

P. D. Edwards, who introduces the Oxford University Press edition of *Aurora Floyd*, claims that there was at least one newspaper source at the time for the character of Aurora Floyd. This would be the high-class prostitute Catherine Walters (better known as "Skittles"), who flaunted her sexual charms in Hyde Park while driving an expensive pony carriage along the Lady's Mile. Skittles became a subject of the daily papers because she was an accomplished horsewoman whose many admirers caused the *Times* to lament the traffic congestion around Hyde Park.

Skittles was a dark and beautiful woman, the mistress of Lord Hartington, and in looks as well as horsemanship, Aurora Floyd resembles her. Skittles was also an unabashedly sexual being and in this too Aurora parallels her. Aurora Floyd's mistake in the novel of the same name is her own lust, fueled by the good looks of her father's groomsman. Thus Aurora falls in love with the lower-class Conyers and marries him before she realizes her error. Conyers is handsome on the outside but base on the inside. Later, Aurora thinks that her first husband has been killed in a racing accident, so she commits (accidentally) her second crime—bigamy—when she marries again. Conyers returns to blackmail her, echoing again the Madeleine Smith case, and then is mysteriously murdered.

Braddon herself called *Lady Audley's Secret* and *Aurora Floyd* her "pair of Bigamy novels," and bigamy certainly sold books in the early 1860s. According to Jeanne Fahnestock, between 1853 and 1863 there were 884 cases of bigamy brought to court in England and 110 in Scotland (p. 58). Bigamy titillated readers; it was adultery without the same level of guilt, and they could vicariously enjoy imagining themselves with alternative spouses.

Of course, the difference between the heroines of Braddon's "pair of Bigamy novels" is that the blond and beautiful Lady Audley commits bigamy for the financial reward. She does not seem sexually attracted to her older second husband, but she deeply desires his money and position. Aurora Floyd, on the other hand, is clearly motivated by sexual pleasure in both her first and second marriages. This drove the critic Margaret Oliphant to comment that "[W]omen who marry their grooms in fits of sensual passion" are depraved women indeed, nothing like the asexual "angel in the house" that the English had been holding up all century as the model of womanhood ("Novels," 1867, p. 263).

Oliphant, who despised sensation novels in general, seemed to reserve her most lethal venom for Braddon. Indeed, Braddon must have been confident indeed to write about bigamy when she herself was committing it with John Maxwell. By the time *Aurora Floyd* appeared, Braddon was pregnant with her second son by Maxwell, whose wife was alive, although mentally unbalanced, and confined to a relative's house in Dublin. Although Maxwell tried to pretend that his first wife was dead and that he and Mary Elizabeth were legitimately married, this was strenuously—and publicly—denied by Maxwell's brother-in-law. Thus, many people, including Oliphant, knew that Braddon was an unmarried woman living with a married man, even as she was making

a fortune on her bigamy novels. In her savage review of *Aurora Floyd,* Oliphant wrote that the bigamous plot was "an invention which could only have been possible to an Englishwoman knowing the attraction of impropriety, and yet loving the shelter of the law" (*Blackwood's,* 1867, p. 273).

For readers, Aurora Floyd was a deliciously powerful heroine. Unlike the stealthily evil Lady Audley, whose crimes are finally punished when Robert Audley has her committed to a Belgian mental asylum for the rest of her days, Aurora Floyd is a bold, confident, outspoken heroine. She's powerful and masculine in her sense of self-worth. In fact, she not only masters horses, but men. Aurora exerts control over her father, her two husbands, and the one suitor she rejects. She even goes so far as to horsewhip a cruel but feeble-minded stable boy in the novel's most shocking and fascinating scene.

As Edwards explains, "The crucial exercise of Aurora's power consists in the total trust, and total subordination of their will to hers, that she demands of both her suitors as a matter of right. . . . She wields her power, moreover, with apparently unequivocal support from the narrator, and presumably from Braddon herself" (p. xix). After the novel came out, some of Braddon's friends began to call her "Aurora," and Edwards believes that Aurora Floyd as well as Lady Audley represent aspects of Braddon herself.

First, Braddon was living bigamously with John Maxwell when she wrote her bigamy novels. Second, Maxwell's wife was confined in the equivalent of a lunatic asylum and, like Lady Audley, that was where she ultimately died. Edwards thinks that Braddon could not have avoided thinking about Maxwell's first wife and her situation, hence the numerous references to insanity and incarceration in asylums that conclude *Lady Audley's Secret* and appear in the first thirty pages of *Aurora Floyd*. Edwards concludes:

> In sum, there is ample evidence that, albeit in ways Braddon can hardly have been fully conscious of, Lady Audley and Aurora Floyd are imaginatively embellished and disguised versions of her self, and of her perception of herself: Lady Audley a projection of her guilt, no doubt largely suppressed;

Aurora of her sense of power—power to sweep aside all the obstacles raised by her disadvantaged girlhood, by her sex, and even by her own scruples of conscience

(pp. xxi–xxii).

REWRITING MADAME BOVARY: THE DOCTOR'S WIFE

Braddon followed the success of *Aurora Floyd* with two more enormously popular sensation novels, *John Marchmont's Legacy* and *Eleanor's Victory* (both published in volume form in 1863). Braddon knew that these popular novels made money, but she also hoped to write something more purely literary, something that might qualify as art as opposed to merely entertainment. Thus, even as she composed the serial installments of her 1863 novels, she wrote to her mentor Bulwer-Lytton:

If I live to complete these two I shall have earned enough to keep me & my mother for the rest of our lives, & I will then try and write for Fame and do something more worthy to be laid upon your altar.
(13 April 1863)

That worthy offering turned out to be *The Doctor's Wife* (1864), a retelling of Gustave Flaubert's *Madame Bovary* (1857), a book that had caused a scandal when it came out in France but was not yet well-known in England. Flaubert's tale, which is now recognized as a classic among nineteenth-century novels, focuses on the adulterous escapades of the wife of a provincial doctor. Of course, though Braddon borrowed the plot, there are many differences between her novel and Flaubert's, not least of all the fact that Madame Bovary revels in her sensuality, whereas Braddon's heroine, Isabel Gilbert, is simply a romanticist who lives in a dream world of books. Further, Isabel never actually commits adultery, whereas Emma Bovary indulges her physical desires with not one, but two lovers. Indeed, Emma Bovary continually mistakes her lust for sex and material goods for love; as Flaubert puts it, "in the heat of her desire she confounded heart's happiness with the sensual pleasures of luxury, true refinement with elegance of manners" (p. 55).

Isabel Gilbert, on the other hand, is ethereal to the point of being a virtual airhead. Braddon describes her: "Isabel Gilbert was not a woman of the world. She had read novels while other people perused the Sunday papers . . . she believed in a phantasmal universe, created out of the pages of poets and romancers" (p. 253). According to Lyn Pykett, Isabel differs sharply from Emma because "her love of fine things is presented as a form of aestheticism rather than a merely materialist or acquisitive love of luxurious objects" (p. xiii).

Where the novels are similar is in their portrayal of two middle-class doctors' wives who are intensely dissatisfied with their lives in the provinces. As sensation novels did throughout the 1860s, *The Doctor's Wife* charts the unhappiness of middle-class women who feel trapped by their marriages and have no real "work" to occupy them. Furthermore, both Emma and Isabel have a reading problem. In a charge that was frequently leveled at sensation novelists, Isabel's addiction to literary romance novels has made her unfit for her everyday domestic life. Emma Bovary takes that unfitness to a deeper level: the books she reads, with their adulterous heroines, incite her to commit a little adultery of her own. In the end, Madame Bovary is brought down by the immoral tales she is reading, whereas Isabel Gilbert moves beyond romances and poetry to "graver books," including those mentally nourishing genres of nonfiction—science, history and philosophy.

Emma Bovary's ultimate death by self-administered arsenic—the only way she can see out of a sordid situation complicated by debt, deception, and blackmail—is far more sensational than anything that happens in *The Doctor's Wife*. Instead, Braddon avoids adultery and its consequences altogether. Pykett believes that Braddon was trying to escape her reputation as a "bigamy novelist" by avoiding immoral sexuality altogether. (Indeed, one wonders if there is any sex at all in Isabel Gilbert's life: not only does she resist the charms of the aristocratic Roland Lansdell, she and her doctor husband never have any children of their own.) Braddon, attempting to rise above her critics' charges of immorality and "fleshly inclinations," focuses on Isabel's romantic dreams, dreams that first harm her but ultimately redeem her.

In a letter to Bulwer Lytton, Braddon explains what she tried to do with the character of Isabel Gilbert. "This study of a silly girl's romantic passion is not a story which I would care to place in the hands of "the young person," but I defy any critic—however nice, or however nasty—to point to one page or one paragraph in that book . . . which contains the lurking poison of sensuality" (September 1867). Alas, Isabel's excessive purity struck the *Saturday Review*'s critic as unrealistic: "It may be questioned whether a personage so exclusively embodying a single idea could ever by possibility exist and continue acting in real life in anything like the fashion of Isabel in the fiction" (5 November 1864, p. 571). The *Spectator* reviewer, though he also thought Isabel an unbelievable character, nevertheless praised Braddon for "at last contribut[ing] something to fiction which will be remembered" (22 October 1864, p. 1214).

For modern critics, *The Doctor's Wife* is particularly intriguing because one of Braddon's main characters is Sigismund Smith, a sensation novelist. (Originally "Sam Smith," but he changed his name for literary effect.) Braddon's first major biographer, Robert Lee Wolff, notes that Sigismund's views on writing sensation fiction are so close to Braddon's own that he serves as "an authorial mouthpiece" (p. 126). Mouthpiece or no, Sigismund is a delightful character who appears again in another of her novels (*The Lady's Mile*, 1866). Sigismund, who trained as a lawyer, has found his calling as a writer of "highly-spiced fictions, which enjoyed an immense popularity amongst the classes who like their literature as they like their tobacco—very strong" (p. 11). Braddon wrote to Bulwer Lytton of her own "penny bloods" (sensation fiction sold in penny parts to working-class readers):

> This work is most piratical stuff, & would make your hair stand on end, if you were to see it. The amount of crime, treachery, murder, slow poisoning, & general infamy required by the Half penny reader is something terrible.
>
> (December 1862?)

Sigismund Smith's career, then, parallels Mary Elizabeth Braddon's, and in the course of *The Doctor's Wife,* he progresses from the penny bloods to sensational three-volume novels. Further, like Braddon, he is not above borrowing other people's plots (just as Braddon is doing with *Madame Bovary* in this very novel): "[T]he next best thing you can do if you haven't got ideas of your own . . . is to steal other people's ideas in an impartial manner. Don't empty one man's pocket, but take a little bit all around" (p. 45).

Nevertheless, Sigismund Smith never confuses fiction with real life (something sensation novelists were accused of making readers do), though Isabel (his landlady's daughter) is completely addicted to the fantasy lives she has discovered in novels. Braddon contrasts these characters: "Sigismund wrote romantic fictions by wholesale, and yet was as unromantic as the prosiest butcher who ever entered a cattle-market. He sold his imagination, and Isabel lived upon hers. . . . She wanted her life to be like her books; she wanted to be a heroine,—unhappy perhaps, and dying early" (p. 28). Sigismund tries to warn Isabel that the novels she is reading are "dangerously beautiful" with "opium inside the sugar" (p. 24). And he even confides in his friend George Gilbert, who is already smitten with Isabel's beautiful dark looks, that she reads too many novels: "No wise man or woman was ever the worse for reading novels. Novels are only dangerous for those poor foolish girls who read nothing else, and think that their lives are to be paraphrases of their favourite books" (p. 30).

Unfortunately, Isabel is a foolish girl, and George Gilbert, the good country doctor, is in love with her despite it. Interestingly, much later in the book, after Isabel and George are married, and Isabel, half-mad with boredom, falls in love with Roland Lansdell, the local aristocrat, it is Sigismund Smith who intervenes. Smith tells Isabel how much George loves her, even though "he isn't one of your demonstrative fellows," and advises her "to occupy herself a little more" to combat the dullness of provincial life. The best idea he can give her is the one that's always worked for him (not to mention his creator): he tells Isabel to write a novel. "Since I've taken to writing novels, I don't think I've a desire unsatisfied," he tells her.

> There's nothing I haven't done—on paper. . . . And if I were a young lady, and—and had a kind of romantic fancy for a person I ought not to care about, I'll tell you what I'd do with him—I'd put him into a novel, Izzie, and work him out in three volumes; and if I wasn't heartily sick of him by the time I got to the last chapter, nothing on earth would cure me.
>
> (pp. 229–230)

Braddon always considered *The Doctor's Wife* her best novel, but it did not give her the fame or the universal critical approval she had hoped for. The reviewer at the *Athenaeum* thought the book "immoral and foolish," and Margaret Oliphant, ever hostile to Braddon, pointed out that the tale was "plagiarized . . . from a French story" ("Sensation Novels," in *Blackwood's*, 1862, p. 569). Perhaps the most damning remarks came from W. Fraser Rae in the *North British Review,* who began his review by praising *The Doctor's Wife* for possessing "fewer artistic faults" than any of her other novels, but then qualified his compliment by saying that this improvement only served to demonstrate "how very nearly Miss Braddon has missed being a novelist whom we might respect and praise without reserve" ("Sensation Novelists: Mrs. Braddon," p. 197).

Clearly, the experience of publishing *The Doctor's Wife* did not cure Mary Elizabeth Braddon of her desire to write sensational novels. Although her career spanned several more decades, and she went beyond the genre in her later fiction, for the rest of the 1860s—the heyday of the sensation craze—Braddon returned to what she (and her alter ego, Sigismund) did best.

DEATH, DESPAIR, SCANDAL

Braddon no doubt felt distressed by her compromised position, living with Maxwell, whose wife was still alive. Maxwell's attempt to scotch those rumors in 1864—by announcing in the society pages of several papers that he and Braddon were married, an assertion flatly contradicted by Maxwell's brother-in-law—did not make her situation any easier. The more famous she became as a novelist, the more difficult it became to hide the irregularities of her home life. Her mother lived with them, but even she did not tell Braddon's other siblings (Maggie, who had married an Italian in 1860 and moved to his native country, and Edward in India) that Mary was not married to Maxwell, much less that she had had several children by him.

English critics, however, certainly knew, and they took every opportunity to point out that the immorality of her fiction derived from the immorality of her own life. One of the nastiest barbs came from a review of *John Marchmont's Legacy* in the *Athenaeum*. The anonymous reviewer, catching an error in the portrayal of a marriage ceremony in the novel, tartly remarked: "When Miss Braddon knows more about the Marriage Service than she does at present, she will know that these words are uttered by the bridegroom,—not the bride" (12 December 1863, p. 792). In fact, it was probably this review that prompted John Maxwell, two months later, to publicly announce that he and Mary were legally wed.

If that announcement and its subsequent denial made a bad situation worse, Maxwell's decision in 1866 to launch a new magazine, with Mary as editor, improved things considerably. Mary, as the editor of the new magazine *Belgravia*, now had a forum from which she could defend herself. For his part, Maxwell now had his star authoress in the driver's seat of his new publication. (Maxwell, whose business practices were often criticized by his contemporaries, knew a gold mine when he met Mary.) Her novels made his publishing ventures a success and supported their family in a luxurious style. *Belgravia*, aimed at a middle-class audience, brought in more money than the cheaper magazines aimed at poorer readers; with Braddon at the helm it sold well, too. She edited the magazine from its inception in 1866 until Maxwell sold it to another publisher in 1876.

MARY ELIZABETH BRADDON

Almost all of Braddon's novels for the next decade, beginning with *Birds of Prey* in 1866–1867, first appeared as serial installments in *Belgravia*. Braddon could also employ writers to defend her work—and that of other sensation novelists—in the pages of her magazine. Her friend George Augustus Sala took up the cudgels on Braddon's behalf, and his essays were directly aimed at Margaret Oliphant, "the poor canting creature" who had made such a stink about Braddon in the pages of *Blackwood's*. Neither Sala nor Braddon knew that Oliphant was the individual attacking Braddon because *Blackwood's,* like other major magazines, published their reviews anonymously. Nevertheless, they were pretty sure that the critic could not be a fellow novelist—no other fiction writer could be so narrow-minded as to damn a popular novel because it did not live up to "moral" standards. Thus, Sala pointed out that the nasty reviewer at *Blackwood's* must be suffering from an acute case of creative envy:

> Hatred and jealousy and spite towards one of the most successful novelists of the age—ill-nature and ill-feeling toward the author of *Aurora Floyd* and a dozen more capital novels shine in every page of the lucubrations of this agreeable soul.
>
> ("The Cant of Modern Criticism," in *Belgravia* 4, November 1867, p. 54)

Sala's and other defenses of her work must have made Braddon feel somewhat vindicated, but then a series of tragedies cast their shadows on her life. First, her young son Francis died in 1866. Then her sister, Maggie, fell ill in Italy, prompting her brother, Edward, to return to Europe after many years in India. Edward first visited Maggie in Italy, then came to England to see his other sister and his mother. On this visit, in the summer of 1868, he discovered that Mary was not married to Maxwell but had borne him several illegitimate children. Edward blew up, and the siblings were estranged for many years to come. Meanwhile, Mary blamed Edward's outburst for making their mother sick.

In the autumn of 1868, Maggie finally died in Italy, followed by a worse blow for Mary: her mother died suddenly at the age of sixty-four.

Mary was inconsolable, writing to Bulwer Lytton: "I cannot tell you how I loved her . . . Thus ends thirty years of the most perfect union, I believe, that ever existed between two human beings of the same sex" (3 November 1868). Braddon's grief was so deep that she could not even write; Maxwell had to find someone else to complete *Bound to John Company,* the serial running in *Belgravia* at the time of Fanny Braddon's death. Those who disliked Maxwell and his sharp business practices (Braddon was the only one of his authors who earned decent wages) observed that the loud and ruddy Irishman had finally gotten his comeuppance. Braddon, thought by many to be Maxwell's cash cow, had suddenly run dry.

As it happens, Braddon wrote very little for the next couple of years. The death of her mother followed quickly by the birth of her fifth child, Rosalie, prompted a nervous breakdown complicated by puerperal fever. In a strange case of life imitating art, Lady Audley's secret (the deepest one) is that she is insane. When Robert Audley finally corners her and gets her to confess that she pushed George Talboys down a well, she screams, "I killed him because I AM MAD. . . . my mind, never properly balanced, utterly lost its balance; and I WAS MAD" (p. 293). Lady Audley reveals that the "taint" in her blood is hereditary: her mother died in a madhouse, a victim of puerperal fever (an illness of new mothers that we know in our era as "post-partum depression"). Lady Audley, it is revealed, suffered the same illness after the birth of her son Georgy (p. 17), and her lack of interest in the child (the illness is marked by a deep aversion to the newborn and the newborn's father) prompts her to abandon him to the care of his tipsy grandfather.

Elaine Showalter, in *The Female Malady* (1985), cites the fact that 7 to 10 percent of female asylum admissions in the mid-nineteenth century were diagnosed as puerperal insanity cases (p. 57). John Maxwell's first wife succumbed to puerperal fever after the birth of their last child, hence her confinement in Dublin, away from him and her children. Robert Lee Wolff, Braddon's first biographer, observes that Maxwell was terrified that Mary Elizabeth, like Mary

Anne, might become permanently insane (p. 228). Luckily, that did not happen. She began to come out of the deepest part of her depression in 1869, and by the spring of 1870 she had begun to write again. Nevertheless, her illness had marked her, and she described to Bulwer Lytton how different she felt when she finally returned from the hallucinatory realm of her long illness:

> When that unreal world faded the actual world seemed strangely dull & empty and my own brain utterly emptied out—swept clean of every thought. My first efforts to write after that time were beyond measure feeble, and I thought imagination was dead—but, thank Heaven, the knack of copy-spinning, at least, has returned.
>
> (13 June 1872)

New novels were soon flowing as easily from her pen as they ever had, but in September 1874, the crowning blow struck the Maxwell household. (By this time the family was living in a mansion—Lichfield House in Richmond—furnished with antiques and valuable paintings and financed by Braddon's many bestsellers.) Maxwell's first wife, Mary Anne, died at the age of forty-eight, at the home of her brother. Maxwell, according to Jennifer Carnell, "handled the situation badly" (p. 181). He telegraphed her brother that he planned to come to the funeral, and to pay for it, and then he sent another telegram backing out and urging his brother-in-law "not to advertise [the] death, as I shall do whatever is necessary" (p. 181). Outraged, Mary Anne's family *did* advertise the death of John Maxwell's wife, and soon enough letters of condolence were appearing at Lichfield House, because people thought Braddon had died. Meanwhile, Maxwell's children by his first wife were disappointed that their father did not bother to attend their mother's funeral. Much as they loved their stepmother, they felt their father had treated their real mother disrespectfully. In fact, many years later, when Maxwell's children reminisced about their parents in either interviews or their own memoirs, not one of them remembered their father with fondness. They gave him credit for being financially generous, but found him loud, overbearing, and embarrassing.

After Mary Anne's death, Braddon had to endure another round of damage to her reputation. Almost all of the servants at Lichfield House, upon the discovery that they had been working for a bigamist and his consort, handed in their resignations. According to Carnell, the scandal was so intense that the family had to move to Chelsea for a year to live it down (p. 183). Not surprisingly, as soon as they possibly could, Mary Elizabeth Braddon and John Maxwell were legally married.

BRADDON'S LATER CAREER

Braddon's career as a novelist did not end with the sensational Sixties, although her works from that era lived on for decades—*Lady Audley's Secret* went through dozens of editions, was performed (in pirated versions) onstage for the rest of the nineteenth century, and was only rivaled by its sister novel, *Aurora Floyd,* for enduring popularity. The latter novel also went through numerous editions and stage versions and was also made into a silent film—which Braddon actually saw in 1913.

Some of Braddon's success also came from changes in printing and cheaper paper. (Prime Minister Gladstone had repealed paper taxes, enabling the existence of many new publications, hence the sudden blooming of English periodicals in the 1860s.) Perhaps most important, Braddon's work appealed to the patrons of Mudie's Circulating Library, a powerful arbiter of Victorian values. According to Richard Altick, Charles Edward Mudie "could make or break an author's career by his acceptance or rejection of a new book" (*Victorian Ideas and People,* p. 196). Mudie's had subscribers in the tens of thousands in England, and it is significant that at no time did he ever ban Braddon's books from his list of offerings—even though Mudie made a point of allowing only fiction suitable for the entire family and had indeed banned other novels and novelists from his shelves. Instead, Braddon was one of Mudie's most popular authors, and the phrase "Queen of the circulating libraries" was printed on advertisements for her novels.

MARY ELIZABETH BRADDON

When the popularity of the sensation novel waned at the end of the 1860s, Braddon adapted; she began to write more novels in the realist vein of Balzac (whom she greatly admired), Zola, and Flaubert. In 1875, she published a novel on a topic she knew well from her stage days—the translating (frequently whitewashing) of French plays to make them appeal to an English audience. What she had done with Flaubert in *The Doctor's Wife,* the characters of *Hostages to Fortune* do with a French play. She was also interested, like Zola, in theories of genetic inheritance. Her novel *The Golden Calf* (1883) treats the effect of an alcoholic man on his family. Another Zola-inspired novel, and the one that her first biographer, Robert Lee Wolff, considered her best work, was *Ishmael* (1884). This novel takes place in the tumultuous period surrounding the ascension of Louis Napoleon in France. Ishmael goes to Paris as a young man and finds his friends among the militant working class. After initially espousing Marxism, in middle age he repudiates his youthful beliefs and advocates a return to paternalism.

All her life, Braddon retained an interest in French literature. She spoke French fluently, kept up with French novels, and traveled frequently to Paris. She also admired much German literature; in 1891 she wrote a strange novel titled *Gerard; or, The World, the Flesh, and the Devil,* that mixes Goethe's *Faust* with Balzac's *La Peau de chagrin* and is set in decadent 1890s London.

Braddon also contributed a great deal to that emergent genre of literature the detective novel. Some critics think she is the first woman to write a detective novel (citing the amateur sleuthing of Robert Audley in *Lady Audley's Secret*), and it's a genre at which she excelled. Many of her best novels of the 1880s and 1890s are detective stories, including *Wyllard's Weird* (1885), *Cut by the County* (1886), *The Day Will Come* (1889), *Rough Justice* (1898), and *His Darling Sin* (1899). As sensation fiction had been the most popular genre of light reading in the 1860s, detective fiction was the most popular in the 1880s and 1890s. All of these books feature a detective—either amateur or professional—as the major character.

Jennifer Carnell, in her biographical study of Braddon, points out the major difference between sensation fiction and detective fiction, the genre into which it segued:

> If detective fiction is the exposé of the solution of a puzzle, the whodunit in a crime or murder, sensation fiction is instead the revelation of secrets, and how the suppression of secrets affects the security of the family
>
> (p. 272)

Braddon continued to write and to be read until well into the twentieth century. Meanwhile, in her private life, she had finally weathered the scandal of her illegitimate relationship with John Maxwell. By the 1880s she mixed in high society, and she and her husband were civic leaders in Richmond. Braddon and Maxwell also owned a second home near Lyndhurst that they called Annesley Bank. This was a large property that enabled Braddon to indulge her love of fox and deer hunting. As often as three times a week she took long gallops on her mares, Peggy and Vixen.

In 1883, a sure sign that Braddon had left the scandals of the past behind her appeared in the shape of a painting by William Powell Frith exhibited at the Royal Academy. This painting depicted the most important personages of the day, and Braddon was included with Browning, Gladstone, Anthony Trollope, Angela Burdett-Coutts, and Oscar Wilde. In 1895, after a long illness and a brief period of dementia, John Maxwell died. After his death, Braddon wrote less but socialized more. In addition to the detective novels, Braddon penned several historical novels, including *London Pride* (1896), *The Infidel* (1900), and *The Rose of Life* (1905), based on her friend Oscar Wilde. Having begun her career on the cusp of the American Civil War in 1861, Braddon died at the beginning of the First World War in 1915.

Although she wrote more than eighty novels and her career spanned the better part of sixty years, Mary Elizabeth Braddon will always be best known for some of the earliest novels she wrote. She was credited in her own day for instigating—and producing the best of—the sensation novel genre, and most of the criticism devoted to her in our own day continues to focus on her work in that realm.

CRITICAL ASSESSMENTS

As mentioned in the course of this essay, sensation fiction appeared in a decade that the Victorians themselves saw as sensational. The theater, thanks to new special-effects techniques, could produce amazing spectacles onstage, including full-scale battle scenes with fires, stampeding horses, and sinking ships. The legal court, meanwhile, produced its own sensational thrills by putting the "secret theatre of home" on public view with spectacular murder trials. These trials, with their often apparently respectable defendants, were either witnessed by Victorians in packed galleries or read about in obsessively detailed newspaper reports. Not surprisingly, then, sensational fiction joined the other forms of the day and became itself one of the major sensations of the 1860s. It was recognized immediately as a cultural phenomenon. One of the first reviewers, in the *Quarterly,* observed that "the sensation novel, be it mere trash or something worse, is usually a tale of our own time," and added, "it is necessary to be near a mine to be blown up by its explosion" (Hughes, p. 18).

In their own era, sensation novels were both avidly read and actively deplored for their immorality, particularly that of their heroines. By the end of the nineteenth century, there were still living writers (notably Henry James and Thomas Hardy) who remembered avidly reading *Lady Audley's Secret* in their youth, but the novel and the genre was not known to young people in that era and had faded from memory in another generation. Those books remained in obscurity until the 1970s, when feminist critics rediscovered them.

In our era, it was the rebellious and immoral heroines that they had once been critically damned for that brought the novels—particularly those by Mary E. Braddon—back to life and publication. Feminist critics of the 1970s, including Elaine Showalter, Sally Mitchell, and Nina Auerbach focused on the subversive quality of these novels for Victorian women readers. In their zeal to point out the way these heroines defied patriarchal authority (and encouraged their female readers to follow suit), Showalter and the other feminists ignored the orthodoxy of the novels. For example, though *Lady Audley's Secret* features a murderous villainess as its main character, said rebellious heroine is also severely punished for her crimes, committed to an insane asylum where she ultimately dies. Any celebration of subversion occasioned by her lawless activities is certainly dampened by the novel's ending.

After feminists broke the critical ground, Marxists began to till the soil. These 1980s theorists were interested in "historicizing" literature, and they read Braddon's enormously popular novels as useful filters through which to view the period and the culture in which they appeared. One of the notable essays of this period is Jonathan Loesberg's "The Ideology of Narrative Form in Sensation Fiction." Loesberg focuses on what he describes as a Victorian fear of "changing" classes and thus losing one's legal and class identity. He links this fear to the initial parliamentary debates in the late 1850s on the Second Reform Bill, not passed until 1867, which was to improve conditions for factory laborers and the working class. His idea is interesting but limited because the reform bill was not a major topic of conversation in England until the mid-1860s, by which time Braddon and the other major sensation novelists had already published their best-known works.

Richard Altick, who published two important books on sensation fiction (*Victorian Studies in Scarlet*, 1970, and *Deadly Encounters*, 1986), takes a different tack and connects the novels to sensational murder trials of the period. Like Loesberg and Showalter, Altick's ideas are also valuable but too limited in focusing on one cause for the broad-ranging effects of sensation fiction.

Perhaps the best book from the 1980s that treats the sensational phenomenon in Great Britain is that written by a practicing detective novelist: *Black Swine in the Sewers of Hampstead: Beneath the Surface of Victorian Sensationalism* (1989), by Thomas Boyle. Other books that provide good overviews to the genre are

Winifred Hughes's *The Maniac in the Cellar* (1980), which makes important links between stage melodrama and sensation novels, and Lyn Pykett's slender *The Sensation Novel* (1994) from the Writers and Their Work series published by Northcote House and the British Council. There are also now two good biographies of Braddon, the original by Robert Lee Wolff (*Sensational Victorian,* 1979), and a later one by Jennifer Carnell that adds much new material about Braddon's years on the English stage (*The Literary Lives of Mary Elizabeth Braddon,* 2000).

Nevertheless, as *Beyond Sensation: Mary Elizabeth Braddon in Context* (2000) shows (despite its title), criticism by the turn of the twenty-first century had still not ranged far beyond Braddon's work as a sensation novelist. The essays in this volume echo the kind of "combination story" that the sensation novel was famous for, by mixing cultural history with feminism; such assessments locate her novels in the nineteenth-century discourses about female sexuality, madness, medical, and legal issues. Discussions of class and gender figure prominently in these essays, and Victorian marriage and divorce laws are scrutinized, as are publishing practices and consumer behavior. Historical events are not ignored, and there is treatment here of the effect of the American Civil War on Braddon's fiction and the impact of British imperialism, not least of all the Indian mutiny of 1857.

In addition to these, many other important books and articles about Braddon have appeared since the 1970s and are listed below in the bibliography.

SELECTED BIBLIOGRAPHY

I. NOVELS. *The Black Band; or, The Mysteries of Midnight* (*Halfpenny Journal,* 1861–1862; repr. Hastings, U.K., 1998); *The Trail of the Serpent* (London, 1861); *The Octoroon; or, The Lily of Louisiana* (*Halfpenny Journal,* 1861–1862; repr. Hastings, U.K., 1999); *Lady Audley's Secret* (London, 1862; repr. Harmondsworth, U.K., 1985; Oxford and New York, 1987); *The Lady Lisle* (London, 1862); *Aurora Floyd* (London, 1863; repr. Oxford and New York, 1996); *Eleanor's Victory* (London, 1863; repr. Stroud, U.K., 1996); *John Marchmont's Legacy* (London, 1863; repr. Oxford and New York, 1999); *Henry Dunbar* (London,

1864); *The Doctor's Wife* (London, 1864; repr. Oxford and New York, 1998); *Only a Clod* (London, 1865); *Sir Jasper's Tenant* (London, 1865); *The Lady's Mile* (London, 1866), *Birds of Prey* (London, 1867); *Dead Sea Fruit* (London, 1868); *Charlotte's Inheritance* (London, 1868); *Run to Earth* (London, 1868); *Fenton's Quest* (London, 1871); *The Lovels of Arden* (London, 1871); *Bound to John Company* (serialized in *Belgravia,* July 1868–October 1869; Braddon fell ill after the first five installments and another writer completed the serial; she replaced these in the book edition, and also changed the title), later *Robert Ainsleigh* (London, 1872); *Strangers and Pilgrims* (London, 1873); *Lost for Love* (London, 1874); *A Strange World* (London, 1875); *Hostages to Fortune* (London, 1875); *Dead Men's Shoes* (London, 1876); *Joshua Haggard's Daughter* (London, 1876); *An Open Verdict* (London, 1878); *Vixen* (London, 1879; repr. Stroud, U.K., and Dover, N.H., 1993); *The Cloven Foot* (London, 1879); *The Story of Barbara* (serialized in the *World* as *Her Splendid Misery,* July 1879–June 1880; published in book form, London, 1880); *Just As I Am* (London, 1880); *Asphodel* (London, 1881); *Mount Royal* (London, 1882; New York, 1885); *The Golden Calf* (London, 1883); *Phantom Fortune* (London, 1883); *Ishmael* (London, 1884); *Wyllard's Weird* (London, 1885); *One Thing Needful* (London and New York, 1886); *Cut By the County* (London, 1886); *Mohawks* (London, 1886); *Like and Unlike* (London and New York, 1887); *The Fatal Three* (London, 1888; repr. Stroud, U.K., 1997); *The Day Will Come* (London, 1889); *Gerard* (syndicated in various newspapers, including the *Sheffield Weekly Telegraph,* from January to June 1891, as *The World, the Flesh, & the Devil;* published in book form, London 1891); *The Venetians* (London and New York, 1892); *Thou Art the Man* (London, 1894); *Sons of Fire* (London, 1895); *London Pride* (London, 1896); *Rough Justice* (London, 1898); *His Darling Sin* (London, 1899); *The Infidel* (London, 1900); *The Conflict* (London, 1903); *A Lost Eden* (London, 1904); *The Rose of Life* (London, 1905); *The White House* (London, 1906); *Dead Love Has Chains* (London, 1907); *Her Convict* (London, 1907); *During Her Majesty's Pleasure* (London, 1908); *Our Adversary* (London, 1909); *Beyond These Voices* (London, 1910); *The Green Curtain* (London, 1911); *Miranda* (London, 1913); *Mary* (London, 1916).

II. SHORT STORY COLLECTIONS. (The stories contained in each collection originally appeared in magazines such as *The Welcome Guest, Belgravia, All the Year Round,* and Braddon's Christmas annual, *Mistletoe Bough.*) *Ralph the Bailiff and Other Tales* (London, 1867); *The Summer Tourist: A Book for Long or Short Journeys by Rail, Road, or River* (London, 1871); *Milly Darrell and Other Tales* (London, 1873); *Weavers and Weft* (London, 1877); *Flower and Weed and Other Tales* (London, 1884); *Under the Red Flag and Other Tales* (London, 1886); *All Along the River* (London, 1893).

III. DRAMA. (All of the plays listed here were performed in London, Brighton, or Liverpool, but some were never published.) *The Loves of Arcadia* (unpublished, 1860); *The Model Husband* (London, 1868); *Griselda; or, The Patient Wife* (1873); *The Missing Witness* (1880); *Margery Daw* (1881); *For Better, for Worse* (unpublished, 1890).

IV. POETRY COLLECTION. (Braddon published poems in a variety of newspapers and magazines throughout her life, but only one collection in book form.) *Garibaldi and Other Poems* (London, 1861).

V. PARODIES AND NONFICTION. A full listing of Braddon's nonfiction articles on subjects as diverse as cruelty to horses, French novels, hot dinners in elementary schools, European travel, Lord Byron, Bulwer Lytton, and a variety of reviews of books and plays, may be found in Carnell, pp. 421–427 (see "Biographies" below).

VI. UNPUBLISHED MEMOIR. *Before the Knowledge of Evil* (1914). This unpublished memoir as well as a great deal of other unpublished material by Mary Elizabeth Braddon may be found in the Robert Lee Wolff Collection of Victorian Fiction, Harry Ransom Humanities Research Center, University of Texas at Austin.

VII. LETTERS. Robert Lee Wolff, ed., "Devoted Disciple: The Letters of Mary Elizabeth Braddon to Sir Edward Bulwer Lytton, 1862–1873," in *Harvard Library Bulletin* 12 (1974). Other letters may be found in the Bram Stoker Correspondence, Brotherton Library, University of Leeds; in the T. H. S. Escott papers at the British Library; and in the A. P. Watt Collection of General and Literary Manuscripts in the Wilson Library, University of North Carolina at Chapel Hill.

VIII. BIOGRAPHIES. Robert Lee Wolff, *Sensational Victorian: The Life and Fiction of Mary Elizabeth Braddon* (New York, 1979); Jennifer Carnell, *The Literary Lives of Mary Elizabeth Braddon: A Study of Her Life and Work* (Hastings, U.K., 2000).

IX. CRITICAL STUDIES. Richard D. Altick, *Victorian Studies in Scarlet* (New York, 1970) and *Victorian Ideas and People* (New York, 1973); P. D. Edwards, *Some Mid-Victorian Thrillers: The Sensation Novel, Its Friends and Foes* (Queensland, 1971); Mary S. Hartman, *Victorian Murderesses* (London, 1977, 1985); Elaine Showalter, *A Literature of Their Own: British Women Novelists from Brontë to Lessing* (Princeton, N.J., 1977; new rev. ed., London, 1982); Winifred Hughes, *The Maniac in the Cellar: Sensation Novels of the 1860s* (Princeton, N.J., 1980); Patricia Craig and Mary Cadogan, *The Lady Investigates: Women Detectives and Spies in Fiction* (London, 1981; Oxford, 1986); Nina Auerbach, *Woman and the Demon* (Cambridge, Mass., 1982); Patrick Brantlinger, "What is 'Sensational' About the 'Sensation Novel'?" in *Nineteenth-Century Fiction* 37 (1982). Jonathan Loesberg, "The Ideology of Narrative Form in Sensation Fiction," in *Representations* 13 (winter 1986); Jenny Bourne Taylor, *In the Secret Theatre of Home: Wilkie Collins, Sensation Narrative, and Nineteenth-Century Psychology* (London, 1988); Thomas Boyle, *Black Swine in the Sewers of Hampstead: Beneath the Surface of Victorian Sensationalism* (New York, 1989); Claire Tomalin, *The Invisible Woman: The Story of Nellie Ternan and Charles Dickens* (London and New York, 1990); Ann Cvetkovich, *Mixed Feelings: Feminism, Mass Culture, and Victorian Sensationalism* (New Brunswick, N.J., 1992); Lyn Pykett, *The "Improper" Feminine: The Women's Sensation Novel and the New Woman Writing* (London and New York, 1992), and *The Sensation Novel from "The Woman in White" to "The Moonstone"* (Plymouth, U.K., 1994); Marlene Tromp et al., eds., *Beyond Sensation: Mary Elizabeth Braddon in Context* (Albany, N.Y., 2000).

BARBARA COMYNS

(1907-1992)

Julie Hearn

IN 1959, THE publisher William Heinemann sent a copy of Barbara Comyns' *The Vet's Daughter* to Graham Greene, hoping for a quote. Greene's response was both swift and perfunctory: "Will you please send me no more books by lady novelists. I'm sick of them. No more." The following day, he sent a telegram: "This writer is marvellous." Comyns, according to the writer Jane Gardam, was delighted by this accolade, "... for there is something that she shared with Greene and she knew it—the sense of wreckage and of evil in the air" (*The Guardian*, 4 August 1992).

Seven Comyns novels were published between 1947 and 1967. Each one can be seen, retrospectively, as an intriguing commentary on the contradictory demands being made of, and by, women in postwar Britain. At the time, however, no one knew quite what to make of them. Her style—"Beryl Bainbridge on acid" according to Celia Brayfield (introduction to *Sisters by a River*, 2000, p. vi)—was too quirky for a literary world which had yet to embrace magic realism. Many critics considered her work distasteful, even though it haunted them.

Her third book, *Who was Changed and Who was Dead* (1954) was banned in Ireland under the Censorship of Publications Act—condemned for its portrayal of madness and savagery in a village stricken by ergot-poisoning. *The Skin Chairs* (1962), in which a 10-year-old narrator cuts through the hypocrisy of the adult world, was only slightly less disturbing. What strange mind, after all, could conceive of the General's chairs? ("'He brought them back from the Boer War, isn't it horrible? Five of them are black men's skins and one white. I believe if you look carefully you can see the difference. He used to adore them, silly old man,'" [p. 19.]) Or of the grotesque Mrs. Alexander, who talks of Italian lovers but whose head, beneath a mauve silk turban, is pitted with scabs? ("That holey head! It reminded me of an ugly thing an old woman had once given my father, a man's head made of china. He was bald and had an awful laugh on his face and his head was full of holes to contain matches," pp. 136–137).

Barbara Comyns was too peculiar; her work was too uneasily situated between literature and popular fiction to attract either critical acclaim or a particularly wide readership. Although *The Vet's Daughter* was serialized by BBC Radio, and turned into a musical, "The Clapham Wonder" (1978) by Sandy Wilson, her reputation flourished no further, and her novels slipped out of circulation.

Then, in the 1980s, Virago republished six of her novels with new introductions by Ursula Holden and Patricia Craig. Inspired by this resurgence of interest, Comyns wrote *The Juniper Tree* (1985), *Mr Fox* (1987) and *The House of Dolls* (1989). All three received respectful reviews. Comyns, by now in her eighties, was delighted and bemused by such an unexpected renaissance. Ursula Holden remembers her at publishers' parties, making the kind of idiosyncratic observations that added charm to her books ("That meat looked as if it had been shredded by tigers...")

Literary studies—even those that focus specifically on postwar women writers—have tended to overlook Comyns and her work. Niamh Baker includes analyses of *Our Spoons Came From Woolworths*, *Who was Changed and Who was Dead*, and *Sisters by a River* in *Happily Ever After? Women's Fiction in Postwar Britain 1945–60* (1989), and there is an entry for Comyns in the *Dictionary of British Women Writers* edited by Janet Todd (1989, repr. 1991). Readers consulting *The Oxford Companion to English*

Literature (2000), however, will find that Compton-Burnett is followed by Conan Doyle.

Jill Foulston, an editor at Virago, remains convinced that Barbara Comyns will shortly take her place among such writers as Barbara Pym, Elizabeth Taylor, Elizabeth Bowen, and Penelope Mortimer as an important woman writer in the decades immediately after the Second World War. Behind the deceptive simplicity of a Comyns novel, maintains Foulston, lie important messages relating to women's roles in both the public and private spheres during the 1940s and 1950s. Indeed, Comyns could be said to epitomise the "serious woman novelist" identified by critic Anthea Zeman:

> She uses the novel as a manual to her sisters, as a reference book for those who have not yet heard the news [...] behind the plot, conversation, description and other luggage there will be found to lie an up-to-date statement of the law, written and unwritten, as it relates to women at that time; these novels are monitoring reports on new freedoms, lost ground, new dangers, new possibilities of emotional tax evasion, and up-to-date reminders of those bills which still have to be paid.
>
> (Zeman, p. 2)

In October 2000, *Sisters by a River*, *Our Spoons Came From Woolworths* and *The Vet's Daughter* were reissued as Virago Modern Classics.

CHILDHOOD

Comyns' childhood, as recalled in her quasi-autobiographical *Sisters by a River* (1947) appears as strange, and enchanting, as a tale by the Brothers Grimm. Her father was an industrialist and landlord of a small cottage where a widow, of Irish descent, lived with her young daughter. According to family legend, while collecting the rent one day, he saw the daughter skipping in the garden and made up his mind to marry her when she was old enough to bake a cake. Years passed, the girl turned seventeen, and duly became the landlord's wife, moving with her aging mother into the "big house" on the banks of the River Avon in Warwickshire.

Six children—a boy and five girls—were born in rapid succession. Barbara, the fourth, arrived on 26 December 1907 (since she habitually knocked a few years of her age, in later life, the year 1909 is frequently given). Her mother lost her hearing while in labor with her last child and remained profoundly deaf for the rest of her life. "I remember her best," Comyns wrote, "lying in a shaded hammock on one of the lawns, reading and eating cherries... or in the winter sitting by the morning room fire and opening and shutting her hands before the blaze as if to store the heat. Her pet monkey sitting on the fender would be doing the same" (introduction to *The Vet's Daughter*, 1980, p. i).

The children's father turned increasingly to drink, as his business enterprises failed. An impatient, violent man, who alternately spoiled and terrified his family, he may well have been Comyns' prototype for the bullying fathers and egotistical husbands who swagger through her fiction like trolls.

Comyns started writing stories at the age of ten, but received little praise or encouragement. Her brother was sent to boarding school, but she and her sisters were sporadically educated by a series of poorly qualified governesses.

> Running wild the curious pack of girls extracted a different kind of education from their decaying estate. Photographs reveal well-stocked herbaceous borders and an immaculate stripe-mowed lawn but Barbara's writing evokes a magical warren of attics and glory-holes crumbling in the midst of a wilderness patrolled by a peacock called Philip who wore a gold chain around his neck.
>
> (Celia Brayfield, introduction to *Sisters by a River*, p. vi)

This sense of disintegration, behind a facade, is a theme Comyns returned to again and again in her novels. Marriages and houses fall apart, slowly. Young girls earning a meager living in post-war London struggle to keep up appearances. Sisters Blanche and Vicky in *A Touch of Mistletoe*, for example, dress their own pale and hungry selves in the colors used to disguise their dingy one-room flat:

> Living in a blue and orange 'complete home in miniature' began to affect us in various ways. For one thing, everything I painted became blue and orange and it also got into our clothes. We bought some vivid blue and orange shantung and I made an orange dress trimmed with blue and Blanche a blue dress trimmed with orange. We cut the necks too large and the collars would not sit properly. We wore these shining dresses for the first time on a sunny spring day when we were lunching with the Scobys and, as we walked down the hill that led to their house, we felt people staring at us and we heard people say , 'Spaniards I suppose'. We looked at our dresses with the sun on them and they were so bright they seemed to be beating.

> (p. 63)

But it was Comyns' ability to see the world from a child's perspective that, more than anything, gave her writing an incisive and frequently startling edge. Her narrators speak with foreshortened understanding, yet are capable of profound insights which alternately delight and unnerve the reader. The world of childhood, with all its terrors and imaginings, is beautifully articulated, as in the following extract from *The Skin Chairs* in which young Frances recalls having to stay with "horsey relatives" following the death of her father:

> One night I dreamt that Mother's head had been severed and made into a pork pie. Although it was a pork pie, I could see it was a dead head. There was another fearful dream that Father was floating down the canal, all enlarged with water, and that eels were living in him [...] To keep myself awake and to calm myself I would go through each room at home so that it almost seemed as if I was there. I tried to recall everything they contained: the yellow rug in the drawing room, which we used to cut pieces from to make doll's wigs; the faded morning-room curtains with monkeys climbing up them [...] The smaller the detail I could remember, the happier I felt—which of the doors that led from the kitchen had latches and which had handles, for instance. Once a guinea pig had died in the kitchen and one of the maids had held a small mirror to its mouth to see if its breath left a mark, and ever after I seemed to see the mark of the guinea pig's last breath on it.

> (pp. 29–30)

Sisters by a River was serialized in the magazine *Lilliput*, then published by Eyre & Spottiswood (1947). The text was left unpunctuated and poorly spelled, just as Comyns had written it— the publishers even added a few more mistakes, to enhance the text's Daisy Ashford charm. Some readers have found this irritating (see Baker, p. 134) but it could also be seen as subversive. Doris Lessing, in *The Golden Notebook*, frequently omitted connectives and neglected correct grammatical structures in order to destabilize language, as an ordering mechanism, and open a space within which to express previously marginalized female subjectivities. *Sisters by a River*, in presenting a child's-eye view of the world in an authentically childlike voice, could be said to break not only the rules of spelling and grammar but also the greater rules of male-centered culture which define the correct way for little girls to speak and behave. The narrator's naiveté both belies and enhances her powers of perception. Beneath their apparent surface simplicity, childlike observations speak volumes about loveless relationships and the disintegration of family life. The style loses some of its authenticity towards the end of the book, when it becomes apparent that this is not a child writing but an adult re-entering a child's world. Still, it remains an effective means of both recording, and challenging, the effects of callous or unthinking adult behavior on the very young.

MARRIAGE

Comyns' father died when she was fifteen, leaving mountainous debts and a widow on the verge of a nervous breakdown. The family home was sold, and Comyns went to art schools—first in Stratford-on-Avon then Hatherley's in London. When she could no longer afford to study, she found a job in an animation studio, drawing cartoons. Living on a pittance in a grim part of London, she spent most of her free time in public libraries. "I was almost drunk on books," she recalled in later life, "but my own writing suffered and became imitative and self-conscious. In the end, with great strength of mind, I destroyed all the stories and half-written novels I'd written over the years when I left my dank bed-sitting room to get married" (introduction to *The Vet's Daughter*, p. iii).

Comyns' first marriage, to fellow artist John Pemberton, was not a happy one. A son, Julian, and a daughter, Caroline, were born but money was tight and the couple, still only in their twenties, found domesticity a strain. Years later, the story of this marriage appeared, lightly fictionalized, in *Our Spoons Came From Woolworths* (1950)—a tragi-comic novel set in a bohemian part of London during the 1930s.

Sophia, the novel's narrator, appears throughout as a passive victim of circumstance. This effect is heightened by the faux-naif style of her narrative—a style which worked well in *Sisters by a River* as a vehicle for childhood reminiscences, but seems an odd voice with which to reflect upon marriage, motherhood, and an affair with an aging art critic.

The reader's sympathies are engaged from the very first paragraph: "I told Helen my story and she went home and cried. In the evening her husband came to see me and brought some strawberries; he mended my bicycle, too, and was kind, but he needn't have been, because it all happened eight years ago, and I'm not unhappy now" (p. 9).

Having cast herself in the role of innocent victim and the reader as another "Helen," to be moved to tears, perhaps, as "the story" unfolds, Sophia continues to manipulate the reader's response as we follow her through one personal crisis after another. It is a narrative technique Comyns uses in other novels, notably *A Touch of Mistletoe*, *Birds in Tiny Cages*, and *Mr Fox*, to elicit sympathy for women trapped in damaging relationships with husbands or lovers. At face value, it seems a trite stratagem—one that portrays women as little more than passive recipients of good or bad fortune. Niamh Baker has said:

I find it difficult to believe that Barbara Comyns was unaware of what she was doing, but I am unsure where her own sympathies lie. Perhaps she too, like Sophia, hides from herself her own anger, or perhaps she is, more subtly, portraying a woman who could play the helpless victim, while cunningly ensuring that even if she was trapped, others should not escape guilt-free.

(*Happily Ever After?* p. 52)

Close analysis of Sophia's character and of the transparency of her narrative suggest that Comyns was indeed being subtle. In chapter eight, Sophia makes what appears to be a casual reference to the contents of popular women's magazines:

Ann had known she was going to be an aunt for some time, and she kept showering me with motherly magazines published by the firm she worked for. They—the magazines, not the firm—were very sentimental and called babies "little treasures", and the walking ones were "toddlers". There were pages about the glories of motherhood. Also there were letters from mothers asking advice—"Was it true that if you eat apples before your baby was born, you would have a dwarf?" Or "Why does my baby cry after eating sardines?" There were stories, too, telling how much more men loved their wives if they were domesticated and had some children. In some of the stories the wives used to prefer going to work every day ... The husbands always left these selfish wives, but just at the last minute before anything drastic happened the wife would become all domesticated or find she was having a "little treasure" and the husband would come back.

(p. 48)

These stories, concludes Sophia, all had happy endings, "which was a good thing." She herself never makes a comparison between her own situation and the ideology being peddled by the media. It is left to the reader to make that connection—and it is easily done. Sophia's husband, Charles, is more than happy for her to be the main breadwinner since it leaves him free to paint. When she becomes pregnant he is horrified, and his response to the first sight of his "little treasure" in a charity hospital is chilling:

When he returned he said there was an awfully nice baby rather like a Japanese, with lots of black hair.

He said he wouldn't have minded that one so much, but ours was rather grim, very thin and red with red hair and an awful look of himself about it. I asked if it felt cold and he said he hadn't touched it, although the nurse had tried to make him hold it.

(p. 71)

When Sophia becomes pregnant for a second time, Charles persuades her to have an abortion, then uses her poor physical and emotional health as an excuse to send their son, Sandro, to stay with relatives. In chapter 22, Sophia recalls visiting the child—a trip only made possible by a male friend with a borrowed car ("I told Charles and at first he said he didn't want to come in case I made a scene about leaving Sandro behind …," p. 127). The visit is remembered dispassionately:

I asked Charles's aunt, who was a very plain woman with a flat chest and hair on her chin, if I could see Sandro now. I had asked before, but she said he was resting after his lunch, but this time she said she supposed I could. The night nursery was upstairs on the right. I found it easily because the door was open and I saw the nurse lifting him out of a cot. He was still only half awake and when he saw me he started to cry. The nurse said children don't like to see strangers when they first wake up.

(p. 129)

This passage typifies Sophia's tone, which remains strangely neutral, whether she is recalling a spring day, or a personal tragedy. Even allowing for the fact that this is a retrospective account, and Sophia is "not unhappy now," it seems excessively disengaged. Why? Sophia, it appears, is refusing to acknowledge the emotional, physical, and psychological damage she has suffered at the hands of men. Maybe she cannot, since to do so would expose her own complicity. Far easier, perhaps, to distance herself from the whole sorry mess than admit to never having had the courage to break away from these men, or the conventions binding her to them.

It is important, at this point, to consider how feminist literary criticism reveals the gaps and tears in women's writing, so that what appears conformist can be seen as deeply ambiguous. Comyns was writing at a time when society was clinging to conservative values, and British fiction was marked by a sense of nostalgia for a prewar world perceived, retrospectively as utopian. It was not the best time to be questioning traditional roles assigned to women—at least, not openly.

A number of contemporary critics (see Niamh Baker, Elizabeth Maslen, Magali Cornier Michael, Deborah Philips and Ian Haywood, and Elizabeth Wilson) have noted contradictions in the way women were perceived during the immediate postwar years. New legal and economic freedoms had been hard won, yet were being pushed aside in a drive to get women back into the home. Elevating the notion of the "happy housewife", however, conflicted with a labor shortage so acute that, in 1947, the Labour government launched a campaign to bring more women into the workforce. Women—particularly those who had worked during the war—were in a bind. Should they work? Did they want to? Could they juggle work, marriage, and motherhood? Were men, who had been either absent or marginal to their lives during the war, worth giving up their independence for?

Our Spoons, although set in the 1930s, cuts straight to the heart of these concerns. Sophia's husband, we are left in no doubt, was barely worth a second glance let alone years of commitment. The marriage finally ends yet, having swallowed the myth of matrimony as the be all and end all of female existence, Sophia can envisage no other way of being happy. After a time spent working as a cook in the country she meets and marries Rollo—a rich and well-established artist. All seems well, but so adept is Comyns at clouding her happy-ever-after endings that she manages, even through first person narrative, to suggest that Sophia has made a mistake.

In an intriguing few passages, the newly engaged Sophia abandons her beloved pet fox cub in the woods, because Rollo has insisted she get rid of him:

I took him a long way away, several miles. I carried him all the way. There was a heavy dew and all the birds were singing. When we came to the place where they reared pheasants I put him down, and I put a large piece of the Redheads' joint beside him, but he wasn't interested; he kept skipping about and sniffing the birds and quite forgot me, so I went away and felt too sad to cry. I felt guilty like the father in Hans and Gretel.

(p. 218)

Whether "Foxy" represents the free-spirit in Sophia, or the cunning she has so far needed in order to survive, letting him go is a pivotal event. From this moment on, the fairy tale marriage that was supposed to be her salvation will stifle her, in all kinds of ways ("We would have liked to have eaten our lunch in the garden ... but I thought the maid wouldn't approve" p. 222).

In the final chapter Sophia's narrative becomes languorous as she waits for Rollo to come home. "Everything seemed to be still and waiting for his return, even the bathwater seemed to come out of the taps all hushed" (p. 222). Images from nature—ants "dashing about with large eggs" the goldfish having "black children"—contrast with Sophia's turpitude as she sits in her garden, waiting. Her visitor, Helen, is trying to ride her old bicycle. She keeps falling off, but perseveres. Sophia finds simply watching her tiresome. She herself has no need, now, to persevere at anything. "I was delighted," she says, "when the brake became bent and prevented the wheels going round any more" (p. 222). The bicycle—symbolic of Sophia's independence—is broken now, and going nowhere.

"I'm not unhappy now," Sophia said, at the beginning of her story—not "I'm blissfully happy now" or even "I'm a lot happier now" but "I'm not unhappy now." These words, so clearly understated, were deliberately chosen for their resonance.

Clouded happy endings are a hallmark of Comyns' work. Most of her protagonists marry—often more than once—only to find themselves, like Sophia, unable to hang onto a sense of their own identities. Vicky, in *A Touch of Mistletoe*, marries twice for love and a third time for security. All three relationships are disastrous—the first two because Vicky is blinded by romantic idealism to the true natures of her men, the third because she sees her husband's failings all too clearly. Her first husband, Gene, suffers from bouts of chronic depression and can think of no

one but himself; her second, Tony, is a feckless alcoholic. Because both these men have an easy charm, Vicky is spellbound. Her narrative, like Sophia's, seems oblivious, even in hindsight, to the extent of her self-abnegation:

> Now, as soon as we finished dinner, he'd rush upstairs to his writing room and I'd follow with a Thermos of coffee, then spend the rest of the evening alone. It was well worth the dull evenings because Tony was so much happier when he was writing, feeling guilty and bored when he wasn't doing creative work. He would leave what he had written for me to type the next day, often scrapping half of it when he returned in the evening.
>
> (p. 160)

A few lines later, we are reminded of Vicky's own wasted talent as an illustrator: "I went to the film place where I used to work and found it deserted, just a few drawing pins left on the walls and a pile of rubbish and an old broom in the corner"(pp. 160–161). What Comyns is doing here is placing the reader in a dichotomous position—the confiding tone of Vicky's narrative encourages identification, yet the transparent naiveté of it makes us want to shake her.

As a young girl, at the beginning of the novel, Vicky spent a purgatorial time in Holland looking after some defective bull terriers for a couple who treated her appallingly. Back in London, she put up with the poverty and cabbage smells of one-room living, while waiting for her prince to come. These interludes, dismal as they were, were leavened with humor, optimism, and a strong sense of the narrator's self reliance—all of which are lost by the time Vicky reaches her forties and is contemplating marriage to a man who makes her heart sink.

It is a touch of near genius that Comyns chose to portray Vicky's third husband, the kindly yet ponderous E. M. Dadds, so much more vividly than the other two. His infuriating habits are nowhere near as damaging to Vicky as her experiences with Gene and Tony—which is precisely why, perhaps, she is able to dwell on them:

> Sometimes he went through the contents of the dustbin and pointed out food that had been needlessly thrown away among the tea-leaves and ashes—

slices of lemon that had decorated the fish or chicken's gizzards which could have been used in soup. When the winter ended, he drained off the antifreeze to use again next year and he stuck paper over all the holes but two on the scouring powder tins so that I didn't sprinkle out too much at once. Often when a kettle was boiling in the kitchen, he'd sense it and come in to see that I hadn't filled it with more water than I needed. Sometimes when he wasn't there, I'd boil up kettles and leave them to get cold.

(pp. 203–204).

Although Vicky claims she went into this marriage with no illusions, Comyns leaves us in no doubt that she remains as much as ever a victim of romantic ideology. In the following passage, having decided to marry "for security and friendship, not for love" Vicky conforms to stereotypical images of seductive womanhood:

I longed for beautiful clothes, to make the best of my looks while they lasted. I tried out new hairstyles and manicured my hands, wearing gloves of rubber or cotton when I was working at home, and I put my breasts in a black uplift bra which made them ache at first. I was still at the aching stage when E. M. Dadds came into The Chinghai ...

(p. 197)

The critic and writer Daphne Watson has said:

Fiction which presents women as happy victims of dominant and egotistic men does neither sex any favours. We need fiction which paints the world in shades of grey, not black and white [...] We need fiction that does not delude us into making the fatal mistake of the romantic idealist, that of projecting our dreams of an ideal lover on to some hapless, ordinary but complex and interesting real person. For too long we have laid the blame at men's doors; it is women who are their own worst enemies.

(*Their Own Worst Enemies: Women Writers of Women's Fiction*, p. 131)

Comyns' women may feign happiness, but it is nearly always illusory, or undermined. Guilty as most of them are of idealizing unworthy men, they appear to know, at some level, that the men themselves are not wholly to blame for the disappointment that inevitably follows.

Birds in Tiny Cages (1964), although the least well-known of Comyns' novels, is worth studying for its astute portrayal of a young wife who rebels against domesticity but, in the end, turns it into a virtue. The metaphorical implications of the title are underlined on the very first page, as Flora Elliot, watching other windows from her eighth-floor flat in Barcelona, sees "brown men wearing bleached white vests and their mothers, sisters and wives fluttering round them" (p. 1).

Flora's life, we are told, is "rather lonely and aimless" (p. 1). Her husband, Leo, is a workaholic and absent from most of the story. In the first chapter, the couple explores the tatty outskirts of Barcelona: "Leo would hurry away from the stench of decaying vegetables and other virulent smells, but Flora was fascinated by the large blue morning-glories which blazed away among the filth ..." (p. 7). Flora, it appears, will see the best in everything, even a rubbish heap. When she meets Parker, a local sculptor, she sees a knight in shining armor.

Bad housekeeping becomes synonymous with sexual deviance as Flora embarks on an affair:

Some mornings Flora would attack the housework in a fury, sweeping the tiled floors with her witch-like broom and, if there was enough water, scrubbing the soiled shirts and sheets as if they were her enemies [...] Her washing did not have the professional look of the other flapping linen and she often hung handkerchiefs and teacloths over the bad places—the pillow-case marked with lipstick, the rather grimy patch in the centre of the sheets, the table-cloth with the wine stain.

(p. 69)

Flora models for Parker, but is shocked to discover, in an optician's window, a cheap reproduction of the sculpture he made of her head, "the face faintly smiling behind violet-coloured sunglasses" (p. 108). Like the vineyard of stunted vines "black and twisted, like Dali moustaches" (p. 51) and the boxy little villas "like Japanese dog-kennels" along the coast (p. 118) the head in the window is a great disappointment, and not at all what Flora expected to see. Before long, she discovers that Parker is involved with his best friend's wife, and he too starts looking tawdry.

Resigned to making the best of her marriage, Flora becomes robotic in her determination to be a good housewife. The following passage depicts a very different Flora to the one who hung her dirty linen in public and banged a "witch-like broom" around: "Flora returned to the stove and took the lemon meringue pie out of the oven with a sigh of relief: it had only slightly browned and looked like an advertisement in an American magazine" (p. 146). This woman is still in her "tiny cage"—but submissively.

Comyns met her second husband, Richard Comyns Carr, in 1940. They got married at the end of the war and spent their honeymoon in a cottage by a waterfall in Wales where Comyns wrote an outline for *The Vet's Daughter*, but put it aside to write a biography of the pre-Raphaelite painter Leigh Hunt. The biography never found a publisher and was abandoned unfinished. Comyns, herself, was to become a painter of some distinction, exhibiting at The London Group, which showed the Vorticists. Her art, like her writing, was surreal and slightly Gothic—a link recognized by a number of critics who admired her novels:

> Everything in the books is envisaged precisely, perhaps through a way of seeing derived from an art school training—sometimes her work recalls the illustrator Harold Jones's, in its subtlety and charm, and sometimes it takes on a Rackham-like outlandishness—and the clearest possible outline is imposed on the narrative material.
>
> (Patricia Craig, introduction to *A Touch of Mistletoe*, 1988, p. ix)

As Comyns returned to fiction-writing, the likeness of her prose to the strange, sometimes discomfiting illustrations of Arthur Rackham came very much into play.

SOMETHING STRANGE

Comyns' work is not easily categorised; beneath its apparently simple surface it has the power to shock, amaze and horrify without obvious effort or contrivance

> (Peter Parker, ed. *The Reader's Companion to the Twentieth Century Novel*, p. 357)

The idea for *Who was Changed and Who was Dead* came to Comyns when she read about an outbreak of ergot poisoning in a French village during August 1951. She transposed the event to a Warwickshire village and the summer of 1914, thus linking it allegorically to the outbreak of war.

Written, unusually for Comyns, in the third person, this novel is concerned with the fragility of boundaries. From the very first page, when the river bursts its banks, we are in a world where the familiar has been turned upside down:

> The ducks swam through the drawing-room windows. The weight of the water had forced the windows open; So the ducks swam in. Round the room they sailed, quacking their approval; then they sailed out again to explore the wonderful new world that had come in the night. Old Ives stood on the verandah steps beating his red bucket with a stick while he called to them, but today they ignored him and floated away white and shining towards the tennis court. Swans were there, their long necks excavating under the dark, muddy water. All around there was a wheezy creaking noise as the water soaked into unaccustomed places, and in the distance a roar and above it the shouts of men trying to rescue animals from the low-lying fields.
>
> (p. 1)

Drowned peacocks on the lawn are a sinister omen. As the floodwaters recede, Comyns defines village life as a shifting, volatile thing; as likely as the river to go beyond the limits that curb and contain it. The local baker decides to make a few loaves of rye bread "as an experiment" (p. 35), and the bread, tainted with ergot (a disease of cereals and other grasses, caused by fungi) begins to make its way through the village.

The villagers are recognizable stereotypes—a sleepy clergyman, three old maids, the village bachelor, the local hussy—but none are clichéd. Comyns' character sketches, however brief, are always beautifully wrought. The clergyman's mother, for example, "was a little frightened bird of a woman, who held her twisted, claw-like hands clasped near her face, as if she was praying. This made it rather difficult for her to play cards and they would fall around her like petals from a dying flower"(p. 23).

Tradition and a sense of common history bind the villagers together. Generations of butchers have sharpened their knives on the stones of the Norman bridge. Old men swap reminiscences at "The Mason's Arms." The paper round the baker's bread is stamped with the family name and reproductions of his medals. It is a typically close-knit English community in which ignorance and superstition are only lightly concealed beneath outward appearances and group dynamics.

At Mrs. Hatt's funeral: "The midday sun burned down on the black group of people. They looked like bloated, sleepy flies at the end of the season." (p. 43). Social and moral boundaries collapse altogether, as the poisoned bread claims victim after victim. Through it all, the Willoweed children cling to the rituals of childhood, and Old Ives sits in his potting shed, like a god on Mount Olympus, casting judgement on other people's lives as he plans their funeral wreaths:

> … a wreath of roses and thyme for Mrs Hatt's grave —full bloom roses because she was a full blown woman, although she never had a child. Ives liked to choose suitable flowers for his wreaths. He often planned the one he would make for Grandmother Willoweed:—thistles and hogwart and grey-green holly—sometimes he would grant her one yellow dandelion. Ebin was to have one of bindweed and tobacco plants. Quite often people would die when the flowers he had chosen for them were not in season. Then he made a temporary wreath for them, and months later they received the real one.
>
> (p. 32)

Who was Changed and Who was Dead was not widely liked, or admired. Disappointed, but undeterred, Comyns went on to produce her best-known and most highly acclaimed work, *The Vet's Daughter*.

In this, her fourth book, naive fantasy has matured into magic realism—a powerful technique with which to explore a young girl's struggle against domestic, sexual, and socio-cultural oppression. There is a foretaste, here, of Angela Carter's work, but the quirky off-beat charm of the narrative remains Comyns' own ("her face worked in an odd way, like knitting coming undone" [p. 165] … "'Do you know, they have Snow White and the Seven Dwarfs all made of soap in the window of a chemist in Lavender Hill. […] Just imagine rubbing a dwarf's beard on your flannel!'" [p. 87]).

Alice, the vet's daughter, lives in a dreary London suburb with her dying mother and callous father:

> I entered the house. It was my home and it smelt of animals, although there was lino on the floor. In the brown hall my mother was standing, and she looked at me with her sad eyes half-covered by their heavy lids, but did not speak. She just stood there. Her bones were small and her shoulders sloped; her teeth were not straight either; so, if she had been a dog, my father would have destroyed her.
>
> (pp. 1–2)

Naive and unprotected, young Alice is preyed upon by men who wish to control and/or abuse her. Taken to the comparative safety of Hampshire by her dull suitor "Blinkers" she falls in love with a handsome young sailor and is devastated when his attention turns to another woman.

It is significant that Alice is completely happy only when she is alone, contemplating nature: "The air was very fresh, yet soft against my face, and suddenly I was filled with hope and not at all anxious" (p. 103). …"When I went outside, the sun had just risen and it was very light. The garden was large and open, and beyond it lay the water, shimmering between the pine trees […] I stood there overcome with peace and happiness, oblivious of the cold" (pp. 114–115).

This identification with nature recurs persistently in Comyns novels and can be read as far more than the occasional peaceful interlude in the lives of her troubled protagonists. Annis Pratt, in her study *Archetypal Patterns in Women's Fiction* (1981), argues that women's novels often constitute "literary variations on preliterary folk practices that are available in the realm of the imagination even when they have long been absent from day-to-day life" (p. 178). Moments of naturistic epiphany, according to Pratt, represent a sense of fulfilment denied to women within a male culture: "Taking possession of nature, she possesses *herself*" (p. 17). Hence, perhaps, the popularity of Elizabeth Goudge's romantic novels, including *The White Witch* (1958) and *The Scent of Water* (1963) in which archetypal female figures are truly at one with nature.

The principal archetypes defined by Pratt as recurrent in women's fiction—the green-world epiphany, the green-world lover, the rape trauma, enclosure and rebirth—are all to be found in *The Vet's Daughter*. Levitation—the ability to literally rise above her situation—is the only way Alice can regain control over her body and her circumstances. When her father discovers this strange talent, he makes immediate moves to exploit it at a public demonstration on Clapham Common.

The novel's final scenes are quasi-mystical and loaded with sacrificial imagery. Alice wears a white dress and flowers in her hair and observes everything she passes—the old church with the blue-faced clock; dandelions in the sodden grass, old men playing chess in the shelter— with the startling perception of someone either seeing them afresh or for the last time. The air through which she levitates is "stuffy and sickening" and the crowd below roars like an animal (p. 188).

Grace Stewart, in *A New Mythos: The Novel of the Artist as Heroine 1877–1977* (1981), writes of flight as a prevalent theme in novels dealing with society's confinement of artistic/non-conformist women. Such women, suggests Stewart, cannot truly soar without losing society's approval and being brought down, Icarus-like, with scorched wings. Many dream of freedom while feeling suffocated:

> Because this polarity between woman and artist persists, the flight imagery in their journeys is distinctive. The means of flight receive special emphases. Jong describes Isadora's wings as "borrowed" and attaches her heroine to a husband named "Wing". In *Lady Oracle* Atwood describes her heroine's wings as ludicrous attachments to an Earth Mother figure or as skimpy wings on a Fat Lady. For the heroines of Richardson, Sinclair and Lessing, flying is possible only in a dream or a trance, and the return necessitates a death-in-life of woman or artist.
>
> (p. 176)

When the vet's daughter returns to earth she is trampled to death by a panic-stricken crowd. "Then I could feel nothing. I simply thought, 'This is it; this is how one dies.' Rosa had ceased to scream, and for the first time in my life I was not afraid" (p. 189).

Death, then, appears inevitable, even horribly welcome for a girl who would never have felt at home in a patriarchal culture where even her one strange talent has been appropriated by a man for his own financial gain. A newspaper report—brief, detached, and inaccurate—provides closure for Alice's life and the novel.

The Skin Chairs (1962) explores a child's need to make sense of a world in which the death of her father and her family's subsequent struggle to keep up appearances mirror social concerns about the erosion of tradition and class privilege between the wars. Aunt Lawrence, with her delusions of grandeur, could have been conjured by Dickens:

> Aunt Lawrence had given us a goose and came round later in the day to smell it. We were each presented with a pair of grey woollen gloves, even Clare who only had one hand. I knew these gloves well, because one of Old Nanny's tasks was to knit them for the poor of the village. [...] Aunt Lawrence said how fortunate we were to have such a comfortable home and we must all help our little mother as much as possible. She pulled Clare's lower eyelids down so that they looked ugly and said she was anaemic, and that I should have my hair cut short because it was too long and curly to be healthy, and that Polly should wear a snood. Then she kissed us all with her soft lips that smelt of sherry, collected her walking-stick and husband, and walked away into the rat-coloured December dusk.
>
> (p. 81)

As the story progresses, young Frances becomes less of an observer and more of a participant, performing rituals to exorcise fear and guilt. She and her sister bury a pornographic book in the garden because it frightens them. Later, the younger children dig it up "and it had become beautiful, all spotted with pink and green" (p. 88). The General's skin chairs are less easily dealt with. Personified, they gather dismally round a table "perfectly still and quiet but glowering" (p. 199). In what has to be the strangest scene Comyns ever wrote, Frances baptizes the chairs, then reads the Order for the Burial of the Dead over them, so that they may rest in peace up in the loft. Since five of the chairs are made of black skins, the irony of a Christian baptism and burial service is implicit. Frances decides to name each chair after famous English poets, thus compounding, in all innocence, the imperial notion of white superiority and the right to define the "other":

> It took some time to choose names that suited the chairs and appealed to me, but I eventually decided on Percy Shelley. I didn't care for the name Percy but I liked Shelley and decided that the chair with the lighter skin should be called after him. George Byron was a chair with something slightly wrong with one foot so that it wobbled a bit. Edgar Poe had a mysterious mark running across his skin, as if from a scar. The last three chairs had no distinguishing marks. I called one Alfred Lord Tennyson because it was a good sound name, another William Yeats because he was still alive and I had only recently discovered him, and the third Anon Circa, who seemed to have died a very long time ago.
>
> (p. 200)

LATER LIFE AND WORK

Miss Comyns is a novelist of exceptional gifts, and her style has the luminous clarity of a painting on glass.

(Selina Hastings, *The Daily Telegraph*, 26 April 1985.)

By the time *The Vet's Daughter* was published, Comyns and her husband were living in Spain. They had left England to avoid a scandal after Richard's boss at the Foreign Office was exposed as a spy. The Mediterranean climate and way of life suited them so well they stayed for eighteen years.

Comyns' *Out of the Red, into the Blue* (1960) gives an account of the move and the trials and tribulations of setting up home abroad. Compared to her other books, this is not a memorable read. Whether she felt constrained by the need to protect the privacy or feelings of her family and friends, or whether her problems with Spanish drains and troublesome dogs are simply not as compelling as the events of her strange childhood, *Out of the Red, into the Blue* lacks the charm of *Sisters by a River* and remains the least known of her works.

After finishing *A Touch of Mistletoe* Comyns helped her husband with his work as a journalist and translator. As the years passed and no more novels appeared, it seemed as if her publishing days were over. Eventually, the couple returned to England, settling in a succession of houses around Richmond. Then, in 1981, Virago reissued *The Vet's Daughter*, followed by *Our Spoons Came From Woolworths*, *Sisters by a River*, *The Skin Chairs*, *Who was Changed and Who was Dead* and *A Touch of Mistletoe*.

Journalists visiting this "forgotten" writer found a delightfully eccentric woman with a resilience and strength of purpose that belied her fragile appearance. Caroline Moorehead, of *The Times*, wrote: "She talks as she writes, with a throwaway deceptively plain style, but without flippancy, choosing words with care and marking them all with a strong and always surprising individual touch" (28 January 1981).

When *The Juniper Tree* was published in April 1985, it was hailed by reviewers as "tantalising" (*The Observer*), "curiously moving" (*The Sunday Telegraph*), and "as welcome as spring" (*The Financial Times*). Based on a story by the Brothers Grimm, *The Juniper Tree* is a masterly intertwining of fairy tale and social realism, all woven together in Comyns' deceptively simple style:

> Quite soon after I left Richmond station I turned into a quiet street where the snow was almost undisturbed and, climbing higher, I came to a road that appeared to be deserted. Then I noticed a beautiful fair woman standing in the courtyard outside her house like a statue, standing there so still. As I drew nearer I saw that her hands were moving. She was paring an apple out there in the snow and as I passed, looking at her out of the

BARBARA COMYNS

sides of my eyes, the knife slipped, and suddenly there was blood on the snow.

(p. 7)

The snow, the courtyard, the apple, the drops of blood—all these are recognizable elements of a fairy tale. But the speaker, Bella, has just left Richmond station. She is about to land an enviable job running an antique shop. She is a single mother—and happily so. She does not, in other words, fit the Perrault, Grimm, or Anderson stereotype of storybook heroine for she is neither asleep, imprisoned, or waiting passively at home for her prince to come.

Still, entrenched mythologies are not easily kicked away. The more Bella feels drawn towards Gertrude and Bernard Forbes, and the apparent idyll of their marriage, the less self-sufficient she becomes. When Gertrude dies in childbirth, Bella agrees to marry Bernard, although she knows full well that her heart is ruling her head:

> Mary came round to the shop some days later and the two of us sat on some rather shaky Regency chairs, drinking instant coffee and talking about how impossible it was for me to marry Bernard. 'You will lose everything if you did, your freedom, the shop and your individuality,' Mary said with great emphasis, and I agreed.[...] We could find no reason for marrying Bernard except the luxury of a bath every day [...] I was half laughing and half crying and figures had little meaning. I couldn't remember why the petty cash was so heavy in September or how much it had cost to replace a sofa's leg. I said, 'Oh, Mary, he sometimes calls me *Bel-Gazou*.'

(p. 138)

By the time Bernard's spoiled son is killed, and Bella buries him beneath the Juniper tree, Comyns has painted a bleak enough picture of married life, and of Bella's fragile psychological state, for the reader to wonder just how accidental the child's death actually was. Bella, however, cannot be stereotyped as "wicked stepmother" any more than as "passive heroine" for, as the narrator of her own story, she escapes objective definition.

In *Feminist Alternatives: Irony and Fantasy in the Contemporary Novel by Women* (1990),

Nancy A. Walker defines fiction as being as disparate as Fay Weldon's parodies and Toni Morrison's tragedies, as being "equally relentless in deconstructing the received wisdom of a culture by revealing the terrible ironic distance between official cultural images and pronouncements and actual human realities" (p. 186). Such writers avoid utopian visions, creating instead characters whose inability to fully script their own lives testifies to the difficulty of transcending received tradition. Comyns deserves her own place in this particular canon for managing to subvert a fairy tale without losing sight of its enduring ideological power. As Walker states, and as Comyns appears to have been aware: "To acknowledge the power of old texts, old scripts, is simultaneously to claim power for the text one is writing, and when [...] the old texts are viewed ironically, the power they lose in the process is transferred to the new texts, as the ironist claims superiority over the subject of her irony" (*Feminist Alternatives*, p. 187).

Mr Fox (1987) takes us back to the world of Comyns' earlier novels (1940s London) via a recognizable narrator (young, blinkered, middle-class) who throws in her lot with an archetypal slacker rather than remain alone with her daughter as England drifts towards war. According to the publisher (Methuen), Comyns wrote this book soon after the war, but mislaid the manuscript. Mary Wesley, writing for *The London Daily News*, declared "whoever found it deserves a medal," adding "Barbara Comyns had me by the throat in that chokey state between laughter and tears given us by all too few writers." (*The London Daily News*, 17 June 1987).

Critic Rosemary Hill found Comyns' style ambiguous: "With its cliches half-grasped, obvious points apparently missed and rather acute ones made, this sort of faux-naive style is a tricky one to handle at length. It risks at one extreme becoming arch, and at the other merely inadequate. It can be as irritating as a precocious child, as hilarious and as moving." At its best, she concedes, Comyns' narrative resembles the "talking voice" of Stevie Smith: "*Mr Fox* can take the likely comparison with its contemporary

Novel on Yellow Paper without disgrace. It is an extremely funny book" (*Literary Review*, May 1987).

THE HOUSE OF DOLLS

'Amy Doll, are you telling me that all those old girls upstairs are tarts?' 'Well, not exactly tarts, Doris, but they have gentlemen friends, who pay them, you know. It's not very nice, but they say they couldn't manage the rent otherwise.'

So begins *The House of Dolls*, published by Methuen in 1989, when Comyns was into her eighties. There were always glimmers, in Comyns' fiction, of her wicked sense of fun and in this, her last published novel, she gave it full rein. Her elderly bawds are marvellous comic creations, with that touch of pathos that saves them from becoming mere caricatures. Age, reduced circumstances, and socio-cultural definitions of "correct" post-menopausal behaviour all conspire to bring down these women but never quite succeed. Even at the end of the novel when Berti and Evelyn move to a flat in Highgate ("handy for funerals") they take the gaudy little tables and carved mirrors from their disbanded salon, just in case... (p. 204).

One cannot help wondering how aware Comyns was of the contrast between these sexually liberated, endlessly optimistic, vibrant old women and the young protagonists of her earlier novels whose emotional ties preclude true happiness and independence. It could simply be that Comyns wanted to cover old age, just as she had covered childhood, marriage, and motherhood in her writing. There remains, however, a tantalizing thread running through several of her earlier novels, hinting at the autonomy and contentment of remaining unattached.

In *A Touch of Mistletoe* an apparently minor character, the servant Marcella Murphy, crops up far more than one would expect in such a self-absorbed narrative as Vicky's. Marcella, we learn, is single, in service, and unattractive. Yet she clearly finds pleasure in the minutae of life and is "blissfully happy" in London, which is more than Vicky is (p. 127). When Marcella dies,

Vicky is surprised at how much she misses her, and even more surprised to have been left her life savings of £300.

In *The Juniper Tree* it is Miss Murray, the owner of an antique shop on Richmond Hill, who haunts the narrative as a symbol of women's self-determination. Bella, like Vicky, fails to see beyond this woman's physical appearance or her lowly status as an old maid. From time to time, though, Miss Murray appears "like a fairy godmother" (p. 88) at Bella's shop to sell slightly damaged china. In one telling scene the two discuss the merits of Italian cups decorated with cupids. To Bella they seem perfect. Miss Murray does not agree. These cups are clearly love symbols, and there are three of them:

'...No one wants three cups, it's six or perhaps four or even two. I know, sell them as a pair and keep the odd one for yourself.' I smiled and said I'd keep one for my early morning cup of tea, and I drank from it for many mornings. It is strange how that Italian cup comforted me and helped me back on the right track again.

(p. 88)

Miss Murray dies suddenly, leaving Bella the entire contents of her shop. It appears that Bella has a choice—to be an "odd one," like the cup and Miss Murray, or to marry Bernard. We know her fate is sealed when she tells us "Bernard was against me accepting the legacy; he thought everything should go to the brother. So I rather bravely telephoned the lawyers and said I was prepared to give up my claim ..." (p. 130).

Comyns herself once said it must be awful to be an old maid (*Out of the Red, into the Blue*, p. 78) and that to be old and alone would be ghastly too (*ibid.*, p. 65). Still, the old maids haunt her narratives and we must wonder, in the end, whether their lives might have been far richer and more content than the turbulent existences of Comyns' narrators, through whose biased viewpoint they are occasionally glimpsed.

So multi-faceted is Comyns' work that it is possible to read her novels time and again, seeing something new on each reading. Jane Gardam, recalling a visit to Comyns' home, has written:

It was a light, airy house full of fragile glassy knick-knacks that seemed like art nouveau until you saw that they somehow were not. [...] her paintings stood about the floor and they too at first seemed very child-like: and then again you saw that they were not.

(*Guardian*, 4 August 1992)

Precisely the same can be said of Comyns' fiction: at first it seems straightforward and then you see that it is not.

When Comyns' health began to fail she moved to her daughter's house in Shropshire. On good days she would sit in the sun, nursing a white hen on her lap and watching cows go by. "I love them passing twice a day—but they are doomed" she wrote to Ursula Holden, her imagination seizing, still, on the flipside of an idyll.

Comyns died on 14 July 14 1992. Later, Holden wrote a tribute in which she described Comyns as a writer ahead of her time: a writer who captured all the freshness and foreboding of a child's world like no other, and whose prose, with its blending of horror, absurdity and lyricism was quite unique. *The London Magazine* rejected the piece on the grounds that Barbara Comyns was not that important a novelist. Apart from Jane Gardam's obituary in *The Times*, her death went unremarked. "She was a brave, serious writer, never interested in fame," Gardam wrote. "Yet her work was ahead of most. *The Vet's Daughter* is likely to be remembered when most of the rest of us are forgotten."

SELECTED BIBLIOGRAPHY

I. NOVELS. *Sisters by a River* (London, 1947; repr. 2000); *Our Spoons Came From Woolworths* (London, 1950; repr. 1986); *Who was Changed and Who was Dead* (London, 1954; repr. 1987); *The Vet's Daughter* (London, 1959; repr. 1981); *The Skin Chairs* (London, 1962); *Birds in Tiny Cages* (London, 1964); *A Touch of Mistletoe* (1967; repr. 1989); *The Juniper Tree* (London, 1985; repr. 1993); *Mr Fox* (London 1987; repr. 1993); *The House of Dolls* (London, 1989; repr. 1991).

II. AUTOBIOGRAPHY. *Out of the Red, into the Blue* (London, 1960).

III. INTERVIEWS AND ARTICLES ABOUT COMYNS. Caroline Moorhead, "Afloat, with a down-to-earth girl called Alice," *The Times*, 28 January 1981; Isabel Quigly, review of "The Juniper Tree," *The Financial Times*, 13 April 1985; unattributed review of "The Juniper Tree," *The Sunday Telegraph*, 14 April 1985; Selina Hastings, "Recent Fiction," *The Daily Telegraph*, 26 April 1985; Margaret Walters, review of "The Juniper Tree," *The Observer*, 21 April 1985; Rosemary Hill, "Ethel in Wartime," *Literary Review*, May 1987; Mary Wesley, "Bliss among the bombs," *The London Daily News*, 17 June 1987; Jane Gardam, "Novelist levitated," *The Guardian*, 4 August 1992.

IV. SECONDARY SOURCES. Anthea Zeman, *Presumptuous Girls: Women and their World in the Serious Woman's Novel* (London, 1977); Elizabeth Wilson, *Only Halfway To Paradise: Women in Postwar Britain 1945–1968* (London and New York, 1980); Annis Pratt, *Archetypal Patterns in Women's Fiction* (Bloomington, Ind., and Brighton, Sussex, U.K.,1981); Grace Stewart, *A New Mythos: The Novel of the Artist as Heroine 1877–1977* (St. Albans, Vt., 1979; Montreal 1981); Marjorie Ferguson, *Forever Feminine: Women's Magazines and the Cult of Femininity* (London and Exeter, N.H., 1983); Niamh Baker, *Happily Ever After? Women's Fiction in Postwar Britain 1945–60* (London and New York, 1989); Janet Todd (ed.), *Dictionary of British Women Writers* (London and New York, 1989; repr. 1991); Nancy A. Walker, *Feminist Alternatives: Irony and Fantasy in the Contemporary Novel by Women* (Jackson, Miss., and London, 1990); Peter Parker, ed., *The Reader's Companion to the Twentieth Century Novel* (Oxford, 1994; New York, 1995); Daphne Watson, *Their Own Worst Enemies: Women Writers of Women's Fiction* (London and Boulder, Colo., 1994); Magali Cornier Michael, *Feminism and the Postmodern Impulse: Post-World War II Fiction* (Albany, N.Y., 1996); Deborah Philips and Ian Haywood, *Brave New Causes: Women in British Postwar Fictions* (London and Washington, D.C., 1998); Elizabeth Maslen, *Political and Social Issues in British Women's Fiction 1928–1968* (Houndmills, Basingstoke, U.K., and New York, 2001). I am grateful to the writer Ursula Holden for permission to quote from an unpublished tribute to Barbara Comyns, 1997.

WENDY COPE

(1945   )

Gerry Cambridge

WENDY COPE IS one of Britain's most popular living poets. Up until 31 March 2001, her first major collection, *Making Cocoa for Kingsley Amis,* published in 1986, had sold a remarkable 117,377 copies. Her second, *Serious Concerns,* published in 1992, had sales figures of 97,901 to the same date. *If I Don't Know,* published on 4 June 2001, seemed set to repeat those trends. Within three months it had sold around 21,000 copies.

Cope's popularity is therefore only outstripped by literary phenomena such as Ted Hughes's *Birthday Letters*, which achieved best-seller status partly because of its context. Her audience has found a congenial match in Cope's persona as a modern, sexual, practical woman, full of common sense, given to debunking the foibles of men, witty, scathing, exasperated, and yet finally affectionate where they are concerned, and recording all this in impeccably constructed rhyming poems. Her popularity, meanwhile, has raised a sort of literary snobbery among some reviewers, snobbery which demonstrates a schism between a somewhat rarefied view of literature and that audience still willing to purchase a book in its thousands simply because they enjoy reading it—a readership that still exists for contemporary novels but is largely lost to poetry.

Cope's first book showed her as an already accomplished parodist of the male canon; her development since has been, to an extent, toward a more personal poetry of relationships, a verse by turns angry, elegiac, or unabashedly romantic. It seems likely that a sizable proportion of her readership consists of women who find their own concerns and preoccupations mirrored in her work.

While it would be mistaken to compare her with major poets—in a way, her work, predicated on modesty, would reject such comparisons— Cope is a far more sophisticated writer than her critics believe. Her popularity results not just from the combination of shrewd marketing and biographical happenstance that have given her an almost journalistic acuteness to what a contemporary reader will find engaging, but also from sheer literary skill. She is one of the nimblest makers of formal poems now writing.

LIFE

Wendy Mary Cope was born on 21 July 1945 in Erith, Kent, the eldest daughter of Fred Stanley Cope and Alice Mary Cope (née Hand), known as Elsie. Cope's sister, Marian Lydbrook, was born three years later, in January 1948. Cope's parents had married in January 1944. They were both from relatively impoverished backgrounds, and both had left school at the age of fourteen. They had met through employment: Fred Cope, offered a job in the department store Mitchells of Erith, eventually became chairman and managing director. His future wife was his secretary. She was thirty-one years younger than her husband.

The poet's father was sixty when she was born, and Cope's mother—perhaps because her own father had died of tuberculosis when she was nine—kept the house scrupulously clean. It was a difficult environment for a little girl to be raised in. As often happens, their own lack of formal education meant that Cope's parents were determined to have their daughters properly—which in their eyes meant privately—educated. Following an initial brief period at a local Roman Catholic school (which seems to have ended after Cope came home one day and asked her Anglican mother for a set of rosary beads), at seven she was sent to Ashford School for girls in Kent. Traditionally, such public school boarding is a painful experience for young children; however, perhaps because of her rigorous home environment, the young Cope was not altogether unhappy. At the age of twelve she went to Farringtons School for Girls at Chislehurst, Kent; there she sat her O levels and Oxford entrance exam, leaving in December 1962.

Cope had been reasonably happy too at Farringtons. Its particular strength was its music teaching. The child discovered a love of singing and church music, and played piano and violin—interests which were perhaps to influence her later liking for pattern and rhyme in her poetry. While she enjoyed English, it was her history teacher, Miss Elsie Smith, who proved most influential. Miss Smith believed in her young student and perceived that she lacked confidence. As Cope has written in a letter, "On one occasion she sat me down in her study and said, 'You do realise, don't you, that you are *very* intelligent—easily the most intelligent person in your year.' "

This was encouragement she needed when, after working in a clerical job and spending two months at a Bavarian language school improving her German, she entered St. Hilda's College, Oxford, in September 1963. The future poet studied history.

Oxford, with its class-consciousness and snobbery, proved an intimidating and unhappy experience for the shy youngster, one she later debunked when she implied, in a biographical note, that all she had learned there was how to play the guitar. She has observed, with characteristic wit, that her emotional life at Oxford, if written, would be a novel; her intellectual life, an epigram. With their eccentricities and liking for the rich and exceptionally gifted, "The history tutors," Cope later wrote, "frightened me." Many years later she became aware that the curious mix of her background—privately educated, yet with parents who worked in the retail trade—perhaps made it harder for her to align herself socially than was the case for students from a straightforwardly working-class background. In her second year she became extremely depressed, though she managed, to an extent, to treat herself by reading psychology books. (She would later enter psychoanalysis.)

Cope graduated in 1966. Her experiences at Oxford dissuaded her from becoming a history teacher. Fond of younger children, she opted to take instead a one-year postgraduate course in primary school teaching at Westminster College, Oxford. She felt teaching at this level would be more stimulating.

In 1967, she began her teaching career at Portway Junior School, Newham, London, where the head teacher, perhaps to reduce any pretensions he felt she may have had from her Oxford education, assigned to her a class known to be difficult. By 1969 she had moved to Keyworth Primary School, Southwark, where she taught until 1973. During this period, in 1971, her father died. He was eighty-six. Cope became severely depressed. She entered psychoanalysis late in 1972 and, following what she has described as "a kind of nervous breakdown" in 1973, moved to the more congenial Cobourg Primary School, also in Southwark. (Here she would remain until 1981, becoming deputy head in 1980.)

Meanwhile, in the spring of 1973, when she was twenty-seven, she began writing poems, most probably prompted by three circumstances. One was her psychoanalysis. Another was that she was living alone for the first time. This gave her both the solitude and perhaps the loneliness in which to write poems. The last factor was the creative work in poetry and music she was conducting with her pupils. Her teaching experiences may also have given her a tendency to prize clarity and the ability to keep an audience's attention—qualities she would later use to good effect in her poetry.

Every beginning poet needs some level of communication with her peers. In October 1976, Cope joined a writing class run by the poet-critic Blake Morrison at Goldsmiths College, London. The previous year she had also begun attending courses run by Britain's Arvon Foundation. These weeklong residential writing courses, which consist of a dozen or so students tutored by two established writers, were held at that time only in Devon and Yorkshire. One of her tutors for the Arvon course she took at Totleigh Barton, Devon, in summer 1978 was the poet and novelist D. M. Thomas. In a discussion after dinner one evening, he asked the group to write a cleri-hew a brief yet disciplined rhyming form. Cope wrote six. She discovered her facility for writing tightly structured poems.

By 1979 she had begun to have work accepted in literary magazines, and a game of inventing pseudonyms had led to her creation of the poet Jason Strugnell. The politically incorrect, bibulous, somewhat seedy, ambitious-beyond-his-reach and blunderingly comic Strugnell was to become a key figure in Cope's earlier writing. D. M. Thomas suggested she have Strugnell write in Shakespearean sonnets. When the poet-critic Craig Raine—later to be Cope's editor at Faber and Faber—published some of them in the literary journal *Quarto,* a radio producer for BBC Radio 3, Fraser Steel, noticed them. He commissioned her to write a half-hour program about Strugnell. Titled *Shall I Call Thee Bard: A Portrait of Jason Strugnell,* it was broadcast in January 1982.

It was heady stuff for a poet who had yet to publish a full collection. Meanwhile Cope had become arts and reviews editor for the Inner London Education Authority's newspaper, *Contact,* where she worked from 1982 until July of 1984. She was now beginning to get some freelance work—readings, school visits, and reviewing—and supplemented this by teaching music at Brindishe Primary School from the autumn of 1984 until 1986. It seemed a relatively happy and creative time for Cope; as she later observed, she felt part of a community of poets.

This was to change quite dramatically with the publication of *Making Cocoa for Kingsley Amis* in 1986. It was published by Faber and Faber, Britain's foremost poetry publisher, whose poetry list was then under the rigorous and individual editorship of Craig Raine. Raine took on very few new poets. Like any opinionated literary figure in a position of power, he had numerous enemies among London's poetic fraternity.

Making Cocoa for Kingsley Amis became an unexpected best-seller. Even Amis himself, whom Cope had not then met, turned up at the book's London launch. (Perhaps fortunately, he approved of her work.) The volume's success, however, meant that Cope also experienced the less attrac-tive side of the contemporary poetry world—its jealousies, rivalries, and petty rancors. As she observed in the poetry journal *The Dark Horse* (no. 2, winter 1995–1996):

> Suddenly, a lot of poets turned against me. People who'd told me how much they'd liked my work started shooting me down in print. That's an extreme example, but there is at least one person of whom this is absolutely true. I couldn't believe it—someone who'd sidle up to me at parties and tell me how much he liked my work, after I was published by Faber, and got on the best-seller list, wrote about me as if I were the absolute dregs.
>
> (p. 24)

Success, however, also had its positive side. Cope became a freelance writer and much in demand for readings. She was appointed in 1986 as the TV critic for the English magazine *The Spectator,* a position she would hold until 1990. The year following the publication of her first book she was awarded a Cholmondely Award for poetry.

She also was able to put her more recent inside knowledge of the literary scene to poetic use. In 1991 she published *The River Girl,* ostensibly classed as a children's book, a long narrative poem notable in part for its sharp delineation of male poetic society. Then, in 1992—a year in which she was also elected a fellow of the Royal Society of Literature—came her second collection for adults, *Serious Concerns.* Although its poems had been written—as genuine poems are—out of their own pressure, the collection was published because Cope, as she frankly admitted, wanted the money. Her negative experiences after the publication of her first book had made her chary of issuing a second collection. In fact, the book sold faster than its predecessor. By 1995, three years after its publication, it had sold 60,000 copies, and the poet had moved from London to Winchester, Hampshire, where she still lives with the fine poet-critic Lachlan Mackinnon—a move that seems to have marked a new stability in her emotional life. By 1995 she had withdrawn considerably from the modern poetry scene, dismayed by its rancors. She remained, however, a regular contributor to BBC Radio 4, a reviewer of children's books for *The*

Daily Telegraph, and a reader much in demand for performances of her own work. In 1995 she also won the Michael Braude Award for Light Verse, administered by the American Academy of Arts and Letters. While accepting the award, she also pointed out her reservations about the term "light verse." As Cope observed in an interview:

> I *detest* the expression "Light Verse." I think it's an unhelpful distinction, often used as an insult or a put down. The word "light" seems to imply that such verse can't be about anything important or deeply felt. Many of my poems, even if they contain jokes, are about things I think are important.
>
> (*The Dark Horse* 2, p. 28)

While she was to continue editing and reviewing throughout the 1990s, nine years were to pass before the publication of her third collection for adults, *If I Don't Know,* a book marked by a new emotional stability. Her impressive sales mean that Cope can afford not to be overly concerned with the snipings of her critics. Despite or perhaps because of her popularity, she has always been, at some level, a poetic maverick ready to subvert received poetic wisdom, as seen even in her spirited editing of anthologies of, respectively, funny and happy poems—qualities not traditionally associated with the gravitas of literature.

MAKING COCOA FOR KINGSLEY AMIS

Cope's first collection is an exceptionally shrewd book. Even in the 1980s, the London literary establishment and English verse tradition was a predominantly male one, and any woman poet could either choose to approach it on its own terms or run the risk of being a marginal figure. Fleur Adcock, in her edition of *The Faber Book of 20th Century Women's Poetry,* put it as follows:

> The danger is that women's poetry will be shunted into a ghetto, occupying the "Women's" section of the bookshop rather than the poetry section, and taught in "Women's Studies" courses at universities rather than literature courses. Part of this could be blamed on women themselves, or certain women writers, who take a radically separatist attitude,

rejecting "patriarchal standards" and "the language of the oppressors," claiming that men do not understand the tones of voice in which women express themselves, and addressing their work exclusively to other women.

> (p. 2)

Cope's method was both astute and subtly subversive. Her first book revealed her considerable skills as a parodist of everyone from Christopher Smart to Ted Hughes and Seamus Heaney. Parody is, traditionally, literary criticism in its most amiable and digestible form. By writing such parody of established, often contemporary, male poets, Cope cleverly achieved a number of things: she proved that she could write in particular styles and poetic forms; she was able to both debunk and express affection and admiration for the objects of her parodies; and she helped to ensure, by writing about the literary establishment, that that establishment, and its readership, would read her.

The book's title poem is a prime example of the poet's shrewdness. Only four lines long, it closes the volume, and is given a section all to itself. To make cocoa for Kingsley Amis, the poem's narrator tells us, was a recent dream. "I knew it wouldn't be much of a poem" she concludes, "but I love the title" (p. 69). The book's cover shows a young person of indeterminate sex heartily drinking a mug of cocoa. The title, image, and the concept shimmer with suggestion. Mothers may make cocoa for children at bedtime, lovers may make it for lovers. Cope's alignment of herself with the senior, male writer is decidedly ambiguous. The image on the book's cover seems to reinforce the possibility that the narrator of Cope's poem is positioning herself as a sort of matriarchal indulger of the famous author. He is really only a child, could be one implication; all men are really only children, a number of the poems in the volume imply. Having Amis's name in the book's title was also clever marketing. He was a popular novelist as well as poet, author of such classics as *Lucky Jim* (1953), whose novels sold in many thousands. His name and its ambiguous setting would have helped catch browsers' attention among the bookshelves.

WENDY COPE

This poem apart, the volume comprises two sections. The first consists of love poems and parodies in the poet's "own" voice. The second section is given over to the works of Jason Strugnell, Cope's invented male poet.

The volume opens with "Engineer's Corner," a fine example of one of Cope's poetic procedures. She will take a seemingly innocuous statement and lampoon it mercilessly, often by taking it extremely literally, in this case an advertisement in the London *Times* placed by the Engineering Council: "Why isn't there an Engineer's Corner in Westminster Abbey? In Britain we've always made more fuss of a ballad than a blueprint. . . . How many schoolchildren dream of becoming great engineers?"

Cope makes scathing use of this, concentrating on pecuniary differences between poets and engineers:

We make more fuss of ballads than of blueprints—
That's why so many poets end up rich,
While engineers scrape by in cheerless garrets.
Who needs a bridge or dam? Who needs a ditch?

Whereas the person who can write a sonnet
Has got it made . . .

(p. 13)

Later, amusingly, "Well-heeled poets ride around in Daimlers." This poem is an early example of her fascination with poetry's contemporary social status; she is interested in the whole business of contemporary poetry, its personalities and the aura of its practice as much as its literary productions. As sales of her work have proven, there is still some residual glamour around the idea of "the poet" in contemporary society—a glamour which would be later of some advantage to Cope herself.

The volume's opening section also established her voice as that of a fine formal poet. Only five of its twenty-one poems were in free verse, and two of them are parodies. She seems to have found the villanelle, a form notoriously difficult to write well because of its pattern of repetition, especially congenial. An example such as "Reading Scheme" shows her ability to come up with entirely new content for the form. Couched in

the manner of a child's reading book, the poem begins innocently:

Here is Peter. Here is Jane. They like fun.
Jane has a big doll. Peter has a ball.
Look, Jane, look! Look at the dog! See him run!

(p. 17)

"Mummy" is then introduced and the milkman arrives, who "likes Mummy." The poem transmutes into a description of adultery, complete with the arrival of the vengeful husband and father, and concludes:

Daddy looks very cross. Has he a gun?
Up milkman! Up milkman! Over the wall!
Here is Peter. Here is Jane. They like fun.
Look, Jane, look! Look at the dog! See him run!

(p. 17)

Staccato statements, simplicity of language, and the poem's context and exclamation points all give a cartoonish touch to grim proceedings. The use of childish language to describe the adult world, and of puns such as that on "dog," which refers literally to the animal but which, by the poem's close, has also become a slang term for the milkman, endow the poem with heavy irony.

Cope also makes her debut here as a fine poet of relationships, of sexual infatuation and disenchantment. She was attracted to repetitious forms such as the villanelle and *rondeau redoublé* perhaps because they helped exemplify in their structures the obsessiveness and relentlessness which sometimes formed her poetry's real subject. "Rondeau Redoublé," for instance, begins:

There are so many kinds of awful men—
One can't avoid them all. She often said
She'd never make the same mistake again:
She always made a new mistake instead.

(p. 39)

Each line of this opening stanza then forms the final line of each of the following four stanzas which describe, with grim hilarity, the varieties of "awful men": "the chinless type," "the practised charmer," "the half-crazed hippy," and so on.

Elsewhere, in the ten-part poem "June to December," which denotes the progress of a love affair in a series of lively vignettes, Cope uses the repetitions of the villanelle to denote sexual obsession and malice, though the sequence is many-toned. In its second poem, "A Serious Person," she expresses her impatience with that type of man given to ponderous exposition and hypocritical divagation:

It's nice to meet serious people
And hear them exchange their views:
Your concern for the rights of women
Is especially welcome news.

(p. 31)

The man addressed may want to sleep with the poem's speaker, but he is bumblingly uncertain about how to make plain his intention. Refreshingly, this formidable narrator, who ends by asking her hapless subject, "Now can we go to bed?" has little patience with the man's habit of talking around the subject. She plays his game, taking him at his word: reflected back at him, his solemnity and statements regarding "the rights of women" appear laughable. What is most notable here is not the verse's formal accomplishment, but its delineation of a situation not commonly expressed in poetry.

Yet Cope's persona in this instance, while broadly feminist, is far from doctrinaire. One cannot imagine her adopting the extreme feminist position of rejecting men altogether. She is too fond of them—exasperated, sometimes, maddened, cynical and angry, yet in the main regarding men with a necessary indulgence. The men in her poems tend to be flawed obsessives, often older than the narrator, yet she treats them with a certain schoolteacherish forbearance. This may be one reason why male readers do not reject her work out of hand.

A case in point is her wonderful "My Lover," a fifty-eight-line parody of the eighteenth-century religious poet and classical scholar Christopher Smart's lines to his cat, Jeoffry, from his *Jubilate Agno* (literally, "rejoice in the Lamb," that is, in Jesus, the Lamb of God). Smart's famous work was written around 1760 while he was confined for insanity in St. Luke's Hospital, London. As excerpted, it is seventy-three lines beginning "For," and forms a paean of indulgent praise to his pet, "the servant of the Living God." The animal is praised in terms as follows:

For he will not do destruction if he is well-fed, neither will he spit without provocation.
For he purrs in thankfulness when God tells him he's a good Cat.

. . .

For he is an instrument for the children to learn benevolence upon. . . .
For, though he cannot fly, he is an excellent clamberer.

(*Norton Anthology,* p. 471)

Cope uses her model to hilarious and touching effect. "My Lover," is an extended love poem. If Smart was judged insane when his poem was written, the author of "My Lover" too is somewhat deranged—but by Eros. Smart addressed his pet with both affection and a certain homocentric condescension; Cope's narrator does likewise. She tells us with the doting attention to detail of the besotted that her nameless forty-nine-year-old lover can imitate "five different kinds of lorry changing gear on a hill;" he is an ardent football supporter obsessed with sex. Here, Cope narrates the early part of their relationship:

For sixthly he invites himself round for a drink one evening.
For seventhly you consume two bottles of wine between you.
For eightly he stays the night.
For ninthly you cannot wait to see him again.
For tenthly this does not happen for several days.
For having achieved his object he turns again to his other interests.
For he will not miss his evening class or his choir practice for a woman.
For he is out nearly all the time.
For you cannot even get him on the telephone.
For he is the kind of man who has been driving women round the bend for generations.
For, sad to say, this thought does not bring you to your senses.

(p. 37)

Deftly written, thoroughly contemporary, and highly witty, a poem such as this explains Cope's popularity with what used to be called the "general reader." While the poem has a literary context that deepens one's appreciation, one need not know that context to enjoy Cope's poem. Her rhetorical technique is also impeccable. Lines 3–7 quoted above gradually increase in length, a method repeated in lines 8–10, where line 8 has eight words containing nine syllables, line 9, nine words containing thirteen syllables, and line 10, seventeen words containing twenty two syllables. The effect is to confirm the narrator's tone of increasing exasperation and frustration with the lover. The technique is not present in its model.

Section 1 of *Making Cocoa* also parodies Wordsworth and T. S. Eliot. Intriguingly, however, the one poem about a woman poet, "Emily Dickinson," avoids parody; instead, it is a double dactyl, a verse form invented in 1951 by Anthony Hecht and Paul Pascal. Cope's poem points out the role of critics and editors "nowadays" in disallowing such eccentricities of punctuation as Dickinson employed. While it seems to imply that Dickinson did not suffer from such constraints—she did—it is interesting that Cope uses the one poem about a woman writer not for a parody, as with her male models, but for making a literary point about editorial restrictions on a woman writer's style.

The book's opening section also contains some free verse poems that sound a gentler, elegiac note—one which will recur throughout Cope's writing. "On Finding an Old Photograph" is a touching poem about her dead father, pictured happily in an image taken in an orchard thirty-three years before Cope was born. Facing it is "Tich Miller," an elegy for a school contemporary. Cope recounts the humiliating procedure by which she and Tich Miller, the least favored choices for sporting teams, would find themselves last to be chosen. The poem closes:

At eleven we went to different schools.
In time I learned to get my own back,
Sneering at hockey players who couldn't spell.
Tich died when she was twelve.

(p. 29)

In this modest and affecting poem, Cope simply presents documentary detail. The reader is left to make of it what they will. An elegiac strain has been present in her work from the first, often missed, or dismissed, by her critics.

Cope's experience of men, as exemplified by the relationship poems in section 1 of *Making Cocoa,* stood her in good stead for the invention of Jason, sometimes Jake, Strugnell—a surname she picked out of a phone directory. Barring its opening poem, the whole of section 2 is given over to the works of Strugnell, either parodying or haplessly imitating poets including Ted Hughes, Seamus Heaney, Craig Raine, Peter Porter, and Geoffrey Hill. Strugnell—the name has a comic echo of "struggle"—is the self-elected bard of Tulse Hill, an unfashionable region of London. His emotional biography is delineated in some of the poems. As a repressed and unattractive adolescent and younger man, he had few sexual experiences—a lack he has tried to make up for in middle age, before it is too late, using poetry to attract women. He has discovered that they "love a bard, however dire."

Cope's portrait of this bleak yet comic midlife-crisis man is not only nonjudgmental but displays her tolerant insight into the less wholesome aspects of male psychology. In the section's opening poem, "Mr. Strugnell"—a pastiche of Philip Larkin's "Mr. Bleaney"—her invention seems similar to Larkin himself. When Strugnell speaks directly, it is through the voices and styles of famous poets. This procedure is comic insofar as the preoccupations—mainly drink, sex, poetic fame, and the lack of all three—remain his own. A case in point is "Strugnell's Sonnets," seven sonnets which, while not strict parodies of Shakespeare's, conjure that famous sequence by parodying the opening line of a Shakespeare sonnet in each. While the latter deals at times with spiritual love and the capacity of verse to preserve a loved one, Strugnell, "still randy as an adolescent," writes a verse distinctly lower in register. He parodies the opening of Shakespeare's sonnet 129, "The expense of spirit in a waste of shame / Is lust in action," a poem about extreme sexual guilt, with "The expense of spirits is a crying shame, / So is the cost of wine," then launches into a poem about the expense of plying women with drink in order to bed them:

I had this bird called Sharon, fond of gin—
Could knock back six or seven. At the price
I paid a high wage for each hour of sin
And that was why I only had her twice.
Then there was Tracy, who drank rum and coke,
So beautiful I didn't mind at first
But love grows colder. Now some other bloke
Is subsidising Tracy and her thirst.
I need a woman, honest and sincere,
Who'll come across on half a pint of beer.

(p. 59)

The technique is finely judged: the slanginess of terms like "bird," "bloke," and "knock back" within the formal constraints of the sonnet, particularly in the light of its illustrious forebear, increase the humor. The inexorable "But love grows colder" with its three repeated "o" sounds giving it a mock-dolorous cast and enjambed from the previous line, exemplifies Strugnell's resolution to dump the fortunate Tracy after his methods prove unsuccessful.

Cope is no less deft in parodies of contemporary poets. A note tells us that "God and the Jolly Bored Bog-Mouse," a fictional narrative poem in four four-line stanzas, was Strugnell's entry to the first Arvon/Observer poetry competition in Britain in 1980, judged by Ted Hughes, Philip Larkin, Seamus Heaney, and Charles Causley. The poem is taken usually as a simple parody of Ted Hughes. In fact, however, the first line of each stanza parodies Hughes, the second, Larkin, the third, Heaney, and the last, Causley. Elsewhere, Strugnell mimics, hilariously, Seamus Heaney in "Usquebaugh"—a parody about the perils of overindulgence in whiskey. As with the best examples, Cope's parody follows certain lines of her model closely, while wholly changing the context. Thus Heaney, for example, in his poem "Oysters," a complex meditation on the history of that bivalve as a food emblematic of privilege, describes "Millions of them ripped and shucked and scattered" (*New Selected Poems,* 1990, p. 92). Cope parodies with "Gallons of it, / Sipped and swigged and swallowed." Heaney, known to be fond of a dram, writes at the end of "Glanmore Sonnet" number 3 (p. 111) that the breeze through trees "Is cadences." Cope observes that the clatter of a bucket in the yard, during a whiskey-induced hangover, "Is agony."

Other parodies mimic the Geoffrey Hill of *Mercian Hymns,* in which that sequence's historical king, "Offa," is replaced by Strugnell's own, "Duffa," with the obvious pun on the British slang "duffer." In Strugnell's "The Lavatory Attendant," Cope parodies the Martian School of Poetry, a 1980s poetic movement in Britain named after a seminal poem by one of the movement's founders, Craig Raine (coincidentally Cope's poetry editor at Faber). Titled "A Martian Sends a Postcard Home," the poem uses unusual metaphors to encourage the reader to see the world afresh, often setting poems in commonplace surroundings (*A Martian Sends a Postcard Home,* 1979. pp. 1–2.). Strugnell takes the method to customary extremes, setting his poem in a public toilet. His parody closes:

When evening comes he sluices a thin tide
Across sand-coloured lino,
Turns Medusa on her head
And wipes the floor with her.

(p. 49)

The mop becomes the goddess who turns men at a glance to stone; she is defeated in Strugnell's wishful thinking.

Such parodies provided a means for Cope to prove her literary skill. While it perhaps contributed to her early success and reputation, parody would come to seem less important to her in future collections.

THE RIVER GIRL

Five years passed before the appearance of Cope's next collection, which was commissioned by Gren Middleton of the Movingstage Marionette Company for performance on a floating barge on the river Thames. Middleton also gave Cope a plot outline: *The River Girl* was intended for a family audience. A narrative poem in quatrains throughout, in which each second line rhymes with each fourth line, its 528 iambic pentameter lines tell the story of John Didde, a young poet unable to write, who falls in love with Isis, the immortal daughter of the river king,

WENDY COPE

Father Thames. It is love at first sight for them both; Isis returns to her father and begs permission to enter the upper world to be with her lover, which her father grants, giving her also the ability to transform herself at will into other creatures. She returns to the upper world, and she and John Didde marry. He writes fluently and well thereafter, is published by Britain's foremost poetry publisher, "Tite and Snobbo," and becomes a fêted poet. This leads him to neglect his wife, the source of his inspiration. He writes less, drinks more, and finally Isis returns permanently to the world of the river, leaving the poet to grieve in her absence.

The book is pleasingly illustrated with brush drawings by Nicholas Garland, and both they and the narrative are enlivened by sly touches of humor. The drawing of Clinton Thunder, for example, editor of "Tite and Snobbo," plainly resembles Cope's literary friend and encourager Craig Raine, during his time as poetry editor at Faber and Faber. The clarity of Cope's style also makes for engaging reading. The narrative contains color doubtless gleaned from the poet's own experience after the success of her first book. When Didde's book is published, he and Isis

Spend every other evening at some party,

Where he is lionized by men and women:

"John Didde! Congratulations! Lovely book!"
"John Didde! I have been desperate to meet you.
I, too, write poems. Would you take a look?"

"Excuse me. I must have a word with John here.
Sometime soon, could I do an interview?"
"Of course. Now here's my wife. I'll introduce you."
She looks at Isis coldly. "How do you do?"

(pp. 27–28)

The grim and ultimately shallow world of networking and fawning literati, of status-seeking and sexual opportunism, is strongly evoked. Isis, while extraordinary in her immortality, can also be seen as representative of that dailiness of life to which the whole literary scene is a rarefied irrelevance—a perception Cope never loses sight of. Isis has nothing in common with that—predominantly male—world. She is not directly

creative herself. She serves as muse to her husband—an interesting situation that serves to differentiate Cope's position from a more extreme feminist one.

Didde's success changes the couple's home life. Parties are frequent, Didde drinks too much, flirts, and argues passionately about poetic reputations. Cope's eye for such literary shenanigans is unfailingly acute:

"You're telling me, John—are you—quite sincerely,
You think Clint Thunder's *good*? I disagree,"
Says one, in drunken tones. "I hate the bastard.
If he knew anything, he'd publish *me*."

(p. 36)

The perspective Cope brings to this kind of *vers de societé* is very much her own: that of a middle-class woman both involved in the literary world and somewhat mocking of its more solemn and competitive elements.

SERIOUS CONCERNS

It was those elements that made her reluctant to publish her second major collection, *Serious Concerns,* the title of which is an ironic reference to the poet's love life. When it did appear, in 1992, it showed a considerable development from Cope's first volume. For one, she was now something of a "name," as the American poet-critic Dana Gioia pointed out in an essay in *Poetry Review*:

Cope has achieved that modest notoriety that publishers, programmers, and journalists occasionally bestow on living poets. She has become—like Larkin or Betjeman, Sexton or Plath before her—a brand name in a literary marketplace where most poetry is dully generic.

(Gioia, p. 57)

One effect of this was that she now had a sense of audience. The temptation could have been to go on producing parodies and to further develop the persona of Jason Strugnell. However, while Strugnell does survive into the second book, and Cope's skill at parody and lampoon remain unblunted, *Serious Concerns* instead developed the unfolding story of its author's emotional life. Its six sections—which seemed somewhat arbitrary—began with a batch of ten personal poems largely about her position as an unmarried and childless woman in her forties, still looking for love. The collection kicks off with the exasperated "Bloody Men," of which this is the first stanza:

Bloody men are like bloody buses—
You wait for about a year
And as soon as one approaches your stop
Two or three others appear.

(p. 3)

The poems range in tone from the angry to the lyrical; "Bloody Men" is followed, for instance, by the lyric "Flowers," in which a lover almost brings the poem's narrator flowers, but either the shop was closed or he decides against it, telling himself she might not want them. The narrator, recalling this after the relationship has ended, finds that the "almost flowers," by not being actual, are not subject to decay. They brighten her memory in this elegy for the better part of a relationship.

Serious Concerns was interestingly received. One reviewer, Robert Potts, writing in the *Times Literary Supplement,* referred to Cope's "copious reiteration of limited themes" and her "ill-advised forays into sentimentality," putting her use of repetitive forms such as rondeaux, villanelles, and triolets down to her having little to say. Clearly, however, her readership thought otherwise; *Serious Concerns* sold faster than its predecessor. Its success, when placed beside the belittling of a critic such as Potts, showed that those members of a reading public willing to pay money for a book of poems were looking for something other than such a reviewer felt they should. Whereas Potts called her approach "unadventurous," ordinary readers, baffled by the limitless adventurousness-turned-obscurity of modernism and postmodernism, seemed relieved to find a poet who wrote of everyday affairs of the heart in memorable rhyming forms. They showed their appreciation accordingly. Cope's work may well seem undistinguished to literary critics trained in teasing out multiple allusions and elucidating complexities in dense verse. Her popularity, however, reminds us that the audience for poetry doesn't consist solely of such literary critics.

Nonetheless, her work conceals considerably artistry. Even a slight poem such as her "Valentine," a triolet that closes the book's first section, shows her expertise in handling this terse form. Originating in France, the triolet's eight lines repeat the first two lines as the last two; line 4 is also line 1 and line 7. Technically it is a taut, brief form that relies on the writer's skill at manipulating nuance and tone. "Valentine" is a poem of wistful absorption in a potential lover. It begins: "My heart has made its mind up / And I'm afraid it's you" (p. 12). The "afraid" starts off as a colloquialism, a mere manner of speech, in line 2; by the time it recurs at the poem's end it has taken on a cast of resigned dread, buttressed by the sense of inevitability emphasized by the poem's repetitions. Cope's use of set poetic forms often exemplifies a poem's emotional subtext.

Another example is the flippantly titled "Roger Bear's Philosophical Pantoum." (Roger Bear appears on the book's cover, reading T. S. Eliot's *Notes Towards the Definition of Culture,* another example of Cope's orientation toward the literary world.) The poem is spoken by Roger Bear himself and deftly uses the repetitions inherent in the pantoum, a form that originated in Malaysia. A pantoum may be of any length, but lines 2 and 4 of a stanza recur as lines 1 and 3 of the following stanza. The closing stanza repeats, as lines 2 and 4, lines 1 and 3 from the opening stanza, thus closing the form's circle. Cope's pantoum is a poem of existential angst bleakly confirmed by the poem's repetitions. Here are stanzas 3 to 5 of this nine-stanza poem:

I am keen on reflection,
Like old Aristotle—
I prefer introspection
To hitting the bottle.

Like old Aristotle,
I rarely descend
To hitting the bottle—
My arms will not bend.

I rarely descend
As far as the floor.

My arms will not bend—
Sometimes life is a bore.

(p. 27)

At first reading, with its jaunty two-beat lines, which are often anapestic in rhythm, the poem seems almost lighthearted. On further readings its sense of claustrophobia becomes suffocating. The jaunty rhythm comes to seem heavily ironic, the gaiety of the condemned, a sort of gallows humor.

Heavily ironic too is the title of another poem, "Some More Light Verse," a monologue spoken by a woman on a self-improvement regimen. In this poem the staccato sentences and the circularity of the poem's invented form—two ten-line stanzas, repeating the rhymes in its couplets—emphasize the manic nature of the speaker. Both poems demonstrate what the poet-critic Robert Nye meant when he observed that the poems in *Serious Concerns* had been written out of "deep despair." It is an observation that Cope, dismayed at being dismissed as a poetic lightweight, has been keen to confirm.

Other poems in *Serious Concerns,* however, prove that she has not lost her humor or her instinct for lampoon. "The Concerned Adolescent" mocks acutely the lack of self-knowledge and the solemnity and untried idealism of adolescence. The poem's narrator, the adolescent, writes of "HUMAN BEINGS" that they:

will not live in peace and love
and care for the little helpless creatures who share the
  planet with them.

....

They pollute the world, they kill and eat the animals.
Everywhere there is blood and the stench of death.
Human beings make war and hate one another.
They do not understand their young, they reject their
  ideals,
They make them come home early from the disco.
They are doomed.

(pp. 22–23)

Among all the solemnity, the querulous note struck by the reference to being made to come home early from the disco is richly comic. Cope's

implicit ridicule of the notion of the Creation consisting of "little helpless creatures" indicates her refusal to idealize the natural world; the tendency throughout her work had been, in fact, distrust of nature. Thoroughly urban, she can be quick to ridicule any simple dichotomy that sees the natural world as pure and the human world as corrupt.

A case in point is the volume's next poem, "Goldfish Nation," penned by Jason Strugnell. The poem is a parody of a book-length, prosy free-verse poem called *Whale Nation* by Heathcote Williams, published in a coffee-table format with photographs in 1988. A poem of awe that, to some extent, erroneously elevates the great whale into a kind of cetacean saint, it enjoyed considerable popularity following its publication.

Cope, always sensitive to the romantic portrayal of nature at the expense of people, picked up something of the tone of sanctimonious piety in Williams' original. Her response, via Strugnell's incompetent efforts, is withering:

Goldfish are intelligent.
They answer to their names.
Go out and sprinkle
Just a pinch of fish food
As you call to them
And see them rising from the muddy depths
To greet you. Sunshine. Goldy.
Flipper. Bertrand Russell.
Maharishi. Name your goldfish
After holy men and sages.
It is appropriate.

(pp. 23–24)

Lofty sentiments and imperatives, contrasted with the banality of the context—the mundanity of a goldfish contrasted to a great whale—serve to ridicule the original and by extension that tone of self-satisfied proselytizing which at times creeps into contemporary nature writing. Cope's sense of comic timing is well honed: note the gradually increasing absurdity of the names given to the goldfish. Such a parody is less successful only insofar as its model, unlike some others chosen by Cope, may not survive to provide the humor or implicit criticism of context.

Strugnell reappears elsewhere in *Serious Concerns,* though his presence is less marked than in

Cope's first book. He writes pastiches of works by the French poet René Char, of the performance instructions to musicians of the German composer Karlheinz Stockhausen, and, in "Strugnell's Christian Songs," gets religion. The latter provide a comic indictment of the Christian belief of salvation in an afterlife. In the third song, for instance, prayer obtains a parking space for a car owner. Religious devotion becomes mere projection of self-interest:

His eternal car park
Is hidden from our eyes.
Trust in Him and you will have
A space beyond the skies.

Jesus, in His goodness and grace,
Wants to find you a parking space.
Ask Him now to reserve a place!
Sound the horn and praise him.

(p. 62)

The Christian belief is lampooned as an extension of selfish earthly impulses. That Strugnell is unaware of how he comes across only increases the irony, which is made more powerful by the comparison of the presumed nobility of being "saved" with the banality of the car owner's desire.

Another continuation of themes from Cope's first book is her acerbic observations on the obsessiveness of male behavior, such as found in "Men and Their Boring Arguments," "Poem Composed in Santa Barbara," and "So Much Depends." The last of these carries an epigraph from an anonymous lover: "And another thing: I gave in far too easily over William Carlos Williams." This poem, which mocks a man desperate to win an argument with a woman about the writer, takes its title from the first line of Williams' imagistic poem "The Red Wheelbarrow," a piece, ironically, about the primacy of the physical world.

As Cope increased in confidence and her sense of audience, this kind of poem grew in forthrightness and gusto; a new tone became apparent in, for instance, the knockabout vigor of "Tumps," which begins:

Don't ask him the time of day. He won't know it,
For he's the abstracted sort.

In fact, he's a typically useless male poet.
We'll call him a tump for short.

A tump isn't punctual or smart or efficient,
He probably can't drive a car
Or follow a map, though he's very proficient
At finding his way to the bar.

He may have great talent, and not just for writing—
For drawing, or playing the drums.
But don't let him loose on accounts—that's inviting
Disaster. A tump can't do sums.

(p. 34)

The narrator's reference to the "tump" in the third person, while addressing an unnamed listener, and her use of the first-person plural "We'll," in line 4, helps set up a conspiratorial tone in the poem: an indication that Cope was by now very sure of her audience. The predominantly anapestic beat of the verse increases its rhythmic energy and helps reinforce the note of mockery. Cope increases the humor by using reductive language: "accounts," for the narrator, becomes the tump's "sums." Women poets, the narrator has it, are "businesslike," exemplary in their common sense and practicality. In contrast, the gifts of tumps extend only as far as "drawing, or playing the drums," both dispensable activities in the eyes of this practical woman. Cope's lampoon, however, has an affectionate bass note. The tumps are held to be the victims of their foibles. The tone is, arguably, one of exasperation, not malice. If a genuine tump would be unlikely to be offended at this portrayal it is because the extremity of the description invests the character type with a kind of cartoonish glamour; it provides a license not to change. The male poet described could escape into this portrayal. The settled description of him as "typically useless" avoids the need for him to be anything else.

Cope had by now achieved some measure of distance from the younger writer she had been, in love with poetry. Her "Exchange of Letters" was prompted by an advertisement in the New York Review of Books: "A man who is a serious novel would like to hear from a woman who is a poem." Here she wittily teases out the metaphor for both the man and the woman. When the feyly

78

named "Song of the First Snowdrop" replies to the advertisement, her response is the opposite of *tey.*

> My first husband was a cheap romance; the second was *Wisden's Cricketers' Almanac.* Most of the men I meet nowadays are autobiographies, but a substantial minority are books about photography or trains.
>
> (p. 70)

She confesses to having always wanted a relationship "with an upmarket work of fiction."

"Death of the Zeitgeist" replies, calling himself "an important 150,000 word comment on the dreams and dilemmas of twentieth-century Man" who is anxious to be read "from cover to cover." There the correspondence closes. Cope's satire on this points up her insight into what are, arguably, certain fundamental differences between many men and women. The woman is most interested in emotion, in the characters of the men she has known; her male respondent is caught up in his own intellectualism; he sees the woman purely as a mirror for himself. Cope uses her humor to debunk male intellectual pretension.

Serious Concerns closes with a group of eleven poems mainly on relationships; two of the pieces were prompted by the death of her maternal grandmother, Eliza Lily. These return to the elegiac note struck in "On Finding an Old Photograph" and "Tich Miller" in *Making Cocoa.* Both of these poems in *Serious Concerns* are in free verse, as if Cope felt her usual rhyming forms would compromise her tone of elegy. "Names" seems the strongest because it escapes into a wider relevance from the purely personal; it is in part a catalog of the various, mainly informal, names her grandmother was called by at different stages of her life. Her informal names, those used by the family, are not "in her file"— both the hospital's file and perhaps her own mental file. Called "Eliza" as a baby, she returns to being "Eliza" in her "last bewildered weeks" in the geriatric ward. The poem has an understated air of sad resignation. The name "Eliza" is emblematic of the circular pattern of the old lady's life; she returns to what she was at the beginning.

Cope's persona as a lovelorn forty-something woman writing sardonically of her troubles with men and given to overindulgence in alcohol struck a chord with her wide readership; if there was perhaps a danger in this as aesthetic strategy, the nine years that passed before Cope's third collection, *If I Don't Know,* went some way to helping the poet develop beyond its reach.

IF I DON'T KNOW

Following the publication of *If I Don't Know* in 2001, it became apparent that Cope had become a considerably different poet from the parodist and creator of Jason Strugnell. The new book showed the continuing evolution seen in *Serious Concerns* away from parody toward a more personal lyric voice. Most probably the change was connected with her changed personal circumstances. In 1994 the poet had relocated to Winchester, Hampshire, at an address not far from Winchester Cathedral and near the water meadows that provided inspiration for Keats when he wrote, on Sunday, 19 September 1819, "Ode to Autumn." She had moved in with her partner, Lachlan Mackinnon, a considerable poet and critic in his own right, who teaches at nearby Winchester College, the independent boys' school. *If I Don't Know* is dedicated to him, "with love and thanks."

In this book her creation Jason Strugnell, "a man in all senses of the word sad," as the poet laureate Andrew Motion has described him, is notable by his absence. Either realizing that she was now too considerable a figure to need to mediate through an invented male voice, or simply wearying of Strugnell's foibles, the poet appears in this collection to speak entirely in her own, recognizably lyric persona. Further, the volume's only parody of a named writer is the somewhat halfhearted "Reading Berryman's Dream Songs at the Writer's Retreat," one of four poems she wrote during a month's residence at Hawthornden Castle, outside Edinburgh, in 1993. The handful of poems with recognizable models are written in the spirit of emulation; the urge to debunk seems largely to have disappeared.

This is obvious from a poem such as "The Christmas Life," the second in the volume. Whereas Christmas-themed poems by Cope in *Serious Concerns,* for instance, were grim squibs often about the unhappiness of the single person at that season, "The Christmas Life" is a beautiful celebration. It takes as its *donnée* a remark made by Lachlan Mackinnon's eight-year-old daughter when she was visiting her divorced father and Cope: "If you don't have a real tree, you don't bring the Christmas life into the house." Cope adapts the little girl's last seven words to form a line that repeats both as line 4 and the final line of this poem of a dozen lines, each of which begins with the simple imperative, "Bring." The repetition conveys an undertone not of obsession or relentlessness but of ritual; it is indicative of an affirming force, almost a chant. The poem is a tableau of gorgeous images: "Bring winter jasmine as its buds unfold," it tells us. The piece closes:

Bring in your memories of Christmas past.
Bring in your tears for all that you have lost.

Bring in the Shepherd Boy, the ox and ass,
Bring in the stillness of an icy night,
Bring in a birth, of hope and love and light,
Bring the Christmas life into this house.

(p. 4)

The poem acknowledges sadness in its eighth line while refusing to be overwhelmed by it. The poem progresses from homely domestic details in its first six lines to a sonorous delineation of traditional Christian iconography in the closing stanza. The progression develops the emotional trajectory of the poem: it becomes a resonant statement of desire for the spirit of the nativity. Cope's use of commas rather than end-stopped lines in the final stanza, in which the phrases build upon one another, increases the sense of emotional crescendo. That Cope can write with convincing freshness on such a potentially hackneyed subject is surely one reason for her popularity.

It is perhaps characteristic of Cope that she should follow this piece immediately with "30 December," which expresses a wish that that day of sunlight and swans flying overhead be Christ-mas, instead of the "muddle / Of turkey bones and muted quarrelling" it in fact was. Yet the note of celebration, of the calm enjoyment of the present moment, continues elsewhere in pieces such as "On a Train," or "Idyll," a poem so close in sentiment to U. A. Fanthorpe's poem of the same name as to be a close imitation. These poems extend Cope's tendency to use free verse for a quiet lyric voice, in particular in poems relating directly to her immediate relationships— poems about family and lover. In "Being Boring," however, a sardonically witty piece with the Chinese curse "May you live in interesting times" as an epigraph, she reverts to a jaunty eight-line formal stanza to reflect on her past and present. The poem closes:

I don't go to parties. Well, what are they for,
If you don't need to find a new lover?
You drink and you listen and drink a bit more
And you take the next day to recover.
Someone to stay home with was all my desire
And, now I've found a safe mooring,
I've just one ambition in life: I aspire
To go on and on being boring.

(p. 9)

Ostensibly lighthearted, behind this piece hovers a serious point. The poet is not "bored," but "boring." Cope is commenting implicitly on a certain expectation that well-known poets, male or female, be outrageous, "interesting," colorful, and chaotic in their personal lives. Dylan Thomas quite possibly died of this expectation on behalf of his audience. In this scenario the poet becomes a sacrificial projection of the suppressed desires of his or her readership. While playing this part may be good for a poet's public persona and profile, it will almost certainly be damaging and dangerous to the private self that produces the poems. Cope's apparently flippant declaration shows a new determination to put that private self first, a desire to develop a new poetic strategy.

It is a desire that another poem in the book's opening pages, "Present"—a title that could be taken in at least three senses—seems to affirm. The poet discovers on the flyleaf of her confirmation present an inscription from her "Nanna," Eliza Lily, which notes at its close, simply,

"Psalm 98." When the poet finally looks it up, she finds it is *Cantate Domino*—"Sing to the Lord." Knowing the first two verses, she simply skims the rest. Thirty-five years later, at Evensong in Winchester Cathedral, which Cope has taken to attending, "the choir sing Nanna's psalm." The poet hears the entire psalm she had missed: beginning "Sing to the Lord / A new song." After some armorial and crusading sentiments in the first two verses, it becomes, from the fourth verse on, an invocation to praise God, advocating thankfulness and rejoicing. "Nanna, / It is just what I wanted," the poet tells her dead grandmother at the poem's close.

Not that the Cope of previous collections has entirely disappeared. It is rather that her satire is gentler. In the four-line "Timekeeping," her partner comes home late, keen to disguise his drunkenness. Attempting to explain his tardiness, " 'The Pob Cluck,' he begins, / And knows he is sunk." From the "many kinds of awful men" in *Making Cocoa*, her attitude has altered. The second of two "Fireworks Poems," commissioned by a festival in Salisbury, England, and displayed in fireworks, makes this plain. It reads:

Write it in fire across the night:
Some men are more or less all right.

(p. 10)

Allied to this recognition is that, now having gained an emotional stability, she has that stability to lose. An elegiac note sounds for the fragility of current happiness. "An Ending" reflects on the month she spent in 1993 at Hawthornden Castle:

Don't want to leave this place,
This time, this happiness:
Loud water, muddy tracks,
Trees rooted in pink rocks,
Our lush steep-sided glen,
Friends I may see again,
But certainly not here,
Not in this world we were.

(p. 30)

The poet employs para-rhyme, emphasizing assonance, rather than full rhyme, to increase the muted note of elegy. The last three words of the poem's opening line are repeated as the poem's last words: the narrator's regret at leaving is enclosed by departure's necessity.

Also present in the shorter poems that make up the first part of the book is a new acceptance of, and even interest in, the rural, especially flora. In "The Squirrel and the Crow," written in a ballad stanza, the poet wishes she could write like that poet of country existence Edward Thomas; she looks up the names of wildflowers in an identification guide. This relative change of approach extends too to that strand of her work that has always been interested in the sociological aspect of the world of poetry. In "A Poem on the Theme of Humour," dedicated to the witty British poet Gavin Ewart, she can still write a poem decrying the po-facedness of judges who debar humor as a theme for poems in a poetry competition, and here she does this directly, to point out the message this gives to the reading public: "Real poetry is no fun at all." It is a directness she uses too in "A Reading," a villanelle. Here the form's repetitions are mimetic of the tedium of the occasion, though the poem itself is far from tedious: its narrator's brazen honesty is highly amusing. The villanelle describes an event likely to be overly familiar to any literary audience:

Everybody in this room is bored.
The poems drag, the voice and gestures irk.
He can't be interrupted or ignored.

Poor fools, we came here of our own accord
And some of us have paid to hear this jerk.
Everybody in the room is bored.

The silent cry goes up, "How long, O Lord?"
But nobody will scream or go berserk. . . .

(p. 44)

The clarity of Cope's style here helps emphasize the difficulty of writing about some of her work: her poems are frequently self-explanatory. This may explain both her general popularity and her neglect by critics. The difficulties of her work more often have to do with her position in regard to the male literary tradition and with emotional subtext than in difficulties thrown up in elucidating a poem's allusiveness or recondite references. The style is often as pellucid as water. Cope frequently has the artistic courage to write very simply: she is never likely to spawn legions of academic commentators as have, say, T. S. Eliot or Sylvia Plath. Further, she is inclined to mock the pretensions of the literary establishment, committing the sin of not taking it, or the world of poetry, too seriously. In the first book this appeared as acceptable parody. "A Reading" may be, if anything, too forthright for that establishment. Cope's work points out the gulf between the highbrow literary—and, by extension, perhaps, the academic world—and the world of the "common reader." She is most obviously on the side of the latter, yet the artifice and subtle craft of the best of her poems make her difficult to dismiss by the former as a poetaster. Her position in this respect is perhaps unique among British poets.

"John Clare," an elegy for that unfortunate figure, illustrates both her unobtrusive literary art and her altered approach in *If I Don't Know* to writing about poetry and its makers. Clare (1793–1864) spent the last twenty-three years of his life incarcerated at Northampton County Asylum; taken up at first by a literati keen to patronize "peasant poetry," he sank into obscurity for the last thirty or more years of his life, though his reputation increased in the twentieth century. Where Cope once employed parody, here she turns to something more akin to homage; the poem is a terse lyric of three five-line stanzas of primarily iambic trimeter. Its intricate rhyme pattern and sonorous broad vowels—"carolling," "woods," "showers," "throat," "true," "loving"— help exemplify the musicality of John Clare's work, which is in part the poem's subject. In the first stanza, perhaps with the insight garnered from what she has felt to be her own literary marginalization, she empathizes with Clare's life. Stanza 2 describes the experience of reading him. By the end of the closing stanza, the poem's narrator cries not with sorrow—as she did in stanza 1—at the poet's situation, but with delight for his achievement. Interestingly, the sole non-rhyming line, line 7, is "I heard you with my eyes": in a poet of lesser skill, this could be taken as a

stylistic tic; in a poem so much concerned with the aural pleasures of Clare's work, the deliberate avoidance of rhyme subtly consolidates the line's content.

Semantic compression is another of the qualities of Cope's writing. A modest short poem such as "The Sorrow of Socks," a variation on the triolet, shows her ability to endow particulars with a wide relevance and her gift for following Robert Frost's dictum that the best poems come from experiences everyone has had but are seldom written about. Cope's poem describes, lightly, the irritating tendency of socks to go missing; the poem becomes by extension a piece on contemporary relationships. It begins: Some socks are loners— / They can't live in pairs (p. 37). Puzzling their owners, they prefer being solitary. But by the poem's close, "They won't live in pairs." Inability hardens into choice, or the appearance of choice. The poem can be read as being about that type of solitary man most likely to lose socks and unable to commit himself to a relationship—a Jason Strugnell figure. The human meaning hovers behind the literal one; even the basic situation posits a male environment. Cope presents this without further explication.

One of the finest poems in the book's first section, "Traditional Prize Country Pigs," continues the aesthetic strategy of being able to be read on at least two levels. Ostensibly a description, in ten sections, of the varieties of pig—"Wessex Saddleback," "Cornish Lop-eared," "Lincolnshire Curly Coat," and "Dorset Gold Tip," among them—the descriptions could also function as accounts of various human types. Much of the poem's comedy comes from this understated superimposition of human and animal. Traditional prize country pigs are a comic bunch, large-eared, rooting, fleshy epitomes of physicality—qualities the poet uses to good effect in her descriptions. Of the "Oxfordshire Sandy and Black," for instance, after elucidating its remarkable pedigree on farms in the English Midlands, Cope writes:

But she knows nothing of her line,
And lives like any other sow,

Taking care of little swine,
Imprisoned in the here and now.

(p. 16)

Cope had previously shown an interest in narrative in her book-length poem *The River Girl*. The whole of section 2 of *If I Don't Know* consists of a further narrative, "The Teacher's Tale," commissioned for publication in 2000 to mark the 600th anniversary of the death of Geoffrey Chaucer in 1400. Its twenty-one pages of rhyming iambic pentameter couplets imitate, to a degree, Chaucer's style. The poem tells the story of Paul, born in 1961, the son of Gus Skinner and "Mrs. Skinner." (We are not told her Christian name, as if to emphasize the cold formality of her character, as the poem's narrator delineates it.) The parents are respectable, non-swearing, disapproving of any form of gaiety. They—especially Paul's mother—raise the boy in an atmosphere of claustrophobic, life-denying strictness. In due course he rebels as a teenager, gets into the company of the rowdy Wayne and Keith, and finally is caught shoplifting, to the horror of his parents—again, especially that of his mother. The crisis, however, precipitates a change in his behavior: he develops a new sense of selfhood, sees that any attempt to please his impossible mother is futile, and resolves to both alter his attitude and work hard at school. He leaves home finally at sixteen and later becomes a teacher. There the story ends, with the poem's narrator wishing him "all / The best that life can bring."

A central theme of the poem is the psychological damage, even in the absence of other factors such as poverty, that parents can wreak upon their children. Some of the poem's edge in regard to the restrictions of Paul's home life may have had echoes in Cope's own—her father's age meant that she and her sister were unable, perhaps, to be as rambunctious as little girls naturally might be. This personal relevance would certainly help account for the depth of emotion in the poem: the narrator plainly has great sympathy for what she considers the plight of its central character, Paul. She is careful to try and disarm the tendency on a reader's part, considering what terrible lives some children do have, to dismiss

Paul's situation as unworthy of the seriousness with which she invests it:

being nicely dressed and clean
With interested parents doesn't mean
That everything is easy for a child.
Paul irritated them—so meek and mild,
When they liked kids with spirit. Or they thought
That he was privileged and that they ought
To take care of the disadvantaged kids,
Whose families had really hit the skids,
With dads in prison, dead or gone away,
And mums who had to struggle through each day.
Don't get me wrong. Those children needed all
The help that they could get. But so did Paul.

(p. 55)

The narrative is cleanly written in a straightforward, plain style; the rhyming couplets give an aural cohesion to the verse, but the poem never draws attention to itself as an artifact: the focus is on the story. Its delineation of the central characters is strong, although the portrayal of Mrs. Skinner can be seen as wholly one-dimensional, and the narrative is full of local color. Cope's description of peer pressure and the school atmosphere are compelling. Certain aspects of the poet's own school life appear to have gotten into the poem: on page 61 is an episode in which Mr. Browning, in Paul's final year of primary school, detains him after class and compliments him, telling him he's "very bright / And very likeable"—a direct echo of Cope's own experience. The poem is never less than engaging, though some readers may find Paul's plight overemphasized by the narrator. Almost as interesting as his situation is the significance the narrator places on its gravity.

"The Teacher's Tale" concludes *If I Don't Know*. Reviewers were divided on the book's merit and occasionally showed considerable misreadings. Mark Lawson, on a BBC 2 *Newsnight* program (25 May 2001), thought that Cope was praising the virtues of boredom; in fact, she does the opposite. On the other hand, the poet Sophie Hannah, whom some critics regard as a younger version of Wendy Cope, perhaps overpraised the book's qualities in *Poetry Review*, Britain's highest-circulation poetry magazine. It remains, however, a considerable collection. It was short-listed for a Whitbread Poetry Award in November 2001—an indication perhaps that Cope's literary stock may be on the rise.

Wendy Cope's poetic progress has been a fascinating one. She has developed from a poet to whom parody was important to a poet of lyric gifts, retaining an impressive audience at least on a par numerically, if not greater than, that of an acknowledged literary great such as Seamus Heaney. Her poem "Spared," which appeared in the *Observer* of 14 October 2001 in the wake of the World Trade Center atrocity in New York, shows her increasing confidence in writing about events of massive public import in a personal lyric voice.

While it is difficult to predict how her work will develop, it seems possible that its tone will deepen in timbre as the poet approaches the age of sixty—though it seems unlikely she will ever entirely abandon the witty observations in rhyming forms that constitute a large part of her work's appeal for readers. In England, at least, she has become something of a public institution. Although she addresses a broad audience, she has been, largely, critically neglected. At this writing, for instance, no sites are devoted to her work on the Internet. And almost no serious evaluations of her work have been written. This may well say more, however, about the preconceptions of some literary critics than about the quality of her writing—a body of work that at its best is scrupulous, irreverent, witty, humane, and memorable.

SELECTED BIBLIOGRAPHY

I. POETRY. *Across the City* (Berkhamsted, U.K., 1980); *Making Cocoa for Kingsley Amis* (London and Boston, 1986); *Poem from a Colour Chart of House Paints* (Berkhamstead, U.K., 1987); *Does She Like Word Games?* (London, 1988); *Men and Their Boring Arguments* (Winchester, U.K., 1988); *Twiddling Your Thumbs: Hand Rhymes,* ill. by Sally Kindberg (London and Boston, 1988); *The River Girl,* ill. by Nicholas Garland, (London and Boston, 1991); *Serious Concerns* (London and Boston, 1992); *If I Don't Know* (London, 2001).

II. EDITED WORKS. *Is That the New Moon?: Poems by Women Poets* (London, 1989); *The Orchard Book of Funny Poems* (London 1993); *The Funny Side: 101 Humorous Poems* (London 1998); *The Faber Book of Bedtime Stories* (for children), (London, 2000); *Heaven on Earth: 101 Happy Poems* (London, 2001).

III. INTERVIEWS AND PROFILES. Miranda France, "Thoroughly Modern Wendy," in *Scotland on Sunday* (4 August 1991); Jane E. Dickson, "Wendy Winds 'em Up," in *Sunday Times* (15 March 1992); Gerry Cambridge, "Wendy Cope in Conversation," in *Dark Horse* 2 (Autumn 1995); Paula Weik, "I Don't Mean To Be Funny," in (Jordan) *Star* (8 June 2000); Emma Brockes, "Laughter in the Dark," in *Guardian* (26 May 2001); Robert McCrum, "Happiness Writes Good Poems," in *Observer* (3 June 2001).

IV. REVIEWS. Christopher Reid, "Here Comes Amy," in *Times Literary Supplement* (17 April 1986); John Lucas, "More To It Than Saying 'Bollocks,' " in *New Statesman* (2 May 1986); Bernard O'Donoghue, "Light Cakes, Thin Ale," in *Times Literary Supplement* (6 June 1986); Peter Riley, "Making Money," in *PN Review* 51 vol. 13, no. 1 (1987); Gavin Ewart, "The Muse Who Cooks," in *Observer* (30 June 1991); George Szirtes, "A Loitering Poet and His Watery Muse," in *Times Literary Supplement* (12 July 1991); Robert Potts, "A Risky Business," in *Times Literary Supplement* (27 March 1992); Elizabeth Burns, "Rolling Round Heaven," in *Scotsman* (25 April 1992); Dana Gioia, "La Prima Donna Assoluta," *Poetry Review* 82, no. 4 (winter 1992–1993); Lloyd Evans, "On the Theme of Humour," in *Daily Telegraph* (2 June 2001); Kate Kellaway, "Of Headless Squirrels and Men," in *Observer* (3 June 2001); Adam Newey, "Funny Business," in *New Statesman* (25 June 2001); Sophie Hannah, "Delight Is the Emotion," in *Poetry Review* 91, no. 2 (summer 2001).

V. CRITICAL STUDIES. Peter Childs, in *The Twentieth Century in Poetry: A Critical Survey* (London and New York, 1999); Marta Pérez Novales, "Wendy Cope's Use of Parody in *Making Cocoa for Kingsley Amis,*" in *Miscelánea: A Journal of English and American Studies* 15 (1994).

A. E. COPPARD

(1878–1957)

N. S. Thompson

IN THE UNITED States in 1951 the Book-of-the-Month Club conferred its signal honor of selection on *The Collected Tales of A. E. Coppard* (1948), the crowning point for an English writer who devoted himself solely to the short story. At the time that Coppard was writing, there were many acclaimed practitioners in this field, including Rudyard Kipling, Henry James, James Joyce, and Ernest Hemingway among whose work Coppard's stands equal, if not unique. Moreover, at the height of the Georgian poetry anthologies, Coppard's poetry was selected by T. S. Eliot for the *Egoist* in 1917 and, in the next decade, his work was solicited by Ford Madox Ford for the *Transatlantic Review,* the literary venture that, although short lived (1924–1925), gave a voice to the group of expatriate writers that Gertrude Stein is credited with dubbing the "lost generation." In June 1924 the review published one of Coppard's most celebrated stories, "The Higgler."

Coppard's success was not limited to the *Transatlantic Review*: his work was also featured in major American and British magazines such as the *Dial, English Review*, and *Metropolitan*. If some of his work was rightly seen as avant-garde, he was also published by such famous mainstream titles as the *Manchester Guardian* and the monthly *London Mercury* as a master craftsman in the tradition of Thomas Hardy and his rural tales. When Coppard came to publish in book form, his first collection, *Adam and Eve and Pinch Me* (1921), was issued by the groundbreaking publishing cooperative the Golden Cockerel Press, later famous for its fine-press editions and woodcut illustrations, but initially a precursor to the independent presses founded after World War II, such as New Directions and City Lights.

Successful as he was in literary terms, the boom years of short fiction in the Edwardian and early Georgian periods came to an end and, with outlets scarce, Coppard later found work difficult to place. By the time of his death in 1957, he was still well considered, even if his best work lay in the distant 1920s. The decade following his death saw influential television adaptations of his best-known tales, which brought him a new readership and respect as one of the most original British short story writers in a golden age of the form. The following account of his life is based on Coppard's autobiography, *It's Me O Lord!* (1957), an enjoyably rambling account of the writer's first forty-four years that offers many detours and divagations along the way. It contains excellent vignettes of his early life and of Oxford during the years of World War I, but says virtually nothing about his first wife, his marriage and its breakup, the sequence of events that led to his first literary successes, nor indeed the genesis of the short stories that he had written up to that date. Published posthumously, it was perhaps a draft that could have been improved with time, and Coppard certainly intended to write a second volume to continue the story. To supplement the autobiography, this essay relied on an unpublished doctoral thesis by Jean-Louis Magniont, and assistance from Coppard's son and daughter.

LIFE

Alfred Edgar Coppard was born on 4 January 1878 in Folkestone, Kent, an important South Coast passenger port on the English Channel, with the rolling countryside of the North Downs lying behind it. His father, George Coppard, was a tailor; he had married Emily Southwell, a housemaid, three years earlier. After the birth of Alfred, there followed three daughters: Nell (born 1881), Mary (born 1885), and Emily (born 1888). As a late Victorian family, it was not large, but

George's lack of permanent work made for a precarious existence in two rooms rented from a carpenter at 35 St. John's Street. One day, without giving any notice, George Coppard left Folkestone; the family heard nothing from him until he contacted them from the seaside resort of Brighton, one hundred miles west along the coast, where he had found better freelance work among the officers and men of the elegant cavalry regiments, who were stationed at Brighton before shipping abroad. Coppard's father was a freethinker, atheist, amateur naturalist, frequenter of public houses, and reciter of ballads—jaunty of outlook and full of natural vivacity as he was, however, he died of tuberculosis in 1887 at the age of thirty-eight. The Coppard family then sank into poverty, and Coppard's vivacious mother, Emily, was forced to work twelve-hour shifts as a presser in a laundry while raising her four children. The family was able to obtain some relief from the parish, and for all its trials and indignities poverty did not seem to leave an indelible scar on the writer. Indeed, in *It's Me, O Lord!* Coppard speaks tenderly of his mother's plight and, using the excuse of careless childhood, often admits to contributing to her trials.

During his father's illness, Alfred's formal education had been necessarily curtailed. His mother had paid a penny a week to send him to a board school in Fairlight Place, but he was a slow learner, especially in math, and recalls his time in school more for his misdemeanors than his scholarly triumphs. In any case, as his father's health grew worse, his mother had a doctor declare Alfred unfit for compulsory education (introduced in 1870 in the United Kingdom), and the young boy was put to work helping a street vendor sell kerosene and firewood, shouting the man's wares from street to street; he also aided his ailing father in making uniforms for the local police force.

The family was surrounded by many relatives in Brighton, as both George and Emily had been born and raised there, and it was his father's eldest brother, a railroad worker in London, who offered to take the boy, after George's death, into a household with four adult cousins and three lodgers. The young Coppard became an errand boy for and apprentice to a tailor in Whitechapel, where he had to walk each morning from Victoria Park, alarmed at the bustle and hurry of the metropolis, but proud to be able to send money back to his mother in Brighton. His two years with "Mr. Alabaster," the Jewish tailor of London's East End, is vividly described in the story "The Presser" (in *Silver Circus*, 1928). After this, he found work as a messenger boy with Reuter's Telegraph Agency, of which he writes, in *It's Me, O Lord!*:

> Life was pleasant then. Well clad in a uniform of grey with green facings and a hat resembling those worn by the soldiers in Monet's Maximilian picture, I was warm and proud and moreover able to buy myself agreeable food with the tips and bonuses I got but never divulged to my aunt, who previously had collared all my wages except a weekly sixpence which she grimly exhorted me to save.
>
> (p. 49)

This fortunate form of street life came to an end on Whit Monday 1891, when on a holiday excursion to see his mother, the boy "wept and begged" (p. 54) to be allowed to stay with her; his mother consented. This behavior on the part of boy and mother was seen as an act of treachery by his aunt and, Coppard reports, it caused a rift between the two homes for over thirty years. By turns, Alfred then became an office boy to a firm of realtors, and a junior clerk, first for a food wholesaler, then for the local depot of the Sunlight Soap company, then for a large carrier that distributed wholesale goods in horse-drawn vans. He finally landed a more secure position as departmental clerk at the Reason Manufacturing Company, a new engineering works opposite the barracks that had once supplied his father with work. After a short time, he rose to cashier, then bookkeeper, much to his own amazement as a boy who had struggled with sums at school.

During these years in Brighton (1891–1906), Coppard began educating himself in English letters. Despite his sluggish performance at school, he developed an avid taste for reading, after first beginning with the popular fiction of the day (Wild West tales "of Deadwood Dick and Calamity Jane") at his uncle's house in London, but progressing quickly to all eras of English literature. Although he had access to the Brighton public library, where he read through *Johnson's Lives of the Poets* and translations from Greek and Latin, the young man's task was less easy when it came to purchasing editions of his own. He was helped in this regard by a developing talent for competitive sport. His father had introduced him early to the countryside, an enthusiasm his son shared, taking long hikes on the South Downs. From this emerged his collateral interest in football, cricket, boxing, and sprinting, but he also tried competition running, or "pedestrianism" as it was then known. There were several local races that Coppard entered because they offered cash prizes. Every Boxing Day there was the Lewes Road Handicap—a five-mile road race organized by the company for which he worked—which he once won, and many others of the shorter distances he preferred. The prize money helped him purchase a collected Shakespeare, J. W. Mackail's translation of *The Odyssey*, Hardy's *Poems of the Past and the Present*, and William Morris's *The Earthly Paradise*.

He gained further access to books by winning literary competitions. In 1898 his entry of a piece of descriptive prose in the *West Sussex Gazette* gained him the prize of Walter W. Skeat's student edition of Geoffrey Chaucer. Later, he composed "My Luncheon Hour," published in 1903 in the *Academy and Literature*, a popular weekly which paid him a guinea (one pound and one shilling), a helpful sum when he was earning only two pounds a week. Naturally, his interest in books was not popular at home.

> My mother, still working at the laundry, was scornful of me because I always "had my head in a book." How she abused me, but all the same mended my down-at-heel boots herself! I was tyrannical and ruthless too, for I demanded complete silence for the brief time of an evening when we were all together at home, and the loud-ticking clock whose noise exacerbated my dainty nerves had to be removed from the mantelpiece and put out on the stairs.
>
> (*It's Me, O Lord!*, p. 85)

Coppard acknowledged that this preparation left him "undisciplined, self-willed, opinionated, and intolerant." But his literary isolation came to an end in the company of a young stenographer with whom he worked, Lily Anne Richardson. The daughter of a plumber, she was a cultivated young woman who played the piano and enjoyed literature, even, like Coppard, writing poetry. Despite opposition from Lily Anne's father, the couple married in 1906 and moved into rooms in Burgess Hill.

Not long afterward, Coppard was offered a position as bookkeeper at the Eagle Ironworks in Oxford, a medium-sized business on the canal to the west of the city. The Coppards moved in early 1907, taking rooms in Jericho near the canal, then in Iffley, before renting a small stone cottage in the nearby village of Islip in 1910. Coppard's years in Oxford were energetic and, ultimately, it was here that he began his literary career in earnest. The ancient university city was still very much the privileged seat of learning for Britain's upper classes, as depicted in Evelyn Waugh's *Brideshead Revisited* (1945), but despite the social taboos and snobbery, the personable young man found friends among both dons (university professors) and students, joining clubs and societies and attending public lectures. Thanks to the help of two young dons, he even managed to obtain reading privileges at the Bodleian Library, although he had to limit himself to its Radcliffe Camera annex.

His entry into the university world was accomplished mainly as a result of his involvement in socialism, then a burgeoning movement. He became secretary of the local Independent Labour Party (the more radical forerunner of the Labour Party) and attended meetings at Ruskin College, which had been recently founded to provide university courses for working-class students. He was introduced to music, plays, and much serious reading, although he found his knowledge of contemporary poetry superior to his better-educated friends. For the two years that he and Lily Anne lived in Islip village, Coppard also pursued his usual pattern of mixing with the locals, organizing and taking part in sports, even accepting the secretaryship of a local credit union. These distractions came to a stop in 1913 when, following their practice of never living more than two years in the same place, they moved to Combe, near Woodstock, and Coppard began to take his writing more seriously. In 1912 he completed his first short story, "Fleet," a loosely autobiographical tale based on himself and his wife, which he sent to Austin Harrison at the *English Review*, but at twelve thousand words it was considered too long to be published and full of infelicities, although passages were salvaged for inclusion in later works. Away from the distractions and pleasures of English village life, Coppard was able to write his first successful stories—"Piffingcap," "Weep Not My Wanton," "Clorinda Walks in Heaven"—together with three poems—"The Lock," "Country Sunday," and "Nocturne"—all of which were eventually published in the serious literary journals of the day. His first published story was "Communion," taken by a university magazine, the *Varsity,* in May 1916.

By this time, many young men were losing their lives in the carnage of the western front, as soldiers in World War I (1914–1918). Although Coppard was in restricted employment, his work in the ironworks being protected by ministerial decree—especially when the factory began to produce munitions—he was called before a military tribunal during a drive for recruitment. Needless to say, his protected status was upheld, but the clerk who had to perform the cross-examination was his considerably agitated wife, who had taken on the job for the war effort, little thinking her own husband would come before her.

During the war, the Coppards lived in several locations in the very center of Oxford, one recalled in "Arabesque—The Mouse," and it was here that he enjoyed his first successes with both fiction and poetry. In 1917 T. S. Eliot accepted his poems "The Lock" and "The Oracle" for the *Egoist* (July), while the next year "Piffingcap" was published in *Pearson's Magazine* (July), and "Dusky Ruth" in the *English Review* (November), together with "Weep Not My Wanton" in the *Saturday Westminster* (September) and several journalistic pieces in the *Manchester Guardian,* resulting from his first holiday trip to Ireland in 1915.

In *It's Me, O Lord!* the writer gives four reasons why, after the end of the war, he left his respectable position in the ironworks: his first literary success, the low cost to sustain himself afforded by his vegetarian diet, his wife's decision to continue working and supporting herself as a secretary, and perhaps most importantly, according to Coppard, a serious disagreement with the directors of the ironworks about his salary. In a fit of anger he gave in his notice and on 1 April 1919 (All Fools Day, he noted) he began his career as a professional man of letters. He moved alone into a tiny cottage named Shepherd's Pit, north of Oxford on the road to Stanton St. John, and at the age of forty-one embarked upon a bohemian life, which did not end until he married his second wife some years later.

Life at Shepherd's Pit was sparse, with no amenities, and Coppard had to bathe outside in a brook, come rain or shine. Nevertheless, he continued to frequent and receive visits from his friends in Oxford, to read as widely as ever, and to visit Lily Anne on weekends. However, despite finding the solitude he craved, the writing was painfully slow, with acceptances equally tardy in appearing. In a logbook he kept in 1919, Coppard recorded five acceptances, twenty-seven rejections, and no payments. The next year, he earned a total of £65 (a story typically paid around £5), compared with his annual salary of £212 at the Ironworks, supplemented by his wife's earnings.

He soon had a collection of stories ready, which was promptly rejected by the major London publishers. One day, however, Coppard was visited by a young man named Harold Taylor, who was looking to found a publishing cooperative. Having admired Coppard's work and hearing that he had a manuscript on offer, Taylor offered to issue the book as the first publication of the Golden Cockerel Press. Thus *Adam and Eve and Pinch Me* appeared in April 1921, to exceedingly favorable reviews. Coppard was soon considered a master of his craft, applauded and appreciated on both sides of the Atlantic. An American edition of *Adam and Eve and Pinch Me* was issued by Knopf in 1922, the same year that Golden Cockerel brought out Coppard's first book of poems, *Hips and Haws*. With Golden Cockerel, he published another short story collection, *Clorinda Walks In Heaven* (1922) and one of verse, *Pelagea and other Poems* (1926); his later collections were published by established London houses. Nevertheless, the famous private press he helped to launch continued to publish fine-press editions of single stories under the direction of Robert Gibbings, who bought the company from Taylor in 1924 and continued to manage it until 1933, when it was sold again. The press issued a special edition of Coppard's *The Hundredth Story* in 1931, with engravings by Gibbings and a special typeface designed by the Golden Cockerel's illustrious engraver Eric Gill.

Despite the beginnings of a solid reputation, with stories accepted by the *Dial* and *Metropolitan* in the United States, Coppard's personal life in the early 1920s continued to be somewhat uncertain. Lily Anne went to Italy for a time as secretary to the American editor Edward J. O'Brien, who regularly published Coppard in his series *The Best Short Stories*. The couple then moved together to a house in Chinnor, Oxfordshire, in 1922; Coppard also took a lease on a small gamekeeper's lodge in Little Poynotts (near Henley-on-Thames) to be near Waltham St. Lawrence, in Berkshire, where Taylor had his press. It was here that he began a long affair with Taylor's wife, Gay, who bought a caravan in Kimble Wood, near Chinnor. After Coppard visited Lily Anne again in Italy in 1923, the marriage had effectively broken down. His wife eventually moved back to Oxford, where she died of a pulmonary embolism in 1932. The affair with Gay Taylor continued until 1929 and was recorded in unvarnished terms in her novel *No Goodness in the Worm* (1930).

At this time there were other affairs, such that the author J. B. Priestley, living nearby, later stated in a letter to Jean-Louis Magniont (4 August 1969) that there was "a touch of the rural Casanova about [Coppard]." Stability came in sight, if not in actual fact, when Havelock Ellis, the famous psychologist who lived near Kimble Wood, introduced the writer to Winifred de Kok (1893–1969), a young South African woman who was studying at the London School of Medicine for Women. As Lily Anne would not grant a divorce, the couple eventually set up house together in Barnes in 1927, when their daughter Julia was born, with their son Christopher following in 1929 while they lived in Long Wittenham, Berkshire. After the death of Lily Anne in 1932, the family moved to Walberswick, on the Suffolk coast; their daughter Julia remembers that during this journey her parents stopped off to get married. Among the witnesses was one of Coppard's old Oxford friends, Eldred Hitchcock, who drove them to their new residence. In Walberswick, Coppard became active in public life. By now, he had seven collections of short stories to his name, as well as a collected works titled *Fares Please! An Omnibus* (1931), and took part in several conferences and symposia on writers and writing, such as The Artists and the World Today, organized by the *Bookman* in May 1934. In the same year, he was elected chairman of the parish council and entered practical politics for three years, as well as organizing (and playing in) sports, participating in local drama, and frequenting local pubs.

With the outbreak of war approaching in 1939, the Coppards moved to Great Easton, near Dunmow in Essex. With family finances under strain, Winifred took a job as the assistant county medical officer for the Essex county council. Coppard continued to write, producing three more collections: *You Never Know, Do You? and Other Tales* (1939), *Ugly Anna and Other Tales* (1944), and *Dark-Eyed Lady* (1947). At the same time, Penguin issued a paperback of *Fisherman's Fiddle* (1941), then *Adam and Eve and Pinch Me* (1946) while Jonathan Cape published a *Selected Tales* (also 1946). After the war, the family moved to nearby Duton Hill and Coppard later enjoyed the financial benefit that resulted from his *Collected Tales of A. E. Coppard*, first published by Knopf in 1948, having been selected by the Book-of-the-Month Club in 1951. As a lifelong socialist, and supporter of the Soviet Union, he enjoyed a visit there with other writers in 1950. To celebrate his seventy-fifth birthday in 1953, C. Day Lewis (then professor of poetry) and others organized a reception and dinner in

Oxford, where the writer was able to meet old Oxford friends such as Louis Golding, Richard Hughes, and Rex Warner, as well as his former office boy at the Eagle Ironworks, who was now its director. A final collection of stories was published, *Lucy In Her Pink Jacket* (1954), but Coppard's last work was his autobiography, *It's Me, O Lord!*, published the year he died, its title not so much a reflection of the author's anticipation of meeting his maker as an exclamation of Coppard's own very singular nature. Coppard was diagnosed with a gastric ulcer in December 1956, and after undergoing an unsuccessful operation, he died on 13 January 1957. After his body was cremated in London, his wife and family scattered his ashes on Mount Harry, in the South Downs above Lewes.

Although Coppard's later collections received little attention, owing to a perceptible decline in quality, there was renewed interest in his work after several of his best tales were adapted for television, some by his son Christopher ("Kit"). In 1967 a BBC *Omnibus* program successfully dramatized "The Field of Mustard," "Adam and Eve and Pinch Me," and "Dusky Ruth," while Granada Television ran a series in 1972 entitled *Country Matters* that included "The Watercress Girl," "Crippled Bloom," "The Sullens Sisters," "Craven Arms," "The Black Dog," and "The Higgler." As a result, Jonathan Cape published a *Selected Stories* (1972) with an introduction by Doris Lessing, which became a successful Penguin Books edition as *Dusky Ruth and Other Stories* (1974, 1975). In 1994 a selection of seventeen of Coppard's stories was published as *The Higgler and Other Tales* by Robert Hale.

THE SHORT STORY AND ITS MARKET

When Coppard began writing, the short story was a relative newcomer among the forms of prose fiction. Although there is a long tradition of short narratives going back to the Bible, folktales, medieval fabliaux and *novelle*, the modern short story presents its material through a highly developed consciousness that has its origins in the work of Edgar Allan Poe, who brought an immediacy and reality to the form that made the material unified and believable, no matter how fantastic the content. This mixture of the fantastic and the real was picked up by Hardy, James, Robert Louis Stevenson, and Joseph Conrad—among many others—such that by the end of the nineteenth century there was a firm expectation that the content of a short story would involve some form of action or consciousness in an extreme situation. This would in turn be accompanied by an irony of circumstance or psychology, or even the supernatural, whereby might lie a twist in the tale. The most famous practitioner in this field was O. Henry, whose popularity in the magazine market in the years before World War I was unchallenged. His success led to a polarity in expectations. As the American writer Katherine Ann Porter made clear in her essay "No Plot, My Dear, No Story" (collected in *The Days Before*, 1952), there were editors and readers who demanded that narrative be driven by plot, and those who were satisfied more by impressionistic and suggestive effects.

Writing during World War I, Coppard responded to this cultural state of affairs in his eclecticism and search for a market. When he made his career break, there was still the memory of the late Victorian and Edwardian writers who had earned a good deal of their income from publishing work in literary and popular journals. But they were all writers who worked in the longer form of the novel, besides writing in other areas such as travel accounts, journalism, and poetry. In specializing as he did in short fiction, it was inevitable that Coppard would run into difficulties. In a note entered in his writer's logbook, 28 August 1920, he expressed exasperation at his lack of success in getting enough work accepted by the reviews: "Apparently I am too lit for the 'Lits' and not enough pop for the 'Pops'." He mentions that the *English Review*, one of the most highly regarded literary journals of its day, suggested that he try the more popular *Windsor Magazine*, which in turn sent him back to the literary journals. If Coppard's work falls between these two camps, it is here that his uniqueness lies and where his work has a special appeal. On the other hand, his concentration on the form of the short story inevitably led him to overproduction, with a consequent weakening of his particular gifts, roughly after his sixth collection, *Silver Circus,* published in 1928.

Although he wrote many reviews for the *Manchester Guardian*, he never attempted a work of literary criticism and his two attempts at a novel—on the invitation of his London publisher, Jonathan Cape—both remained unfinished. If he enjoyed a modest success as a poet, this was not in the scope of a professional career. In all, he published fourteen collections of short stories, some of which were regrouped in omnibus or selected editions; a work for children, *Pink Furniture* (1930); three volumes of poems he later grouped in *The Collected Poems of A. E. Coppard* (1928); and, finally, his autobiography, detailing the events of his life to the year 1922. There were also several fine-press editions of individual stories and poems.

But what was considered a classic short story in this golden age of large-circulation popular magazines and prestigious literary reviews? Writing in his text *The English Short Story* (II) in 1967, T. O. Beachcroft characterized such a work as follows: "It is a single incident; it has a vivid pictorial setting dominated by one mood. Though it has significant action, it has no cleverness of plot. Above all, it has no personal narrator; it springs from no essay or conversation; it simply happens before one's eyes" (p. 8).

If Coppard exhibits all these characteristics, he also allows his narratives to be dominated by several moods, to exhibit a twist of plot, to be related by a personal narrator and, though everything happens simply before the reader's eyes, stories may spring from conversations—indeed, they may consist solely of a conversation. But what is most striking about his best work is the quality that he himself found in Hardy. Speaking of his own literary origins in *Beginnings*, edited by Adrian Alington (1935), Coppard talks of Hardy's *Life's Little Ironies* (1894) as "poetry in prose"; the same quality may be said to characterize Coppard's own works. In the compass of a short story, it is necessary to weigh every word in the same way as in a poem. Length restrictions do not allow for full description and explication, therefore much is relayed through suggestion and implication. It was here that Coppard was a master, gauging his dialogue with the same precision as his narration and, like Hardy, giving the impression of rural and urban dialects rather than a full representation. On the one hand he was able to create plot-driven narratives requiring a twist in the tale, especially in the story's end; on the other, he was able to create impressionistic pieces describing moods, views, conversations, and states of mind. He was able to write the perfectly concrete narrative replete with realistic detail as much as he was able to create quasi-allegory and quasi-fairy tale and, different again, pieces characterized by mood. His work is consequently difficult to categorize. Many tales reflect the influence of Hardy, recounting the lives of simple country folk, others the worlds of H. G. Wells and Somerset Maugham, dealing with cities, travel, and cosmopolitan scenarios. Furthermore, Coppard was able to turn his hand to the supernatural and eventually collected those narratives in *Fearful Pleasures* (1951). Given this diversity, it is not surprising that he quickly gained a reputation as a master storyteller, but equally not surprising that this plurality was hard to sustain. This study will therefore concentrate on the writer's best work in the short story, while briefly discussing his later collections of short fiction and the children's book, as well as his poetry.

THE TALES

Given that he began publishing relatively late in life, Coppard came onto the literary scene having thought a great deal about his craft. Thus his first work is already significantly mature. Of the twelve tales in his first collection, *Adam and Eve and Pinch Me* (1921; Penguin 1946), six are in the fantastic vein, the rest in a closely observed realistic style of significant events or passing impressions.

"Marching to Zion" visits the very roots of narrative in a quasi-allegorical tale in which the narrator, Michael Fionnguisa, finds himself on a journey similar to that of Christian in John Bunyan's *Pilgrim's Progress*. Out on the highway of life he meets characters who approximate allegorical personifications, but not quite. The most important is Monk, who kills three successive perpetrators of dreadful crimes, then shocks the narrator when he owns up to stealing money off the corpses to pay for the journey's expenses. The two travelers then meet Mary, who tells them that she is not making the journey alone, as they assume, but is accompanied by her soul. When the sceptical Monk declares that "soul is just but the chain of eternal mortality," the girl counters that it is "the little garment which sometime God will take upon him." As the three continue on together, Michael reveals that he is a poet; he writes verses about Mary's beauty, the identification with the biblical Mary, the mother of Christ, becoming more evident until she vanishes, leaving "me and Monk very lonely in the world." The evocation of Mary's beauty is delicate and convincing, so much so that Coppard appears to substitute an aesthetic underpinning for the spiritual, except that the tale ends with a sense of desolation at her loss that admits both values. In many later tales, a similar tension is set up between a larger sense of being and a smaller, but—again like Hardy—Coppard's personal scepticism never allows him to use the spiritual plane to view the worldly one, although very often he wishes there were a greater sense of goodness and charity to redeem the wrongs of this world.

Beauty and spirituality are again conflated in "The Angel and the Sweep" which begins with lowlife characters talking in a pub. One of them relates a time when he was living rough in the woods with his mate. They were visited by a chimney sweep whom the second character insulted and abused, leaving him horribly beaten under some bushes. When they returned to the scene in the morning, the sweep had vanished, but nearby a beautiful female angel lay naked. Where his mate simply bolted, afraid, the speaker's small act of kindness to the apparently dead figure brought him some small rewards in return. The characters listening to the speaker react variously to the tale they have heard, either taking it seriously or with a pinch of salt.

If "Marching to Zion" and "The Angel and the Sweep" are cast in the allegorical mold, then "Piffingcap" follows the traditions of the fairy tale. Piffingcap, the barber of Bagwood, is left a cup of lead by "a queer-minded man." It possesses four qualities: it will bring about the "doom of half a million beards," but also contains a "test of virtue," "a choice of fortunes" and a "triple calamity." When the barber finds that its use stops the beards of Bagwood from growing, he throws it in the stream and the three prophetic events are worked out among the barber's three daughters and a little girl, so that Piffingcap is eventually forced to melt the object to be rid of its influence. If these actions reveal hidden secrets among the protagonists, the application to human behavior is not as clearly marked as in a traditional folk tale such as "The Three Wishes."

"The King of the World" and "The Princess of Kingdom Gone" are also fairy tales, the first in the form of a biblical story about an Assyrian captain who falls for a phantom lover in the same way as the knight-at-arms in John Keats's poem "La Belle Dame sans Merci"—one of Coppard's favorite poems—whereas the second reverses the situation and a princess ends up mourning for the phantom Narcissus with whom she falls in love. The delicacy and original evocation of love and purity in these tales is striking, but nowhere near that of the collection's title story, which relates a strange first-person narrative of what appears to be a ghost observing his former wife and three children—especially Gabriel, the youngest—as they continue life without him. Finding himself invisible and without substance, he becomes increasingly frustrated at remaining unnoticed as he observes the children at play, until his wife calls him to supper and normality returns. He asks after their three children, Adam and Eve and Gabriel, to be reminded they have only two, but that his wife has just had some good news about a third on the way. The narrative ends with the protagonist about to relate the events of his strange experience to his wife. The horrific feeling of suddenly finding oneself a ghost is well conveyed and cleverly offset by an ending that charms without succumbing to a clichéd, "it-was-only-a-dream" dénouement, the title referring to the children's rhyme about pinching, which is also the well-known test for dreaming.

A. E. COPPARD

Love in two other guises is seen in "Dusky Ruth," in which a traveler arranges a tryst with the serving maid of the inn in which he is staying, only to find that she is not the easy conquest he had perhaps assumed, while "The Quiet Woman" relates the case of a young man who falls in love with a beautiful young Russian woman who is deaf and dumb. But Coppard's talent really lies in the creation of vivid realistic scenes from everyday life that tell a greater story, especially when the subject is a child. "Weep Not My Wanton" is a good example of the kind. In this tale, an itinerant laborer and his family are traveling along the Downs at sunset, listening to the sound of squealing pigs being gelded on a nearby farm. As they walk, the young son is beaten and upbraided by his giant of a father for having lost sixpence. When the man's anger and energy finally abate, the boy turns his bloodied face up to his mother and surreptitiously pushes the coin into his mother's hand. Although no explanation for the act is given, a great deal is communicated about what the laborer does with his wages, as well as what the young son has undergone to save a little money for the family. This modernist presentation of a rural family has a powerful effect: we are given the "thisness" of the situation with no comment or moralizing beyond the chorus of young squealing boars on the farm. On a lighter level, in "Communion," a young boy of low status in the community finds himself locked in the village church overnight, having been ejected earlier by the sexton because of his unbelieving family. Curious of the rituals, the boy managed to sneak back, whereupon he observed the sexton fawning over a lady of good standing (whose long prayers suggest perhaps her sins). Once locked inside the church, the boy imitates the lady by going to the alter, but knowing no prayers, he can only recite the calendar rhyme beginning "Thirty days hath September." Finding half a loaf in the vestry, he eats it, and drinks the Communion wine, then falls asleep on a pile of hassocks. When he is found the next morning, the vicar ejects him forcibly by the ear with the cry of "you beast!" This short narrative makes a strong point about a church organized for propriety and privilege, having long forgotten that it was founded for the purpose of charity; it is woefully unable to fulfill its mission, failing to help the young waif so drawn to it.

In Coppard's next collection, the title story of *Clorinda Walks in Heaven* (1922) is again a short quasi-allegorical narrative. Miss Clorinda Smith walks a dream landscape in the afterlife, in which she is accosted, it appears, by husbands from past lives as if from a series of reincarnations. She then comes across an angel who says he is her "unrealized desires," an image of her virginity, but Clorinda's virginal status—we come to learn—has been brought about by pride, which has caused her to reject the long series of suitors she has encountered. The dream then fades to an image of a woman in a coma, whose beauty was famous, but who rejected all would-be lovers and "became one of those faded grey old maids who wear their virginity like antiquated armour." This ethereal admonition against a cloistered life contrasts with the realistic pathos of "The Hurly Burly." Phemy Madigan is the servant of the farmer Glastonbury ("Glas") Weetman, who is put in jail for one month after assaulting a workman. Left to run the farm, Phemy relishes both the freedom and the responsibility of being in charge, her quiet control in marked contrast to the "hurly-burly" of Glas's ways, which had made all work mere drudgery. When the farmer is released from prison, in a rare moment of tenderness and desire he takes Phemy as his mistress, even though he is engaged to Rosa Beauchamp. When Phemy declares she is pregnant, Glas vows that he will do the honorable thing and marry her. The drudgery imposed by Glas soon returns, while the farmer also continues to court his former fiancée. After the child is stillborn, Glas sourly bemoans his noble gesture toward Phemy, but soon afterward she contracts blood poisoning and from her deathbed rues her fate: "'Nurse,' moaned the dying girl, 'what was I born into the world at all for?'" While this outburst stirs compassion for the poor orphan "charity girl" sent from the workhouse to the farm at age fourteen, it is perhaps too final a judgment for a narrative that presents merely drudgery as opposed to the cruel torsion Hardy depicts in *Tess of the D'Urbervilles*, in which the heroine suffers her last and final humiliation on the gallows.

At the heart of what Coppard wrote in tales like "The Hurly Burly" and many others is a desire for a better world, a world less cruel, less unjust. As a socialist, he might have been expected to write in sociological terms about the fate of the proletariat, about politics, about social reform, but instead preferred to write more objectively about individuals trapped by circumstance, twisted by fate, and often authors of their own misfortune. Having said this, as a moralist, he was hampered by having no real touchstone of goodness to embrace other than individual acts of kindness. Having no greater dispensation to draw on than a Hardyesque "fate" meant that, as a whole, Coppard's universe appears a malevolent one, even if occasionally redeemed. Although, of course, it is sufficient to portray kindness in contrast to the world's ills, and these actions create wonderful small epiphanies in his tales, the reader also has the feeling that they are but brief moments in lives of unrelieved misery.

A good example that obviously draws on the author's own experience is "The Cherry Tree" in *Clorinda Walks in Heaven,* a superbly written short narrative of a small family brought up in poverty, who try to re-create the marvelous cherry tree their mother remembers from her youth by decking out, on her birthday, a miserable bush in the "dull little den" of their garden with an enormous quantity of fresh cherries. This tale introduces the character of Johnny Flynn, the author's alter ego (and nickname preferred by his second wife) who reappears elsewhere, notably in "The Presser" (collected in *The Silver Circus*).

His third collection, *The Black Dog* (1923), also contains another story forged from personal experience, "Luxury," a vignette about his time struggling to write in Shepherd's Pit, where a decision to share some precious bananas with a group of street urchins becomes an act that frees his creativity. In contrast, the world's unfathomable cruelty reappears in a longer tale called "The Poor Man." This time the protagonist is Dan Pavey, a poor woodworker who is gradually stripped of his few worldly comforts when harried by the Reverend Scroope, who is out to stop Dan's poaching, his sideline in betting, even his singing in the church choir. When Dan loses his illegitimate son while serving a prison sentence, the light goes out of his world forever. If the steady grinding down of this hearty man is mechanical, the characters are fully rounded real-life portrayals, especially the Reverend Scroope. Also in this collection, "The Tiger" is a tale with a twist that revolves improbably around a baleful tiger with a vindictive attitude toward its tamer, the circus manager with an eye for another performer, Marie the Cossack. When the tamer succeeds in seducing the drunken Marie one night, the next morning she lets the animal out of its cage and steps in as the tiger leaps out on the unfortunate tamer. A tale in the style of O. Henry, it was what the popular market was considered to want. A much more highly developed narrative is the title story, "The Black Dog." It recounts a believable tragedy that unfolds when a woman returns to the home of her innkeeper father and ousts a humble young woman whom she discovers has been living with him since she and her mother left several years before. Unable to face her father on her own, Orianda enlists the help of a gentleman of private means, who accompanies her and whose presence in the ménage complicates the events of the tale, which ends tragically for the innkeeper's young woman. Although relaying a savage turn of events, the tale is balanced in its effects and subtle, though powerful, in its portrayal of devious machinations, with fine descriptions of character and countryside:

Small frills of willow curving on the river brink, and elsewhere a temple of lofty elms, offered the only refuge from sun or storm. Store cattle roamed unchecked from field to field, and in the shade of gaunt rascally bushes sheep were nestling.

(p. 71)

As testimony to Coppard's range, *The Black Dog* also includes an amusing story of a young clerk sent to extract a long-standing debt from a socialite Oxford student, who embroils the patient clerk in a long evening of shenanigans that ends with his carrying off a pretty chorus girl ("The Ballet Girl"). In a similar vein "Alas, Poor Bollington!" relates the ridiculous adventures of a couple whose prolonged marriage consists in each trying to leave the other, with neither able to agree on who is running away from whom. The trials and tribulations of country people are also seen in a mordant vein in "The Wife of Ted Wickham" and "Mordecai and Cocking."

Fishmonger's Fiddle (1925) contains more vignettes of country life in such tales as "At Laban's Well," as well as tales of marital discord in "Italian Whirligig" and "A Wildgoose Chase," evidently rooted in Coppard's own visits to his first wife in Italy. But the three narratives that stand out portray the frustrations of young women, two in rural settings, one in an Edwardian seaside town. In the title story, "Fishmonger's Fiddle," an abandoned wife is taken in by the absconder's puritanical aunt and uncle who, while caring for her as a daughter, continue to squash the hope that the young woman has in the love of a young musician who plays daily in an orchestra on the pier. "The Watercress Girl" is an overtly macabre story involving a young woman who is seduced and abandoned by a man, Frank Oppidan and—unknown to him—mother to their stillborn child. As an act of revenge, she throws acid in the face of Oppidan's new love. When she is given a lenient prison sentence of six months, Oppidan determines to wreak the same vengeance on her when she is set free, but relents in a crisis of conscience when she finally tells him the events of the secret birth. The fact that the couple continues on as before is poignant in showing the limited lives they lead, but the story never resolves the issue of the disfigured rival.

The most successful story in this collection, and one of Coppard's best, is "The Higgler," told with all the relish that Coppard reserved for his stories of country folk and the countryside, yet unforgiving in its view of humanity. *Higgler* is a pejorative expression for a market trader, defined by the *Oxford English Dictionary* as "an itinerant dealer," especially "a carrier or huckster who buys up poultry and dairy produce, and supplies in exchange petty commodities from the shops in town." In this instance, Harvey Witlow is a young man, a veteran of World War I, whose high hopes of a return to country life as a market trader are qualified by the precarious economic conditions of the postwar world. Nevertheless, he finds a suitable supplier in a lone farm owned by a widow and her daughter and is successful in selling the farm's produce at a reasonable profit. Given that shrewdness and wariness are the very essence of his work, he is highly suspicious when the widow offers her silent daughter in marriage, with the farm to come as a future legacy and added inducement. Unable to believe in his good fortune, thinking there is some serious catch, he marries instead the slatternly girl he has been courting. Due to the depressed postwar economy, he soon finds his business tumbling, so that he is forced to approach the wealthy widow for a loan. Having now to borrow a horse for his cart, he sets off, only to find that the widow has died that night. As Harvey helps the widow's daughter lay out the corpse, the shy young girl openly declares that it was she who persuaded her mother to offer her hand in marriage. Desperate now that her mother is dead, she can only offer Harvey the post of bailiff. The reader is left to speculate on the outcome of his taking this position.

If Coppard's short narratives focus on unrelenting misfortune, they also show the adverse effects of not grasping good fortune with open hands. The higgler's calculating brain is his own worst enemy, even if the conditions in which he lives almost demand that he is wary and shrewd to a degree. Coppard's best effects thus depict the claustrophobia and small-minded mentality of country folk, set against the rolling countryside that invites but seldom elicits a wider view.

The writer's most successful collection commercially and critically was *The Field of Mustard* (1926), where his subjects include young urban couples demonstrating varying degrees of sophistication, as well as those familiar from his ironic country tales. Coppard's variety is often underestimated and, while it is short narratives such as "The Black Dog" and "The Higgler" that communicate most successfully to the reader, his narratives set in the city are also full of sharp-eyed observations of people and the passing scene. In many ways they reflect the first rebellion of youth after World War I against the strictures and prohibitions of the Edwardian world, in the same way that Coppard himself defied respectability in the 1920s.

"Christine's Letter" concerns a young woman who has left her weak and selfish husband and works as a waitress to support herself in an age when such behavior amounted to a considerable breach of propriety. The sanctimonious and self-exculpatory letter that she receives from her husband fully justifies her desperate measure, however, and the reader can only wish her luck. A downtrodden railway clerk in "The Funnel" patents a nondrip funnel and earns a small fortune, but is asked by his self-sufficient young wife to leave. Although she wants none of his money, he secretly sends it to her. When she dies suddenly, he inherits nothing because of her liaison with a seaman. The story is resolved by means of an amusing plot twist.

In "Fifty Pounds," a sudden legacy enables a young woman to give that sum as an anonymous gift "from an admirer" to the struggling young writer with whom she lives. When he neither shares with her nor otherwise celebrates the news of his good fortune, she rightly perceives his arrogance and self-centered nature and leaves, considering the money well spent in exposing his true nature. Another writer, living in a caravan, causes rivalry between two sisters in "The Man from the Caravan," a tale based loosely on Coppard's own intrigues in the Chilterns. With strong fables of the supernatural in "The Bogy Man" and of country life in "The Truant Hart," the collection spans the full range of Coppard's themes. Of these, the most outstanding is the title story, "The Field of Mustard," in which three women return from gathering brushwood and reminisce on the men in their lives. The stoicism with which they face the future and old age is masterfully portrayed. It is a powerful evocation of women's lives in the limited compass of the country, poignant and humorous by turns as two women find they both shared the love of the same man out of wedlock:

"...he used to make fine little slippers out of reeds."

"Yes," Rose concurred, "he made me a pair."

"You!" Dinah cried. "What—were you...?" Rose turned her head away.

"We was all cheap to him," she said softly, "cheap as old rags; we was like chaff before him."

(Penguin, p. 216)

On a different social plane are the two spinsters in "Olive and Camilla," who—as lifelong companions—similarly discover each other's foibles in old age. In "Judith," the romantic entanglement between a young schoolmaster and an aristocratic woman could have been devised by D. H. Lawrence, but "Judith" takes a turn into murder and relates the crushing fate of the schoolmaster, who is implicated in the death of a young itinerant worker when he is prevented from giving the full truth of his whereabouts at the time of the crime. His lover, Lady Leeward, shrinks from declaring the truth in order to defend herself rather than her socialist lover. The more generous space for descriptions here and, indeed, greater narrative pace make one wish that Coppard had persisted in his attempts at longer prose fiction.

The stories in *Silver Circus* (1928) largely reveal the anecdotal quality and mechanical irony that unfortunately characterize a good deal of Coppard's later work, which was primarily aimed at capturing a popular market. The title story is a scarcely credible tale of two rivals in love who find themselves sewn into animal skins and billed to fight as lion and tiger for a Vienna circus show. The contest becomes horribly real when the protagonists discover each other's identity under the costumes and a savage death ensues. "Fine Feathers" concerns a brewery clerk's aspiration to own a dress suit; he gets his come-uppance when the brewery owner's daughter invites him to a ball—not, as he initially thinks, as a guest, but to act as a steward. "The Third Prize" recalls Coppard's days of pedestrianism in the Edwardian era, and "Purl and Plain" is about the rivalry of an Anglican vicar and Catholic priest for the right to baptize a child.

Silver Circus does contain, however, another of Coppard's masterpieces in "The Presser." Relating the adventures of a young boy who works for a Jewish tailor in London's East End, it obviously draws on the author's own experiences of nearly forty years earlier. The solicitous behavior of Mr. Alabaster to young Johnny Flynn is contrasted with the affair that Flynn witnesses between the presser and one of the sewing girls, as well as his own precarious existence as a small boy on the streets of the great Victorian metropolis. The reader cannot help but share both Johnny Flynn's every twinge of fear and his sudden, gratefully accepted windfalls.

LATER WORK

After *Silver Circus*, Coppard published a further seven collections of stories and one book for children, *Pink Furniture* (1930). The best of his later work was published in the late 1940s in *The Collected Tales of A. E. Coppard*, but generally it suffers from an anecdotal quality, such as the loosely autobiographical "My Hundredth Tale" (originally collected in *Nixey's Harlequin,* 1931) about a writer and his amours. Nevertheless, the thirty-eight stories in *Collected Tales* provide the best introduction to Coppard's work as a whole, as they include his rural masterpieces, his anecdotal tales, his stories of young people in seaside towns, and his tales of the fantastic.

The best of his later work in the supernatural and fantastic mode was also collected in *Fearful Pleasures* (1946, 1951), which included early tales such as "Clorinda Walks in Heaven," "The Tiger," and "Simple Simon" from *The Black Dog*. But again, the anecdotal or mechanical nature of the tales allows for very little tension. A good example is "Ahoy, Sailor Boy!" (collected in *Dunky Fitlow*, 1933), in which a sailor in an amorous mood meets an elegant lady on a park bench only to be told that she is a ghost. The only way she can prove this to him is by taking off her clothes. When the sailor goes into the bushes looking for her, he finds only her clothes, and then, when he looks again, even the clothes are gone. When he takes out a handkerchief to mop his brow, that too is whisked from his sight. Again, it was a tall story to amuse the popular magazine market.

His last collection was *Lucy in Her Pink Jacket* (1954), in which oddball characters and conversations revisit many of his earlier narrative haunts, as the title story reveals. A rambler and amateur painter in the Lake District meets an attractive young woman with a hoe on a remote part of a field. He asks if she lives nearby and if he may have a cup of tea. He accompanies her to the tiny cottage she shares with her crippled father, is invited to spend the night in her bed, then finds out the next morning from her irate father that she is actually married to a sailor who has all but abandoned her. The rambler then continues his tour, whistling "a sort of thoughtful, plaintive, museful air." Delightful as Lucy is in her pink jacket, with nothing underneath, the story evokes none of the pathos that Coppard was able to wrest from the brief encounter relayed in "Dusky Ruth."

Coppard's only work for children, *Pink Furniture* is an episodic adventure story in picaresque fashion. Its hero is Toby Tottell, a young boy who leaves home to find some pink furniture, that which is "only allowed for gentlemen who have got noble natures" (p. 13). In the course of his journeys he meets a miller named Cobbs, who tells him a story about a farmer. He then comes across a forester who tells him a story about Cobbs. After falling asleep and dreaming, he finds himself on the Island of Purganda, where after a little detective work, he recovers a prince's much-prized missing marble. Via an episode on a pirate ship, he travels to the land of Patcat, where he becomes involved in the races run by giant animals, encounters a human giant, reads a wonderful tale about a golden cage, then finally discovers a book in a temple, called *Open and Ask Me,* that leads him to a sudden maturity and the conclusion of his quest.

An interesting mixture of narratives, from boy's adventure to fairy story to *Alice in Wonderland, Pink Furniture* contains an imaginative sequence of events with several truly magical stories embedded in its framework, but Coppard failed in this work to create a unified whole. The answer to the boy's quest—that he had pink furniture all the time, if only he could see it—is the typical paradoxical ending of a folktale.

A. E. COPPARD

THE POEMS

If Coppard's main literary education came by his reading of English poetry from Chaucer to Hardy and beyond, his own poetry achieved little success beyond publication in the journals of the day and was abandoned after the publication of the sixty-five poems that make up his *Collected Poems* (1928). His first volume of poems was *Hips and Haws* (1922), published by the Golden Cockerell Press, followed by *Pelagea and Other Poems* (1926). The two were published together in America as *Yokohama Garland* (1926); then, with the addition of several new poems, Jonathan Cape issued a collected edition two years later.

Stylistically, Coppard's poems follow the fashion of Georgian poetry, where abstract pastoral landscapes elicit thoughts in free verse of idealized beauty or melancholy, interspersed with one or two hearty lyrics about rural characters and scenes in short quatrains. Edward Thomas, Robert Frost, and D. H. Lawrence were able to create lasting poetry out of such a climate, with Rupert Brooke, Walter De la Mare, and John Masefield providing a second rank in the field. The former trio was able to particularize the subject matter and make it evoke a real sense of time and place, only vaguely suggested by the second. Coppard, whose prose was distinguished by authentic speech and the depiction of local setting, tended to generalize in his verse and frequently employed fin de siècle inversions that would have been perceived as clichéd even in Coppard's own time: "where blooms an acacia tree" ("The Streams"), for example, and "Easy is unhappiness, difficult is joy" ("The Lock"). Titles such as "Autumn Song," "Country Sabbath," "Dusk," and "Eclipse" provide some idea of his poetry as a whole, with one of the most successful scenes being that depicted in "Winter Field":

> Sorrow on the acres,
>   Wind in the thorn,
> And an old man ploughing
>   Through the frosty morn.
>
> A flock of the dark birds,
>   Rooks and their wives,
> Follow the plough team
>   The old man drives;

And troops of starlings,
  A-tittle-tat and prim,
Follow the rooks
  That follow him.

CONCLUSION

To the chronicles of lower-class rural and urban life, and of low tragedies of the dispossessed, A. E. Coppard brought an intensity and a poetry that—for the age in which he wrote—was unexpectedly realistic, avoided melodrama, and let the moral speak for itself. He was unparalleled at giving voice to country people who in other fiction might have occupied only walk-on parts, the people usually considered too uneducated or coarse to bear great drama or passion in their lives, but who are discovered to live an intense everyday tragedy in the shorter compass of a short story's events. In the best of his tales, Coppard's sympathy for the rural underclass, his depiction of women struggling for independence against class strictures and propriety, and his deft handling of the psychology of unsophisticated people show how often a sense of possibility opens up in their lives, only for the individuals to create a prison around themselves of their own making. In other tales, the forces massed against the individual are such that they do not stand a chance against the cruel twists of fate and the reader is left not on a knife edge, but with a view of the execution block. Elsewhere, in his many allegories and fairy tales, Coppard writes as if out of Christian judgment and mercy, but ultimately sees a universe unredeemed by either God or man, lit only sporadically by brief lights of kindness and charity. But in the scope of the short story, only a hint or a suggestion is necessary, and in this Coppard was a master whose best tales will continue to find a place in anthologies.

SELECTED BIBLIOGRAPHY

I. COLLECTED WORKS. *Collected Poems* (London, 1928); *Fares, Please! An Omnibus* (London, 1931); *Fearful Pleasures* (Sauk City, Wis., 1946; London, 1951); *Selected Tales, from his Twelve Volumes Published Between the Wars* (London, 1946); *The Collected Tales of A. E. Coppard* (New

York, 1948); *Selected Stories,* with an introduction by Doris Lessing (London, 1972); *Dusky Ruth and Other Stories,* with an Introduction by Doris Lessing (Harmondsworth, 1974); *The Higgler and Other Tales* (London, 1994).

II. SHORT STORIES. *Adam and Eve and Pinch Me* (Waltham Saint Lawrence, 1921); *Clorinda Walks in Heaven* (Waltham Saint Lawrence and New York, 1922); *The Black Dog and Other Stories* (London, 1923); *Fishmonger's Fiddle* (London, 1925); *The Field of Mustard* (London, 1926); *Count Stefan, with a portrait and decorations by Robert Gibbings* (Waltham Saint Lawrence, 1928); *Silver Circus* (London, 1928); *The Higgler* (New York, 1930); *The Man from Kilsheelan* (London, 1930); *The Hundredth Story of A. E. Coppard* (Waltham Saint Lawrence, 1931); *Nixey's Harlequin* (London, 1931); *Crotty Shinkwin* (Waltham Saint Lawrence, 1932); *Dunky Fitlow* (London, 1933); *Ring the Bells of Heaven* (London, 1933); *Emergency Exit* (New York, 1934); *Polly Oliver* (London, 1935); *Ninepenny Flute* (London, 1937); *Tapster's Tapestry* (London, 1938); *You Never Know, Do You? and Other Tales* (London, 1939); *Ugly Anna and Other Tales* (London, 1944); *Dark-Eyed Lady* (London, 1947); *Lucy in Her Pink Jacket* (London, 1954).

III. POETRY. *Hips and Haws* (Waltham Saint Lawrence, 1922); *Pelagea and Other Poems* (Waltham Saint Lawrence, 1926); *Yokohama Garland and Other Poems* (Philadelphia, 1926).

IV. OTHER WORKS. *Pink Furniture: A Tale for Lovely Children with Noble Natures* (London, 1930); *It's Me, O Lord! An Abstract and Brief Chronicle of Some of the Life with Some of the Opinions of A. E. Coppard, Written by Himself* (London, 1957).

V. BIBLIOGRAPHIES. Jacob Schwarz, *The Writings of A. E. Coppard: A Bibliography with Foreword and Notes by A. E. Coppard* (London, 1931); Gilbert H. Fabes, *The First Editions of A. E. Coppard, A. P. Herbert and Charles Morgan, with values and bibliographical points* (London, 1933).

VI. BIOGRAPHICAL AND CRITICAL STUDIES. Journal articles. J. B. Chapman, "A Teller of Tales," in *Bookman* 78 (May 1930); B. K. Seymour, "A. E. Coppard as Author of the Month," in *Woman's Journal,* June 1930; Louise Morgan, "A. E. Coppard on How to Write Short Stories," in *Everyman* 4 (22 January 1931); Adrian Alington and L.E.O. Charlton, eds., *Beginnings* (London, 1935); Frank O'Connor, "A. E. Coppard," in *Pacific Spectator* 10 (fall 1956); Arsiné Schmavonian, "The A. E. Coppard Papers at Syracuse," in *Courier* 9, no. 3, Syracuse University Library Associates Courier (1972); Jean-Louis Magniont, "Introduction à la lecture de A. E. Coppard," in *Les Langues Modernes,* no. 3, (1972); Jean-Louis Magniont, "Les Contes de A. E. Coppard," in *Etudes Anglaises* 27, no. 2 (1974). Jean-Louis Magniont, *A. E. Coppard (1878–1957): L'homme et l'oeuvre*, Ph.D. thesis, Université de la Sorbonne Nouvelle, Paris III. In works on the short story. H. E. Bates, *The Modern Short Story: A Critical Survey* (London, 1941; repr. 1972, Chapter VI: 'Katherine Mansfield and A. E. Coppard'); Frank O'Connor, *The Lonely Voice: A Study of the Short Story* (Cleveland, 1963; London, 1965, Chapter 9: 'The Price of Freedom'); T. O. Beachcroft, *The English Short Story II* (London, 1969); T. O. Beachcroft, *The Modest Art: A Survey of the Short Story in English* (London and New York, 1968, Chapter XV: 'The Twenties and Thirties'); Valerie Shaw, *The Short Story: A Critical Introduction* (London and New York, 1983, Chapter 7: 'Subject Matter')Walter Allen, *The Short Story in English* (Oxford, 1981, Chapter IV, iv: 'T. F. Powys, Coppard').

MAJOR MANUSCRIPT COLLECTION. A. E. Coppard Papers at the Harry Ransom Humanities Research Center, University of Texas at Austin.

FRANCES CORNFORD

(1886–1960)

Philip Hobsbaum

FRANCES CONFORD WAS born on 30 March 1886, in Cambridge. A poet and translator, hers was one of the most illustrious families ever to have graced the annals of English intellectual life. Her paternal grandfather, Charles Darwin (1809–1882), ranks with Isaac Newton as being one of the Englishmen who changed the world picture, notably by his book *On the Origin of Species* (1859), which consolidated the evolutionary theory of life and, probably without intention, dealt a blow to the biblical view of creation.

Darwin had five sons, four of whom achieved a degree of eminence as scientists. Cornford's father, Sir Francis Darwin (1848–1925), was a botanist who served as his father's editor and biographer; he was a lecturer at Cambridge and a fellow of the prestigious scientific academy, the Royal Society of London. Her mother was Ellen Crofts (1856–1903), Francis Darwin's second wife, who was a lecturer in English literature at Newnham College.

Born Frances Crofts Darwin, Cornford spent her life in Cambridge, which formed the setting of many of her poems. She grew up in an agnostic household at Wychfield, a large house with a large garden, situated on the Huntingdon Road. Many relatives from her father's side of the family lived nearby. Indeed, her mother may have felt a little too surrounded by Darwins; she certainly seems to have been of a melancholic temperament. Frances's father, Sir Francis, was something of a valetudinarian, and lacked vaulting ambition. Sir Francis refused, for example, to be considered for the chair of botany at Cambridge, on the grounds that this position should go to a younger man who might be more in need of it. The young Frances was less affected by this domestic lack of high spirits than might have been supposed. She is remembered by her cousin Gwen Raverat, in the charming autobiographical sketch *Period Piece: A Cambridge Childhood* (1952), as something of a tomboy. She never went to school but was taught by a governess, Ada Sharpley, who encouraged her early interest in poetry.

FLUX AMID PERMANANCE: MARRIED LIFE AND EARLY POEMS

Cornford characteristically refers to Cambridge as a place of permanency and tradition. The place itself, set in the flat, damp country of the Fens, remained at the heart of a rich agricultural area. Despite the university's ascendancy, it was essentially a market town, employing domestic servants and laborers. The motorcar had not yet taken over private transport. It was a setting that her grandfather would have recognized.

However, there was a degree of flux. From being a place where men passed time before they became country squires, barristers, or clergymen, the university mutated into a practical institution in which pursuing the vocation of an academic was a career, and where subjects such as natural science could be studied. As interest in the sciences grew, teaching moved out of the colleges. The university was able to pull in grants to establish laboratories that even the richest of colleges, Trinity—of which Cornford's father was a fellow—could not afford to maintain. At the same time, organized games, college clubs, and competitive examinations became norms of a culturally useful background. Though the structure remained apparently tranquil, it was in the process of development. From 1878, fellows of colleges had been allowed to marry, so Frances Cornford and her cousins were among the first generation of academics' children born into a university community that was still small and exclusive.

FRANCES CORNFORD

By marriage as well as heredity Cornford was near the center of a proliferating intellectual circle. In 1909 she married Francis Macdonald Cornford (1874–1943), a lecturer in classics at Cambridge who became a professor of ancient philosophy. She got to know him well during an amateur production of John Milton's *Comus* with which they were both associated and in which Francis played the leading part, with Rupert Brooke as the Attendant Spirit. Francis Cornford was an eminent Platonist who is remembered by nonclassicists for his good-humored satire on university politics, *Microcosmographia Academica* (1908).

Frances Cornford fulfilled the destiny of a university wife, first in a house in Chesterton Road, then in one built by her father especially for her purposes further out, along the Madingley Road. She had five children between 1914 and 1924: Helena Darwin, Rupert John, Christopher Francis, Hugh Wordsworth, and Ruth Clare. She had told Rupert Brooke that she wanted a dwelling where people would come in naturally when they would, not just "a dead suburban castle with a smell of repulsion and distrust in the hall" (Hassall, p. 214). He helped her in her inclinations, and she and her husband had a name for being hospitable. Their house was frequented by writers, artists, and musicians; it was a place of refuge as well as social gatherings.

Even so, she demonstrably found time to write. Her first collection of verse, *Poems,* appeared in 1910, more or less privately issued by the Priory Press at Hampstead—"a humble little publisher," as she called it. She more usually claimed as her first book *Spring Morning* (1915), published by The Poetry Bookshop—well known among aficionados of contemporary verse—five years later. Indeed, the two collections have several poems in common, and among them are a number of her best: "Autumn Morning at Cambridge," "Autumn Evening," "The Watch," "Dawn," and "To a Fat Lady Seen from the Train." This last is printed here in its entirety.

> O why do you walk through the fields in gloves,
>   Missing so much and so much?
> O fat white woman whom nobody loves,
> Why do you walk through the fields in gloves,

> When the grass is soft as the breast of doves
>   And shivering sweet to the touch?
> O why do you walk through the fields in gloves,
>   Missing so much and so much?

This is perhaps the best-known example in English of a metrical form known as the triolet. It was also for many years Cornford's prime anthology piece. The poem is catchy, but also somewhat eerie. The coldly critical view of the "fat white woman whom nobody loves" is equated with a lack of sensuality, "missing so much and so much." The evocation of the grass—"shivering sweet"—is romantically opposed to the shutting off of experience, walking through the fields in gloves. This is a quaint vignette, owing everything to authentic experience, it would seem, yet strangely haunting. This poem used to be proffered to schoolchildren as presentably modern, as distinct from the verse of T. S. Eliot, which was deemed obscure.

Yet it dates, at latest, from 1910, and the triolet itself had been revived as a form by poets thought decadent in the 1890s. This suggests a curious traditionalism in Cornford that nevertheless reaches forward into the twentieth century. It is partly her absence of cant and afflatus that recommend her, and also her terse and quirky wit.

Another piece common to both *Poems* and *Spring Morning,* also to be found in twentieth-century anthologies, including that edited by the poet Philip Larkin, is "The Watch":

> I wakened on my hot, hard bed;
> Upon the pillow lay my head;
> Beneath the pillow I could hear
> My little watch was ticking clear.
> I thought the throbbing of it went
> Like my continual discontent;
> I thought it said in every tick:
> I am so sick, so sick, so sick;
> O death, come quick, come quick, come quick,
> Come quick, come quick, come quick, come quick.

The poem is something of a verbal trick, perhaps prompted by the accidental resemblance of the watch ticking to the sound of the phrase *come quick.* And what is to "come quick" if not death? But there is also the far-from-coincidental fact that the sound of the watch resembles the beating of the heart, and this itself tells the passage of time, and hence of life. However young you are, in a few seconds you are appreciably nearer death, and the watch counts out those seconds to minutes and minutes to hours. Even this does not quite explain the ironic charm of the poem. The bed is hot and hard, and the little watch is signaling an end to discomfiture.

Readers must have sensed an uncomfortable sort of talent here, even though in both *Poems* and *Spring Morning* there are pieces that, on the surface at least, seem reassuring. "Autumn Evening," for instance, appears to be the portrait of a person at ease:

The shadows flickering, the daylight dying,
And I upon the old red sofa lying,
The great brown shadows leaping up the wall,
The sparrows twittering; and that is all.

The person tries to send her soul "to far-off lands," to "an enchanted town." But it is too happy and too warm at home. The poem personifies quiescence by more or less repeating in the last two lines of the third stanza the last two lines of the first stanza: "With just the shadows leaping up the wall, / The sparrows twittering; and that is all." There is a sense here of powers unused. It goes along with a sense of dissatisfaction with existence, as though the ordered middle-class existence of a university town was not quite enough.

A degree of exuberance may be found at the beginning of "Autumn Morning at Cambridge," written in 1902, when the author was sixteen: "I ran out in the morning, when the air was clean and new, / And all the grass was glittering, and grey with autumn dew . . ." Yet the speaker is somehow not totally engaged with the scene. Others are sweeping up the old leaves to let the people pass. She is not herself active; she is watching. Amid that which she watches are "the men [who] go to lecture with the wind in their gowns." It is these others who are engaged in life.

It is death that sharpens her attention, here as elsewhere. One of the more striking poems is "A Recollection," in which she remembers a friend of her father's coming round, pink-cheeked,

laughing, talking to her. Within the week, she hears that he has died. This gives her a sense of guilt, but also of self-importance: "Deep in my heart I thought with pride, / 'I know a person who has died.'" The poem is one spoken by a child and, in a sense, it is a child's poem. This interest in childhood guaranteed Frances Cornford a secure place in school anthologies.

It is a child who "gashed and defaced" the precious hours in "A Wasted Day" (*Spring Morning*). In the poem entitled "Dawn" (in *Poems*) it is a child's day that begins, albeit the day of a growing child: "Quiet as a flower / In this first gray hour." When the speaker is an adult, it is often a child who is being addressed, as in these lines from "Mountains": "Child unknown who shall be mine hereafter, / Your heart, too, shall leap at sight of the mountains." A little girl, asking about old age, is reassured in "Youth and Age," but only with a measure of irony: "Shall I be trembling and querulous of tongue? / You shall be wiser than anybody young." Characteristics of this early style are simplicity of vocabulary, a fairly strict adherence to traditional rhymes and meter, a sense of atmosphere—particularly that associated with English lyrical-descriptive poetry in the line of Robert Herrick and William Wordsworth and indeed with the Georgian school of poetry itself, discussed later.

This period also marks the appearance of *Death and the Princess* (1912), a piece fit to be performed in a college for decorous young ladies. It may have grown out of the Darwin family ritual of the Christmas Play, written and performed in their houses on Christmas Eve by Frances and her cousins when they were children. The present dramatic work is styled "a morality," and the author is careful to tell us in a prefatory note what she means by this: "Whereas any medieval Morality could suggest the whole conception of life and death belonging to the great religion behind it, *Death and the Princess* can only convey one side (as a lyric might do) of the belief of some people to-day."

The story is rather like an English version of William Butler Yeats's celebrated *The Countess Cathleen* (1892), without, however, the latter's political implications. The peasants of a secluded valley are menaced by a threatening figure variously termed "the Dragon," "the Evil One," "the Bull-God," and "the Horned One," but who turns out to be "the King of the Wood." They cry upon the princess to assume the role of the Holy Maid who, it is prophesied, shall come forth as their Great Deliverer and, of her own free will, die to save them. Although skeptics among the peasants declare that the Princess cares nothing for her people, in fact she appears secretively, together with her hunched dwarf Sardonyx, in search of

> the King of the Woods,
> They write of in old books—that brown-faced king,
> Making the butterflies dance in empty glades,
> Where the sweet shadows lay.

As this will suggest, much of the "morality" is written in a pleasantly pastoral verse. The rest of it is in rhythmic prose. As might have been foreseen, at the end of the play the princess joins the King of the Woods and goes with him into his cavern, first saying:

> I know that death is easy as a sleep,
> The simple end of all earth's creatures. This
> Your wisdom taught me. But for man alone
> Death can be more—a triumph . . .

Though *Death and the Princess* should not be taken too seriously, these lines share something of the attitude of Cornford's early lyrics: the feeling that death can be a shrugging off of the heat and botheration of the waking day.

CORNFORD AND THE GEORGIAN POETS

The Poetry Bookshop, which had published *Spring Morning,* also published a companion volume, *Autumn Midnight* (1923). By the time of its publication Cornford had become tolerably well known, because The Poetry Bookshop, directed by Harold Monro, was the publisher of a series of influential anthologies edited by Edward Marsh, *Georgian Poetry.* There were five volumes in all, issued between 1911 and 1922, and featuring such poets as Rupert Brooke, Sir John Collings Squire, Edmund Blunden, Robert Graves, William Henry Davies, and Walter De la Mare.

By this time, the style of Cornford's poetic style in some ways resembled the work of the last two, while the first two—Brooke and Squire—attempted to persuade Marsh to include Cornford's poetry in his anthologies. This was the case even though Brooke, struck by the brevity of her lyrics, had dubbed Cornford the leader of the Heart-Cry School of Poetry—"short, simple, naïve" (Hassall, p. 276). Their pleas for Cornford's inclusion were in vain, however: the only women ever to contribute to *Georgian Poetry* were Fredegond Shove, wife of an academic acquaintance of Marsh, and, in the final volume, Victoria Sackville-West. The series remained an overwhelmingly masculine affair.

Yet Cornford's poetry was well known to Marsh, and on several occasions she acknowledged his help. Her *Collected Poems* of thirty years later is dedicated to Marsh's memory. This suggests that she harbored no resentment about her exclusion. Further, during this period the key phase of modernist poetry appears to have occurred, from *Des Imagistes* (1914), edited by Ezra Pound, to *The Waste Land* (1922), written by T. S. Eliot. To many readers, it must have seemed that the Georgians represented a defense of the English tradition against the surrealistic effects and free versification of these American-led young moderns. Indeed, in Cambridge circles it was felt that Cornford herself stood for the poetic establishment against alien incursions.

Modernism could best be described as the breakdown or even suppression of plot in a poem—suppressed in favor of an associative play of imagery, termed "phanopoeia" by Pound. Take, for example, Pound's poem "The Return," published in his collection *Ripostes* (1912); it begins as follows:

> See, they return; ah, see the tentative
>   Movements, and the slow feet,
>   The trouble in the pace and the uncertain
>   Wavering!
>
> See, they return, one, and by one,
> With fear, as half-awakened;
> As if the snow should hesitate
> And murmur in the wind,
>   and half-turn back;

These were the "Wing'd-with-Awe",
Inviolable . . .

Part of the charm is an invitation to the reader to decode what the poet is writing about. The implication seems to be that some people, unidentified explicitly, are returning, presumably home, in a subdued and unthreatening way. Their movements are tentative, their feet slow, they appear to be afraid. They may be inferred to have had a heroic past, these "Wing'd-with-Awe," who seem to have been "Inviolable." The impression by now must have grown upon us that the characters of whom the poet speaks are something akin to soldiers coming back from a battle in which they have been vanquished, perhaps ingloriously. But the message is not explicitly stated. The mode remains that of an impression.

How different from this is the approach evinced by Cornford in her poem found in *Autumn Midnight,* "No Immortality?," later retitled "Contemporaries." Although the opening is couched in the form of a question, we can deduce without too much trouble that somebody beautiful and well remembered—though dead—is being evoked with clarity and precision.

Can it be possible, when we grow old
And Time destroys us, that the image of you,
Who brought to all, serenely, like a gift,
The eternal beauty of youth—as though you had lain,
A moment since, in English grass by the river,
Thinking and dreaming under the fresh sky
When May was in the hedges—can it be
This unique image of you, you yourself, your smile,
(Which kept a secret sweetness like a child's,
Though you might be most sad), your frowning eyes,
Must, when we die, in the vast air of Time
Be swallowed . . . ?

It is the sentiment of Walter De la Mare, in his poem "An Epitaph," which ends

But beauty vanishes; beauty passes;
However rare—rare it be;
And when I crumble, who will remember
This lady of the West Country?

One can find parallels throughout the Georgian anthologies: "Babylon" by Ralph Hodgson, "Not Dead" by Robert Graves, "Littleholme" by Gordon Bottomley.

The exclusion of Cornford from *Georgian Poetry* remains a mystery. It could be argued that *Autumn Midnight* is a dilution of the possibilities evinced in the preceding volume of lyrics. But any dilution takes us nearer to the generic Georgian style—pastoral, whimsical, backward-looking—rather than nearer to the individual note of which the earlier Cornford was capable. Pieces such as the title poem, "On the Dunes," and "The Country Bedroom" could have been composed by any of the more minor Georgians. And with such a poem as "Hope"—not subsequently reprinted—Cornford confronts the major ones:

"There never will be peace till Hope is dead,"
A torn Heart said.
"Die, Hope, and plead no more. I cannot bear,
Each time you fall defeated, this despair."

But Hope replied: "Without me none can live.
I must creep back to you, torn Heart, forgive!
I must creep back, and sleep, and then recover
And you, O Heart, torn Heart, shall be my lover."

That breathes the same air as Robert Graves, a poet somewhat younger than herself whom Cornford hugely admired. Behind such verse is that of Robert Louis Stevenson and A. E. Housman. And it went on to influence a number of especially women poets, who formed a kind of buried stream running below the more spectacular achievements of the twentieth century. A semblance of Cornford may be traced in such writers as Ruth Pitter, Frances Bellerby, Joan Barton, and E. J. Scovell, all of whom were encouraged by Walter De la Mare.

DIFFERENT DAYS *AND* MOUNTAINS AND MOLEHILLS

The situation seems all the more complex when one reflects that, where *Autumn Midnight* came out under the imprint of The Poetry Bookshop, which published *Georgian Poetry,* Cornford's next volume, *Different Days* (1928), was issued by the Hogarth Press, whose proprietors were Virginia and Leonard Woolf, icons of the Bloomsbury group. They had already published the key text of modernist poetry, Eliot's *The Waste Land*. *Different Days* represents no particular advance upon the body of verse that Cornford had already assembled. It would escape the epithet of being Georgian—beginning to be slighting by this time—because of a singular chastity of style, not given to sentimentality or overstatement:

> . . . The figure of a scholar carrying back
> Books to the library—absorbed, content,
> Seeming as everlasting as the elms
> Bark-wrinkled, puddled round their roots, the bells,
> And the far shouting in the football fields . . .
>
> ("A Glimpse")

In some ways, this is a retreat from the early verse. It is as though she is keeping the landscape in place by sheer willpower. In the face of the hundreds of thousands of young men slaughtered in World War I, some of them her friends and acquaintances, she writes at the opening of "The Glimpse" of her beloved Cambridge, "O grasses wet with dew, yellow fallen leaves, / Smooth-shadowed waters Milton loved" and at the poem's end, "The same since I was born, the same to be / When all my children's children grow old men."

Much of the book seems to be a celebration of an unchanging, essentially English, way of life. "Cambridgeshire," in spite of the upheavals of the First World War, through which the poet lived, is celebrated as an entity that is there to stay:

> Nothing is changed. The farmer's gig goes by
> Against the horizon. Surely, the same sky,
> So vast and so familiar, grey and mild,
> And streaked with light like music . . .

The secret, of course, is that these poems are essentially atavistic. In this one, gently introspective as it is, Cornford is speaking of her youth. The stanza continues

> I, a child,
> Lifted my face from leaf-edged lanes to see,
> Late-coming home, to bread-and-butter tea.

It does not take too acute an ear to pick up the willed quality that shapes this apparently pastoral description.

Scene after scene may be said to have that essentially "English" quality. The tiles of the old roof, mellow and gray-red, are evoked in "Lincolnshire Remembered." The rocks and waves provide a source of imagery for her children, Helena and Christopher, in "Cornish April." She remembers her far-off North of England roots in "Ancestors": "They lived in stone houses, under the black-shadowing sycamores." Inevitably, there is the sense of death; for Cornford was an accomplished elegist. In a quatrain called "The Dead One," later, "The Old Friend," the reproof is gentle: "The wrong you have done is very quiet, just / Not being there." She remembers her great-aunt Sara in a poem called "At the End": "She was more quiet than the brown, ploughed fields that lay outside." Whoever it was that is commemorated in "The Dead Painter" has "passed this day to us the cup of life, / That differently we might drink together." The "difference" in *Different Days* presages a degree of sameness.

This quality, almost approaching quiescence, may have annoyed a younger generation, as can be seen in the correspondence between Cornford and her brilliant young son, John. Their letters are reproduced in a selection from John's writings called *Understand the Weapon Understand the Wound* (1976), edited by Jonathan Galassi. A good many of the letters exchanged between mother and son consist of a picking over of each other's verses. Several poems by Cornford that went on to be collected in *Mountains and Molehills* (1934) were discussed in this way. In 1932 John Cornford quotes his mother as having said to him during a school holiday that the most any poet could do was to write a few individual lines for himself in every poem "and let the tradition he writes in write the rest" (Galassi, p. 153). In a letter of 27 November 1931 she suggested that "nobody at [the age of] fifteen can hope to be doing really original work" (Galassi, p. 144), but she seems also to have applied this dictum to older poets. Certainly, and in the teeth of modernist critics, "originality" cannot be accepted as a value in its own right. Nevertheless, there is a gap between the advocacy of originality for the sake of originality and the acceptance of a preset style that is to perform the bulk of the writing process

The poems collected in *Mountains and Molehills* are very much the mixture as before. Perhaps individual people are more evident:

> . . . Even the old,
> Old labourer sunning in a windsor chair,
> Patient as tree-roots and the stubbled fields,
> With pink and purple asters at his door,
> Whom but to pass this morning, stirred awake,
> Heart-deep, my father's fathers' loyalties—
> Our joint familiar never-spoken loves—
> Even his image is too hard to hold,
> Lapped as I lie in this Lethean gold . . .
>
> ("Cambridge Autumn")

The speaker of "Cambridge Autumn" has been lying out all afternoon in "sun-receiving fields." However, the experience is relayed through images that are, perhaps, too familiar: "stubbled fields," "Lethean gold." There is an absence of pressure. Even the sense that the old laborer must "fare / Alone into the dark of death" need not disturb us. There will be plenty of old laborers, in postures similar to his own, to replace him.

It is not that this book is slipshod or, indeed, clumsy in any way. It is that the writing is so expected; everything settled down into an iambic norm. What may be significant is that the best poem in the book is a translation—granted, a brilliant and fairly free one—of "La servante au grand coeur . . ." by Charles Baudelaire:

> I cannot but believe, though you were dead,
> Lying stone-still, and I came in and said
> Having been out perhaps in storm and rain:
> "Oh dear, O look, I have torn my skirt again,"
> That you would rise with the old simple ease,
> And say, "Yes, child," and come to me . . .
>
> ("Nurse," later retitled "The Old Servant")

There are details crisply expressed that redeem the poem from being merely derivative: "your white crackling apron" and "quick hands, rough with the washing-up." The quality of the verse may be assessed if contrasted with the semi-official—though, it must be agreed, far closer—translation, by Joanna Richardson:

> Great-hearted nurse who earned your jealousy:
> Beneath the sward she sleeps on, quietly.
> Yes, we should take her flowers for times gone.
> The poor dead know their desolation. . . .

However, even "Nurse" does not achieve quite the alertness of the very early poems, such as "The Watch" and "Autumn Morning at Cambridge."

Other poems that retain a degree of interest include the one placed first in the book, "Mountain Path." This contains some descriptive verse that displays a characteristic fastidiousness of language: "These dark hieratic trees their branches raise / And lift their burnished cones." What should be said is that the scene described does not grip the poet with so much interest as to avoid a fancy that "an old dwarf . . . with humpèd back" will descend "the rocky winding way" in order to locate and examine his "little safe-tied bags / Of leather."

There are several characteristic child-pieces in *Mountains and Molehills*: "Fool's Song," "Mother to Child Asleep," "The Madman and the Child." And there are a number of pieces, in a mode now familiar, concerned with death: "Constant," "The End," and "Neighbours." This last begins:

> Old Mrs Thompson down the road is dead.
> The maids knew first from what the milkman said,
> (He heard on Sunday she was very bad)
> And as they work they are sorry, stirred and glad . . .

The speaker points out that she will inevitably meet the same fate as old Mrs. Thompson, with a similar, dispassionate effect felt by another set of maids: "They will know first, because the fish-boy heard; / And as they dust, be sorry, glad, and stirred." One finds a redeeming wryness here. Certainly, there is nothing sentimental about Cornford's view of death, her own or that of anybody else. It is symptomatic, however, that so often this writer's work tends to be defined in negatives.

WAR, LOSS, AND THE LIMITS OF TRADITION

Cornford's *Mountains and Molehills* was written at a time when fascism was on the rise, when workers were disaffected and unemployed, when socialism was advancing upon Europe, when the ills consequent upon the Treaty of Versailles were becoming noticeable—and noticed. We cannot blame Cornford for failing explicitly to acknowledge contemporary events in her poems. There is, though, an absence of a pressure that might have been required behind the verse.

The scenes described exist for their own sake, as though to provide the opportunity for good, just, exact writing, and no more. Of course, a poet may be limited by his or her range, and the performance of a writer such as Cornford could leave an audience wanting more. We need not be surprised, then, that the discourse between Cornford and her son John turns upon "tradition." Young John, away at school in 1932, wrote the following:

> I wonder, how much of your poetry is shaped by tradition: are the poems that you write really your most important experiences? or has your view of poetry been so much moulded by the traditional view that the more important experiences are too repressed to occur in poem-form at all? . . . it always seems to me that you have a great deal that needs to be said more urgently but can't because of the limitations of your view of poetry—because I should guess (though I don't know) that until fairly recently you would have denied (and perhaps still do) that every subject is equally "poetical."
>
> (Galassi, p. 147).

The issue is one of form as much as subject matter. Cornford had previously written to her son, "The irregular rhyming metre has failed. It was meant to represent recitative in music, mixed with bits of typical melody" (Galassi, p. 145). She appears to be referring to an experiment of her own, but it is clear that she expects her strictures to be applied to the world of verse at large. John had already made a bonfire of the old, trusted Victorians that his mother so admired: "I detest nearly all Browning and I am more annoyed by artificiality and Victorianism than I enjoy his occasional really good verses" (Galassi, p. 127). He even discounts Victorian admirations from the past, such as the seventeenth-century lyricist Robert Herrick.

Yet mother and son concur in appreciating Robert Graves. She wrote to him on 20 February 1931, "I'm glad you're getting Graves" (Galassi, p. 133)—meaning, presumably, that she is glad he is understanding that poet and picking up some of his traits of style. And he writes back to her, "I found them [Graves's poems] exceedingly good, though intensely obscure. . . . They are in his later and more intellectual style, and the simplest need a good deal of hard work, but all, at least all that I have so far been able to understand have been well worth it" (Galassi, p. 135). Given the period, the poems to which these letters refer must be those in Graves's *Poems (1926–1930)*. This collection includes poems such as "Castle," "Railway Carriage" (later known as "Welsh Incident"), "In Broken Images," and best of all, "O Love in Me" (later known as "Sick Love"):

O love, be fed with apples while you may,
And feel the sun and go in royal array,
A smiling innocent on the heavenly causeway. . . .

For many, this will remain the quintessential Graves—Romantic in feeling, purged in diction.

However, this was by no means the only exciting influence. Early on in his correspondence with his mother, while praising W. H. Auden, John admits that he finds him "difficult" and has rewritten one of his easier pieces "as a romantic poem." Exactly which piece this is may be hard to identify, since most of John Cornford's slender verse output reads like Auden rewritten in this way:

At least to know the sun rising each morning
And see at least a sunset's punctual glory
Is at least something. And at least to hear
Water over a rock, all night dripping,
And at least sometimes to walk the mountains all day
On rock above running water . . .

(Galassi, p. 25)

But the way is not that of John Cornford's most famous poem, his anthology piece.

This is one of the best-known love poems of the twentieth century, usually called "To Margot Heinemann," after its recipient. Here the young poet sheds all the modernist trappings and writes a lyric that Herrick would have recognized and that readily could have taken its place in the traditionalist anthologies that succeeded *Georgian Poetry*. It begins

Heart of the heartless world,
Dear heart, the thought of you
Is the pain at my side,
The shadow that chills my view.

The wind rises in the evening,
Reminds that autumn's near.
I am afraid to lose you,
I am afraid of my fear . . .

(Galassi, p. 40)

Shortly after writing this, in December 1936, John Cornford was killed in battle above the village of Lopera on the Cordoba front of the Spanish Civil War. He had just turned twenty-one. It is eerie. His first name was Rupert, called after that handsome figure from Cambridge, Rupert Brooke, who died prematurely in World War I and who may well be the romantic hero evoked in "No Immortality?," that poem found in *Autumn Midnight*. Like his namesake, before volunteering to fight on the Republican side in the Spanish Civil War, Rupert John Cornford had lived life to the full. He had won a scholarship in history to his father's college, Trinity, and also enrolled at the London School of Economics. He took first-class honors in both parts of the history tripos at Cambridge, joined the Communist Party, and fathered a child out of wedlock with Ray Peters, a fellow political activist. Toward the end of his short life, his thoughts were running to politics rather than poetry. However, one cannot doubt that, whatever line of action he adopted, his intellectual energy would have taken him to the top. His was a loss to the world, and one can only imagine what damage it did his mother already clinically depressed. To make matters worse for her, her husband of thirty-four years, F. M. Cornford, died of pneumonia in 1943.

POETRY IN TRANSLATION

Perhaps the dates of her books give a clue. There was no volume of original verse between 1934, when *Mountains and Molehills* was published—by the Cambridge University Press, no less—and 1948, when a highly autumnal volume, *Travelling Home,* was issued by the Cresset Press. What may have helped eventually to break the silence was the friendship between Frances Cornford and two Russian writers, Nicholas Bachtin and Esther Polianowsky Salaman. With the latter, not having a word of Russian herself, she produced a volume, *Poems from the Russian* (1943), published by the leading poetry firm, Faber and Faber. Cornford and Salaman produced versions of poems by, among others, Alexandr Sergeyevich Pushkin, Mikhail Yuryevich Lermontov, Fyodor Ivanovich Tyutchev, Aleksander Aleksandrovich Blok, and Anna Akhmatova. Akhmatova, born in 1889, was almost the exact contemporary of Cornford. Not surprisingly, Cornford had a good deal of sympathy with Akhmatova's stand against Blok and the symbolists. She quotes her as saying, "We want to admire a rose because it is beautiful, not because it is a symbol of mystical purity." This could really be part of Cornford's own credo. She says approvingly of Akhmatova that she writes with perfect economy, straight out of personal experience, and as only a woman could. She quotes Sir Edward Marsh as maintaining that no poem can be represented by a piece of verse that does not stand on its own legs in its own language. There is no translatese, no forced language, here. Many of these poems could pass for genuine pieces from Cornford's own hand. Keeping to Akhmatova, we find:

Noiseless they moved about the house,
    No hope was in their eyes.
They brought me to the dying man
    I could not recognize.

"Thank God!" he said. Then more remote
    And sunk in thought he grew.
"I know it's time I went; but first
    I had to wait for you;

"For every word you ever said
    Through my delirium ran—

Tell me: of course you can't forgive?"
  I looked, and said: "I can" . . .
             ("The End")

The poem goes on, but already we experience the admixture of death and hope, and the terse, clear unsentimental accents. There is not a forced phrase, here or in the rest of the book. This particular poem ends:

 Then, all at once, the last strength leapt
  In those blue eyes half-blind:
 "It's good that you will let me go:
  You were not always kind."

 Again I recognized the face,
  Grown younger for release.
 I said: "Thy servant lettest Thou,
  O Lord, depart in peace."

It is as though there were some well of experience in Cornford that could be tapped to vitalize subjects not immediately of her own choosing.

One finds a similar phenomenon when she and her collaborator turn their attention to Tyutchev. There is a singularly beautiful—one might almost say Cornfordian—poem, "The Night Wind." Here we have a dexterous use of what John Ruskin, whom Cornford's father greatly admired, called "the pathetic fallacy." By this Ruskin appears to have meant the attribution to nature of human feelings. In this case, the author recognizes that the wind does not itself have feelings but is capable of inspiring them, and that this can be a dangerous practice.

Wind in the night, on your mysterious way,
Why do you grieve, why do you moan and call?
What does your voice, wind of the darkness, say?
Whispering now, and now maniacal?

How clear, in speech the heart can comprehend,
Of pain incomprehensible it cries
Again and then again without an end,
Till in the breast the answering storms arise.

Oh, do not let those shuddering songs begin,
Which lay the old, the native Chaos bare!
How greedily my world of night within
Harks to the loved and luring voices there,

And from the bounded heart aspires to leap,
With the Unbounded craving to unite.

Oh, do not wake the tempests from their sleep!
Beneath is Chaos, stirring in the night.

There is not a willed rhyme in this poem. The plot may be attributed to Tyutchev, but the verbal expression is that of the translators. Their efficacy may be seen if the poem as they render it is compared with the version by an English poet of a generation younger than that of Cornford, Charles Tomlinson (in *Versions from Fyodor Tyutchev*). This is how it starts:

Excluded stranger, easeless beast
Fretful in alternation of loud on low,
Who shall interpret your nocturnal frenzy?
Only the heart can read unreason,
And, as your unintelligible voice
Burrows beneath its dark, the heart replies
Drawn to the dialogue of formless pain. . . .

The first thing the reader is likely to notice here is the ugliness in sound of the verse. Words made up of consonantal clusters, such as *excluded, fretful, nocturnal,* and *unintelligible,* are singularly difficult to accommodate in the formal plasm of English meter. Also, the verse is almost totally devoid of mimetic quality. The wind comes at us with an undifferentiated harshness. The almost raucous internal rhymes—"easeless beast," "interpret"/"nocturnal"—get little across other than harshness and noise. The effect of near-functionless dysphony is accentuated by all those sibilant *t*s and *s*es.

Now that may be a fair representation of this poem by Tyutchev. If so, the translation is no very welcome addition to poetry in English. Tomlinson certainly knows more Russian than did Cornford. But he is unlikely to have known more than Salaman, who was a native speaker and who coauthored this Faber selection of Russian verse in English translation. It is surprising how like Cornford some of these versions of major Russian poets sound. It is as though we have a set of unexpected additions to the poet's already ascertained oeuvre. Certainly these poems deserve to be better known, not least as specimens of English verse. We find in a version of Pushkin, "Outlived Desire," the quietly disillusioned cadence of

So, stricken by the early cold,
The whistling, bitter gales of grief,
Still the autumnal branches hold
One shuddering leaf.

A very different poet, Lermentov, is rendered in a poem titled "The Testament," through a masculine voice in accents that we can nevertheless recognize as Cornfordian elegy:

Tell her what's happened, plain and bare;
That empty heart you need not spare;
Just let her cry and have her say;
Tears cost her nothing, anyway.

Celebrating the onset of spring in a poem of that name, there are verses based on some by Afanasy Afanasyevich Fet which might well take their place among Cornford's more familiar nature poems. She gives them her characteristic cadence: a fusion of wit and, not altogether unelegiac, hope:

To tell how over every thing
    Delight is blowing on the air—
I know not yet what I shall sing;
    I only know the song is there.

It might almost be an allegory concerned with writing poetry. Indeed, Cornford achieves, when seeking to translate that hardly congenial genius, the mighty Blok, a convincing image of the Muse in a poem called "The Stranger":

But every evening at the fated hour—
Or is it just my dream?—
A figure moves across the misted window,
A girl in silks that gleam. . . .

. . . Her silken waist, her hat of sable feathers,
Her narrow hand with rings,
Seem to exhale a breath of long-forgotten
And legendary things . . .

Of this poem, in a postscriptive note, Cornford and her collaborator comment: "Blok was thrown back into a more personal mysticism . . . by a process of semiconscious falsification [wherein] a local prostitute is transformed into the Stranger—herself an echo of *La Belle Dame*." Though what Cornford and Salaman have in mind is an earlier sequence of poems by Blok, it is impossible for an anglophone reader not to bear in mind the spectral beauty envisaged by John Keats in his poem "La Belle Dame sans Merci" and, behind him, a host of balladeers specializing in the eerie.

Cornford and Salaman's *Poems from the Russian* is perhaps best regarded as a book of imitations, in the manner that was to be notoriously followed by Robert Lowell some twenty years later. What one can say is that this forms a distinguished collection of poems in its own right. It served to tide Cornford over what must have been a uniquely difficult period in her life.

LATER WORKS

Travelling Home (1948) was the first book of original verse Cornford published after a break of fourteen years. It is very much a war book. Some of the best poems in it are redolent of the armed struggle with Germany that had ended only three years earlier. There is a feeling of guilt upon the enjoyment of German music, the liede of Franz Schubert, in "For M.S. Singing *Frühlingsglaube* in 1945." There is the poem "Autumn Blitz" which, after the chaos of the night, welcomes another day. "Soldiers on the Platform" celebrates the "young, bare, bullock faces" that nevertheless share a secret—that even in their animal vitality they stand within reach of death.

None of these poems embodies great truths or startling originality, either in subject matter or in mode. The jacket copy, which may well have been written by the author, attests an intention that is also an effect: "Pity and irony are her most affecting modes of expression, the one revealing her compassionate tenderness, the other her keen sense of proportion." This suggests what the reader may well find, a kind of stripped-down wit, as it might be that of epigram. Though the book as a whole may not alter one's preconceptions—nor would the author herself have recognized that in itself as a value—individual pieces strike home with a sharp-edged authenticity born of their classic simplicity of expression. Several have, as a result, found a home in anthologies of modern verse: this one, "Parting in War-Time," in particular.

How long ago Hector took off his plume,
Not wanting that his little son should cry,
Then kissed his sad Andromache goodbye—
And now we three in Euston waiting-room.

This is poetry stripped down to its bare essentials. Such was the mode Cornford favored in her later years. The inspiration may have come fitfully, and it certainly came in short, sharp incursions.

As one might have expected, a favored theme is old age. "The Old Woman in Spring" tells of an envy felt for the ancient oak tree, which may be contorted in its bole but can still proclaim a youthfulness of heart because it is capable of putting forth green leaves. That is the difference between a tree and an old woman, who may be happy in her heart but has only her twisted hands and wrinkled brow as semblance.

There is a truly magical epigram—and more and more Cornford's verse tended to epigram—which in surprisingly short space manages to proclaim the continuity of life in spite of age and even death. It is called "All Souls Night."

My love came back to me
Under the November tree
Shelterless and dim.
He put his hand upon my shoulder,
He did not think me strange or older,
Nor I, him.

Perhaps the best poem in this autumnal book, and a possible candidate for being the best in all Cornford's output, is "Childhood." Like much of her best verse, it relies upon a childhood perception. Its crispness of utterance and indeed utter disillusion places it in the front rank of anthology pieces.

I used to think that grown-up people chose
To have stiff backs and wrinkles round their nose,
And veins like small fat snakes on either hand,
On purpose to be grand.
Till through the bannisters I watched one day
My great-aunt Etty's friend who was going away,
And how her onyx beads had come unstrung.
I saw her grope to find them as they rolled;

And then I knew that she was helplessly old,
As I was helplessly young.

One can see how this ties in with the early piece, "A Recollection" (*Spring Morning*), when the author recalls a friend of her father who died a week after she met him. Almost half a century separate these two poems. They have in common a deftness in versification and phrasing, but the later work, while as witty as the earlier, is demonstrably more in earnest. There is, beneath the lyric wit, a grim apprehension that the end of life has all the helplessness of its beginning, without the advantages of hope and promise. There is the recognition that the last few years of anyone's biography are liable to be grim ones. The recognition is made all the more persuasive by the fact that, as ever in her best writing, Cornford's control over vocabulary and meter is such as to render the verse wholly natural in phrasing, an example of the speaking voice in poetry.

Cornford's *Collected Poems* came out in 1954. This should be regarded as her central text, even though it was somewhat heavily edited by the author in collaboration with John Hayward, and not all the emendations were improvements. It takes poems from the six previous books. With her usual fastidiousness, Cornford omits poems that many lesser authors would have included. Notable absentees from this final file are "Autumn Evening" and that strangely Gravesian poem "Hope." On the other hand, every poem that appears in *Travelling Home*, except for "The Betrayer," is included. Like many poets, Cornford valued most highly her more recent work. Her *Collected Poems* was a great success and was the choice of the Poetry Book Society. In addition to those poems that had already appeared in volume form, there was a section of recent poems ("Poems 1948–1953") substantial enough to be regarded as a whole new book, twenty-nine in all, as well as seven jeux d'esprit termed "occasional verses."

One would not expect, at this stage, any considerable change in style, but there are, as might have been expected, some new pieces worthy of notice. There is a charming idyll, "The Spanish Maids in England." It shows Ascención clasping her washing in the courtyard and calling up to Salomé in her attic, all the doors of the house open, the women turning that rare, English sunny day into the sun-bright dazzle of their native Spain. More characteristic, perhaps, at this period are the purged, stripped epigrams, facing childhood or death with equal steadiness. "Two Years Old" is a quatrain that perceives, as the child cannot, his "soft-nosed" innocence. There is an epitaph for the ballet dancer, Nijinsky—"A panther ready, or an arrow drawn"—perhaps to make up for the longer and more pretentious commemoration, "Grand Ballet," that has been dropped. Charlotte Brontë also gets her epitaph: a contrast between "the children of [her] fiery heart and brain"—that is to say, the characters in her books—and the stark gynecolog facts of her life, "I died, because my body could not bear / A mortal child." There is "The Scholar," which seems to be an elegy for her husband, F. M. Cornford, quiet and restrained in tone, perhaps befitting its subject: "You spoke to Plato. You were native there."

She has made the quatrain, in particular, her own special art form. This can be grave, as in "The Quarrel":

How simple is my burden every day
    Now you have died, till I am also dead,
The words "Forgive me," that I could not say,
    The words "I am sorry," that you might
    have said.

Or the quatrain can be witty, as in this spiced gibe, "Epitaph for a Reviewer":

Who so maintains that I am humbled now
    (Who wait the Awful Day) is still a liar;
I hope to meet my Maker brow to brow
    And find my own the higher.

The final volume, On a Calm Shore, came out in 1960, the year of the author's death from a chronic heart condition. That took place, like her life, in circumstances of quietness and resignation, on 19 August, in Cambridge. In this last book, deftness of versification takes the place of wit, and a judicial air of summing up replaces the wisdom and atmosphere of earlier poems. Both may be found, in place of any more remark-

able attributes, in a quatrain such as this, entitled "Two Old Men Outside an Inn":

Somewhat their shoulders have begun to bow
As if in deference to earth, who now
May any day invite them to be done
Quite quietly with bench and beer and sun.

There is an air of epigram, and the phrasing is neat enough, but nothing of genuine wit is said. Indeed, there is a tendency to reach, however succinctly, for the commonplace, as in "East Anglian Church-yard":

How many souls departing have enriched
The ways they trod, the fields they hedged and
    ditched,
The rounded ricks and daily skies above,
And all this level land with obstinate love.

The redeeming phrase here is *obstinate love.* Otherwise the proximity of "departing" and "souls," like that of "hedged" and "ditched," takes us perilously near cliché.

Short the earlier poems may have been, but they were well formed and did not demand to be longer. In the poems of On a Calm Shore, there is an air of fragmentariness. Occasionally this gives us a sense of a further, more frightening, world, as with "Waiting in Hospital," where there is actually an epigraph from the dangerously subversive Eliot—"These fragments I have shored against my ruin"—

This dominant machine,
These forms, these files,
This self-assured routine,
Cylindered oxygen for gasping breath,
White antiseptic tiles,
Clattering heels and smiles,
Each fragment of this regulated hour
Innocent man has shored against the power
Of ruinous death.

There is certainly a glimpse of something after death, that undiscovered country. However, whatever glimpse there is seems to be tidied away behind the acceptable diction. That rhyme of "breath" and "death" would seem to have been used too many times, by Cornford herself, and her multitudinous predecessors.

Of course, there are individual poems one would like to rescue and, perhaps, anthologize. Their merits lie in apt phrasing rather than specific pressure behind the achieved generalities, as in "He Says Goodbye in November":

You say you know that nature never grieves:
I also see the acquiescent leaves
Fall down and rot
As down the derelict statue runs the rain;
But you believe that spring will come again
And I do not.

But one has only, with a degree of unfairness, to compare this phrasing with Hardy's in his "During Wind and Rain"—"Down their carved names the rain-drop ploughs"—to see where the deficiency lies. Cornford's pessimism, it could be said, is too easily achieved. One could never call her poetry glib, but there is something too ready about the comparison in "Missing":

With what an absolute reproach
   Lost things lie,
Dead soldiers or unposted letters
   Watched by the sky.

"You dropped us," say our fallen letters
   Innocently clear.
The corpses: "Your indifference
   Laid us here."

It is as though the technique has taken command over the subject matter. There is that in the reader's sensibility which would require—rather than demand—a little more responsibility, a degree of showing us why we should take an interest in such things. The comparison of accidentally discarded letters with soldiers presumably killed in battle is not so inevitable as the suave phrasing makes it, momentarily, appear.

On A Calm Shore includes yet another memory of Nijinsky. There are also, inevitably, several glimpses of old age; in spring, summer, in autumn—"I know how this beatitude must thin / And different days begin." That poem, "September Soliloquy," even has the echo of a title evinced more than thirty years previously, when Cornford was contributing poems to forgotten periodicals, valid in their time, such as the *Adel-*

phi, the *New Leader,* the *Chap-Book.* The vignettes of children recur: "a child's absolute gold"; "these small epitomes of sin"; "their concrete joys have such fragility." There is Cornford's abiding love of music, seen at its most epigrammatic in "The Guitarist Tunes Up":

With what attentive courtesy he bent
Over his instrument;
Not as a lordly conqueror who could
Command both wire and wood,
But as a man with a loved woman might,
Inquiring with delight
What slight essential things she had to say
Before they started, he and she, to play.

Yet this will not altogether stand comparison with the poem by Seamus Heaney, "Victorian Guitar," in which the speaker, almost erotically, sees the instrument "trim as a girl in stays" and suggests that the man who is playing it now is "giving it the time of its life."

The stage is cleared; the veteran poet is taking her well-deserved bow. Appropriately, the final poem in the book is "Exeunt Omnes":

For now both high and low at curtain-fall
Each playing perfectly his equal part
Convey the evanescence of us all.

Perhaps an augmented *Collected Poems* is overdue. It would not only include some of the better poems published after the 1954 edition but several of the better earlier poems which the fastidiousness of this poet caused to be left out.

Fastidious is the word: it would be all too easy to sum up the art of Cornford in terms that are overnegative. She is not obscure; she does not overstate; she keeps clear of the surrealism and exaggeration that were stylistic faults of the 1930s and 1940s; she waves no flags, makes no claim upon our political loyalties; never raises her voice; cannot be accused of sentimentality. The reality, however, is much more positive than this would suggest. That there is a concealed program here is reasonably certain. Cornford is at the head of a tendency, largely propelled by female writers, that has acted as something of a counterpoint to more spectacular efforts in verse. Long before the necessary spring-cleaning effected by the young male poets of the 1950s, such as Philip Larkin and Kingsley Amis, authors of her persuasion were writing poems that had shape, scene, plot—attributes which were not necessarily those of the apparently dominant modernist school.

Cornford could be reproached for what she did not do. There are no experiments in her work, not even what would have been reasonably tentative ones involving pararhyme, in which vowels at line-endings vary in agreement, or sprung verse, in which the basic meter is variegated by the addition of extra syllables. However, there are a surprising number of achieved poems; none the less achieved for being quiet in tone and sedate in phrasing—characteristics that would sound somewhat tame were it not for the presence of a redeeming wit. It is gratifying to find how frequently one can return to these poems. Behind the verbal assurance is a degree of sanity welcome in these intermittently preposterous times. She does not seem to have had a religious faith, but her sense of tradition, feeling for topography, and love of her surroundings do duty in its stead.

At a time when England is in danger of losing its sense of identity, owing to deprivation of a world role and failure to maintain equilibrium in a multi-cultural society, this unapologetically Cambridge figure holds her own. That is not only a question of remembering and indeed celebrating the past. It is a matter of bringing that sense of the past into the present; of recognizing that, amid the flux of war and development, certain inalienable values persist. This is true, not only of a way of life, but of a sense of language, and of what language can do for us.

SELECTED BIBLIOGRAPHY

I. COLLECTED WORKS. *Collected Poems* (London, 1954); *Selected Poems,* ed. by Jane Dowson (London, 1996).

II. POETRY. *Poems* (London, 1910); *Spring Morning* (London, 1915); *Death and the Princess: A Morality* (Cambridge, 1915); *Autumn Midnight* (London, 1923); *Different Days* (London, 1928); *Mountains and Molehills* (Cambridge, 1934); *Travelling Home* (London, 1948); *On a Calm Shore* (London, 1960).

III. POETRY TRANSLATIONS. *Poems from the Russian,* with Esther Polianowsky Salaman (London, 1943); Paul Éluard, *Le Dur Désir de Durer,* with Stephen Spender, illustrated by Marc Chagall (Philadelphia, 1950).

IV. BIBLIOGRAPHY. Alan Anderson, *A Bibliography of the Writings of Frances Cornford* (Edinburgh, 1975).

V. BIOGRAPHICAL STUDIES. Gwen Raverat, *Period Piece: A Cambridge Childhood* (London, 1952); Christopher Hassall, *Rupert Brooke: A Biography* (London, 1964); Jonathan Galassi, ed., *Understand the Weapon Understand the Wound: Selected Writings of John Cornford, with Some Letters of Frances Cornford* (Manchester, 1976); *The Neo-Pagans: Rupert Brooke and the Ordeal of Youth* (New York, 1985); Helen Fowler, chapter on Frances Cornford in *Cambridge Women: Twelve Portraits,* ed. by Edward Shils and Carmen Blacker (Cambridge, 1996); Hugh Cornford, "A Memoir," in Frances Cornford, *Selected Poems,* ed. by Jane Dowson (London, 1996).

VI. CRITICAL WORKS. Timothy Rogers, "Frances Cornford 1886–1960," *London Magazine* 32, nos. 5–6 (August/September 1992); Jane Dowson, "The Importance of Frances Cornford," in *Charleston Magazine* no. 9 (spring/summer 1994).

WILLIAM DUNBAR

(c. 1460–c. 1522)

Sandie Byrne

WE KNOW VERY little for certain about Dunbar's life. Like much of our information, the conjectural date of his birth, 1460–1461, is derived from the section of Dunbar's "The Flyting of Dunbar and Kennedie" attributed to fellow poet Walter Kennedy. Kennedy says that Dunbar was conceived during "the grete eclips" ("The Flyting of Dunbar and Kennedie" l. 489. [All references are to Bawcutt's edition]), which scholars have taken to be the eclipse of July 1460, though a number of others occurred during the period 1445–1465. He makes an attack on the history of the earls of Dunbar and March, which suggests that Dunbar was born into that house, perhaps a member of a junior branch. Scholars such as David Laing have suggested that he was born in East Lothian, the most prosperous region of Scotland at the time, to a family well-off enough to pay his university fees, possibly the grandson of Sir Patrick Dunbar of Biel or Bele, in East Lothian, and the son of another William. Certainly Dunbar was what we would now call a raging snob, and no democrat, as "To the King: Complane I Wald" shows, but he also satirized the corruption of the day that enabled the upper and merchant classes to live in luxury while the peasants starved in rags.

A William Dunbar is registered as a determinant (bachelor of arts) of St. Andrew's University in 1477, and as a licentiate (master of arts) in 1479. That Dunbar is often referred to as "Maister" suggests that he did have a master's degree, which would have entitled him to teach. His education would have been in the medieval curriculum based on the study of religious texts, Latin, grammar, and rhetoric, followed by logic and natural philosophy. As well as reading Aristotle's works on ethics, politics, and metaphysics, he would have studied more recent philosophers and theologians, medieval school men such as Albert the Great, St. Thomas Aquinas, Duns Scotus, and William of Ockham.

His movements between the years 1479 and 1500 are obscure. Some scholars have inferred from references in the poetry that he became a novice in the Franciscan order, others that he used the dress of a mendicant friar to travel and beg. Subsequently he joined the court of King James IV of Scotland as a clerk or envoy. He may have traveled on a diplomatic mission or missions to France and Scandinavia, for which he received a pension (annual salary) from 1500. In 1501, Dunbar traveled to England as part of a mission to negotiate a marriage settlement between James IV (reigned 1488–1513) and Margaret Tudor, daughter of Henry VII and sister of the future Henry VIII. It may have been during this visit that Dunbar composed "London thow art of Townys A per se" (though the attribution is not proven), and he may have been the "Rhymer of Scotland" to whom Henry VII gave £6 13s 4d as a reward. Sometime around March 1503, Dunbar was probably ordained as a priest, since, as was traditional, the king offered seven crowns (£4 14s) for his first mass at that time. He was not a professional or laureate poet, though he did produce poems commemorating state occasions that were possibly commissioned or semi-official. His employment at court was probably as a scribe and occasionally as an advocate, and his poems reveal familiarity with legal procedures and terms.

Dependent on patronage, Dunbar became a favorite of the queen but clearly felt that the king undervalued his talents, since several poems are humorous petitions for money, such as "Sanct Salvatour! Send Silver Sorrow" and "Schir at this feist of benefice."

He alludes to his unbeneficed state and allegedly increasing decrepitude in tones that range from the humorous to the scolding in this untitled poem (usually called "Schir, yit remember..."):

Schir, yit remember as befoir
How that my youthe is done forloir
In your service with pane and greiff.
Gud conscience cryis reward thairfoir:
Exces of thocht dois me mischeif.

(Sir, remember as in the past
How my youth has been lost
In your service with pain and grief.
Good conscience demands reward for this.
Excessive thought does me mischief.)
　　　　(Bawcutt, ed., *Selected Poems*, pp. 287–288)

His pension was raised from £10 to £20 in 1507, and quadrupled to £80 (with the stipulation that it would cease if he obtained a benefice of £100) in 1510. This compares well with the latest pension awarded to Geoffrey Chaucer, £20. The last mention of Dunbar in the court records is on 14 May 1513, but there is a gap in these records following the battle of Flodden (September 1513), in which the king died. Poems attributed to him in manuscripts of the time suggest that Dunbar may have survived into the reign of James V, but there is no evidence that he did.

Dunbar's reputation among his contemporaries was high. Gavin Douglas included him in the Court of the Muses in his *Palice of Honour,* and David Lindsay appreciated Dunbar's "language at large" in *Papyngo,* yet no full scholarly edition of his work appeared until 1834.

EDITIONS

We have no manuscripts in Dunbar's own hand. The only known printed source from Dunbar's lifetime is Chepman and Myllar (1508)—black-letter prints produced by Walter Chepman, an Edinburgh wood and textile merchant, and Androw Myllar, a printer, who were granted a patent by James IV. This includes "The Goldyn Targe," "The Flyting of Dunbar and Kennedie," "The Lament for the Makaris," and "The Ballade of Barnard Stewart." This edition is as close as we have to a copy text, since it may have been overseen by Dunbar himself. No other printed witnesses of

Dunbar's writing survive until Allan Ramsay published some poems from the Bannatyne MS in his *Ever Green* of 1724. (For other important manuscript sources, see the bibliography following this essay.)

Dunbar's canon is not fully established. Successive editors have attributed a varying number of poems to him, from James Kinsley's eighty-three, W. Mackay Mackenzie's eighty-four with nine attributions, to J. Schipper's ninety-one with a supplement of twelve, and John Small's ninety, with eleven attributions. Patricia Bawcutt includes eighty-four poems, including a number that are problematic. The chronology of the poems' composition also cannot be established, apart from occasional poems such as "The Thrissil and the Rois" (1503) and those collected by Chepman and Myllar (references to this edition often modernize the names to Chapman and Millar), which must have been written before 1508, though scholars have suggested dates for certain poems. J. W. Baxter, for example (in *William Dunbar: A Biographical Study*), makes a good case for a date near the beginning of James IV's reign for the "New Year's Gift to the King" and "The Wowing of the King quhen he wes in Dumfermeling" (pp. 50–51). Most of the titles by which the poems are known today were given by eighteenth- and nineteenth-century editors, and many come from the poems' first line (incipit) or refrain, though a few derive from early manuscript sources, for example, *The Goldyn Targe* and "The Flyting."

In his preface to *The Poems of William Dunbar,* James Kinsley remarks that he had hoped to produce an edition "less quaintly antique than the Victorian volumes of the Scottish Text Society and less slap-dash than Mackenzie's [of 1932]" (p. v). The Scottish Text Society was unsatisfactory to Kinsley, who found the transcriptions careless, the collation spasmodic, the commentary, though learned, garrulous and outmoded, and the glossary inadequate. He found Mackay Mackenzie's edition an improvement, but it was "an emergency job to meet urgent student needs" and rested on Scottish Text Society transcripts rather than manuscripts. Kinsley found the Dunbar corpus both a nightmare and a challenge: "these 6,000 lines have cost me more anguish, textually, than the 65,000 of Dryden's verse and critical prose. The demands made on the editor as exegetist and lexicographer have been as heavy" (p. vii).

Priscilla Bawcutt notes that the editor of Dunbar "is confronted with many problems and difficult decisions," not least because "many of the witnesses containing Dunbar's poems have suffered the destructive effects of time and neglect: the pages of the Maitland Folio are often damp-stained and difficult to read, and some texts in other prints and manuscripts are fragmentary, or dislocated" (*Poems of William Dunbar*, vol. 1, p. 10). Successive copyists and editors have altered Dunbar's verse through error, to "improve" the meter, to shorten the text, to modernize spelling, syntax, or vocabulary, to eradicate alliteration, or, in the case of "The Tabill of Confessioun," to fit Protestant orthodoxy. Dunbar was well aware of the dangers to literary integrity of unauthorized copying. In "Schir, I complayne off iniuris" (Sir, I complain of injuries), he refers to "That fulle" (fool) who has "dismemberit" (dismembered) his verses. Priscilla Bawcutt attempts to restore the meter and the diction in the most recent, thorough, and scholarly edition of the poems, *The Poems of William Dunbar* (1998). Bawcutt also edited the most useful and accessible single-volume selected edition, *William Dunbar, Selected Poems* (1996), which collects seventy of Dunbar's poems and from which quotations in this article, unless otherwise indicated, are taken.

INFLUENCE AND TRADITION

The terms most associated with Dunbar are "makar" and "Scottish Chaucerian." A makar is a poet: a craftsman who creates. Dunbar envisaged himself as the rightful inheritor of a long line of Scottish makars, such as Robert Henryson and John Holland but disassociates himself from the Gaelic Bardic tradition: "Bot wondir laith wer I to be ane baird," "I was reluctant to be a bard" ("The Flyting," p. 264). Like Dunbar, many of his contemporaries acknowledged a debt to Geoffrey Chaucer whom Dunbar (in *The Goldyn Targe*, p. 244) called the "rose of rethoris all" and "of makaris the triumph riall" (rose of rhetoric and of makers worthy of royal honors). The first major Scottish poem in Chaucerian style is *The Kingis Quhair*, attributed to James I of Scotland and said to have been composed during the king's long imprisonment in England. Scottish Chaucerians of the second wave include Robert Henryson (1450–c.1505) and Gavin Douglas (1476–1522), best known for his translation of *The Aeneid*. The playwright Sir David Lyndsay (c.1486–1555) could also be included. Although Chaucer's influence is important, in some ways Dunbar more closely resembles François Villon, and the medieval goliardic or *clerici vagantes* tradition.

The Scottish Chaucerians were admirers of Chaucer but not slavish imitators. Chaucer's influence on Dunbar is sometimes direct, but the two poets often develop themes and forms from common sources—French, Italian, and Latin traditions to which Dunbar often gives a fresh slant. His courtly poetry uses a variant of the traditional "rhyme royal" (ten syllables to a line, seven lines, rhyming *ababbcc*) and lengthens it to nine lines. He produces the expected decorative flourishes but is more sparing than his predecessors. He introduces colloquial Scots words to undercut the formality, and north European weather to counteract the balmy climes of courtly poetry, interspersing conventional tropes with vivid images. He exploits the lyric stanzas of the Provençal troubadour tradition but brings his own mastery of the refrain, whether comic, assertive, or haunting. His use of allegory comes from Romance and stories of *amour courtois* (courtly love) such as the important *Roman de la Rose*, and his aureate poems (that is, written in highly decorated language) and heraldic symbolism come from the French school known as *Les Grands Rhetoriqueurs*. The more robust stories, however, owe more to the earthier tradition of the *fabliaux* (traditional fables). The satires and complaints are of course homoletic and didactic, like the sermons Dunbar may have preached, and many of these poems convey a sense of the preacher's voice: exhorting, scolding, dramatic. At another extreme, "This Lang Lentern Makis me Lene" resembles a goliardic drinking song. As Tom Scott says, "the warp and weft of medieval life not merely are present in all his work . . . they are, in fact, its subject-matter" (Scott, p. 37).

Like Chaucer, Dunbar can delight in the rambunctious, licentious, or even vulgar, but poems such as *Tretis of the Tua Mariit Wemen and the Wedo* show that he had a wide knowledge of the peccadilloes of humankind and a Chaucerian delight in and sympathy for their follies and absurdities. This is quite different from the attitude toward corruption evident in the more serious satirical poems, which is anything but accepting and suggests that Dunbar could have had some sympathy with the position of women in his time.

While the aureate diction and rhyme schemes come from the Romance and courtly traditions, his use of alliteration and caesura (a break in the line) ultimately come from Teutonic, Old English poetry, though these features persisted into Middle English poetry in texts such as the West Midlands dialect poem *Sir Gawain and the Green Knight,* and *Piers Plowman.* In his *Dunbar: A Critical Exposition of the Poems,* Tom Scott shows how the Old English and Romantic metric systems are blended in Dunbar's writing.

Doun throu the ryce // a ryuir ran wyth stremys
So lustily agayn thai lykand lemys
That all the lake as lamp did leme of licht

(Down through the branches a river ran with streams
So lustily facing those pleasing rays of light
That all the lake like a lamp gleamed with light.)
(*The Goldyn Targe, Selected Poems,* p. 185)

STYLE AND SUBJECT MATTER

In his *English Literature in the Sixteenth Century,* C. S. Lewis wrote of Dunbar:

> when you are in the mood for it, his poetry has a sweep and volume of sound and an assured virility which (while the mood lasts) makes most other poets seem a little faint and tentative and half-

hearted. If you like half-tones and nuances you will not enjoy Dunbar; he will deafen you.

(p. 98)

Dunbar's preferred term for his own writings was "ballattis," which usually connoted short, lyric, secular poems. Even his longer works are shorter than the contemporary norm; the dream poem *The Goldyn Targe* is, at 27,911 words, shorter than was usual, and his longest poem, *Tretis of the Tua Mariit Wemen and the Wedo,* is only 53,011. He was a virtuoso with an enormously wide range, able to write on almost any subject and in any mood, from his headache to a technical treatise on penance; from a devout expression of faith to a burlesque satire. Although the tone and style of his writing is adjusted to fit its matter, and his diction is often colloquial and even profane, he also employs the aureate language considered appropriate for courtly poetry during the later Middle Ages. Dunbar's language is colloquial Middle Scots with a lexicon augmented by Latin and French. This is the language of lowland Scotland, and is more closely related to that of contemporary Northern England than to the Gaelic (or Erse) spoken by Highland Scots.

Dunbar experimented with many genres: beast fable, dream, elegy, epistle, panegyric, and satire. His dream poems are characteristically varied: the most famous is *The Goldyn Targe,* a complex dream poem of courtly allegory in which love triumphs over reason; another is a vision of the Crucifixion in the tradition of the Mystery plays; and several others, grotesque in style and satirical in purpose, might better be described as nightmares. Dunbar is also an accomplished metrist. *Tretis of the Tua Mariit Wemen and the Wedo* shows his mastery of the by then old-fashioned form of unrhymed alliterative verse, but he also employs a variety of stanzas, ranging from rhyme royal to the popular carol. In his essay "Dunbar's Metrical Technique," J. Derrick McClure asserts:

> If the roll-call of Scotland's poets contains one figure who has, by universal consent, earned the epithet "virtuoso," he is William Dunbar. . . . Dunbar stands supreme for his mastery in the handling of words: he has, perhaps, equals in emotional

intensity and in descriptive and evocative power, and superiors in intellectual profundity, human sympathy and capacity for sustained efforts; but no one who matches and very few who can even approach him in sheer technical skill.

(in Mapstone, ed., "*The Nobill Poyet,*" p. 150)

While many of the poems are conventional exercises in popular forms, others experiment with those forms, or arise from commissions, or are responses to people and occasions. Poets in Dunbar's time performed a social function; they ornamented a court and showed the taste and cultivation of its patron, and they provided entertainment (*gam*) through jests (*bourdes*) as well as occasional poetry, such as elegies and panagyrics, to mark festivals and important events. He exhibits a strong sense of himself as a makar and as an artist whose work was important. His chief complaint about his headache is not that it is painful, but that it made composition difficult, and in "Schir, I complane of injuris" (p. 259) he expresses outrage at the mutilating of his meter by a "refing sonne of rakyng Muris" (a thieving son of roaming Mure). He seems to have been granted considerable license, for a number of poems mock not only recognizable members of the court but the king himself. There may, however, have been limits to the license; perhaps the influence of the clergy whom Dunbar satirizes so mercilessly prevailed upon the king to deny Dunbar the benefice he craved. Dunbar's work is considered unusually individual for his time, revealing details of his personal appearance, experience, and feelings. The "I" in his poetry is not always a character, however, but, especially in the didactic works, more a mouthpiece of conventional pieties. In other poems, such as "In to thir dirk and drublie days" and "I that in heill wes" (conventionally given the title "The Lament for the Makaris"), we can find poignant glimpses of a real personality. That personality had both its light and dark sides: iconoclastic and with a keen eye for the ridiculous, Dunbar also broods on mortality and the corruption of human nature, and the energy of his quick-fire phrases and rapid pacing can seem demoniac.

One of his earliest known poems, the courtly allegory *The Thrissill and the Rois,* commemorates the marriage of James IV and Margaret Tudor in August 1503. The form, rhyme royal, comes from a French tradition, *chant-royal,* used by Chaucer and by James I of Scotland in his *Kingis Quair.* As befits a poem concerning an alliance between royal houses, the poem employs an aureate diction and heraldic symbolism, in which Margaret is represented by the rose "of cullour reid and quhyt," the Tudor rose, and James by the thistle of Scotland. The king is also given emblems of his three roles, governor (lion), lawgiver (eagle), and war leader (thistle). Both theme and style are stylized and conventional. The bridal pair adopt the roles of *dame* (highborn lady) and *ami* (languishing lover) of *amour courtois,* and the language lacks the vivacity and realism of other poems, but Dunbar's idiosyncratic Scots voice can occasionally be heard. Clearly poets were allowed some degree of license at the Scottish court, since Dunbar almost browbeats the king in his demands for virtuous, continent behavior from the royal groom.

> And, sen thow art a king, thow be discreit.
>   Herb without vertew hald nocht of sic pryce
> As herb of vertew and of odor sweit,
>   And lat no nettil vyle, and full of vyce,
>   Hir fallow to the gudly flour delyce;
>   Nor latt no wyld weid, full of churlichness
>   Compair hir till the lilleis nobilnes.

> (And since thou art a king, see thou be discreet;
> A herb without virtue hold not of such price
> As herb of virtue and of odour sweet;
> And let no vile nettle, full of vice,
> Follow the godly fleur-de-lys
> Nor let wild weed, full of churlishness
> Be compared to the nobility of that lily.)

(ll. 134–140, p. 206)

A number of poems are concerned with festive events of James's reign, such as the Tournament of the Black Lady (1507), the arrival of the French envoy Bernard Stewart in 1508, and the queen's visit to Aberdeen in 1511. The court of James IV was sophisticated and cosmopolitan, the home of artists and scholars such as John

Major, with powerful links to France and northern Europe (though the king himself appears to have been more interested in doctors and alchemists than in poets). But it was also a place of suspicion, envy, and intrigue, satirized by Dunbar, and it was surrounded by poverty, disease, and squalor among the poor and corruption among the rich. Dunbar's critique of his times is wide-ranging, and not even the king is spared. "Renounce thy God" is an excoriating attack on the cheating and hypocrisy that Dunbar finds in the guilds; "Sic Tydingis Hard I at the Sessioun" focuses on the law courts; "Thir Lady is Fair" is about women who exchange sexual favors for a desired judgment; "A General Satyre" ranges across all classes of society, finding corruption everywhere. "Eftir Geving I Speik of Taking" complains that clerics care nothing for the souls of the poor but only for the money to be made from them; that merchants care for nothing but profit; that the barons rob the poor of their harvest, making them beggars; and that there is no redress from the law. "Discretioun in Taking" similarly complains that only the poor are condemned for criminal acts, while the rich prosper.

Grit men for taking and oppressioun
Ar sett full famous at the Sessioun,
Quhair small takaris ar hangit hie,
Schamit for evir and thair successioun:
In taking sowld descretioun be.

(Great men for thieving and oppression
Become famous in the courts' Session
Where petty thieves are hanged,
Shamed for ever and their succession:
There should in taking be discretion.)
(ll. 36–49, in Bawcutt, *Poems of William Dunbar,* vol. 1, p. 148)

"Schir, Ye have mony Servitouris" complains that among those whom the king rewards for their services, whether deserving (lawyers, courtiers, carpenters, doctors, philosophers) or undeserving (flatterers, boasters, and hangers-on), there is a notable omission: Dunbar. When he sees himself overlooked and these undeserving rewarded, "Than on this fals warld I cry fy" (l. 68, *Selected*

Poems, p. 285). He even dares to upbraid the king for his wenching among the wives and daughters of his subjects, in "This Hinder Nicht in Dunfermeling."

The poem known as "Dunbar at Oxinfurde" (the title was given by the editors of the Maitland text, who conjectured that Dunbar visited Oxford while on the diplomatic mission to England in 1501) expresses contemporary moral conventions. Just as medieval scholars habitually cited "authorities," established canonical thinkers and writers, as exemplars of intellectual wisdom, so theologians cited canonical moral and doctrinal texts, primarily the Bible, as mirrors of spiritual wisdom, and distinguished between the two. The former, "waurdly wissdome," is "accumilacioune of honoris, dignities, riches, gud fortoune and happiness, and jt js oftymes na wissdome bot foly, *quia Sapienca huius mundi stulticia est apud deum*" (accumulation of honors, dignities, riches, good fortune, and happiness, and is often not wisdom but folly). Real wisdom is "gotten throu gud lif & clene consciens, for the [thorn] devin sapiens sais: *Jn animan maliuolam non introibo neque jn corpore subdito peccatis,*" (gotten through a good life and clean conscience, for the devine wisdom says) (in Johannes de Irlandia, *The Meroure of Wyssdome,* Scottish Text Society 12, Edinburgh, 1926; quoted in Ross, *William Dunbar,* pp. 130–131). Dunbar's poem exhorts those in orders to find true wisdom, and become mirrors to the rest of society.

Quhairfoir ye clarkis grittest off constance,
  Fullest of science and off knawlegeing,
To us be myrrouris in your governance
  And in owr darknes be lamps in schyining,
  Or than in frustrar is your lang leirning.
Giff to your sawis your deidis contrair be,
  Your maist accusar is your awin cunning.
A paralus seiknes is vane prosperite.

(Wherefore the clerks of greatest devotion [to learning],
Fullest of science and of erudition
Are mirrors to us in our self-governance
And in our darkness are lamps shining
Your long learning is in vain
If your deeds are contrary to your sayings

Your greatest accuser is your own cunning.
A perilous sickness is vain prosperity.)
(ll. 16–24, Selected Poems, p. 332)

The makar should be a mirror and a lamp, a penetrating light that illuminates the darkness and corruption of his world, and the provider of moral exemplars. Dunbar did not always write in this ideal mode, however. "On His Heid-Ake," describing a commonplace experience with wry humor, gives twenty-first-century readers an imaginative link to this poet remote in time:

My heid did yak zester-nicht,
This day to mak that I na micht.
So sair the magryme dois me menyie,
Perseing my brow as ony ganyie
That scant I luik may on the licht.

And now, schir, laitlie, efter mes,
To dyt thocht I begowthe to dres,
The sentence lay full evill till find,
Unsleipit in my heid behind,
Dullit in dulnes and distress.

Full oft at morrow I upryse,
Quhen that my curage sleipeing lyis,
For mirth, for mestrallie and play,
For din nor danceing nor deray,
It will nocht walkin me no wise.

(My head did ache yester-night
So that today I could not write.
So sore the migraine hurt me,
Piercing my brow like any dart
That barely can I look on light.

And now, sire, not long since, after mass,
To compose I thought to make ready.
But the topic lay full difficult to get out,
I having not slept, from the back of my head,
Made dull in gloominess and distress.

Often in the morning I arise,
When my creativity sleeping lies,
Not mirth, nor minstrelsy, nor play,
Noise, nor dancing, nor revelry,
Will not awaken me, no way.)

(pp. 150–151)

The Goldyn Targe, an allegorical poem containing brilliant imagery in aureate language, and

The Tretis of the Tua Mariit Wemen and the Wedo, an uninhibited, bawdy debate by three women on the nature of marriage, written in unrhymed alliterative verse, display two extremes of Dunbar's courtly art. Both use the framing device of an eavesdropper and/or voyeur common in *chanson d'aventure* poems, whose significance for contemporary audiences Helen Phillips explores in her essay "Frames and Narrators in Chaucerian Poetry":

> The detached narrator may hide: in the *Belle Dame* watching from behind a trellis, in Dunbar's Goldyn Targe from behind leaves . . . These hiding-places are the border between heterodiegetic and homodiegetic narrative levels, a border which the narrators of framed narrative often cross. Such devices, giving the narrator temporarily an external standpoint, reflect the sense in which the medieval first-person narrator (originating in an age of oral performance of texts) frequently represents an aspect of the mode of reception: a part written for the performer of the poem. Long into a period when reading was taking over from oral performance, Chaucerian frames often dramatize this ancient detachment of the narrator-presenter from the narrative: the unsought dream, the involuntary overhearing, the aimless wandering and so on.
>
> (in Cooper and Mapstone, eds., p. 80)

The language is lapidary to the extent that the lexical field of the man-made and highly wrought extends even to descriptions of nature, which seems to have come from a jeweler's shop:

The cristall air, the sapher firmament,
The ruby skyes of the orient,
Kest beriall bemes on emerant bewis grene;
The rosy garth depaynt and redolent
With purpur, azure, gold, and goulis gent

(The crystal air, the sapphire firmament,
The ruby skies of the orient,
Cast beryl beams on emerald green boughs;
The rosy field painted and redolent
With purple, azure, gold, and beautiful reds)

(ll. 36–40, p. 234)

Tom Scott suggests that *The Goldyn Targe* is a parody of the *amour courtois* tradition—using the conventional aureate style and concerned with the traditional subject, but also interrogating the tradition and demonstrating its incompatibility with reason (pp. 40–41). The poem is in seven parts, of which the first is a prologue in five stanzas setting the scene in strongly visual terms. Scott describes the aureate writing ("goldyn candill matutyne"; "stern of day [sun]") as "rather overlarded." He finds the passage typical of *amour courtois,* but "the sheer realism of the description is at odds with that tired convention: even the crystal tears of 'Aurora,' hanging on the boughs as 'Phoebus' as she parts, take on a comparative concreteness in the setting" (p. 41). The action is developed over the next seven stanzas, as the poet falls asleep and dreams of the approach of a ship. From the ship disembark a hundred beautiful ladies, all emblematic figures: goddesses, nymphs, and personifications, among them Nature, Venus, Aurora, Flora, Juno, Proserpina, Diana, Clio, Thetis, Pallas and Minerva (two names for the same divinity), Fortune and Lucina (another name for Diana), and Apollo (a god). Scott remarks: "Dunbar's knowledge of classical mythology is either very shaky or he is pulling our legs" (p. 42). In the ladies' train, described in a two-stanza third section, is a court composed of Cupid, Mars, Saturn, Mercury, Priapus, Phanus, Janus, Neptune, Bacchus, and Pluto.

In the main section of the poem, comprising eleven stanzas, Venus discovers the hidden poet and sends her archers against him. Attacked by Beauty, Fair Behaving, Fine Portraiture, Pleasance, he is defended by Reason with her shield of spotless gold, the "targe" of the title. Tender Youth, Green Innocence, Shameful Abasement, Dread, and Humble Obedience come to him, but not with violence. Then Sweet Womanhood assaults him with her weaponry, Nurture, Good Fame, Continence, Patience, Discretion, Steadfastness, and Soberness. But again, Reason defends the poet. The next wave of attack comes from High Degree, with her allies Estate, Dignity, Honour, and so on, but again, Reason's shield holds them off. At this, Venus calls upon Dissimulation, Presence, Fair Saying, and Cherishing. When Presence throws a powder into Reason's eyes, he staggers, and the poet is wounded. Beauty takes him prisoner and delivers him to Hevynesse. Eolus' bugle, however, brings a blast of cold wind, and knowledge of reality.

The fifth section, also of two stanzas, describes the laying waste of the fair garden by the cold wind, the retreat of the ladies to their ship, and its departure. The firing of the departing ship's guns wakes the poet from his dream and leads into the sixth section, which is a beautiful stanza describing the reality of a lovely May morning. The final section (described by Scott as "unnecessary and unconvincing," [p. 43]) is a coda in which the poet addresses his poetic predecessors Chaucer, Gower, and Lydgate, in flattering terms, and bids his own work be humble and submissive before such men of learning.

The poem deals in oppositions: between reality and dream, concrete and ideal/abstract, sanity and insanity. The goldyn targe (shield) of reason is Dunbar's defense against the dream or nightmare and the insanity. It is a statement of allegiance to a new kind of poetry, middle-class and realist, which, while not entirely replacing the old upper-class allegorical Romance, will be Dunbar's preferred mode of writing in the future.

The Tretis of Tua Mariitt Wemen and the Wedo also uses the *chanson d'adventure* form of an overheard conversation, opening with a delightful description of Midsummer Eve. Wandering through a conventional idealized garden after midnight on Midsummer's Eve, listening to the birds and enjoying the scent of flowers, the poet overhears three ladies conversing in an arbor. He conceals himself and listens, as the wine sinks lower in the cups and the talk becomes more and more unguarded. The widow asks the two married women if they are happy in their married lives: If they had the chance again, would they choose differently? Abruptly the tone changes, and those listeners lulled into expecting a courtly debate receive a rude shock. The poem is another parody, and the description of the women, stylized and idealized, is a parody of the conventional descriptions of unattainable high-born women who serve as the focus of unrequited courtly love. These women, however, are all too attainable. The formal courtly *chanson d'aventure* becomes a *chanson de mal mariée,* that is, a bawdy song of bad marriage. The expected formal debate about the nature of love becomes a forthright and lewd treatise on deceit. The first wife answers:

It that ye call the blist band that bindis so fast
Is bair of blis and bailfull and greit barrat wirkis.
Ye speir, had I fre chois, gif I wald cheis bettir?
Chenyeis ay ar to eschew and changeis ar sweit.

(This so-called blessed band that binds so fast
Is without joy and wretched and causes great strife
You ask, had I free choice if I would choose better?
Chains are to be avoided and changes are sweet.)

(ll. 50–53, p. 37)

She would prefer to be like the birds, which do not marry for life, but can choose a new mate each year. If she had the chance:

Than suld I cast me to keik in kirk and in markat
And all the cuntre about, kyngis court and uther,
Quhair I ane galland micht get aganis the nixt yeir
For to perfurneis furth the werk quhen failyeit the
  tother.

(Then should I look about me in church and market
All the country around; king's court and elsewhere,
Where I might get a gallant against the next year
To perform the work when the other failed.)

(ll. 81–84, p. 38)

Her husband (pp. 89–93) is "ane wallidrag, ane worme, ane auld wobat carle" (a slob, a worm, an old churl of a caterpillar); "Ane skabbit scarth" (a scabby monster, with disgusting habits); "To see him scart his awin skyn grit scunner" (To see him scratch his own skin is very disgusting). His bristly skin scours her cheek "with his hard hurcheone scyn sa heklis he my chekis" ("hurcheone" meaning "hedgehog"). Referring to him as "larbar" (impotent) and "carybald" (monstrous), she describes how she makes him promise her expensive gifts before she will grant him any favors.

The second wife is glad to be able to unburden herself of a "ragment fra rute of my hert,' a catalog of heartfelt grievances. She hates her husband for consorting with prostitutes:

My husband wes a hur maister, the hugeast in erd,
Tharfor I hait him with my hert, sa help me our Lord.

(My husband was a whore-master, the biggest on
  earth,
Therefore I hate him with all my heart, so help me
  Our Lord.)

(ll. 168–170, p. 42)

His dissipation has aged him prematurely (l. 176): "His lume is waxit larbar and lyis in to swoune" (His tool has grown weak and lies in a swoon). If she were given the chance to choose again, she would (l. 209, p. 44) "haif a fresch feir to fang in myn armys" (have a fresh mate to take in my arms).

The widow then advises the younger women to profit by her example, and learn to live a double life (l. 263): "Be dragonis baith and dowis ay in double forme" (Be both dragons and doves in double form). While she kept her first, old, husband sweet "With kissing and clapping" (l. 283), she also kept "a lufsummar leid my lust for to slokyn" (a good-looking lad to slake my lust). She managed her second husband, a wealthy merchant, by constantly reminding him of the difference between them socially. Now that he is dead, she enjoys an untrammeled life:

Deid is now that dyvour and dollin in erd
With him deit all my dule and drery thoghtis.

(Dead is now that bankrupt and buried in earth
With him died all my sad and dreary thoughts.)

(ll. 410–411, p. 52)

But she maintains a front of a grieving widow, carrying a sponge in order to wet her cheeks as if with tears. After a night of carousal, the ladies go home, and the poet immediately records their conversation. Finally, he addresses his audience to ask a pointed question:

Ye auditoris most honorable, that eris has gevin
Onto this uncouth aventur, quhilk airly me happinit,
Of thir thre wantoun wiffis, that I haif written heir,
Quhilk wald ye waill to your wif, gif ye suld wed
  one?

(You most distinguished auditors who have given your
  ears
To this extraordinary adventure which happened to me
  early one day,

Of the three wanton wives that I have written about here,
Which would you choose to be your wife, if you had to wed one?)

(ll. 527–531, p. 57)

Felicity Riddy points out that *The Tua Marriit Wemen and the Wedo* is an inversion of a common medieval theme, the harlot's progress.

> The harlot's progress, in which progression is inevitably downwards, must have been one among several narratives about female sexuality available in the fifteenth century; its obverse is the story of the harlot's success which underlies Dunbar's *Tretis of the Tua Mariit Wemen and the Wedo*. The narrative of ruin lurks in the mid-fifteenth-century advice poem "Thewis of Gud Women," in which young girls are warned that painting the face and keeping bad company are "giglotrye," the first step on the path to the loss of all social identity.
>
> ("Henryson's Testament of Cresseid," in Cooper and Mapstone, p. 241)

In the case of Dunbar's women, their giglotrye assures them a social identity.

We should not assume that Dunbar condemns the women, or even, as A. D. Hope points out, that they are presented as realistic portraits. With their uniform appearance in green mantles over green kirtles, their hair, in defiance of convention, loose, they could be fays or other traditional figures. They are surrounded by a hawthorn hedge, and holly, both associated with the fairies. They appear as if from nowhere in the middle of their feast. Most significantly, the setting of their conversation on Midsummer's Eve, associated with pagan beliefs and more recent superstitions, could mark the poet's experience as a dream of an Otherworld (Hope, pp. 13–23).

Dunbar's range is equally wide in his occasional poems. The fierce invective of satirical pieces such as the "General Satyre," "Tidings from the Sessioun," and "To the Merchants of Edinburgh" seems to express passionate outrage, while "The Ballad of Kynd Kittok" is more comic in tone and theme. "Fasternis Eve in Hell" is fantastical in language and hurly-burly in pace. The devil Mahound (Mahommet) summons unshriven sinners to a *danse macabre* with his fiends and the seven deadly sins. He calls for Highlanders to dance a fling, but the Scots make such a terrible noise that not even the devil can stand it.

Than cryd Mahound for heleand padyane.
Syne ran a feynd to feche Makfadyane,
  Far northwart in a nuke.
Be he the correnoch had done schout
Erschemen so gadderit him abowt,
  In hell grit rowme thay tuke.
Thae tarmegantis with tag and tatter
Full lowd in Ersche begowth to clatter
  And rowp lyk revin and ruke.
The devil sa devit we with thair yell
That in the deepest pot of hell
  He smorit thame with suke.

(The Mahomet cried for a Highland entertainment.
A fiend ran to fetch MacFadean,
  Far northwards in a nook.
After the loud outcry was done
Highlanders gathered about him,
  They took up a lot of space in Hell.
Those devils in rags and tatters
Began to chatter full loudly in [Scots] Gaelic
  And croaked like ravens and rooks.
The devil was so deafened by their yell
That in the deepest pit of hell
  He smothered them with smoke.)

(ll.100–120, pp. 184–185)

"The Flyting of Dunbar and Kennedie" is a wonderful example of the Scots tradition of "flyting," a ritualized exchange of insults in ever more hyperbolic and scurrilous invective. Although the form is related to the Provençal *tenson,* Dunbar uses it to exploit to the full the resources of Middle Scots. His opponent is fellow Makar Walter Kennedy, and their poetic contest is conducted according to the strict ritualized forms of the duel. The first poem in the series is addressed to Dunbar's "second," John Ross, inviting him to the flyting and adverting to Kennedy's alleged offence: outrageous self-praise. As second, Ross was clearly intended to convey this to the adversary as a challenge in the manner of the flung glove. Kennedy replies in three stanzas of escalating abuse and threat. Preliminary shots having been fired, each opponent launches a sustained attack in a lengthy section. Kennedy derides Dunbar's lack of height; Dunbar, Kennedy's gauntness; Dunbar suggests that Kennedy's ancestry is Irish and his background rude and rustic (Highland), while Dunbar's own is of the "Inglis" area (the term "Scottish" was not applied to the speech of Lowland Scotland until the 1490s). Kennedy asserts that Dunbar's scholarship is as negligible as his height and as threadbare as his gown (though the significance of "Hillhouse" is unclear):

Maunch muttoun, byt buttoun, peilit gluttoun, air to Hilhous,
Rank beggar, ostir-dregar, flay-fleggar in the flet.
Chittirlilling, ruch rilling, lik-schilling in the milhous,
Baird rehator, theif of nator, fals tratour, feyindis gett.

Maggoty mutton, bite-button, destitute glutton, heir to Hillhouse
Rank beggar, oyster-dredger, flea-chaser in the hall.
Pig's innards, rough rilling-wearer, licker of husks in the mill
Villainous bard, thief by nature, false traitor, fiend begot.

(ll. 241–243, p. 276)

The climax of Dunbar's sections is described by Baildon (p. 259) as "a miracle of literary Billingsgate." In metrics no less than in lexicon it is a bravura display. Each line has both end-rhyme and three internal rhymes, so that each eight-line stanza contains thirty-two rhyme words, as well as alliterating words.

Perhaps Dunbar's most touching poem is his "Lament for the Makaris," though, as with other of his poems, the title was bestowed by a later (eighteenth-century) editor. Dunbar is said to have written it during a time of sickness, when his mortality was starkly clear to him. A meditation on the transitory nature of life and on death as leveler gives way to the naming of individuals, a roll-call of twenty-three departed poets, twenty of them Scots, which shows that Dunbar placed himself within a long tradition of Makars. A number of those named are now forgotten, or not known as poets, but among those whom history has remembered are Andrew Wyntoun, author of a verse chronicle of Scottish history; "Stobo" (John Reid); John Barbour, who composed *The Bruce*; as well as Blind Harry, the author of *Wallace*; Robert Henryson; and Dunbar's flyting partner, Walter Kennedy (here described affectionately as "Gud Maister"). The form of the poem is the old French *kyriell*, four-line stanzas (twenty-five of them, making a total of 100 lines), rhyming in couplets with a refrain. The liturgical Latin *Timor mortis conturbat me* means "the fear of death crowds in on me," "conturbat" having associations of confusion, oppression, and distraction. It resonates like a knell, punctuating Dunbar's enumeration of his "brothers" whom death has claimed, and underlining his unspoken knowledge that he will be next.

I that in heill wes and gladnes
Am trublit now with gret seiknes,
And feblit with infermite:
  Timor mortis conturbat me.

Our plesance heir is all vane glory,
This fals world is bot transitory,
The flesche is brukle, the Fend is sle:
  Timor mortis conturbat me.

(I that in health was and gladness
Am troubled now with great sickness
And enfeebled with infirmity:
  The fear of death oppresses me.

Our pleasure here is all vainglory,
This false world is but transitory
The flesh is frail, the fiend is sly
  The fear of death oppresses me.)

...

He has done petuouslie devour,
The noble Chaucer, of makaris flour,
The monk of Bery, and Gower, all thre;
Timor mortis conturbat me.

(Death has piteously devoured
Noble Chaucer, of makers the flower,
The Monk of Bury (Lydgate), and Gower, all three;
  The fear of death oppresses me.)

...

Sen he hes all my brether tane
He will nocht lat me lif alane;
On forse I man his nyxt pray be:
  Timor mortis conturbat me.

Sen for the deid remeid is none,
Best is that we for dede dispone,
Eftir our deid that lif may we:
Timor mortis conturbat me.

(Since he has all my brethren taken
He will not let me live alone;
Of necessity I must his next prey be
The fear of death oppresses me.

Since for this death there is no remedy
Best is that we for death are disposed
That after our death we may live eternally
The fear of death oppresses me.)
(ll. 1–8, 49–52, 93–100; pp. 106, 108, 110)

DEVOTIONAL VERSE

Much of Dunbar's religious poetry is macaronic, in other words, it mixes vernacular and Latin phrases. A poem on the Nativity takes as its title the well-known Latin phrase *Et Nobis Puer Natus Est* (The Noble Child is Born), while an Easter poem whose refrain is the Latin *Surrexit dominus de sepulchro* (The Lord is risen from the tomb) has the arrestingly colloquial opening line: "Done is a battell on the dragon blak." The latter depicts Christ's descent into hell to wrestle with the devil for the souls of those born before his coming as a heroic struggle between man's champion, Christ, and a serpent or dragon, the devil, and it becomes a triumphal hymn of victory.

The fo is chasit, the battell is done ceis,
The presone brokin, the jevellouris fleit and flemit,
The weir is gon, confermit is the peis,
The fetteris lowsit and the dungeoun temit,
The ransoun maid, the presoneris redemit,
The feild is win, ourcumin is the fo,
Dispulit of the tresur that he yemit:
Surrexit dominus de sepulchro.

(The foe is chased, the battle is ceased,
The prison broken, the gaolers fled and banished,
The war is gone, the peace is confirmed,
The fetters loosed, and the dungeons emptied,
The field is won, the foe is overcome,
Despoiled of the treasure that he held:
Risen is the Lord from the tomb.)
(ll. 33–40, p. 79)

"Hale, sterne superne," also known as "Ane Ballat of Our Lady," is described by Kinsley as "one of Dunbar's most accomplished pieces of virtuosity" (p. 225). The aureate diction and internal rhymes are characteristic of medieval Marian poetry, and Dunbar calls upon a long-established lexicon of Marian emblems derived from biblical and other traditional sources. Douglas Gray (in "'Hale, sterne superne' and Its Literary Background") follows Priscilla Bawcutt in finding models for the lexical and rhyme patterns of the poem in Latin hymns. He also finds another element in the Latin tradition relevant to "Hale, sterne superne," Books of Hours:

> those immensely popular personal prayer books (in which the Little office of the Virgin Mary—itself a most illuminating background to Dunbar's poem—is central) contain a number of prose prayers to the Virgin which list her titles in an ecstatic rhythmical style. . . . Such prayers easily become a kind of litany. . . . The heavily repetitive style, liturgical in origin, has a striking aural effect, and the repetition has cumulative force of a kind that was popular in late medieval rhetorical writing.
>
> (in Mapstone, *The Nobill Poyet,* pp. 200–201)

The structure of the poem is complex, using triple internal rhyme and alliteration round an *Ave Maria, gracia plena* anaphora (a figure in rhetoric, when the same word or words are repeated at the beginning of two or more succeeding verses or clauses of a sentence) at line 9 of each of the seven stanzas. Alliteration is marked by italics, internal rhyme by bold, and lower-case letters show the rhyme-scheme:

*H*ale, *s*terne *s*uperne; *h*ale, in e**terne**	*a*
In Godis sicht for to schyne;	*b*
Lu**cerne** in *d*erne for to *d*is**cerne**	*a*
Be *g*lory and *g*race devyne;	*b*
Hodi**erne**, mod**ern**, sempit**ern**	*a*
Angelicall regyne:	*b*
Our **tern** inf**erne** for to disp**ern**	*a*
Help, *r*ialest *r*osyne.	*b*
Ave Maria, gracia plena:	[unrhymed anaphora]
Hail, *f*resche *f*loure *f*emynyne:	b
Yerne, us gub**erne**, virgin mat**ern**	a
Of *r*euth baith *r*ute and *r*yne.	b

(Hail, star on high; hail, in eternity
  Shining in God's sight
Lantern in darkness by which we see
  By glory and grace divine;
For the present, today, for ever
  Of the angels queen:
To drive away our infernal gloom,
  Help, most royal rose.
Hail Mary, full of grace:
  Hail, fresh flower of femininity:
Have compassion, govern us, virgin mother
  Of pity both root and rind [the perfect example of
  pity.])

(p. 86)

Gray observes that we are conscious of the poem's indebtedness to the tradition of Marian poetry that prizes intricate ornament, rhetorical display, and elaborate musical patterns, but asserts that "somehow even the closest parallels do not seem to have Dunbar's sustained dynamic force and energy" (p. 207). He asks what really distinguishes the poem from the tradition, and finds an imaginative handling of the traditional matter, and an imaginative control. The unrhymed Latin salutation forms a kernel of each stanza and of the poem.

> The striking difference in the rhythm gives the sense of a pause, and ensures that the aural pattern is not a simple one. This is supported by the variation in the diction, with . . . the alternation of "aureate" and simpler common words. . . . The spectacular opening lines culminate in a petition embodied in the simple monosyllable "helpe," making them a fine intricate late medieval piece of verbal music.
>
> (p. 207)

Although the poem does not develop an argument through logical stages, it has a devotional and emotional structure. Gray finds interwoven patterns of imagery and ideas, especially imagery associated with light and with flowers, which are announced in the first stanza and found in almost every subsequent one. In the third stanza, the imagery of lines 1 and 2 ("bricht be sicht," "day sterne orientale")

are expanded, very meaningfully, in lines 3-4: "Our licht most richt in clud of nycht, / Our dirknes for to scale" (27-8). Here "scale" ("scatter," a word used sometimes in a military sense of making a body of armed men to scatter or retreat in disorder) picks up the idea found in the word "dispern" (drive away) in the first stanza, and stresses the active power of the Virgin Mary (who is not a star shining with a simply passive beauty), introducing the bold idea of her as a warrior—"wicht in ficht," "puttar to flicht"—in lines 28-9.

(p. 208)

This image is in accordance with the representation of the Virgin as Empress of Heaven as well as "leman" (sweetheart), Mother, and "oratrice" (one who listens) of mankind.

As Priscilla Bawcutt says, "Despite the lapse of five centuries, Dunbar has a remarkable power to excite, amuse, and indeed infuriate readers—his attitudes to women and Highlanders, for instance, are far from politically correct" (introduction to *Selected Poems*, p. 1). Yet "Dunbar's finest poems are neither parochial nor dated, but treat of perennial themes. An intelligent but not a profoundly intellectual poet, he excels in the vividness of his imagination and in the intense energy of his expression. No other poet of his time is so rhythmically adroit or so sensitive to the connotations of a word or a phrase."

SELECTED BIBLIOGRAPHY

I. EARLY MANUSCRIPT SOURCES. Aberdeen Sasine Register, vol. 2 (1502–1507) and vol. 3 (1507–1513), City Charter Room, Town House, Aberdeen (three poems); Chepman and Millar (1508), National Library of Scotland, and anthology of miscellaneous pieces. See William Beattie, ed., *The Chepman and Millar Prints.* Edinburgh Bibliographical Society (1950); Asloan MS (c.1515–1525), Edinburgh, National Library of Scotland MS 16500 [A] (four poems), see W. A. Craigie, ed., 2 vols., Scottish Text Society (1923–1924); Arundel MS, British Museum MS Arundel 285 [Ar] (three poems), see J. A. W. Bennett, *Devotional Pieces in Verse and Prose,* Scottish Text Society (1955); British Museum Royal MS 58, appendix (early sixteenth-century, with one poem by Dunbar); Bannatyne MS, Edinburgh, National Library of Scotland, MS Adv. I.I. 6 [B, Bd], a large miscellany of early Scottish poetry collected by the Edinburgh merchant George Bannatyne and completed "in tyme of pest" in 1568 (45 poems by Dunbar), see W. Tod Ritchie, ed., 4 vols., Scottish Text Society (1928–1934); Maitland Folio (c.1570), Pepys Library, Magdalene College Cambridge, MS 2553 [MF] (59 of Dunbar's poems), see W. A. Craigie, 2 vols., Scottish Text Society, (1919, 1927); Osborn Manuscript, New Haven, Conn., Beinecke Rare Book and Manuscript Library, Yale University, Music MS 13 [O] (one poem); Reidpath MS, University Library, Cambridge, Moore LL.v.10, a partial transcript of the Maitland Folio c.1622 (eight poems).

II. NINETEENTH- AND TWENTIETH-CENTURY EDITIONS. *The Poems of William Dunbar*, ed. by David Laing, 2 vols. (Edinburgh, 1834, supplement 1865); *The Poems of William Dunbar*, ed. by J. Schipper (Vienna, 1892–1894); *The Poems of William Dunbar,* ed. by W. Mackay Mackenzie (Edinburgh, 1932; rev. ed. 1960); *William Dunbar: Poems*, ed. by James Kingsley (Oxford, 1958); *The Poems of William Dunbar*, ed. by James Kinsley (Oxford and New York, 1979); *Selected Poems of Henryson and Dunbar*, ed. by Priscilla Bawcutt and Felicity Riddy (Edinburgh, 1992); *William Dunbar: Selected Poems,* ed. by Priscilla Bawcutt (London, 1996); *The Poems of William Dunbar*, ed. by Priscilla Bawcutt, vols. 27 and 28 of *Association for Scottish Literary Studies* (Glasgow, 1997–1998); *William Dunbar: Selected Poems*, ed. by Harriet Harvey Wood (Manchester, 1999).

III. CRITICAL STUDIES. J. W. Baxter, *William Dunbar: A Biographical Study* (Edinburgh, 1952); James Kingsley, *"The Tretis of the Tua Mariit Wemen and the Wedo,"* in *Medium Aevum* 23 (1954); Tom Scott, *Dunbar: A Critical Exposition of the Poems* (Edinburgh and London, 1966); C. S. Lewis, *English Literature in the Sixteenth Century* (Oxford, 1968); A. D. Hope, *A Midsummer Eve's Dream: Variations on a Theme by William Dunbar* (Canberra, Australia, 1970); John MacQueen and Winifred MacQueen, eds., *A Choice of Scottish Verse, 1470–1570* (London, 1972); R. J. Lyall, "Moral Allegory in Dunbar's 'Goldyn Targe,' " in *Studies in Scottish Literature* 11 (1974), and "Politics and Poetry in Fifteenth- and Sixteenth-Century Scotland," in *Scottish Literary Journal* 3, no. 2 (1976); Adam J. Aitken et al., eds., *Bards and Makars: Scottish Language and Literature: Medieval and Renaissance* (Glasgow, 1977); Edmund Reiss, *William Dunbar* (Boston, Mass., 1979; R. J.

Pearcy, "The Genre of William Dunbar's *Tretis of the Tua Mariit Wemen and the Wedo,"* in *Speculum* 55 (1980); Priscilla Bawcutt, "The Text and Interpretation of Dunbar," in *Medium Aevum* 50 (1981); R. J. Lyall and Felicity Riddy, eds., *Proceedings of the Third International Conference on Scottish Language and Literature (Medieval and Renaissance)* (Stirling and Glasgow, 1981); Roy J. Percy, "William Dunbar's *Tretis of the Tua Mariit Wemen and the Wedo,"* in *Studies in Scottish Literature* 16 (1981); Ian Simpson Ross, *William Dunbar* (Leiden, 1981); Elizabeth Roth, "Criticism and Taste: Readings of Dunbar's *Treti*" in *Scottish Literary Journal* 15 (1981); Shaun McCarthy, " 'Syne maryit I a marchand': Dunbar's *Mariit Wemen* and their Audience," in *Studies in Scottish Literature* 18 (1983); J. Derrick McClure, ed., *Scotland and the Lowland Tongue, Studies in the Language and Literature of Lowland Scotland, Presented to David D. Murison* (Aberdeen, 1983); Walter Scheps and J. Anna Looney, eds., *Middle Scots Poetry: A Reference Guide to James I of Scotland, Robert Henryson, William Dunbar, and Gavin Douglas* (Boston, 1986); R. D. S. Jack, ed., *The History of Scottish Literature,* vol I: *Origins to 1660* (Aberdeen, 1988); J. Derrick McClure and M. R. G. Spiller, eds., *Brycht Lanternis: Essays on the Language and Literature of Medieval and Renaissance Scotland* (Aberdeen, 1989); Patricia Bawcutt, "The Earliest Texts of Dunbar," in *Regionalism in Late Medieval Manuscripts and Texts,* ed. by Felicity Riddy (Cambridge and Rochester, N.Y., 1991); Joanne S. Norman, "A Postmodern Look at a Medieval Poet: The Case of William Dunbar," in *Studies in Scottish Literature* 26 (1991); Priscilla Bawcutt, *Dunbar the Makar* (Oxford and New York, 1992); Priscilla Bawcutt, "Images of Women in the Poetry of Dunbar," in *Etudes Ecossaisses* 1 (1992); Helen Cooper and Sally Mapstone, eds., *The Long Fifteenth Century* (Oxford, 1997); Sally Mapstone, ed., *William Dunbar, "The Nobill Poyet": Essays in Honour of Priscilla Bawcutt* (East Lothian, Scotland, 2001).

ROBERT GREENE

(1558–1592)

Dan Brayton

IN 1592 A London writer attacked an up-and-coming playwright with a striking insult, calling the latter "an upstart Crow, beautified with our feathers, that with his *Tygers hart wrapt in a Players hyde,* supposes he is as well able to bombast out a blanke verse as the best of you: and beeing an absolute *Iohannes fac totum,* is in his owne conceit the onely Shake-scene in a countery." The specific choice of words in this insult points to the playwright's identity, for they are borrowed from the playwright himself: William Shakespeare. The young Shakespeare had recently described Joan of Arc as having a "woman's hart wrapped in a tiger's hide" in a play called *The Second Part of King Henry VI.* In a slight alteration of line, the critic indicates the malefactor's identity through ridicule. The insult contains a snobbish barb: to have a heart, even a tiger's heart, "wrapped in a player's hide" was no enviable condition, for players in the Elizabethan period were of dubious social status. The critic who found the young Shakespeare so objectionable was Robert Greene, a prolific writer whose life was going in the opposite direction to Shakespeare's. The passage appears in *Greene's Groatsworth of Wit* (p. 46), a work of prose that would be one of the last written before its author's death. It was not the only work written by Robert Greene to contain the author's name in the title, which suggests that, by the end of his life, Greene had become at least somewhat famous—or infamous. The passage above has been immortalized as some of the most emphatic evidence that Shakespeare was in fact a successful—if resented—playwright on the London scene by the early 1590s.

Today Robert Greene is perhaps most often remembered for the vivacity and wit of the above attack, and, hence, as a footnote to Shakespeare. Yet, as the tone of his harangue indicates, in 1592 Greene had ample reason to consider himself the more accomplished writer of the two. Greene had written five plays, a large number of prose romances, a good deal of what would today be considered journalism, and some fine poems before Shakespeare arrived on the literary and theatrical scene. At this moment, Shakespeare was just getting started and had most likely written only one or two plays. Greene had a university education, having earned his bachelor's and master's degrees from Cambridge. Shakespeare had earned neither. Moreover, Greene could legitimately impute that Shakespeare's work was derivative, for the latter made good use of the blank verse and the romantic comedy that Greene pioneered for the stage. Shakespeare would later make use of at least one plot from Greene's fiction (*Pandosto,* the basis for *The Winter's Tale*). To some extent, then, Greene's harangue seems legitimate.

While his writings were popular and, in the case of some works, well received in his lifetime, Greene never achieved a fraction of Shakespeare's success. Part of Greene's misfortune was to live in an era when modern conceptions of authorship—and their attendant benefits of wealth, fame (for the fortunate), and credit for one's creations—had not yet been established as legal institutions or social conventions. Living in a time when intellectual property was anything but private and plagiarism was not a developed idea, much less a problem, Greene was acutely aware of his marginal, threatened social position as a creator of literary fictions. Even today scholars variously consider him both a major writer and something of a literary hack, a frenzied producer of prose works and a skilled dramatist who wrote both good and bad plays. Greene's animosity toward Shakespeare and, more significantly, his pioneering fictional writings ensured him a significant place in the history of English literature; they were also part of a notorious, miserable, and relatively short life.

LIFE AND EDUCATION

Because Greene's favorite topics were bad behavior and himself, especially the two together, a major part of his biography comes down to us in the form of autobiography. Much of the story of his life derives from his own, final works: *Greene's Groatesworth of Wit* and *The Repentance of Robert Greene*. Sensationalism sells, and Greene was in the business of selling books. The story he fashioned out of his own life is the narrative of a prodigal. Others contributed to this story. Contemporaneous writers, including the likes of Thomas Nashe (1567–1601), a writer who admired Greene, and Gabriel Harvey, an intellectual who did not, readily took up the topic of their unfortunate colleague. A considerable amount of myth has inevitably been built around the name of Robert Greene, and the colorful narratives in which he is both hero and villain are abundant. We would do well, therefore, to maintain a healthy skepticism about what we think we know. For information about his life, then, we have little to go on but the works of opinionated and gifted writers of fiction. We must rely on his late writings (colorful stories), the title pages of his works (often quite descriptive), the writings of both friends and enemies (much of it posthumous), and whatever interior evidence we can glean from his other writings (copious but uncertain).

Robert Greene was born in Norwich, the largest city in East Anglia, located about a hundred miles mile to the northeast of London, the second largest in England at the time. He was baptized on 11 July 1558; he died in London on 3 September 1592. Since there is nothing unusual about the name, scholars have found difficulty in deciding which Robert Greene on record in fact became the writer we remember today. We do know that Norwich in the middle decades of the sixteenth century was a hotbed of religious dissent, thus an apt place of birth for such an irreverent writer. He matriculated at St. John's College of Cambridge University—not far from the city of his birth—on 26 November 1575. He received his first degree in 1578, and in 1583 he entered Clare Hall, also at Cambridge, from which he later earned a master of arts degree.

Greene himself was a sizar, a student attending the university on a scholarship, which means that he came from a less wealthy background than most of his fellow students. The tensions and opportunities created when young men with a familial background "in trade" found themselves in a community of privileged youths had a great impact on the careers of many writers. Several other students enrolled at the universities of Oxford and Cambridge at the same time, and also destined for literary careers, including Christopher Marlowe, Thomas Lodge, and George Peele (Greene came to be known as a University Wit), came from relatively humble backgrounds. So too did other great writers who did not have the opportunity for university study, most notably Benjamin Jonson and William Shakespeare.

Cambridge was not simply an austere place of learning during the reign of Elizabeth I. Students could be riotous and ungovernable; they certainly caused the university elders much worry. Their penchant for aping the aristocracy—particularly in their clothing—had become a serious issue by 1578. In that year Lord Burghley, then chancellor of Cambridge University, wrote about his worries concerning some students' growing habit of dressing like their wealthier peers (Crupi, p. 5). Burghley's anxiety was quite common among people in power in Elizabethan times: unruliness, sartorial or otherwise, caused anxiety in many quarters. The concern for maintaining a dress code was not unique to the university context, for "sumptuary laws," which governed what people could and could not wear, were common in the Elizabethan era (1558–1603). In a hierarchical society such as that which existed in Elizabethan England, transgression of the codes that determined one's social identity was cause for punishment. The fact that such laws had to be made, however, suggests that Elizabethans often chose to wear whatever they liked. The two groups most often associated with wearing what they should not have were prostitutes and actors, both groups that Greene would associate with for most of his adult life.

After his Cambridge years, if the *Life and Death of Robert Greene* (often attributed to Greene, but uncertain) is to be credited, the young writer traveled on the European continent. There he putatively indulged all of his vices and returned a worse man than he left:

> For being at the Vniuersitie of Cambridge, I /light amongst wags as lewd as my selfe, with whome I consumed the flower of my youth, who drew mee to trauell into Italy, and Spaine, in which places I sawe and practizde such villainie as is abhominable to declare. Thus by their counsaile I sought to furnish my selfe with coine, which I procured by cunning sleights from my Father and my friends, and my Mother pampered me so long, and secretly helped mee to the oyle of Angels, that I grew thereby prone to all mischiefe: so that beeing then conuersant with notable Braggarts, boon companions and ordinary spend-thrifts, that practized sundry superficiall studeis, I became as a Sien grafted into the same stocke, whereby I did absolutely participate in their nature and qualities.
>
> (*Repentance*, p. 20)

Of his years abroad, little is known for certain, but Greene describes himself as the stereotype of the atheistic English fop returning from a sinful jaunt in the vice-ridden realms of Italy and Spain.

In England again, in his own words, things went from bad to worse. Greene portrays himself at this time in theatrical terms as a Malcontent, a stock character on the stage who rails against others even as he commits crimes himself.

> At my return into England, I ruffeled outin my silks, in the habit of Malcontent, and seemed so discontent, that no place would please me to abide in, nor no vocation cause mee to stay my selfe in: but after I had be degrees proceeded Maister of Arts, I left the Vniuersitie and away to London, where (after I had continued dome short time, & driuen my slef out of credit with sundry of my frends) I became an Author of Playes, and a penner of Loue Pamphlets, so that I soone grew famous in that qualitie, that who for that trade growne so ordinary about London as Robin Greene. Yong yet in yeares, though olde in wickednes, I began to resolue that there was noth-

ing bad, that was profitable: whereupon I grew so rooted in all mischiefe, that I had so great a delight in wickednesse, as sundrie hath in godlinesse: and as much felicitie, I took in villainy, as others had in honesty. . . . From whordome I grew to drunkennes, from drunkennes to swearing and blaspheming the name of God, hereof grew quarrels, frayes, and continual controuersies, which are now as wormes in my conscience gnawing incessantly.

> (*Repentance*, pp. 20–22).

Here the repentant Greene writes of his own life as a kind of Rake's Progress, a descent into iniquity caused by the company he kept and closely related to his identity as a writer. Greene portrays his younger self in a manner consistent with an Italian proverb of the time, *Inglese italianato, diavolo incarnato* (an Italianate Englishman is the Devil incarnate). Later in life, the repentant Greene invokes this expression when he protests, "I am English born, and I have English thoughts, not a devil incarnate because I am Italianate, but hating the pride of Italie, because I know their peevishness" (*Cony-Catching*, p. 8). He protests too much.

Greene received a second master's degree—this time from Oxford—in July 1588. He married in 1585 or 1586 but later abandoned both his wife and children, choosing instead to spend his time in the taverns and bawdy-houses of London. The specifics elude our knowledge; not much remains to tell us about Greene's wife. Since the writer most responsible for Greene's reputation as a dissolute man of great literary talent was Robert Greene himself, it seems reasonable to consider the mythological Robert Greene as a historical narrative in its own right, the story of a wayward writer with immense literary ability and little concern for appearing decorous. Greene was his own harshest critic, fictionalizing himself in more than one of his works and adding a good deal to the genre of repentance literature.

Greene comes down to us as one of the most colorful of Elizabethans. Nearly all the accounts of his life and death paint a vivid picture of him as a witty writer, at times acerbic, at times confessional, always opportunistic, critical, prolific, and full of wit. By all accounts, Greene's adult life was dissolute and at times desperate. He died in poverty, and for most of his life he lived in it, too. Friends and foes alike wrote of his faults, which included drinking, whoring, and keeping bad company. Thomas Nashe, a friend and in many ways the writer who most resembled Greene, claimed that "Hee inherited more vertues than vices. Debt and deadly sinne, who is not subject to? With any notorious crime I never knew him tainted" (Jordan, p. 2). But Nashe scarcely seems credible (he, too wrote fiction). The tantalizing terms "debt" and "deadly sinne" suggest a good deal about Greene's life; by reading between Nashe's lines we glimpse the strong possibility that Greene needed some defending. The actual extent of Greene's sins and transgressions has been the talk of readers, writers, and critics ever since his much-written-about death.

In the introduction to *The Repentance of Robert Greene,* the printer, whose name is inscribed on the title-page as "Cutbert Berbie," sensationalizes the pages to follow.

> Gentlemen, I know that you ar not vnacquainted with the death of Robert Greene, whose pen in his life time pleased you as well on the Stage, as in the Stationers shops: And to speake truth, although his loose life was odious to God and offensiue to men, yet forasmuch as at his last end he found it most grieuous to himselve (as appeareth by this his repentant discourse) I doubt not but he shall for the same deserue fauour both of God and men.

Here Greene's life is introduced as worthy of study because it represents the moral exemplum of a repentant man seeking expiation for his sins.

Are we really supposed to read the following text for its morally instructive aspects, or are we being invited to entertain ourselves with scandal? The kinds of scandal mentioned in the rest of the introduction appear designed to entice readers.

> And considering Gentlemen that Venus hath her charmes to inchaunt; that Fancie is a Sorceresse bewitching the Senses, and follie the onely enemie to all vertuous actions. And forasmuch as the purest glasse is the most brickle [brittle], the finest Lawne [cloth] the soonest staind, the highest Oake most subject to the wind, and the quickest wit the more easily woone by folly: I doubt not but you will with regarde forget his follies, and like to the Bee gather hony out of the good counsels of him, who was

wise, learned and polliticke, had not his lasciuious life withdrawen him from those studies which had been far more pro/fitable to him.

> (*Repentance,* pp. 3–4)

What better way to sell a book than by depicting its author as a talented man who, having gone down the wrong path in life, decided at the end to repent? The rhetoric of this passage resembles the prose of John Lyly and of Greene himself; it certainly attempts to sensationalize the material that it is meant to introduce, and the moralizing tone adds a certain dimension of titillation to the framing of the narrative. Indeed, such a preface is worthy of Greene himself.

PROSE FICTION

Like the social order itself, literature in the Elizabethan era was understood in hierarchical terms: poetry ranked higher than prose, and certain forms of poetry—epic poetry in particular—ranked higher than others. Greene was a talented poet, but his poems were occasional and relatively few; most of his work was in prose, and prose was considered a lowly medium for fiction. The fact that Greene also wrote for the public stage tells us that he was much more interested in making a profit by his writing than he was in finding everlasting fame. Greene's commitment to the less exalted branches of literature was so complete that he appears as something of a historical foil to more ambitious writers of his day, such as Edmund Spenser, author of the verse epic *The Faerie Queene* (1590/1596). Even Shakespeare, who wrote for the relatively lowly public stage, made an effort to elevate his own literary reputation by writing two epic poems on classical themes and a sonnet sequence. Greene took no such pains to distinguish himself as a highbrow writer.

Greene's early career as a writer was devoted to prose romances, the literary precursors of the novel. Greene lived at a time when the novel was only just in the process of being invented in Spain and still had not made its way to England. Miguel de Cervantes would write his immensely popular and influential *Don Quixote* over a decade after the death of Greene, and English writers would not begin writing novels of any note for over a century after that. Prose fiction did exist in late sixteenth-century England, but for the most part only in episodic tales of adventure and courtly love. Like their precursors, the medieval verse narratives that recounted the exploits of the Knights of the Round Table, of Charlemagne and Roland, Renaissance prose romances tended to deal with courtship and courtly love. The latter, however, tended to focus more on love and intrigue than on the chivalric code. Less tightly plotted than the novel and less concerned with the internal development of a protagonist, the prose romance often strikes modern readers as unstructured and superficial. They were, nevertheless, quite popular among Elizabethan and Jacobean readers, and they often sold well.

Greene's prose romances were strongly influenced by the writings of John Lyly, known for his "euphuism," or elaborately florid and bombastic rhetoric, and Sir Philip Sidney, a poet, soldier, and hero known for his sonnets and for his prose work *Arcadia*. Lyly's romances, *Euphues, the Anatomy of Wit* (1579) and *Euphues and his England* (1580), immediately became immensely popular and widely imitated. The distinctive, artificial, bombastic, and elevated rhetorical style of these works made a powerful impression on readers and writers of the time. The plot acts as an excuse to discourse on conduct, courtly love, and education; it was the highly affected style that distinguished these works. The heavy— excessive, to modern tastes—use of mythical themes, balanced antithesis, and alliteration make euphuistic writing difficult for modern readers to enjoy. Some Elizabethan readers too parodied euphuism, but more chose to employ it themselves. Greene and Thomas Lodge were the two most notable imitators of Lyly, and the rhetorical bombast of some of Greene's euphuistic works stands in contrast to his more direct and less florid writings later on.

Greene's first publication, *Mamillia: A Mirror, or Looking-Glasse for the Ladies of England,* falls into the category of "rogue literature," or what the author himself called "love-pamphlets," which were popular in England at the time. These prose works are largely confessional; the exposure of scandal, sin, and criminality motivate the plot (and, no doubt, the reader). The plot involves two characters, Mamillia and Florion, who correspond on the topic of love. After leaving the court on Florion's advice, and retiring to her father's house, Mamillia is eventually seduced by a deceiver. The plot and much of the rhetoric owe a good deal to Lyly's *Euphues,* but with a crucial difference, as an astute reader has pointed out:

> Greene's story thus suggests a disjunction between precept and experience quite foreign to Euphues. In Lyly's novel passion overturns precept and nature upsets nurture, but, if successfully adhered to, precept and nurture would guard one against the dangers of love. In Greene precept and nurture are equally irrelevant, and virtue, however resolute, provides no defense against vice. Virtue and vice are alike pawns in the hand of all-governing fortune, and in some stories fortune dispenses altogether with the instrument of passion, creating disorder by mere natural accident.
>
> (Helgerson, p. 81)

This apt summary not only describes *Mamillia,* but, as we will see, goes a long way toward explaining the particularly grim perspective on fortune and human passions that characterizes one of Greene's most important works, *Pandosto.*

After *Mamillia,* Greene wrote three more works that were highly successful, *Pandosto* (1588), *Menaphon* (1589), and *Ciceronis Amor: Tullies Love* (1589). All three were popular for much of the late-sixteenth and early-seventeenth centuries; they would each go through multiple editions in the decades immediately following their composition. Greene published nearly thirty of these prose tracts, some better than others. One of the best known of Greene's prose works today because of its influence on Shakespeare, *Pandosto; or, The Triumph of Time* (also called *The History of Dorastus and Fawni)* was an extremely popular and influential prose romance. Shakespeare based his late play *The Winter's Tale* (1611) on *Pandosto*, and numerous editions and translations were published during Greene's lifetime and after his death.

Pandosto is constructed as a lively third-person narrative punctuated with melodramatic monologues on elevated and abstract subjects spoken by the major players in the story, with little dialogue. Greene's stylistic register also includes numerous moralizing speeches on the natural world, the vagaries of Fortune, and the healing power of Time. This last theme is signaled, of course, by the novel's subtitle, "The Triumph of Time." A brief advertisement following the title on the frontispiece of the 1588 first edition offers a succinct statement of Greene's moral and philosophical message about Time:

> Wherein is discovered by a pleasant History, that although by the means of sinister fortune Truth may be concealed yet by Time in spite of fortune it is most manifestly revealed. Pleasant for age to avoid drowsy thoughts, profitable for youth to eschew other wanton pastimes, and bringing to both a desired content.
>
> (*Pandosto,* p. xxiii)

Not only can time heal the wounds inflicted by Fortune, but "age" and "youth," two generations that are separated by time, can both find pleasure in the same text and hence are brought into some semblance of harmony. The statement on the title page thus becomes a prefiguration of a central theme within the text: the resolution of tension between the generations, represented by Pandosto and Egistus on the one hand and their children Dorastus and Fawnia on the other.

The play opens with Pandosto, the king of Bohemia (roughly the modern-day Czech Republic), and his wife, Bellaria, entertaining Pandosto's childhood friend Egistus, the king of Sicilia. Bellaria, out of her great love for her husband, treats Egistus with great respect and affection, which awakens in Pandosto intense jealousy. He soon convinces himself that Bellaria and Egistus are lovers. While Greene is explicit later in the tale that Bellaria and Egistus are entirely innocent of adultery, he offers ambiguous representations of their actions early in the story which, though articulated in blunt third-person narration, seem to come from Pandosto's overheated imagination:

> Bellaria . . . used him [Egistus] likewise so familiarly that her countenance bewrayed [betrayed] how her mind was affected towards him, oftentimes coming herself into his bed chamber to see that nothing could be amiss to mislike him. This honest familiarity increased daily more and more betwixt them . . . there grew such a secret uniting of their affections, that the one could not well be without the company of the other.
>
> (p. 5)

The mention of a "secret uniting" and the reference to Egistus' bedchamber are followed immediately by the first awakening of Pandosto's jealously, as if the narrative replicates the psychological trajectory of Pandosto's thinking. Later in the story, when both Bellaria and the narrator (and a divine intervention) make it clear that there has been no adultery, the earlier description of their intense affection opens the way for a reading of their relationship as a kind of emotional and intellectual adultery.

Consumed with jealously, Pandosto orders his servant Franion to poison Egistus or be killed himself. Franion embarks upon an internal ethical debate that raises crucial themes of servitude and economic power:

> Thou art [he says to himself] servant to a king and must obey at command; yet . . . against law and conscience it is not good to resist a tyrant with arms, nor to please an unjust king with obedience. What shalt thou do? . . . Egistus is a stranger to thee, and Pandosto thy soverign. . . . Think this, Franion, that a pound of gold is worth a ton of lead: great gifts are little Gods; and preferment to a mean man is a whetstone to courage: there is nothing sweeter than promotion. . . . Kings are known to command, servants are blameless to consent: fear not thou then to lift at [kill] Egistus; Pandosto shall bear the burthen. Yea but, Franion, conscience is a worm that ever biteth, but never ceaseth. . . . Prefer thy content before riches, and a clear mind before dignity; so being poor thou shalt have rich peace.
>
> (p. 10)

Having talked himself out of murdering Egistus, Franion resolves to warn him of Pandosto's plans. Egistus at first disbelieves Franion, thinking Pandosto innocent and the tale to be a Bohemian plot to overthrow Sicilia by first murdering its king; eventually Egistus is convinced, and he and Franion sail secretly away from Bohemia. This enrages both Pandosto and the Bohemians, who consider the act to be a signal of treason. Greene thus makes it clear that, while the story is largely personal and psychological, the actions of kings and queens have unavoidable political consequences.

Pandosto now throws his wife into prison and publicly accuses her of adultery and treason (again, the personal and the political intertwine). While in prison she gives birth to a second child, a girl; Pandosto orders the infant to be set afloat on the sea alone in a rough boat. Bellaria is then called for a formal trial, where she asks that Apollo's oracle at Delphi be consulted to prove her innocence. Several of the king's lords return with a message from the oracle: "Suspicion is no proof: jealousy is an unequal judge: Bellaria is Chaste: Egistus blameless: Franion a true subject: Pandosto treacherous: His babe an innocent; and the king shall live without an heir, if that which is lost be not found" (p. 26). This unequivocal message from the gods causes Pandosto to repent, but just as he begs his wife for forgiveness, news is brought to the court that their son, Garinter, has been killed, and Bellaria falls dead. Pandosto raises a noble tomb for her, and the first half of the tale ends.

The second half of the romance follows the infant daughter of Pandosto and Bellaria as she is washed up on the shores of Sicilia and adopted by a poor shepherd and his wife. Fawnia, as the peasants name the infant, grows up into a beautiful young woman whose "natural disposition did bewray [betray] that she was born of some high parentage" (pp. 37–38). One day as she tends her sheep she encounters a beautiful young man, Dorastus, and the two immediately fall in love. Dorastus is the son and heir of Egistus, and, status-conscious, he attempts to raise Fawnia's social status by inviting her to the court. She refuses, praising the pastoral pleasures of the shepherd's life and asking Dorastus to become a shepherd. He does so, with many regrets for his princely dignity, and the two make plans to elope. The couple set sail, but a storm blows them off course and they are forced to land in Bohemia, where they are brought before Pandosto. Dorastus, knowing the old animosity between his father

and Pandosto, lies about his identity; Pandosto disbelieves Dorastus and tosses him into prison. During Dorastus' imprisonment, Pandosto becomes enamored of Fawnia (who, though he does not know it, is his daughter) and propositions her. She refuses him, declaring her devotion to Dorastus, and Pandosto threatens to make her his mistress by force.

Meanwhile, Egistus discovers his son's elopement and his imprisonment by Pandosto. Egistus sends servants to Pandosto, demanding the release of Dorastus and the execution of Fawnia (whom Egistus holds responsible for his son's elopement). The servants of Egistus arrive in Bohemia and reveal Dorastus' true identity to Pandosto, who releases him and agrees to order the execution of Fawnia. Just before their execution, Fawnia's adoptive father (the shepherd) produces the jeweled chain and explains the circumstances of Fawnia's discovery and adoption. Pandosto recognizes his daughter at last and everyone sets off for Sicilia to celebrate the marriage of Dorastus and Fawnia. Just after the marriage, however, Pandosto is overcome by remorse and melancholy for his many misdeeds: the original false accusation of Bellaria, his plans to murder his friend Egistus, and his incestuous love for his own daughter. He commits suicide and the comic marriage ending of the novel is transformed briefly into tragedy.

In his late play *The Winter's Tale,* Shakespeare borrows a great deal from *Pandosto,* making the jealous, murderous husband the king of Sicily (Leontes) and, crucially, resurrecting the falsely accused wife, whom Shakespeare names Hermione (her death is only feigned in Shakespeare's rendition). Although Shakespeare does not replicate the majority of Greene's rhetorical or stylistic techniques, he does borrow entire phrases from Greene, and Shakespeare does a great deal with the central importance of time in the play. Shakespeare also violates the theatrical unities of time and place in spectacular fashion by having the action of the play take up nearly seventeen years, and makes the character Perdita, the daughter of Leontes and Hermione, the embodiment of time's triumph. In the end, Perdita and Florizel (based on Dorastus and Fawnia) are married with their parents' blessing, and Leontes and Hermione are reunited.

If Shakespeare borrowed the plot of his drama from Greene, Greene himself borrowed from prior sources. The source for Greene's rendition of the story is thought to come from a historical event, the subject of local ballads, which took place in fourteenth-century Poland. A duke, falsely accusing his wife of adultery, has her strangled in prison after the birth of a son who is smuggled away to be raised by a local peasant woman. The duke eventually repents and his son is restored to him. Another source of the story comes from the myth of *Alcestis* and from other earlier prose and verse texts.

The influence of Sir Philip Sidney, the great Elizabethan poet-aristocrat who wrote the prose narrative *Arcadia,* can be seen in Greene's romance, *Menaphon,* which was popular enough to be reprinted as *Greene's Arcadia.* Sidney exercised a good deal of influence on writers of his day, but as much as *Menaphon* derives inspiration from it, the latter is resolutely Greene's own. Published in 1589, *Menaphon* is as well known for itself as for its incendiary preface, written by the young Thomas Nashe. In defending his friend Greene's literary merits, Nashe vociferously attacked Greene's rival writers—especially those who drew excessively on ancient authors for plot devices. Nashe's defense of Greene embroiled Nashe in a lengthy written battle with other contemporary authors. The plot of *Menaphon* contains many similarities to *Pandosto*: an oracle, disguised royal figures, parents separated from their children, incestuous desire, estranged and reunited lovers, and an overarching contrast between the world of the court and the world of shepherds. Unlike *Pandosto,* the prose narration of *Menaphon* is frequently interspersed with lively lyric poems.

Menaphon begins in Arcadia, a bucolic region of Greece plagued by a "noisome pestilence." The king, Democles, receives a typically abstruse pronouncement from Apollo's oracle at Delphi hinting that Arcadia will finally be healed of its woes. We are introduced to the pastoral beauties of Arcadia by a shepherd, Menaphon, who glories in the splendors of the natural world but refuses

to recognize the importance of love; in one of the narrative's more entertaining lyrics Menaphon discourses on the folly of love:

Some say Love,
Foolish Love,
Doth rule and govern all the gods.
I say Love,
Inconstant Love,
Sets men's sense far at odds.
Some swear Love,
Smooth'd-face Love,
Is sweetest sweet that men can have.
I say Love,
Sour Love,
Makes virtue yield as beauty's slave.
A bitter sweet, a folly worst of all,
That forceth wisdom to be folly's thrall.

Love is sweet.
Wherein sweet?
In fading pleasures that do pain.
Beauty sweet.
Is that sweet
That yieldeth sorrow for a gain?
If Love's sweet,
Herein sweet,
That minutes' joys are monthly woes.
'Tis not sweet
That is sweet
Nowhere but where repentance grows.
Then love who list if beauty be so sour.
Labor for me! Love, rest in prince's bower.

This brief song testifies to Greene's talents as a lyric poet; he showcases his poetic abilities in many of his prose works, and many of these poems are excellent (more about Greene as poet below).

Given the traditional associations of the pastoral with idyllic love, Menaphon must be punished for his one-sided understanding of the genre. Immediately after his song, he sees three survivors of a shipwreck, an old man and a beautiful young woman carrying a young infant. Menaphon falls in love with the young woman and provides the trio shelter in his rustic cottage. The young woman is Sephestia, the daughter of King Democles, but she has been cast out (along with her infant son, her uncle, and her husband, Maximus) by her father. Believing her husband to have died in the shipwreck, and desiring to hide her identity, she tells Menaphon that her name is Samela and begins a new life as a shepherdess—a life that suits her extremely well. As in numerous romances that rely heavily on the pastoral, the country life becomes an idealized and temporary retreat from the power politics of city and court. Among the many shepherds who succumb to Samela's charms is one Melicertus, who is Maximus in disguise. Samela and Melicertus unaccountably fail to recognize one another but fall in love because each perceives intense similarities to their (supposedly) dead spouse in the other.

As in *Pandosto*, the second generation too must become embroiled in a sequence of mistaken identities and estrangements. Samela's son Pleusidippus, when he has grown into a beautiful boy, is kidnapped by a pirate and taken as a gift to the king of Thessaly, who (perceiving the innate regality of the child's bearing) adopts Pleusidippus as his heir. When Pleusidippus is a young man, he hears tales about Arcadia's lovely shepherdesses and sees a picture of Samela, whose beauty has made her famous. Not recognizing her as his mother, Pleusidippus sets off for Arcadia, fired with passion. Meanwhile, King Democles has also heard tales of a beautiful shepherdess living in his kingdom and leaves the court for the rural life. The two men, Samela's son and Samela's father, meet in the fields, both dressed as shepherds and both seeking Samela. Pleusidippus finds her first, and courts her; when she rebukes him, Democles encourages Pleusidippus to kidnap her, which he does. She is taken to a castle owned by Democles and subjected to advances first by her son (whom she does not recognize), and then her father (whom she does recognize, but to whom she does not reveal herself). Melicertus (Maximus) arrives at the castle to save her and challenges Pleusidippus (his own son) to a duel; the two fight but are so evenly matched that they become exhausted, whereupon Democles has them both thrown into prison. Democles renews his advances to Samela, who declares her devotion to Melicertus; in a rage, Democles condemns both Samela and Melicertus to death.

At the moment of their execution an old woman steps out of the crowd and reveals the truth of the assorted tangled relationships, and the romance ends with the recognition and reconciliation of husband and wife, mother and son, father and son, and father and daughter. Fate now begins to reveal itself, much as it did in *Pandosto*. The oracle's pronouncement with which the narrative began is understood to be logical after all, and harmony is restored to Arcadia. Menaphon hears the truth about his love's identity, and, "seeing his passions were too aspiring and that he bark'd against the moon, he left such lettice as were too fine for his lips and courted his old love Pesana" (*Life and Complete Works*, vol. 6). This mixture of metaphors appropriately describes the facility with which the convoluted love plot untangles itself and brings peace and harmony back to Arcadia.

GREENE AS PLAYWRIGHT

Greene was a talented, innovative, and—although he wrote only a handful of plays—influential playwright. He wrote two plays that are generally considered quite good; he also wrote three mediocre plays. The bulk of his works consists of prose, and it was in this realm that his greatest talents lay. As few in number as his plays were, they had a significant influence on the work of later, greater playwrights (most notably Shakespeare). One of them, *Friar Bacon and Friar Bungay,* has a good deal of dramatic merit. It also had a significant impact on the development of Elizabethan and Jacobean drama, and makes for enjoyable reading.

Greene's first play, *Alphonsus, King of Aragon* (1588), baldly imitates Christopher Marlowe's highly successful tragedy, *Tamburlaine the Great.* Marlowe had created a spectacular character in Tamburlaine, a ferocious and ambitious warrior who conquers much of the world and speaks in lofty flights of blank verse (unrhymed iambic pentameter), and his two plays of that name were both big hits with London audiences. Greene's Alphonsus resembles Marlowe's Tamburlaine all too much, and the trajectories of the two warrior-leaders' careers are all too similar. The plot mimics Marlowe's, with Alphonsus achieving military victories and the power to bestow crowns and lands on his supporters and, ultimately, marrying his enemy's daughter. While many Elizabethan playwrights—indeed, writers of all kinds—borrowed plots and lifted elements from the writings of others, the parallels between these two plays are so numerous and obvious as to be comical.

Some readers have suggested that *Alphonsus* is a play that parodies, rather than imitates, *Tamburlaine*; true or not, this response speaks worlds about how bad a play Greene wrote. Not only does the action hobble stumblingly along; the blank verse does too. The only redeeming feature of the play is its spectacular use of the technology of the stage. Three trumpet calls announce the start of the play, at which time the opening stage direction instructs, "after you have sounded thrice, let Venus be let down from the top of the stage." The closing stage direction comes full circle: "Exit Venus, or if you can conveniently, let a chair come down from the top of the stage and draw her up." There is a Ghost that appears and disappears through the trapdoor in the stage (a useful feature of Elizabethan theaters), and at one point a brass head spouting fire appears "in the middle of the place behind the stage," that is, in the so-called "discovery space." Greene makes much better theatrical use of a brazen head in a later play, *Friar Bacon and Friar Bungay*; he also showcases his talents more effectively there.

Greene wrote the second of his plays, *A Looking-Glasse For London and England* (1590), in collaboration with Thomas Lodge, another of the University Wits. This play deals with biblical themes—the sins and threatened destruction of Nineveh and the story of Jonah. Greene and Lodge represent Nineveh as a warning for Londoners. The play is thus didactic, and it recalls the morality plays of the Middle Ages that were the precursors to the early modern drama of the Elizabethan era. Its only strength as a play lies in comical scenes with Adam the clown. When Greene turns his attention from the exotic to the domestic, then, his work as a playwright improves a good deal.

The third of Greene's plays, *The History of Orlando Furioso* (1591), is consistent with the first two, and barely worth reading, although, because it appears to be a clear burlesque of both *Tamburlaine* and Thomas Kyd's *The Spanish Tragedy,* it may have been enjoyable to view on the stage. In this play Greene takes his subject matter from Lodovico Ariosto's (1474–1533) great narrative poem chronicling the exploits of the paladin Orlando (Italian for Roland). Orlando runs mad for much of the play (hence the title, which can be translated as "Mad Orlando"), committing such ridiculous deeds as tearing a shepherd apart (offstage) and fighting with soldiers when he is armed only with a club. In a mad moment, Orlando knights his lady love, Angelica, believing her to be a squire; he also "arms" a group of rural characters as soldiers with kitchenware. The action of the play is ridiculous in the extreme, and it seems certain that Greene meant it to be so.

Friar Bacon and Friar Bungay (1591), Greene's most famous play and possibly his best, is about the shape of the nation and the means of overcoming spatial constraints on power and knowledge. Its two major themes are magic and love. Considered by many to be the first successful romantic comedy written in English (although it is also a chronicle history play), it was immensely influential on subsequent playwrights, in particular the young William Shakespeare, whose comedies rely heavily on it. *Bacon* also resembles Marlowe's great—and nearly contemporaneous—play *Dr. Faustus*. But whereas Marlowe wrote the story of an overly ambitious scholar as a tragedy, Greene wrote it as a comedy. And while Marlowe's protagonist is a German scholar of legend, Greene's is an English magician whose story is told in a folk book.

Greene depicts England as a political body unified by the central intelligence of Edward Plantagenet, the prince of Wales, whose access to Friar Bacon's magic tricks gives him the power of observing far-removed events in his own country. The play connects necromancy (magic) with national geography in ways that could not have been possible before the completion of Christopher Saxton's *Atlas of Britain* (1576).

When Edward and his cohorts pay a visit to the Oxford "nigromancer," Bacon offers the prince a look in his crystal ball (1.1.93). The lovelorn Edward watches from Brasenose (Brass-nose) College in Oxford as his proxy suitor, Lacy, the earl of Lincoln, betrays the prince by falling in love with Margaret of Fressingfield—his lover in far-off Suffolk.

Theatrical and geographical space are both at issue in this play. Margaret's very name designates her as a regional character; she is "of Fressingfield" and the stereotype of the English country lass. Edward intervenes in Margaret and Lacy's budding love-affair by way of Bacon's magical ability to transport people from county to county. Bacon then transports his rival, Friar Bungay—enlisted to marry Margaret and Lacy—all the way to Oxfordshire. Greene's vision of national space is what Elizabethans understood as "chorographic," that is, based on the separate identities of the English counties (or shires). The two sites of Suffolk and Oxford organize the action of the play.

Into this mix we must include the ludic and ludicrous character of Rafe Simnell, Edward's fool. When Simnell impersonates the prince, he cleverly represents his simulated powers in geographical terms:

> Doctors, whose doting nightcaps are not capable of my ingenious dignity, know that I am Edward Plantagent, whom If you displease, will make a ship that shall hold all your colleges, and so carry away the Niniversity with a fair wind to Bankside in Southwark.
>
> (Scenevii , lines 69–73 pp. 43–44).

In this passage, impersonation accompanies the power to transport (or deport) one's adversaries. The Oxford University, with all of its stone colleges and weighty doctors, becomes a Niniversity, a ship of fools that is no match for Simnell. To transport the university from Oxford to Southwark is to turn the world upside-down by relocating the preeminent site of learning to the site of the playhouses. Southwark was a "liberty," a sort of Renaissance red light district and home to bear-baiting and bull-baiting theaters, "bawdy houses" (houses of prostitution), and the public playing houses (later the Globe would be erected there).

The Rose Theatre, in which this play was first successfully performed in 1589 or 1590 (the dating is uncertain), was itself located in Southwark. (Philip Henslowe records the play's revival at the Rose in February 1592 and again in April 1594.) This fact that the play refers to its own performance at the Rose, which could not have been lost on the Elizabethan audience, gives the Fool's claim to magical powers a commercial overtone. The Fool's joke is a provocative metatheatrical statement, for Simnell is most emphatically not Edward Plantagenet, and the actor reciting his lines is not Edward's fool either. Nor was the actor playing the role of Simnell at Oxford; he was, in fact, reciting his lines in Southwark. These lines thus signal the embodiment of an actor in the role of Rafe Simnell, who is himself impersonating the prince. This is the kind of metatheatrical humor that Shakespeare would later exploit to its fullest in his own romantic comedies.

Bacon is also a political play. If political authority in the Renaissance was intimately linked with the ability to put on a show (as many scholars have noted), then the spectacular nature of sovereignty itself becomes subject to the Fool's (and Greene's) mockery. Simnell also apes the geographical—as well as the spectacular—basis of royal power, for the king's ability to banish becomes a playful threat to put the serious dons of Oxford on the stage to be looked at and laughed at. The borders of the ultimate political body, that of the nation, become part of the plot's ludic and at times ludicrous high jinks. Friar Bacon's magnum opus is the creation of a great brass head that his diabolical arts have invested with magical power. At the proper hour, the Brazen Head is to emit magical incantations which will, in turn, reveal to Bacon how to encircle the nation with a brass wall. This would make the nation an enclosure of Bacon's—and the Devil's—devising.

With seven years' tossing nigromantic charms
Poring upon dark Hecate's Principles,
I have framed out a monstrous head of brass,
That, by th'enchanting forces of the devil,

Shall tell out strange and uncouth aphorisms,
And girt fair England with a wall of brass

(xi, 15–20)

The image of an England ringed round by a wall of brass created by the magical words of a brazen image gives form to a nationalistic dream of an impermeable and uniform kingdom. Greene places the protection of the geographical integrity of the nation as the highest goal of the scholarly and magical arts. This project fails when Miles, Bacon's clumsy apprentice, forgets to awaken the magus at the Brazen Head's hour of speech.

What might be the relationship between a massive brass head and a brass wall encircling the nation? Greene seems to be making fun of learning. But this is not all, for Friar Bacon is not so much the object of fun in the play as its instrument: it is the immense learning that resides in Bacon's head that promises to girdle England. It is no accident that Bacon's idol to esoteric knowledge is a head. The image of national containment puts this play in dialogue with the cartographic projects that were burgeoning in Elizabethan England and on the continent. This was the age of Gerard Mercator and Abraham Ortelius, the great European mapmakers who were redrawing the shape of the known world and vastly transforming the European geographical imagination. This is the historical moment when the magus becomes replaced by the engineer, the forerunner to the modern scientist who deploys reason and technology where the sorcerer had used magic and alchemy. Bacon is, then, a Copernicus or a Mercator—but an English one.

Greene's other play of any quality, *James IV*, unfortunately survives in poor form, the folio exemplifying the difficulties of textual transmission from an age when the printing of dramatic literature was not always carefully overseen. *James IV* is generally considered to be a forerunner of an important development in Elizabethan drama, the tragicomedy, and it rather deftly interweaves plot elements from Scottish history, Italian romance, and English folklore. Like most Elizabethan plays that deal with historical subjects, historical accuracy is not its strong point. This romantic comedy takes a story from Cinthio's *Ecatommiti* and adapts it to a Scottish

context. Its political themes—the necessity of a strong monarchy and the dangers of fawning courtiers—suggest a contemporary social commentary, but no more so than was standard fare for the drama of the time. Many of the play's themes find their way in one form or another into Shakespeare's comedies. *As You Like It, The Tempest,* and *A Midsummer Night's Dream* each owe a debt to Greene's *James IV,* and in the characters Bohan and Oberon can be seen a good deal of Shakespeare's Jaques (from *As You Like It*).

GREENE AS POET

The Elizabethan era was an age of great poets and poetic compendia. The age of print was in full swing in England, and ballads, songbooks, and poetic miscellanies abounded. English poets imitated the great Italian sonneteers by writing sonnet sequences, schoolboys memorized rhetorical tropes and figures, the queen herself dabbled in verse, and her courtiers competed to flatter her with clever verse compositions. Works of drama and of prose frequently contained poems; the pastoral romances at which Greene excelled provided an excellent opportunity for the prose stylist to interject poems at suitable points in the narrative. In fact, Greene wrote numerous poems and songs (there was little or no distinction between the two), and in this respect, his romances depart from the model established by Lyly in the two volumes of *Euphues*; Sidney's *Arcadia* was more of a model for Greene in its use of verse. Thomas Lodge's *Rosalynde* outdoes Greene's romances in its use of poetry, but few other similar works do. Although Greene only published a single volume of nondramatic poetry (*A Maiden's Dream,* 1591), the sum total of his poetry is quite large. Most of his poems are rightly acknowledged as excellent. They certainly span a great variety of subjects and moods. Several of them will be quoted here in their entirety in order to emphasize the range and musical quality of Greene's poetic creations.

A brief example of Greene's abilities as a poet appears in his *Morando, the Tritameron of Love*

(1587). Known by its first line, this poem is a conventional statement about the uncertainty of fortune.

> The fickle seat whereon proud Fortune sits,
>   The restless globe whereon the Fury stands,
> Bewrays her fond and far inconstant fits;
>   The fruitful horn she handleth in her hands
> Bides all beware to fear her flattering smiles,
>   That giveth most when most she meaneth guiles.
> The wheel that runing never taketh rest,
>   The top whereof fond worldlings count their bliss,
> Within a minute makes a black exchange,
>   And then the vild and lowest better is;
> Which emblem tells us the inconstant state
>   Of such as trust to Fortune or to Fate.
>   (Rollins, p. 380)

An example of emblem literature, a type of visually based writing which was extremely popular among Renaissance writers, this poem represents the vicissitudes of Fortune in terms of Fortune's ancient symbol, the wheel.

One of Greene's finest poems, "Sephestia's Song to Her Child," appeared in *Menaphon*. It is an elegant lullaby with a simple refrain formed by a heroic couplet (two lines of iambic pentameter rhyming *aa*):

> Weep not, my wanton, smile upon my knee.
> When you art old there's grief enough for thee.
> Mother's wag, pretty boy,
> Father's sorrow, father's joy.
> When thy father first did see
> Such a boy by him and me
> He was glad, I was wo.
> Fortune chang'd made him so,
> When he left his pretty boy,
> Last his sorrow, first his joy.
>
> Weep not, my wanton, smile upon my knee.
> When thou art old there's grief enough for thee.
> Streaming tears that never stint,
> Like pearl drops from a flint,
> Fell by course from his eyes
> That one another's place supplies.
> Thus he griev'd in every part,
> Tears of blood fell from his heart,
> When he left his pretty boy,
> Father's sorrow, father's joy.
>
> Weep not, my wanton, smile upon my knee.
> When thou art old, there's grief enough for thee.

> The wanton smil'd, father wept,
> Mother cried, baby lept;
> More he crow'd, more we cried,
> Nature could not sorrow hide.
> He must go, he must kiss
> Child and mother, baby bliss.
> For he left his pretty boy,
> Father's sorrow, father's joy.
>
> Weep not, my wanton, smile upon my knee,
> When thou art old there's grief enough for thee.
>   (Collins, pp. 250–251)

This poem attests to Greene's talents as a versifier, and its elegant simplicity suits the subject matter—a father's abandonment of his wife and infant son (which we cannot help recalling was Greene's own experience as a father and husband)—beautifully and with poignancy.

Greene's talents as a poet varied, and not all of his poems strike the same note as the one above. Far from it. In *Ciceronis Amor* (1589), the poem, known by its first line, makes a statement about female beauty.

> When gods had fram'd the sweet of women's face,
>   And lock'd men's looks within their golden hair,
> That Phoebus blush'd to see their matchless grace,
>   And heavenly gods on earth did make repair,
>   To quip fair Venus' overweening pride
>   Love's happy thoughts to jealousy were tied;
>
> Then grew a wrinkle on fair Venus' brow,
>   The amber sweet of love was turn'd to gall;
> Gloomy was heaven; bright Phoebus did avow
>   He could be coy and would not love at all,
>   Swearing no greater mischief could be wrought
>   Then love united to a jealous thought.

Here again Greene employs iambic pentameter, but the rhyme scheme that runs through these two brief stanzas, *ababcc*, is somewhat more sophisticated—and appropriately so—than the couplets of the lullaby above.

PROTO-JOURNALISM

Criminality in Elizabethan England is a fascinating topic, and a significant one, for the fact is that thousands of displaced, dispossessed, vagrant, vagabond, and "masterless" men and women formed a large underclass in the London of the late-sixteenth century. This urban underclass developed sophisticated methods of separating the more fortunate from their money and goods, and some banded together and formed criminal societies. Greene's late works examine the Elizabethan underworld—purse-snatchers, cardsharpers, con men, and prostitutes—that he must have known intimately. His interest lay in the specific methods used by criminals to cheat people of their money, and he professed a desire to expose these tricks out of a sense of patriotic duty and personal repentance. We should keep in mind that Greene displays a thorough knowledge of these practices and that his "discoveries" or exposures of them were a means of selling books for a profit.

Practices of criminal deception by which unsuspecting citizens lost their money or property were known as "coney-catching," a phrase derived from the practice of trapping hares and rabbits by tricks and ruses. These works form a fascinating contribution to the sociology of Renaissance England. Variously labeled "rogue literature," "journalistic narratives," and "proto-journalism," they make for the some of the most interesting reading in Greene's oeuvre. The coney, also spelled "cunnie," "cony," and "conny," and also referred to as a "gull," was a dupe or unwitting person to be cheated, often a merchant, apprentice, yeoman, or country bumpkin, with money to lose. Their deceivers, the coney-catchers, developed a specialized dialect which writers took up on occasion. Greene uses such specialized terms as "the foist, the nip, the stale, the snap" as methods of purse-cutting, and "the Setter, the Verser, and the Barnackle" as roles for con men (*Conny-Catching*, pp. 11, 17). In the middle of one such work, Greene provides "a table of the owrds of art, used in the effecting these base villanies" (p. 37). In this Greene exposes the vocabulary of "cozeners," or con men—the terms for their various roles as criminals as well as the verbs that describe their criminal techniques.

The title-page of one such work is worth quoting at length in order to understand why these writings sold well. In 1591, Greene published a work of prose called "A Notable Discovery of Cosenage," the title page of which reads as follows:

A / Notable Difcovery of Coofnage. / Now daily practifed by fundry lewd perfons, called Conniecatchers, and Croffe-biters. / Plainely laying open thofe pernitious fleights that hath brought many ignorant men to confufion. / *Written for the general benefit of all Gentlement, Citizens, Aprentifes, Countrey Farmers and yeomen, that may hap to fall into the company of fuch coofening companions. / With a delightfull difcoucourfe of the coofnagve of colliers.* / Nafcimur pro patria. By R. Greene, Maifter of Arts.

(Collins, pp. 263–264).

This blatantly appeals to the curiosity of Londoners who might have been anxious about being separated from their wealth. The rhetorical posturing as advice or conduct literature is also striking; the pamphlet was "written for the general benefit" of the kinds of Londoners most likely to worry about losing what they had. The illustration on the title page depicts a large hare (a "cony") holding a card in each hand, one clubs, the other spades. At the hare's feet are two dice, and on either side are a bowl and a jug. This illustration emblematizes the phrase "cony-catching," conning or cheating people, and it displays the common devices for doing so.

The text deals with two kinds of cheat, which Greene calls "coney catching" and "cross-biting." The first of these impostures was "a deceit at Cardes"; robbery by a pimp and robbery by a prostitute (p. 9). *The Second Part of Conny-Catching* (1592) follows up the first with further anecdotes of criminality, "laws" of the art or trade of coney-catching, and moralizing addresses to its readers. In both works, Greene's method is to narrate both general and particular examples of such cheats; the entire pamphlet consists of a series of narratives that follow one another closely. Thus, immediately upon telling the story of an unfortunate Welshman who has been duped in London, he launches into another about a shoemaker who gets his revenge upon a man who has fleeced him. Greene indulges his propensity for yarn-spinning by creating representative scenarios that read like fictions of criminality in which the narrator seems to take a certain amount of pleasure.

LIFE AFTER DEATH

Greene died young—at thirty-four he cannot have been considered old, even by Elizabethan standards—in circumstances that have caused a great deal of discussion in his own day and in ours. The major feature in the accounts of his death has been the writer's descent into debauchery and his relationship to the Elizabethan world of criminals. Not long after his death, Greene became the subject of several narratives, including Henry Chettle's *Kind-Heart's Dream* (1592), *Greene's News both from Heaven and Hell* (1593), by one B. R., and John Dickenson's *Greene in Conceit* (1598). In these works—for his sins and his desire to expose sin—Greene cannot quite make his way into heaven or hell. Instead he dwells in literature, an appropriate fate for such a prolific writer. In this century, Virginia Woolf changed Greene's first name and gave him a role in her delightful novel *Orlando*. Here, "Nicholas" Greene appears first as a witty and impecunious Elizabethan writer and later (traveling in time like the eponymous Orlando), as a Victorian publisher. His defining characteristics are wit and a desire to turn a profit from literature. He becomes the figure of that historically emergent identity, the professional writer, the author whose very being is determined by the production and dissemination of narratives— preferably scandalous ones.

One recent study of Elizabethan literature, *Elizabethan Prodigals,* by Richard Helgerson, explains the peculiar combination of self-promotion and self-chastisement that characterizes much of Greene's work and the dominant features of his reputation:

Why is so much Elizabethan fiction autobiographical? Part of the reason is self-advertizement, but part too may be guilt. . . . As his guilt increased, so did [Greene's] attention to himself, until, in one of the most remarkable passages in sixteenth-century fiction, he breaks off his *Groatsworth of Wit* to confess that he and his protagonist are one.

(p. 80)

Part of Greene's achievement as a writer was to write himself into a popular Elizabethan narrative of prodigality, of transgression and repentance, that was not only strikingly consistent with the bulk of his work but also extremely appealing to a wide variety of readers. In the early twentieth century, Felix E. Schilling summed up the conventional image of Greene's death in striking fashion. "Degraded with sin, pinched with want, starving and dying in the street, except for the charity of a shoemaker's wife, almost a beggar like himself, he had reached the end of a short and wasted life, and now too late lay repentant in the agony of hopeless humiliation" (Crupi, p. 2). This kind of maudlin account provides a sense of Greene's enduring fascination for students of the English Renaissance. The portrait of a brilliant but injudicious hack living in an age of great writers has appealed to readers for over four centuries.

SELECTED BIBLIOGRAPHY

I. COLLECTED WORKS. *The Plays and Poems of Robert Greene*, ed. by J. Churten Collins. 2 vols. (Oxford: Clarendon Press, 1905); *The Dramatic and Poetical Works of Robert Greene and George Peele,* ed. by Alexander Dyce. (London: Routledge and Sons, 1861); *The Life and Complete Works in Prose and Verse of Robert Greene,* ed. by Alexander B. Grosart, 15 vols. (New York, 1881–1886; repr. 1964).

II. PROSE, POETRY, DRAMA. *Pandosto,* ed. by P. G. Thomas (London, 1907), also in Paul Salzman, ed., *An Anthology of Elizabethan Prose Fiction* (Oxford, 1987); *Ciceronis Amor: Tullies Love* (Gainesville, Fla., 1954); *A Quip for an Upstart Courtier* (Gainesville, Fla., 1954); *A Notable Discovery of Coosnage* (London, 1923); *The Second Part of Conny-Catching* (London, 1923); *The Repentance of Robert Greene* (New York, 1970); *Friar Bacon and Friar Bungay,* ed. by Daniel Seltzer (Lincoln, Neb., 1963); *Groats-Worth of Witte, bought with a million of Repentance* (West Port, Conn., 1979); *The Scottish History of James the Fourth.* ed. by J. A. Lavin. (New Mermaids, London: Ernest Benn, 1967); *A Critical Edition of Robert Green's Cicesanis And: Tullies Love.* ed. by Charles Howard Larson. *Elizabeth and Renaissance Studies,* no. 36. (Salzburg: Universität, Salzburg, 1974).

III. OTHER PRIMARY TEXTS. Gabriel Harvey, *Fovre Letters and certeine Sonnets, especially touching Robert Greene and other parties by him abused,* ed. by G. B. Harrison (London, 1922); *Henslowe's Diary*, ed. by R. A. Foakes and R. T. Rickert. (Cambridge, 2002).

IV. CRITICAL STUDIES. John Clark Jordan, *Robert Greene* (New York, 1915; repr. 1965); Tetsumaro Hayashi, *Robert Greene Criticism: A Comprehensive Bibliography* (Metuchen, N.J., 1971); Richard Helgerson, *The Elizabethan Prodigals* (Berkeley and Los Angeles, 1976); Cecile Williamson Cary, "The Iconography of Food and the Motif of World Order in Friar Bacon and Friar Bungay," in *Comparative Drama* 13 (1979); A. C. Hamilton, "Elizabethan Romance: The Example of Prose Fiction," in *ELH* 49, no. 2 (1982); James Seay Dean, *Robert Greene: A Reference Guide* (Boston, 1984); Charles W. Crupi, *Robert Greene* (Boston, 1986); Darryll Grantley, "*The Winter's Tale* and Early Religious Drama," in *Comparative Drama* 20 (1986); Phillip Parotti, "Having It Both Ways: Renaissance Traditions in Robert Greene's 'Mars and Venus,' " in *Explorations in Renaissance Culture* 12 (1986); Allen D. Carroll, "The Badger in Greene's *Groats-Worth of Witte* and in Shakespeare," in *Studies in Philology* 84, no. 4 (1987); Douglas L. Peterson, "Lyly, Greene, and Shakespeare and the Recreations of Princes," in J. Leeds Barrol, ed., *Shakespeare Studies* (New York, 1988); W. W. Barker, "Rhetorical Romance: The 'Frivolous Toyes' of Robert Greene," and Robert B. Heilman, "Greene's Euphuism and Some Congeneric Styles," in George M. Logan and Gordon Teskey, eds., *Unfolded Tales: Essays on Renaissance Romance* (Ithaca, N.Y., 1989); Kevin J. Donovan, "Recent Studies in Robert Greene," in *English Literary Renaissance* 20, no.1 (1990); Constance Relihan, "The Narrative Strategies of Robert Greene's Cony-catching Pamphlets," in *Cahiers Elizabethains* 37 (April 1990); Paula M. Woods, "Greene's Conny-Catching Courtesans: The Moral Ambiguity of Prostitution," in *Explorations in Renaissance Culture* 18 (1992); D. Allen Carroll, ed., *Greene's Groatesworth of Wit* (Binghamton, N.Y., 1994); Brenda Cantar, "The Player-Patron in Greene's *Groatesworth of Wit* (1592)," in *Studies in Philology* 91 (1994); Lori Humphrey Newcomb, " 'Social Things': The Production of Popular Culture in the Reception of Robert Greene's *Pandosto*," in *ELH* 61 (1994); W. Ron Hess, "Robert Greene's Wit Re-Evaluated," in *Elizabethan Review* 4, no. 2 (1996); Lori Humphrey Newcomb, "The Triumph of Time: The Fortunate Readers of Robert Greene's *Pandosto*," in Cedric Brown and Arthur Marotti, eds., *Texts and Cultural Change in Early Modern England* (New York, 1997); Brenda Cantar, " 'Silenced but for the Word': The Discourse of Incest in Greene's *Pandosto* and *Menaphon*," in *English Studies in Canada* 23, no. 1 (1997); Tetsumaro Hayashi, *The Poetry of Robert Greene* (Muncie, Ind., 1997); J. Clinton Crumley, "Anachronism and Historical Romance in Renaissance Drama: *James IV*," in *Explorations in Renaissance Culture* 24 (1998); Anne Lake Prescott, "Through the Cultural Chunnel: The (Robert) Greeneing of Louise Labe," in Peter Hermann, ed., *Opening the Borders: Inclusivity in Early Modern Studies* (Newark, N.J., and London, 1999); Bryan Reynolds, *Becoming Criminal: Transversal Performance and Cultural Dissidence in Early Modern England* (Baltimore and London: The John Hopkins University Press, 2002).

V. FURTHER READING. Gamhi Salgado, *The Elizabethan Underworld* (London: J.M. Dent and Sons, Ltd., 1977); Michael Hattaway, *Elizabethan Popular Theatre* (London and Boston, 1982); Peter Stallybrass and Allon White, *The Politics and Poetics of Transgression* (Ithaca, N.Y., 1986); Christopher Hill, *The World Turned Upside-Down* (London and New York, 1991); Wendy Wall, *The Imprint of Gender: Authorship and Publication in the English Renaissance* (Ithaca and London, 1993); Elizabeth L. Eisenstein, *The Printing Revolution in Early Modern Europe* (Cambridge, 1996); Steven Mullaney, *The Place of the Stage: License, Play, and Power in Renaissance England* (Ann Arbor, Mich., 1998); Linda Woodbridge, *Vagrancy, Homelessness, and English Renaissance Literature* (Urbana and Chicago: University of Illinois Press, 2001).

SARAH KANE

(1971–1999)

Philip Parry

ALTHOUGH IN THE opinion of many enthusiastic admirers of modern theater Sarah Kane is the most powerful British dramatist of the 1990s, her plays have generated a great deal of controversy but very little reasoned debate. Those newspaper reviewers who vigorously disapproved of *Blasted* in 1995 too often trivialized the issue of stage violence by blunting the distinction between events in the real world and their dramatic representation. Ian's blinding is truly horrible, but not more so than Gloster's ("Out vile jelly") in *King Lear,* and both blindings are much less horrible than—and are horrible in a different way from—the real-life blinding of an undercover policeman by a soccer racist, which was Kane's inspiration. Because life and art are different, real violence and stage violence are also different. The really shocking but entirely predictable thing about the violence in Kane's plays is how rapidly it has ceased to shock. That is not in any sense Kane's fault; it flows from pre-publicity (so that we know what to expect) and from repetition (so that we judge one performance against another).

But those who have risen to the defense of *Blasted* have blurred important distinctions too. Kane is a deeply moral writer who is morally neutral; she is a politically engaged dramatist who hides her politics; she has something to teach us but offers no instruction; she packs her plays with violence because violence is an un-ignorable part of our world; she forces us to face up to the violence that we seek to ignore; she is wholly new and deeply indebted to earlier dramatists. And this last confusion is one to which Kane herself was susceptible. "If there's a precedent, I don't want to do it," she once said. But she also said that the first third of *Blasted* was influenced by Pinter and Ibsen, the middle third by Brecht, the ending by Samuel Beckett, and its dialogue by the terse example of Edward Bond's *Saved.*

The voice (we must not simply equate it with Kane herself) to which *4.48 Psychosis* gives expression declares itself "last in a long line of literary kleptomaniacs" (p. 213).

LIFE AND DEATH

Sarah Kane was born on 3 February 1971 in Brentwood, Essex. Her mother was a schoolteacher and her father was a journalist who worked as the East Anglian correspondent for the *Daily Mirror.* In her early and mid-teens Kane embraced the born-again evangelical Christianity of her parents, but she had lost faith in it and had begun to turn against it violently by the time she was ready to study drama at the University of Bristol in 1989. She never entirely left her childhood behind, however, and her taste for violent imagery of war and rape and cruelty was, she claimed, directly derived from her early reading of Scripture. She might have been amused (or appalled, or both) had she lived long enough to find support for this view in unexpected quarters: in a meditation upon her suicide printed just a few days after her death, the author of a Catholic parish newsletter claimed that the uninstructed reading of the Bible is a dangerous activity that "can cause wars, and as we can see in Sarah Kane's sad case, it can take individual lives."

Although by her own account she was a contentious and not always conscientious student, Kane graduated from Bristol with a first-class honors degree in 1992 and then moved to the University of Birmingham to take up a place on its newly established one-year master's course in playwriting. This course, which was directed by David Edgar, himself a highly respected and productive playwright, was intended to encourage would-be dramatists to bridge the gap between the lonely experience of writing and the cooperative venture of play-production. It has worked well, Edgar says, pointing out that a third of its graduates are now professionally connected with the theater. But Kane thought the course unduly academic and was bored with discussions of three-act structure and other sterile technicalities of play-making. The early scenes of *Blasted*—the part of the play where Ian and Cate are in the hotel room before the intervention of the Soldier—were developed as her project work for the course and were given a workshop performance on 3 July 1992. One of her tutors, perhaps with the benefit of hindsight, claimed to have found in the embryonic piece the only evidence that year of real dramatic talent.

Kane developed *Blasted* further while she was associated in a semi-formal way with the Bush Theatre in London, where she was appointed a literary associate in March 1994. On 29 January 1994 a rehearsed reading of the play was directed by James Macdonald at the Royal Court Theatre, and in January 1995, Macdonald staged the first production of the completed play there. Kane's association with the Court was appropriate, for it is a theater which has twice in the twentieth century been a home for radical and innovative British theater: first between 1904 and 1907, when George Bernard Shaw was its leading dramatist, and again from 1956 onward, when it was leased to the English Stage Company. Apart from introducing British audiences to modern European classics (both Brecht and Beckett), the ESC has a policy of encouraging new writing: John Osborne is the most famous of the playwrights whose talents it has fostered. In 1965 the theater was plunged into notorious controversy when Edward Bond's *Saved,* in which a baby is stoned to death, forced its licensees to apply for a temporary change of status in order to avoid the censorship which at that date attached to public performances.

Sarah Kane maintained an association with the Court. *Cleansed* was premiered by the company in 1998, and, in somewhat controversial circumstances, so was her last play, the posthumously produced *4.48 Psychosis,* in 2000. But she also worked for other companies. *Phaedra's Love*

(1996) was commissioned by the Gate Theatre in Notting Hill and was the only one of her plays that she herself directed. Later in 1996 she became writer-in-residence for Paines Plough, a company that specializes in generating new work. Under the pseudonym of Marie Kelvedon, assumed so as to avoid the controversy associated with the author of *Blasted,* she had *Crave* presented as a lunchtime reading at the company's Bridewell Theatre. Its performance premiere (this time under her real name) was at the Traverse Theatre in Edinburgh—another venue with a long history of presenting new and experimental work—during the Edinburgh Festival. It was an immensely successful production that brought Kane real acclaim and the hope that she might shed the burden of earlier controversy. Her final play, *4.48 Psychosis,* was commissioned by the Actors Touring Company (better known as ATC). Intended as an adaptation of Goethe's *The Sorrows of Young Werther,* a novel about suicide that was supposed to have made suicide fashionable, it soon outgrew its source and developed into a strange, semi-dramatized and scarcely performable work.

Just after completing *4.48 Psychosis,* Kane, who had a history of depression and emotional instability, tried to kill herself and was taken to Kings College Hospital in London. There, a few days later, on 20 February 1999, she hanged herself by her bootlaces in a lavatory. Her parents were initially reluctant (for obvious reasons, granted its exceptionally painful subject matter) to give permission for *4.48 Psychosis* to be performed, but eventually relented. However, they removed it from ATC, for whom it had been written but who had not secured legal possession of it, and had it premiered instead at the Royal Court.

Sarah Kane wrote also one brief television screenplay. Commissioned by Channel 4, generally the most innovative and daring of Britain's terrestrial channels, *Skin* (1997) was promoted on the back of the hugely controversial *Blasted.* Inevitably, much more so than her stage work, it observes the naturalistic conventions of television drama, but it challenges these in many interesting ways.

SARAH KANE

PROBLEMS AND CONTROVERSIES

A death that is early and recent poses problems that anyone who now writes about Sarah Kane must seek to resolve or minimize. No cumulative tradition of response was able to form in her brief lifetime and no substantial critical tradition has had time to form since her death, so that there have not yet been developed those standard scholarly tools that critics depend upon even while protesting that they do not.

As of 2002, for example, there was still no professionally edited collection of her plays. All texts—play scripts even more than other kinds of text—are inherently unstable. The Methuen Contemporary Dramatists edition of *Complete Plays,* introduced by David Greig, prefaces each of the plays (except *Skin* and the posthumously produced *4.48 Psychosis*) with a note telling us that Kane's post-performance revisions have been incorporated into the Methuen text, so that what is now printed "should . . . be regarded as the definitive version in all respects." But a truly definitive text (assuming one is possible) will list rejected readings as well as those that have been accepted, because of the possibility that the relationship between both sets of readings will itself be significant. What is at stake here—just how much weight even the tiniest details sometimes have to bear—can be shown from a seemingly minor alteration (the substitution of a dash for a period) in scene 3 of *Blasted.* Our appreciation of context, as is so often the case with Kane's work, proves crucial. At this point in the play, the Soldier, whose relationship with Ian is a puzzling mixture of intimacy and brutality, has been questioning him about his latest sexual encounter with Cate:

> SOLDIER: When? I know it was recent, smell it, remember.
> IAN: Last night. I think.
> SOLDIER: Good?
> IAN: Don't know. I was pissed. Probably not.
> SOLDIER: Three of us—
> IAN: Don't tell me.
> SOLDIER: Went to a house just outside town.

The Soldier then tells Ian (and us) the first of his horrifying stories of rape and atrocity. But in the earlier version of the text (printed in *Frontline Intelligence 2* in 1995 and reprinted in Methuen's 1996 text of *Blasted* and *Phaedra's Love)* after "Three of us" there is a period ("of us.") rather than a dash ("of us—"). The problem is that neither text fully captures Kane's intention, and one needs to compare them in order to develop a feeling for what is really happening. It is possible to interpret the revised punctuation as ensuring that these three words merely introduce the horror story that follows. Ian, anxious to stop the story, interrupts a speech that, had it not been interrupted, would have flowed on. ("Three of us [three soldiers] went to a house.") But how does Ian know that a story of wartime atrocity is to follow? The earlier version, by contrast, gives Ian cause for protest because it makes the "three of us" refer back to Ian and Cate and the Soldier, who is hinting at a three-way sex session. Ian's response ("Don't tell me" can be paraphrased as "Don't suggest what I think you're going to suggest") is deliberately intended to reject the Soldier's proposal by cutting it short. The Soldier's story then represents a diversion or an improvisation that is also a punishment and a scarcely veiled threat. What these two readings when they are put together indicate are both the Soldier's eagerness for sexual activity and his violent reaction to the thwarting of that eagerness. It is a pattern repeated throughout the play. (The only thing that truly irritated Kane in rehearsals and read-throughs were, Lyn Gardner, the *Guardian's* critic, has said, actors who ignored her punctuation: "If they don't do that fucking comma properly, I'm going to kill them." In the extract from *Blasted* just cited, notice the difference in weight between Ian's "Last night. I think" and the more usual, and much more casual, "Last night, I think."

There is also no biography of Sarah Kane and—granted the shortness of her life, the extreme sensitivity of some of the material that she wrote, and the complex and distressing relationships that exist between her art and her life—producing a reliable and informative biography that is more than an anodyne or adulatory memoir will be a task of considerable delicacy. T. S. Eliot, whose poems are echoed throughout *Crave,* once famously declared that in any successful artist there has to be a distance between the man who suffers and the mind which creates. That distance is easily blurred when one reads Kane's work; for, as one can never forget, she died by her own hand as the result of long-standing depressive illness. This may well be the most grievous burden under which criticism labors. "My mind is the subject of these bewildered fragments" (p. 210). There is a temptation, almost impossible to resist when dealing with *4.48 Psychosis,* to assess everything that she wrote in the light of her death and to treat it as an imaginative anticipation of, or step along the road toward, her calamitous end. But if Sarah Kane merits her inclusion in this series of essays, she does so because she is a playwright, not because she was one. However premature her death, both her life and the body of work that resulted from it must be judged to be complete.

There is no volume of her *Collected Letters,* very few books and articles, no "casebook" of critical essays, not even a readily accessible collection of the early newspaper articles and reviews. In consequence the scholarly apparatus at the end of this essay is unavoidably thin.

STAGECRAFT

When we have to deal with a new writer—whether a novelist or poet or playwright—around whom judgment has not had time to consolidate, our first task is to work out, approximately and provisionally (for critical judgment alters with the passing of time), what kind of novelist or poet or playwright we are dealing with. In order to do this we often make use of a rather crude set of critical terms: plays are naturalistic, non-naturalistic, "well-made," imagist, symbolist. Judgments that invoke these terms will need to be refined, for no play falls entirely under such simple headings, but they are an essential first step towards critical assessment. Some dramatists seek to create onstage an exact image—as exact as theater can manage—of contemporary life; others seek to move their audiences toward a better understanding of political or social issues; others construct strong and intricate plots that are amusing or exciting in themselves; others concentrate on the relationships between the characters that they create. But there are still others—Sarah Kane among them—who work up their plays from incidents and images and symbols that are often brought into violent or seemingly random proximity to other incidents, images, and symbols. This kind of dramatist writes plays that are hard to interpret since they need to be decoded much as one might decode an imagist poem. These plays are metaphorical, but in *4.48 Psychosis,* Kane reminds us that "the defining feature of a metaphor is that it's real" (p. 211). They are plays in which, in words taken once again from *4.48 Psychosis,* "every act is a symbol" (p. 226).

There is a very good example of Kane's imaginative processes at work in an incident in *Crave.* This is a play for four "characters," though they are not characters as we ordinarily encounter them in conventional drama. Instead they are identified merely by letters of the alphabet ("A," "B," "C," and "M"). We can be reasonably (though not absolutely) certain that "A" and "B" are men, and "A" is (or says he is) a pedophile. "A" tells the following disconcerting story (disconcerting because it reminds us that child molesters are likely to be extremely knowledgeable about the needs and weaknesses of children):

> A small girl becomes increasingly paralysed by her parents' frequently violent rows. Sometimes she would spend hours standing completely still in the toilet, simply because that was where she happened to be when the fight began. Finally, in moments of calm, she would take bottles of milk from the fridge or doorstep and leave them in places where she may later become trapped. Her parents were unable to understand why they found bottles of sour milk in every room in the house.
>
> (p. 185)

Why are there bottles of sour milk in every room in the house? What do these bottles mean? One explanation that might appeal to rather foolish parents is that their house is home to a poltergeist, and they might seek the services of an exorcist. But perhaps this exorcist is a wise man who decides that what haunts this house is of natural origin. "A" gives us an explanation that forces us to see these milk bottles as evidence of—and also symbols of the distorting effect of these parents upon that child: unintended but real abuse. Once this story is lodged with us, these bottles can never again be simply bottles, for they have moved across from life (where things can merely happen) to art (where, because everything is deliberate, nothing is without meaning). In a way the little girl is a kind of poet (who gives symbolic expression to her distress); and so is Sarah Kane (when she divines the meaning behind the symbol); and so are we (when we interpret the story that Kane has told us).

In the plays written before *Crave* and *4.48 Psychosis,* Kane's symbols are actions on a stage rather than words in a story. In *Blasted* (the end of scene 2), at the beginning of his strange, thwarted relationship with Ian, the Soldier "reaches out to touch Ian's face but stops short of physical contact." (Compare this with *4.48 Psychosis,* p. 215: "No one touches me, no one gets near me.") Ian, already shown to be homophobic in his earlier exchanges with Cate, cuts the gesture short with characteristic vulgarity ("You taking the piss?"). The Soldier smiles, asserts his dominance ("Our town now") and gives literal expression to Ian's words ("He stands on the bed and urinates over the pillows"). In a gentler world pillows are where you lay your head and dream your dreams: here—because, as the Greek origin of the word makes clear, a "theater" is a place where we go to see things—we see dreams being besmirched and defiled. Kane's theater is, as perhaps theater at its best must always be, intensely physical: a space where the human body—at rest or in motion, clothed or naked, beautiful or ugly, whole or broken—is the chief generator of drama's symbolic life. Oscar Wilde, the nineteenth-century wit, critic, and playwright, wrote in *The Portrait of Mr. W. H.* of "that strange mimicry of life by the living which is the mode and method of theatric art." He was saying that theater is an art form in which one human being stands in for—or presents or represents—another. The actor both is (imaginatively, for the duration of the performance) and is not (truly is not) the character that he impersonates, but he is always, Wilde stresses, "the medium through which alone the Drama can truly reveal itself." This is a statement in which Wilde nails his colors to the mast: the true student of drama reads the human body.

What Wilde says is universally true of theater and is a truth which, in making her own very different plays, Sarah Kane observes and exploits (in the plays that precede *Crave*; perhaps in *Crave* itself; but perhaps not in *4.48 Psychosis*). Actors, moving about and speaking on a stage, are the medium in which theater operates. But, limited by their humanity, these real human bodies that are really there in front us impose—much more so than computer-generated images in cinema—significant constraints upon what audiences can be shown. Indeed it is in the inevitable gap between the "what" of representation and the "how" that theater lives. Nowhere is this gap more obvious or of greater consequence for a true understanding of Kane's work than when it involves the theatrical representation of physical and sexual violence. In *Cleansed,* in many ways her most violent play, there are scenes of brutal torture and mutilation (and flamboyantly eccentric action) that require a representational treatment very different from cinematic realism. When Tinker "produces a large pair of scissors and cuts off Carl's tongue" (scene 4) or "takes Carl by the arms and cuts off his hands" (scene 8), or "forces Carl to the ground and cuts off his feet" (scene 13), and when these feet are carried offstage by rats, Kane is presenting her directors with challenges to their ingenuity to which they can only respond symbolically: for at the curtain call the actor who is Carl must appear intact and unhurt, a living embodiment of the truth that theater is an art of pretense. Nils Tabert, Kane's German translator, has noted her dislike of a Berlin production of *Blasted*. She was, he says, very prudish about her own work and found the production "offensive, cool and stylised, like Tarantino, whom she detested." The German production "was true to the text, but it lacked the metaphorical quality, the poetry, and that's what she hated" (Hattenstone, *Guardian,* 1 July 2000).

You can always give two accounts, parallel but different, of what happens in a play. One is an account of the play as a plot or fiction and is couched in terms of what characters do: they fall in love, or lose all their money, or die. The other tells us what actors do: they cross downstage or drop a handkerchief or exit stage left. Stage directions too observe this distinction. When Ian "takes a sandwich and eats it" (scene 1), the actor who impersonates him might reasonably mime eating or might genuinely eat the sandwich; but when Cate "bites [Ian's] penis as hard as she can," or the Soldier "pulls down Ian's trousers, undoes his own and rapes him" (scene 3), we can be as certain as in the *Cleansed* instances that in the sane world of performance actors do not do these things. Sometimes, then, actors represent actions by performing the same action, and sometimes they represent them by performing other actions. Kane was well aware of this basic distinction and also of how easily it breaks down. No theatrical action is ever an exact replica of the action that it imitates: the actress who is Desdemona deliberately drops the handkerchief that Desdemona accidentally drops. In short, we need to remember what perhaps the early hostile reviewers of *Blasted* forgot: that drama is always a symbolic art.

Since it is not possible to comply, directly or literally, with many of Kane's stage directions (an actor cannot simply be dropped from a vast height onto the surface of the stage, nor can that same stage suddenly sprout daffodils), some critics have concluded that she is essentially a writer who disregards or is unresponsive to the limitations of live theatrical performance. The argument from her stage directions is for the most part not true: the most extreme of these test the ingenuity of her directors certainly, but not against the standards of cinematic realism. One direction at the end of *Blasted*, and the whole of *Crave* and *4.48 Psychosis,* do, however, keep the issue open.

BLASTED

On 12 January 1995, the first London performance of *Blasted* led to a furious critical reaction in both populist and more serious newspapers that threatened to burgeon out of control. Not since 1988, when Howard Brenton's *The Romans in Britain*, staged at the National Theatre in London, was censured for its copious displays of male nudity, an explicit scene of sodomitical penetration, and its equation of rape and political exploitation, has a new play provoked as much outrage. Yet within a very few years, reassessed in the light of her later work and of her suicide, *Blasted* was being vigorously reclaimed for mainstream theater. And on the Continent, where British newspaper controversy has merely served to excite a positive interest in her work, her reputation has always been a strong one, and all of her plays are frequently performed.

"Initially I was stunned by the play's excesses," the critic Michael Billington explained in a highly public act of retraction and contrition that was his review of the revival of *Blasted* in March 2001. Billington's public change of mind is significant because he was the most highly respected of those theater critics who had reviled and dismissed the play when it first appeared. Its excesses, listed in his hostile review, were "scenes of masturbation, fellatio, frottage, micturition, defecation . . . homosexual rape, eye-gouging, and cannibalism." This list, though frequently repeated, is not wholly accurate: Ian's eyes are sucked out of his head and eaten but they are not gouged out. Other newspaper reports were more exaggerated: the Soldier does not urinate into Ian's mouth, and this latter act was neither performed nor simulated in the play's first production. Nor is Cate "naive, epileptic and underage" (*Independent*, 5 April 2001): according to Kane's opening stage direction (though nothing that we see or hear makes clear how old she is) Cate is twenty-one. Kane had complete freedom to choose Cate's age and she chose to put her above the age of consent. This does not mean that Cate consents to what Ian does to her: she is naive and epileptic, but she is not ("absolutely not," Kane insisted in an interview) simple-minded. It does mean, though, that the issue of consent cannot be automatically resolved by appealing to her age.

Kane's death merely compounded the inaccuracy that has surrounded her most famous play. In an obituary notice (27 February 1999) the *Daily Telegraph* added a nonexistent incident of tongue-munching to Billington's catalog of horrors. Much more seriously, Richard Eyre and Nicholas Wright in *Changing Stages,* generally a reliable and invigorating survey of twentieth-century theater, say that the play "starts with an abusive sexual relationship between father and daughter" (p. 374). But it does not. The error perhaps stems from the fact that both Kane's father and Ian are tabloid journalists, or perhaps from a feeling that Ian's attractiveness for Cate (Why does she agree to visit him at the hotel?) is not sufficiently explained. What is it that locks them together in a relationship to which one of them, at any rate, does not wish to give sexual expression? Apparently, as Aleks Sierz tells us in *In-Yer-Face Theatre,* Peter Whelan, a fellow dramatist, also feels that the play makes more sense if Ian and Cate are father and daughter (p. 104).

Kane's own description of *Blasted* is utterly uncompromising ("middle-aged male journo rapes his girlfriend and gets buggered by a soldier who sucks his eyes out") but is in part a protest against the view that the play can be adequately summarized solely in terms of its plot ("a list of a play's contents is not a review"). Perhaps it too glibly brings together the two very different halves of the play, for it is the relationship between the scenes Kane had sketched out in Birmingham and the war scenes she added to complete the play that lies at the heart of genuine critical disquiet over what she has done. Her account is a candid one: having produced scenes set in a Leeds hotel, which she thought too good to jettison, she lost interest in the play and wanted instead to write something about the war in Bosnia that was just beginning to hit the headlines. She united these two tasks (one completed, the other yet to be written) by arguing that "the logical conclusion of the attitude that produces an isolated rape in England is the rape camps in Bosnia, and the logical conclusion to the way society expects men to behave is war" (Sierz, p. 104).

But this argument raises two issues—about how we interpret what happens to Cate and about the nationality of the Soldier—that have not been adequately discussed. At the very beginning of *Blasted,* as part of the hospitality package that one buys into when one pays for an expensive hotel room, there is "a large bouquet of flowers." At the end of the first scene, in order to win Cate round after she has told him that she does not love him, Ian "sees the bouquet of flowers and picks it up" and offers it to her. "These are for you," he says, though Kane leaves it for a director to decide whether Cate accepts them or not. But at the beginning of scene 2 (set "very early the following morning" in the same room) a stage direction tells us that the bouquet of flowers is now ripped apart and scattered around the room. The torn-apart bunch of flowers symbolizes Ian's violent sexual session with Cate. Unusually in a play famed for its explicitness and from a dramatist who claimed to see no point in the offstage violence of classical Greek theater ("Why pay £10 not to see it? Why not stay at home?"), Kane does not portray this crucial bit of action directly but inserts it into the space between the first and second scenes. Moreover, in an interview with Aleks Sierz, Kane complained of a production in which this second scene began with Cate naked, spread-eagled and bleeding (Sierz, p. 105). Perhaps the offending director was simply anxious to emphasize that what had happened offstage was rape; for central to this second scene is an episode in which Cate initiates sexual activity, controls it throughout, and bites Ian's penis hard when he climaxes (which he does as he completes the sentence "I / Am / A / Killer"). This she does, Ian believes, in revenge for his oral overenthusiasm during the night. ("You bit me. It's still bleeding.") From this one might conclude that their relationship is imprisoning and abusive but also a relationship in which (and, if so, *Skin* is relevant here) abuse and exploitation are reciprocated.

The question that Kane had to be able to answer in order to complete *Blasted* was, "What could possibly be the connection between a common rape in a Leeds bedroom and what's happening in Bosnia?" But, though her response to the emerging Balkan atrocities undoubtedly fueled the plays last three acts, this is not in itself an explanation of why (or whether) the Soldier is Bosnian. Perhaps, indeed, he is not: certainly there is not on the page any attempt to locate him by means of accent or speech patterns. What matters, it might be argued, is that we witness not simply the horrors of war but, more specifically, the super-heated horrors of civil war. Civil war, what an earlier age termed (in an expression that yokes together the body and the body politic) "intestinal strife," is an appropriate source for Kane's imagery because she wishes by means of it to symbolize personal disorder and internal strife. This point seems to be basic and may precede the choice of the Balkan wars as image-source, for there is an aspect of Ian's characterization that is otherwise hard to explain. His first name is Scottish (Ian is the Scottish form of the name that is John in English, Ieuan or Sion in Welsh, and Sean in Irish), but he is a Welshman (Ian Jones) who has lived so long in Leeds that he sounds completely English. ("Welsh born but lived in Leeds much of his life and picked up the accent.") Just as with Cate's age, Kane has absolute freedom to make Ian whatever she wants him to be. He is an Englishman, a Scotsman, and a Welshman. It sounds like an old joke, but where is the missing Irishman? In Northern Ireland, whose divided population looks ambivalently toward Eire and Great Britain, there has been a particularly nasty episode of civil strife that has lasted thirty years and has claimed many thousands of lives. Interestingly (but is it just coincidence?) the actors who played the Soldier in both the 1995 and 2001 productions had Irish names (Dermot Kerrigan and Tom Jordan Murphy, respectively). Kane wished, countless reviewers have claimed, to bring home to an apathetic and morally deadened public the horrors of Bosnia; by a grim irony it may be that, for British audiences and a British playwright, Northern Ireland is too close to home to be brought home to us.

One should probably not try to pin down the action too much: when the Soldier tells Ian that he sounds English, Ian's explanation ("I live there") suggests that the irruption of the Soldier and the mortar bomb attack have blasted the action (perhaps one of the meanings of the play's title) way out of Leeds ("I live there," not "I live here") into some mental landscape in which our most horrible imaginings are matched by the realities of war. It is also the point when the play takes leave of those naturalistic conventions that, however strained they have been, have held sway over the play's first two scenes.

Blasted is a short play comprising five scenes, none of which is very long and which get shorter as the play proceeds. The two-hour running time that seems now to be normal for the piece (reviewers noted that the 2001 revival was much slower than the 1995 production) is the result of treating the stage action very slowly and deliberately and separating it off from the dialogue, so that we are presented with alternating blocks of action and of dialogue. Of course this is not always the case (Ian keeps up a flow of conversation while Cate makes love to him during scene 2), but it is the case often enough to be a distinctive feature of the play, and it is a feature that is established right from the outset. Perhaps the clearest instance of this technique occurs in scene 3 where "the Soldier looks at Ian for a very long time, saying nothing. Ian is uncomfortable." And not just Ian; audiences too find long silences in the theater disconcerting. "Eventually," the stage direction tells us, Ian responds, but with just a single word (What?"). The Soldier's reply is sinister but noncommittal; having said nothing, he then says "Nothing." There is then further "silence" and "Ian is uneasy again." Clearly this pattern of silence, embarrassment, and constrained and inhibited speech is deliberately constructed by Kane and is part of the tortured and torturing relationship that rapidly develops between Ian and the Soldier.

It is not just theatrical texts that change through time. Performance, too, is notoriously unstable, for every play that is regularly performed lives on from one performance to the next and alters with each performance: such variability is the defining mark of a live-performance art. This kind of more or less unconscious evolution has not had time to operate in Kane's case, but there have been some deliberate performance developments that are perhaps worth questioning before they harden into a tradition. One of the strongest moments in *Blasted,* and certainly one of its most controversial moments, is when the Soldier, who has trapped Ian in his hotel bedroom, blinds him (scene 3). Here is what Kane's text tells us:

The Soldier grips Ian's head in his hands.
He puts his mouth over one of Ian's eyes, sucks it out, bites it off and eats it.
He does the same to the other eye.

A recent touring production altered this in order to have the Soldier remove Ian's eyes with a corkscrew. This perhaps brings what an audience sees closer to the scene in Edward Bond's *Lear* (itself an adaptation of its Shakespearean original) in which Warrington's eyes are removed by means of a mechanical instrument, but it does so at some cost. The Soldier's actions, though unforgivably and shockingly brutal, are often ambiguous; he rapes Ian with his "eyes closed and smelling Ian's hair." And his way of blinding him begins with an action that could look like an amorous one: as is so often the case in Kane's plays, a sexual act rapidly degenerates into a violent and a dismembering one. This act both looks back to a sentence in the Soldier's immediately preceding description of wartime atrocities ("insides of people's heads came out of their eyes") and forward to a passage in *Psychosis 4.48,* which is also about wartime atrocities: "I gassed the Jews, I killed the Kurds, I bombed the Arabs . . . I'll suck your fucking eyes out send them to your mother in a box" (p. 227). Ian and his tormentor have something in common: in Kane's cruel world it is the cruelty of love that binds them together. Immediately after the blinding there is a brief blackout (appropriately enough) and then the lights come up to reveal that "the Soldier lies close to Ian, the revolver in his hand. He has blown his own brain out." And at the end of the play Ian is left "crying, huge bloody tears": "He is hugging the Soldier's body for comfort."

It is not just in this respect that *Blasted* ends very oddly indeed; yet none of the play's reviewers seems to have commented on its oddity. Indeed it is possible that no one noticed it, and that itself is a strange state of affairs. At the end of the play, having suffered what we might well think of as the torments of the damned, Ian—a stage direction tells us—"dies with relief." It then starts to rain on him and ("eventually") he responds with an expletive ("Shit"). This one-word reaction, noted the reviewer from the *Daily Telegraph* (5 April 2001), reduced the house "to hysterics," perhaps no more than the nervous laughter of an audience seeking emotional release. Much harder to determine is whether either the audience or the reviewer had grasped that Ian had died. How, after all, could they have done so? The information is tucked away in a stage direction, and Ian continues to speak and eat after his death. What kind of death is this? You "can't die and come back," Ian has told Cate in the previous scene: "That's not dying, it's fainting. When you die, it's the end." Ian's death can register fully only with the play's readers.

That is a very strange situation indeed for a practicing dramatist to contrive, but it resonates with other elements in Kane's work. She herself said, an obituarist noted, that because of the way she was brought up, she was left with "a dilemma in my head about when life begins and ends" (*Daily Telegraph,* 27 February 1999). What might initially seem like a reference to the moral debates that surround abortion and euthanasia expands so as to include the possibility that even larger issues—including survival into an afterlife—are involved. Among many sinister moments in *4.48 Psychosis* is one in which its principal voice says that it is fear "that keeps me away from the train tracks. I just hope to God that death is the fucking end" (p. 211). Here is an occasion when both profanity and obscenity are justified. What state of turmoil must one be in to pray for one's own extinction to a God whose existence, if he exists, will keep one alive? And extinction is imagined, in a grim pun, as an escape from the sexual demands of human living. But the real fear is not of extinction but of revival and survival. And it may be that it is theater itself that supplies a precise symbolic rendering of this fear: every character that dies in every play revives at the next performance.

SARAH KANE

PHAEDRA'S LOVE

Kane's *Phaedra's Love,* which opened at the Gate Theatre in London in May 1996, is her least-known play. Poised uneasily between *Blasted* (itself uneasily divided between naturalism and its negation) and *Cleansed,* it ends with scenes of rape, violence, mutilation, and murder that are more flamboyant than anything in *Blasted* and which anticipate the still more flamboyant (but artistically more assured) atrocities of *Cleansed.* It was, however, the only one of her plays that Kane herself directed, and she discusses the play in an interview that is reproduced in Heide Stephenson and Natasha Langridge's *Rage and Reason.* It is a play about the experience of depression and its consequences, and (as in the Soldier's relationship with Ian) it links opposites in a deadly union:

> Through being very, very low comes an ability to live in the moment because there isn't anything else. What do you do if you feel the truth is behind you? . . . You can't have faith without doubt, and what are you left with when you can't have love without hate?

The play's opening scene, though set in a royal palace, is a sordid domestic tableau in which Hippolytus, surrounded by the rubbish of his idle but expensive life, pleasures himself by masturbating into a sock. This is an image, graphic in a way that we now recognize is typical of Kane, of his self-absorption and inertia. A doctor whom Phaedra, his stepmother, has consulted diagnoses depression. But despite the fact that Hippolytus smells (so does Ian, though for different reasons), is fat, will not move, and mistreats every women that he has ever had, Phaedra has fallen in love with him and wants a sexual union. Instead of adding to the despised gifts that the populace brings him on his birthday, she decides (scene 4) to make a present of herself. This Hippolytus accepts but then (as Phaedra's daughter, drawing upon her own experience of him, had foretold) he rejects her. Humiliated and thwarted, Phaedra kills herself and leaves a note in which she accuses him of having raped her. Despite the play's title, it is Hippolytus' reaction to this potentially very dangerous accusation that really forms the meat of the play. However unpleasant his treatment of Phaedra, he has not, as Kane points out in the interview, really raped her: "What Hippolytus does to Phaedra is not rape—but the English language doesn't contain the words to describe the emotional decimation he inflicts." The word "decimation" carries a good deal of weight here. Originally it meant the killing of one-tenth of a subject population—usually in, or as a consequence of, war—by way of punishment or retribution; now it is used to mean any kind of mass slaughter. But in using it here Kane is, as in *Blasted,* linking interior hurt with massive social disruption.

Hippolytus, however, thinks that being known as a rapist gives him dignity and glamour and a role in life that he otherwise lacks. It is Phaedra's dangerous accusation rather than her sexual self-offering that is, he concludes, the true gift that she has brought him and the genuine fruit of her love. Faithful to his perception of his newly found purpose in life, he voluntarily enters a prison ("I'm turning myself in"); refuses the reforming blandishments of a priest (scene 6); and in the final scene, as he is being taken to execution, breaks free from his guard and hurls himself into the crowd that is baying for his blood. He is castrated and disemboweled and kicked and stoned and is left (stage directions tell us three times) "completely motionless," "motionless," and "completely still." But then—"eventually" (one of Kane's favorite directions)—he opens his eyes, looks at the sky, speaks ("If there could have been more moments like this"), and only then (a direction informs us) "dies." Here Kane's use of directions cannot be faulted: perhaps, using Ian's terminology, Hippolytus faints under torture and revives in order to die. Nonetheless the similarity between the endings of *Blasted* and *Phaedra's Love* is worth noting. Theseus, having raped and murdered his stepdaughter, "cuts his own throat and bleeds to death." We are left with three bodies onstage and are bound to think that the play is ended. Then ("eventually") Hippolytus opens his eyes and speaks. The play's real ending stretches out beyond its presumed ending, and this is also exactly what happens in *Blasted.*

SKIN

Skin, which was commissioned by Channel 4 Television on the back of the controversy that greeted *Blasted*, is Kane's only screenplay. Though very short, it nonetheless throws an interesting light upon her stage plays precisely because the conventions of television performance imposed limitations upon what she could do, which force the film into broader conformity with the canons of naturalistic representation than she usually allowed herself, and which allow her persistent oddities to shine forth by contrast.

It is on first viewing a simple work: twenty-four brief scenes about a skinhead called Billy who, despite his racist beliefs and actions, is sexually attracted to a black woman (Marcia); they have an affair in which he becomes the victim of her violence and sadism. The coexistence of repulsion and attraction within an abusive relationship is old territory for Kane, but her script is more complex than a too simple summary might suggest, and it is worthwhile listing some of its incongruities. In the first scene we see Billy asleep under a duvet in his bedroom. At the foot of the bed is a cuddly polar bear. Elsewhere in the room a stage direction alerts us to a photograph of a smiling middle-aged woman, a baseball bat, and, in the center of the room, a castlelike structure made out of empty cigarette packets and boxes of mushroom soup.

The polar bear is a child's toy (though Billy is scarcely a child) but an unusual one: not the more common teddy bear but a bear that is white (a loaded word in a skinhead's vocabulary) and one that lives among ice and snow (also white and cold and, by extension, emotionally withdrawn). In scene 2, when Billy is failing to eat breakfast in a dive in South London (and this failure to eat—a lack of appetite—is itself a repeated motif), a small boy of mixed race who carries an identical bear presses his face up against the café window, laughs when Billy shows him a swastika drawn on his fist, and runs away laughing and with no sign of fear. What connects Billy, the polar bear, and the boy of mixed race? (In scene 3 it is a mixed-race wedding that Billy and the other skinheads disrupt outside a church in Brix-ton; the groom is white but wears black, the bride is black but wears white.)

The middle-aged woman in the photograph is never identified but is perhaps the "Mum" to whom Billy appeals in scene 16 after he has slowly dressed himself in Marcia's clothes, and is perhaps also the MOTHER who leaves him an answering-machine message at the end of the opening scene ("William, it's me. Mum. I'm very worried about you"). But the only MOTHER that we see in the play, who appears briefly in scene 2, is a café owner, "a big man with a fag in his mouth." It is in his café that other skinheads tease Billy in a smutty way that calls his sexual orthodoxy into question. From the entirely innocent "Get some meat on your bones" (Billy, a stage direction tells us, is "painfully thin"), they proceed by indecent stages to "[Get] your mouth round some meat" while waving in his face "a sausage that he doesn't take." They then add a taunt that is in context ambiguous and strangely threatening: "I do hope you're not turning into a vegetarian, Billy."

Acts of dressing and undressing punctuate the screenplay. For much of the time Billy is naked, most notably at the beginning and end of the play: he is a skinhead whose skin we are forced to inspect. In scene 5, a scene set in Billy's flat in which the only words uttered are two answering-machine messages, we watch him dressing in the regulation skinhead costume of "tight blue jeans, white tee-shirt, red braces and cherry red docs"[Doc Marten boots]: the red, white, and blue of the Union flag that is also the unofficial emblem of the British National Party. But when Marcia, from the window of a flat opposite, beckons to him to join her, he must change his clothes (though we do not see him doing so) since in the next scene he runs down the stairs wearing black baggy jeans and a black denim jacket (this unusual costume, we are told, excites the interest of Neville, an old black man who eventually saves Billy's life). When (scene 16) Billy knocks on Marcia's door, however, he is greeted by Kath, a shaven-headed white woman who wears "tight blue jeans, white tee-shirt, red braces and cherry red docs." Her dog stands next to her (and this dog, we shall see, matters). Later (scene 22), after Marcia has sexually abused Billy (by tying him up in his own Union Jack boxer shorts) and thrown him out, Kath—"fully clothed"—gets into bed with Marcia and "wraps her arms around her from behind." What then are we to make of this complex pattern of dressing and undressing and cross-dressing? And of sexual aggression and submission and ambiguity?

Since baseball is scarcely ever played in Britain, the baseball bat has a much more sinister significance: it is a standard weapon of racist gangs. And this point is also picked up later: when, in scene 8, Marcia asks Billy whether he has ever touched a black woman before, his reply is "Only with a baseball bat." The model castle in the middle of Billy's room (a fortress protecting him from what?) is both example and symbol of unhealthy habits (the empty cigarette packets) and an inadequate diet (the boxes of mushroom-flavored soup). It is matched in Scene 8 by a pyramid of tin cans in Marcia's room. These cans, we learn, contain dog food (for Kath's dog presumably). In scene 11, Billy is forced to crouch naked on the floor while Marcia tips an opened tin of dog food into a bowl in front of him. In scene 17, the scene where Marcia rejects Billy, he looks at the dog bowl, which is now empty.

What is obvious is that *Skin* is not the straightforward piece of dramatized reportage of a day in the life of a skinhead that at first it might appear to be. In many ways, despite the constraints of television, it raises themes and questions common to all of Kane's plays.

CLEANSED

Sigmund Freud claimed that a distinctive feature of the way in which the imaginative power that puts our dreams together operates is that it analyzes everyday utterance into its component parts, interprets these parts literally, and then gives visual expression to them. So love, via the commonplace expression "You look so good that I could eat you," might be imaged in a dream as an act of cannibalism, an act which in waking life is strongly tabooed. Jokes operate in the same

way, and what both dreams and jokes express by this means is the dark counterpart that is repressed from our consciousness and from our serious (non-joking) utterance. Related to this point is Freud's further claim that in the visual language of dreams we cannot express a negative, so that what we in our waking lives accept and what we reject are equivalently imaged in a dream.

This absence of the negative is, indeed, a feature of any picture language. If someone tells you to imagine a field that does not have a tree in it, you cannot do so without imagining a tree; we summon up the tree mentally in order to disregard it. Kane's particular malfunction—and this is a critical rather than a psychological point—is that she could not disregard what her imagination presented to her. Harold Pinter, a keen admirer and defender of her work, says that, unlike the rest of us, having had her vision Kane could not "compromise with it." She simply could not edit down the flood of violent images with which every one of us is bombarded, could not put her awareness of physical horror "on the shelf" or out of mind (Hattenstone, *Guardian*, 1 July 2000). Kane herself makes the point even more tellingly: "Many people feel depression is about emptiness, but actually it's about being so full that everything cancels itself out." Or, adopting the language of parable, the life of a depressive is a ship that sinks because, though it rides low in the water and a storm rages, its captain refuses to throw anything overboard.

In Kane's work in general, and in *Cleansed* in particular, the everyday turn of phrase to which the play gives dreamlike or nightmarish or literal or imaginative or, in Freud's rather specialized use of the term, joking expression is that "love is tearing me apart." *Cleansed* begins with a rare joke (an entirely conscious one). One of the fiercest of the critics of *Blasted* was Jack Tinker, who reviewed the play for the *Daily Mail*, and who tore into it and wrenched it apart. In *Cleansed* he gives his name to the madly destructive psychiatrist whose cruelties abound in this most ostentatiously violent work. The relationship between Carl and Rod best illustrates this point. Their relationship is a homosexual one that must be repressed in pursuit of normality, and this is what

Tinker persistently does. When Carl tries to speak, Tinker cuts out his tongue (scene 4); when he tries to write, he cuts off his hands (scene 8), when he tries to dance (his "dance of love for Rod") he cuts off his feet (scene 16); and (also in scene 16) when, despite these torments, Rod and Carl are reconciled to each other, Tinker cuts Rod's throat. What is given physical enactment here is granted verbal expression in *4.48 Psychosis*:

Cut out my tongue,
tear out my hair
cut off my limbs
but leave me my love
I would rather have lost my legs
pulled out my teeth
gouged out my eyes
than lost my love

(p. 230)

This violence is, of course, extreme even by the standards of *Blasted*, but the nature of the violence and the stylization that is required if it is to be represented onstage means that we never lose sense of its theatricality or of its symbolic force. Indeed hostile critics noted this point but then turned it against the play. The director James Macdonald's elegant fulfillment of Kane's impossible stage directions (where colored streamers were used to suggest the blood flowing from amputated limbs) shocked greatly by not being shocking enough.

CRAVE AND 4.48 PSYCHOSIS

The most obvious thing to say about *Crave* and *4.48 Psychosis* (which are often presented in tandem) is not just that they are unlike Kane's other plays (there are, in fact, striking similarities) but rather that they are not really like plays at all. In *Blasted* Kane blew up the naturalistic stage-setting, but in *Crave* and *4.48 Psychosis* her dismantling activity is much more radical.

Crave is a piece for four actors who, as mentioned earlier, are identified for a reader's benefit by the four letters of the alphabet "A," "B," "C," and "M." They do not refer to one another by these letters, however; stage direc-

tions are minimal ("emits a short one syllable scream") and, because we do not know whether the theatrical convention whereby each speaker responds to the immediately preceding speaker is operating, we cannot be sure of who is addressing whom. In performance, no doubt, decisions of this kind have to be made: a production in which each speaker speaks in uncommunicative isolation and nobody addresses anybody might have some symbolic point but would be impossibly tiring. But the decisions made in one production will be unmade and remade in the next: Kane provides almost no constraints upon a director's, reader's, or performer's freedom of interpretation. And in *4.48 Psychosis* not even this much is given us. James Macdonald, who directed its first performance on 23 June 2000, chose three actors (one man and two women), but this decision once again cannot be binding. One can attach, it is true, labels with which to identify speakers in question-and-answer sequences like the following:

PSYCHIATRIST: Have you made any plans?
PATIENT: Take an overdose, slash my wrists then hang myself.
PSYCHIATRIST: All those things together?
PATIENT: It couldn't possibly be misconstrued as a cry for help. (*Silence.*)
PSYCHIATRIST: It wouldn't work.
PATIENT: Of course it would.

(p. 210)

But perhaps in pursuit of a sterner ending to the sequence we choose to suppose that the silence breaks the alternating pattern of the dialogue:

(*Silence.*)
Patient It wouldn't work.
Psychiatrist Of course it would.

The point is that we do the choosing; at a very fundamental level Kane's text of *4.48 Psychosis* keeps our interpretative options open.

How stageable are Kane's last plays? One simple and perfectly proper way of answering this question is by listing the very large number of productions that have appeared in theaters all over the world. Clearly plays staged this often are not plays that are impossible to stage. But the worry that underlies the question is not an empty one, and it does help us to ask what kind of thing (play or poem or performance or text) *Crave* or *4.48 Psychosis* is. The best place in which to appreciate this point is scene 15 of *Cleansed*. Although mild by the standards of the cruelty that Tinker exhibits elsewhere, this is a harrowing scene. Robin, who is an insecure, poorly educated, and deeply vulnerable young man, has bought a box of chocolates for Grace. These chocolates are, like so many presents, both a gift and a declaration of love. Tinker, as always happens when he sees love about to blossom, reacts violently. He tosses the chocolates one by one to Robin and forces him to eat them until the box is empty. The repetitive nature of the act perfectly symbolizes Tinker's obsessional personality—throwing the entire box at Robin would be petulant rather than scheming and deliberately cruel—and we see this obsessiveness when we watch the play. But we also see it (in a different meaning of the verb) when we notice how Kane sets out her stage direction. She prints

> TINKER *throws him another.*
> ROBIN *eats it.*

twenty-four times (with only an occasional minor variation). Set out this way, so as to take up a page and a half of print, the direction is extraordinarily wasteful of paper and is theatrically quite unnecessary; for the important point is that Tinker keeps on going until the box is empty, not that he repeats the action precisely twenty-four times. But the extended and repetitive direction does give physical expression—on the paper itself—to that obsessional nature to which performance gives alternative and more properly dramatic expression. One is reminded of concrete poetry, where the shape of the words on the page is part of the poem's meaning, or of a line from *4.48 Psychosis*: "Just a word on the page and there is the drama" (p. 213).

But in this chocolate-box example the theatrical equivalent of the point that is being made typographically is easily located: all that an actor need do is follow the direction. There are large parts of *4.48 Psychosis,* however, where the text seems to work typographically but not theatri-cally, rather than typographically as well as theatrically. How it ends (pp. 244–245) is a good example. As the voice that speaks (or voices that speak) runs (or run) out of words, the text thins out until more and more white paper surrounds and suggests the isolation of less and less ink. The last page has just two small blocks of print, twenty-one words in all (rather than the three hundred words that cram themselves onto a crowded page). This is a powerful, and power-fully visual, image, but one for which there is no obvious visual equivalent in performance.

Perhaps, though, what a director needs to find is a visual equivalent that is valid without being obvious. Kane, whether she was aware that these were to be her final plays or not, knew that they were a radical departure from her earlier work and recognized that they were structurally ambiguous, but she still thought of them as plays. "I wanted to find out how good a poet I could be while still writing something dramatic" was her own account of *Crave*. As was the case when he first saw *Blasted,* though this time more in sorrow than in anger, Michael Billington felt he had to express dissent. Of *4.48 Psychosis* he wrote ruefully that "the play is as much a literary as a theatrical event" (*Guardian*, 30 June 2000).

BIBLIOGRAPHY

I. COLLECTED WORKS. *Complete Plays*, intro. by David Greig, Methuen Contemporary Dramatists (London, 2001). This is the standard modern edition from which quotations in this essay have been taken.

II. OTHER EDITIONS. *Blasted*, in *Frontline Intelligence 2: New Plays for the Nineties* (London, 1994); *Blasted and Phaedra's Love* (London, 1996).

III. INTERVIEWS. Heide Stephenson and Natasha Langridge, *Rage and Reason: Women Playwrights on Playwriting* (London, 1997); Peter Buse, "Sarah Kane: In and On Media," in *Nach dem Film* 2 (December 2000).

IV. CRITICAL STUDIES. Tom Sellar, "Truth and Dare: Sarah Kane's *Blasted,*" in *Theater* 27, no. 1 (1996); Aleks Sierz, "Cool Britannia? 'In-Yer-Face' Writing in the British Theatre Today," in *New Theatre Quarterly* 56 (November 1998); James Hansford, "Sarah Kane," in Thomas Riggs, ed., *Contemporary Dramatists* (Detroit and New York, 1999); Dan Rebellato, "Sarah Kane: An Appreciation," in *New Theatre Quarterly* 15, no. 59 (August 1999); Dominic Dromgoole, *The Full Room: An A-Z of Contemporary Playwriting* (London, 2000); Richard Eyre and Nicholas Wright, *Changing Stages: A View of British Theatre in the Twentieth Century* (London, 2000); Peter Morris, "The Brand of

Kane," in *Areté* 4 (winter 2000); Aleks Sierz, *In-Yer-Face Theatre: British Drama Today* (London, 2000); Stefani Brusberg-Kiermeier, "Re-writing Seneca: Sarah Kane's *Phaedra's Love,"* Annette Pankratz, "Greek to Us? Appropriations of Myths in Contemporary British and Irish Drama," and Heiner Zimmermann, "Theatrical Transgression in Totalitarian and Democratic Societies: Shakespeare as a Trojan Horse and the Scandal of Sarah Kane," in Bernhard Reitz and Alyce von Rothkirch, eds., *Crossing Borders: Intercultural Drama and Theatre at the Turn of the Millennium* (Trier, Germany, 2001); Aleks Sierz, "The Element That Most Outrages: Morality, Censorship, and Sarah Kane's *Blasted,"* in Edward Batley and David Bradby, *Justice and Morality: Visions of Change in European Theatre* (Amsterdam, 2001); Aleks Sierz, "NTQ Checklist: Sarah Kane," in *New Theatre Quarterly* 67 (August 2001); Peter Buse, *Drama + Theory: Critical Approaches to Modern British Drama* (Manchester and New York, 2002); Graham Saunders, *"Love Me or Kill Me": Sarah Kane and the Theatre of Extremes* (Manchester and New York, 2002).

V. NEWSPAPER REVIEWS AND ARTICLES. Robin Stringer, *Evening Standard* (19 January 1995); Mike Ellison and Alex Bellos, *Guardian* (20 January 1995); Michael Billington, *Guardian* (20 January 1995); David Benedict, *Independent* (22 January 1995); John Gross, *Sunday Telegraph* (22 January 1995); James Macdonald, *Observer* (22 January 1995); Jonathan Miller, *Sunday Times* (22 January 1995); Clare Bayley, *Independent* (23 January 1995); Tom Morris, *Guardian* (25 January 1995); Patricia Holland, *Independent* (27 January 1995); Edward Bond, *Guardian* (28 January 1995); Tom Morris, *Sunday Times* (29 January 1995); Snoo Wilson, *New Statesman* (3 February 1995); Ruth James, *Socialist Review* 184 (March 1995); Sarah Hemming, *Financial Times* (18 November 1995); David Benedict, *Independent* (15 May 1996); Aleks Sierz, *Independent* (9 April 1997); Alison Boshoff, *Daily Telegraph* (16 June 1997);

James Christopher, *Observer* (2 November 1997); Lyn Gardner, *Guardian* (13 March 1998); Kate Stratton, *Time Out* (15 March 1998), *Theatre Record* (23 April–6 May 1998); Simon Fanshawe, *Sunday Times* (26 April 1998); Claire Armitstead, *Guardian* (29 April 1998); James Christopher, *Independent* (4 May 1998); David Benedict, *Independent* (13 August 1998); Caroline Egan, *Guardian* (21 September 1998). Lyn Gardner, *Guardian* (23 February 1999); Mark Ravenhill, *Independent* (obituary, 23 February 1999); Paul Taylor, *Independent* (24 February, 1999); *Independent* (24 February 1999); David Greig, *Herald* (obituary, 27 February 1999); *Daily Telegraph* (obituary, 27 February 1999); James Macdonald, *Guardian* (28 February 1999); James Macdonald, *Observer* (obituary, 28 February 1999); Jackie McGloan, *Scotsman* (obituary, 13 March 1999); John Mortimer, *New Statesman* (26 April 1999); Fiachra Gibbons, *Guardian* (20 September 1999); Aleks Sierz, *Daily Telegraph* (27 May 2000); Michael Billington, *Guardian* (30 June 2000); Simon Hattenstone, *Guardian* (1 July 2000); Susannah Clapp, *Observer* (2 July 2000); Dominic Cavendish, *Time Out* (5 July 2000); Matt Wolf, *Variety* (10 July 2000); Michael Billington, *Guardian* (5 April 2001); Charles Spencer, *Daily Telegraph* (5 April 2001); *Independent* (5 April 2001); *Financial Times* (6 April 2001); Andrew Smith, *Observer* (8 April 2001); Dominic Dromgoole, *New Statesman* (3 September 2001).

VI. BACKGROUND READING. Richard Findlater, ed., *At the Royal Court: Twenty-Five Years of the English Stage Company* (Ambergate, U.K., and New York, 1981); Philip Roberts, *The Royal Court Theatre, 1965–1972* (London and New York, 1986) and *The Royal Court Theatre and the Modern Stage* (Cambridge, 1999); Dominic Shellard, *British Theatre Since the War* (New Haven, Conn., 1999); Michelene Wandor, *Post-War British Drama: Looking Back in Gender* (London and New York, 2001).

MICHAEL LONGLEY

(1939–)

John Redmond

TROUBLINGLY SHADOWED BY a history of political violence, Northern Irish culture has seen a remarkable flowering of poets during the last thirty tears, including Seamus Heaney, Derek Mahon, Paul Muldoon and Medbh McGuckian. Of all these poets, the one who has been the least interested in extremes of form and subject-matter, and more modestly concerned with issues of scale and proportion, has been Michael Longley. Described by Seamus Deane as "the most civil" of Northern Irish poets, his technically adroit poems have pursued formal equilibrium, deepening, over the years, with the inclusion of more personal material (Deane, p. 243).

The image projected by Longley's poetic world is a readily identifiable one—a world of otters and lapwings, of sandy expanses and wild flowers, of clouds shuffling shadows on the bog between the mountains. While its concerns are universal, it is a private world well removed from media sensationalism, a world where an ever-deepening familiarity forces significant changes in perspective. There is no doubt that Longley is a poetic conservative—his writing has been characterized by a constant reworking, rendering the same material over and over again with steadily increasing assurance. Although he has relied heavily on a relatively limited set of devices including, for example, the animal-poem, the one-sentence poem, and the list-poem, he has used these devices in increasingly subtle ways. His development is less the result of conscious experiment as it is making the most of his own poetic limitations.

Longley has found himself suspended between a number of provocative contrasts. A poet of urban Belfast who repeatedly writes about the rural landscape of the West of Ireland, an Ulster Protestant who feels close to the Irish Republic, he is very scrupulous about defining entities, from the smallest to the largest, through their relationships with each other. Avoiding rigid concepts of identity has proved fruitful with respect to the distorted political entity where he grew up and to which, despite its evident drawbacks, he has continued to be loyal:

> [Ulster is] one of the most interesting, if heartbreaking, places in the world. It's like living in three places at once; Ulster is a province of Ireland, it's a province of the UK and it's also its own awkward self. It's been a privilege.
>
> (*Irish Times*, 9 March 2000)

Within his poetry, questions of intricate political relationship are absorbed into larger questions of relationship about the nature of all relationships, of entities which can only be defined by their relationship to others. The poem "A Questionnaire for Walter Mitty," for instance, which appeared in his first book *No Continuing City*, takes as its theme the relationship of desire to fiction and to reality. Since Mitty is given to daydreaming, the poem ponders whether or not he might experience real self-transformation in, and through, his fantasies. The question, however, is left unanswered. Instead it is asked in a variety of different ways and the possible definitions are arranged at suggestive angles to each other. In a way typical of Longley's later poetry, Mitty is left suspended between rival identities:

> At which side of the glass does Mitty stand
> In his epiphany—in front? behind?
> Or both—the hero with the also-ran?
>
> And, Walter Mitty, how would you define
> The water-walker who made the water wine—
> Was it Christ the god? Was it Christ the Man?
>
> (p. 12)

The poem ends as it began in a series of contrasts: contrasting positions, "front" and "behind";

contrasting types, "hero" and "also-ran"; contrasting elements, "water" and "wine"; contrasting spirits, "God" and "Man."

Growing up in Ulster as the son of English parents, Longley was in the habit of assuming multiple identities from an early age, alternating for example between an English accent spoken in the home and a Belfast accent spoken in the schoolyard. As a result, he has been acutely conscious of the subtle ebb and flow of allegiance in response to social and political pressures. Commenting positively on political accords that had recently been signed in Northern Ireland, he spoke about the feelings of relief which have come in their wake:

> The Good Friday Agreement and the power-sharing executive are triumphs of the political imagination. They allow me to feel more Irish, more British and just as importantly, more neither.
>
> (*Irish Times*, 9 March 2000)

Michael Longley, like his fellow Northern Irish poet, Seamus Heaney, was born in 1939, the year when W. B. Yeats died. Longley remembers his father, Richard, as a kind and gentle character, who retained the aura of a colourful past. Richard Longley, who was known to some in Northern Ireland as "the Major" (although he did not like the title) had fought in both world wars. His military memories, which included the extraordinarily destructive Battle of the Somme, were a major influence on Longley's poetic sensibility. A successful soldier, he had become a captain by the age of twenty. Repelled by the snobbery of ranking officers, however, he left the military for an adventurous spell of mining in Africa. Themes of disappearance and erasure are prominent in Longley's poetry, and this original family migration is one of their influences. Not all disappearances in the family history were as positive. Longley's maternal grandfather, George, who regaled the boy with fantasies of having fought in the Boer War, contrived never to mention his own retarded son who had disappeared in the First World War. In retrospect, Longley recognized that this occlusion, like many others in Northern Ireland, was rooted in the tragic intersection of family and conflict:

> The tragedy of the Somme affects all of Ulster.... My father's own experiences, which he recounted vividly on only a couple of occasions, have allowed me to participate in the community's glum pride. My mother's mentally retarded brother disappeared in the Trenches—and from family conversation. His vanishing act haunted my childhood much more than the vaster catastrophe ever did.
>
> (in Healy, p. 130)

By the time he returned to Clapham in England at the age of thirty, Richard Longley had a glamorous allure and soon met his future wife, Connie. He was now a commercial traveler for a firm of furniture manufacturers, and his work took him to Ireland with which he promptly fell in love. Together with his wife he came over from Clapham and they settled in Belfast in 1927.

Longley's childhood, shared with one sister, Wendy, and his twin brother, Peter, was by no means idyllic. Although both parents were depressive, there was a severe contrast between their personalities. His mother, the victim both of a traumatic childhood and a hip malformation which made her limp, was given to sudden moodswings. Indeed, Longley discovered near the time when she died in 1979, that she had tried to have the twins aborted. She transferred her feelings of anxiety on to her children, a turbulence which Michael struggled to forgive:

> Like my father, she [Longley's mother] was a depressive, and the latter part of Peter's and my childhood probably coincided with her menopause. By that time she would have been well into her forties, my father in his mid-fifties. They withdrew into themselves still further, and Wendy, a maturing teenager who at sixteen had already fallen in love with her future husband, Ernie Clegg, started to fill the emotional gaps.
>
> (*Tuppenny Stung*, p. 21)

Another mark of difference which made Longley self-conscious about his identity was his school. In an area which had many working-class families, he found that, compared to the other children, he was comfortably middle-class. His cultural formation at school was resolutely Unionist. Anti-Catholic sentiment was a common feature, and Longley recalls much lurid propaganda about the other religion being shared amongst his peers. The curriculum of both his primary school and his grammar school little reflected that the students were living on the island of Ireland (*Tuppenny Stung*, p. 27). Significantly, in view of the Homeric structures in his later poetry, Longley had gravitated towards the classics, which he would go on to specialize in at university when he went to Trinity College, Dublin, in 1958.

Longley's first important literary friendship was with Derek Mahon, a fellow Protestant, who attended the same school as Longley: the Royal Belfast Academical Institution. Because of the gap in age (Mahon was Longley's junior by two years), the two did not meet properly until university. Although Longley was on the editorial board of the college literary magazine, *Icarus*, he was ambivalent about his desire to write, describing himself, in retrospect, as "an aesthete in private, a hearty in public who briefly made it on the 1st XV [the rugby team]" (*Tuppenny Stung*, p. 33). Mahon, though younger, was at that stage far ahead of his friend in terms of literary sophistication, and so Longley's decision to befriend him was made with mixed feelings:

> ... poets, because they should never completely grow up, must continually come of age. I began to come of age—or come of age for the first time—when I decided to embrace the pain of friendship with a younger poet who seemed already to have arrived while I was just setting out.
>
> (*Tuppenny Stung*, p. 35)

The friendship prospered. Together they read contemporary poetry voraciously, swapped poems and criticized each other's work. After graduation, they shared a flat in Dublin's Merrion Square. Longley was making ends meet with a job he enjoyed, teaching Latin at a school in Blackrock.

Since 1960, the year when his father died, Longley had been courting Edna Broderick, the daughter of the professor of pure mathematics at Trinity, who would become one of Ireland's major literary critics. When Edna acquired a job in Belfast, Longley followed her there and found another job as a schoolteacher. The pair were married the day before New Year's Eve, 1964. Along with Mahon (who was best man at the wedding), Longley's circle of literary friendships and connections was significantly expanding. Through his wife he met the English literary critic, Philip Hobsbaum, a visiting lecturer at Queen's and the dominant presence in the fabled "Belfast Group." The Group met regularly to discuss poems and included many young writers and artists, including Seamus Heaney. The value of the Group to its various participants has since been disputed. It was probably more important for Heaney whose approach to poetry found favor with Hobsbaum. As Longley remarked, "Hobsbaum's aesthetic demanded gritty particularity, an unrhetorical utterance" (*Tuppenny Stung*, p. 40). Longley's style, which was more oblique and polished, quickly put him at odds with Hobsbaum. Nevertheless, Longley had entered an important literary circle and the friendships he made with Heaney and others endured.

Longley's first book *No Continuing City* (1969) emerged at the onset of the Troubles. It was a difficult time for him personally, as he pondered his future, and experienced what he later characterized as a minor mid-life crisis (in Ní Anluain, ed., p. 127). Around this time, he began to visit the West of Ireland for the first time, beginning an association with a landscape that would come to dominate his work. The uncertainty of his career in teaching was ended by his decision to join the Arts Council of Northern Ireland, the main plank of his non-literary career, and a job he would hold for twenty-one years. Longley got into the job through his interest in painting—his reviews alerted the attention of the council director, Kenneth Jamison, which resulted in an offer of a job as temporary Exhibitions Officer. While this led him in his first year to supervising the hanging of exhibition paintings, Longley also edited an anthology of poems by young people called *Causeway*. At a time of increasing sectarian violence, the title revealed his typically strong sense of civic responsibility, as he explained in his introduction to the volume:

> In one of the dictionaries I consulted 'causeway' is defined as a path of stepping stones. This is, I think, a fair description of the role played by the arts in any society: it defines what should reasonably be

expected of them in all civilised countries, but especially in a troubled community like our own.

(*Causeway*, p. 9)

Although a native of Belfast he spends about two weeks of every year holidaying in the townland of Carrigskeewaun in County Mayo, and from this landscape are drawn the animals and plants which populate much of his work. Although he spends only two weeks out of every year there, so many of his poems are set there, one might think that he was there all year round. Longley's poems about landscape are to some extent those of an outsider. And he is conscious of this fact.

The cottage in Mayo to which the Longleys go each year belongs to David Cabot, naturalist, author, and film-maker, who was responsible (together with Michael Viney) for a television documentary on the poet. *The Corner Of The Eye* begins with a great purple-blue slice of Connemara tracked by its panning camera, a few tawny cows nosing through the foreground, then closes in on a little white cottage, and then on the face of its occupant, Michael Longley. As he talks not quite to camera, Longley describes the process of exploring a place in a manner which the film's opening sequence seeks to imitate. He describes how, as a native of Belfast, he started to spend holidays in Carrigskeewaun just when the Troubles were breaking out in Northern Ireland and what first impressed him was the horizon, the sense of unlimited space, the lines of hills. Then, gradually, he became more aware of the middle distance of walls and trees and roads until finally, his love affair with the landscape ended on his hands and knees as he looked "into the faces of small flowers."

Between his job in Belfast and his holidays in Mayo, Longley entered a settled period of his life. The Mayo landscape provided him with a pastoral counterpoint to his feelings about the violence in Northern Ireland, feelings which dominate his next three books, *An Exploded View*, (1973) *Man Lying On A Wall*, (1976) and, perhaps his best book, *The Echo Gate*, (1979). Longley's connections through the Arts Council, particularly with pivotal senior figures of the cultural scene like Estyn Evans and John Hewitt, helped to deepen his understanding of the regional Ulster traditions which derived from both communities. Many of these traditions remained contentious. In the 1970s, for example, during the time of some of worst sectarian tit-for-tat murders, he went on tour with Irish folk musicians, a perilous activity given the cultural prejudices of certain audiences:

So far as Protestant paramilitaries were concerned, all Irish musicians were part of a pan-Celtic conspiracy and would have been legitimate targets. In certain locations I was aware of a rather spooky and frightening antagonism in the audiences, and so were the musicians.... For me this was an education, a belated education in Irish music.

(in Ní Anluain, p. 130)

Longley's administrative career resulted in other achievements as he established for the first time writers-in-residence (including writers in the Irish language) at the University of Ulster, Coleraine and at Queen's University, Belfast. He did not, however, enjoy the increasing bureaucracy of his job, and the latter half of his career in the 1980s was an unhappy time, although his commitment to cross-community understanding remained and he helped set up the Cultural Traditions Group in 1988. The unpleasant demands of his job coincided with a fallow period in his poetic career, and Longley did not produce a new collection for twelve years. He did not emerge again until *Gorse Fires* appeared in 1991, a volume which won him the Whitbread Poetry Award. The new book saw him under Homeric influences, as he began to connect the tragic experience of Northern Ireland with motifs in Latin and Greek poetry. The soft and mollified outlines of Longley's later poetry brings to mind another image from David Cabot's documentary of the poet staring out to sea in a peat-coloured coat, his ankles in the Atlanic, his trousers rolled up to his knee, holding a pair of wellington boots. The image is of a self-conscious kind of calm, of a personality entirely at ease within its own boundaries. Longley's late books have won him increasing recognition, and he is certainly one of the most prominent of all contemporary poets. His book *The Weather in Japan* won the T. S. Eliot prize in 2001 and later the same year he won the Queen's Gold Medal for Poetry.

NO CONTINUING CITY

Longley's early poetry is open to many influences, including the formalism and wit of Auden and Louis MacNeice. Terence Brown describes it as

> ... the work of a self-conscious, urban sophisticate for whom Ireland as a possible poetic subject scarcely exists. Indeed his first volume, *No Continuing City* (1969), contained only one poem on an explicitly Irish subject. In that collection we enter a world of private associations, of wit, intelligence and formal relations.
>
> (Brown, p. 201)

One can extend Brown's reasonable observations to say that not only does Ireland scarcely exist as a poetic subject in *No Continuing City,* the poetic subjects themselves exist very much in a shadowy, secondary way; wit, intelligence and formal relations are the poem's most prominent characteristics. Brown emphasizes the technical character of the volume because the characters in so many of the poems, like "Emily Dickinson" and "Words for Jazz Perhaps," are either literary or musical technicians, and because the characters in some of the other poems, like "Odyssey" and "Circe," merely aid the poet's advancement of his technique. Throughout *No Continuing City,* the poet's personality is deliberately withheld from the reader.

For Longley it seems to have been helpful that poems about animals can be written without revealing much about oneself, a practice utilized by Ted Hughes, particularly in the volume *Lupercal,* of which Longley has spoken highly ("The State of Poetry," pp. 3–75). Animals extend Longley's opportunity to deploy contrast because their characteristics can be played off against the characteristics of the human world. In this respect individual phrases and passages owe a good deal to *Lupercal.* Consider the way in which Hughes ends a poem like "Mayday on Holderness":

Curded to beastings, broached my palate,
The expressionless gaze of the leopard,

The coils of the sleeping anaconda,
The nightlong frenzy of shrews.

(*Lupercal,* Faber, 1960, p. 12)

Here the animals do not dominate the poem—as they often do in *Lupercal*—but rather provide an illuminating contrast to the human element as represented by the shadowy narrator. Human society is freshly seen when juxtaposed with the animal kingdom. In this way the poem, by claiming less importance for itself as a specifically human document, seems more measured and balanced. This kind of extra-social animal poem in *Lupercal* is clearly behind a poem like Longley's "Christopher At Birth":

Although there is such a story to unfold
—Whether as forecast or reminder—
Of cattle steaming in their byres, and sheep
Beneath a hedge, arranged against the cold,
Our cat at home blinking by the fender,
The wolf treading its circuit towards sleep.

(*No Continuing City,* p. 43)

There are strong resemblances here to "Mayday on Holderness." In the penultimate line, for instance, an image of animal quiescence is contrasted, as in the Hughes poem, with a final image of animal ferocity. The lack of enjambment towards the end of each stanza is also tellingly similar. Many of the poems in *Lupercal* allow the animals to suggest ways in which human beings might live (and die): to be extremely cruel ("Hawk Roosting"); to be immensely adaptable ("An Otter"); to be as nothing in death ("View of a Pig"). They represent ways of being in the world, which are obviously not confined to animals.

A clearly related concern is Longley's melancholy attitude towards mortality, projected on to other biological creatures. The poem, "To Three Irish Poets," for example, indicates an early fascination with the theme of erasure—animals are creatures which like ourselves can be read through the temporary marks they leave behind, but these readings are provisional and, like their subjects, already beginning to vanish:

The approximate untold barks
Of the otters we call water-dogs,

\\A dim reflection of ourselves,
A muddy forepaw that dissolves.

(An Exploded View, p. 32)

Not all poems in *No Continuing City* are as oblique, and Longley sometimes makes the narrator an actor, although the stance remains mostly impersonal. A more integrated poem from the volume is called "The Hebrides." The action, this time, takes place in a recognizable landscape rather than a metaphysical ante-room, and the musings of the poet are projected more dramatically on the scene. Birds, again, are used to balance the human element:

> Between wind and wave this holiday
> The cormorant,
> The oyster-catcher and osprey
> Proceed and keep in line
> While I, hands in my pockets, hesitant,
> Am in two minds.
>
> (p. 27)

Just as the holiday is balanced between wind and wave, just as the poet's human response is balanced by the presence of the natural creatures, his mind is balanced between two choices. When the nature of his choice is finally revealed to us, it appears in very vague and abstract terms. The poem concludes:

> Granting the trawlers far below their stance,
> Their anchorage,
> I fight all the way for balance—
> In the mountain's shadow
> Losing foothold, covet the privilege
> Of vertigo.
>
> (p. 29)

The stanza is memorable because, to an extent which is unusual in *No Continuing City*, its unfolding play of abstractions balances the formal and dramatic dimensions. The unvoiced fricatives of "fight" and "foothold" give way, at the most urgent point of the narrator's struggle, to the sumptuous, resonantly voiced fricatives of "covet," "privilege," and "vertigo." Ultimately though, the poem rests too heavily on the mere balance of abstractions.

Because of the central role of contrast in these early poems, metaphysical values are frequently juxtaposed with physical states. For instance, in "The Ornithological Section," the dead, stuffed birds on a physical level are balanced between stillness and flux, while, on a metaphysical level, their representations are balanced between what might be broadly described as a "cold," scientific outlook and a "warm," imaginative one. While Longley recognizes the birds' stillness, the inescapable, scientific fact of their death, he balances this with a kind of imaginative empathy, which can see them as moving things, that is, in flux. Longley is torn between an empirical rendering of the birds as they are and an imaginative rendering of what they might have been:

> while winging it through fable,
> Fuse all we hope with what we know—
> Their fate incontrovertible,
> Their vanished bodies flying still.
>
> (p. 16)

A further focus of attention, which becomes increasingly important, collection by collection, is the theme of war. Only embryonically present in *No Continuing City*, the topic of war features in two poems, "The Centaurs" and "In Memoriam." "The Centaurs" is a surreal fable, related to the hazy allegories of "The Hebrides" and "Camouflage." Politically, it is a good example of Longley's consistent moderation, as he puts his point in the communal (and impersonal) first person plural:

> Into the water our youth is spilled.
> We make on the causeways our last stands.
> Because of the bridges we did not build
> Our whole army fights for balance.
>
> (p. 36)

"Fighting for balance," a phrase also used in "The Hebrides," takes on a deeper meaning in this poem, for Longley relates it to the divisions in Northern Irish society. The poem ends with a utopian vision of reconciliation:

> our nightmare now a mystery tour,
> At ease along the river's edges
> Each cavalry man becomes a centaur,
> The causeways growing into bridges.
>
> (p. 37)

This very schematic poem tries to combine opposites and to squeeze out differences. The soldier, like a scion of the Great War, representing the loss of Georgian innocence, and the centaur, as though escaped from the arboreal mists of some Georgian pastoral, seem welded together at the point of the horse's saddle into a composite creature. Such a blend as this, in Longley's first book, of pre-war innocence and post-war anxiety, can be seen still in *Gorse Fires* (1991), in a poem like "Stone-In-Oxney," showing the continuity of his poetic obsessions.

In contrast to the fabular distance of "The Centaurs," another poem from *No Continuing City*, "In Memoriam" crisply records the experiences of Longley's father in The Great War. It balances the wartime horror of "shrapnel shards that sliced your testicle" with his father's post-war efforts to verify his sexual potency with "chorus girls and countesses." At the end of the poem, Longley summons these girls into his own imagination:

Now those lost wives as recreated brides
Take shape before me, materialise.
On the verge of light and happy legend
They lift their skirts like blinds across your eyes.

(p. 42)

Here Longley's style advances beyond the point of manipulating abstractions like "balance" and "vertigo." He deploys a grimly realistic style which graduates towards a moment of lyrical release. The poem ends neatly in a lyric brightening, although so emphatic here as to be more in the nature of a neat conclusion than the kind of meaningful occlusion which can be found, for example, in Philip Larkin's "High Windows."

In view of the detachment of so many poems in *No Continuing City*, "In Memoriam" was an important poem for Longley, who described it as "certainly some kind of descent from the ivory tower" (in Healy, p. 131). But for the most part, Longley's early poems had no great theme, no animating centre. All that he had was an obvious desire to write and to write well—combined with a less tangible desire for "balance." But, if one has no great theme, what does one write about? Longley could at least create, with the aid of his sound technique, considerable aesthetic impact. That is why he makes such use of contrast in *No*

Continuing City and why he includes so many animals in the book. He sees them as opportunities for technical displays, especially as opportunities for the use of contrast.

AN EXPLODED VIEW

Longley's second volume, *An Exploded View* (1973), is generally seen as a more personal work than *No Continuing City*. The poems are shorter and rather more oblique. There are fewer full-blown allegories and there is greater use of metonymy. Animals are still used, however, very much in the manner of *No Continuing City*, and Longley's basic poetic posture—not so much sitting on the fence, as sitting on the central hub from which all fences radiate—is maintained. In a poem like "The Corner of the Eye," for instance, Longley shows various aspects of his persistent desire for balance:

> *kingfisher*

> a knife-thrower
> hurling himself, a rainbow
> fractured against
> the plate glass of winter

(p. 26)

In this poem, the kingfisher is delicately poised between air and water, in the same way as it seems to be suspended, because of the clever line-break before the verb, between stillness and flux. It is also suspended, in an intriguing way, between versions of itself. The trope of self-manipulation, represented by the phrase "hurling himself" is significant.

Christopher Ricks has noted that this trope, in Marvell's England and in Northern Ireland, may reflect the pressures of civil war, as it "simultaneously acknowledges the opposing forces and yearns to reconcile them" (Ricks, p. 55).

Longley's kingfisher splits from himself under pressure, as well as acting "amphibiously"—balancing itself between different elements. In a poem which deals more directly with the historical pressure on him, "Kindertotenlieder," Longley abandons the conspicuously self-confident tone of his first volume and attempts something more understated:

There can be no songs for dead children
Near the crazy circle of explosions,
The splintering tangent of the ricochet,

No songs for the children who have become
My unrestricted tenants, fingerprints
Everywhere, teethmarks on this and that.

(p. 42)

The frequent, almost obsessive use of marks of every kind is one of the hallmarks of Longley's poetry and this use is especially obvious in *An Exploded View*: fingerprints, fingernails, footprints, toenails, toothmarks, cattle tracks. These fragments of creatures and things, like the relatively short poems of his second volume, underline the slightly altered nature of Longley's poetic ambitions. Because the most significant difference if not, perhaps, the most obvious one between *No Continuing City* and *An Exploded View* is the shift from the allegorical to the metonymical. Brian McIlroy has speculated on the reasons for the increased reliance on metonymy:

> ... in Michael Longley's poetry there is a discernible fascination with parts because no one whole is available. It is as if we are given parts to assemble into some pattern, into some unified subject, which perforce must remain anonymous, nameless, or simply pluralist.

(McIlroy, p. 61)

McIlroy goes on to identify the political ramifications of Longley's attachment to parts and to the rendering of parts, connecting it with the Ulster Protestant's habitual sensitivity to external pressures, the so-called "siege mentality" ("Poetry Imagery as Political Fetishism," p. 60). On another level, Longley's poetry represents the problems of a part, like Northern Ireland, which is or has been subject to various attempts to reorient itself in relation to larger wholes, like the Republic of Ireland, the United Kingdom, and Europe. Like Northern Ireland, it is not always clear what his parts are part of. They might be as much a part of one thing as another—and seem

balanced *between* the various options. Alan Peacock notes the way in which Longley, like MacNeice, has little trouble writing from within a British cultural framework while at the same time being happy to describe himself as "Irish" (Peacock, p. 263). Discussing MacNeice's cultural identity, Longley describes Ulster as "a limbo between two (three?) cultures"—and here the question mark is surely indicative of a markedly unresolved identity (in Dunn, ed., p. 99).

Longley's metonymical poetic objects, which are widely distributed throughout *An Exploded View*, are on the whole suggestive rather than descriptive. They encourage the reader to imagine and infer rather in the way that an excavated bone can allow a paleontologist to picture a dinosaur. Such delicacy can be seen, for instance in "Love Poem":

I

You define with your perfume
Infinitely shifting zones
And print in falls of talcum
The shadow of your foot.

2

Gossamers spun from your teeth,
So many light constructions
Describing as with wet wings
The gully under my tongue.

3

These wide migrations begin
In our seamier districts—
A slumdweller's pigeons
Released from creaking baskets.

(p. 15)

There is no trace here of the heavy abstractions which dominated *No Continuing City*. The poem makes its point through the quiet manipulation of suggestive parallelisms. The lover is imagined not as a whole, but in the context of various parts: "teeth," "feet," "wings," "tongue." This miniaturisation is also reflected in the polysyllabic words: "infinitely," "constructions," "migrations." The crammed light syllables evoke small spaces rather than large abstractions. The poem ends with the sudden brightness (the release of pigeons in the air), which is so often associated with lyrical release in the poets. The suggestive contract of the last stanza undermines the slightly over-absorbed world of the lovers.

Longley's tendency in *No Continuing City* to extend metaphors is thus severely curtailed in *An Exploded View*. The use of such extended metaphors (allegory, fable) had given an impression of trying to control his material in too complete a way. After all, if one tries to substitute a fable for a social situation, as he had tried to do in "The Centaurs," one must have—or appear to have—a deep understanding of the social situation. Allegory, in other words, demands that the observer is in complete command of that which he surveys and that he can represent it in terms of something else, of which he must also be in complete command.

Metonymy, on the other hand, is uncommanding. It suggests that because you only represent a part of something, you are only able to represent part of it, that there is something inhibiting a complete treatment of your subject. This is especially the case where the poet appears not to be playing games with the reader. This style suited the increasingly more casual tone of Longley's work.

Stephen Spender has remarked of the Thirties poetic generation that it owed its fascination with the works of such poets as Wilfred Owen to the fact that its parent's generation lived (and died) during the Great War (*Love-Hate Relations: A Study of Anglo-American Sensibilities*, 1974, p. 144). As Longley and Hughes both had fathers who fought in that war, it is no surprise that they too are both very interested in twentieth-century war poets, particularly Wilfred Owen, Edward Thomas, and Keith Douglas. Paul Fussell, in *The Great War and Modern Memory*, noticed similarities of approach to the issue of the Great War in the poetry of both Longley and Hughes and deals with both poets side by side. He points out the significance to Longley's canon of the poem "Wounds" in *An Exploded View* and observes that Longley, like Hughes, "derives his images not from experience but from mythic narrative" (Fussell, p. 324). "Wounds" is in a direct line of

development from the poem "In Memoriam" and deals, in a grimly realistic way, with the experiences of his father, at one point imagining his burial:

> with military honours of a kind
> With his badges, his medals like rainbows,
> His spinning compass, I bury beside him
> Three teenage soldiers, bellies full of
> Bullets and Irish beer, their flies undone.
>
> (p. 40)

The passage shows the increasing delicacy of Longley's verse, in particular, the emotional emphasis which is placed on small objects like "badges" and "flies."

Fussell also makes a useful observation that bears on the trope of self-manipulation, examined above. The way in which this trope appears to be a response to enormous pressure agrees with Fussell's observation of an effect that the war had on its soldiers:

> Seeing warfare as theater provides a psychic escape for the participant: with a sufficient sense of theater, he can perform his duties without implicating his "real" self and without impairing his innermost conviction that the world is still a rational place.
>
> (p. 192)

Another poem which confirms the advance made by Longley in *An Exploded View* is the quiet and subtle "Swans Mating":

> Even now I wish that you had been there
> Sitting beside me on the riverbank:
> The cob and his pen sailing in rhythm
> Until their small heads met and the final
> Heraldic moment dissolved in ripples.
>
> This was a marriage and a baptism,
> A holding of breath, nearly a drowning,
> Wings spread wide for balance where he trod,
> Her feathers full of water and her neck
> Under the water like a bar of light.
>
> (p. 22)

Here the most important lines are the first and the last. The phrase "Even now..." with its faintly exhausted and belated air sets the tone immediately. It parallels in an interesting way the opening phrase of Derek Mahon's most well-known poem, "A Disused Shed In Co. Wexford": "Even now there are places a thought might grow." Each phrase seems to assert that something positive has already been lost while holding out the possibility of either reclaiming or replacing it. Like the trope of self-manipulation, the phrase suggests that the poem's action is taking place in spite of some great unidentified pressure.

The middle part of "Swans Mating" depends, to a disappointing extent, on clichéd juxtapositions like "sailing in rhythm" and "This was a marriage and a baptism." But the poem is rescued by its conclusion. The last line is particularly evocative because, as in "The Ornithological Section," it embodies a contrast between the aridly scientific and the warmly imaginative ways of seeing. The phrase "bar of light" ambiguously combines these qualities. The word "bar" has undertones of the scientific and the rational, in the sense that it can be used to describe a metal rod and also because it forms parts of words which are used to measure natural phenomena, like "isobar" and "millibar." Meanwhile, by the end of the poem we are given the expected lyric blur with its associations with transcendence and epiphany. Longley's "bar of light" suggestively combines associations with the mechanical and the natural worlds. The use of mechanical imagery to describe natural things reminds us that our world, the world of machines, always tends to undermine Nature. Thus the phrase, which climaxes the poem, also holds it in careful balance. It reminds us that any natural idyll is always under pressure, just as Longley's poetic procedures are always under pressure from natural and historical events.

MAN LYING ON A WALL

Longley's third collection, *Man Lying On A Wall* (1976), is a consolidation, rather than an advance, on the successful practices of *An Exploded View*. The title poem returns us, insistently, to the theme of balance:

You could draw a straight line from the heels,
Through calves, buttocks and shoulderblades
To the back of the head: pressure points
That bear the enormous weight of the sky.
Should you take away the supporting structure
The result would be a miracle or
An extremely clever conjuring trick.
As it is, the man lying on the wall
Is wearing the serious expression
Of popes and kings in their final slumber

(p. 42)

Here are all the familiar concerns: the emphasis on body parts and the emphasis on the pressure, which the poem's subject is coming under. The concern with a still body, so important in Northern Irish poetry is one which Longley will extend in his next collection, *The Echo Gate*.

On the back cover of *Man Lying on a Wall*, there is the following quote from Longley:

This is my most personal book to date. Certainly its privacies were not conceived in reaction to the political and more public utterances of its predecessor, *An Exploded View*: both books grew out of similar preoccupations and pressures. The man lying on the wall might be resting between sleep and waking, dream and reality, life and death.

Evidently, the importance of balance has not diminished for Longley. The difference between *Man Lying on a Wall* and the poems of his first collection is that the assembled contrasts of the blurb above would have been stated in the poem rather than suggested by it.

Another poem of some importance to this collection is "The Goose." Like "Man Lying on a Wall" it deals with a still body; indeed, it deals with its dismemberment:

I thought of you through the operation
And covered the unmolested head,
The pink eyes that had persisted in
An expression of disappointment.

It was right to hesitate before
I punctured the skin, made incisions
And broached with my reluctant fingers
The chill of its intestines

(p. 11)

Although this is merely a domestic scene, the preparation of a goose for cooking, it is shot through with a sense of violence on a grander scale. Somewhat more amplified in its intimation of exterior pressures than "Swans Mating,", it nevertheless acts like that poem in a fundamentally suggestive manner. McIlroy uses it as an example of how Longley, in a troubling manner, fetishizes parts, so the poem can be read as a distant displacement of political violence ("Poetry Imagery as Political Fetishism," p. 62). The poem from Hughes's canon which it brings to mind is "View of a Pig" from *Lupercal*:

The pig lay on a barrow dead.
It weighed, they said, as much as three men.
Its eyes closed, pink white eyelashes.
Its trotters stuck straight out.

...

Too deadly factual. Its weight
Oppressed me—how could it be moved?
And the trouble of cutting it up!
The gash in its throat was shocking, but not pathetic.

(*Lupercal*, p. 40)

There are clear similarities: the use of an overtly pretty colour, pink, in an ugly context; the cold emphasis on body parts; the mild reluctance of the dismembering party. Hughes's detached stare could, one feels, issue from anyone who destroys life, from a trench-soldier to a death-camp doctor. The only real difference between Longley and Hughes, in this case, is that Hughes wants to bring us face to face with this violent extremity, while Longley is forced to do the same under pressure.

THE ECHO GATE

The pressure seems even stronger in Longley's fourth and possibly best collection, *The Echo Gate* (1979). The emphasis on objectified body parts is extended until it becomes reminiscent of Seamus Heaney's procedures in *North*. In a poem like "Oliver Plunkett," for instance, Longley dwells on minute parts of the body; the emphasis on weight and fingernails is most reminiscent of Heaney's "The Tollund Man":

His thigh bones and shoulder blades are scales
That a speck of dust would tilt, making him

Walk with a limp or become a hunchback.

He has been buried under the fingernails
Of his executioners, until they too fade
Like the lightning flash of their instruments.

(p. 11)

Here the terror, which was only present by implication in "The Goose," is made explicit by the word "executioners." The contrast between scientific objectification and imaginative love that runs through so many of Longley's poems continues here. Just as the "bar of light" in "Swans Mating" embodies this contrast, here the same function is carried out by the phrase "the lightning flash of their instruments," a strange lyric intensification, where the evil and mechanical instruments are poised ambiguously with the vital freedom of the lightning flash. Does the flash cancel the instruments or do the instruments simply cancel the flash? The reader is balanced between the options.

Throughout *The Echo Gate* the war motif continues to play an important role. Just as Longley in "Wounds" placed the poems in the historical context provided by the First World War, in *The Echo Gate*, he juxtaposes poems about the conflict in Northern Ireland like the sequence "Wreaths" with poems which deal with the violence in Flanders like "Last Requests" and "Second Sight." This is done to such an extent that when Longley writes a poem called "The War Poets," the word "war" has an intentionally global resonance:

It was rushes of air that took the breath away
As though curtains were drawn suddenly aside
And darkness streamed into the dormitory
Where everybody talked about the war ending
And always it would be the last week of the war.

(p. 34)

Once one realizes that Longley, in this stanza, is referring to more than one "war," it recalls the half-serious historical remark that World War I and World War II were in reality one "Giant War" with a twenty-year ceasefire in the middle. Longley's poems in *The Echo Gate* and elsewhere would seem to extend this "Giant War" into the

Troubles of Northern Ireland. The effect is remarkably similar to Heaney's juxtaposition of contemporary violence in *North* with the violence of Iron Age communities. Longley, like Heaney, mythologizes the conflict; instead of investigating its real historical causes, he makes it seem contiguous with the violence of another time, of the First World War, just a Heaney made it seem contiguous with the violence of the Iron Age. This demonstrates that the processes of the two poets are very similar.

The major achievement of *The Echo Gate* comes in a sequence where Longley shows a little-used talent for projecting himself into alternative lives. Previously, Longley's creation's of imagined speakers were exercises in wish-fulfilment in which he became, say, a more cosmopolitan or bohemian version of himself. In a remarkable sequence of four poems entitled "Mayo Monologues," however, he catches the desperation of rural existences, lives which he would not want to occupy:

They have locked me up in the institute
Because I made love to the animals.
I'd sooner stand barefoot, without a cap
And take in the acres from a distance,
From the rocky hilltops or the seashore,
From the purgatory of the windy gaps.

This sequence could be put alongside some of the best of Frost's poems such as "A Servant to Servants" or "The Death of The Hired Man" or Patrick Kavanagh's "The Great Hunger." The scorching pessimism of these poems is rare in Longley's work, perhaps because the poems have usually moved away from extremes of emotion towards an accepting calm, the mood in which Longley's late poetry is saturated.

GORSE FIRES

In *Gorse Fires* (1991), a collection which came out after a hiatus of a dozen years, Longley extends the devices which proved successful in the past, while terminating some of his less productive styles, making for an even, conspicuously correct collection. The book inaugurates his late phase—poetry characterized by a renewed confidence in its minimalist means. Indeed, it attempts to make those means more minimal still. For the first time a Japanese influence is felt in the poems. Longley also establishes more meaningful relationships between Latin and Greek myths on the one hand and contemporary Northern Irish conflict on the other.

Many of the techniques of the book remain familiar. Animals, in *Gorse Fires*, are still used to create reflection and contrast with the human world. They continue to make suggestive, metonymical marks in poems such as "Otters":

An upturned currach at Allaran Point
And a breaking wave are holt and hover
Until the otter, on wet sand in between,
Engraves its own reflection and departure.

(p. 6)

But the use of animals is now marked by a new self-consciousness in which Longley seems to recast the techniques of his earlier poems. A further effect is that Longley has made himself so comfortable and at home within his own techniques that the feelings of security are transmitted to the reader. The new confidence within his own methods is combined with an intensified tendency to collapse distinctions between outside and inside, art and nature, as in "Remembering Carrigskeewaun":

Home is a hollow between the waves,
A clump of nettles, feathery winds,
And memory no longer than a day
When the animals come back to me
From the townland of Carrigskeewaun,
From a page lit by the Milky Way.

(p. 12)

The "in-between-ness" and "balance" of the otter here is repeated in an elegy for a friend entitled "Between Hovers":

I watched a dying otter gaze right through me
At the islands in Clew Bay, as though it were only
Between hovers and not too far from the holt.

(p. 5)

The plangent diffidence of these poems results in a kind of tenderness, where the fastidious desire for balance seems to become an ethical principle in itself. Longley, unlike Heaney, has not pushed his gifts to an extreme of utterance; he has merely shed manners for which he has no gift, like the fables and allegories of *No Continuing City*. Poems in *Gorse Fires* have a determinedly elusive quality. Consider a poem to which I alluded earlier, "Stone-In-Oxney":

At a table which seems to take root on the lawn
We breakfast late to a single propellor's drone,
The ghost of a Spitfire over Stone-in-Oxney
Or a Stuka, its turning circle that cloud-gap
Or wherever you point to show me a bird; its dive
Low as the ceiling-beams in Chapel Cottage.
We bump against pilots who hang out of the sky.

(p. 47)

The poem, like many in *Gorse Fires*, subtly blends a kind of Georgian nature poetry with a post-war despondency and melancholia. The first line opens with a blurring of the distinctions between civilization and nature. Gradually, the opposition between what man finds in nature (trees and birds) and what man builds from nature (tables and planes) dissolves. The poem suggests that, although what man finds in nature is a cause for wonder and delight, what man builds from nature threatens everything that he finds. The ambiguity of the tone is deepened by the seventh line, which suggests pilots parachuting to safety or else, since "hang" is more passive than "fall," hanging down stationary and perhaps dead. "Stone-In-Oxney" ends:

Someone's hand is overshadowing the place-names,
Tracking the migration of wheatears and blackcaps
Who cross the channel and make their landfall here.
Let him spread his fingers on a broken wing, now
Reed warblers are singing at Wittersham Levels
And at Small Hythe and Peening Quarter nightingales.

(p. 47)

The eerie, obliterating hand is obviously running across a map, a made thing, following lines which have been made in the Second World War by birds and planes. The poem invests much ambiguity in the phrase "broken wing"—for what kind of wing is it? Does it belong to a bird or a plane? Longley's poems are very rarely argumentative, and the poem works by being suggestive, rather than discursive, by leaving the mark of the writer's style on the reader, rather than by persuading the reader of a particular proposition.

THE GHOST ORCHID

For all their personality and accommodation of pain, the poems in *The Ghost Orchid* are never really shattered, their composure is never broken. It is as if they had anticipated every kind of emotional disturbance and arranged themselves accordingly. Virtually all the poems deal with large themes, although their treatment may be relatively oblique. Through a variety of subjects—poems about painting and form, Greek myths, women's sexuality, Japan and China, war poems, post-war poems, metaphysical poems about death (plus a rare factual reminiscence of student days)—the evenness of tone is consistent and remarkable. "The oars, heavy with seaweed, at rest in humid mists"—this, the beautifully drowsy opening to "The Ship of The Wind" (partly a translation of a poem by Karel van de Woestijne) is typically mellow (p. 21). The poem, like many others, seems to be articulated slowly and deliberately, an almost diplomatic act in which every word is carefully weighted, and nothing is hazarded or unjustified.

Much of *The Ghost Orchid* is a story of miniaturization, of small poems, some no more than two lines long, and images of tiny objects, eggs, tears, snowflakes, of equations which can be written on the back of postage stamps, and names which can be written on a grain of rice. The title poem, for example, renders the delicate life of the small flower with a sharp sense of its fragility:

Adding to its few remaining sites will be the stanza
I compose about leaves like flake of skin, a colour
Dithering between pink and yellow, and then the root
That grows like coral among shadows and leaf-litter.
Just touching the petals bruises them into darkness.

(p. 52)

The emotional effects are generated by the narrator of the poem constantly approaching, but never completing the process of, erasure. To become familiar is in a sense to shrink, to become so *au fait* with a place or a person that one knows about every detail, able to number every hair, map every freckle, whereas as strangers we survey the big shapes. In "A Gift of Boxes," these concerns are related to a lover's relationship:

> You make a gift of boxes by putting boxes inside
> Boxes, each one containing the Japanese air you
>   breathe,
> More and more of it diminishing boxes, smallness
> Condensing in the end to two boxes the size of tears.
>
> (p. 17)

The poems maintain a balancing act between the greatly reduced (the tiny objects) and the greatly enlarged (the references to distant times and cultures). The speaker connects himself to the microscopic scales while being prepared to focus the poem on China or ancient Greece. As if to balance the feather-lightness of such a vision, the poems talk quite a lot about weight. "The Scales," for example, is about the Last Judgement, and the inventive elegy "Sun & Moon" begins: "Could water take the weight of your illness ever …" (pp. 43, 50).

Like Louis MacNeice, Longley has mostly chosen not to exploit Irish mythology, especially those mythological characters like Cuchulainn who are associated with the Irish Literary Revival. This is a trait which he shares to some extent with Derek Mahon, his closest poetic contemporary. Longley's later books have been content to exploit Latin and Greek mythology. Sometimes he makes a link between the contemporary background and the mythical foreground through the use of Ulster dialect words. This process can take uncomfortably self-conscious forms, as in "The Helmet":

> When shiny Hector reached out for his son, the wean
> Squirmed and buried his head between his nurse's
>   breasts
> And howled, terrorised by his father, by flashing
>   bronze
> And the nightmarish nodding of his horse-hair crest.
>
> His daddy laughed, his mammy laughed, and his
>   daddy
> Took off his helmet and laid it on the ground to gleam,

> Then kissed the babbie and dandled him in his arms
>   and
> Prayed that his son might grown up bloodier than
>   him.
>
> (p. 38)

In *The Ghost Orchid*, where death and beginnings are stark obsessions, all the parts of his earlier volumes return in a version of what Harold Bloom likes to call *apophrades*, the return of the dead voices. Falling through the poems like the snow at the end of Joyce's short story "The Dead,", the parts come back like sand-grains long subject to the whitening friction of the sea, blown about in the wind with feathers and grains of rice:

> Thick as the snowflakes on a wintry day when God
> Comes down as snow and shows mankind his arsenal,
> Putting the winds to sleep, blanketing in snowdrifts
> Hill-tops, rocky promontories, pasture, turning
> Jetties and beaches white …
>
> ("The Scales," p. 43)

Of course, to signpost larger realities in this way runs the risk of the poems emptying themselves to the point of insubstantiality. How do you orient the part so that it points accurately to the whole? Longley usually accomplishes this by pace; his poems proceed with an even solemnity, like soldiers at a state funeral. One feels there must be something more serious going on, and one busies oneself in a search for significances. Actions are anticipated by ceremonial verbal formulae, which emphasize the importance of consciously dignified movements: "I want to wash the hagi petals in my bowl, then balance / Before your lips an offering of crabs' brains on a shiso leaf" ("A Gift of Boxes," p. 17). Often these actions serve to elevate seemingly unremarkable events: "I'll hand to you six duck eggs Orla Murphy gave me / In a beechwood bowl Ted O'Driscoll turned …" ("Phoenix," p. 30). The liturgical atmosphere suits the gravity of those poems where Longley imagines his corpse blending slowly into the landscape which sustains it:

> With the three parts of water in my bones and tissues
> Coloured blue; two eyes like sea-stars; my forehead

(The driest part) wrinkly, a carbon-copy of the earth's
Crust; my soul at sea making waves: have I the sense
To describe every day two circles—the merry-go-
Round around the sun and the roundabout of death.

> ("Sorescu's Circles," p. 46)

THE WEATHER IN JAPAN

Even more elegiac in tone than the two preceding volumes, *The Weather In Japan* more explicitly associates Longley with minimalist techniques. The percentage of very short poems is high, like the two-line title poem:

Make bead-curtains of the rain
Of the mist a paper screen.

> (p. 7)

With haiku-like brevity, Longley again suggests a collapsing of the division between art and nature, between what is inside the home, the domestic space, and what is outside. The human subject is simultaneously enlarged, by being implicated in all natural actions, and diminished, by the absorption of these actions. The imperative mood of the title poem also suggests the poet's confidence in his craft, as the paper screen ambiguously evokes the artisitic process.

The tact with which these poems tackle difficult subjects, like the experiences of Longley's father, becomes their main point. The deepest emotions are left unstated, implicit, although we are aware that they must be present, as in "January 12, 1996":

He would have been a hundred today, my father,
So I write to him in the trenches and describe
How he lifts with tongs from the brazier an ember
And in its glow reads my words and sets them aside.

> (p. 25)

We are not told what the father reads into Longley's words, nor indeed what we should read into the father's readings. Where another poet might have chosen to begin a much-longer work, Longley's poem abruptly ends, as though to make his feelings explicit and unambiguous would be to injure them.

Longley's consistent, although not exclusive, use of the one-sentence poem has made him more inventive and confident with the form. He has succeeded in perfecting the technique of holding the main action of the poem, often a fanciful variation on reality, within subordinate clauses, while the main clause often has the subject performing a simple action like seeing, thinking, or imagining. Holding all the action within one sentence also allows Longley to convey simultaneity, the complex, though often unnoticed, interrelationship of events at the same time. As the speaker's individuality is distributed among these collective happenings, many of the poems (including the first three) end in a plural noun suggestive of that collective identity: lives, eyes, tongues, stars, leaves, trees, horses. These features are all combined in what may be the book's best poem, "Pale Butterwort":

Pale butterwort's smoky blue colours your eyes:
I thought of this when I tried to put together
Your every feature, but a buzzard distracted me
As it quartered the tree-tops and added its skraik
And screel to the papery purr of the dragonflies'
Love-flight, and with so much happening overhead
I forgot the pale butterwort there on the ground
Spreading its leaves like a starfish and digesting
Insects that squirm on each adhesive tongue and
Feed the terror in your eyes, your smoky blue eyes.

> (p. 2)

In a book appealingly suffused with goodwill, the harmonious convergence of activities taking place on different scales, this poem has a darker edge, reminiscent of Frost's "Design." Longley's later poems are usually reluctant to close on such a threatening note.

The valedictory note is strong in Longley's later collections, and he has anticipated how he will be remembered after his death numerous times. He is in the relatively unusual position of having written a number of competing epitaphs. The concern with how he will be seen after he is dead leads him to write poems reminiscent of Patrick Kavanagh's Canal Bank sonnets. Longley asserts his own place in the contemporary canon:

If you were to read my poems, all of them, I mean,
My life's work, at the one sitting, in the one place,
Let it be here by this half-hearted waterfall
That allows each pebbly basin its separate say,

Damp stones and syllables, then, as it grows dark
And you go home past overgrown vineyards and
Chestnut trees, suppliers once of crossbeams, moon-
Shaped nuts, flour and crackly stuffing for mattresses,
Leave them here, on the page, in your mind's eye, lit
Like the fireflies at the waterfall, a wall of stars.

("The Waterfall," p. 65)

CONCLUSION

Through their technical polish, Longley's early poems achieved pleasing formal symmetries. Affecting cosmopolitan and sophisticated airs, they remained at a remove from the emotional center of Longley's personality. Gradually more personal themes, especially conflict, mortality, and identity, worked their way into the poems' tight technical structures. Longley's relationship with the west of Ireland landscape put him in touch with an inexhaustible source of motifs and images—the landscape acting as a pastoral counterweight to his growing concerns with communal conflict. His poetry has gradually refined itself, extending techniques for which he had an aptitude, erasing techniques for which he did not. His range of styles and of subjects has been small. The deceptively modest poems from the second half of his career are especially concentrated. At once confident and self-conscious, they reflect the hard-won contentment of Longley's retirement, revisiting the themes of his earlier poems with sharper technique and judgement.

SELECTED BIBLIOGRAPHY

I. POETRY. *No Continuing City* (Dublin, London, and Chester Springs, Penn., 1969); *An Exploded View* (London, 1973); *Man Lying on a Wall* (London, 1976); *The Echo Gate* (London, 1979); *Gorse Fires* (London and Winston-Salem, N.C., 1991); *The Ghost Orchid* (London, 1995; Winston-Salem, N.C, 1996); *The Weather in Japan* (London and Winston-Salem, N.C, 2000).

II. AUTOBIOGRAPHY. *Tuppenny Stung: Autobiographical Chapters* (Belfast, 1994).

III. EDITED WORKS. *Causeway: The Arts in Ulster* (Belfast, 1971); *Under the Moon, Over the Stars* (Belfast, 1971); *Selected Poems of Louis MacNeice* (London, 1988 and Winston-Salem, N.C, 1990); *Poems, W. R. Rodgers* (Oldcastle, 1993).

IV. OTHER WORKS. "The State of Poetry—A Symposium" (participant) in *Review* 29, no. 30 (1972); "The Neolithic Light—A Note on the Irishness of Louis MacNeice," in Dunn, ed., *Two Decades of Irish Writing* (Cheadle U.K., and Chester Springs, Penn., 1975).

V. INTERVIEWS. Eileen Battersby, "Blooming Lately," in *Irish Times* (9 March 2000); Dermot Healy, "An Interview with Michael Longley" in *Force 10 in Mayo* (Castlebar, Ireland, 1991); Mike Murphy, "Interview with Michael Longley" in Clíodhna Ní Anluain, ed., *Reading the Future: Irish Writers in Conversation with Mike Murphy* (Dublin, 2000).

VI. TV DOCUMENTARY. Michael Viney and David Cabot, *The Corner of The Eye* (RTE, 1989)

VII. CRITICAL STUDIES. Terence Brown, *Northern Voices: Poets From Ulster* (Dublin and Totowa, N. J., 1975); Seamus Deane, *A Short History of Irish Literature* (London and Notre Dame, Ind., 1986); Paul Fussell, *The Great War And Modern Memory* (Oxford and New York, 1975); Christopher Ricks, *The Force of Poetry* (Oxford and New York, 1984); Brian McIlroy, "Poetry Imagery as Political Fetishism: The Example of Michael Longley" in *The Canadian Journal of Irish Studies* 16, no. 1 (July 1990); Alan Peacock, "Michael Longley: Poet Between Worlds" in Michael Kenneally, ed., *Poetry in Contemporary Irish Literature* (Gerrards Cross, 1995); Alan Peacock and Kathleen Devine, eds., *The Poetry of Michael Longley* (Gerrards Cross, 2000).

JAMES MACPHERSON

(1736–1796)

Scott Ashley

AT THE AGE of ten, James Macpherson witnessed the violent end of a culture that had lasted centuries and in which his ancestors had played a leading role for generations. On 16 April 1746 the British army, commanded by the Duke of Cumberland, destroyed the Scottish Jacobite army of Charles Edward Stuart, the Young Pretender, on Culloden Moor, near Inverness. The battle ended the Forty-five, the last rebellion aimed at restoring the Stuart dynasty to the crowns of Great Britain and Ireland, and rang the death knell for the world of the Highlands and its ancient social system, based on kinship, loyalty, and a Gaelic oral culture. With the Highland clans proving staunch supporters of the Stuart cause in the rebellions of 1715 and 1745–1746, the British government had been engaged in a harsh military occupation of the north long before Culloden, building barracks and forts while forcing roads through the mountains and glens to keep the soldiers supplied. After Culloden, the entire social structure and culture of the clans began to be dismantled.

Macpherson was born in the Scottish Highlands on 27 October 1736 at Ruthven, in the Badenoch region of Inverness-shire, the son of Andrew and Ellen Macpherson, who farmed at Invertromie, in the valley of the River Spey. Through both historical situation and family connections, James's early years were lived in a landscape of rebellion and oppression. His father appears to have been first cousin (through an illegitimate line) to the clan chief at the time of Culloden, Ewan Macpherson of Cluny. There had been an army barracks at Ruthven since the Jacobite uprising of 1715, and the main road leading out of Badenoch had been newly constructed by the British forces in an attempt to order the Highlands. In 1745 Ewan Macpherson followed Prince Charles Edward Stuart's army south into England,

and when the Jacobite army turned north again on the road to Culloden, it stopped off at Ruthven to besiege and then burn the English garrison. The response of the British government to these acts of revolt was swift and brutal. The commander of the royal forces, "Butcher" Cumberland, began a notorious program of suppression of the Highlands through uncontrolled violence, and in Badenoch the Macpherson clan was disarmed and then humiliated as Cluny Castle, the seat of their chief, was burned to the ground. Cluny himself had gone into hiding in the mountains above Ruthven, where he remained for the next nine years, supplied and protected by his clansmen, before finally escaping to France in 1755. During those years government troops poured into Badenoch to search for Cluny; although the hunt was to prove unsuccessful, there is evidence that it generated profound fears among the local population. Across the Highlands the clans had their weapons taken away, their traditional dress prohibited, and their lands dispersed. Macpherson's formative years were ones in which he saw his close kin hunted down, his locality ravaged, and his community demoralized.

These early and traumatic events provide the key to understanding Macpherson's future development, both as a man and as an author. His ambivalent relationship with Scotland and the Highlands, seeing them simultaneously as backward provinces and as sites of purity and sentiment, stems from the paradox of Scottish history in the eighteenth century. The British government set out to "improve" and "civilize" the Highlands, but it set out to achieve these ends by the violent destruction of the cultures already there. Throughout his life Macpherson seems to have felt an aversion to the social and economic poverty of the Highlands typical of the age; but he could never square this with the fact that "improvement" was synonymous with Anglicization. Equally, his literary career, from the early poems of the late 1750s to the histories of the 1770s, is concerned with the nature of what it means to be Scottish and how that identity relates to its new "British" context. His most famous productions, the *Ossian* poems of the 1760s, are acutely concerned with the twilight of a heroic Scottish Gaelic culture both in subject matter and structural apparatus. But the genuine Gaelic ballads surviving in the Highlands from the Middle Ages were not good enough for him, of course, and he had to recreate his own epics, an Ossian more suited to the prevailing models of English taste. Whether that constituted "forgery," the accusation leveled at Macpherson by contemporaries and posterity, remains to be seen. The immediate point to remember is that the profitable complexities of Macpherson's attitude to his literary materials had at its root a lived experience.

These tensions were only exacerbated by his education. Macpherson clearly was well schooled at the local institutions in Badenoch, because in 1752 he left Ruthven for the University of Aberdeen. During the 1750s Aberdeen was a place undergoing rapid change, both intellectual and economic. Once a small fishing town, the city was experiencing a boom in textiles and commerce, resulting in unprecedented prosperity. Matching this effervescence in the town, new ideas and methods were being developed in the university that were to play a major part in that distinctive movement known to historians as the Scottish Enlightenment. While a student at Aberdeen, Macpherson would certainly have been introduced to the ideas of Thomas Blackwell, an expert in Greek literature and one of the most influential scholars there. Blackwell's ideas on Homer seem to have registered with Macpherson, especially his belief that poetic genius flourished most fully in times of violence and civil unrest, and his primitivist theory that archaic or "unpolished" language provided the best form for the most ancient genre of literature, epic poetry. Perhaps recognizing something of ravaged, Gaelic-speaking Badenoch in Blackwell's vision of Homeric Greece, Macpherson's own work of the 1750s and 1760s was underpinned

by many of the assumptions he imbibed at Aberdeen. In his emphasis on the superiority of epic, his association of war with natural genius, and his use of a self-consciously primitive style in the *Ossian* poems, Macpherson had learned his lessons well.

But as well as offering powerful models for sympathetic understanding of his native culture, Macpherson's experience at Aberdeen also confirmed that the defeated Highlands were places that needed to be left behind. Although it contained a primitivist strain, the Scottish Enlightenment was profoundly interested in social advancement, progress, and improvement. Blackwell's own student, Alexander Gerard, was teaching in Aberdeen that noble savages were merely savage, with little in the way of nobility, lacking refinement of taste and preferring vice over virtue. For Gerard, ancient Greece was the home not of wild and untutored original genius but of poets who selected, rearranged, and refined material to meet the canons of taste. In 1754 Macpherson transferred from the older (and more expensive) King's College in Old Aberdeen to Marischal College, in the New Town, where Gerard was a tutor. This alternative vision, as applicable to the condition of the Highlands as Blackwell's, also seems to have given Macpherson pause for thought. In 1756 he returned to Ruthven after a short spell in Edinburgh without a degree, but with enough learning in Latin and Greek to take up a post as a teacher in the school where he had himself been a pupil. The ambivalent attitudes toward the Highlands encapsulated by Blackwell's and Gerard's analyses of ancient Greece made it hard for Macpherson to settle down. Several years later in London he was to tell James Boswell that he always wanted to "have something in perfection: either the noble rudeness of barbarous manners or the highest relish of polished society. There is no medium. In a little town you have the advantage of neither" (Boswell, *London Journal*, ed. by Pottle, pp. 73–74). The scraps of evidence surviving from this period of Macpherson's life suggest a melancholic young man, ambitious but frustrated as to how his talents might be unlocked in Ruthven.

Macpherson had developed something of a reputation for writing comic verse while at Aberdeen, and apparently he also wrote more serious poetry. Back at Ruthven, the idea of a literary career seemed both vocation and escape route. His first publication, "To a Friend mourning the Death of Miss—" an imitation of an ode by the Roman poet Horace, appeared in the *Scots Magazine* in May 1755. The poem is chiefly interesting for the seeds of the future contained within it, particularly the fact that it is a loose translation of an ancient poet, modernized to suit contemporary taste. The forces that drove Macpherson into the arms of the modern world while pledging his love for the distant past are as evident in this first tentative step into the literary arena as they are in the poems of *Ossian* a few years later. The *Scots Magazine* took another poem in 1758, "On the Death of Marshal Keith," a lament for the Scottish Jacobite soldier, exiled to Prussia after the failure of the 1715 rebellion. Again, the work demands attention only for the light it sheds on Macpherson's slow development toward the themes and tone of *Ossian*. Already the death of the Scottish hero is represented as more than a personal tragedy, as symbolic of the end of an entire bloodline and the decay of a culture:

See! the proud halls they once possessed, decayed,
The spiral tow'rs depend the lofty head;
Wild ivy creeps along the mould'ring walls,
And with each gust of wind a fragment falls;
While birds obscene at noon of night deplore,
Where mighty heroes kept the watch before.
    (*Poems of Ossian*, vol. 2, ed. by Laing, p. 589)

The concern with ruins and endings and the preoccupation with how even the strongest are laid low by death to survive only in the memory of the poet-bard prove the defining characteristics of Macpherson's work on the *Ossian* poems in the 1760s.

As well as producing these shorter pieces for the *Scots Magazine* (there are a handful of others sometimes attributed to him on questionable grounds), Macpherson was working on more ambitious poetic projects. On his death, manuscript copies of two long poems written while he was a schoolmaster at Ruthven were discovered and eventually published in 1805. The first of these was a work of some five hundred lines

entitled "Death," a morbid piece in the tradition of contemporary works like Robert Blair's *The Grave* (1743), Edward Young's *Night Thoughts* (1745), or even Thomas Gray's *Elegy in a Country Churchyard* (1751), though he seems to have had a low opinion of the last. Macpherson seems not to have thought "Death" worthy of publication, a verdict supported by generations of editors and critics who have seen it as an inept, rambling piece trading on a mid-eighteenth-century vogue for melancholic sentimentality. More interesting is the second work found in the manuscript notebook, a long poem in ten cantos given the title of "The Hunter" by its first editor. Again, although the work lacks focus and is still an apprentice piece, Macpherson moves for the first time into the epic genre so favored by the intellectuals at Aberdeen. The poem tells the story of Donald, a Highlander, who, visited by ambitious visions brought on by a vengeful fairy, is driven to the city, rescues the kingdom from English invaders, and wins the king's daughter and, by implication, perhaps the kingdom.

The importance of "The Hunter" was that it provided the draft for Macpherson's first venture into book-length publication when *The Highlander* appeared in Edinburgh in 1758. This poem can best be described as a slimmed-down and historicized second draft of "The Hunter," telling the story of Duffus (originally known as Alpin), a young Highland warrior who saves the kingdom of Scotland from a Viking invasion by the Danish warlords Sueno and Magnus. Like Donald in the earlier "epic," Duffus-Alpin succeeds in winning the hand of the king's daughter, Culena, but the rags-to-riches motif is more fully elaborated in *The Highlander* when the hero is discovered to be the lost son of the previous king. Thankfully, the incumbent of the throne dies, allowing Duffus and Culena to restore order and harmony to Scotland, a device that was to be used with greater sophistication by another Scottish writer influenced by *Ossian*, Sir Walter Scott. Indeed, in its patriotic themes, sublime language, and epic ambitions, *The Highlander* looks forward both to *Ossian* and more generally to the romantic literature of the Highlands exemplified by Scott after 1800. Its epic narrative structure resembles *Fingal*, Macpherson's first Ossianic epic of 1761, in several ways. Both works begin abruptly in the middle of the action, *The Highlander* with the death of Alpin's father and the hero's journey to the Scottish court, *Fingal* with the Cuchullin sitting under his tree, alone with his thoughts of past wars. Immediately both jolt into life as Viking invasion begins to determine the course of the narrative, with warriors coming from outside the boundaries of the kingdom to rescue the besieged royal forces. In the earlier work, this is the Highlander coming from the north to the civilized court, in the latter Macpherson created a more patriotic flavor, as we shall see, by having Fingal, the King of Morvern, come from Scotland as the savior of the Irish army of Cuchullin. In their irreligious fervor for a glorious death and in the related concern with keeping the memory of those heroic dead alive in the communal memory through the power of poetry, the rather stereotyped and two-dimensional figures who move through *The Highlander* are the lineal descendants of the equally underdeveloped but somehow more mysterious and wraithlike population of the *Ossian* poems. In its attempt to mythologize the figure of the Highland warrior, and then isolate that strand of the past as a dominant one in the identity of Scotland, Macpherson's first, faltering steps in epic signal the opening up of the Highlands as a profitable literary landscape as they ceased to be a dangerous political and military one. But Duffus's easy and almost inevitable incorporation into the norms of Lowland civilized life at the end of the poem demonstrates how that redistribution of imaginative resources did little to empower the Highlands themselves. Edinburgh, Glasgow, and urban Scotland—and behind them England—determined how the Highlands were seen and how they were to see themselves. Recognition of this fact was to take James Macpherson away from Ruthven and into a wider world.

FRAGMENTS OF ANCIENT POETRY

Macpherson was sowing the seeds of the future in the poems he was writing at Ruthven between 1756 and 1758. But, scarce though the evidence is, there is a suggestion that something even more momentous began to take shape in those years. After Macpherson's death, one of his pupils noted how his old teacher started to write down Gaelic songs and ballads from the old men of the Badenoch region in the years after his return from Aberdeen, from a desire to find amusement that gave way to a growing historical interest. The extent of Macpherson's knowledge of the Gaelic language has been a matter of prolonged debate ever since the publication of the first *Ossian* poems. It is still common to read that he knew little or no Gaelic and that such collections made in the Highlands were little more than garbled records of authentic poetry or, at worst, forgeries. To accept this view entails overlooking the fact that Badenoch was a Gaelic-speaking area of Scotland during Macpherson's time and that Gaelic would have been the first language of his parents and peers. Undoubtedly, Macpherson learned English early at the Ruthven school he attended and became skilled in the use of it. Equally, like all Highlanders for whom Gaelic was predominantly a spoken language, he had problems reading some of the medieval manuscripts containing genuine Ossianic poetry, with their complex orthography and paleography. (How many of us today could easily read a fifteenth-century English manuscript?) There is no good reason for continuing to assert that Macpherson could not have understood the songs and ballads he heard from the natives of Badenoch and the Highlands. Research by Derick S. Thomson and Donald Meek suggests rather the opposite; that Macpherson's knowledge of the Gaelic tradition was not only sound but, given the contemporary context, extensive.

In 1758, the year *The Highlander* was published—to little acclaim—Macpherson managed to escape Ruthven and moved to Edinburgh as tutor to the young son of Thomas Graham, of Balgowan. The Graham family connections began to move Macpherson ever closer to the literary fame he evidently desired. There is a suggestion that he visited the home of the eminent Scottish philosopher and fellow Highlander Adam Ferguson early in 1759. It may have been through Ferguson's interest in the young poet that Macpherson was invited to the meeting that changed his life and brought into being the poems of Ossian. In the autumn of 1759 he met the playwright John Home, author of a recent patriotic tragedy, *Douglas* (1756), on the bowling green in the Scottish spa town of Moffat. Although he knew not a word of Gaelic, Home had been intrigued by reports that an oral poetic tradition survived in the Highlands, and on meeting Macpherson demanded that he translate some of the pieces from his collection into English. Although Macpherson declined at first, within a few days Home was presented with the first of the Ossianic fragments, "The Death of Oscur" (Fragment XIII). Over the next few days Macpherson brought two or three more poems, to the astonishment and delight of Home. Macpherson was introduced to Alexander Carlyle, another prominent member of the Edinburgh literati, and together Home and Carlyle set about publicizing their finds around the literary circles of the Scottish capital. All were impressed, but none more so than Hugh Blair, then writing a series of lectures on literature and belles-lettres and soon to be appointed professor of the same subject at the University of Edinburgh. He immediately set about persuading Macpherson to produce enough translations for publication in a small book, a commission eventually undertaken only with the greatest reluctance, the poet being convinced that no translation of his could do justice to the originals. Research into Macpherson's Gaelic sources for *Fragments* (incomplete as it is, attention tending to focus on the "epic" *Fingal*) points to the use of some genuine ballad material, in Fragment VI or Fragment XIV, for example. This has then been yoked together with poems for which there are no known sources, such as Fragment I, the whole reworked to fit more closely mid-century ideas of sublime and melancholic bardic poetry. Macpherson was never a faithful translator, bringing an original Gaelic poem into English word for word. But then such a method not only was thought undesirable by eighteenth-century standards, it was nearly impossible, given the differences between the two languages. It is all a long way from the image, often repeated, of Macpherson the impudent forger, pulling the wool over the eyes of a credulous public for fame

and financial fortune. With pressure being asserted from the Edinburgh literati, and with the attention of English writers such as Thomas Gray and Horace Walpole directed north of the border by Blair, Macpherson kept going, and in June 1760 *Fragments of Ancient Poetry,* collected in the *Highlands of Scotland* appeared, with a preface by Blair.

The first edition of *Fragments* consisted of fifteen short prose pieces, increased to sixteen with minor revisions when a second edition was needed only four months later. There was no mention of Macpherson in either edition. "There can be no doubt that these poems are to be ascribed to the Bards"; "Oscian" [*sic*] was merely described as "the principal personage in several of the following fragments" (*Poems of Ossian*, ed. by Gaskill and Stafford, p. 5). Despite the apparent modesty of the publication, the subtext of *Fragments* was grandiose indeed. Blair's preface worked hard to determine the responses of the first readers, assuring the public that not only were the poems genuine remains of Scottish Gaelic poetry but that they were derived from the most remote antiquity of the country and could be dated to "the very infancy of Christianity in Scotland" (*Poems of Ossian*, ed. by Gaskill and Stafford, p. 5). Blair claimed that the *Fragments* were originally part of a greater epic poem of the Highlands, now lost, concerning the heroic deeds of Fingal (identified as Oscian/Ossian's father), which, clearly on the advice of Macpherson, he suggested would have as its subject the wars against the Danish invaders of Ireland. Such hints were calculated to stimulate further excitement in a literary climate based upon appreciation of Homer, Virgil, and the ancient epics. Like Thomas Blackwell in Aberdeen, Blair was convinced that epic was a superior genre, created out of sublime emotions, imaginative, noble, and childlike in their vehemence and passion. The notion of a lost Scottish epic behind the *Fragments* looked set both to confirm Blair's theories and to be a bestseller. Hence his confident assertion that "there is reason to hope that one work of considerable length, and which deserves to be styled an heroic poem, might be recovered and translated, if encouragement were given to such an undertaking." (*Poems of Ossian*, ed. by Gaskill and Stafford, p. 6). Macpherson's own education at Aberdeen seems to have brought him into sympathy with Blair's vision, and he appears to have regarded the extant poems and ballads collected in Ruthven and worked into *Fragments* as the corrupted and broken ruins of a purer, primitive culture. The translator's job was to try to restore something of the lost qualities of the poems, stripping away what had become attached to the originals over time. What Macpherson had found in Ruthven were lichen-covered blocks fallen from a once great building; he was to scrape off the moss and put the ruins back together again. It was a perspective on history that must also have made sense to a young man who had witnessed the Forty-five and Culloden and felt its aftermath firsthand.

Although by the second edition in October 1760 the recovery of the forgotten epic was advertised as under way, it remained purely an object of speculation for the time being, and readers had to rely on the *Fragments* themselves. Blair announced that the public must decide whether they had literary merit, and for a time the public responded positively. These disjointed and, by contemporary standards, bizarrely written prose poems appealed so strongly to mid-eighteenth-century taste that even that great skeptic and philosopher of "common sense" David Hume was moved to describe them, on first appearance, as wildflowers plucked from the Highlands of Scotland. But are the *Fragments of Ancient Poetry* still worth reading? There is undoubtedly a narrowness of theme and of tone in the sixteen pieces that eventually made up the second edition, being almost exclusively concerned with stories of tragic death, usually bound in with tales of tragic love. The style strives to convey the voices of the bards, often through the use of overtly dramatic form, but the register barely varies between melancholic nostalgia and defeated whisper. Yet each episode builds on the next to evoke a world where landscape and people, both living and dead, are connected organically by the repetition of natural images: rock, oak, moon, sun, deer, wind, storm, cloud. As the reader moves through the book, the ac-

cumulation of these images produces the sense of pervading gloom and pessimism that Macpherson is aiming for. When warriors are compared to oak trees or when silence is said to fill the mountains we know tragedy is imminent; we have seen similar warriors felled and know that the silence surrounds hilltop tombs in previous fragments. Macpherson imitates the supposedly primitive, nonabstract vocabulary of the ancient poet to create an almost hypnotic effect, and narrowness is part of the overall effect desired.

Evocation takes precedence over concrete description; the world that the bardic voices call upon is one that is gone beyond recovery, the heroes and maidens existing only in memory as ghostly shapes, their presence in the Highland landscape negatively defined by their absence from it. Most of the fragments end with voices faltering into silence as the bard sits by the tombs of the dead, now little more than grassy mounds, or as the survivors listen for ghosts, promising to commemorate the glorious deeds of the past as they themselves fade into old age and death. There is no future in Macpherson's ancient Caledonia, only the endless repetition of lost triumphs and tragedies. Time seems to have frozen in the minds of Oscian and the bards with the passing of the previous generation, leaving only decline and death. The season is perpetual autumn, although constant references to the north winds evoke the coming of the final winter. The dominant narrative subject of thwarted and destructive love furthers this mood, each couple marshaled to their doom without the chance to produce children. As Fiona Stafford writes, "Instead of normal sexual activity, the lovers are united only in violent death, sleeping together not in bed, but in the grave" (*Sublime Savage*, p. 105).

The relish with which the twenty-three-year-old Macpherson seems to dispatch his youthful heroic characters and the affinity he seems to have with the debilitated and fading bards makes greater sense when seen in the context of mid-eighteenth-century Britain. As a Highlander by birth, from a clan directly implicated in Jacobitism and deeply affected by the brutal aftermath of Culloden, the *Fragments* can be read as Macpherson's elegies for the dying culture of

Gaelic Scotland, with Fingal, Oscur, Connal, and the rest standing in for contemporary "heroes"—no matter how ambiguous their historical position—like Cluny Macpherson or Marshall Keith. In the aftermath of the Forty-five, with martial law, estates forfeited to the Crown, and clan chiefs no longer able or willing to fulfil their traditional roles as leaders of the community, a kind of emptiness and silence did indeed settle on the north—a silence that would spread and deepen at the end of Macpherson's life as the population disappeared in large-scale clearances, to be replaced by sheep. That sterility and decay should characterize the *Fragments*, and that Ossian should be the last of the race, seems appropriate to the situation around Badenoch, and to the Highlands more generally, in which they were first conceived. It would nevertheless be wrong to see in his work a lament for the world of the ordinary men and women of the Highlands who suffered most under the new Hanoverian order brought to northern Scotland after 1746. In 1762 Boswell recorded Macpherson's contempt for "'a parcel of damned rascals that did nething but plough the land and saw corn.' He considered that fighters only should be celebrated" (*London Journal*, ed. by Pottle, p. 110). The vision underpinning all the poems is an aristocratic one, glorying in the actions of a warrior elite that is mysteriously self-sustaining, liberated from the vulgar reliance on the labor of others to feed and clothe it: peasants, laborers, and the poor have no role in *Ossian*. Macpherson wanted not only to look back through the corrupt Gaelic sources to the purity that lay beneath them but also to uncover a more noble culture than the one dominated by want and paternalistic exploitation in which he had grown up. Blair had concluded his preface to *Fragments* with the modest observation that any recovered Highland epic "might serve to throw considerable light upon the Scottish and Irish antiquities" (*Poems of Ossian*, ed. by Gaskill & Stafford, p. 6). Although it did indeed stimulate an entire field of antiquarian and ethnographic investigation in Great Britain and Ireland, the society Macpherson imagined in *Ossian* was one that did not exist, and never could have existed.

FINGAL

Fragments of Ancient Poetry appeared at exactly the right time to appeal to the Edinburgh literati on whom Macpherson's immediate chances of fame relied. The Scottish *philosophes* Hugh Blair, John Home, David Hume, Alexander Carlyle, and Adam Ferguson had for several decades been involved in a general movement to improve the position of the arts in their homeland. Their patriotism was sharpened by traditional English hostility to Scotland, hostility that was to reach new peaks in the early 1760s with the Wilkes and Liberty agitation that began with attacks on George III's Scottish first minister—and patron of Macpherson's epic works—the earl of Bute. But in 1760–1762 it was the question of a Scottish militia that provided the context for embracing *Ossian*. Scots wanted to raise a local guard to defend against external enemies and internal tyranny, but such an ambition had been regarded with suspicion by the government at Westminster since the Jacobite uprisings. Many of the intellectuals who promoted Macpherson, including Home and Carlyle, who had "discovered" him at Moffat, were active supporters of a Scottish militia bill. Poems that seemed to prove the existence of a Caledonian Homer—Ossian is also said to be blind—and which demonstrated the honorable and valiant use of arms by a Scottish nobility were guaranteed to pique the interest of the Edinburgh elite in 1760.

In August of that year a dinner was held to raise funds and rally support for a trip to the Highlands and the Hebrides by Macpherson to find the lost epic of Fingal. He set out later that month in the company of a kinsman, Lachlan Macpherson of Strathmasie, a good Gaelic scholar and a considerable poet in his own right. They spent the late summer and autumn traveling through the Highlands to Inverness, to the Isle of Skye, and then on to the Outer Hebridean islands of North and South Uist and Benbecula. Macpherson hoped to find the purest forms of the ancient Gaelic poems there, as well as obtain any medieval manuscripts he could lay his hands on. Clan connections evidently helped Macpherson in Skye. There he met another relation, Dr. John Macpherson of Sleat, an authority on Celtic antiquities, whose *Critical Dissertations on the*

Caledonians (1768) bears a striking resemblance to the Ossianic theories, suggesting a mutual influence. His recording of the fleeting oral performance, so characteristic of genuine Gaelic poetry, was aided by his meeting with Ewan Macpherson, tutor to Dr. John Macpherson's sons and knowledgeable in Highland linguistics. He was also directed to Alexander Macpherson, a blacksmith, who not only could recite Ossianic poems but owned a manuscript of them. On Benbecula Macpherson spent time with the MacMhuirich family, hereditary bards to the Clanranald lords of the island, and owners of more precious manuscript material. In all he managed to collect a number of Gaelic manuscripts (nineteen were delivered to the Highland Society on his death, and there may have been more), of which by far the most important was the early sixteenth-century *Book of the Dean of Lismore*. If the ethics of Macpherson's methods of gathering these books remains debated—he may well have bullied the owners to hand over their property—the fact that he arrived in Ruthven in October 1760 with a substantial body of authentic Gaelic poetry in both manuscript and oral transcription is not.

With the help of Strathmasie and another friend, the Reverend Andrew Gallie, Macpherson set about reducing these eclectic and often opaque sources into a Scottish epic. It was obviously not an easy task, complicated by the difficulty of reading the late-medieval manuscripts and by Macpherson's conviction that time and unskilled bards had fundamentally corrupted both these written redactions and the contemporary oral versions. Gallie recorded Macpherson's frustration when trying to recover what he believed to be the true third-century original:

> I remember Mr Macpherson reading the MSS. found in Clanronald's, execrating the bard himself who dictated to the amanuensis, saying, "D—n the scoundrel, it is himself that now speaks, and not Ossian."
>
> (Mackenzie, ed., *Report of . . . the Highland Society*, p. 44)

By early 1761 Macpherson was back in Edinburgh, living in lodgings immediately below those of Blair, who was rapidly becoming his greatest champion. He kept working at his Ossi-anic materials, interrupted by a visit to London in February to court the publishers of the capital, and by another Highland tour in June, this time across Argyll to the island of Mull in June, accompanied by John Home. In December 1761 the long-awaited epic was revealed to the world, the full title giving an accurate description of the work itself, less so of Macpherson's contribution to it: *Fingal, an Epic Poem, in Six Books: Together with several other Poems, composed by Ossian the Son of Fingal. Translated from the Galic Language by James Macpherson.* Unlike the *Fragments,* this was a complete example of ancient Scottish Gaelic poetry by a single bard, Ossian, and in contrast to the earlier anonymous pamphlet, responsibility for the handsome quarto publication was awarded to James Macpherson.

Of all Ossianic poems produced by Macpherson, it was *Fingal* that bore the closest relationship to the Gaelic originals collected in Badenoch and during the Highland tours of 1760–1761. Derick S. Thomson first systematically tried to identify the sources used in constructing the epic in 1952, reaching the conclusion that Macpherson had used two main Gaelic traditions for the outline of his main plot, the "Garbh mac Stairn" ballads in Book I and the "Magnus" ballads in Books II, IV, V, and VI. He also utilized another three ballads for the main episodes, "Fingal's Visit to Norway" and "The Maid of Craca" in Book III and "The Courtship of Ossian" in Book IV. These range from quite close translations, as in the "Courtship" ballad, to general resemblances. In addition, Thomson found echoes of several other Gaelic texts in *Fingal,* though whether these were used directly or secondhand remains unclear. Donald Meek has recently supplemented this with the suggestion that Macpherson's epic theme of war and invasion in *Fingal* may have been influenced by exposure to the Gaelic "Battle of Ventry" tales, in both prose and verse, which survived in the latter form in the *Book of the Dean of Lismore.* As a result, Meek has suggested that from a position inside the Gaelic literary tradition, Macpherson's "search for an 'epic', established within a manuscript tradition, may have been much less misguided than is commonly thought" (*Ossian Revisited,* ed. by Gaskill, pp. 40–41).

The various editions of *Fingal* certainly looked like those of a real epic, containing by 1765 a preface, a dissertation on the antiquity of the work, extensive historical and linguistic footnotes, and some sixteen miscellaneous poems concerning Fingal and his era. Macpherson added to the scholarly character of his work by emphasizing the connections between the original *Fragments of Ancient Poetry* and his new work, including revisions of Fragments XIV, XV, and XIV in *Fingal*, reinforcing the authenticity of his first book and implying that he had discovered new and better versions of the originals during his Highland tours. Indeed, perhaps he had, if the reworking of the "Maid of Craca" ballad from *Fragments* (VI) to *Fingal,* Book III, really does hint at exposure to an alternative tradition sometime after 1760, as suggested by Thomson. We should not automatically assume that, just because *Ossian* was not everything Macpherson claimed it to be, all of his literary moves are spurious and disingenuous.

Whatever the truth of the matter, *Fingal* opens with the poem that appeared as Fragment XIV in 1760, with the name of the Viking warlord altered from the more correct Garve to Swaran (a change already anticipated in Blair's preface of 1760):

Cuchullin sat by Tura's wall; by the tree of the rustling leaf. — His spear leaned against the mossy rock. His shield lay by him on the grass. As he thought of mighty Carbar, a hero whom he slew in war; the scout of the ocean came, Moran, the son of Fithil.

Rise, said the youth, Cuchullin, rise; I see the ships of Swaran. Cuchullin, many are the foe: many the heroes of the dark-rolling sea.

(*Poems of Ossian*, ed. by Gaskill & Stafford, p. 55)

From this striking and vigorous opening, the action unfolds into the story of the invasion of Ireland by Swaran, King of Lochlin, the brave but unsuccessful efforts of Cuchullin and the Irish army to defend their homeland, the appearance of Fingal, King of Morvern, and his forces from Scotland, and their triumphant and noble victory over the Vikings (an anachronism derived from the original sources). This basic narrative regularly pauses to relate a number of episodes—

often the most authentic Gaelic part—that serve not to advance the main thrust of the story but to add a sense of depth and underlying tragedy. There is a case to be made that such episodes do little except dissipate narrative tension and create confusion for the reader, with the figures who exist only as subjects of a bardic performance seeming as real and important as Cuchullin, Swaran, or Fingal. Stafford accurately characterizes the effect as one that "leaves the reader uncertain as to which characters have actually appeared in the main action and which survive only in the memories of the protagonists" (*Sublime Savage*, pp. 140–141). But in evoking atmosphere and an illusion of other tales, perhaps even other epics, lying behind that being told in *Fingal*, the digressions do work to facilitate the suspension of disbelief. Authentic early epics, such as the Anglo-Saxon *Beowulf*, contain a number of bardic recitations within the main poem for precisely this reason. Equally, the dead, either as ghosts or as vital remembrance, have an active role to play throughout the entire *Ossian* corpus, functioning as symbols of human transience and as reminders to the living of what has gone before and what is to come. It is difficult to distinguish between the ancient dead and the living in the poems because Macpherson has created an Ossian who finds such distinctions almost impossible himself. To the bard, *all* of his protagonists are dead, for he himself is the last of the race:

Often have I fought, and often won in battles of the spear. But blind, and tearful, and forlorn I now walk with little men. O Fingal, with thy race of battle I now behold thee not.

Battles! where I often fought; but now I fight no more. The fame of my former actions is ceased; and I sit forlorn at the tombs of my friends.

(*Poems of Ossian*, ed. by Gaskill and Stafford, pp. 79, 104)

Fingal is less an epic about the wars between Swaran, Cuchullin, and Fingal than a poem about the elderly Ossian's memories of it; and his mind is apt to wander.

But Ossian's memory is of course determined by Macpherson's concerns and prejudices. The Scottish militia bill has already been mentioned as one such issue that was drawn into the orbit of

Ossian, and if Macpherson was not implicated in the controversy surrounding it directly, his work reflected several of the themes that energized it. The structure of *Fingal* is provided by the story of invasion of a part of the British Isles, specifically the north of Ireland, by external enemies. When the book appeared, Great Britain was at war with France and on the brink of war with Spain. A fear of maritime adventures by the French into Britain's exposed western Irish and northern Scottish flanks was an ongoing theme of eighteenth-century military strategy, and Macpherson's vision of a united Celtic response to invasion certainly had contemporary resonance. Fingal's noble and triumphant intervention in favor of Cuchullin and the Irish seemed to present a model for the reconciliation of old rivalries, as well as offering reassurances that the Scots had both the valor and the virtue to become trusted and loyal Britons. This defense of the *patria* against external foes is also a major theme in the associated poems, "Comála," for example, telling of the defeat by Fingal of the Roman emperor, Caracul (Caracalla), supposedly in A.D. 211. Interestingly, like much eighteenth-century patriotism, this preoccupation with the Scottish martial spirit looked in more than one direction. It was on the one hand centripetal in tendency, working toward a more unified British identity, focusing its energies against threats from overseas. But on the other, a potentially centrifugal current ran deep within it, a not fully articulated warning to English interlopers that Scotland could and would defend itself. The Roman legions in "Comála" did not come from Italy but from Britain, south of Hadrian's Wall. With England identifying itself both culturally and politically as a kind of modern-day Rome, ambiguities creep in at the edges. On some level Macpherson is refighting in poetry the battles England won and awarding the laurels to the other side. *Fingal* tells of Scottish victories over Scandinavian kings and Roman emperors: had not the victor of Culloden himself, William Augustus, Duke of Cumberland, gloried in the names both of a Viking-descended conqueror from Normandy and the first and most famous of emperors?

If there was a strong element of anti-Scottish prejudice in English culture, manifested both in the political sphere and in the response to *Ossian* during the 1760s, there was also undoubtedly a prejudiced streak in Macpherson. Boswell relates a number of anti-English gibes made by Macpherson in London at this period; more serious and relevant to understanding *Fingal* and the later Ossianic works was his ingrained dislike of Ireland. Despite all the claims made by critics that the work engages with the contemporary drive toward a cohesive Britishness, we should never forget that the basic narrative of *Fingal* proper tells how an Irish army is defeated by foreigners and rescued by heroic Scots. The image of Cuchullin hiding in a cave at the end of Book VI, magnificently patronized by Fingal, who invites him to the feast to cheer his spirits rather than because his high rank as regent of Ireland entitles him to be there, was guaranteed to enrage patriotic Irish antiquarians. Macpherson's comments in his preface and "Dissertation" were equally provocative. Contrary to the claims of the Irish, Ossian was a Scotsman: "The bards of Ireland, by ascribing to Ossian compositions which are evidently their own, have occasioned a general belief, in that country, that Fingal was of Irish extraction, and not of the ancient Caledonians, as is said in the genuine poems of Ossian" (*Poems of Ossian*, ed. by Gaskill and Stafford, p. 37). And rather than the Irish colonizing Scotland, the true history of the peopling of the islands ran in the opposite direction: "Some adventurers passing over from those parts of Britain that are within sight of Ireland were the founders of the Irish nation" (*Poems of Ossian*, ed. by Gaskill and Stafford, p. 44). In his latter claim, modern scholarship has proven Macpherson wrong; in his former, half-right, there being a genuine and longstanding Scottish Ossianic tradition, though the earliest material does indeed come from Ireland. What matters in this context, though, is that the publication of *Fingal* sparked a long-running dispute between the pro-Ossianic Scottish literati and their Irish counterparts (aided by English "allies" such as Samuel Johnson) regarding the authenticity of the work, and gave renewed impetus to ongoing rivalries over the early history of the respective nations that was to last into the nineteenth century. Macpherson's epic was more than just a poem, whether genuine or not, by the time it was reprinted, along with *Temora,* in the 1765 *Works of Ossian.* It had become the centerpiece in a highly charged and bruising cultural politics that required all the constituent parts of the British Isles to look at their own identities and each other's.

TEMORA

Fingal made Macpherson famous, not only in Scotland but throughout Great Britain and beyond. By 1763 the first epic was translated into Italian, and from there an Ossianic vogue spread rapidly across Europe and over the Atlantic to North America. Macpherson traveled to London, where he was feted by the literary circles of the capital and threw himself into a round of parties, socializing, and amorous liaisons, though he does not seem to have been entirely happy in it. Boswell has left a picture of Macpherson in his journal for the years 1762–1763 that portrays a man divided between fascination with and abiding contempt for mid-eighteenth-century civilization. Keen to play the fashionable part of the melancholic and sentimental male, a role given new energy by *Ossian,* he was also attracted to more earthy and plain-speaking conduct—also a model for life that could be derived from the Ossianic culture he had created. No matter what direction he decided to take in his personal life, there was pressure to "translate" another epic, what with Blair lecturing on Ossian at Edinburgh University (the material was published early in 1763 as *Critical Dissertation on the Poems of Ossian*) and the mounting success of *Fingal.* Macpherson had included as one of the supplementary poems in that book a piece entitled "Temora: an Epic Poem," described tantalizingly in the notes as little more than the opening of a longer poem that appeared "from the story of it, which is still preserv'd, to have been one of the greatest of Ossian's compositions" (*Poems of Ossian,* ed. by Gaskill and Stafford, p. 456). Over the next year

he got to work on the bard's second epic.

The response to *Fingal* had exceeded all expectations, most of the audience responding to it as a new kind of poetry, sublime and romantic, and not worrying too much about how genuine it was or how much historical veracity Macpherson's surrounding apparatus could claim. Dissenting scholarly voices, however, were being raised both in private and in public. Doubts had been raised even before the publication of *Fragments of Ancient Poetry* as to such poems' authenticity, but the modesty of that publication tended to deflect attention from the issue. The more heavyweight and frankly aggressive style of *Fingal* was a direct challenge and could not be avoided. The earliest published response seems to have been Ferdinando Warner's *Remarks on the History of Fingal,* which appeared in February 1762. Warner, however, believed *Fingal* and Ossian generally to be the genuine productions of a third-century bard; his complaint was that they were Irish, not Scottish. A sense of uncertainty as to how to respond to Ossian characterized this phase of the controversy; a sharpening of the conflict took place only after the publication of *Temora.* During 1762 David Hume, an early defender of Macpherson, began to express fears not about the authenticity of *Fingal* but about the excessive claims to literary merit being made for it by Blair. Even Horace Walpole, an inveterate enemy of Ossian in later years, wrote late in 1761:

> *Fingal* is come out—I have not yet got through it—not but it is very fine . . . I will trust you with a secret, but you must not disclose it, I should be ruined with my Scotch friends—in short, I cannot believe it to be genuine—I cannot believe a regular poem of six books has been preserved, uncorrupted, by oral tradition, from times before Christianity was introduced into the island.
>
> (*Selected Letters of Horace Walpole,* ed. by Lewis, p. 103)

Walpole's mixture of skepticism and admiration is typical of many early responses to Ossian, which similarly distinguished between authenticity and literary quality.

Macpherson seems to have been protective of his honor and attempted to respond to the skeptics early in 1762 by exhibiting the "originals" of *Fingal* in his publisher's shop-window in London, an event that was advertised as far away as Paris. What exactly these were remains a matter of debate. Were they some of the Gaelic manuscripts that Macpherson had collected during his Highland tours in 1760–1761? Were they transcriptions of these genuine Ossianic sources, or something else entirely? The most recent examination by Howard Gaskill concludes that what was most likely to have been displayed were back-translations of *Fingal* into Gaelic made by Macpherson himself in 1760–1761. Macpherson certainly had pretensions to write in his native tongue: pseudo-Gaelic "originals" from his pen were eventually published in 1807; there was also a Gaelic "specimen" of *Temora* published with the first edition in March 1763, clearly translated retrospectively from English. By then it was too late, however, as the appearance of the second epic unleashed a flood of attacks on Macpherson from English, Irish, and even some Scottish critics that were to determine popular perceptions of his character and achievement until the present day.

The reaction to *Temora, an Ancient Epic Poem* by critics, both contemporary and modern, has been generally hostile. English and Irish commentators found the arrogant and bullying tone of the preliminary "Dissertation" and notes off-putting, while the eight books of the poem itself have been found to lack the narrative focus of *Fingal*'s six and to be repetitive, incoherent, and, in the words of Derick Thomson, "a much more vague and bodiless production" (*Gaelic Sources of Macpherson's "Ossian,"* p. 59). Following Thomson's argument, the reason most often adduced is Macpherson's demonstrable failure to use real Gaelic sources as a means of restraining his own imagination. Whereas Thomson discovered twelve passages in *Fingal* where Macpherson had used genuine Ossianic material, in *Temora* there is only one, and that in Book I, originally published with the first epic in 1761. Macpherson adapted a version of a set of Gaelic ballads on the Battle of Gabhra to tell of the death of Oscar, Ossian's son, at the hands of the usurper Cairbar. Apart from that, and perhaps a few hints as to royal genealogies reworked from Irish historians, the rest seems to be of Macpherson's invention. He came close to admitting as much in the prefatory essay:

> The second book, and several other episodes, have only fallen into my hands lately. The story of the poem, with which I have been long acquainted, enabled me to reduce the broken members of the piece into the order in which they now appear. ... As to the merit of the poem I shall not anticipate the judgment of the public. My impartiality might be suspected, in my accounts of a work, which, in some measure, is become my own.
>
> (*Poems of Ossian*, ed. by Gaskill and Stafford, p. 215)

It seems not unlikely that at one point Macpherson did truly believe that an Ossianic epic existed in the Scottish Highlands and Islands, but such a belief had clearly faded by 1763. By *Temora* he was playing down his role as passive "translator" of Ossian and emphasizing his own creative input. A famous man after the publication of *Fingal*, Macpherson's ambitions seem to have driven him to attempt an escape from the bardic persona that had transmuted the lead of *The Highlander* into the gold of *Ossian*.

Nevertheless, there are several things of interest in *Temora*. Macpherson was not content simply to repeat the formulae of *Fingal* and tried to extend both the narrative range and the motivations of his characters. Just as Homer's two epics told of the heroic climax of the Greeks in the *Iliad* and then of the aftermath and homecoming in the morally ambiguous *Odyssey*, so Ossian, the Scottish Homer, developed a more nuanced and ambivalent story in "his" second long work. *Temora* is essentially the story of the beginnings of the dissolution of the age of heroes and of Fingal's last battle, a process begun by his intervention in a great civil war in Ireland raging between the Firbolg inhabitants and the descendants of the Caledonians. Cairbar, a Firbolgian chieftain, has murdered the young king Cormac, for whom Cuchullin was regent in the previous epic, but who has now become Fingal's kinsman. Fingal and his army leave Morvern for Ireland once again to revenge Cormac but suffer a reversal when Oscar, killing Cairbar, is in turn killed. Fingal's spirit is troubled, and authority devolves to Fingal's follower, Gaul. The remaining seven books are filled with the fluctuating fortunes of battle, again punctuated by digressive episodes, and the death of Fingal's son and Ossian's brother, Fillan, before the inevitable Caledonian victory, the defeat of the noble villain, Cathmor, and Fingal's restoration of peace. In the last scene the aged king hands over his spear to Ossian and resigns his command for good, telling him to look to the example of his forefathers. Given that the death of Oscar has deprived Ossian of an heir, and given that the reader knows that the line of Fingal has a past but no future, this is a poignant moment.

Despite the glorious ending, the war has seen the death of one of Fingal's sons and his grandson and a weakening of the royal line that will leave Ossian lamenting his lonely fate as the last of the race. *Fingal* is concerned with the vigorous height of the Ossianic world, *Temora* with the moment when it begins to falter and decline into old age. Fingal's own motives seem less straightforwardly heroic too, his invasion of Ireland driven as much by the need to avenge the slight to his own family as by a disinterested desire to protect the Celts from foreign invasion. In the second edition of his *Critical Dissertation on the Poems of Ossian* (1765), Blair wrote, "Temora has less fire than the other epic poem; but in return it has more variety, more tenderness, and more magnificence" (*Poems of Ossian*, ed. by Gaskill and Stafford, p. 370). The insight proved true to a whole generation of readers who came to Macpherson's works not for historical information but for literary experiences beyond that offered by some of the more staid works of eighteenth-century classicism. With an even greater emphasis than in *Fingal* on beautiful feeling and sentiment, sublime grandeur of scenery and action, and a melancholy recognition of dissolution and endings, *Temora* was in many ways the defining work in the Ossianic canon that set the terms by which the Celtic peoples and their literature were to be judged until well into the twentieth century.

LATER LIFE AND WRITINGS

After the publication of *Temora* Macpherson found himself in possession of wealth, literary fame, powerful connections, and a black reputation. The coy dedication of *Fingal* to "a certain noble person" (*Poems of Ossian*, ed. by Gaskill and Stafford, p. 33) had by 1763 been replaced by an open acknowledgment of the patronage of the Earl of Bute, at the very moment when the flow of criticism against Bute's ministry swelled to a torrent of abuse, led by John Wilkes and the poet Charles Churchill. Bute resigned as George III's first minister less than a month after *Temora* appeared; Macpherson's association with the Scottish lord did not go unnoticed, and his standing as a writer suffered as a result. In addition, the historical speculations with which he had surrounded the two epics had successfully insulted both Irish and Welsh scholars, aggravated the patriotism of English critics, and raised the suspicions of some of his Scottish supporters. David Hume's early enthusiasm had given way to concern, which by the summer of 1763 had become open anxiety. He urged Blair to undertake a thorough investigation into the provenance of Ossian and to collect testimonies from the Highlands regarding the authenticity of the poems. Blair did so, including many of the positive responses he received in an appendix to the second edition of his *Critical Dissertation*, but Hume still could not shake off his feeling that "the whole is strange, passing strange" (*Ossian Revisited*, ed. by Gaskill, p. 151), and his confidence gradually ebbed away.

But by this time Macpherson had been off the literary and political scene for more than a year. Blossoming connections with the wealthy and influential and growing impatience with playing second fiddle to Ossian—a dissatisfaction plain by the publication of *Temora*—resulted in Macpherson's own priorities shifting away from Gaelic poetry and toward a political career. In June 1764 Bute secured him a post as provincial secretary to the governor of West Florida, but Macpherson seems to have found colonial responsibility difficult and tiresome and returned to London at the end of 1765, in time to see the publication of his revised two-volume edition of the *Works of Ossian*, essentially *Fingal* and *Temora* bound together with Blair's *Critical Dissertation*. After this uncertain start Macpherson began to thrive as a political figure, using his literary skills to produce propaganda for the ministry first of Lord Shelburne and then of Lord North. He also developed something of a reputation as a writer of histories, a natural extension of the concerns with the ancient Scottish past that had fed into *Ossian* and its accompanying panoply of footnotes and antiquarian essays. His first effort was *An Introduction to the History of Great Britain and Ireland*, published in 1771, a frankly partisan text that glorified the Celtic Caledonians at the expense of their Irish and Welsh neighbors while celebrating the civil and religious liberties embodied in the British institutional tradition passed down both from the Germans of Tacitus and the vanished world of Fingal and Ossian. It was attacked in the press by antagonistic reviewers but sold well enough that a second and then a third edition were produced in 1772 and 1773. In 1775 another historical work issued from Macpherson's pen, the *History of Great Britain from the Restoration to the Accession of the House of Hanover*, a continuation of his erstwhile supporter David Hume's *History of Great Britain*. This was supplemented by *Original Papers, containing the Secret History of Great Britain from the Restoration to the Accession of the House of Hanover* (1775), the fruits of his research in London, Edinburgh, and Paris into the papers of the Jacobite historian Thomas Carte. Again, the work was savaged by reviewers, especially by those who identified themselves with the values of the early eighteenth-century Whig party, whom Macpherson had shown in a bad light, and accusations of forgery and misrepresentation surfaced again in familiar mode. And, again, it sold well, and the *Original Papers* are still consulted by historians; Macpherson's vocal critics continued to be confounded by the silent nonpartisan majority who bought, read, and enjoyed his books.

The only failure at this period was his abortive return to poetry, with a translation of Homer's *Iliad* into Ossianic-style prose (1773). The work was poorly received in literary circles and failed to replace Alexander Pope's majestic *Iliad* (1715–1720) in the public imagination. Nevertheless, in its use of archaic prose and interest in the historical Homer, Macpherson's version does look forward to some of the concerns of nineteenth- and twentieth-century Homeric translation. The disappointment over the *Iliad* was swiftly put behind him when, the same year, Macpherson supervised a heavily revised two-volume *Poems of Ossian*, an eternal money-spinner. He attempted with this edition to emphasize his own role in the production of the poems, and announced that they were now consigned to their fate. Ossian would not go away quietly, however: Samuel Johnson and James Boswell promptly undertook their famous tour to the Highlands and Hebrides reigniting the authenticity controversy.

Johnson had long held Ossian in contempt, partly because he thought it a fraud and partly because Macpherson was a Scotsman. Although wholly ignorant about Scottish Gaelic culture, hopelessly misguided about the nature of oral tradition, and favoring mistaken Irish interpretations of the early history of the British Isles, it was typical of Johnson to feel qualified to hold forth about matters Ossianic. In January 1775 Macpherson caught wind of the fact that Johnson's account of his travels, *A Journey to the Western Islands of Scotland*—to be published in a matter of days—contained some serious critical allegations against his integrity:

> I suppose my opinion of the poems of Ossian is already discovered. I believe they never existed in any form than that which we have seen. The editor, or author, never could show the original; nor can it be shown by any other; to revenge reasonable incredulity by refusing evidence is a degree of insolence with which the world is not yet acquainted; and stubborn audacity is the last refuge of guilt.
> (Johnson, *Journey to the Western Islands of Scotland*, ed. by Levi, p. 118)

Macpherson responded through his and Johnson's publisher, William Strahan, demanding that the doctor delete reference to "insolence," "audacity," and "guilt," but as to "his want of belief on the subject I have not the smallest objection" (Saunders, *Life and Letters*, p. 246). Johnson made soothing noises through Strahan, but nothing was done, and the *Journey* appeared unedited. To make matters worse, a second edition was already in press, and when Macpherson discovered this, he sent an angry letter (now lost) to Johnson, accusing him of being a liar. Boswell, Macpherson's one-time drinking companion, preserves Johnson's theatrical reply for literary history, with its overblown fears of physical attack from a man now referred to as a cheat and a ruffian. Although undoubtedly furious, Macpherson let the matter drop in public, what with both the *History of Great Britain* and the *Original Papers* set to appear and with his interest in Ossian on the wane. Neither man let the matter go in private however, and both may well have anonymously contributed passages of critical and personal abuse to treatises reopening the "Ossian wars" in the years following.

Although his sense of personal honor had been offended, Macpherson's career was little affected by the feud with Johnson. The *History* and *Original Papers* were financially successful, several eminent critics jumped to his defense against Johnson and his ill-informed and prejudiced attacks on the entire Scottish Gaelic literary tradition, and by 1776 he had another widely read political pamphlet published, the *Rights of Great Britain asserted against the Claims of America*. Two years later he became the London agent to the enormously wealthy Indian prince the Nawab of Arcot, thanks to the dubious dealings and clan connections of John Macpherson (son of Dr. John Macpherson of Sleat and future governor general of India). Despite labyrinthine political maneuverings, scandals, and charges surrounding the East India Company, the role of both Macphersons, and the debts of the Nawab, James sailed through the troubled waters to a seat in Parliament in 1780, which he held until the end of his life, and a hefty reward from the "Arcot interest" for his justifications of their cause in his propagandist *History and Management of the East India Company* (1779). Offered the forfeited lands of "Cluny" Macpherson in 1783 for services to government, he refused, but the next year he purchased land in Badenoch only a few miles from Ruthven, where he built a great house,

Belleville, and carved out a Highland estate for himself. There he enjoyed life to the full, bringing up his five illegitimate children—he never married—and creating a social round of parties and amusements far removed from the poor and oppressed Badenoch he had left in the 1750s.

Wherever Macpherson went Ossian haunted him. Ever since Johnson's attack in 1775, Macpherson's friends had been urging him to settle the matter once and for all by publishing the originals. Naturally, he had equivocated, explaining that though he wished to do so, the publication of the orginals would be too expensive for him to undertake. Unfortunately, in 1783 some of his friends from the East India Company provided £1000 to cover the costs of the project. Macpherson would once again be under suspicion if he did not comply, and he set to work collating sources, rummaging through trunks unopened for twenty years, and translating some thousands of lines of the Ossianic epics back into a kind of pseudo-Gaelic, which at one point he actually contemplated presenting in Greek characters. Despite working at the "originals" until his death, it was a huge and ultimately quixotic task, and nothing appeared until 1807, when the Highland Society of London published a three-volume *Poems of Ossian, in the Original Gaelic* partly funded by a donation in Macpherson's will. He had fallen into poor health in 1793—reputedly the result of too much fast living—and eventually died at Belleville, on 17 February 1796. True to his double nature as both Highlander and cosmopolitan Briton, his will left instructions that he was to be buried not in Scotland but in Westminster Abbey. Eighteen days later he achieved his last triumph over the critics and was laid to rest in that shrine to British literary and political fame.

CONCLUSION

It is always well to bear in mind the comment by Richard Sher that "no epic poem like *Fingal* or its still less authentic sequel of 1763, *Temora*, has ever been known to exist in the Scottish Highlands" (Sher, *Church and University*, p. 249). This does not mean that we should thereby accept the judgment of Hugh Trevor-Roper, rivaled only by Johnson's in its cavalier disregard for facts, that James Macpherson and John Macpherson of Sleat were "two insolent pretenders" who in *Ossian* and *Critical Dissertations on the Caledonians* constructed a "bold forgery" that "in so far as [it] had any connection with reality, had been stolen from the Irish" (Trevor-Roper, "Invention of Tradition," p. 17). The authenticity question has been settled in outline since the Highland Society's *Report* on the matter in 1805; genuine names, events, ballads, and histories were used as the basis for the works of Ossian, of which James Macpherson was the only begetter. But this question is coming to seem one of the least interesting that can be asked. It is time that Macpherson began to be "normalized," to become less than a unique literary wizard, fooling half of Europe, and more than a forger. He had his influences, his biographical determinants, his successes, and his failures, just like any author, and these should be uncovered. Research on Macpherson and the Ossian books in the last two decades has made us look again at what made his work so popular throughout Europe and America, entrancing such luminaries of the age as Thomas Jefferson and Napoleon Bonaparte, Goethe and Diderot, Ingres and Mendelssohn. It has sent critics back to the long unread epic poems to assess what we can learn from them about mid-eighteenth-century Britain, its cults of sensibility and sentimentality, its love of the primitive and worship of the civilized, its destructive and constructive elements. Philosophers and historians have enriched our understanding by placing Macpherson back into his contexts within the Scottish and European Enlightenments. The contribution of the Ossianic controversy to the development of ethnographic studies in Britain and Ireland is only just beginning to be uncovered. And Gaelic scholars still stumble across fragments and echoes of the real medieval Oisín in the eighteenth-century Ossian. If it is difficult for readers today to fully appreciate the shock and delight with which contemporaries first responded to *Fragments of Ancient Poetry*, *Fingal*, and *Temora*, it is a sign of the abiding achievement of Macpherson that literary

merit and importance are once again being separated from the question of authenticity, restoring to the canon "the words of the bards in the days of song; when the king heard the music of harps, and the tales of other times" (*Poems of Ossian*, ed. by Gaskill and Stafford, p. 170).

SELECTED BIBLIOGRAPHY

I. FIRST EDITIONS OF INDIVIDUAL WORKS. *The Highlander* (Edinburgh, 1758); *Fragments of Ancient Poetry* (Edinburgh, 1760); *Fingal* (London, 1762); *Temora* (London, 1763); *An Introduction to the History of Great Britain and Ireland* (London, 1771); *The Iliad of Homer* (London, 1773); *Original Papers, containing the Secret History of Great Britain from the Restoration to the Accession of the House of Hanover*, 2 vols. (London, 1775); *The History of Great Britain from the Restoration to the Accession of the House of Hanover*, 2 vols. (London, 1775); *The Rights of Great Britain asserted against the Claims of America* (London, 1776); *The History and Management of the East India Company* (London, 1779); *A Short History of the Opposition during the Last Session* (London, 1779).

II. FIRST COLLECTED POETIC WORKS. *The Works of Ossian, the Son of Fingal. Translated from the Galic Language by James Macpherson*, 2 vols. (London, 1765); *The Poems of Ossian, containing the Poetical Works of James Macpherson*, 2 vols., ed. by Malcolm Laing (Edinburgh, 1805; repr. 2 vols., ed. by John MacQueen, Edinburgh, 1971).

III. MODERN COLLECTED POETIC WORKS. *The Poems of Ossian and Related Works*, ed. by Howard Gaskill and Fiona Stafford (Edinburgh, 1996).

IV. MODERN SELECTED POETIC WORKS. Mark Akenside, James Macpherson, and Andrew Young, *Selected Poetry*, ed. by S. H. Clark (Manchester, 1994).

V. BIBLIOGRAPHY. George F. Black, *Macpherson's Ossian and the Ossianic Controversy* (New York, 1926); John J. Dunn, "Macpherson's Ossian and the Ossianic Controversy: A Supplementary Bibliography," in *Bulletin of the New York Public Library* 75 (1971), pp. 465–473; Richard B. Sher & Dafydd Moore, "Selected Bibliography: James Macpherson and Ossian," *www.c18.org/biblio/macpherson.html*.

VI. BIOGRAPHY. Bailey Saunders, *Life and Letters of James Macpherson* (London, 1894); Fiona J. Stafford, *The Sublime Savage: James Macpherson and the Poems of Ossian* (Edinburgh, 1988); Paul J. deGategno, *James Macpherson* (Boston, 1989); Paul J. deGategno, "The Sublime Savage in America: James 'Ossian' Macpherson's Tour of Duty in West Florida," in *Scotia* 16 (1992), pp. 1–20.

VII. SELECTED CONTEMPORARY RESPONSES. Hugh Blair, *A Critical Dissertation on the Poems of Ossian, the son of Fingal* (London, 1763; repr. in *Poems of Ossian*, ed. by Gaskill and Stafford, 1996); James Boswell, *Life of Johnson* (London, 1791); Henry Mackenzie, ed., *Report of the Committee of the Highland Society of Scotland, appointed to Inquire into the Nature and Authenticity of the Poems of Ossian* (Edinburgh, 1805); James Boswell, *London

Journal, 1762–1763, ed. by Frederick A. Pottle (New Haven, 1950); Horace Walpole, *Selected Letters of Horace Walpole*, ed. W. S. Lewis (New Haven, 1973); Samuel Johnson and James Boswell, *Journey to the Western Islands of Scotland and Journal of a Tour to the Hebrides*, ed. by Peter Levi (Harmondsworth, 1984).

VIII. CRITICAL WORKS. John S. Smart, *James Macpherson: An Episode in Literature* (London, 1905; repr. New York, 1973); Edward D. Snyder, *The Celtic Revival in English Literature, 1760—1800* (Cambridge, Mass., 1923); Frederic I. Carpenter, "The Vogue of Ossian in America: A Study in Taste," *American Literature* 2 (1931), pp. 405–417; Derick S. Thomson, *The Gaelic Sources of Macpherson's "Ossian"* (Edinburgh, 1952); Henry Okun, "Ossian in Painting," in *Journal of the Warburg and Courtauld Institute* 30 (1967), pp. 327–356; Malcolm Chapman, *The Gaelic Vision in Scottish Culture* (London, 1978); M. M. Rubel, *Savage and Barbarian: Historical Attitudes in the Criticism of Homer and Ossian in Britain, 1760—1800* (Amsterdam, 1978); Josef Bysveen, *Epic Tradition and Innovation in James Macpherson's "Fingal"* (Atlantic Highlands, N.J., 1982); Richard B. Sher, "'Those Scotch Imposters and their Cabal': Ossian and the Scottish Enlightenment," in *Man and Nature: Proceedings of the Canadian Society for Eighteenth-Century Studies*, ed. by R. L. Emerson (London, Ont., 1982), pp. 55–63; Hugh Trevor-Roper, "The Invention of Tradition: The Highland Tradition of Scotland," in Eric Hobsbawm and Terence Ranger, eds., *The Invention of Tradition* (Cambridge, 1983), pp. 15–41; Richard B. Sher, *Church and University in the Scottish Enlightenment* (Edinburgh, 1985); Howard Gaskill, "'Ossian' Macpherson: Towards a Rehabilitation," in *Comparative Criticism* 8 (1986), pp. 113–146; Peter T. Murphy, "Fool's Gold: The Highland Treasures of Macpherson's Ossian," in *English Literary History* 53 (1986), pp. 567–591; Jennifer J. Carter and Joan H. Pittock, eds., *Aberdeen and the Enlightenment* (Aberdeen, 1987); Leah Leneman, "Ossian and the Enlightenment," in *Scotia* 11 (1987), pp. 13–29; Clare O'Halloran, "Irish Re-creations of the Gaelic Past: The Challenge of Macpherson's Ossian,"

in *Past and Present* 124 (1989), pp. 69–94; Fiona Stafford, "Dr. Johnson and the Ruffian: New Evidence in the Dispute between Samuel Johnson and James Macpherson," in *Notes and Queries*, new series 36 (1989), pp. 70–77; Peter Womack, *Improvement and Romance: Constructing the Myth of the Highlands* (Basingstoke, 1989); Howard Gaskill, "What did James Macpherson Really Leave on Display at his Publisher's Shop in 1762?" in *Scottish Gaelic Studies* 16 (1990), pp. 67–89; Howard Gaskill, ed., *Ossian Revisited* (Edinburgh, 1991); Adam Potkay, "Virtue and Manners in Macpherson's *Poems of Ossian*," in *Proceedings of the Modern Language Association* 107 (1992), pp. 120–130; Colin Kidd, *Subverting Scotland's Past: Scottish Whig Historians and the Creation of an Anglo-British Identity, 1689–1830* (Cambridge, 1993); Howard D. Weinbrot, *Britannia's Issue: The Rise of British Literature from Dryden to Ossian* (Cambridge, 1993); Howard Gaskill, "Ossian in Europe," in *Canadian Review of Comparative Literature* 21 (1994), pp. 643–675; Murray Pittock, *Poetry and Jacobite Politics in Eighteenth-Century Britain and Ireland* (Cambridge, 1994); Terence Brown, ed., *Celticism* (Amsterdam, 1996); Nick Groom, "Celts, Goths, and the Nature of the Literary Source" in Alvaro Ribeiro, SJ, and James G. Basker, eds., *Tradition in Transition: Women Writers, Marginal Texts, and the Eighteenth-Century Canon* (Oxford, 1996), pp. 275–296; Murray Pittock, *Inventing and Resisting Britain: Cultural Identities in Britain and Ireland, 1685–1789* (London, 1997); Katie Trumpener, *Bardic Nationalism: The Romantic Novel and the British Empire* (Princeton, 1997); Fiona Stafford and Howard Gaskill, eds., *From Gaelic to Romantic: Ossianic Translations* (Amsterdam, 1998); Sebastian Mitchell, "James Macpherson's *Ossian* and the Empire of Sentiment," in *British Journal for Eighteenth-Century Studies* 22 (1999), pp. 155–171; Dafydd Moore, "*Ossian*, Chivalry and the Politics of Genre: the Case of *Fingal King of Morvern, a Knight-Errant*," in *British Journal of Eighteenth-Century Studies* 23 (2000), pp. 21–35.

CHARLES ROBERT MATURIN

(1780–1824)

Melissa Knox

CHARLES ROBERT MATURIN has been called a master of the Gothic novel, a term requiring clarification because "gothic" refers both to literature and architecture, and to emotions associated with the ruins of Gothic monasteries and castles that frequently appear in literary works to which the label of "Gothic" is applied. The architectural style was associated with the Catholic church and Catholic doctrine, but many if not most novels grouped under the rubric of "gothic" are flagrantly anti-Catholic. Protestant novelists— who comprise the majority among those writing "Gothics"— drew connections between the Gothic architectural style and practices deemed grotesque or immoral by reform churches. Maturin, who wrote *Five Sermons on the Errors of the Roman Catholic Church*, was typical in this regard of Protestant Gothic novelists, although he was nonetheless intrigued and inspired by Catholic doctrine. Other early practitioners were M. G. Lewis (1775–1818) and Ann Radcliffe (1764–1823).

The hallmark of the Gothic novel is whatever seems contrary to nature, conceived of either as what actually exists in the physical world or what ought to exist from a traditional Christian moral standpoint. Gothic novels often feature supernatural creatures like vampires, or like Maturin's Melmoth the Wanderer, whose dealings with the devil allow him to break the "natural" span of human life. Also typical are events transgressing moral boundaries of human nature, such as incest, bizarre torture, or necrophilia. Bram Stoker's *Dracula* (1897), one of the best-known gothics, includes all of the above. Mary Shelley's *Frankenstein* (1818) combines the "unnatural" collection of dead body parts and their gruesome electrical charging to produce a grisly living creature in a laboratory. The genre was sufficiently established by 1818 for Jane Austen to spoof it in *Northanger Abbey*, in which her heroine discovers a mysterious manuscript in an old black cabinet—mysterious manuscripts being an essential stock-in-trade of the Gothic novel— but the document turns out to be neither tragic nor shocking, only a laundry list.

Dread and terror, forming the emotional climate of the Gothic novel, sharply contrast to the standard domestic and familial themes of the Victorian novel, and are often amplified by extreme disruptions in nature, such as violent storms and hurricanes, staples of *Melmoth* and other works. *Melmoth*, written at a time of great personal catastrophe that allowed Maturin to magnify these emotions, was a culmination of Gothic horror and narrative. Balzac, Baudelaire, Goethe, Poe, Thackeray, Rossetti, Mario Praz, Leslie Fiedler, and Andre Breton all praised *Melmoth* (Shirley Clay Scott, *Myths of Consciousness in the Novels of Charles Robert Maturin,* p. 28).

The book was published in 1820, a year that also saw the publicaton of John Keats's "Ode to a Nightingale," Percy Bysshe Shelley's "Prometheus Unbound," and Sir Walter Scott's *Ivanho*e, as well as considerable political unrest. The Jesuit order of priests, which receives harsh criticism in Maturin's deeply Protestant novel, and which has always been a controversial order even within Catholicism, was thrown out of Rome. Meanwhile, revolutions erupted in Spain, where King Ferdinand VII was compelled to restore the Constitution of 1812, and in Portugal, where pressure for a constitution grew. These countries are particularly important in *Melmoth the Wanderer*, because they are Catholic and, therefore, deserving of having many spiritual abuses undermined. As Maturin's chief biographer, Niilo Idman, observed in 1923, "Many of the most characteristic passages in Maturin's writings can be explained by the fact that he was fond of imagining his own family to have been a victim of religious persecution" (*Charles Robert Maturin: His Life and Works*, p. 4). Maturin believed his family to have been descended from a Huguenot priest who had been a foundling raised in the Catholic faith, and who spent twenty-six years imprisoned in the Bastille for his beliefs (Idman, p. 4; Dale Kramer, *Charles Robert Maturin*, p. 11). Idman adds that the "time in which Maturin lived . . . was the most remarkable in the political history of Ireland" and details relevant facts such as the establishment of Ireland as a nation during that period, the workings of the Irish parliament to reconcile with England, and the establishment—if only briefly—of Dublin as "one of the liveliest capitals in Europe" (p. 8). Dublin had for some time been a cultural center; Handel's *Messiah* was first performed there, on 13 April 1742.

In his classic *The Romantic Agony* (1933), Mario Praz describes how Melmoth, "a kind of Wandering Jew crossed with a Byronic vampire ('ce pâle et ennuyè Melmoth', Balzac called him)[,] interrupts a wedding feast and terrifies everybody with the horrible fascination of his preternatural gaze: soon after the bride dies and the bridegroom goes mad" (pp. 78–79). The Wandering Jew is a mythic figure supposed to have mocked Christ on the cross, and who is as a punishment condemned to wander the earth without rest until Judgment Day. Praz evokes Maturin's mastery of the terror tale: "The novel abounds in frightful descriptions of tortures both physical and moral. There is a long story of a forced monastic vow derived from Diderot's *Religieuse* and elaborated with a subtlety of penetration into the terrors of the soul such as is elsewhere only found in Poe; there is a parricide who recognizes his own sister in the woman whom he has been pleased to starve to death with her lover; there is a mother who pretends that her son is the fruit of an adulterous union, in order to avoid his marrying a poor cousin whom he is thus persuaded to think is his sister; there is a trial of the Inquisition, a mysterious personage being present . . . there is a whole family reduced to desperation and hunger through the avarice of the priests, and a youth who sells his own blood to support them" (p. 121).

The novel has been called a "gothic blockbuster" (Jacqueline Pearson, "Masculinizing the Novel," p. 635). Yet even the many critics who praise it lavishly often find fault with its complexity; with the seemingly built-in chaos of the many stories and stories within stories that comprise it. Dale Kramer refers to *Melmoth* as a "marred masterpiece" that "mingles inconsistencies and bombast among splendidly realized passages of perversity and terror"; however, he compares it favorably to its chief gothic predecessors—Mary Shelley's *Frankenstein*, John Polidori's *The Vampyre*, Lord Byron's heroic dramas, Anne Radcliffe's *The Mysteries of Udolpho*, and the stories of Monk Lewis. He notes Maturin's skillful use of European folklore, and writes that Melmoth's "history and behavior endow him with the legendary qualities of Satan, Adam-Eve, Cain, Faust; Maturin, he says, "draws upon both Goethe's and Marlowe's Faust" (pp. 94, 96–97).

Melmoth achieved fame and notoriety not just from its lurid psychodrama and gripping narration—it maintains a hysterical surrealism throughout—but through its association with the Irish wit, playwright, and literary critic Oscar Wilde. Following his traumatic two-year prison sentence for homosexual acts, Wilde adopted as a pseudonym the name of Sebastian Melmoth. The surname was in honor of Charles Maturin, Wilde's great-uncle. On 29 May 1897, Wilde wrote in a letter, "Melmoth is the name of that curious novel of my grand-uncle . . . the book is now an extinct volcano, but I come from it like Empedocles, I hope, if the Gods prove kind to one who denied them" (*More Letters of Oscar Wilde*, ed. by Rupert Hart-Davis, p. 148). Empedocles—who appears as a romantic hero in Matthew Arnold's poem "Empedocles on Etna"—was a philosopher who plunged into the volcanic crater on Mouth Etna in an attempt to prove his divinity. Similarly, Maturin's Melmoth spends the final night of his long life (a hundred and fifty years!) dreaming of a fiery hell that resembles a volcano into which he either falls or feels himelf flung:

He dreamed that he stood on the summit of a precipice, whose downward height no eye could have measured, but for the fearful waves of a fiery ocean that lashed, and blazed, and roared at its bottom, sending its burning spray far up, so as to drench the dreamer with its sulphurous rain. The whole glowing ocean below was alive—every billow bore an agonizing soul. . . . Suddenly the Wanderer felt himself flung half-way down the precipice. He stood, in his dream, tottering on a crag midway down the precipice . . . he fell . . . burning waves boomed over his sinking head.

(*Melmoth the Wanderer*, ed. by Victor Sage, pp. 602–603; all further references are to this edition)

This final dive into a volcano of sorts is forshadowed in Maturin's imagery: at the conclusion of the first tale-within-a-tale in the novel, that of the Englishman Stanton, the manuscript upon which it is written is, we are told, suddenly illegible just at the point where Stanton is on the verge of some terrible choice forced upon him by the Wanderer, implicitly concerning the perdition of Stanton's soul, and then Maturin's narrative resumes with this commentary on illegibility: "No antiquarian, unfolding with trembling hands the calcined leaves of an Herculaneum manuscript, and hoping to discover some lost lines of the Æneis in Vergil's own autograph . . . ever pored with more luckless diligence . . . over his task" (*Melmoth*, ed. by Sage, pp. 65–66). A "Herculaneum" manuscript was one from the town of Herculaneum, which was destroyed by the eruption of Mount Vesuvius in A.D. 79 (*MELMOTH*, ED. BY SAGE, NOTE, P. 619).

Wilde's choice of "Sebastian" as the other portion of his pseudonym has hardly been remarked upon in connection with Maturin's novel, but it is relevant: Wilde had from his youth identitified himself with Saint Sebastian shot full of arrows, and the name suggests one of the most poignant features of Maturin's Melmoth, namely, his suffering. Although Maturin portrays his Wanderer as a tempter and a tormentor of innocent souls, a man whose supernatural powers come from his pact with the devil, Melmoth remains tortured and suffers even as he torments others and causes their suffering. The image of Melmoth jumping to his fiery fate of eternal flames seems to have haunted Maturin's famous nephew, Wilde, who spoke of the poet John Keats as a "lovely Sebastian killed by the arrows of a lying and unjust tongue" (*More Letters*, ed. by Davis, p. 41) and who knew that Keats had himself remarked, "I would jump down Aetna for any great public good—but I hate a mawkish popularity" (*Life and Letters of Keats*, ed. by Richard Monckton Milnes, London, 1867, pp. 76–77). Wilde's mother, who was Maturin's niece, had in one of her many melodramatic letters proclaimed that she was "first cousin to Aetna and half-sister to Vesuvius" (Mellisa Knox, *Oscar Wilde: A Long and Lovely Suicide*, p. 5). The nightmarish vision of self-immolation and the fantasy of rising, Phoenix-like, from an "extinct volcano" seems to have inflamed the imaginations of Maturin and his descendants, and indeed Maturin's strongest and most memorable characters in his novels and his plays are invariably those whose penchant for torturing others is equaled by their own deep and obvious pain, self-torture, and eloquent inability to experience pleasure.

Another experience Maturin's heroes have in common with both their creator and with Oscar Wilde and his mother is his extreme ambivalence toward Catholicism. Similarly, Oscar Wilde's mother, like her uncle Maturin, was of Anglo-Irish, and hence Calvinist stock. The possible literary influence of Maturin upon Oscar Wilde has been noted by a few critics. Like Maturin, Wilde produced a novel with many gothic elements, *The Picture of Dorian Gray*. Both Wilde's novel and Melmoth the Wanderer contain portraits of a figure who has made a mysterious transaction with the devil, who in each novel has accepted the protagonist's soul in exchange for prolonged (or in the case of Dorian, theoretically eternal) youth. Melmoth's portrait has apparently had some life of its own like Dorian's portrait, for the eyes in the portrait of Melmoth move. When Dorian stabs his portrait, which is the only evidence of his aging and of his evil deeds, he dies, but when the portrait of Melmoth is slashed, Melmoth appears in a dream or a vision to his descendent, young Melmoth, whispering, "You have burned me then; but those are flames I can survivie.—I am alive,—I am beside you" (Fowler 532; Maturin, 68). When the young man awakes, he has black and blue marks on his wrist that appear to come from the stronger grip of another hand.

LIFE

Charles Maturin was born on 25 August 1780 (one source claims 1782) in Dublin to William Maturin and Fidelia Watson. William Maturin was originally in clerical service, but left it and began working for the post office. He was appointed "Clerc [sic] of the Munster Road" (Idman, p. 5), a position that became lucrative, and lived prosperously for the last two decades of the eighteenth century. He was apparently fascinated by the mysterious past of his Huguenot ancestor, Gabriel Maturin, whose life might indeed have formed part of the plot of a Gothic mystery. The ancestor Gabriel Maturin was a founding and, according to Idman, a Huguenot priest "to whom life in [France] was made impossible." Telling the story, Idman cautions that Maturin believed it to be true, but took pleasure in the idea of being descended from a man suffering from religious persecution. Idman then provides Maturin's way of "telling the legend" of a Catholic "lady of rank" discovering a "child lying in the street" who was "richly drest" but unidentified. She raised him as a strict Catholic, and "being puzzled by a name for him, she borrowed one from a religious community, les Maturins, of whom there is mention in the Jewish Spy, and who were then of sufficient importance to give their name to a street in Paris, La Rue des Mathurins." But in spite of the lady's efforts, "my ancestor was perverse enough to turn protestant, and became pastor to a hugonot [sic] community in Paris. . . . about the time of the revocation of the edict of Nantz [sic] Maturin was shut up in The Bastille, where he was left for twenty six years" (Idman, p. 4). The gruesome dungeons of the Spanish Inquisition in Maturin's *Melmoth* therefore have a certain autobiographical basis, as does his tale of Monçada, the boy forced into the Jesuit priesthood who experiences many years of mental and physical anguish for desiring to leave the order.

From 1805 until his death in 1824, Maturin, an ordained minister in the Anglican church of Ireland, was a poorly paid curate, first at Loughrea, a rural parish, and later at St. Peter's parish in Dublin. At the age of twenty-three, he married Henrietta Kingsbury, like Maturin from an established Protestant family; her grandfather was Oscar Wilde's mother's great-grandfather, and "it was Miss Kingsbury's grandfather to whom [Jonathan] Swift is supposed to have uttered his last words before the light of his powerful mind was darkened for ever" (Idman, p. 10). Although Maturin was a gifted preacher, his literary imagination often came into conflict with the moral strictures of the time, his successful works harming his status in the church. For his first book, *The Fatal Revenge; or, The Family of Montorio* (1807) a Gothic thriller, he took the pseudonym Dennis Jasper Murphy (Idman, p. 14). Since Gothicism was already somewhat disreputable, Maturin defended it in his preface with the psychologically penetrating remark that he questioned "whether there be a source of emotion in the whole mental frame so powerful or so universal as the fear arising from objects of invisible terror" (Idman, p. 15). This perceptiveness about human fears guided his best work artistically, while constant financial distress filled him with an urgent need to produce. As numerous critics observe, nearly all Maturin's surviving letters—and there are not many—allude to his embarrassed finances, and often beg for a loan or assistance. On the few occasions when substantial sums came his way, he disposed of them extravagantly, partying or buying his wife expensive clothes. By the time his final novel and greatest work, *Melmoth,* was written, Maturin was attempting to support four children and his wife on his meager salary as a curate. Many factors influenced his inability to make a living, chiefly that he was raised as a pampered, adored gentleman's son and never expected to need to work. His extravagant personality and his literary tastes earned him the disapproval of those who might have given him preferment in the church.

From about 1810 on, Maturin enjoyed a close friendship with the novelist Sir Walter Scott, who had recognized the talent in Maturin's first novel and given it favorable mention in the *Quarterly Review* (Scott, p. 4). In 1813, Scott loaned Maturin fifty pounds, which Maturin's financial distress prevented him from ever repaying. By 1828, Maturin's third novel, *The Milesian Chief*, was so well known that the French novelist Balzac published a translation of it. The money from this book must have helped Maturin with the support of his growing family and aging father, who had lost his job in 1809 (Scott, p. 8). The cause of Maturin's death, on 30 October 1824, is not known, but poverty and extreme financial distress appear to have hastened his demise. He was only forty-four years old, and had been sickly for years. He and his wife had lost a child shortly after its birth in 1821. Idman writes only that Maturin's "last months were, by all accounts, about the gloomiest in his existence," since many anxieties preyed on him, and that sitting up all night writing *The Albigenses* broke his health "completely. . . . In the beginning of October 1924 Maturin was seized by an acute malady which the physicians, considering his impaired health in general, apprehended to be mortal" (p. 308).

MELMOTH THE WANDERER

Melmoth the Wanderer opens in the year 1816 with the return of John Melmoth, a university student in Dublin who is descended from the novel's anti-hero, the Wanderer, to the crumbling estate of a dying uncle. John Melmoth arrives to find the house a shambles, the servants sitting around the kitchen drinking and eating up most of the larder while his uncle raves on his deathbed that he is actually dying of fright, because the original of the figure in a mysterious portrait dated 1646 and hidden in his wine cellar is still alive. The uncle dies, the nephew indeed sees "the living original of the portrait" (p. 23), none other than Melmoth the Wanderer, and the uncle's will bequeathes John a moldering manuscript, urging him to burn it. Naturally John Melmoth does nothing of the kind, but instead reads it by candlelight after midnight, while wind and rain outside rattle the windows.

By this point, the gothic mood is well established, and it deepens as the nephew immerses himself in the manuscript's liver-spotted pages. The first tale, about a man named Stanton, is dated 1677, and concerns an Englishman traveling in Spain, where he first sees Melmoth the Wanderer. It is another dark and stormy night, and Stanton is abandoned "by a cowardly guide" (p. 33) but continues down a lonely road, admiring Roman ruins in the moonlight. His reveries are interrupted by the sight of two persons carrying the body of a young girl who has been struck dead by lightning. To add to the horror, just as two other figures emerge from the murk carrying the "blasted and blackened figure of what had once been a man" (p. 35)—the dead girl's newly married husband—a "person" suddenly appears, whose diabolic quality is broadcast by his calmness. This mysterious being bursts "into a laugh so loud, wild and protracted" (p. 35) that he frightens away the peasants bearing the dead bodies.

At this suspenseful moment, the manuscript John Melmoth is reading becomes illegible. Pages are turned and many more legible episodes occur, but the manuscript has a way of disintegrating at key moments. Among the more important readable cliffhangers are those between the Wanderer and Stanton at a point when Stanton has been confined in a madhouse by an unscrupulous relative, and hovers on the borderline between insanity and despair for pages, during which time the Wanderer visits and tempts him with an awful proposition, never named, which Stanton manages to resist, and then to escape from the madhouse. Every tale that follows includes the descent into madness or despair of an important character, but for the moment the narrative returns to young John Melmoth, who busies himself burning Stanton's manuscript as well as the portrait of the Wanderer.

The next night, during a terrible storm, a ship is wrecked off the coast of Melmoth's crumbling Irish estate (a scene repeated with striking similarities in Maturin's other major work, the drama *Bertram*). The sole survivor is Alonzo Monçada, the illegitimate son of a Spanish duke, who had been forced to join the Jesuit order years before, and had been visited and tempted by the Wanderer during the many terrible ordeals arising in his life with the Jesuits and his capture and interrogation in the custody of the Inquisition, the formal tribunal in the Roman Cathlic Church directed at the supression of heresy. John Melmoth falls into the sea while chasing the Wanderer, who has appeared on a precipice uttering his familiar, bone-chilling laugh at the sight of a tragedy, and Monçada manages to rescue him, but shortly thereafter collapses into a near-catatonic stupor upon learning that he is being sheltered in the home of the descendant of the Wanderer.

All following narratives in *Melmoth the Wanderer* are splintered from the main tale within the John Melmoth frame, which is Monçada's harrowing life story—referred to as the Tale of the Spaniard, apparently circa 1800—and Maturin's lengthy attack upon the Catholic Church as experienced by Monçada and by victims of the Inquisition. The illegitimate child of a nobleman and a guilt-ridden woman who describes herself as "of rank far beneath your father" (p. 100), Monçada has been promised to the Jesuit order since before his birth, as his mother's means of penance. Although he entreats both parents not to force him into this monastic life, for which he feels no vocation, he finds himself a virtual prisoner of the order, whose monastery boasts every abuse of Catholicism that a Calvinist Irish clergyman like Maturin could dream up: cynical lying, sadistic beatings and tortures, being confined to a reptile-ridden dungeon, starvation, sexual perversions, not spelled out, but implicating the Virgin Mary, whispered into Monçada's ear as he sleeps, a terrifying escape through an underground maze, led by a parricide who gloats over various torments he has in the past inflicted on lovers, and who subsequently stabs to death Monçada's devoted brother. The parricide has his own tale within the tale of Monçada, which terminates with the parricide's gruesome death by stoning at the hands of an angry mob in the subsequent tale. Briefly, the parricide's tale, circa 1796, reveals his delight in tormenting Monçada, whom he is assisting in an escape from the monastery and who is his captive audience, with

tales of how he murdered his father and how he locked two lovers in an underground vault, thrilling to the sound of their hunger agonies and discovering, upon opening the vault after their death, that the woman is his own sister. In the course of his and Monçada's journey through the dank labyrinthine tunnels beneath the monastery, the parricide takes full advantage of the silence, darkness, and built-in despair of their surroundings to amplify the horrors of his confession.

It is at Monçada's moment of deepest despair, after his brother's death and when he finds himself a prisoner of the Inquisition, that the Wanderer, true to form, appears to tempt him to sell his soul for freedom. Monçada declines, miraculously escapes the seemingly inevitable auto-da-fé at which he would be burned, and finds himself running through another labyrinth hiding the homes of some Jews who are also concealing themselves from the Inquisition. Ultimately Monçada takes refuge with another mysteriously old man, the Jew Adonijah (one critic, Kathleen Fowler, identifies him as the biblical prophet Elijah), and is put to work translating and transcribing a lengthy manuscript concerning Melmoth the Wanderer and other victims tempted by him, who have also resisted him.

Three more tales emerge from the intricate manuscript of Adonijah. "The Tale of the Indians" (1676) details the life of the Eve-like Immalee, abandoned as an infant on an uninhabited island in the Indian Ocean, and visited and tempted by Melmoth, who, after her unexplained return to her family in Spain, where she is known as Isidora, ultimately marries her in the midst of a violent storm, the church a ruin, the cold hands of the clergyman—unbeknownst to her—in reality those of a corpse. This tale, the longest one in the novel, achieves its poignancy from the deep and wholehearted love of Immalee for the Wanderer, who reluctantly, indeed to his horror, loves her back with an increasing sense of rage and despair. It is in this tale that the depth of the Wanderer's suffering seems most to equal the degree of suffering he doles out. Falling in love against his will, he "viewed that lovely and helpless being . . . with a look, that, for the first time, intimated compassion." She becomes "the first of his intended victims he had ever beheld with compunction," and her joy in his visits "almost brought back human feelings to a heart that had long renounced them" (*Melmoth the Wanderer*, p. 316). Idman observes, "the impression made upon Immalee by the conversations of Melmoth is very different from what he intended. She sheds tears and suffers with the sufferers, but nevertheless she is seized with a longing towards the world" (Idman, pp. 239–240). Ultimately her feeling of being "sheltered" (Idman, p. 240) whenever she is near him draws him toward her and creates a deep conflict between his desire to tempt and his longing to be near her. Tender feelings develop for her, which remain a torture to the Wanderer.

The Wanderer takes it upon himself to instruct her in the religions of the world, dwelling on their cruelty and hypocrisy, providing her with a telescope so that she can witness victims throwing themselves beneath an Indian juggernaut, an idol of the Hindu god Krishna pulled on wheels, and countless others torturing themselves. Immalee declares herself a Christian and says Christ shall be her god, and the Wanderer flees but finds himself unable to stay away from her. She is miraculously returned to Spain, where she pines for her Wanderer amid the confines of her spiritually cold family, elopes with him, is married, and carries his child, who spends its few days in a prison of the Inquisition with her. Once she knows that she will be confined to prison for the rest of her life and the child taken away from her, the child is found dead in her arms with "a black mark" around her throat, apparently strangled (*Melmoth the Wanderer*, p. 593). It remains unclear who did the strangling: Idman writes that Immalee (now known as Isidora) strangles the baby "when the officals have come to take it from her" (Idman, p. 248). Isidora herself claims that she is not guilty of the death of her infant, but that Melmoth had come to her cell the night before; she implies that he killed the child (*Melmoth the Wanderer*, p. 594). She cannot help continuing to love Melmoth, and when she thinks with her dying breath of a

heavenly paradise following death, she cries: "Will he be there?" (*Melmoth the Wanderer*, p. 596).

The long story of Immalee/Isidora is interrupted by "The Tale of Guzman" (pre-1676) and "The Lover's Tale" (1600s). "The Tale of Guzman" has long been thought to be a hidden portrait of some of the financial reverses suffered by Maturin's own family. Guzman is a Spanish Catholic who never appears within the story but who sends word to his sister, who has married a German Protestant, that he will leave the family his large fortune. The sister and her family come to Spain, she hoping to see her brother before he dies and heal their estranged relations, but although he provides lavishly for this family, which up to that point had lived frugally on the husband's income as a musician, he refuses to see them. When he dies, the family is informed that Guzman's will leaves them nothing, but donates all his considerable wealth to the Catholic Church. The family comes close to starvation, the father enraged and almost maddened by hunger, to the point of attempting to murder his children, and the reader almost expects a repetition of the gruesome scene in the tale of the parricide, in which the lovers entombed in a crypt fall into ravenous despair, the man taking a bite out of his beloved's shoulder before they fall down dead. In fact, the son of the musician grows unnaturally pale in a manner suggesting some nefarious misdeed, and turns out to have been selling his blood to a surgeon to support the family. One of his sisters narrowly resists the temptation to become a prostitute. Melmoth appears at the father's moment of greatest desperation when he considers the likelihood that his children will starve to death, but he manages to resist the diabolical offer. Only when the family is at death's door does the fact of the Catholic church having falsified the will become known, and the money purloined by that insitutution given to Guzman's heirs.

"The Lover's Tale" concerns an ill-fated couple in England, who are on the verge of having their wedding foiled by the groom's money-mad mother, who discovers that her son John will inherit only five thousand pounds if he marries

Elinor. The mother then lies to John, telling him that Elinor is his half-sister, so he leaves her pining at the altar and marries her cousin Margaret, who dies giving birth to twins. John goes mad, his mother's falsehood becomes known, and Elinor nurses him for the rest of his gloomy days. Melmoth appears to tempt Elinor, but to no avail.

The novel ends with a return to the frame story of John Melmoth, after the death of Immalee/Isidora in the prison of the Inquisition. Monçada, who has been trying to conclude his lengthy narrative, gets interrupted by the entrance of Melmoth the Wanderer, who has, however, reappeared not to tempt but to die. The Wanderer then experiences the terrible nightmare of falling into the volcanic pit, detailed above, and awakens from it dramatically aged. He tells Monçada and young Melmoth that his hour has come, and that no matter what they must not enter his room. From the corridor they listen to "terrible" sounds, and obey the Wanderer's admonition. When silence falls, they finally do enter, but he is nowhere to be found. They find "traces of footsteps" leading them to a rocky crag over the ocean, and clinging to the crag is "the handkerchief which the Wanderer had worn about his neck the preceding night—that was the last trace of the Wanderer!" (*Melmoth the Wanderer*, pp. 606, 607).

In the rather limited range of literary commentary that exists, critics of Maturin's best novel tend to gravitate toward analyses of its complex structure, which many describe as being like Chinese boxes or nesting boxes (Kathleen Fowler, "Hieroglyphics in Fire," p. 524; Richard Haslam, "Maturin and the 'Calvinist Sublime,' " p. 49), in which one story opens into another, the narratives and narrating points of view not infrequently confusingly blended or impossible to distinguish. Typically, one critic has called the novel a "layered narrative; structurally, it resembles a series of Russian dolls, each containing a smaller one inside" (Joseph W. Lew, "Unprepared for Sudden Transformations," p. 176). This structure is often perceived as problematic by critics. Nicola J. Watson has remarked on the novel's "extraordinary formal extravagance, disintegrative excess, and bewildering

multiplicity of narratives, some embedded within each other to the extent that they are buried up to three levels below the outer frame narrative, making it virtually impossible to remember any story's provenance" (*Revolution and the Form of the British Novel, 1790–1825*, p. 158). David Morse compares the novel to "a spinning globe suddenly arrested by the malignant author" (*Romanticism: A Structural Analysis*, p. 85).

One critic defends the book's apparent difficulties and structure as one of the main sources of the book's ability to "move its readers powerfully" (Fowler, p. 521). Katherine Fowler's observations break new ground by arguing that the confusions experienced by Maturin's readers are intended by him, and are not the result of carelessness. She writes: "the novel's multiplicity of stories and unusual narrative structure do mightily vex and bewilder the reader. . . . The novel moves steadily into the interior of a labyrinth. The reader expects that ultimately he will be led out again. Instead, he is abandoned somewhere within the maze seemingly without a map, or even a thread." She goes on to observe that the narratives are deliberately left without closure, "internally incomplete"; the omissions are part of Maturin's artistic design. The manuscript of Adonijah, she point out, has been written in Spanish and then transcribed into Greek characters, and is therefore "little better than hierogyphics. . . . To force this manuscript to yield up its secrets, the reader must possess both languages." This strange manuscript is the paradigm for interpreting Maturin's novel, whose fundamental source, Fowler argues, is the biblical Book of Job. Each of Maturin's many narratives within the novel contains, like the Book of Job, an "archetypal sufferer undergoing temptation." Other parallels abound, for instance, that "It is only the righteous who are tempted by Melmoth to blaspheme and to renounce God." Melmoth himself resembles the figure of Satan in the Book of Job: "Like Job's Satan, Melmoth fails to part his victims from God not because he is weak, but because they are strong ("Hieroglyphics in Fire," pp. 525–528).

Fowler's insightful and original commentary nevertheless fails to develop the similarities that she perceives between Job's Satan and Job himself. The Wanderer's problem is that he must tempt a soul to take his place in order to avoid eternal damnation and the volcanic fiery pit into which he dreams of falling at the novel's end. The Wanderer is himself a figure filled with torment and dread. What has received insufficient commentary is Maturin's deeply psychological creation of character and interpretation of motive.

BERTRAM

Maturin's drama *Bertram; or, The Castle of St. Aldobrand; A Tragedy in Five Acts* (1816), which enjoyed a long run on the London stage and was his only theatrical success, has the distinction of having aroused the extreme jealousy of the Romantic poet and literary critic Samuel Taylor Coleridge, whose play *Remorse*, appearing at the same time as *Bertram*, fared nowhere near as well with audiences or critics. Initially rejected by Covent Garden, *Remorse* had a brief run of only twenty nights and—compared to *Bertram*—a paltry three editions. *Bertram* enjoyed a run of sixty nights; seven editions of it were published. It went through three editions in one year, while *Bertram* lasted sixty nights and went through seven editions. So incensed was Coleridge that he devoted an entire chapter of his most important critical work, *Biographia Literaria* (1817), to a scathing critique of *Bertram*.

Bertram is as Gothic as the genre gets. The opening setting is described as follows: "Night, a Gallery in a convent, a large Gothic window in the extremity, through which lightning is seen flashing. Two monks enter in terror" (*Bertram*, p. 1). The monks are terrified by the sight of a storm and a shipwreck, and when their prior attempts to console them with the idea that God is watching over the storm, one monk asserts that this is "no earthly storm," but a sign of the "strife of fiends," that the "glare of hell is in these sulpherous lightnings" (*Bertram*, p. 3). Such inflated rhetoric deepens the mood of melodramatic suspense. By the third scene, the sole survivor has been led into the monastery and asks where he is. Told that he is in a monastery near the castle of Lord Aldobrand, he identifies himself with Gothic gloom as a "man of woe" (*Bertram*, p. 7), and, questioned why he has this woe, he answers only, "Because I live," and tries to throw off the monks who are trying to help him.

In the next scene, the lives of the women at St. Aldobrand's castle unfold, and it develops that the wife of Aldobrand, Imogine, has for years been pining over the very man who has, unbeknownst to her, just been rescued from the watery grave that doomed all his shipmates. Gazing at Bertram's picture, Imogine laments, "Th'Elysian dreams of lovers, when they loved— / Who shall restore them?" (*Bertram*, p. 11). Clotilda, her maid, enters, and Imogine confesses her love for Bertram under the guise of telling a tale of true love. She identifies Bertram as a fugitive—"With desperate men in desperate ways he dealt"— whose own mother rejects him: "she that bore him had recoiled from him" (*Bertram*, p. 14). Imogine then reveals that she loves Bertram. A monk enters, requesting shelter for the victims of the shipwreck, and Imogine grants it.

The second act opens with the prior watching Bertram's troubled sleep and waking him. Bertram—Count Bertram, it turns out—identifies himself, and the prior informs him that the shipwreck has landed him "Hard by . . . the halls of Aldobrand / (Thy mortal enemy and cause of fall)" (*Bertram*, p. 22).

Bertram gloats at the thought of murdering Aldobrand, horrifying the prior, although, strangely enough, the prior, knowing that Bertram and Aldobrand remain mortal enemies, has just taken care to assure Bertram that no one will reveal Bertram's identity. In the next scene, Bertram's band of men is welcomed into the castle, and in the next, Imogine is up on the castle ramparts in the moonlight, sighing over Bertram. Clotilda comes up to tell her the men have arrived, and of one among them with a "wild and terrible grandeur" (*Bertram*, p. 28). This is of course Bertram, who has asked to see Imogine. Bertram enters; she does not recognize him. His self-description pegs him as a moral twin of Melmoth the Wanderer:

The wretched have no country: that dear name
Comprizes home, kind kindred, fostering friends,

Protecting laws, all that binds man to man—
But none of these are mine; I have no country
And for my race, the last dread trump shall wake
The sheeted relics of mine ancestry . . .

(Bertram, p. 30)

Tottering toward him, Imogine recognizes him, and he confesses that if he looks on her longer, the sight of her pale cheeks "will make me human." Imogine falls at his feet, confessing that she married Aldobrand only to save her "famishing father," and Bertram rages, "could a father love thee / As I have loved?" (*Bertram*, pp. 31–33). Imogine, having begged him to leave, now begs him to stay, and he rushes out after kissing her child.

In the next scene, Imogine comes to the cloister, confessing to the prior that she is "withering with unholy love" for Bertram (*Bertram*, p. 42). The prior forbids her to see Bertram, urging her to do penance and sending her away, and at just that moment Aldobrand arrives home. Bertram finds Imogine praying, and begs for an hour alone with her, which she grants him.

In act 4, Bertram, whose affinity with Melmoth seems accentuated as the play goes on, appears in an agitated state under the castle walls, extending his arms in the direction of Imogine's room, and apparently regretting his seduction of her: "Beneath the black cope of this starless night / There lurks no darker soul— / My fiend-like glory hath departed from me." He regrets not having slain Aldobrand, and instead having "stol'n upon his secret bower of peace / And breathed a serpent's venom on his flower" (*Bertram*, p. 49).

Aldobrand returns home, and the guilt-ridden Imogine refuses his bed, slinking away to do penance, having no suspicions even when she murmurs,

I'm dying, Aldobrand, a malady
Preys on my heart that medicine cannot reach,
Invisible and cureless—look not on me
With looks of love, for then it stings me deepest

(Bertram, p. 59)

Aldobrand leaves her to her prayers, and Bertram enters with a dagger and asks her where her husband's bedroom is, since, as he puts it, "This morning must not see us both alive" (*Bertram*, p. 62). Imogine screams. They argue and she falls at his feet, "writhing like a worm" (*Bertram*, p. 64). At this point, Imogine and Bertram utter lines that turn them into embodiments of good and evil. She cries, "By heaven and all its host, he shall not perish," and Bertram replies, "By hell and all its host he shall not live" (*Bertram*, p. 64). By the end of the fourth act, Bertrand and his band of men have slain Aldobrand.

Meanwhile, back at the monastery in act 5, the prior has been having horrible visions of a "brinded wolf" tearing a "struggling lion" while a "cowed lioness stood trembling by" (*Bertram*, p. 72). Imogine rushes in with her child, her hair disheveled, her dress bloody, and begs to be saved, saying, "He hath no father—we have murdered him" (*Bertram*, p. 75). She clings to the prior, who rebuffs her violently. She runs out with the child. Enter Bertram, covered with blood, announcing that he has come "to yield— but not to be subdued" (*Bertram*, p. 81). Bertram is led away in chains, and the prior remonstrates with him to confess before his upcoming "awful death" (*Bertram*, p. 87). Imogine is heard shrieking and rushes out of a cave asking for death; her child is dead, and the only likely culprit is herself. Bertram rushes toward her, then watches her die slowly, apparently mad, in Clotilda's arms. Then, taking his cue from Othello, he stabs himself, crying: "I died no felon death / A warrior's weapon freed a warrior's soul" (*Bertram*, p. 91).

Dale Kramer has commented on the status of Bertram as a "Gothic hero-villain," remarking that Bertram is "an individual portrait, even though he follows certain patterns of the genre. His characterization has a vitality of development lacking in most Gothic villains, although his posturings and heroic speeches obscure the nature of this change. Most characters in Gothic drama are static. They have either committed their sins . . . or they commit them shortly after the play opens. . . . The despair . . . connecting Bertram with the Gothic tradition is not motivated by guilt, as is the despair of almost every Gothic hero-villain, but by a burning unrest of spirit and by an insatiable hatred of Aldobrand that it seems impossible to relive by an act of revenge" (*Charles Robert Maturin*, p. 67).

MINOR WRITINGS

Maturin's minor writings greatly outnumber his two literary successes. He was a prolific, though largely unsuccessful, author. He wrote five other novels besides *Melmoth the Wanderer*: *The Fatal Revenge: The Family of Montorio* (1807), *The Wild Irish Boy* (1808), *The Milesian Chief* (1812), *Women: Or, Pour et Contre* (1818), and *The Albigenses* (1824). He wrote two other plays besides *Bertram*: *Manuel* (1817) and *Fredolfo* (1819) He produced a popular document, *Five Sermons on the Errors of the Roman Catholic Church* (1824).

The Fatal Revenge is an incredibly complicated affair, set in Naples and involving the usual ingredients: deception, poison, family hatreds, incest, monasteries, murders, and, as one critic quoted by Idman remarked, "sufficient sparkle and movement for half a dozen ordinary romances" (Idman, p. 32). The plot concerns two brothers, one good and one evil, or rather one happy and unsuspecting and the other pathologically envious and desirous of stealing his successful brother's wife, castle, and fortune. The bad brother is fondly regarded by Orazio, his doting, unsuspecting brother, until he has managed to frame Orazio's preternaturally chaste wife, Erminia, as an adulteress, and induce Orazio to murder her supposed lover before her eyes, a sight that kills her. This tragedy sends Orazio into turmoils of travel and exotic mystical studies, culminating in his disguising himself as a monk in order to wreak revenge upon his brother, which brings disaster upon himself. Despite the bubbling melodrama, it "is almost intolerable to read Montorio from beginning to end," despite "many impressive passages" (Idman, p. 33).

The Wild Irish Boy, an epistolary romance, differs vastly from the bulk of Maturin's work; in the words of one critic, "Maturin is bent on reaching metaphysical and moral conclusions that would satisfy the most determined rationalist or the most pious puritan"; the book so goes against the author's grain, however, "that there is scarcely a page for which anyone would take responsibility" (Shirley Clay Scott, pp. 103, 105). In need of cash, Maturin titled his novel with the idea of suggesting a sequel or counterpart to a successful romance by Lady Morgan, *The Wild Irish Girl*; Maturin's novel was "calculated to please all—except the author himself" (Idman, p. 46).

The Milesian Chief opens with a mysterious young Englishwoman living in Naples, the daughter of one Lord Montclare, an English noblewoman. She is said to unite "in mind and form the charms of all the muses and all the graces" (*The Milesian Chief*, p. 2), but something always prevents her from exhibiting her talents. A monk is for some reason pursuing her father, producing "terrible effects," and when the father appears with the monk, the latter remarks of the daughter—whose every ability has been cultivated by her father and a collection of masters hired by him—that "Splendid talents often cause more uneasiness than triumph: she has too much genius, perhaps too much pride, to be happy: her talents and her sensibility have been refined till neither her own excellence or the applause of others afford her any further pleasure" (*The Milesian Chief*, p. 5). Again, Maturin's psychological bent is prominent.

Women; or, Pour Et Contre, opens with a young man, Charles de Courcey, walking in the dark on the outskirts of Dublin because his carriage has broken down. He hears what he takes to be the despairing howls of an abducted girl in a carriage going by, and immediately sets out to pursue and rescue her. He finds her in a dead swoon in the home of an apparently insane old woman. The girl, Eva, is then, through de Courcy's efforts, picked up by a man who is apparently her uncle and who takes her away without explaining what has happened to her. De Courcey collapses and has to be nursed back to health. One Sunday in a Methodist chapel (where else?), he happens to meet Eva again, and falls even more madly in love with her. The stage is set for star-crossed lovers' agonies, in which Charles falls in love with a gorgeously mysterious actress, Zaira, also known as Madame Dalmatiani, who turns out to be none other than the long-lost mother of the saintly Eva, who has been languishing for weeks, and now dies beautifully just as this secret is being aired and just before Zaira gets to visit her. De Courcey also dies.

The Albigenses, an historical novel, was probably inspired by the encouragement and success of Maturin's friend Sir Walter Scott. Idman comments, "That most contemporary critics . . . hailed *The Albigenses* as Maturin's best work only proves their partiality for the style in which it was written; of later judges even his greatest admirer admits that Maturin's attempt to 'marry history to fiction' turned out a failure" (p. 284). The Albigenses were a religious sect originating in Provence. They believed in an endless struggle of good and evil derived from ancient Manichean sects, and practiced extreme asceticism—for example, starvation to the point of suicide. Regarded as heretics by the Catholic church, many were executed and more persecuted.

The hero of Maturin's novel, which opens in the year 1216, is a young knight named Sir Paladour de la Croix Sanglante, who is tricked by a maniac into believing that his bride is his mortal enemy, and urged to slaughter her on their wedding night. He tries to stab himself instead, leading to a hairbreadth escape of the two lovers. The girl, who is disguised as a boy, is accidentally wounded when Sir Paladour tries to stab himself and she struggles for the knife. Political and love intrigues abound in this overheated tale.

Manuel, which proved a complete box office failure, concerns a Spanish count with a son, Alonzo, born in his old age. The play opens on "a Street in the city of Cordova" (*Manuel*, p. 2) with the requisite "Gothic gate in the background," which fronts a monastery. Family conflicts and violent hatreds ensue but are developed in a dismally undramatic way. A knight in black armor and a dagger emblazoned with the name of a murderer are other gothic elements whose dramatic possibilities go undeveloped.

Fredolfo has been characterized by Idman as romantic "in the highest degree," and he considers it "not only the best of Maturin's dramatic compositions, but a work of considerable poetic value" (pp. 180, 181). Kramer disagrees, remarking that "the plot's coherence is seriously rent by uncreative devices intended to sustain interest . . . . numerous redundant, abject pleas for mercy by the heroine Urilda, and Wallenberg's nefarious schemings." This is a pity, since, he remarks, the initial dramatic situation "is the most promising of all Maturin's plays. The play employs the social background of the Swiss struggle in the fourteenth century for independence from Austria; several characters trapped in situations not worthy of their essential natures; and the suspenseful threat of malign poitical and personal persecution" (p. 76).

Maturin's *Five Sermons on the Errors of the Roman Catholic Church* uses biblical material to undercut the Roman Catholic belief in the validity of the temporal body, and to dismiss the traditional Catholic sacraments, except for baptism and marriage (which are also Protestant sacraments). He argues also that the Catholic church is not apostolic (Kramer, p. 145). The sermons were preached on Lent of the year 1824, and proved extremely popular.

Several other minor works were orginally attributed to Maturin, but the authorship is now known to be false or doubtful: the 1815 prize poem at Trinity College, Dublin, "Lines on the Battle of Waterloo," may or may not have been his (Kramer, p. 157). "The Universe: A Poem," published in London in 1821, has Maturin's name on the title page, but—according to Kramer—the sons of the Rev. John Mills claimed that their father wrote the poem. Idman has the name of the "real" poet as "Mr. John Wills," not "Mills," however (p. 270). In any case, all authorities agree that the poem is negligible.

MATURIN AND CONTEMPORARY CRITICS

Maturin's work, especially *Melmoth the Wanderer*, continues to engage critics and to speak to many current critical interests, among them postcolonial studies, identity politics, and feminism. Heinz Kosok remarks that *Melmoth* "contains, in the 'Tale of the Indians,' one of the fiercest attacks on colonialism to be found in nineteenth century literature" ("Charles Robert Maturin and

Colonialism," p. 228). He compares Maturin's attack on European vessels invading the islands to that of Jonathan Swift in *Gulliver's Travels*, and suggests that Maturin's "personal experience of a colonialist situation in pre-and post-Union Irelsand [is] reflected in those of his novels that have a contemporary Irish setting [as well as in] . . . one of his plays, [*Fredolfo*]" (p. 232).

In "'Unprepared for Sudden Transformations': Identity and Politics in *Melmoth the Wanderer*," Joseph W. Lew characterizes the novel as "political allegory. It is literally about Civil War England, Spain under the Inquisition, and life on an Indian island, but also about contemporary Ireland" (p. 175). He points out that the novel "continually presents characters with more than one identity" (173) and relates this propensity to Maturin's "own compromised position as an Anglo-Irish curate out of political favor. In the guise of its Spanish Gothic and exotic East Indian settings, Melmoth explores problems of cultural and personal identity and assimilation—a problem particularly acute for the English in Ireland during Maturin's lifetime but also becoming increasingly important in Great Britain's colonial holdings" (p. 174). These characters with more than one identity—for instance, Immalee, the Eve-like daughter of nature is also the highborn Spanish Catholic Isidora and Antonio, son of the hidden Jew Adonijah, is really Menassah-ben-Solomon, forced like his father to masquerade as a Catholic—are reminiscent of the Irish, who were compelled to adopt English ways and the English language. The Anglo-Irish, like Maturin and his famous descendant, Oscar Wilde, belonged uneasily to both English and Irish culture, and also belonged to neither. The complications of identity in *Melmoth* speak to this cultural disease.

In "Masculinizing the Novel: Women Writers and Intertextuality in Charles Robert Maturin's *The Wild Irish Boy*," Jacqueline Pearson derides the propensity of many critics to criticize this novel as a carelessly plagiarized work, arguing that "to accuse him of plagiarism is to misunderstand his intertextual practices and those of his age" (p. 635). Incidentally, contemporary literary criticism of Oscar Wilde points toward a related thesis; Dierdre Toomey remarks that the Irish oral tradition was misperceived by English critics as plagiarism. The cultural differences between English and Irish aesthetics are not the primary concern of Pearson, however, who theorizes that Maturin deliberately borrows from and resists, as well as remakes, "female-authored novels," an interesting thesis, because the Gothic novel was dominated by several prominent female writers, the mistress of the genre being, as we have seen, Ann Radcliffe. Women, Pearson observes, were in the late eighteenth and early nineteenth century—that is, in the heyday of the Gothic novel—prominent "as both producers and consumers of literature" (p. 635), a remark that might describe the current market, insofar as today women remain the most prominent consumers of romantic and gothic novels written in the style of Danielle Steele, and popularly known as "bodice-rippers."

Pearson describes the female-dominated genre of the novel form in Maturin's day, observing that as a Gothic novelist he was "treading in the footsteps of Ann Radcliffe; as a writer of Irish 'national tales' . . . he was working in a mode dominated by Maria Edgeworth and Sydney Orenson Morgan; as a novelist of society life . . . he was aware of the example of Edgworth and probably . . . of Frances Burney." He was, Pearson concludes, feeling "an anxiety of influence in a particularly gendered way" (p. 637).

SELECTED BIBLIOGRAPHY

I. NOVELS. *Fatal Revenge: or, The Family of Montorio: A Romance*, by Dennis Jaspar Murphy, pseudonym (London, 1807); *The Wild Irish Boy* (London, 1808); *The Milesian Chief: A Romance* (London, 1812); *Women: or, Pour et Contre* (Edinburgh and London, 1818); *Melmoth the Wanderer*, ed. by Victor Sage (London, 2000 [1820]); *Melmoth the Wanderer*, ed. by Douglas Grant (New York and Oxford, 1989); *Melmoth the Wanderer: A Tale.* (Edinburgh and London, 1820); *The Albigenses: A Romance* (London and Edinburgh, 1824).

II. PLAYS. *Bertram; or, The Castle of St. Aldobrand* (Oxford and New York, 1992 [1816]); *Manuel: A Tragedy* (London, 1817); *Fredolfo: A Tragedy* (London, 1819).

III. SERMONS. *Sermons* (Edinburgh and London, 1819); *Five Sermons on the Errors of the Roman Catholic Church* (1826 [1824]).

IV. BIOGRAPHY. *More Letters of Oscar Wilde*, ed. by Rupert Hart-Davis (New York, 1885); Niilo Idman, *Charles*

Robert Maturin: His Life and Works (London, 1923; includes criticism); Melissa Knox, *Oscar Wilde: A Long and Lovely Suicide* (New Haven, 1994).

V. CRITICAL STUDIES. Mario Praz, *The Romantic Agony*, 2nd ed., trans. by Angus Davidson (New York and Oxford, 1920); Willem Scholten, *Charles Robert Maturin: The Terror Novelist* (Amsterdam, 1933); Robert Kiely, *The Romantic Novel in England* (Cambridge, Mass., 1972); Dale Kramer, *Charles Robert Maturin* (New York, 1973); Shirely Scott Clay, *Myths of Consciousness in the Novels of Charles Robert Maturin* (New York, 1980); Rosemary Lloyd, "*Melmoth the Wanderer*: The Code of Romanticism," in *Beaudelaire, Mallarmé, Valéry*, ed. by Malcolm Bowie, Alison Fairlie, and Alison Finch (New York and Cambridge, 1982); David Morse, *Romanticism: A Structural Analysis* (London, 1982); Samuel Taylor Coleridge, *Biographia Literaria*, ed. by James Engell and W. Jackson Bate (Princeton, 1983); Kathleen Fowler, "Hieroglyphics in Fire: *Melmoth the Wanderer*," in *Studies in Romanticism* vol. 25, no. 4 (winter 1986); Charles Swann, "Poe and Maturin: A Possible Debt," in *Notes and Queries*, vol. 235, no. 4, of the continuous series (New Series, Vol. 37; Oxford, 1990); J. Th. Leerssen, "Fiction Poetics and Cultural Stereotype: Local Colour in Scott, Morgan, and Maturin," in *Modern Language Review* 86, no. 2 (April 1991); Amy Elizabeth Smith, "Experimentation and 'Horrid Curiosity' in Maturin's *Melmoth the Wanderer*," in *English Studies: A Journal of English Language and Literature* 74, no. 6 (December 1993; Richard Haslam, "Maturin and the 'Calvinist Sublime,' " in Allan Lloyd Smith and Victor Sage, eds., *Gothick Origins and Innovations* (Amsterdam and Atlanta, Ga., 1994); Joseph W. Lew, " 'Unprepared for Sudden Transformations': Identity and Politics in *Melmoth the Wanderer*," in *Studies in the Novel* 26, no. 2 (summer 1994); Nicola J. Watson, *Revolution and the Form of the British Novel, 1790–1825* (Oxford, 1994); Regina B. Oost, " 'Servility and Command': Authorship in *Melmoth the Wanderer*," in *Papers on Language and Literature* 31, no. 3 (summer 1995); Heinz Kosok, "Charles Robert Maturin and Colonialism," in *Literary Inter-Relations: Ireland, Egypt, and the Far East*, ed. by Mary Massoud, *Irish Literary Studies*, 1996); Helen Small, *Love's Madness: Medicine, the Novel, and Female Insanity, 1800–1865* (Oxford, 1996); Jacqueline Pearson, "Masculinizing the Novel: Women Writers and Intertextuality in Charles Robert Maturin's *The Wild Irish Boy*," in *Studies In Romanticism* 36, no. 4 (winter 1997).

NGŨGĨ WA THIONG'O

(1938–)

J. Roger Kurtz

NGŨGĨ WA THIONG'O is the leading name among East Africa's first generation of writers, meaning those Africans who began to write and publish in English at the end of the colonial era. Thanks to his writing and his activism—activities that for him are inveterately linked—Ngũgĩ has been a seminal influence not only on the literature of his Kenyan homeland, but also on the broader world of postcolonial literary studies.

It can be difficult to decide which of Ngũgĩ's numerous accomplishments is most significant. Would it be his ground-breaking fiction, which not only initiated the East African novel as a genre but also laid out much of its thematic repertoire? Or his involvement in Kenyan popular theater, which led to his detention and exile? Or his leading role as intellectual rabble-rouser in arguing for a restructuring of the African educational curriculum or in advocating the use of African language by writers and academics? Whatever the case, it is impossible to separate Ngũgĩ's literary achievements from his committed, often oppositional, stance on political and social issues. "The Making of a Rebel" is Carol Sicherman's subtitle for her study of Ngũgĩ's life and of the influences on his thinking, and it is an apt description, for in a lifetime of writing—which by 2002 had produced six novels, four plays, and seven volumes of cultural commentary—we find a consistently activist and even rebellious social vision. It is a vision that has led to memorable literature but has also required Ngũgĩ to spend half of his adult life exiled from his home in Kenya.

CHILDHOOD AND EDUCATION IN COLONIAL KENYA

Ngũgĩ's life spans a crucial historical period in East African history, from the height of British colonial rule, through the tumultuous independence era, and into the twenty-first century. He was born into a peasant farming family in the so-called "white highlands" of colonial Kenya on 5 January 1938. His father, Thiong'o wa Ndũũcũ, had four wives, and Ngũgĩ is the fifth child of Wanjikũ wa Ngũgĩ, the third of these wives. When he was about ten years old Ngũgĩ's parents separated, and he was raised by his mother. Ngũgĩ excelled in his early studies, especially in English, which allowed him to attend the elite schools of his day, eventually leading to academic posts at top universities in Kenya and abroad, along with his writing career. In short, as Patrick Williams concludes, Ngũgĩ was "exposed to the best and worst faces of British colonial culture simultaneously" (p. 5)—the worst being the often violent injustices of the colonial period, and the best being the high-quality education from which he benefited.

Kamĩrĩĩthu, Ngũgĩ's home village, where he would later return for his experiments in popular theater, sits near the town of Limuru, a small urban center about twenty miles northwest of Nairobi. This area is in the southern part of what is now the administrative region known as Central Province, a region referred to as "Kikuyuland" in colonial shorthand because it was inhabited primarily by the Kikuyu people (spelled Gĩkũyũ in more recent orthography). Under colonial rule—which in Kenya lasted from the chartering of the Imperial British East Africa Company in 1888 until independence in 1963—British settlers confiscated and farmed large swaths of Gĩkũyũ territory, forcing the original inhabitants and their descendants to become landless squatters, sometimes even working on the very land that had been taken from them. "When I was growing up," Ngũgĩ has remembered, "I was very much aware of the physical confronta-

211

tion between foreigners and Kenyans at Limuru. On one side of Limuru was the land controlled by the foreign settlers, and on the other side was the land controlled by peasants and Kenyan landlords" (in Sicherman, *Making of a Rebel,* p. 19).

The Gĩkũyũ are a traditionally agricultural community for whom the land has a crucial, even spiritual function, so that even though the British actually took more land from the Maasai, the "land hunger" of the British settlers (to use a former colonial administrator's phrase—see W. Mcgregor Ross, *Kenya from Within,* 1927), was especially disruptive for the Gĩkũyũ. Ngũgĩ would later come to see the colonial economy of Limuru in Marxian terms: peasants who were alienated from their land were forced to work either on plantations that grew cash crops like coffee, tea, or pyrethrum (chrysanthemums grown for use as insecticides), or else in newly established factories in the area, thereby creating an entire new class of people who no longer controlled the land that was their means of livelihood—in short, a proletariat. Ngũgĩ used Limuru as the setting for many of his novels and stories, loosely disguised under fictional names like "Kipanga" (in *Weep Not, Child*) or "Ilmorog" (in *Petals of Blood* and *Devil on the Cross*).

In his childhood, Ngũgĩ witnessed firsthand some of the strongest opposition to colonial rule in Kenya. Through the colonial period, tribes from all parts of Kenya resisted actions such as the confiscation of land by the crown, the imposition of taxes, and forced labor. But because of their proximity to Nairobi, and because they inhabited much of the colony's most desirable farmland, the Gĩkũyũ were on the front lines of British settlement in the region and consequently also on the front lines of resistance to colonialism. In some areas, the Gĩkũyũ adopted European influences quite readily—they were quicker to embrace Western dress, formal education, and Christianity, for instance, than their neighbors, the pastoralist Maasai. In other areas (such as the issue of female circumcision), they remained at odds with Western demands. But the major factor in inciting resistance to colonialism among the Gĩkũyũ was loss of their land. The Gĩkũyũ led or

dominated most of the significant political pressure groups in the decades preceding independence. These included the Kikuyu Association (KA), founded in 1919; the more radical East Africa Association (EAA), founded in 1921 and banned a year later; the Kikuyu Central Association (KCA), founded in 1924 and banned in 1940, and whose general secretary, Jomo Kenyatta, would later become the first president of independent Kenya; the Kenya African Union (KAU), which formed in 1944 and eventually evolved into the Kenya African National Union (KANU), the political party that would govern independent Kenya; and of course the Mau Mau movement.

Mau Mau is the enigmatic and still unexplained name given to what the Gĩkũyũ called the "land and freedom army," an armed insurgency against the British that arose in Central Province, particularly in the mountainous, forested region around Mount Kenya and the Aberdare range. Despite its historical prominence, Mau Mau was not successful as a military movement; indeed, the martial law enforced by the colonial administration during the 1950s (commonly referred to as "the Emergency") effectively dismantled the Mau Mau threat. It was, however, successful in promoting the political battle for independence. At the same time, the Mau Mau experience was tremendously divisive for the Gĩkũyũ. Just as the community had been deeply divided twenty years earlier over the circumcision issue, so they were finding themselves on two sides in the Mau Mau movement, with "patriots" (those who went to fight in the forests) lined up against the "loyalists" (those who sided or worked for the colonial administration).

Although he was in high school during the height of the Emergency and was not personally involved in the armed struggle, Ngũgĩ was profoundly and closely affected by it. His family home and village were demolished and relocated as part of the government's anti-Mau Mau "villagization" campaign. In the story of Gitogo, in *A Grain of Wheat,* the deaf and mute character who is shot by colonial authorities, is modeled on Ngũgĩ's stepbrother, who was killed in similar circumstances. Like Njoroge in *Weep Not, Child,*

Ngũgĩ had an older brother, Wallace Mwangi, who joined the Mau Mau resistance.

Growing up in the heart of the Gĩkũyũ community, Ngũgĩ was naturally saturated with the traditional cultural influences: "I grew up under the influence of Gĩkũyũ peasant culture—songs, stories, proverbs, riddles around the fireside in the evening—as well as those values that govern human relationships in a peasant community" (in Sicherman, *Making of a Rebel*, p. 19). Ngũgĩ would use aspects of this tradition in his writing, and he would also use the geography of the Limuru area—the ridges and hills of this elevated rural terrain on the edge of the Great Rift Valley—as integral symbolic elements, particularly in his early works.

Ngũgĩ's immediate family was not Christian, but the area where he grew up was within the sphere of influence of the Church of Scotland Mission (CSM), a group that would later become the Presbyterian Church of East Africa. The family's landlord was a CSM elder, and Ngũgĩ began his formal studies at one of the mission's elementary schools in nearby Kamandura. When he was ten, however, Ngũgĩ shifted to a Gĩkũyũ independent school at Maanguũ (Mango). These independent schools arose in the late 1920s as a supplement and alternative to the mission and government schools in colonial Kenya. Independent schools operated on limited resources but had the advantage (for the Gĩkũyũ) of including traditional religion and culture in the curriculum, and they also introduced English at a far earlier stage than schools run by Europeans. Ngũgĩ asserts that attending an independent school gave him a keener awareness of the oppressive nature of colonialism and a concurrent appreciation for traditional Gĩkũyũ culture. The government and some of the missionaries viewed these schools with suspicion and even fear, and Ngũgĩ's school at Maanguũ was later moved and taken over by the government (during the Emergency, this was the fate of all independent schools in Central Province).

For his secondary education (1955–1959), Ngũgĩ earned a rare spot at the elite Alliance High School, where his interest in writing and his political awareness would grow. Run by a consortium of mission agencies, Alliance offered an intellectual haven even as it reinforced a colonial worldview that took European cultural superiority for granted. In several of his novels, Ngũgĩ modeled the fictional Siriana school on Alliance. His fictional headmasters (Reverend Livingstone in *Weep Not, Child* and the less sympathetic Cambridge Fraudsham in *Petals of Blood*) are caricatures of Alliance's influential headmaster, E. Francis Carey, who at one point felt it necessary to warn Ngũgĩ against political agitation (Sicherman, *The Making of a Rebel,* p. 4). At Alliance, Ngũgĩ developed an interest in writing and wrote essays for the school journal. He also came to be a fairly sincere Christian— "rather too serious a Christian," by his own account (in Sicherman, *Making of a Rebel,* p. 4)— but later in life he would reject Christianity and also stop using the Christian name James, with which he had signed his first stories and novels and which he would use for the last time in 1970 with the publication of *This Time Tomorrow*.

HIGHER EDUCATION AND EARLY CAREER

After Alliance, and again because of his outstanding academic performance, Ngũgĩ was admitted to Makerere University College in Uganda, which at the time was the preeminent institution of higher education in East Africa, if not in the entire continent, where the curriculum was established under a special arrangement with the University of London. Ngũgĩ would spend five years there, from 1959 to 1964. Although Makerere's curriculum and ideals were as fundamentally Eurocentric as those at Alliance (David Cook and Michael Okenimpke suggest that Makerere's English syllabus was conservative enough that it "would have looked a little outmoded in the United Kingdom," p. 4), the college's overall atmosphere was somewhat more liberal. The literature curriculum was entirely British, but outside of his coursework Ngũgĩ was exposed for the first time to other African and West Indian writers. He remembers being "overwhelmed" by the Barbadian novelist George Lamming (Sicherman, *The Making of a Rebel,* p. 4).

It was at Makerere that Ngũgĩ began to find success as a creative writer, publishing his first short story ("The Fig Tree") in the English department's literary magazine, *Penpoint*. By virtue of his early publications, Ngũgĩ was invited to attend the Conference of African Writers of English Expression, held at Makerere in June of 1962. Writers from all over the African continent attended the conference, which has since come to be seen as a watershed event in East African literary history, if only because it made the region's writers more aware of the accomplishments of their counterparts in Nigeria and South Africa. In retrospect, Ngũgĩ has also noted the irony that he was invited to attend the conference on the basis of a few publications in English, while other and more accomplished poets and artists, because they did not write in English, were ineligible to attend.

Nevertheless, it was clear by this time that Ngũgĩ was a promising name in African literature. His play *The Black Hermit* was performed as part of Uganda's Independence celebrations in November 1962. He had completed a novel, "The Black Messiah," in December 1961, during his third year at Makerere, and the manuscript won a novel-writing contest sponsored by the East African Literature Bureau. The work was eventually published in 1965 under the title *The River Between,* which has led to the question for critics as to whether this ought to be considered his first novel or whether that honor should go to *Weep Not, Child,* which was written later (in 1962) but published first, in 1964. In any case, by the time he graduated from Makerere, Ngũgĩ had established himself as a leading figure in East African creative writing. He was the first East African to write a novel and the first to have a full-length English-language play produced; he also was contributing a regular column to the Nairobi-based newspaper the *Daily Nation*. In 1965, when Taban lo Liyong issued his famous lament on the barrenness of East African literature, one of the few local stars he could point to was Ngũgĩ. "We need Ngũgĩs in plural," Taban implored in "East Africa, O East Africa" (*Transition* 19, p. 11).

At Makerere, Ngũgĩ had been profoundly influenced by reading D. H. Lawrence and Joseph Conrad, writers whose traces critics later would notice in Ngũgĩ's novels and stories, but at Leeds University in England, where Ngũgĩ studied from 1964 to 1967, a more radical intellectual climate prevailed. He was permitted to write his dissertation on George Lamming and West Indian literature; he was taught and influenced by Arnold Kettle, a leading Marxist critic; and he began to read Lenin, Marx, and Engels, as well as Frantz Fanon, the Martinican psychiatrist famous for his analysis of the devastating psychological dynamics of colonialism. Although he never actually completed his degree at Leeds, by the time he returned to Kenya in 1967, Ngũgĩ had added another layer of experience and ideological concepts—a Marxian social philosophy—to the Gĩkũyũ cultural values, the mission-sponsored Christian education, and the liberal Western academic curriculum that had so far marked his educational experiences.

Back in Kenya, now in his late twenties, Ngũgĩ was appointed lecturer in English at the University of Nairobi, becoming the first African to hold such a position. In 1969, he resigned in protest at government interference in the university and instead taught at Makerere and then Northwestern University. He returned to the University of Nairobi in 1971, where he would remain until 1977 (when he would be arrested by the government and detained without trial). By this stage, Ngũgĩ was firmly convinced of the need to "decolonise" those aspects of Kenyan society that still bore the marks of colonial influence, particularly in the realm of culture. He had made waves with the proposal—coauthored in 1968 with his fellow academics, Taban lo Liyong and Henry Owuor-Anyumba—that the English department be changed in order to make African literatures central to the curriculum. Their proposal argued for "the centrality of Africa in the department," so that students would be presented with "Africa at the center of things, not existing as an appendix or a satellite of other countries and literatures" (*Homecoming,* p. 150). The proposal was in fact a response to some less sweeping curricular changes initially suggested by the department head, James Stewart. In the end, the English Department was renamed the Department of Literature, and a Department of Linguistics and African Languages was also formed. In 1973, Ngũgĩ became acting head of the Department of Literature, which was the first time an African had been appointed to such a post at the university.

As part of his broader vision to "move the center" of literary studies, Ngũgĩ also worked to promote a greater awareness of literature from the African diaspora. He especially promoted the study of Caribbean literatures, which have remained a central feature of the literature curriculum in East African universities ever since. Some of these connections developed personal ties. Ngũgĩ brought the Barbadian poet Edward Brathwaite to Nairobi in 1971; at a ceremony at Ngũgĩ's home, Brathwaite was given a Gĩkũyũ name—Kamau—by Ngũgĩ's grandmother, a name he has used ever since (see Brathwaite's opening essay in Cantalupo, *Ngũgĩ wa Thiong'o: Texts and Contexts*). In 1976, Ngũgĩ also brought to Nairobi George Lamming, the figure who had originally opened his mind to the possibility of a broader literary world back at Makerere.

In another initiative consonant with his desire to decolonize the literary establishment, during his tenure at the University of Nairobi, Ngũgĩ became increasingly outspoken about his belief in the importance of African languages and their promotion. If this notion seems logical or even obvious, it must be remembered that even forty years after independence the overwhelming majority of Kenyan literature is still produced in English; as in most other African nations, leading authors write and publish in European languages, the languages of their former colonizers. The language debate had been alive well before the 1970s, of course. Already at the 1962 Makerere conference, the Nigerian Obiajunwa Wali had argued (in an essay republished in *Transition*, 1963, no. 10) that African literature in non-African languages is both sterile and doomed to failure. Others—particularly those writers who had been publishing in European languages—defended the right of authors to express themselves in any language they wished, including English. Through the 1970s, Ngũgĩ had been writing in English almost exclusively, with the notable exception of the Gĩkũyũ-language play *Ngaahika ndeenda* (I Will Marry When I Want). In 1986, however, he announced that he would no longer write in English and that "from now on it is Gĩkũyũ and Kiswahili all the way" (*Decolonising the Mind*, p. xiv). Carol Sicherman reports that in 1976 Ngũgĩ had begun writing his fifth novel in English (*Making of a Rebel*, p. 5), but after his arrest and detention he revised his storyline, switched to Gĩkũyũ, and completed it on prison toilet paper. The novel was published in 1980 as *Caitaani mũtharaba-ini*, for which Ngũgĩ did his own English translation that appeared two years later as *Devil on the Cross*. Ngũgĩ's sixth novel, *Matigari*, also appeared first in Gĩkũyũ and later in an English translation by Wangui wa Goro.

DETENTION AND LIFE ABROAD

Why was Ngũgĩ detained and later exiled? There is no doubt that his outspoken social criticism, which was becoming increasingly effective as his reputation grew during the 1970s, was angering the political and economic elite. Ngũgĩ's enemies accused him of being both a tribalist (a supporter of Gĩkũyũ nationalism) and a communist. His fourth novel, *Petals of Blood*, appeared in 1977, and while it contains a direct attack on the corruption of government and business in Kenya since independence, it apparently did not cross a certain unspoken line, since then Vice President Mwai Kibaki officiated at ceremonies launching the novel in Nairobi and claimed that his presence signified the depth of the government's commitment to free speech. Six months later, Ngũgĩ was arrested. His detention order was signed by the minister for home affairs, Daniel arap Moi, who would go on to become president of Kenya the following year, and it listed the grounds of his detention as "having engaged yourself in activities and utterances which are dangerous to the good Government of Kenya and its institutions" (*Detained*, p. 230).

It is generally felt that it was Ngũgĩ's involvement with peasant theater, specifically the production of *Ngaahika ndeenda*, that ultimately led to his arrest. In 1976, Ngũgĩ had begun working with a peasant cooperative in his home village—the Kamĩrĩĩthu Community Educational and Cultural Centre—and at first the focus was on literacy and vocational training. Shortly thereafter, Ngũgĩ and a collaborator, Ngũgĩ wa Mĩrĩĩ, were commissioned to write a play that grew out of the literacy classes and that involved the actors and the audience in its creation. *Ngaahika ndeenda,* the result of this collaboration, might be seen as being in the tradition of the radical democratic theater of Bertolt Brecht. Rehearsals took place during the middle of 1977, and the play opened in October, running for six weeks before it was shut down by the district commissioner due to "public security" concerns. The play is critical of government policies and celebrates the power of the peasant proletariat, but most importantly it was performed in Gĩkũyũ, effectively reaching a mass audience rather than only those who could read. This was apparently where the line was crossed. Ngũgĩ was arrested in the early morning hours of 31 December, six days before his fortieth birthday. His detention was announced on New Year's Day of 1978, and he would spend almost the whole year in Kamĩtĩ maximum security prison.

Ngũgĩ's detention drew international attention, and there were protests within Kenya and around the world. He has described the experience in *Detained: A Writer's Prison Diary,* a masterful work in which he is careful to present his story not as the clash of individual wills but as a manifestation of a broader class struggle in postcolonial Kenya. By this account, the performance of *Ngaahika ndeenda* represented the strongest example yet of "the peasant/worker consciousness, struggle, and anti-imperialist challenge" (p. 123). Ngũgĩ was detained along with a number of other political prisoners, and what probably made their eventual release possible was the death of President Kenyatta in August 1978. Moi assumed power, and four months later Ngũgĩ and other political prisoners at Kamĩtĩ were released.

At this point the Kenyan government still viewed Ngũgĩ with suspicion, but he continued his activist ways. He worked with a group of Gĩkũyũ linguists and writers to revise the orthography of the Gĩkũyũ language originally devised by missionaries; he published *Caitaani mũtharaba-inĩ, Ngaahika ndeenda,* and *Detained;* he tried working with Ngũgĩ wa Mĩrĩĩ and the Kamĩrĩĩthu cooperative to produce another play, *Maitũ njugĩra (Mother, Sing for Me),* which was suppressed by the government. In the preface to *Detained,* Ngũgĩ claims that government and university forces were conspiring to deny him employment and thereby drive him to look for work outside Kenya. Going abroad, he defiantly declared, was "an eventuality I have rejected" (p. xii), but the following year he would change his mind. In London for the launch of *Devil on the Cross,* Ngũgĩ heard that he was to be arrested on his return to Kenya and so decided to remain, thus beginning a long period of living, writing, and teaching outside of his homeland. He would deliver papers at various international conferences and university settings, study filmmaking in Sweden, and become involved in organizations with other Kenyan exiles and dissidents. Meanwhile, back in Kenya, he was being accused of leading underground opposition groups whose goal was the overthrow of the government; the Gĩkũyũ version of *Matigari* was suppressed; and the government orchestrated "spontaneous" protests that included burning his effigy.

Now persona non grata in his home country, Ngũgĩ eventually settled in the United States, where he taught at Yale University and, since 1992, in the Department of Comparative Literature at New York University. He continues to be an active proponent of African languages, although his focus has shifted from advocating that writers use their mother tongues to pressuring African studies departments in the United States and Europe to give African languages a more central place in their programs of study. In 1996, along with a number of other Gĩkũyũ academics, Ngũgĩ founded the Gĩkũyũ-language journal *Mũtiiri* (the "Guardian"). In 1998 he published a seventh volume of critical commentary, *Penpoints, Gunpoints, and Dreams: Towards a Critical Theory of the Arts and the State in Africa.* In 2001 he won the international portion of the Nonino Prize, an Italian award for foreign works translated into Italian that was granted on the basis of his sixth essay collection, *Moving the Center*. All the while, Ngũgĩ watchers were anticipating a seventh novel that he had reportedly been working on. As of early 2002, however, the novel had not yet been published.

NGŨGĨ THE WRITER

Given that his writing career stretches from the late 1950s into the twenty-first century, it is to be expected that Ngũgĩ's style and concerns would develop over time, as they do. Nevertheless, through all of his works we find a remarkably consistent set of underlying concerns and ideas. The theme of betrayal features prominently in all of Ngũgĩ's work, as does what Carol Sicherman calls his leitmotif, an exploration of resistance to the injustices that result from betrayals (*Making of a Rebel,* p. xvii). This resistance comes in various forms, including direct, armed resistance to colonialism (which appears, for instance, in his play celebrating the life of the freedom fighter Dedan Kĩmathi). But what seems to interest him even more is resistance on the cultural level.

Like their counterparts in other postcolonial settings, African writers confront a history that has been written about them by outsiders, a set of defining (often derogative) tropes and stories to which they often feel compelled to respond. They need to "remember" a history that his effectively been dismembered as a result of the violent encounter of colonialism. Thus revisiting Kenyan and Gĩkũyũ history plays a central role in Ngũgĩ's works. His first novels are set in the recent colonial past; the middle novels, while set at the time of independence and after, feature extensive flashbacks as an integral part of their structure. Traditional Gĩkũyũ stories, songs, myths, and customs, along with the stories and songs of the resistance movement before and after independence, are also key elements in this urge to recover an obscured or misrepresented past.

Christian imagery and allusions feature prominently in all of Ngũgĩ's work. If this seems surprising from someone who does not call himself a Christian, it must be remembered that, as Ngũgĩ regularly points out, Kenyans and especially the Gĩkũyũ are widely Christianized, and the Bible is probably the one text with which a largely illiterate population is familiar. The Bible thus offers a rich and handy store of characters, events, and symbols for a writer to exploit. Ngũgĩ's cast of characters contains a wealth of Moses, Messiah, and Judas figures alongside allusions and quotations from Psalms, the Old Testament prophets, and Gospel parables.

Many critics argue that there is a marked difference between Ngũgĩ's early works, specifically the novels and stories that he wrote in the 1960s, and those that came later. The early fiction, by this account, fits comfortably within the Western humanist tradition, emphasizing the techniques of realism and the development of an individual consciousness. Numerous critical essays point to the strong Conradian streak in these works, which focus on the psychology of an individual character whose deepest convictions are put to the test. The later works, coming after Ngũgĩ's more radicalized education at Leeds, are more experimental, more willing to break out of the realist mode, more communal in their narrative orientation, more interested in external than internal psychological dilemmas, and much more direct in their social commentary. Those who prefer the early works argue that Ngũgĩ's recent writing is too polemical, sacrificing art for didacticism. Proponents of the later works find them more relevant, more in tune with a distinctively African aesthetic, and suggest that the early Ngũgĩ was entrapped by a Romantic aesthetic that resulted in a certain ideological ambivalence. While these differences may exist, it is also accurate to say that there is in fact no fundamental break between the early and later Ngũgĩs, in the sense that the overarching concerns and approaches in his work have remained constant. Certainly there have been changes in style and presentation, thanks to Ngũgĩ's personal development as well as the historical circumstances in which he wrote. But what can be asserted is that in all of his writing—fiction and nonfiction alike—there is a profound sense that literature must attend to and comment on social conditions.

NGŨGĨ WA THIONG'O

EARLY FICTION

As stated earlier, Ngũgĩ drafted two novels while he was a student at Makerere—*The River Between* in 1961 and *Weep Not, Child* in 1962—but it was the second of these that was published first. The Kenyan critic Abdul JanMohamed believes they should considered in the order of their publication, since *The River Between* contains a "greater stylistic maturity" and a "more satisfactory reworking of the paradoxes" in the plot (p. 298). Peter Nazareth disagrees, arguing that both novels are about the awakening of a sleeping land and a sleeping people, and that *Weep Not, Child* is in fact more mature or developed because at the end of that novel there is a greater, albeit still incomplete, sense of awakening, and that therefore they ought to be placed in the order that they were written (p. 2). Both novels are set in Gĩkũyũ territory during the colonial era, both feature child protagonists, and both are what JanMohamed calls "truncated *bildungsroman*" (p. 194) because of their ambiguously open endings. If we arrange them chronologically in terms of their subject matter, then *The River Between* ought to come first, as it is set in colonial Kenya of the 1930s, while *Weep Not, Child* takes place in the 1940s and 1950s.

As its title suggests, *The River Between* poses an opposition between two historical forces and explores the dynamics of this clash. It highlights two key aspects of Gĩkũyũ history in the 1930s—the role of female circumcision as a rallying point for resistance to colonial rule, and the significance of the Gĩkũyũ independent schools—each of which grows out of the tension between traditional religious practice and mission-sponsored Christianity. Two ridges, Kameno and Makuyu, are separated and yet linked by the "valley of life" and the river Honia that flows between them, whose name "meant cure, or bring-back-to-life" (p. 1). The boy Waiyaki (from Kameno) and the girl Nyambura (from Makuyu) meet in school, where they fall in love, but are kept apart by the antagonism between their families. Nyambura's father, Joshua, is a missionary convert who "always preached in sharp ringing tones that spoke of power and knowledge" (p. 29). His born-again followers on Makuyu ridge oppose Waiyaki's family and others from Kameno, who "remained conservative, loyal to the ways of the land" (p. 28).

Matters become complicated when Joshua's second daughter, Muthoni, insists on being circumcised against her father's wishes. She represents the desire for a compromise between Christians and the traditionalists; Muthoni wants to be "a Christian in the tribe" (p. 53), a symbol of the "river between" that could unite the ridges. Waiyaki also emerges as a potential mediator between these divided forces. He looks to education, through the establishment of independent schools, as a way to unite Kenyans and lead them to prosperity and autonomy. Above all, he wishes to unite the two ridges in order to reclaim their land. For a time Waiyaki's success as a teacher grows, and he even comes to believe what some people are saying, that he might be the fulfillment of a prophecy that a hero would emerge to unite the Gĩkũyũ and drive the white man from the land. In the end, however, these attempts at reconciliation are foiled by extremists on both sides. When it is revealed that Waiyaki, the hero of the traditionalists, intends to marry Nyambura, the uncircumcised daughter of a Christian leader, he is rejected by his people, and *The River Between* closes on an image of darkness, with the two ridges still divided.

Weep Not, Child is the most autobiographical of Ngũgĩ's novels. The young protagonist, Njoroge, is a talented and eager student. He is the first from his family to attend school and hopes to help them to prosperity through his education. As the text makes clear, however, much of his important education occurs in the *thing'ira,* his father's hut, where the stories of Gĩkũyũ history are passed down by his father to the children of Njoroge's generation. These stories include the Gĩkũyũ creation myth but also the more recent story of how Gĩkũyũ land was stolen by the British.

Weep Not, Child shows the misery and disruption brought about by colonialism, and it also shows the range of responses to colonialism and how the Gĩkũyũ were divided in their response. Njoroge is too young to play an active part in the resistance movement, and in any case he seems destined to take what he can from a European education. His brother, however, chooses the way of armed revolution. His father wavers, refusing to take the Mau Mau oath but joining an ill-fated strike against the settler farmers. The novel closes on a symbolically ambiguous note. Following the death of his father and the capture of his brother, Njoroge is dissuaded from hanging himself by the timely appearance of his mother, who finds him standing in the darkness, looping a noose around a tree. "He saw the light she was carrying and falteringly went towards it" (p. 135), but he is plagued by the knowledge of his own weakness and cowardice. In the end, both *The River Between* and *Weep Not, Child* focus on the dilemma of the young intellectual in the face of colonialism, and the comparison between the two protagonists and Ngũgĩ is obvious. Although he was himself too young to participate in Mau Mau or other active struggles against colonialism, it seems inevitable that Ngũgĩ would have felt "some sense of guilt or failure as a noncombatant" (Cook and Okenimkpe, p. 3).

A Grain of Wheat, his third novel, is Ngũgĩ's masterpiece, a portrayal of a vexed nation on the cusp of independence. He wrote the novel while he was a student at Leeds (it was published in 1967, shortly after his return to England and the same year that he began work as a university lecturer), and it contains a sophistication and depth that are no doubt the result of Ngũgĩ's own maturation as a scholar and thinker. *A Grain of Wheat* both continues and transcends the literary project that Ngũgĩ initiated in his first two novels. Chronologically it picks up where *Weep Not, Child* left off, as it is set in 1963 at the moment of Kenyan independence, but it goes beyond the first two novels, because the protagonist is now an adult. It is also far more complex in its structure. As Ngũgĩ explains it, he found the linear plots that he deployed in his first novels insufficient to explain the complexity of Kenya's society at independence.

The actual story takes place over four days, but most of the narrative consists of a series of flashbacks. The protagonist is Mugo, a name recalling the Gĩkũyũ prophet Mugo wa Kibiro, whose prophecies were an integral part of Ngũgĩ's earlier novels. This Mugo, however, is something of an antihero, for although the village reveres him for his supposed involvement in the anticolonial struggle, it soon becomes clear that his role in that movement and the circumstances surrounding his imprisonment and torture are rather more complicated than the villagers realize. In fact, we discover that Mugo betrayed the true hero and freedom fighter, Kihika. Ngũgĩ's brilliant move in this novel was to focus not on a hero of independence, but on a traitor with a conscience, thereby laying out in an unusually complex way the many implications of the independence struggle. We also see, as in all of Ngũgĩ's works, an integration of Christian and traditional imagery. The novel is replete with allusions to Christ figures such as Kihika, who always carries a Bible with him and ends up figuratively crucified, as well as to obvious Judas figures like Mugo. Wrongly assuming that Mugo made heroic sacrifices, the villagers ask him to speak at their Independence Day celebrations. At first he tries to avoid the job then agrees to do it, but when the moment comes, instead of continuing to pose as a hero he confesses his crime against the people and is taken away to be tried.

The various subplots woven through *A Grain of Wheat* further complicate the quest for reconciliation and healing in post-independence Kenya. Gikonyo and Mumbi, whose names evoke the Adam and Eve figures of Gĩkũyũ mythology, are estranged lovers who are moving tentatively toward reconciliation at the end of the novel. There are former Mau Mau freedom fighers who are eager to avenge the death of their comrades. There are Europeans like the research scientist Thompson, who came to Kenya bursting with idealism but ends up torturing Mau Mau detainees. There is the timid Karanja, whom everybody suspects of betraying Kihika, but who gets an unexpected reprieve when Mugo confesses. And there are nefarious Kenyan politicians like the villagers' new member of Parliament who takes over a settler's ranch himself, instead of redistributing the land. While the novel ends on a note of hope, it is a hope tempered with a large dose of uncertainty.

NGŨGĨ WA THIONG'O

In 1986, nine years after its original publication, Ngũgĩ revised parts of *A Grain of Wheat.* Several details were changed to make them more historically accurate—the number of Kenyans killed while protesting the arrest of Harry Thuku is changed from 15 to 150, for instance—and the references to "the party" are changed to "the movement," probably because of Ngũgĩ's disenchantment with the political party KANU in the decade after *A Grain of Wheat* was published. More dramatic is the change to a scene where Mau Mau fighters attack Dr. Lynd, a white woman at the research station. In the original version she is raped, but in the revision they brutally kill her dog. In justifying these sorts of changes, Ngũgĩ argues that one uncovers new insights and revises judgments as one goes.

Ngũgĩ has also revised a number of his short stories through their various manifestations over the years. Although he has published relatively few stories, and most of them date from before 1975, they continue to appear regularly in anthologies and collections of African short stories. As Ngũgĩ tells it, he wrote his first significant short story in 1960 at Makerere when, on a whim, he asked Jonathan Kariara, an older student and the editor of *Penpoint,* to consider a piece he had written for publication in the magazine. When Kariara agreed, Ngũgĩ had to quickly write the tale, which at that point existed only in his mind. It became "The Fig Tree," later retitled "Mugumo" (the Gĩkũyũ name for an indigenous species of ficus that is sacred to the community).

Most of Ngũgĩ's short stories are gathered in *Secret Lives,* a collection that he published in 1975. In the preface Ngũgĩ says these works "form my creative autobiography over the last twelve years and touch on ideas and moods affecting me over the same period" (p. xii). They cover much of the same ground and many of the same ideas that are to be found in his first novels. Especially in the first stories, there are the familiar themes of alienation, betrayal, and frustration in the face of powerful external forces. In the later stories, the focus is on the corruption of a ruthless post-independence society. "Minutes of Glory," for instance, is a story of a prostitute who steals her client's money. Knowing that she will inevitably be punished she returns to the bar she had frequented in order to play the part of a rich and glamorous woman, if only for a day. A friend told Ngũgĩ the tale, who found this idea of a secret life intriguing, giving rise to the title of the whole collection. Some of the stories in *Secret Lives* were new with the collection, and others Ngũgĩ revised for republication, tightening and updating some of the wording: the words "tribe and tribal" are removed in favor of less pejorative terms, and in "The Village Priest" the "witchdoctor" is renamed a "rain-maker."

LATER FICTION

Ngũgĩ's first novel after his return from Leeds, *Petals of Blood,* has the reputation for being his most challenging work, and it is certainly his longest and most structurally complex. He wrote it over a longer period than his other novels, beginning in 1970 while on a one-year teaching post at Northwestern University, continuing the work on it after his return to Nairobi, and adding the final touches in 1975 during a month-long stay in Yalta as a guest of the Soviet Writers Union. This would also be the last novel Ngũgĩ would compose in English.

Petals of Blood is the first of Ngũgĩ's novels in which all the action takes place in independent Kenya. In the opening, it appears to be a simple detective novel, a form that had become immensely popular in Kenya during the early 1970s. Four suspects are being rounded up for questioning in a murder case. Soon, however, it becomes clear that *Petals of Blood* goes well beyond a murder mystery; it is a strong exposé of the corruption and greed made possible by rampant capitalism in post-independence Kenya. The dead men, burned in a brothel fire that was obviously arson, are leading businessmen and politicians. Ngũgĩ emphasizes the city-country conflict to show how a parasitical urban elite in Nairobi profits from the impoverished but dignified peasants who live in Ilmorog. In the end, the teacher Munira confesses to the murder, but it is clear from the investigation that all of the suspects, as well as others in the village, would have ample reason to seek revenge on the dead men.

The ending calls for solidarity among Kenya's oppressed classes, and Ngũgĩ attempts to reinforce a communal, anticapitalist ethic in the very narrative structure of *Petals of Blood*. There is no single protagonist; rather, the four suspects in the case are each major figures whose stories and testimony merge to fill out the narrative. Ngũgĩ also deploys a narrator who speaks in the collective voice—"we" and "us"—which serves to remind the reader of the communal nature of traditional Gĩkũyũ society. These all function to create what David Cook and Michael Okenimkpe describe as a "bold and powerful attempt to combine the intimacy of the traditional novel with a public rhetorical manner in a new and perhaps itself artistically revolutionary amalgam in order to analyse social injustice and the human dilemmas it creates, and to mark out the practicable path to social change" (p. 118).

The overt didacticism of *Petals of Blood* is continued in Ngũgĩ's two later novels, wherein Ngũgĩ continues his shift away from the classical realist form; *Devil on the Cross* and *Matigari* are both written in a more allegorical mode than any of his previous works. These are also the first novels he composed in Gĩkũyũ, which explains why they have the heightened sense of an implied African audience and may also explain why, after a series of novels whose structures are increasingly complex, there is a noticeable return to less complicated narrative schemes.

Ngũgĩ begins his prison diary, *Detained,* with an invocation of "*Warĩĩnga ngatha ya wĩra . . .* Warĩĩnga heroine of toil" (p. 3). Warĩĩnga is the lead character in *Caitaani mũtharaba-inĩ (Devil on the Cross)*, the novel that he is writing in Kamitĩ prison, using the prison toilet paper for stationery. She becomes something of a muse for him, a fictional creation who inspires her creator through her will to resist. In the story, Warĩĩnga has managed to overcome the early interruption of her education (after she had become pregnant by a rich "sugar daddy"), but returns to Ilmorog when a new set of troubles begin. There, she finds herself attending a "feast of thieves and robbers," who turn out to be local capitalists and businessmen celebrating their abilities to exploit their fellow Kenyans. This is the start of a heightened consciousness for Warĩĩnga, who begins to recognize the links between her personal, sexual, and economic exploitation. Realizing that she can no longer be a passive observer, she takes decisive action, shooting the Rich Old Man from Ngorika (her erstwhile "sugar daddy" and the father of her fiancé) and walks out, aware "with all her heart that the hardest struggles of her life's journey lay ahead" (p. 254).

Considering the circumstances of its composition, and given its powerful indictment of Kenyan society, *Devil on the Cross* is a remarkably humorous work. Cook and Okenimkpe call it "savagely comic" (p. 126), and it is certainly Ngũgĩ's most bitingly satirical work. He turns a set of Kenyan tycoons into a remarkably believable convocation of thieves and robbers who use a skewed version of the biblical parable of the talents in their contest to see who has been the most creative and successful in exploiting the masses.

Writing in Gĩkũyũ seems to have freed Ngũgĩ to make greater use of the rhetorical gestures of oral narrative, and the novel directly raises the question of appropriate forms for cultural expression. One of the characters, Gatuiria, is a university professor who is seeking the best form for a genuinely indigenous musical composition, in the same way that Ngũgĩ is seeking to create an authentic but new entity in writing this, the first Gĩkũyũ novel. The result is a narrative infected with the shape and rhythm of oral storytelling, which is introduced by a *gicaandi* player, a self-proclaimed "Prophet of Justice." The book draws on many stock moves from the oral tradition: stylized characters, repetition, and the frequent use of song.

Devil on the Cross suggests that Kenya's ills result from a conspiracy of the privileged, and that their cure can be found through heroic individual acts (in the end, Warĩĩnga takes a dramatic but solitary action). This is the main difference between this and Ngũgĩ's sixth novel, *Matigari,* which, like its predecessor, attacks global capitalism and its local practitioners as the source of Kenya's ills, but also makes clear that the problems are connected to large-scale economic relations and that any resistance or change can only be effective if it results from a communal effort. Even the protagonist himself represents a collective: the name Matigari ma Njirũũngi means "the patriots who survived the bullets," a reference to Mau Mau fighters "and their political offspring." At the beginning of the story, Matigari emerges from the forest having girded himself with a "belt of peace," but he is dismayed at the neocolonial reality he encounters and realizes that he must return to the forest to renew the armed struggle against oppression. His own quest for truth and justice lays bare the machinations of the government's "Ministry of Truth and Justice." Although Matigari himself disappears at the end of the story, swept away in a river while pursued by the police, the child Mũriũki takes up his struggle by returning to the forest and digging up Matigari's weapons. The message is that a new generation must deal with Kenya's new injustices, by using the same tactics of communal resistance that the Mau Mau deployed in the struggle against colonialism.

As a final note on Ngũgĩ's fiction writing, it must be mentioned that in the 1980s he also wrote three children's stories, all of them in Gĩkũyũ and two of which have been translated into English. The "Njamba Nene" stories follow the exploits of a young boy (whose name means "big hero" although he is an impoverished and skinny child) who in his various adventures helps his friends and other revolutionaries oppose the oppressive forces of a government army. Yulisa Maddy and Donnarae MacCann classify these as "liberationist children's tales" (in Nazareth, p. 283).

DRAMA AND FILM

It is generally agreed that his plays are not Ngũgĩ's strongest suit, and it appears that in the later part of his career he has abandoned the genre entirely. He has published four plays on his own and two in conjunction with others, the most recent of them being the Kamĩrĩĩthu collaboration from the 1970s. Despite their artistic shortcomings, several of the plays appeared at

critical moments and are memorable for the role they have played in Kenyan literary history.

The three plays collected in *This Time Tomorrow* are Ngũgĩ's least remarkable. The characters are rigid and underdeveloped, and while we encounter themes similar to those in his early novels, in the plays these ideas are treated in a far less satisfactory and more superficial manner, often leaving an impression of fatalistic melodrama. Ngũgĩ wrote *The Rebels*, the first play in the collection, for a drama competition at Makerere in 1961. It depicts a young man who leaves his village to pursue an education. When he returns home with a fiancée (a woman from a distant Ugandan tribe) he discovers that his family has already picked a bride for him. The second selection, *The Wound in My Heart*, was also produced for a Makerere drama competition, in the following year. It presents the anguish of a returned Mau Mau detainee who discovers that his wife has had a child by a white man. The title piece is the most satisfactory work in the collection, and was commissioned for the BBC Africa Service in 1967. It portrays the effects of a brutal demolition of an urban slum by municipal authorities who consider it an eyesore. Among the slum's residents are former freedom fighters whose loyal sacrifice for their country in the colonial era is now being betrayed in the interest of making the city attractive to foreign tourists and investors.

Another play from Ngũgĩ's Makerere years has had far greater impact. *The Black Hermit* was written on the occasion of Ugandan Independence in 1962 and was first performed by a drama group from Makerere at the Uganda National Theatre that same year. This was the first full-length production in a national theater from an East African writer. As Cook and Okenimkpe note, it also "gained importance because of the shortage for many years of alternative East African material to satisfy the demand for serious indigenous drama in schools, colleges, and society at large" (p. 153). In a preface appended to a later edition of the play in 1968, Ngũgĩ recalls that at the time he composed *The Black Hermit* he believed that tribalism was a central problem for East African society (he would later change his mind and come to see neocolonialism as a much greater evil). The play certainly criticizes the villagers' interests in promoting their narrow political interests over other tribes, but it also highlights the shortcomings of its idealistic and educated young protagonist, who espouses pan-African ideals. The title character is Remi, a young man who falls in love with Thoni, a woman who is unfortunately required to marry his brother. When Remi's brother dies, he must "inherit" his brother's wife according to tradition. He does so, but even though Remi had once loved Thoni, he believes she can no longer love him, and he escapes to the city, where he eventually begins an affair with a white woman. When the elders appeal to Remi to return, he agrees, but his purpose is not reconciliation but rather a chance to upbraid the villagers for their short-sighted tribalism. Thoni commits suicide, and in the end Remi realizes the errors he has made as a result of his blind idealism.

Ngũgĩ recounts that his collaboration with Mĩcere Mũgo on *The Trial of Dedan Kĩmathi,* another historically significant play, grew out of their hallway conversations in the University of Nairobi's literature department. Writing the play became "an act of literary and political intervention" (*Decolonising the Mind,* p. xi). In the preface, Ngũgĩ explains that the Kĩmathi play was envisaged as the first in a series celebrating "the neglected heroes and heroines of the Kenyan masses" (p. vi) that would also include figures like Koitalel, Me Kitilili, Mary Nyanjiru, Waiyaki, and others. Elsewhere, Ngũgĩ explains how he and Mũgo were spurred to write because of another play about the Mau Mau leader by Kenneth Watene, titled simply *Dedan Kimathi.* Watene's version, while sympathetic to Kĩmathi, did not portray him in the suitably heroic role that Ngũgĩ and Mũgo wished, and so they wrote their own version of his story.

Kĩmathi was one of the main leaders of Mau Mau who was captured by the British and died in detention. In Ngũgĩ and Mũgo's version of the story, the focus is not precisely on the actual historical trial of Dedan Kĩmathi (although that frames the story). Rather, it imagines a series of four tests or trials that Kĩmathi undergoes (not unlike Christ's) during his detention. The first is when the judge offers Kĩmathi his life in exchange for a confession. The second is when a trio of businessmen—a European, an Asian, and an African—offer him money if he will give up his struggle. For his third trial, a politician, a priest, and a former radical argue that Kĩmathi's struggle is no longer needed, as Kenyans have prospered. Torture by his captors is Kĩmathi's final trial. Along with Francis Imbuga's *Betrayal in the City, The Trial of Dedan Kĩmathi* was selected to represent Kenya in the 1977 Black and African Festival of Arts and Culture (FESTAC) in Lagos.

Ngaahika ndeenda (I Will Marry When I Want), the last play that Ngũgĩ has published, will always remain a milestone in his career. His involvement in this play returned Ngũgĩ to his home of Kamĩrĩĩthu, where it was conceived and developed along with the members of the village cooperative and in collaboration with Ngũgĩ wa Mĩriĩ (from the University of Nairobi's Institute of Development Studies). At this time Kamĩrĩĩthu was a depressed area, with many of its inhabitants either unemployed or working on nearby tea and coffee plantations or in the Bata shoe factory which was the main employer in the area. The collaborators created a lively story about local profiteers, the directors of a company who connive to take over the small plot of a peasant couple in order to build a pesticide factory. Traditional wisdom and socialist exhortations contrast with Christian platitudes just as the dignity of the working people is contrasted with the barren stinginess of the wealthy. In the end, the peasants lose their land but are eager to join with others in the struggle for justice. The play intersperses the action and dialogue with songs, dances, mime, proverbs, and earthy humor. It functions as what Oliver Lovesey has called "an African morality play, targeting the alliance of capitalism and Christianity as the enemy of cultural integrity and national cooperation" (p. 94).

In *Detained,* Ngũgĩ explains how profoundly the work on *Ngaahika ndeenda* influenced his thinking. The experience represented the highest achievement of his goal of making literature a practical tool of education and emancipation. After his release from detention, he returned to Kamĩrĩĩthu, creating a second collaboration with Ngũgĩ wa Mĩriĩ, the musical *Maitũ njugĩra* (Mother, Sing for Me). This was to be another work in the same tradition as *Ngaahika ndeenda*, although it also attempted to move beyond strictly Gĩkũyũ experience, including songs in eight Kenyan languages. It too was suppressed by authorities, and has never been published (for more on this episode, see Björkman).

Like a number of other African writers, Ngũgĩ has been intrigued by the expressive possibilities of film and video, although he has not produced any major works in this area. His most significant accomplishment to date is a documentary about the life of the Senegalese writer Sembene Ousmane (who also experimented with film). *SembeneOusmane: The Making of African Cinema* (1994) was directed by Ngũgĩ along with Manthia Diawara, a filmmaker and colleague of Ngũgĩ's at New York University.

ESSAYS AND CULTURAL COMMENTARY

Above all else, Ngũgĩ wa Thiong'o is an intellectual and a man of ideas who has always been willing to comment directly on his own and others' works, so that his seven volumes of essays on cultural commentary form a corpus that equals his fiction in substance and significance. The first of these is *Homecoming: Essays on African and Caribbean Literature, Culture, and Politics,* which is part of the first wave of book-length critical studies of literature from the East African region (along with volumes from Taban lo Liyong, Peter Nazareth, and Chris Wanjala). Published in 1972, most of the essays were written in the 1960s and reflect many of the same concerns that appeared in his early novels. The title reflects Ngũgĩ's convictions about putting African culture at the center of academic studies, and uncovering the African links with Caribbean literature forms a kind of homecoming as well. The first section, "On Culture," features essays on nationalism, Mau Mau, racism, and the role of the church in Kenyan culture. The second, "Writers in Africa," examines literary works from

East Africa and Nigeria, while the third section, "Writers from the Caribbean," largely consists of his unfinished postgraduate dissertation from Leeds on George Lamming.

Writers in Politics appeared in 1981, shortly after Ngũgĩ's release from prison, and contains essays written during the 1970s. It reflects Ngũgĩ's quest during this decade to make literature—at the university and in society—relevant to the lives of ordinary people and a force for their liberation. "If the essays are dominated by issues of language and theatre," Ngũgĩ writes in the preface, "it is only because the great ideological battle between a pro-imperialist culture and Kenyan national, patriotic culture has been fought out particularly in the theatre" (p. xi). Part 1, on literature and education, discusses the role of literature in the schools, the racist policies of the Kenya National Theatre, and includes an essay calling for the use of African languages in Kenyan literature. In part 2, "Writers in Politics," Ngũgĩ discusses his own work by connecting it to the Mau Mau struggle and the nationalist efforts of leaders like J. M. Kariũki (who was assassinated in 1975). A third section, "Against Political Repression," connects East African cultural politics with those in South Korea. "I have titled the book, *Writers in Politics,*" Ngũgĩ wrote, "because literature cannot escape from the class power structures that shape our everyday life. . . . Every writer is a writer in politics. The only question is what and whose politics?" (p. xii).

Detained: A Writer's Prison Diary also appeared in 1981, and it contains an often fascinating and sometimes horrific account of Ngũgĩ's detention. He uses the writing of *Caitaani mũtharaba-inĩ* as a sort of running plot to structure the account of his year in prison. Three months before his release there is a chilling moment when the manuscript is confiscated (all but two chapters that were hidden in his Bible), but, writes Ngũgĩ, it is later returned by the chief warder. " 'I see nothing wrong with it,' he said. 'You write in very difficult Kikuyu!' " (p. 165). He also supplies Ngũgĩ with writing paper in place of the toilet paper he had been using. Also of interest in this prison memoir is how Ngũgĩ comes to terms with the fact that he has been jailed by the regime of Jomo Kenyatta, the same Kenyatta who was once his hero. To be betrayed in this way by Kenyatta, a fellow Gĩkũyũ and a father figure in the nationalist struggle, must have been particularly difficult. Toward the end of *Detained,* Ngũgĩ denounces Kenyatta as a leader who is "petty bourgeois to the core, who never consciously rejected that class base" (p. 161). For Ngũgĩ, Kenyatta was a failed Moses figure, who initially led his people toward freedom but who undermined that freedom in the end. Ironically, it was Kenyatta's death that made possible Ngũgĩ's own freedom from prison.

Barrel of a Pen: Resistance to Repression in Neo-Colonial Kenya, published shortly after Ngũgĩ's exile, does not contain a great deal of new material (there are three essays from the early 1980s). Rather, its goal is to expose the repressive nature of the Kenyan government, especially to its Western allies that generally held Kenya as an example of a reasonably (if not fully) fair and responsible regime. The evidence suggests that the government's crackdown on dissenters was reaching unprecedented levels in 1982. The Moi regime had already banned the Kamĩrĩĩthu Community Educational and Cultural Centre, shutting down the rehearsals of *Maitũ njugĩra* and bulldozing the open-air theater in the first part of the year. In June, Ngũgĩ felt compelled to stay abroad, and the government used a foiled coup attempt in August as an excuse for further crackdowns, including the arrest of more university lecturers. *Barrel of a Pen* includes excerpts from several of Ngũgĩ's plays as well as the text of a presentation he gave in October 1982 to political pressure group in London.

Decolonizing the Mind: The Politics of Language in African Culture appeared in 1986 and is probably Ngũgĩ's most successful collection in the sense that its contents have been extensively quoted and reprinted. It contains his major theoretical statements on the issue of African languages in theater and fiction as well as his account of the curriculum debate at the University of Nairobi in the 1970s. The overall tone of the essays is reasoned and scholarly; this, mixed with memorable stories of Ngũgĩ's experiences, gives the volume its richness and power. In a prefatory statement to the collection, Ngũgĩ famously announces his intention of following his own advice and writing only in African languages henceforth.

Perhaps as a result of his exposure to contemporary literary theory at Yale University (during his time there in the late 1980s) and at New York University (starting in the 1990s), Ngũgĩ's later essay collections—*Moving the Centre: The Struggle for Cultural Freedoms* (1993) and *Penpoints, Gunpoints, and Dreams: Towards a Critical Theory of the Arts and the State in Africa* (1998)—contain an awareness of the vocabulary and concepts of postcolonial theory that is not as present in his earlier works. While they never indulge in highly abstract theory, and while they retain a commitment to the basic ideas that have always engaged Ngũgĩ (to the point of repeating some of the same material that appeared in earlier collections), these are the most scholarly of his presentations in their tone and approach.

Moving the Centre is a collection of twenty-one essays from the late 1980s and early 1990s that cover topics like the language question, the role of the intellectual in a postcolonial society, and the necessity for social change. Some of the essays are topical, such as the one on Karen Blixen (a version of a talk in which he surprised some of his Danish audience by arguing that the author of *Out of Africa* was profoundly racist) or the one on Mandela's release from prison. The overall message of the collection is that the existing world's power centers should be shifted—both within nations and between nations—and better yet that there ought to be a multiplicity of centers rather than a monolithic Euro-American domination of world culture.

Penpoints, Gunpoints, and Dreams is a collection of four talks that Ngũgĩ presented as the Clarendon Lectures at Oxford University in 1996. All four deal with tensions between the artist and the state, a complex mixture that Ngũgĩ says are best "suggested through images and hence the overall title" (p. xi). The first term of the title also has the effect of reminding us of Ngũgĩ's (and other emerging East African writers') earliest efforts in the Makerere journal, *Penpoint*.

NGŨGĨ WA THIONG'O

NGŨGĨ AND THE FUTURE

Forty years after Ngũgĩ emerged from Makerere University as a promising name in the developing field of East African literature, he has firmly established himself as the major figure in that field. Indeed, there is now an entire sub-field of Ngũgĩ studies, and the wealth of journal essays and graduate dissertations that have analyzed his work are being joined by a significant number of noteworthy book-length studies. Several such volumes had already appeared in the early 1980s: G. D. Killam provides a balanced and thorough introduction to the early Ngũgĩ, and the study by David Cook and Michael Odenimkpe is enriched by their personal knowledge of Ngũgĩ and his milieu (Cook was a professor at Makerere during Ngũgĩ's time there). More recently, Carol Sicherman has provided two extremely useful references for Ngũgĩ scholars. There are several new monographs on Ngũgĩ or aspects of his works (Patrick Williams' study is especially good as a general introduction, while James Ogude's highlights Ngũgĩ's engagement with history), and there are various new collections of critical essays including one edited by Peter Nazareth, a former Makerere classmate of Ngũgĩ's. As the venerable Ghanaian poet Kofi Anyidoho noted while introducing him as the keynote speaker at the 1997 convention of the African Literature Association, by now Ngũgĩ wa Thiong'o is somebody who needs no introduction.

Will Ngũgĩ ever be able to return to Kenya? The aging President Moi, whose regime has been so hostile to Ngũgĩ, is supposed to leave office in 2002, according to the current version of the Kenyan constitution. Since Ngũgĩ celebrates his sixty-fifth birthday at the beginning of 2003, it is not unthinkable that he might at some point return. If so, it will be a long-awaited and emotional homecoming.

SELECTED BIBLIOGRAPHY

I. NOVELS AND SHORT STORIES. *Weep Not, Child* (London, 1964); *The River Between* (London, 1965); *A Grain of Wheat* (London, 1967); *Secret Lives and Other Stories* (New York, 1975; London, 1976); *Petals of Blood* (London, 1977; New York, 1978); *Caitaani mũtharaba-inĩ* (Nairobi, 1980), trans. by Ngũgĩ wa Thiong'o as *Devil on the Cross* (London, 1982); *Matigari ma Njirũũngi* (Nairobi, 1986), trans. by Wangũi wa Goro as *Matigari* (Oxford, 1989; Trenton, N.J., 1998).

II. PLAYS. *The Black Hermit* (Kampala, 1963; Nairobi and London, 1968); *This Time Tomorrow* (Nairobi, 1970); *The Trial of Dedan Kĩmathi*, coauthored with Mĩcere Mũgo (London, 1976); *Ngaahika ndeenda*, coauthored with Ngũgi wa Mĩriĩ (Nairobi, 1980), trans. by the authors as *I Will Marry When I Want* (London, 1982).

III. CHILDREN'S STORIES. *Njamba Nene na mbaathi ĩ mathagu* (1982), trans. by Wangũi wa Goro as *Njamba Nene and the Flying Bus* (Nairobi, 1986; Trenton, N.J., 1995); *Bathitoora ya Njamba Nene* (1984), trans. by Wangũi wa Goro as *Njamba Nene's Pistol* (Nairobi, 1986); *Njamba Nene na cibũ kĩng'ang'i* (Nairobi, 1986; Trenton, N.J., 1995).

IV. ESSAYS. *Homecoming: Essays on African and Caribbean Literature, Culture, and Politics* (London, 1972); *Detained: A Writer's Prison Diary* (London, 1981); *Writers in Politics* (London and Exeter, N.H., 1981; rev. and enl. ed., Oxford and Portsmouth, N.H., 1997); *Barrel of a Pen: Resistance to Oppression in Neo-Colonial Kenya* (London and Trenton, N.J., 1983); *Decolonising the Mind: The Politics of Language in African Literature* (Nairobi and London, 1986); *Moving the Centre: The Struggle for Cultural Freedoms* (Nairobi, London, and Portsmouth, N.H., 1993); *Penpoints, Gunpoints, and Dreams: Towards a Critical Theory of the Arts and the State in Africa* (Oxford and New York, 1998).

V. CRITICAL STUDIES. Clifford B. Robson, *Ngugi wa Thiong'o* (London, 1979); G. D. Killam, *An Introduction to the Writings of Ngugi* (London and Exeter, N.H., 1980); David Cook and Michael Okenimkpe, *Ngugi wa Thiong'o: An Exploration of His Writing* (London, 1983; 2d ed. Oxford and Portsmouth, N.H., 1997); Abdul R. JanMohamed, *Manichean Aesthetics: The Politics of Literature in Colonial Africa* (Amherst, Mass., 1983); G. D. Killam, ed., *Critical Perspectives on Ngugi wa Thiong'o* (Washington, D.C., 1984); Ingrid Björkman, *"Mother, Sing for Me": People's Theatre in Kenya* (London and Atlantic Highlands, N.J., 1989); Carol Sicherman, *Ngugi wa Thiong'o: A Bibliography of Primary and Secondary Sources, 1957–1987* (London and New York, 1989); Carol Sicherman, ed., *Ngugi wa Thiong'o, the Making of a Rebel: A Sourcebook in Kenyan Literature and Resistance* (London and New York, 1990); Charles Cantalupo, ed., *Ngũgĩ wa Thiong'o: Texts and Contexts* (Trenton, N.J., 1995); Charles Cantalupo, ed., *The World of Ngũgĩ wa Thiong'o* (Trenton, N.J., 1995); F. Odun Balogun, *Ngugi and African Postcolonial Narrative: The Novel as Oral Narrative in Multigenre Performance* (St. Hyacinth, Quebec, 1997); James Ogude, *Ngugi's Novels and African History: Narrating the Nation* (London, 1999); Patrick Williams, *Ngugi wa Thiong'o* (Manchester, U.K., 1999); Bernth Lindfors, ed., *The Writer as Activist: South Asian Perspectives on Ngugi wa Thiong'o* (Trenton, N.J., 2000); Oliver Lovesey, *Ngugi Wa Thiong'o* (New York, 2000); Peter Nazareth, ed., *Critical Essays on Ngũgĩ wa Thiong'o* (New York, 2000); Gicingiri Ndigirigi, *Ngũgĩ wa Thiong'o's Drama and the Kamĩrĩĩthu Popular Theater Experiment* (Trenton, N.J., 2000); Simon Gikandi, *Ngũgĩ wa Thiong'o* (Cambridge, 2001).

OLD NORSE LITERATURE

Paul Bibire

OLD NORSE WAS the language of the Vikings. These were pagan Scandinavian peoples, Norsemen, "North-men," who raided, traded in, conquered, and settled much of northern Europe during a period from the late eighth century until the eleventh century A.D. They reached the Caspian Sea down the Volga, the Black Sea and Byzantine Empire down the Dnieper, the western Mediterranean through the Straits of Gibraltar, and across the Atlantic to Iceland, Greenland, and North America. Starting about the middle of the ninth century, they settled in Russia, the British Isles, specifically the northern and western Isles of Scotland and the northern part of its mainland, the northeastern half of England later called the "Danelaw," and much of Ireland, as well as part of northern France, later named after them as Normandy. They also colonized Iceland, starting around 874 A.D., and Greenland from about 986. This geographic span was organized not by military or political institutions but by trade through Viking towns such as Kaupang (near modern Oslo), Birka (near modern Stockholm), or Hedeby (near modern Schleswig) in Scandinavia; Dublin or Wexford in Ireland; York in England; and Novgorod and probably Kiev in Russia. Slaves, largely from the British Isles and the Baltic, were probably the early staple of this trade, supplying Byzantium and the caliphate of Baghdad, but Viking towns seem rapidly to have developed as industrial centers where skilled artisans produced luxury goods for trade.

The Norsemen spoke a North Germanic language related to Old English and Old High German. This is known from a sparse but continuous sequence of inscriptions in the runic alphabet from about 200 A.D. onward. It can properly be described as a separate language—Old Norse—after a period of rapid change during the seventh century, and it first shows signs of dialect development in the tenth century, into East and West Norse. The modern languages derived from East Norse are Danish and Swedish, both with many dialects. West Norse survives as the many dialects of modern Norwegian, as well as Faroese and Icelandic. Modern Icelandic has altered little since the medieval period, though the other modern languages have changed greatly. In the British Isles, Norse does not survive as such, but modern English, both in its standard form and in the dialects of the north and east, shows so many Norse characteristics that it must be seen as derived from Old Norse in the same way, if not to the same extent, as it is derived from Old English. Modern English is to some extent a Viking language.

On settling in Russia, England, Ireland, and France, the Vikings rapidly adapted to the societies around them and were swiftly Christianized. However, in the empty countries of Iceland and Greenland, which seem not to have had significant preexisting populations, they set up Scandinavian societies. Although the colony in Greenland perished in the fifteenth century, that in Iceland has survived to the present. The Scandinavian homelands were Christianized toward the end of the Viking period: Denmark by the late tenth century, Iceland probably in the year 1000 A.D., Norway in the first decades of the eleventh century, parts of Sweden perhaps as late as the twelfth century. Iceland had developed an extraordinary quasi-republican constitution which lasted until 1262–1264, when the country came under Norwegian and later Danish rule; it did not regain independence until 1944. Conventional unitary monarchies rapidly developed in mainland Scandinavia, and the states of Denmark and Sweden were formed. State formation in Norway was interrupted in the late Middle Ages, when Norway came under Danish and later Swedish rule, and was not completed until the beginning of the twentieth century.

OLD NORSE LITERATURE

With Christianity came the Roman alphabet and conventions for writing Norse in it. Norwegians and Icelanders learned to write the Roman alphabet from the English, so they used Old English special letters, þ for the "th" sound at the beginning of the modern English word "thigh" (only used at the beginning of words), ð for the "th" sound in "thy" (only at the middle or end of words), and æ, used for several sounds similar to the "a" of the English "bad." They also needed other vowel signs, and borrowed or invented œ, ø, and ǫ (these last two often printed as ö), as well as using the acute accent over vowels (for example, á, ý), originally to mark vowel length. Most of these are still used in writing Icelandic; here they are used in Icelandic names, technical terms, and quotations. In mainland Scandinavia the coming of Christian literacy, using the Roman alphabet, formed a cultural break with the pagan past, and the medieval kingdoms of Denmark, Sweden, and Norway adopted the literary forms and conventions of western European writings.

In Iceland, the circumstances of Christianization permitted almost complete cultural continuity, and the country was sufficiently remote from mainland Europe to be able to develop and maintain a distinctive literature. The Icelanders, once they had learned to write Norse in the Roman alphabet, set about recording their own traditions about their pre-Christian past in both poetry and prose. Some of this poetry was ancient, much of it was difficult, and it required prose explanation. Further, as a colonial people, they needed to justify their own existence through "foundation legends." Partly to produce these, they developed an entirely unprecedented literary form, the saga: a large and usually complex prose narrative text often containing poetry. In the period from the twelfth to the fourteenth centuries A.D., though continuing in unbroken tradition thereafter, they wrote a huge number of texts, some very large indeed. These recounted their own legends and history, and those of adjacent polities—Greenland, the kingdoms of Norway and Denmark and the earldom of Orkney, and also to some extent England and Ireland. The Icelanders were also acquainted with mainland European literature

and translated it from Latin, French, and English, not only into Norse but into their own literary forms. When they ran out of existing source material, they composed new. Accordingly, Old Icelandic literature is vast in amount, varied in range, and often extraordinarily original. Not all of it has been studied or even published in modern printed editions. In contrast there is not much original literature known to have been composed in Old Norwegian, and very little in Old Danish or Old Swedish. Old Norse literature, therefore, is largely that recorded and composed in Iceland.

Old Norse poetry in part records the mythology of Norse and Germanic paganism and legends of the remote past—the "Migration Age" of the fourth to sixth centuries A.D., shared by early English. It also commemorates figures of the Viking Age itself. The Icelandic saga at its best probably surpasses in literary quality any previous European prose literatures, including those of ancient Greece and Rome. It is arguably unmatched until the nineteenth-century novel. This literary achievement is the more striking since it was produced by a population probably never exceeding 50,000, stricken then as later with great poverty in a remote land on the edge of human habitation. Such flowering of literary activity in a small space is comparable with that in the Athens of Aeschylus, Sophocles, and Aristophanes, or in the London of Marlowe, Spenser, and Shakespeare.

Old Norse had direct input into English literature. Shakespeare derived the plot of *Hamlet* ultimately from Norse sources, and as its setting in Denmark shows, he was aware of its Scandinavian association. Norse poetry has stimulated later poets as diverse as Thomas Gray, Henry Wadsworth Longfellow and Seamus Heaney, and it continues to form the basis of novels and other literature. The nineteenth-century novel was to some extent modeled on the sagas, which were already known to writers such as Sir Walter Scott and which certainly affected his creation of the historical novel. The sagas also fed not only into the Gothic novel of the late eighteenth century onwards, but into "fantasy" literature from the late nineteenth century onwards, particularly through William Morris. Sagas inspired the romantic nationalism which led to the creation of the modern nations of Norway and Iceland, and quite largely also Scotland, again through Walter Scott. They also described the first certain European discovery and settlement of North America, and so provide "foundation legends" not only for their own societies but for the modern nations of North America. They prefigured the courtroom and political drama popular in the twentieth century. Medieval Norse literature also dealt with major issues that must still concern modern writers, some universal, but some which have reappeared recently: problems of the presence or absence of the author, and of the authorial voice within the text; methods of creating the illusion of actuality and objectivity in prose narrative; methods of characterization and ethical analysis, ethical ambivalence in characterization and hence the antihero; and methods of unifying large narrative structures.

Most of this literature survives in medieval manuscripts (hand-written books) preserved in Copenhagen, through the activities of manuscript-collectors in the sixteenth and seventeenth centuries; many have now been returned to Iceland. The universities of Copenhagen and Iceland are the main centers for their study.

OLD NORSE POETRY: EDDAIC POETRY

Old Norse poetry falls into two fairly well-defined categories, Eddaic (Eddic) and skaldic. Eddaic poetry is so known from a single manuscript, preserved in the Old Royal Library in Copenhagen, known since the seventeenth century as the Elder or Poetic Edda (*Sæmundar Edda*). The manuscript, to judge by its handwriting, was probably written in the third quarter of the thirteenth century in the south of Iceland. It is not now complete: at some stage a few pages fell out of it. It contains two sequences of poems, most of which do not survive elsewhere. The first eleven poems contain mythological and related material from Norse paganism; the second, longer sequence of twenty poems recounts a cycle of heroic legends. A few other poems of similar meter and subject matter, surviving elsewhere, are grouped with these.

The poems of the Elder Edda share a common tradition of meter and poetic language, closely related to those of the early poetry of the other Germanic languages (attested in Old English, Old Saxon, and Old High German). All Norse poetry composed within this tradition is usually and loosely termed "Eddaic." The meters are all alliterative and rhythmic; each line is defined by its rhythmic pattern, and pairs of lines are linked by alliteration on their first accented (stressed) syllables. One meter (*fornyrðislag*, "tune of ancient wording") is almost unchanged from common Germanic meter, and the others are largely formed by regularizing available variants within the older tradition. The most important metrical innovation is that the poetry is divided into verses (strophes), usually of eight or six lines. Specifically poetic diction is largely limited to nouns, and provides varied terms for heroic content. The grammar and syntax of the poetic language differ from those of prose, mostly in ways that seem more archaic.

Eddaic poetry is almost always anonymous, and dating the composition of individual poems is always difficult, often impossible. Older poetry may well have been recomposed in probable oral transmission many times before the written versions that survive. The poems often imply dramatic dialogue, perhaps indicating how they were meant to be performed. They are mostly narrative and recount myths of paganism, or legends of the Germanic Migration Age—the time at the end of the Roman Empire when Germanic peoples spread from the north into most of western, southern, and eastern Europe, including Britain (the English), Gaul (the Franks), north Italy (the Lombards and then the Goths), Spain (the Visigoths), Bulgaria, and the Ukraine (the Goths). Some of these poems may be very ancient, but there were certainly later periods when poets took great interest in the remote past, whether for political, antiquarian, or quasi-romantic reasons. Many such poems are likely to date from the tenth and twelfth centuries and some from much later.

MYTHOLOGICAL AND EDDAIC POEMS

The mythological poems of the Elder Edda are the primary surviving sources for knowledge of Norse mythology, and the major source of written information for Germanic paganism in general.

The first of them, *Vǫluspá* ("The Sibyl's Prophecy"), gives an account of pagan cosmogeny and cosmology—the mythological universe from its creation to its ultimate downfall and destruction and beyond. The poem conveys its imaginative scope and emotional power in near-riddling brevity. It is certainly an Icelandic composition and seems to show Christian elements in late paganism. In particular, its evaluation of the gods—the story it tells of their gradual corruption from within through oath breaking and betrayal to their ultimate tragic end—seems to apply Christian ethics to the heart of paganism itself.

The other mythological poems in the Elder Edda are organized by gods of the pantheon, firstly Óðinn ("Odin," Old English "Woden" as in "Wednesday," and German "Wotan"), who is the central figure of the poems *Hávamál* (Sayings of the High One), *Vafþrúðnismál* (Sayings of Vafþrúðnir), and *Grímnismál* (Sayings of Grímnir). These are mostly "wisdom" poems, dealing with proverbial or mythological knowledge, though they also contain narrative. *Hávamál* is probably a composite text, and some of its content may be very ancient. It describes a dark, cynical, and bitter world of treachery and sudden death, where a man's only hope is to win the fame that alone may outlive him. The other two poems deal with mythological knowledge, set in the context of a "wisdom-contest," where one participant asks the other obscure mythological questions, and he who knows less loses his life. Óðinn plays several such games in myth and legend, always disguised, and only reveals his identity as he asks the final question which only he of living beings can answer. *Skírnismál* (Sayings of Skírnir) deals with the god Freyr and his uncontrollable desire for the giant-maiden Gerðr, for whom he sends his servant Skírnir. Despite its potential for romance and comedy, realized in later Icelandic retellings, the poem itself is magnificently if grimly obscene at its climax, where Skírnir threatens to put a curse on the reluctant giantess if she does not accept Freyr.

Most of the other mythological poems deal with Þórr ("Thor," Old English "Þunor" as in "Thursday," and German "Donner"). Of the poems *Hárbarðsljóð* and *Hymiskviða,* the first is a debate between him and his father, Óðinn, who is disguised as a reluctant ferryman, while the second tells one of many versions of his encounter with his mortal foe, the World Serpent, while out fishing. Details of this myth are corroborated by a number of Viking Age carvings showing the god fishing, and sticking his foot through the bottom of the boat. *Lokasenna* ("Loki's Taunting") is also to some extent about Þórr, since although the malicious god Loki abuses all the rest of the gods in turn, only Þórr finally responds with the violence that ends it. *Þrymskviða* is a lightheartedly comic poem about how Þórr's weapon, a hammer, is stolen by a giant while he sleeps. The giant demands to marry the beautiful goddess Freyja as ransom. Freyja understandably refuses, and so Loki suggests that Þórr himself should dress up as Freyja and go to marry the giant. The god is acutely embarrassed by this cross-dressing, emphasized when Loki gives the excuse of sexual desire to explain Þórr's burning eyes and appetite at the wedding-feast. However, of course, once he recovers his hammer, of course, he employs it upon the unfortunate giant with the usual result. The poem is remarkable not only for its comedy but for its relative restraint: it never degenerates into coarseness.

One poem, *Vǫlundarkviða,* stands outside this sequence: it is the fullest surviving version of the legend of the elf-smith Vǫlundr (English "Wayland"), closely related to the Greek account of Daedalus. Like his Greek parallel, Vǫlundr is captured and maimed by a hostile king and set to work to create marvels for him. In revenge, he entices the king's two young sons to his smithy, slays them, and makes jewel-studded cups for the king from their skulls. He then rapes the king's daughter, leaving her pregnant with a future hero. Afterward he builds wings for himself from the feathers of birds shot by his brother and flies off into the unknown, taunting the unhappy king.

The poem seems to have strong English associations, both in its meter and diction, and in an apparent textual relationship with the Old English poem *Deor.* Details of its narrative also appear in carvings from eighth-century Northumbria, which as part of the area later known as the Danelaw, formed part of the Norse cultural world. The last mythological poem in the Elder Edda, *Alvíssmál* (Sayings of the All-Wise One), tells of a wisdom contest between a learned dwarf and, improbably, Þórr, who is not elsewhere noted for wisdom.

A few similar mythological poems survive outside the Elder Edda. Some of these are certainly late pastiche, but *Baldrs draumar* ("Baldr's Dreams") and *Rígsþula* ("Rígr's Listing") may be early or contain early material. The first deals with the death of Óðinn's son Baldr, also mentioned in *Vǫluspá,* and the second with the obscure and difficult god Heimdallr, here credited as the parent of the orders of mankind, "thrall," "landowning freemen," and "earl."

The mythological poems are the primary surviving written sources for knowledge of Norse paganism and, more widely, the pre-Christian religion of the Germanic peoples, of which they offer tantalizing glimpses, often confusing and contradictory. Only one, *Vǫluspá,* gives any hint of a coherent worldview, and that may be much influenced by Christianity. Much is alien to the modern reader, particularly the lists of obscure and improbable names that often appear in the wisdom poems. Comedy may also seem an unlikely aspect of Norse religious texts, though the humor is usually sardonic, even rather grim. Some scholars have seen this comic aspect as showing late composition by Christians mocking paganism, but such a view is based solely on the assumption that religion must be solemn. Mockery, based perhaps on tensions between cults within paganism, could have formed a common means of religious expression in Norse. The poems are varied in content and in their treatment of that content, though by chance or selection their literary quality is consistently very high: their effects are both immediate and enduring, and despite their brevity they imply far more than they state.

LEGENDARY EDDAIC POEMS

The remaining twenty poems of the Elder Edda recount heroic legends of the Age of Migrations. With one exception, they all deal with a single cycle of legends, known also from rock-carvings, from the *Nibelungenlied* in Middle High German and briefly from Old English, which tells of the dragon-slaying attributed to the hero Sigurðr (German "Siegfried"), his disastrous marriage into the Burgundian royal dynasty, and the fall of that dynasty in conflict with the Huns. The cycle is not complete: legendary material from its beginning is not represented, and there is a substantial gap where some leaves have fallen out of the manuscript. The content of this material is known, however, from a rather dull prose summary of the entire cycle, the legendary *Vǫlsunga saga.* The poems are very disparate and range from picturesquely grotesque contests of abuse between warrior-poets to grieving the lamentations of bereaved women. They also seem very disparate in age and origin: at least two are from Greenland, according to their headings in the manuscript. To judge from evidence such as rock carvings, cross-references in other poetry, and Norse name-giving practices, these legends were widely popular in the tenth century and remained so at least until the thirteenth. They were rediscovered with enthusiasm in the late eighteenth century, and have remained archetypally important ever since. They stand with the Theban cycle, the Greek legends of Oedipus and his children, as statements of heroic tragedy within Western literature.

Some similar heroic poems survive outside the Elder Edda, mostly embedded within sagas. Some of these are certainly late pastiche and have varying literary merit. The legendary *Heiðreks saga* (also known as *Hervarar saga*) contains three heroic poems. The last of these, "The Battle of the Goths and the Huns" (also known as *Hlǫðskviða*), although sadly fragmentary, contains linguistic fossils that seem to indicate very great age—so much so that it may in part date back to the Migration Age itself, and if so, may be the oldest surviving Germanic poetry. It deals with historic events, the fall of a Gothic empire in the Ukraine at the Hunnish invasions of the fifth century A.D., and is the only legendary text surviving in any Germanic language that remembers these events. The other two heroic poems in the saga are probably both of fairly late composition: *Hjálmarr's Death-Song,* in which a dying hero looks back over his rather conventional exploits, and *The Waking of Angantýr,* a very vivid and colorful account of how a heroine arouses her dead father from his barrow to get his sword. Judging from the motifs it uses, this is probably a twelfth- or thirteenth-century composition.

OLD NORSE POETRY: SKALDIC POETRY

Skaldic (scaldic) poetry is so known from the word *skáld,* "poet," and the surviving poetry is mostly attributed to some 260 named Norwegian and Icelandic poets, including women, of the ninth to fourteenth centuries. Earlier in this period these were professional poets, often from families of poets where fathers trained their children. They performed for named patrons, kings and noblemen, who paid them for their praise. This was not, at least within paganism, merely the service of noble vanity; according to *Hávamál,* the only thing to survive a man was the fame that he won, and this fame was enshrined in the imperishable words of poetry. After Christianization, professional poets gradually ceased to be employed, but Norwegian aristocrats themselves composed skaldic poetry at least up to the twelfth century; in Iceland its composition continued throughout the Middle Ages and was not limited to the aristocracy. Evidence for skaldic poetry elsewhere in the Viking world is very limited. Most of this poetry is preserved within prose texts, largely sagas, as supporting evidence or ornament for narrative.

The word *skáld* is of uncertain origin, but it was borrowed into Middle English, giving the Modern English "scold." This is symmetrical with the Old English word for "poet," *scop,* which is also of uncertain origin, but is cognate with Norse *skop,* "mockery." Clearly one major function of these poets was abuse. Abusing a foe is the mirror image of praising a friend. Abuse, *níð,* is fairly well-attested in skaldic poetry; it

served obvious political or military functions but was certainly also used for religious purposes, both within paganism and against the early Christian missionaries. Skaldic poetry could also be used for criticism and complaint, or even political advice, within the relationship between poet and patron. It was entirely unsuited to narrative, and those skaldic lays, verse-sequences discussed below, that attempt to tell stories usually do so by presenting isolated and unrelated glimpses of their story matter, often in a very visual way and sometimes with apparent visual antecedents. So the genre of "shield lays" dealt with narratives depicted upon decorated shields.

Skaldic poetry is composed in a variety of meters based upon *dróttkvætt* ("court spoken [measure]"). Like the Eddaic meters, *dróttkvætt* links pairs of lines through alliteration; it is strophic, where each verse consists of eight lines divided into separate four-line half-strophes. Each line usually contains six syllables, of which commonly three are stressed. Each line contains internal rhyme; odd-numbered lines contain double alliteration and usually consonant rhyme (assonance); even-numbered lines contain single alliteration, almost always on the first syllable, and full rhyme. Line endings are rhythmically invariable and always share the internal rhyme. Most of the variations upon this already complex meter consist of further elaborations. Internal rhyme is the only feature of the meter that has no probable source within Germanic tradition, and some scholars have argued for an Irish origin for this. The earliest known skaldic poetry is arguably just late enough for this explanation to be possible if not plausible.

Skaldic poetry differs in grammar and syntax from both prose and most Eddaic poetry. In particular it has a different system of negation, using a variety of negative suffixes that only survive elsewhere in the language as fossilized elements in obscured compound words. It usually interweaves a number of separate clauses or even sentences within a single half-strophe, either by embedding or interlace: a sort of verbal plaitwork.

To match its metrical and syntactic complexity, skaldic poetry uses diction of far greater difficulty than any other Germanic poetry. It has many more poetic words than appear in Eddaic diction, and although some of them are borrowed, most seem to be ancient within Germanic, thus perhaps giving access to a stratum of Germanic vocabulary not surviving elsewhere.

As well as using rare and difficult noun vocabulary, a skaldic poet was almost required to express important concepts in metaphorical paradox, through the device of the "kenning." Kennings are genitival constructions taking the form "the *x* of *y*." Simple examples are found in other Germanic poetic traditions, so that in Old English "the homeland of the whale" or "the riding place of the swan" are kennings for the sea. The sea is not a "land," a man cannot "ride" upon the sea—yet it is the whale's home, and the swan rides upon it as though it were a road. This simple pattern was taken up by Norse skaldic poets and elaborated beyond measure; it became an entire, riddling worldview encompassing legendary and mythological reference. The sea is the "gull's fen," as St Rǫgnvaldr's ship, the "bowsprit's elk," leaps across it to Bergen in the twelfth century. For Bragi the Old, three centuries earlier, battle is "the eddy of swords" or "the delight of wolves." But kennings can often use narrative reference: Bragi can call a ship "Eynæfir's ski" and the sea "Reifnir's racetrack," after legendary Viking sea kings. Equally, the qualifying noun in the simple kenning can itself be expanded into a secondary kenning, and so on, to an extent only limited by the size of the half-strophe. So Bragi can compose a shield kenning such as "the instep-leaf of Þrúðr's thief." Þrúðr is the daughter of the god Þórr, who was kidnapped by the giant Hrungnir: he is her "thief." When challenged to battle by the god, Hrungnir is tricked into believing that Þórr will attack from beneath, so he stands upon his shield. The "leaf" of his instep is thus the round shield on which he stands. The kenning is an intellectual game, played between the poet and his audience; it requires them to look through multiple layers of understanding. Everything is seen in terms of other things, and the metaphorical relationships of sense are set up by the narratives of myth and legend.

It is tempting to think that the use of mythological kennings shows religious significance for this poetry in paganism; if skaldic poetry were of pagan importance, this might explain any elimination of this part of the poetic tradition elsewhere in the Norse or Germanic worlds. In Norwegian and Icelandic skaldic poetry, mythological kennings are almost completely eliminated after conversion to Christianity, and the poetry is significantly simplified. However, by the end of the eleventh century, poets seemed to feel free to resume use of pagan mythological reference, even when dealing with explicitly Christian content: evidently by then such reference no longer had religious significance. During the course of the twelfth century, scholar-poets undertook the antiquarian study of skaldic poetry, including the pagan myths used in its kennings, while actively continuing to compose and develop this poetry. This culminates in the Icelandic poetic treatises of the thirteenth century, above all *Snorra Edda*, discussed below.

Kennings are hardly ever repeated in the entire surviving corpus, and there seems to have been a notion of poetic copyright, where poets were given credit not for the content of their poetry but for the actual wording that they used. They must deliberately have avoided repetition of kennings, which seems to have been condemned as plagiarism, even though kenning types for common concepts were fairly standard. This implies the concept of the poetic "author" and a value placed on that author's verbal originality. This may explain the habit of attributing skaldic poetry to named poets, unique in any early Germanic vernacular poetic tradition, and it also implies that skaldic poets knew the entire existing corpus at the time when they worked. Medieval Latin poets were usually named, but unlike skaldic poets, they frequently quoted their predecessors, whether Virgil or the Bible or earlier Christian poets, partly to display their learning and literary allegiances but mostly in a deliberate cultivation of "intertextuality," to invoke the meanings and effects of earlier contexts. Skaldic avoidance of verbal repetition is therefore particularly striking, since so strict a requirement for verbal originality seems to be found neither in other vernacular nor Latin poetic traditions of the period.

Skaldic poets accordingly often refer to themselves within their own poetry. These first-person references sometimes seem to be conventions of reportage, but they are by no means generally so. Occasionally within the poetry, and fairly often in accompanying prose narrative, skaldic verses are themselves presented and used as the poet's own self-expression in ways that seem familiar from classical and modern lyric poetry. Instances of such "lyric" self-expression in skaldic poetry sometimes seem suspiciously "romantic" in that one may suspect the influence of Old French troubadour or romance poets upon the narrative presentation, if not on the poetry itself. Such influence upon skaldic poetry can be convincingly demonstrated from the middle of the twelfth century onwards, and in prose narratives probably from the end of that century.

Skaldic poetry seems largely to have been composed as lays: fairly long verse-sequences apparently intended to be performed in a single session. A lay with a refrain was called a *drápa* and had higher status than a lay without a refrain, a *flokkr*. The content of early lays was praise for the poet's patron and condemnation of his enemies—in other words, celebration of the achievements of Viking lords. Through legendary reference in kennings, these ninth- and tenth-century poets could compare their own heroic lords with the heroes of ancient Germanic legend, just as they could relate their lords to the gods of Germanic and Norse paganism through mythological kennings. Already at this stage, however, the sources record many verses that were apparently composed as incidental, occasional comment, so-called "loose verses" (*lausavísur*), and which apparently never formed parts of larger structures. The lays of praise survive into Christian times, but are transferred to Christian subjects, and later lays are composed to praise saints or the Virgin Mary. Meanwhile, composition of occasional verses seems to have been continuingly cultivated as a personal accomplishment.

Most of the poetry included within sagas is in the form of occasional verses, which act as a sideways poetic commentary upon the narrative. They are often presented as giving some sort of evidence for the truthfulness of the prose, as if they were the original words of the characters corroborating the text around them. Since medieval Icelandic historians certainly used genuine verses for this purpose, other instances may also be genuine, and many more must have been intended to be taken as such. Many verses, however, seem to have been composed for their sagas, and although they must be read as part of the overall composition, they are unlikely to have any value in validating the content of the saga. Their effective functions are usually literary.

Modern historians of the Viking Age sometimes attempt to make use of skaldic poetry as textual source evidence for historical events. Even where the poetry is likely to be genuine, its difficulty is a major hindrance, as is the fact that this poetry is unsuited to narrative content. More importantly still, the poets were much less concerned with details of content than with elaboration of its expression.

Complexity of meter and diction has been put forward as a reason for the precise preservation of skaldic poetry: in order to maintain its meter, a verse must be remembered exactly. This is not adequately evident in practice; at least in written transmission some poetry has been corrupted beyond interpretation, though in other instances it sometimes appears almost suspiciously intact. This in turn can lead to doubt whether such poetry is as old as is claimed, or whether it had recently been recomposed by a competent updater.

Dating skaldic poetry can be difficult, especially where its attribution is uncertain or implausible. There are metrical tests: some vowels (φ and ϕ, α, and α) coalesced during the twelfth century but were different earlier, so that lines which rhyme them are probably late. But early rhymes do not prove early composition, since they could always have been produced later by imitating genuinely early poetry. Some literary tests are used, but these mostly depend upon unprovable assumptions. In practice many different indicators, some inherently subjective, can tip the judgment of probability. For instance, *Grettis saga* and *Eyrbyggja saga* both contain much excellent poetry in their accounts of tenth-century events. A few verses in *Grettis saga* use demonstrably late rhymes. But for the present writer, there is the strong impression of a single creative mind behind all the poetry in *Grettis saga,* no matter to whom it is attributed within the saga; the poetry, as it stands, was probably composed or recomposed by a single poet for the saga itself. In contrast, most of the poetry in *Eyrbyggja saga* uses rhymes that would have been acceptable in earlier skaldic poetry, and the verses attributed to different characters differ greatly in style and quality, which may imply different poets. In this case, therefore, the saga probably used preexisting poetry, some of which may genuinely go back to the actual figures depicted within the saga.

An example of fairly simple skaldic poetry is this verse, attributed to the Icelandic poet Arnórr "Earls' Poet" Þórðarson as part of a memorial lay for Earl Þorfinnr of Orkney (died c.1065), echoing tropes also found in *Vǫluspá*. Alliteration is shown in italics, internal rhyme in bold (all vowels alliterate with each other; ǫ rhymes with *a* in l. 4).

Bjǫrt verðr *s*ól at *s*vartri,
*søkk*r fold í mar *døkk*van,
bre**str** *e*rfiði *Au*stra,
*a*llr glymr sær á fj**ǫll**um,
*á*ðr at *E*yjum frí**ðr**i
(*inn*dróttar) Þor**finn**i
(*þeim* hjálpi *Go*ð *gey*mi)
g**œð**ingr myni f**œð**ask.

Bright sun shall blacken,
breaks earth into dark ocean,
Austri's effort shatters,
all sea crashes on mountains,
ere at the Isles a lovelier
lord (court's) than Þorfinnr
(that keeper may God save)
king may come to being.

This translation attempts to reproduce metrical alliteration (even at the cost of accuracy), but only occasionally internal rhyme; it also maintains strained word order, with the tension it generates. *Austri's effort* is a kenning; Austri was a mythological dwarf who helped to hold up the sky, and so that is his "effort." The pagan cosmos shall pass away, land will sink into the sea, the sky will shatter before a lovelier land than Þorfinnr comes to Orkney; may the Christian God keep that prince (at and beyond Judgment) who so kept his own retainers.

OLD NORSE PROSE: EARLY TEXTS

Icelandic prose texts first appear early in the twelfth century, though these already show established spelling conventions and skill in handling the language, so that some eleventh-century writing may have taken place, perhaps sermons and legal documents. According to Ari Þorgilsson "the Wise" (b. 1067–1068, d. 1148), part of the law, previously transmitted orally by trained lawyers, was written in the winter of 1117–1118. Apart from that, Ari's own work is the earliest surviving Norse prose written in the Roman alphabet: *Íslendingabók* ("The Book of the Icelanders"), written by or before 1134. It is a short collection of historical essays on topics such as the Settlement, the calendar, the discovery of Greenland, the Conversion, and the episcopacies of the first two native bishops of Iceland. It has two continuing concerns: the establishment of an internal chronology for Icelandic history, and the development of the Icelandic legal system. Ari is remarkable among medieval historians in that he is constantly concerned for chronological exactness as well as identification of the sources for his material. In both respects he almost certainly modeled his work upon that of Bede. According to his first-person preface, the surviving text is a second, revised edition. But a later description of his work (in the prefaces to *Heimskringla* and *The Separate Saga of St Óláfr*) seems to give an account of a different version that includes information about Norwegian royal history. *Íslendingabók* itself is rather dry, but it almost always shows mastery of language, style, and narrative.

Ari is also plausibly credited with part-authorship of *Landnámabók* ("The Book of Settlements"), a geographically organized, annotated catalog of genealogies, probably originally compiled in the early twelfth century but surviving in several much-expanded later versions. The annotations are mostly fragments of narrative, and some instances can be seen as the seeds of sagas. Blood relationships had narrative implications in their social and legal rights and responsibilities. Personality traits were also believed to be inherited; genealogical narrative was therefore a guide to how subsequent descendents would behave in specific narrative situations. Thus recurrent personality types, genealogically organized, partly account for cyclic narrative patterns within sagas.

Other texts were written at this time. An older contemporary of Ari's, Sæmundr Sigfússon "the Learned" (b. 1054–1056, d. 1133), is frequently cited as a historical authority and is likely to have established a chronology for Norwegian royal history. Scientific texts survive from about the middle of the twelfth century: of these the anonymous *First Grammatical Treatise* is probably the most important. In setting out to reform Icelandic orthography, it gives a phonetic and phonological account of the language unparalleled elsewhere in medieval Europe, using techniques (for example, using "minimal pairs" to show contrast) only rediscovered in the twentieth century. Astronomical work was also undertaken at this time. These treatises are remarkable not only for their astonishing originality but because they were written in Icelandic, not Latin, the language of scholarship elsewhere in western Europe.

OLD NORSE PROSE: THE SAGAS

The sagas, almost all of which are of Icelandic origin and preserved in Icelandic manuscripts, are the dominant literary form of Old Norse. Surviving sagas seem to have been written from the late twelfth century onwards; some major texts may date from as late as the fifteenth century in their present forms. They are conventionally divided by modern scholars into a number of major groups, and there is medieval evidence to support some modern distinctions. Most widely-known are the "Sagas of Icelanders" (*Íslendinga sögur*), sometimes inappropri-

ately called the "Family Sagas." These deal with the semihistorical events of Iceland's "heroic age": the Settlement of Iceland from about 870 A.D. onwards, and the personages of Icelandic society up to and just beyond the Conversion. Icelandic history is continued in the so-called Contemporary Sagas (*samtíðarsögur*), which deal with the period from the early twelfth century to the late thirteenth: some of these may have been composed by eyewitnesses. There is an unexplained gap of about a century (roughly 1020–1120), events of which are not told in sagas but are known from other sources.

Parallel with these are the "Kings' Sagas" (*konunga sögur*), a continuous cycle of sagas from prehistoric legend up to the thirteenth century, dealing with the Norwegian royal dynasty king by king. Similar cycles seem to have been composed for the Danish dynasty, surviving only fragmentarily, and for the earls of Orkney, surviving as the modern compilation *Orkneyinga saga.*

The earlier heroic periods, the Viking Age and before that the Germanic Migration Age, were only known to the Icelanders as heroic legends, from skaldic and Eddaic poetry respectively, and they composed many legendary sagas, "Sagas of Ancient Times" (*fornaldarsögur*), and many further sagas which reworked motifs from genuine or spurious legend into what modern readers must see as fantasy.

The Icelanders encountered the new literary genre of the romance, mostly Arthurian, both directly from Old French and indirectly through Middle High German and Middle English. Some of these romances were translated into Norse prose narrative, especially for the modernizing Norwegian monarchy of the thirteenth century, but the Icelanders composed many more from scratch: these romantic "Sagas of Knights" (*riddarasögur*) proved very popular, again as a fantasy literature.

Biographies of saints (*heilagramanna sögur*) were available: many were translated from Latin, and more were produced for native saints and would-be saints: St Óláfr of Norway; St Magnús and St Rǫgnvaldr of Orkney; St Þorlákr, bishop of Skálholt in the south of Iceland; St Jón, bishop of Hólar in the north of Iceland; bishop Guðmundr "the Good." These overlapped with biographies of Icelandic bishops (*biskupa sögur*), of which an intermittent cycle was produced.

Huge cyclic compilations of foreign legend were also produced or translated, dealing with the legends associated with Theodoric the Ostrogoth (*Þiðreks saga*) and Charlemagne (*Karla-Magnúss saga*). Scholarly Icelanders encountered Dares Phrygius' account of the Trojan War, Walter of Châtillon's *Alexandreis,* and Josephus' *History of the Jews,* and turned them into Norse sagas (*Trójumanna saga, Alexanders saga,* and *Gyðinga saga,* respectively).

At least some of these different kinds of subject matter were treated differently. Romances developed their own distinguishing prose styles and rather ornate vocabulary, as separately did the saints' lives. Scholarly material tended to be expressed in correspondingly Latinate styles. In contrast, legendary sagas tended to use a rather simplified and bare prose style. Romances and legendary sagas used different bodies of motifs and different rules for their assembly. These should not be seen as genre distinctions, however, since individual texts frequently shift from one to another as their subject matter shifts: these are criteria of literary mode rather than of genre. Sagas on similar subjects or of similar mode were also sometimes copied in the same manuscripts.

The saga contributed to the development of the nineteenth-century novel and can be approached from that. Sagas are much more varied in length and structure than novels. They are always primarily narrative prose, but examples can be short, a few printed pages, up to vast composite texts of thousands of pages. They always deal with individual characters, but they may have no single hero, or many. They frequently tell more than one story, sometimes simultaneously. They seem to require narrative "completeness," that is, the ultimate origins and final outcomes of their narratives must be told, often across several generations. Sagas are almost always anonymous and contain no overt authorial voice; they appear to give objective, external accounts of events, without any omniscient narrator to report characters' thoughts or emotions. This is often

mirrored by deceptively simple and transparent narrative prose; they can thereby create a remarkable illusion of reality. They delight in complexities of characterization, usually created by superimposing multiple character types within a single figure. They equally delight in implicit ethical analysis of both character and situation, employing multiple ethical systems—Christian and secular, ancient heroic and medieval chivalric, social, legal, and mercantile—and exploiting their discrepancies. The ambivalences so developed are typically handled with economically ironic understatement, sometimes comic, sometimes bitter, but often more moving than the rhetorical flourishes of romance.

Sagas seem to have been composed and transmitted for entertainment and instruction within a substantially literate secular society. Lay literacy in Iceland seems to have begun early and at the highest social levels; by the mid-twelfth century most major households probably had access to someone who could read and write. Sagas were borrowed and copied for local domestic performance, read aloud, and were adjusted accordingly, to fit the interpretation, taste, and style of the performer and the expectations of the intended audience. Manuscript evidence suggests that most medieval copyists could recompose the saga that they were copying: they were rewriting the text as redactors, rather than mechanically copying it as transcribers. Each redactor contributed to the authorial process, and each medieval redaction can itself be seen as a "performing version," though not simply as the record of a performance. This partly explains the "absence of the author": when everyone involved in saga transmission and performance could share in the creative process, no single person could be the "author." There was indeed no word for "author," and no words for the process of composition other than *setja saman* or *semja,* "to put together, compile." Modern scholars, working within a culture that venerates the creative genius of individual authors to the point of superstition, accordingly find difficulty in discovering the "authorship" of most Icelandic sagas or to reconstruct any original, authorial text. Equally, attempting to date the composition of Icelandic sagas may in many instances be futile if the texts grew during recomposition over many years. For instance, *Grettis saga* refers to *Bandamanna saga* by name, but *Bandamanna saga* seems in part to be based upon *Grettis saga*. This is easily explained if both sagas developed side-by-side.

There was much debate during the twentieth century over the use of preexisting oral tradition in the sagas. This was largely fruitless, since no one could know what, if any, earlier oral traditions had actually existed. An approximate consensus emerged, however, that some sagas might contain some such tradition, but that each case needed to be considered individually. For example, a saga containing old poetry might well have inherited old narrative traditions with that poetry. Few modern scholars would dare to dismiss *Egils saga Skalla-Grímssonar* as mere thirteenth-century invention: it gives the biography of its hero, a grimly pagan tenth-century poet, together with much of his poetry, at least some of which is likely to be as old as its subject. Other sagas, sometimes far more realistic, such as *Bandamanna saga,* have far less corroboratory evidence for their content, and could be invention.

The sagas' truth value, intended and otherwise, has been much discussed. There was no word in Old Norse for the difficult modern concept of "fiction," which may not have arisen in English until the seventeenth century. The only available terms in Norse were *sannr,* "true," (or at least "trustworthy") and *lygi,* "lie." The word "saga" can be used for the equally difficult modern term "history," which is the same word as English "story" and generally had that meaning at least until the eighteenth century. Certainly some sagas must have been intended to be a "true account" of things, or at least an intentionally truthful reconstruction of how things "must have been" or "should have been"; many more must have been intended to seem so. Other ideas of truth may also have been used, for instance, exemplary or allegorical truth, with which any medieval reader of saints' lives was familiar. Sagas often seem to shift disconcertingly between different kinds of truth value, and each instance must be considered individually.

There are between thirty and forty surviving Sagas of Icelanders, organized geographically clockwise around Iceland, starting in the southwest. This organization is already apparent in some medieval saga manuscripts and goes back to *Landnámabók,* later versions of which function as saga summary and index. A few major Sagas of Icelanders are discussed here.

Only one major saga survives from the southwestern plains, the fertile and historically important area around the first bishopric at Skálholt and the early schools there and at Oddi and Haukadalr. Yet this saga is often reckoned the greatest of all: *Njáls saga* ("The Saga of Njáll of the Burning"). It is a large text and has probably absorbed other older and shorter sagas from the district. It is, however, an entirely unified whole. It tells three linked stories. The first of these tells of Gunnarr of Hlíðarendi and his marriage to the beautiful but malevolent Hallgerðr, modeled upon Guðrún in *Laxdœla saga*; she brings about the feuds that lead to Gunnarr's death in a final heroic siege of his farmstead. Gunnarr is both an idealized hero of the old, pre-Christian world, and entirely realistic as a farmer struggling with awkward neighbors. The second story tells of Gunnarr's friend and adviser, Njáll, an elderly lawyer and man of peace; he is cursed with foreknowledge of the future, and specifically of his own death and that of his sons. He attempts to manipulate events to avoid the inevitable, and so brings about what he most feared. A feud breaks out between his sons and his much-loved foster son, whom they kill. In vengeance for this fratricide, and after a long and unsuccessful lawsuit, Njáll and his sons are burned alive in their own home. Only when Njáll is at last able to accept his fate and look beyond it to Christian hope does he finally find peace. Njáll, unlike Gunnarr, is largely a passive, suffering figure; his story includes the Conversion of Iceland, which introduces a new ethical system to the saga. The third story is of Njáll's son-in-law, Kári, who escapes the burning and takes continuing vengeance for Njáll's death; the saga does not end until final reconciliation has put an end to three generations of feud and hatred. Kári, like Gunnarr, is an active, heroic figure, but unlike Gunnarr, he is allowed the possibility of redemptive reconciliation within the new ideology.

All this is set against a huge social backdrop of Iceland and northern Europe: kings of Norway and Ireland and earls of Orkney have bit parts, and the saga is tied into climactic events such as the Battle of Clontarf in Ireland in 1014. The saga addresses metaphysical issues, in particular the relationship between predestination and free will in both secular and Christian terms. It always presents these, however, with awareness of the price paid by the individual caught up within them. It is the Icelandic *War and Peace,* and does not suffer in that comparison.

Most of the sagas from the southern bay on the west coast of Iceland are associated with one fjord at its head, Borgarfjörðr, a little north of modern Reykjavík. There are several important texts from this district concerned with poetry. This may partly reflect thirteenth-century literary activity here, particularly associated with the politician, poet, and historian Snorri Sturluson (d. 1241). The most important is *Egils saga Skalla-Grímssonar* ("The Saga of Egill Skalla-Grímr's Son"), a long and detailed biography of this tenth-century skaldic poet; included or appended is much poetry attributed to him, some of which is of astonishingly high quality. The saga creates a wholly convincing portrait of a figure at once vicious and admirable. Two brothers appear in each generation of his family, the one fair-haired, handsome, and successful, who meets an early death due to a king, the other dark-haired, ugly, and malevolent. This figure is always a poet, and survives. Egill himself fulfils this role in his own time. He is an Óðinn-worshipper who shares some of the attributes of his god, including poetry, runes, and werewolf associations. The saga shows him using these in conflict with the Norwegian king Eiríkr, nicknamed blóðøx ("blood-axe") and the witch-queen Gunnhildr. At times Egill is presented as more horrific than his opponents. In a more-or-less justified duel against a berserk, steel will not bite on his opponent, so Egill leaps upon him and bites his throat out. But he is also given powerfully sympathetic emotions: his grief for his brother's death in battle, or for his son's drowning, are portrayed in the saga

with poetry of great power. Arguably the most memorable part of the saga, however, is its depiction of Egill's bitter old age, blind and impotent, and his rage against the fading of the light.

Two other "sagas of poets" are associated with Borgarfjörðr: *Gunnlaugs saga ormstunga* ("The Saga of Gunnlaugr Serpent-Tongue") and *Bjarnar saga Hítdœlakappa* ("The Saga of Bjǫrn Champion of the Folk of Hít-Dale"). These two, together with two others from Húnaflói in the northwest, *Kormaks saga* and *Hallfreðar saga vandræðaskálds* ("The Saga of Hallfreðr the Awkward Poet"), share the same basic story as *Laxdœla saga.* This story pattern is probably derived from or influenced by the romance of Tristan and Isolde. It tells how a poet falls in love with a woman in Iceland but then goes abroad, asking her to wait for three years. He is delayed, but meanwhile his companion returns and reports—correctly, in most versions of the story—that the poet has an amorous liaison overseas. The companion then marries the woman. The poet subsequently returns, and the two men spend the rest of their lives feuding. *Gunnlaugs saga* is rather oversimplified and sentimental, but *Bjarnar saga* has pleasingly vigorous and well-rounded characters, and a magnificently vitriolic exchange of abuse poetry. *Kormaks saga* fails to make sense of its emotionally incompetent hero, who is nonetheless credited with some of the finest surviving skaldic love poetry. *Hallfreðar saga* combines this story pattern with that of *Fóstbrœðra saga,* since Hallfreðr ends up serving Óláfr Tryggvason, effectively the first Christian king of Norway. The king had difficulty converting his reluctant poet to Christianity, and so Hallfreðr acquired his nickname, the "Awkward Poet." After the king's death, however, Hallfreðr is a changed man and ends his life in Christian reconciliation with his foes.

Two major sagas deal with the history of Breiðafjörðr, the northern bay on the west coast of Iceland, north of the long peninsula of Snæfellsnes. They are *Eyrbyggja saga* ("The Saga of the Shingle-Dwellers") and *Laxdœla saga* ("The Saga of the Folk of Laxdale"), and are closely entwined with each other through the figures of Snorri and

Guðrún. *Eyrbyggja saga* recounts the origins and development of the communities on the north side of Snæfellsnes. Its complex structure probably makes it the most awkward of all the major sagas of Icelanders for a modern reader. It has no single hero and tells many stories in counterpoint, some comic, some tragic, some simply strange and often supernatural. Almost all of these stories, however, are woven around the central figure of Snorri goði ("the chieftain"). Snorri appears in many major sagas, and has, for instance, an important minor rôle in *Njáls saga*. He is always depicted in the same way, as a coldly manipulative politician, successful not in action but in planning and policy; others do the deeds that he has set up for them. He is usually portrayed as ultimately benevolent in that he brings about peace and social order, but he does this only on his own terms. This shared literary treatment may of course represent historical fact, but it also certainly shows the strength of a common literary tradition, probably transmitted through the twelfth-century historian Ari Þorgilsson; one of his named informants was a daughter of Snorri goði. In contrast with its central figure, *Eyrbyggja saga* is characterized by a warm humanity and breadth of sympathy; no other major saga gives so full and diverse a range of characters, each seen not only from his or her own viewpoint but as others around them saw them. Equally, no other major saga gives a comparable sense of individuals and communities getting on with their own lives, as the stories of the saga weave their way together among them.

Laxdæla saga tells the stories of recurrent jealousies, often sexual, between half-brothers within a family descended from the matriarchal first settler, Auðr (Unnr) the Deep-Minded. In each preceding generation these jealousies are defused until the climactic narrative of the saga. As noted above, this tells the same story as the "poets' sagas," though here without poetry. The young and handsome hero, Kjartan, falls in love with a girl, Guðrún Ósvífrsdóttir, but then goes abroad with his much-loved foster brother and cousin, Bolli. While in Norway, Kjartan dallies with the king's sister and overstays the period of three years within which he had promised to return to Guðrún. Bolli returns and reports matters to Guðrún, whom he then marries. Kjartan subsequently returns and marries another woman. Guðrún in long anger stirs up jealousy between Kjartan and her own brothers, and also her husband Bolli, who finally kills Kjartan. The feud continues: Bolli is killed, and in vengeance Guðrún causes the death of one of his slayers. As a widow she becomes the matriarch of the family, but Iceland is now Christian, and in old age she repents of her hatreds and anger.

Guðrún, the "woman of contention" at the center of the feud, becomes the central figure of this saga, and her conflicting emotions of love, anger, jealous hatred and penitence are portrayed with absolute conviction. Guðrún herself clearly echoes the terrible archetypes of legend, Brynhildr and Guðrún Gjúkadóttir, women who in the heroic poems of the Elder Edda cause their husbands or brothers to slay past lovers or husbands, despite the emotional cost to themselves that leads to their own suicides in fire. Yet she is not alone: the central story is as much the tragedy of Bolli, who is forced in fratricide to kill his dearest friend and foster brother, knowing that this will lead to his own death. Elements of romance are present, both in a few notable set-piece descriptive scenes, and in the saga's emphasis upon the destructive power of love. The saga can be seen as the union of Norse heroic legend and French romance, employing the strengths and avoiding the potential weaknesses of each literary form, while reenacting the whole within the realistic setting of tenth- and eleventh-century Iceland.

A few lesser sagas belong to this group. Among them is *Eiríks saga rauða* ("The Saga of Eiríkr the Red"), which tells of the discovery and settlement of Greenland, and the discovery of Vínland, North America. It assumes knowledge of various characters in *Eyrbyggja saga,* with which it also shares an antiquarian interest in the supernatural. *Grœnlendinga saga* ("The Saga of the Greenlanders") tells basically the same stories as *Eiríks saga,* but with substantial differences of detail; the two sagas show how the same traditions developed differently in two separate narrative traditions.

Several sagas are associated with the western Fjords of Iceland, the huge mountainous hand stretched out toward Greenland at the northwestern extremity of the country. The two most important are *Gísla saga Súrssonar* ("The Saga of Gísli Súrr's Son") and *Fóstbrœðra saga* ("The Saga of the Fosterbrothers"). *Gísla saga* tells of its hero's outlawry for a killing justified in his eyes by older heroic values, which have become unacceptable in settled and unheroic Icelandic society. Gísli undergoes a long and purgatorial outlawry, given strong religious implications and recounted with much powerful poetry: his death not only fulfils the demands of the older heroic ethics, but implies a release from them into Christian hope. *Fóstbrœðra saga* recounts the loves of Þormóðr Kolbrúnarskáld ("Coal-brow's Poet"): first, a couple of comic love affairs; second, and more seriously, his comradeship with a hero of the old sort, his foster brother, who takes heroics to their logical conclusion, is killed and avenged; and third, his devotion to the sainted king of Norway, St Óláfr Haraldsson. Þormóðr finally dies with the king at the Battle of Stiklastaðir in 1030, and so by implication is redeemed by the king's sanctity. Again the saga contains much excellent poetry and can be seen as ethical exploration of three kinds of love, with narrative exploration of the kinds of story proper to them.

Húnaflói, the large bay towards the west of Iceland's northern coast, is the setting for several important sagas, including *Grettis saga* and *Bandamanna saga* ("The Saga of the Confederates"). *Grettis saga* is a long and episodic biography of an outlaw, Grettir, who is dogged by bad luck that arises from his own recalcitrant nature and accumulates through the supernatural episodes of the saga until it destroys him. Like Egill, Grettir is a figure both admirable and reprehensible. But unlike Egill, the disasters that befall him are not usually of his own making, and also unlike Egill, he does not survive. He cannot fit into human society because he cannot accept authority: he is the archetypal rebellious teenager. However, beyond the moral, legal, and physical boundaries of ordinary human society, in the difficult borderlands inhabited by outlaws, berserks, trolls, and walking corpses, he can use his violence and huge strength decisively and usually benevolently to protect humanity. In most of these encounters he is cumulatively diminished or damaged, becoming both more vulnerable and less human, more the equivalent of the monsters whom he encounters. Finally, in an ironic role reversal, he is slain like a troll by another character taking the function of hero.

These cyclic episodes are largely told in "legendary saga" mode. Each has its own separate setting and characters, who do not usually reappear in the saga, but the episodes are set within a continuing naturalistic narrative of Icelandic society, with its own recurrent characters. Grettir's killer afterwards goes to Byzantium but is pursued by Grettir's brother, who takes vengeance for him there in an episode told in chivalric mode, using motifs derived directly from the romance of Tristan and Isolde; finally the brother becomes a hermit in a short hagiographic conclusion. The saga is not tragic, and it portrays its grim content with wry wit. Grettir himself is given a sequence of verses, often ironic and sometimes comic, in which he comments upon the narrative with much self-awareness.

Bandamanna saga is social satire. It tells how a group of greedy chieftains band together to prosecute a rich merchant to get his wealth, but are outwitted and mercilessly humiliated by the merchant's estranged father. The old man cynically exploits all the ethical possibilities of the situation, culminating in a scene rather reminiscent of the Eddaic poem *Lokasenna*, where he publicly abuses each of them in turn. The saga is brilliantly and economically effective, but its impact is entirely negative.

Eyjafjörðr, the long, narrow fjord in the center of Iceland's north coast, is associated with several sagas, mostly fairly short. Two of these are *Víga-Glúms saga* ("The Saga of Glúmr of the Slayings") and *Valla-Ljóts saga* ("The Saga of Ljótr from Vellir"). They are mirror images of each other: Glúmr is a rather vicious figure, who is temporarily successful against his neighbors until he disposes of the inherited items, cloak and spear, that embody his family luck; Ljótr is a pleasant and peaceable man who suffers but survives local hostility. The region east of Eyjafjörðr is associated with a few major sagas, of which *Ljósvetninga saga* ("The Saga of the Folk of Bright-Water") is probably the most interesting. It is largely concerned with the chieftain Guðmundr "the Mighty," who is a counter-figure to Snorri goði. Guðmundr is a powerful, magnificent, and rather vain figure whose achievements never quite match up to his pretentions. He is set against a heroic character, Þorkell hákr ("hake"), whom he destroys at the cost of personal humiliation.

The northeast and east of Iceland is associated with many small texts rather than a few large sagas, for instance *Hrafnkels saga,* a political account of the fall and rise of a chieftain, which, in its perfection, seems a little too much an exercise in the craft of saga writing. The fragmented stories of the east contrast with the narrative synthesis of the great sagas of the southwest or of Breiðafjörðr.

The processes of narrative synthesis appear at their fullest in the Kings' Sagas, which for the most part only survive as cycles. The greatest of these is *Heimskringla,* "The Circuit of the World," named after its first sentence, which recounts the history of the Norwegian dynasty from mythic legend down to the mid-twelfth century, ending abruptly in the reign of Magnús Erlendsson (reigned 1164–1184). This point was probably chosen because the account of Magnús' successor, Sverrir, had already been told in *Sverris saga,* attributed to the Icelandic abbot Karl Jónsson, and according to different versions of its preface, partly dictated to Karl by the king before his death in 1202.

The central saga of *Heimskringla* is *Óláfs saga helga* ("The Saga of St Óláfr"), which also survives in a rather fuller separate version. *Heimskringla* is attributed in a late, secondary source to the Icelandic chieftain and poet Snorri Sturluson (d. 1241). This attribution is usually accepted, and certainly stylistic evidence suggests common authorship with the other work attributed to Snorri. *Heimskringla* is a towering literary achievement that compels belief; its cogency and

coherence, its intellectual subtlety and emotional force, disarm source criticism. For these reasons it is greatly distrusted by most modern historians, and it cannot usually be tested as a historical source. Above all, its portrait of the warrior-saint, King Óláfr Haraldsson, is astonishing in its complexity and power. Óláfr is at once an overbearing and cruel tyrant, a sensitive, kind and generous king, and at his death a credibly transcendent saint. The narrative sweep is epic, yet always grounded in gritty reality. Later versions of the cycle expand by adding much extra material, but they rarely alter the substance and presentation of *Heimskringla,* which seems to have achieved classic status within medieval Iceland. Other versions of the cycle, using some of the same sources as *Heimskringla* but not derived from it, survive in *Fagrskinna* and *Morkinskinna.* The account of Sverrir's dynasty is continued in *Hákonar saga Hákonarsonar,* attributed to Snorri's nephew, Sturla Þórðarson (d. 1284).

Sturla Þórðarson is also both a major actor in, and author of the largest component of a huge composite cycle of Contemporary Sagas, *Sturlunga saga* ("The Saga of the Descendants of Sturla"), recounting Icelandic history of the period about 1120–1270. This vast and disparate compilation tells of the increasingly violent feuds, equivalent to civil war, that tore Icelandic society apart during the last century of the Commonwealth, leading to submission to King Hákon Hákonarson the Old of Norway in 1262–1264. It is a remarkable literary anthology of politicians' memoirs, bishops' lives, old-fashioned heroic sagas, and above all, political history, told in great detail and with much passion.

To modern taste, no legendary or romantic saga or saint's life matches the literary achievement of the Sagas of Icelanders or the Kings' Sagas, although they contain much to interest and be admired. As a stylistic tour de force, however, *Alexanders saga* is of unusual quality.

OTHER OLD NORSE PROSE

Large numbers of technical, legal, scientific, rhetorical, and encyclopedic prose texts survive, as well as much of a medieval translation of the Bible. One text, however, is of special importance: *Snorra Edda* (also known as the *Prose* or *Younger Edda*). The manuscript surviving in Uppsala names the text and attributes it to Snorri Sturluson. It is a large treatise on poetry in three main parts. Of these, the third, *Háttatal* ("Reckoning of Meter") was probably composed earliest. It is a long poem of Snorri's own composition, exemplifying every meter, metrical, and rhetorical device known to him. The poem itself is very dull, but it is presented with a detailed prose technical commentary. It is a complete *Ars Poetica* for Norse, and as such is unique in northern medieval Europe. Most of the technical terminology for Germanic poetry is derived from this. To judge from its subject matter, it was composed sometime around or very shortly after 1220. Then, in order to explain Norse poetic diction, and particularly kennings, Snorri composed the second section, *Skáldskaparmál* ("The Language of Poetry"). This tells the stories to which kennings refer, and in so doing, Snorri quotes the earlier poetry containing the kennings. Most of this poetry only survives because Snorri quoted it, and many of the myths and legends are only recounted here. Finally, Snorri provided a narrative context for the myths: an account of Norse pagan cosmology. This he created in what is now the first major section of *Snorra Edda, Gylfaginning* ("The Deluding of Gylfi"). It is set in the form of a wisdom contest, as in the poems of the Elder Edda; a figure called Gylfi (described as a disguised Swedish king, but the name he takes in his disguise, Gangleri, also appears as an Óðinn name) interrogates three figures, Hár, Jafn-Hár, and Þriði ("High," "Equally-High," and "Third"). These names are found elsewhere as Óðinn names and certainly imply a well-attested Óðinn trinity. Gylfi asks questions, often ostensibly naive but often ironic, about the pagan mythological universe, and his three respondents reply with material structured from *Vǫluspá*. Much mythological poetry is quoted, mostly from poems surviving in the Elder Edda, but some not found elsewhere. Certainly Snorri had sources now otherwise lost. However, because he was working more than two centuries after Christianization, he has been suspected of invention or alteration on religious grounds. Where he can be tested, however, he shows remarkable acumen in judging his sources and remarkable fidelity to them in content. His presentation of that content, however, is layered with levels of irony; nothing is ever quite what it seems. *Gylfaginning* is not merely an important source, it is the best and most engaging retelling of Norse and Germanic pagan mythology, ancient or modern.

LATER ICELANDIC LITERATURE

Sagas of most sorts continued to be composed throughout the later medieval period and up to the eighteenth century; some of these are not without merit and may even preserve old narrative content. New meters and poetic forms appear from the fourteenth century onwards, particularly the long, difficult, and ornate romantic poems called *rímur*, which still used the diction of skaldic poetry and continued to be copiously composed up to the early nineteenth century. Some of the *rímur* rework older material, poems or sagas, but many of them take new content: for instance, *Skotlands rímur* recount the conspiracy of the earl of Gowrie against James VI of Scotland in 1600. There is thus direct literary continuity in Icelandic prose and poetry from the earliest medieval texts up to the literary renaissance of the nineteenth century, and so to the present day.

CONCLUSION

Old Norse produced one of the major literatures of Europe, unusual in that it shows direct continuity of culture, history, and literature from prehistory to the present. It has direct associations, both of origin and input, with English literature, and its texts present solutions to many of the problems faced by modern English writers. The same must be said, for instance, of French, German, or Russian. Norse differs from these perhaps in degree, but also above all in an intimacy born of inheritance. Those who speak English are heirs of this literature, in the same way, if not to the same extent, as those who speak the modern Scandinavian languages. This literature is our own.

SELECTED BIBLIOGRAPHY

I. EDITIONS. Semi-scholarly reading editions of the Sagas of Icelanders and some Kings' Sagas, with full introductions and notes in modern Icelandic, are published by Íslensk fornrit, various editors (Reykjavík, 1933–). For a collected popular edition that contains many of the more important surviving sagas, see *Íslendingasagnaútgáfan,* 39 vols., ed. by Guðni Jónsson and Bjarni Vilhjálmsson (Reykjavík, 1946–1954). Scholarly editions of many texts have been produced in series of editions, various editors, under the auspices of Det arnamagnæanske institut, Copenhagen (*Bibliotheca Arnamagnæana*), Samfund til udgivelse af gammel nordisk litteratur, Copenhagen, and Stofnun Árna Magnússonar, Reykjavík.

II. TRANSLATIONS. Viðar Hreinsson, ed., *The Complete Sagas of Icelanders* (Reykjavík, 1997); see also the many excellent translations of Sagas of Icelanders and of *Snorra Edda* published in the *Everyman* series, various translators, and in Penguin Classics, translated by Hermann Pálsson and others.

III. BIBLIOGRAPHIES. Older material is cataloged in the early volumes of *Islandica* (Ithaca, N.Y., 1908–); see also the annual *Bibliography of Old Norse–Icelandic Studies* (Copenhagen, 1963). Ends in 1988 (with the volume for 1981–3).

IV. SECONDARY LITERATURE IN ENGLISH. Gabriel Turville-Petre, *Origins of Icelandic Literature* (Oxford, 1953) and *Scaldic Poetry* (Oxford, 1976); Roberta Frank, *Old Norse Court Poetry: The Dróttkvætt Stanza* (Ithaca, N.Y., 1978); Carol J. Clover and John Lindow, eds, *Old Norse–Icelandic Literature: A Critical Guide* (Ithaca, N.Y., 1985); Jónas Kristjánsson, *Eddas and Sagas*, trans. by Peter Foote (Reykjavík, 1988); Phillip Pulsiano and Kirsten Wolf, eds., *Medieval Scandinavia: an Encyclopedia* (New York, 1993); Vésteinn Ólason, *Dialogues with the Viking Age: Narration and Representation in the Sagas of the Icelanders*, trans. by Andrew Wawn (Reykjavík, 1998).

T. F. POWYS

(1875–1953)

Philip Hobsbaum

THE POWYS FAMILY descended from country gentlemen who had estates on the Welsh borders. Three generations of clergymen, latterly resident in the West Country of England, eventually gave rise to a generation of writers. The Reverend Littleton Powys married Maria Shaw, who died in 1833. Their son, the Reverend Littleton Charles Powys (1798–1871) married a wealthy widow, Amelia Knight. Their son, the Reverend Charles Francis Powys (1843–1923), married a collateral descendant of the poet William Cowper, Mary Johnson—herself a parson's daughter and granddaughter—and they produced eleven children: six boys and five girls. One of them, a daughter, died in childhood. The others mostly lived to old age and achieved a measure of distinction in their various pursuits.

The best known of these are John Cowper Powys (1872–1963), Theodore Francis Powys (1875–1953)—the subject of the present study—and Llewelyn Powys (1884–1939). All were writers and have been studied together, but in fact their work is quite distinct. John Cowper Powys was the author of massive allegorical romances, never using one word where five would do. Llewelyn Powys, chronically ill with tuberculosis through most of his life, produced travel books and autobiographical essays. These show an acute ear for language but lack a cohesive structure. It was the third brother, T. F. Powys, who composed the classic works of fiction *Mr. Weston's Good Wine* (1927) and *No Painted Plumage* (1934), together with a great number of other pieces, some thirty of which set him, along with his near contemporary D. H. Lawrence, among the finest English practitioners in the art of the short story.

The family was, to some extent, dysfunctional. Louis Wilkinson, a lifelong friend of T. F. Powys, refers to "the mental masochism of the mother" and the "repressed ferocity of the father" in his biographical study (written under the pseudonym Louis Marlow) *Welsh Ambassadors: Powys Lives and Letters* (p. 5). It was the mother who was the intellectual, a great reader during the period of quiet which she insisted upon at the end of each day after her arduous chores. The Reverend Charles Powys had been appointed vicar of Shirley in Derbyshire, and it was here that his five eldest children were born. However, on the death of his elder brother, he inherited a substantial fortune and decided to move back to his native West of England, where he eventually became vicar of the Somersetshire village of Montacute.

There, in an imposing house, T. F. Powys (born 20 December 1875) and his siblings grew up. He was sent, when he was ten and very much underage, to Dorchester Grammar School. However, he was a pupil there for only three terms, during which he mostly stayed at home, ill with jaundice. In 1886 he attended Sherborne Preparatory School for an additional three terms, but was off ill again, this time with measles. He appears to have been unhappy while in attendance there. Instead of progressing to Sherborne School itself, as two elder brothers had done, he arrived—considerably overage, as it happened—in 1890 at another preparatory school, Eaton House, Aldeburgh, Suffolk. This was conveniently near the vicarage of his maternal grandfather in Northwold and also that of an uncle who had taken over the parish of Powys's paternal grandfather at Yaxham. Though Powys seems to have been reasonably happy at Eaton House, he remained there only three and a half terms. His formal education ended in 1891. He was then fifteen. Unlike his elder brothers, he did not proceed to university.

Instead, after almost a year at home in Somerset, Powys returned to Suffolk and took up training to be a farmer. For two years he was apprenticed to a relative of his friend Louis Wilkinson at a farm near the village of Rendham. It has been suggested (by R. P. Graves) that he was in love with Wilkinson's sister Christobel, a refined young lady some four years his senior, who died of tuberculosis at the age of twenty-five, an event that may have confirmed a constituional melancholy. By 1895 he was renting a farm on his own account not far away, near Sweffling, where he helped to start a library. Though he took farmwork seriously and was especially interested in sheep rearing, he also read voraciously, chiefly the German mystic Jakob Böhme, the German philosopher Friedrich Nietzsche, the Romantic poet Percy Bysshe Shelley, and such English moralists as Robert Burton, Jeremy Taylor, Sir Thomas Browne, Richard Baxter, William Law, and John Wesley. Law's sharp-edged portraits may have affected him; certainly the pithy narrative of Wesley, to which he frequently refers, did. However, the most enduring influences upon him were, along with the Authorized Version of the Bible, the English writers John Bunyan and Jane Austen. An unpublished essay of this period recommends that we read the earthy details in Bunyan's *Pilgrim's Progress* (1678) in order to apprehend the mystic vision that shines through. This is a clue to appreciating Powys's own fiction.

The more he studied, the more he felt that the farming life was not for him. He decided to become a writer. To that end, he accepted a small allowance his father made him and was resident, first in Studland, the heart of Thomas Hardy's Dorset, and then in 1904, still in Dorset, at East Chaldon, where he settled. Here, in 1905, he married a local girl, Violet Dodds, a barely literate adopted daughter of a solicitor. In 1908 he borrowed enough money to buy the leasehold of a redbrick dwelling called the Nook. It was promptly renamed Beth Car, Hebrew for "the house in the pasture." This was the couple's home until 1940, when they moved to Mappowder, some twenty miles away. They had two sons: Theodore, known as Dickie, born in 1906, and Francis, born in 1909.

AN INTERPRETATION OF GENESIS AND SOLILOQUIES OF A HERMIT

T. F. Powys's apprenticeship as a writer was more difficult than that which he had undergone as a farmer. He was dealing with concepts more complex than those pertaining to cows and sheep. His work may be described as the effort of a man to understand "the moods of God." That is a phrase which echoes through an early work, *Soliloquies of a Hermit*, written in 1915 and published in 1918 (it was published in the United States two years earlier as *The Soliloquy of a Hermit*). It is a collection of essays, oddly similar to some of those by D. H. Lawrence, though that resemblance may be attributed to the common influence of Nietzsche upon both writers. Nietzsche's cult of power must have been at once exciting and disturbing to an introspective personality such as was Powys. One quite often comes across in the German philosopher what seem to be anachronistic—Powysian remarks. For example, "It was subtle of God to learn Greek when he wished to become an author—and not to learn it better" (*Beyond Good and Evil*).

However, that is Nietzsche as translated by Walter Kaufmann, and the copy of *Also Sprach Zarathustra* bought by Powys in 1898 had been translated by one Alexander Tille. Thus Kauffman has, "Some souls one will never discover, unless one invents them first," while Tille has, "Many a soul will never be discovered unless it be first invented." It is Tille rather than Kaufmann that shaped the style of the commentaries on the Old Testament that Powys wrote in 1905 and 1906, even before *Soliloquies of a Hermit*. Only one of these commentaries was given some kind of fugitive distribution, and that was in 1908. *An Interpretation of Genesis* (1929) is written in a breathless sub-biblical style derived from Tille, and is consequently difficult to read. The comment upon Gen. 6:22, "Thus did Noah; according to all that the Truth commanded him, so did he" runs as follows: "Man's death cometh when he ceaseth to live for the Truth. Many there are upon the earth that go about in full health of body and yet are dead. Many there are that have changed into dust and yet live" (p. 20–21). The gloss departs considerably from the original.

Powys's unpublished Old Testament commentaries are part of the Bissell Collection, housed in the Harry Ransom Humanities Research Center, at the University of Texas in Austin. Edward Bissell was a Warwickshire grocer who collected the manuscripts of many authors, especially those of the Powys brothers. Theodore's interpretations of the Bible contain many unexpected angles. For example, the comment on Gen. 41:39–40 denounces Joseph as having worked to enslave the men of Egypt. The jacket copy of another of Powys's early books announced the imminent publication of his commentary on the Book of Job, but this work has in fact never been issued. In the commentary, Powys declares that Job was right in cursing God, and further maintains that Job's reinstatement at the end of the book is an acceptance of falsehood; in short, a complacent selling out.

It is this ceaseless wrestling with the moods of God as evidenced in the Bible that forms the background of *Soliloquies of a Hermit.* This was first published in 1916 in the United States, where it received an enthusiastic notice from Powys's friend, Louis Wilkinson. He declared it—in contradistinction to the novel *Wood and Stone* (1915) by John Cowper Powys—a work of genius that would be read in a hundred years' time. Certainly, *Soliloquies of a Hermit* has its poignant moments, especially when the Nietzschean influence brings the sentiment of Powys near that of Lawrence, thus:

> God takes him up and casts him down, and pitches him from one mood into another, taking care that no mood lasts that the priest can live and feed upon.
> (*Soliloquies of a Hermit,* p. 5)

It is a fearful thing to fall into the hands of the living God. But it is a much more fearful thing to fall out of them.

> D. H. Lawrence, "The Hands of God,"
> in *Last Poems,* 1932

THEMES AND EARLY WRITING LIFE

The insistent moralizing of *An Interpretation of Genesis* and *Soliloquies of a Hermit* does not provide a framework of sustained interest. For all his interest in theology, Powys is no theologian. Instead, his search for a structure brought him closer and closer to that mode of fiction which was to be his peculiar medium.

Peculiar it certainly is. There is the use of a terrain that refers to a fictionalized Dorset but which certainly is not a realistic representation. Villages that the author names Dodder, Madder, or Sheldon may have their prototype in East Chaldon, but a process of refraction has taken place. People speak in stylized dialect and they are driven by strange obsessions. Yet sometimes these obsessions lead to truths not accessible by means of more orthodox methods. There is a mode of foreshortening, as of fable, that some readers may find hard to accommodate alongside their expectations. There is an irony which, though apparently limited, can vary in its extent of complexity and so place the reader at something of a disadvantage.

It is said that Powys's heterodoxies caused his mother considerable grief. He seems to have aspired to the simple faith of his clergyman father but never to have got there. Certainly he appears to have believed in God and also to have credited that God with ultimate benevolence. Yet he regarded the universe as gross and probably evil. The process of his fiction is a struggle to reconcile the evil of the universe with the goodness of its creator.

A complicating factor was what may be called an avid concern with pain. In an autobiographical fragment, "This Is Thyself," published posthumously in 1987 in *The Powys Review,* Powys described how, at the age of about five, he first saw blood. This happened while the young Powys watched a struggling cow being driven by two herdsmen; the cow ultimately smashed its head against a wall.

What is revealing about the fragment is the sensual excitement with which the adult Powys describes his reactions to this event as a child. The narrative is matched to some extent by a fairly late story called "The Hunted Beast," collected in *The White Paternoster*, in which a sedate clergyman finds himself flushed into a quasi-sexual sadism by three children torturing a rabbit. The images of animals under torture that intersperse Powys's various narratives almost to the extent that they become a kind of mannerism suggest a substratum inhibited by worldly retreat. He seems to have recognized impulses in himself which were decidedly antisocial. One near relative declared that Powys suffered from an endogenous depression. Certainly, Theodore Francis calculated his existence in such a way to spare himself the stresses of modern, urban life.

In the earlier years of the twentieth century Powys is described as a gloomy young man, wearing a heavy moustache resembling that of Nietzsche. Though he was a reasonable height—about five feet ten inches—his brothers, long men rather than big men, towered above him. They traveled and were extroverts—John Cowper Powys, indeed, earned his living as an itinerant lecturer—whereas Theodore Francis had withdrawn into a remote village and married an uneducated woman.

A racy description in a story called "God" (collected in *The Two Thieves,* 1932) seems to be based on Violet Powys and might give us some idea of what he saw in her. The girl in question is vivacious, earthy, in touch with the world. There can be little doubt that the thoroughly unliterary Violet's appetite for village gossip fueled her husband's stories, as did, no doubt, the anecdotes of rustic shortcomings retailed in the local newspaper. Like a lot of hermits, he was not as remote as he seemed. In the front room of his house, Beth Car, he wrote for two or three hours daily, drafting and redrafting in longhand. The finished work was put away in a cupboard, to be salvaged, some of it, as occasion served—sometimes at the request of editors in search of material. Yet gradually, as he struggled with the forms of fiction, he began to gather around him various admirers.

The first of these was a sculptor, Stephen Tomlin. He had discovered the village of East Chaldon in 1921, while on a walking tour. When he returned thither, he met Powys and was as much taken by his personality as by his fine head—by

now denuded of its walrus moustache—which he proceeded to portray. Tomlin sang the praises of his new acquaintance to various metropolitan friends. One result was that a letter for Powys arrived from a then little-known story writer, Sylvia Townsend Warner. Townsend Warner herself arrived a few months later. Another friend of Tomlin's was David Garnett, a story writer on the fringes of the influential Bloomsbury Group, who on his first visit to the sculptor was taken round to meet this remarkable neighbor. If Powys can be said to have had analogs, Townsend Warner and Garnett might be so termed. Both excelled at scenes of passion in deceptively pastoral settings. It seems that Garnett was instrumental in getting Powys into print, largely by means of introducing his work to Charles Prentice, an editor at (and later partner in) the established firm of Chatto and Windus. The firm stood by Powys, with certain qualifications, throughout his literary career.

CHARACTERIZATION AND STORYTELLING

The works of Powys were not published in the order in which they were written, and some were not published at all. It was not until 1967, well after Powys's death, that "Tadnol" appeared (in *Two Stories: "Come and Dine" and "Tadnol"*), even though it was written in 1915, a revision of an earlier, unpublished, novel, "Sheep's Clothing." "Tadnol" concerns a squire who in pursuing his own mysterious studies develops an interest in the bones of the dead. The narrative lacks the focus of later stories, the background being more interesting than the foreground. However, several characters are evinced therein which were to figure in various fictional contexts over a period of years.

There is Blacksmith James Croot, who may also be found in the novels *Kindness in a Corner* (1930) and *Mr. Weston's Good Wine*, and such stories as "The Lost Proofs," "King Pim," and "Adders' Brood" (in *The House with the Echo,* 1928), "Mr. Dottery's Trousers" (in *The White Paternoster,* 1930), *Uncle Dottery: A Christmas Story* (1930), "The Tithe Barn" (in *The Tithe Barn and The Dove and the Eagle,* 1932), "Only the Devil," and "The Atheist" (in *Three Short Stories,* 1971), and the novella *Feed My Swine* (1926). The characterization is consistently that of a gullible man, always wanting to be well thought of and sometimes putting himself unduly forward. Usually, as is the case with most of these serial characters, he is given a cameo role or even a mere walk-on part, but in "The Atheist" he is placed center stage and encouraged to make a complete fool of himself. Powys's view of God might have been heterodox, but he seems to have had no doubt of the deity's existence.

Another serial character is Farmer Spenke. He is usually presented as having a number of troublesome daughters, and like most of Powys's farmers is fat, gross, and lazy. He appears in *Kindness in a Corner*, and in the stories "Lady Louisa and the Wallflowers," "The Lost Proofs," "King Pim," "Adders' Brood," *The Left Leg* (1923), *Feed My Swine,* "Mr. Dottery's Trousers," "The Tithe Barn," "The Atheist," and "Circe Truggin" (in *Bottle's Path*, 1946).

There are other character recurrences from "Tadnol" onward, a seeming favorite of Powys's being the hero of "Circe Truggin," Sexton Truggin. He appears in two novels, one unpublished in Powys's lifetime, and in no less than fourteen stories. Mr Truggin is obsessed with the need to bury people, and in "No Room" (in *The House with the Echo,* 1928) he digs the final grave in a cemetery and occupies it himself. Nevertheless, he is on the whole a cheerful personality, knowing his own worth and physically a mirror image of his self-indulgent vicar, Mr. Dottery.

The latter makes an early appearance in "The Tithe Barn," written contemporaneously—about 1915—but not published until 1932, by an Indian admirer, K. S. Bhat and never republished thereafter. The vicar may seem to make fewer appearances than the indispensable Truggin, but nevertheless Dottery is a substantial figure and usually plays the lead. He can be found in one novel and ten stories, characteristically portrayed as a self-indulgent clergyman, eating epicurean dinners prepared by his housekeeper, Mrs. Taste, and writing a history of the kings and queens of England. Powys seems to feel that Dottery does no particular harm. In that respect, he is unlike

quite a number of Powys's clergymen, and perhaps occupies a role which, given a less sensitive conscience, Powys might have played himself.

A surprising number of the stories emanating from this period were relegated to the cupboard, and some were chewed by the mice which, in Violet's cat-ridden household, nevertheless seemed to abound. An early novel, *Mr. Tasker's Gods* (written in 1915–1916), had been considered for publication by the small firm of Andrew Melrose Ltd, which had issued the English edition of *Soliloquies of a Hermit* in 1918 and would go on to publish the sexually explicit *Open the Door!* by D. H. Lawrence's friend Catherine Carswell. However, it seems that *Mr. Tasker's Gods* was a deal too outspoken for Andrew Melrose.

Despite its striking title—Mr. Tasker's gods are his pigs—this novel is something of a mélange. Mr. Tasker, penurious dairyman, occupies only one of its strands of plot. The low adventures of the Reverend Hector Turnbull take up more space, and the proclivities of his two sons, one a fellow clergyman and the other a doctor, have also to be reckoned with. Contrasted with these specimens is the idealistic purity of a third son, Henry, who because the elders of the village consider him to be a threat to industrial relations, is eventually kicked to death. His only friend, a gentle parson, dies in the arms of a sister returned from missionary work in India. Thus the meek in spirit fail to inherit the earth.

Quite the most striking figure in the book is Mr. Tasker's father, who remains unnamed. He is—inexplicably, given the outward respectability of Mr. Tasker—a sturdy tramp who is hired to administer the fatal kicking that dispatches the innocent Henry. However, they that live by the boot shall certainly die a violent death. The tramp ends up being attacked by Mr. Tasker's dog and being mauled by Mr. Tasker's pigs.

There are seventy-three characters in this book, many of them connected with each other only tenuously. Two additional sections not included in the text as published have been discovered, but they do little more than add further items to the mélange. One fleshes out the story of the

Reverend Hector's son, the Reverend John Turnbull, together with that of his equally sensual friend, the Reverend Edward Lester. Another adds a story concerning Rose Netley, a social worker who, in coming to the aid of fallen women, figures as well in the main body of the text.

The book would maintain a degree of integrity whether this missing material were added in or not. It succeeds, if at all, by means of set pieces written with a kind of bright savagery. The Reverend Hector collapses with a heart attack consequent upon chasing round the bed in a low lodging-house a girl he has hired for sexual purposes. The tramp and a drover battle over another girl they have found wandering across a heath. Mr. Tasker himself is always good for a quip, the best one being his comment upon his family—"Too much livestock indoors." But *Mr. Tasker's Gods,* surprising though in many ways it is, would not rank in the first file of Powys's fiction.

David Garnett and Townsend Warner persuaded Chatto and Windus to bring out a group of three long stories in 1923 under the generic title of one of them, a novella or short novel, *The Left Leg.* Alfred Knopf published this group in the United States. It attracted a degree of critical attention. "Hester Dominy," the weakest of the stories, was written in 1918. It concerns the dilemma of a girl as to whether to live in the town or the country. "Abraham Men" was written in 1921 and concerns an idealistic young prophet, Luke Bird. He is similar to the ascetic Father Adam, protagonist of a story of that name, written at this time but not published until many years later. However, it is the title story of this collection that makes it memorable. It takes its name from a nursery rhyme that is the story's epigraph—"There I met an old man / Who would not say his prayers; / I took him by the left leg, / And threw him down the stairs." The old man in this story is Farmer Mew, who wishes to possess and even to devour the countryside and all who live in it. Here we are moving from fiction to allegory. Farmer Mew is opposed by the mythical figure of Tinker Jar, who figures in one novel and ten stories—some of the latter quite long ones. He is, though not the best, the most frequently used representation

in Powys of God wandering among his people on earth. In a plan to blow up the interfering tinker, Farmer Mew succeeds only in destroying himself. It is his left leg, detached from the rest of his anatomy, that falls from the sky, giving the story its title.

The moderate success of this collection of novellas ensured that *Mr. Tasker's Gods* was published in 1924, eight years after its completion, by Chatto and Windus in London and by Alfred Knopf in the United States. It was immediately preceded in 1923 by *Black Bryony,* a novel that had been written in 1917 and that concerned an unluckily adopted baby, and was succeeded by one of the best of these minor novels, *Mark Only,* written in 1922 and published in 1924.

It is in some ways more dispersed than *Mr. Tasker's Gods,* having eighty-seven characters and portraying the little world of Dodderdown. But it is dominated by the figure of Mark Only, so called because his father was insistent that "Mark" alone with no addition should be his Christian name. He is usually seen at a distance and on high, plowing among the hills that overlook the village where abide the folks that plot against him, designing to swindle him out of his inheritance and his future bride. He is not a good plowman—his eyesight is going—but he is engaged to be married to Nellie Holland, who finds his uncouth ways preferable to the silence of his insinuating brother James and to the blandishments of an interloper in the village, Gentleman Charlie Tulk.

Powys being Powys, the good and the meek come to grief. It may be argued that so do some of their persecutors—Gentleman Tulk is found hanging in a barn, victim of a drunken accident—but not before they have had a wantonly cheerful time in the world. One of the persistent images in this strange book is that of a pack of pursuing hounds that betoken death. It is said that Powys had an aversion to dogs and once hid from a bunch of terriers kept by his neighbor, Mrs Ashburnham. She seems to have been the prototype of Miss Pettifer, who figures in three novels and five stories, always in admonitory postures. A clue as to her original identity is given in the fact that at one time she is married to a bishop called Ashbourne.

Immediate successors to this novel are comparatively slight. *Mockery Gap,* written in 1923 and published two years later, is really a collocation of short stories, and indeed three of the better chapters—"An Ugly Thing," "The White Mice," and "Silent Bells"—are based on a story, "The Beautiful Sea" (written in the early 1920s and collected in *Rosie Plum and Other Stories,* 1966). It was a peculiarity of East Chaldon, where Powys lived, that, while it is near the sea, it is not in fact on the coast. A central character in this story is Mrs. Moggs, who appears in one other novel and in eight other stories, usually keeping a shop. Though only half a mile from the shore, she has never been there. While occupied in keeping her shop (which is also the post office) neat, she lives in dread of being found in default with respect to stamps and postal orders. When a defalcation takes place through no fault of her own, she decides at last to go to the sea and, as told in the novel, she steps into it and is drowned.

This is only one of several strands of plot. What holds them together is the advent in this quiet place of a strange fisherman, called by the children "the Nellie-bird." He is more remote even than Mark Only, on one special occasion accorded the privilege of direct speech, and he appears to be an instance in Powys of supernatural manifestation. In this case, his freedom sets him apart from the machinations of the villagers, and he could be taken to be a representation of Jesus Christ. His presence redeems some of them for a time, but when he is gone they resume their former bickering.

Innocent Birds, written at much the same time and published a year later, in 1926, is based on a short story, "In from Spain" (collected in *Rosie Plum and Other Stories*). It concerns a young man, Fred, who is thought to be making his fortune abroad but, when at length returned as a tattered tramp, is not recognized. The expansion of this story into a novel involves an unfurling of narrative over eighty thousand words and something like 156 characters, hinting at the inter-

relationships of a village as it develops. Gradually the conflict emerges between the two young lovers—Fred and Polly, the girl Fred left behind—and the wicked landlord, Mr. Bugby. The bird that hunts this violent lecher to his death seems to be related to the cormorant, Satan in disguise, that sits on the Tree of Life in Milton's *Paradise Lost*. It wheels and flaps its way through half a dozen sightings, until it takes the soul of Mr. Bugby to consort with the damned.

The Market Bell is almost exactly contemporaneous in composition but not published in Powys's lifetime (it appeared in 1991). It is even longer—perhaps a hundred thousand words—and much more inconsequential, with as many as 180 characters. Though there is a central figure, the evil Edward Glen, his story is much interrupted by the cavortings of more colorful personalities. These include the gentle Shepherd Poose, an alter ego of Powys's who appears in a dozen stories, and an especial favorite, Lord Bullman, who hunts and drinks hard in *Mr. Tasker's Gods*, "Yellowskin," "The Unbidden Guest," "The Kingfisher," "The Wrong Name," "The Wine Fed Tree" (in *Rosie Plum and Other Stories*), among other stories and novels, and also the unspeakable Farmer Lord, of "A Papered Parlour," "Rosie Plum," "The Devil and the Good Deed" (in *Rosie Plum and Other Stories*), "Two Chairs," and "The Mother of the World" (the latter two collected in *Mock's Curse: Nineteen Stories,* 1995), who in Chapter 38 is seen attempting to rape a girl he has just purchased at Stonebridge Market.

Powys's art, then, is essentially that of the short story, and certainly some of those mentioned above could be seen as his accredited masterpieces. "A Papered Parlour," for instance, tells of a grotesque domestic situation in which a new wife is not allowed to hang the wallpaper she has destined for her parlor, or indeed to do anything else about the house. The husband, a rabbit catcher, subjects her to his enormous lusts and even offers her to his best friend, the sexton. The unhappy wife papers a grave, induces the sexton to lie in it—never to emerge—and shoots her husband while he is returning home with a sack of rabbits.

This story appears in the posthumous collection *Rosie Plum and Other Stories*. Others, dating most probably from the same period, 1924–1928, remained in manuscript until they were at length collected by Elaine and Barrie Mencher of Brynmill Press under the generic title *Mock's Curse*. That was in 1995, and it remains hard to believe that a story of the quality of, say, "Two Chairs," might never, but for these editors' application, have seen the light of day.

In this story, a man sets out two parlor chairs on a hill in order to convince his friend, an atheist, of the existence of miracles. Since a miracle is, by his friend's definition, something that never happens, the surprise appearance of two domestic chairs outside will demonstrate his case. Subsequently, his house is struck by lightning and burnt down, but he refuses to believe that his wife was within at the time—though she was—and sets off on his travels to find her. In the end, he returns fruitlessly, a tired old man, and sits down on one of the chairs, while she, incredibly occupies the other, dressed as when he first set off, as though she were still alive. His atheist friend, now dying, sees from his bedroom window the old couple sitting hand in hand and side by side, and sighs thankfully, recognizing the miracle.

Powys's stories are emphatically unlike anyone else's. "The Mother of the World," also published posthumously in *Mock's Curse,* speaks about a subject concerning which Powys could be seen as the acknowledged master: bereavement. John Topp, who bears the name of a character figuring in eight other stories, has lost his wife and devotes himself to his cow. The cow appears to mourn for her mistress, and diminishes in scale as the presence of Mrs. Topp is felt more and more substantially. The story ends with all three of them journeying up a lane that leads into the sky.

MR. WESTON'S GOOD WINE

Such stories as "Two Chairs" and "The Mother of the World" tend, it would seem inevitably, to the greatest height Powys was to reach, his novel *Mr. Weston's Good Wine,* a work of the mid-1920s. The range of prose in this novel is extraordinary. It begins, in accordance with its title—a quotation from Jane Austen's *Emma*—with a scene whose cadences echo those of that author.

> A Ford car, of a type that is commonly used in England to deliver goods in rural districts, stood, at half-past three in the afternoon, before the Rod and Lion Hotel at Maidenbridge upon the 20th November 1923.
>
> The town was settled, as was its wont at this time of the year, into its usual autumn sleep that wasn't in the least likely to be disturbed by the arrival in its midst of so common a thing as a tradesman's automobile.
>
> (p. 1)

Yet this apparently matter-of-fact language is an element in a fabric designed to deliver one of the most peculiar messages in English literature. The van belongs to God, who is visiting this quarter of the West Country in the guise of an elderly wine merchant, to see how his people are getting on. He is accompanied by an archangel, a tall and handsome young man named Michael. The real destination is not the town of Maidenbridge but, more remotely, the village of Folly Down.

As with previous novels, the narrative proceeds through the accretion of character. Here, however, accretion is more like development. The characters, it is true, have their own specific stories, but there is more of a meaningful connection between them. The people of Folly Down believe that all evil doings in the parish may be laid at the door of the ugly and deaf sexton, Mr. Grunter, who in a prior suicide attempt, declares of himself that he is nothing. The landlord of the Angel Inn, Mr. Bunce, alone is convinced that God is responsible. Mr. Bunce is also the father of the handsome and sensual Jenny, who is desired by the unworldly preacher, Luke Bird; Bird figures as a kind of holy fool in the earlier stories "Ducky" and "Abraham Men." Jenny Bunce is further linked to the narrative by being maid to the daughter of the Reverend Nicholas Grobe, Tamar, who wishes to be enamored of an angel.

In fact, the narrative develops in terms of its characters' desires. Mr. Vosper, husband of the village procuress, believes that, on the right evening, he might meet God at the village inn. Squire Mumby is at the inn for the purpose of swindling the cattle dealer, Mr. Kiddle, out of a fine calf. Mr. Meek, a shopkeeper, is there to absorb as much warmth from the fire as he can. The landlord resents his clock, because it dallies during the day and races at night. However, on this particular evening, shortly after the entrance of Mr. Grunter, time stops and, as Grunter himself remarks, eternity begins. The characters and all their stories are linked by the presence of Mr. Weston.

None of these people has any apprehension as to who Mr. Weston is. They only know that he seems familiar. He may be a lost brother who got a village girl pregnant; a distant cousin generous in buying drink; an uncle who once bought a secondhand cross for his own grave; a father now resident in heaven. All these semblances carry quaint allusions to the Bible. Though each customer at the inn is under the impression that he knows Mr. Weston, only Mr. Grunter dares to identify the wine merchant to his face. He at first gets it wrong when he calls him "brother-in-law," but there is a moment, much later on in the book, when Mr. Grunter gets it right. The incident takes place inside the village church.

> "And who be thee to command folk?" asked the clerk.
>
> Mr. Weston uncovered his head and looked at him. Until that moment he had kept on his hat.
>
> "Who be thee?" asked Mr. Grunter, in a lower tone. . . .
>
> "I know thee now," said Mr. Grunter.
>
> "Then tell no man," said Mr. Weston.
>
> (pp. 262–263)

Nothing is omitted from this brief quotation; the ellipsis dividing the second and third remarks of Mr. Grunter is that of the author.

Throughout the book, Mr. Weston (a short tubby man with a mane of hair like white wool) is, for the most part, genial. However, there is with him the implication of power held in abeyance; that of a spiritual Pickwick. He has two brands of wine to sell: the light wine of love and the dark wine of death. Landlord Bunce has asked of the teetotaler Luke Bird an impossible dowry

for his daughter: that the well from which Luke drinks be filled with wine. Not only does Mr. Weston fill it thus, but Luke of necessity must drink from it.

Taken as a realistic novel, its prose is deployed with remarkable power. Perhaps especially behind it is that of Jeremy Taylor, an author of the seventeenth century who had more ways of speaking about death than any of his successors, save only T. F. Powys himself. Taylor wrote in a 1650 work, "Funeral Sermon for Lady Carbury," "No man is surer of tomorrow than the weakest of his brethren; and when Lepidus and Aufidius stumbled at the threshold of the Senate and fell down and died, the blow came from heaven in a cloud, but it struck more suddenly than upon the poor slave that made sport upon the Theatre with a premeditated and foredescribed death." Powys represents the Reverend Nicholas Grobe as an ordinary man, who lost his faith after his lovely young wife was killed. Powys writes, "Death is a great master among the artists; though he can be so common and vulgar as to kill everyone, yet he can give each experiment of his such a new colour that, seen by a husband or wife or brother who survives, the blow falls so heavily as to be regarded as utterly unnatural" (p. 104). This is beautifully tuned prose. The very deliberation with which each exquisite brand of pain is recorded carries its own overtone of irony.

> For the Reverend Mr. Grobe there is no future. He is totally without hope.
>
> Upon such an evening, when the right silence reigns, Mr. Grobe's melancholy feeds upon itself; his sorrow lingers and hovers in the dark corners of the room that are away from the light. Mr. Grobe feels then his loss, if such an evening be but long enough, as something that can almost be kind and loving to him. . . . The glorious summer, the hot noon of all the seasons, only dooms his steps to falter; and the harvest saddens him, for that season shows how all things, even a green blade of corn, tend to their end. It is only a long autumn evening that can soothe Mr. Grobe's soul.
>
> (p. 43)

The fathers of the Church represented hell as a sense of infinite loss. Into Grobe's dull life a bright passage intervened, in which he knew sensual joy with his wife. That passage being blocked, he has lost all faith, and Powys shows how he sees this loss as the most terrible thing that could have happened. The clergyman goes through the motions of life, but he is no longer a responsive person. Therefore he is designated a candidate for Mr. Weston's dark wine, the wine of death which is, by implication, the wine of oblivion.

A good many people are judged in Folly Down. Some, like the procuress Mrs. Vosper, are deemed to be beyond redemption. A strange beast drags her down to hell. Squire Mumby's sons are confronted with the mangled and rotting body of a girl they raped. One is terrified into a degree of virtue, the other into imbecility. Luke Bird gains his Jenny Bunce at the cost of entering the ordinary material world. Jenny's employer, Tamara, gains her wish. She is possessed by an angel and transported out of this life and into the skies. Mr. Weston finally vanishes in a cloud of flame that turns into a pillar of smoke.

The novel uses elements of naturalism much as parables do. The characters are emblematic of sins and obsessions at once drawn from reality and tending beyond it. The book, but for its basic good humor, might be called a sermon by example. Certainly it embodies Powys's reading of the paradox that a merciful God can inhabit a malign universe. His own life could have been rendered more simple had he refused to believe in God at all. But in such a case we should not have had the peculiar working out of this paradox in his fiction.

NO PAINTED PLUMAGE

Powys has been treated largely as a novelist but, despite *Mr Weston's Good Wine*, it makes a degree of sense to term him essentially a short story writer. Alongside the great novel, *Mr. Weston's Good Wine,* stands an interconnected book of stories first published as *Fables* in 1929 and republished in 1934 as *No Painted Plumage,* the title under which it is best known today. The narrative appears to have been planned as a cohesive work. Unlike the items in other books of short stories, none of these was published beforehand in a magazine, whereas the stories written between 1918 and 1927, and figuring in *The House with the Echo,* first appeared individually in such periodicals as *The New Leader*—whose editor H. N. Brailsford was a friend of David Garnett's parents—and *The Nation and Athenaeum.* Among them were such effective fictions as "The Lonely Lady," "Thy Beautiful Flock," and "No Room"—this last already mentioned in connection with Sexton Truggin.

Also mentioned herein is the plentiful range of characters that Powys laid out in his fiction. There are 218 in *Mr. Weston's Good Wine,* but the number is bound to remain approximate because in some cases, including that of a group of bears—familiarly referred to—who devoured some naughty children, the numbers are indeterminate. In many instances—there is the rat on Mr. Grobe's hearth rug and the centipede at Mrs. Vosper's—they are, while quite individual, not of the human species. This tendency to include nonhumans in his cast, extending even to humble herbs and roots, grew in Powys's fiction over the years.

When he declared himself devoid of inspiration, it is said that his brother Llewelyn suggested that Powys write about common objects, such as a log of wood or an old boot. This would be very much in the tradition of his collateral ancestor, William Cowper, who began a major poem by singing of a sofa. In Powys's hands, this produces a curiously terse ironic effect, as in the following example:

> A bucket once lay upon its side in a little shed, that was a short way down a by-lane, near to the village of Shelton. This bucket, a large one, had been kicked over by a man who had hanged himself up by the neck, by means of an odd piece of rope that he had tied to a strong beam.
>
> The man's name who had hanged himself was Mr. Dendy, who rented a few pleasant fields that he used to plough happily, and, besides keeping a few good cows, he fattened some nice pigs. . .
>
> (p. 137)

The matter-of-factness of this prose is instantly contradicted by the fact the bucket and the rope in effect narrate the story, and in any case promptly start up a conversation:

"Is it not a little curious, if not altogether surprising," observed the bucket, "that we should have been put to so sad a use in helping our good master to die? Perhaps you can remember as well as I the joyful day when we were first purchased, which happened to be the very day before Mr. Dendy was married".

"He married, as you know, a woman, a creature created to ease a man of the heavy burden of desire, a burden as troublesome to carry as a kicking ass."

"And who also," observed the rope, "was intended to cook and prepare a man's food, to rear his children and to clean his house . . ."

(pp. 138–139)

The reader is made to suspend his or her disbelief and accept that inanimate objects can converse like rational beings. The story from which the above passages are taken, "The Bucket and the Rope" (in *No Painted Plumage*), is a disquisition upon marriage. Powys believed that one should marry for love, and was quoted as saying that, in a loveless marriage, all that grows is the cuckold's horns. Poor Mr. Dendy finds out that his wife is betraying him with her old flame, and his suicide is the result. The bucket and rope, not being human themselves, fail to understand his motivation, but the quality of their discourse enables it to be understood by the reader.

This form of irony suffuses *No Painted Plumage*. Perhaps the most audacious item is "Mr. Pim and the Holy Crumb." This story concerns the skepticism of a church clerk with respect to the clergyman's belief that the Lord God, in the clerk's Dorset parlance, "do change 'Isself into they scrimpy bites of Mr. Johnson's bread that thee do take and eat up at church railings." While seeking to take Holy Communion, Mr. Pim drops a crumb on the church carpet and is accordingly addressed by it. Offered salvation and resurrection, he avers he would rather lie quietly by the side of his friend John Toole, who hanged himself. The Host is distressed by this and wishes he had entered a mouse rather than a man. He has his wish when a veritable church mouse creeps out from under the altar and devours what is left of the holy crumb.

In this down-to-earth way, Powys disposes of the difficult concept of impanation and, in pass-

ing, of the afterlife. His obsession with sextons and graves suggests that he had some notion of immortality as being a quiet crumbling into dust beneath the soil.

No Painted Plumage should be read as a whole. However, stories such as "The Dog and the Lantern," "The Corpse and the Flea," and "The Hassock and the Psalter"—comedy to the near-tragedy of *Mr. Weston's Good Wine*—can be read to considerable effect as detached examples of Powys's ironic art.

THE NOVELLAS

Several of Powys's novellas—published separately—are half in and half out of the stylized fabulation that is the essence of *No Painted Plumage*. Among these are *Feed My Swine, What Lack I Yet?* (1927), *Christ in the Cupboard* (1930), *The Key of the Field* (1930), *Uriah on the Hill* (1930), *The Only Penitent* (1931), *Make Thyself Many* (1935), and *Goat Green; or, The Better Gift* (1937). These were written, so far as can be told, between 1925 and 1931, and, for the aficionado, may represent the consummation of Powys's art outside the two acknowledged masterpieces.

The best-known items of this group were published by Chatto and Windus under the generic title of *The Two Thieves* in 1932. The title story is an attempt to represent extreme sinfulness, but its energetic attempts in that direction are crude by comparison with the suave approach of a story from 1932, "A Suet Pudding." This is included in *Bottle's Path and Other Stories* (1946), Powys's fifth collection, and is a representation of domestic sadism that takes almost to the limit what a reader can be expected to bear.

Unlike the short stories, the novellas are comparatively little known. *Uriah on the Hill* and *Make Thyself Many*—both issued by small presses—have never been reprinted and were not included in any of Powys's collections. Such items, however, represent a great range of expression, even within an individual text.

The Only Penitent, for example, shows an aspect of Powys that has as yet been too little emphasized: that of the humorist. Mr. Hayhoe, vicar of Maids Madder, has decided to open a confessional booth. Joe White's father, a man with a rough beard and a strong hand for a spade, stops Mr. Bunny on his way to the inn, to observe in an extremely melancholy tone his belief that he has done something very ill. Mr. White, it turns out, has forgotten to dung the ground in which his spring onions were planted, causing them to come up very poor. Mr. Bunny is appalled by this dereliction and suggests to Mr. White that he find some excuse to offer the good clergyman—he asks Mr. White if there isn't "anything that mid save thee from the wrath of God."

> "I fear that I can think of nothing," answered Mr. White, rubbing his head in great perplexity, "unless to say that I were drunk every night for a fortnight before I sowed they unlucky seeds, and did go each of they nights out into farmer's meadow with Mrs. Wicks."
>
> "T'wouldn't do to take thik silly tale to church," observed Mr. Bunny, "for God would only make sport of 'ee for telling en."
>
> "Then I be damned," said Mr. White sadly.
>
> (pp. 125–126)

The joke here is that Mr. White has been guilty of what would be thought far greater sins than denying nourishment to his spring onions, but is unconscious that these sins are, in fact, greater—a lack of consciousness shared by his friend, Mr. Bunny. Mr. White therefore does not go to confession and, in fact, the only person who does—other than the blameless wife of the vicar—is Tinker Jar, a character Powys typically used as a simulacrum of God. What God confesses is indeed terrible:

> "I crucified my son," he said. Mr. Hayhoe was silent. "'Twas I who created every terror in the earth, the rack, the plague, all despair, all torment. . . .
>
> I destroy all men with a sword," said Jar. "I cast them down into the pit, they become nothing."
>
> (p. 138)

This last sin becomes his salvation. Mr. Hayhoe is able to forgive God, to confirm Him and strengthen Him in all goodness, and in an astonishing reversal, "Bring [him] to everlasting death" (p. 139). Because God brought death, that ultimate release, into the world He is to be allowed to partake of this dispensation himself. So the story ranges, from rustic comedy to sublimity, and it is only one of the masterpieces that occur towards the end of Powys's writing life.

LATER LIFE AND THE ABANDONMENT OF FICTION

After *Mr. Weston's Good Wine* and *No Painted Plumage,* Powys was beginning to write himself out. Novellas such as *Uriah on the Hill* repeat the gestures of earlier works: Uriah Topp has all too much in common with the character Mark Only. The feeling in these late works is that Powys has said it all before. Neither of the two last novels can be called a success. Nothing much happens in *Kindness in a Corner,* written in 1928–1929 and published in 1930. The central figure, Mr. Dottery, easily disperses the calumnies of his enemies, the Reverend Mr. Dibben and the former Miss Pettifer, who have preposterously declared that he keeps a girl for his pleasure in the study cupboard. "In this corner where I live," he sighs, "I have tried to be kind" (p. 55). The book contains some distinguished writing, chiefly in a chapter called "The Dirt of God," concerning Sexton Truggin and his dealings with the moribund Mr. and Mrs. Turtle. However, this would be better read as an independent short story.

With the last novel to be completed, *Unclay* (1931), the failure is more insidious. The central figure, a representation of death, is gray and withdrawn, as opposed to the exuberant Mr. Weston, and the novel is correspondingly less colorful. It is possible to argue that death is more effectively represented in less central manifestations, such as those in the earlier novels *Mockery Gap* and *Innocent Birds,* or such stories as "The Kingdom of Heaven," (in *Mock's Curse*), "Archdeacon Truggin," (in *The White Paternoster*), and "The Midnight Hour" (in *Three Short Stories*). In any case, Powys was well aware that his apogee as a writer had been reached, and quite deliberately retired from the fray. In an interview with Claude F. Luke published in *John O'London's Weekly* (3 October 1936), he stated, "I have abandoned writing . . . because I felt spiritually urged to do so. . . . It is simply that I have reached a state of doubt and an inclination to do other things."

Though Powys attempted to avoid the stresses of life, much happened around him. The intimacies of his younger brother, Llewelyn—who stayed for a time in East Chaldon—in themselves provided a series of contingent dramas. Some of these concerned Powys's role at the epicenter of two intersecting sets of triangular relationships. One set involved Llewelyn, his wife Alyse Gregory, and his lover who was the American poet Gamel Woolsey, half-sister of the judge who decriminalized James Joyce's *Ulysses*. Another involved Gerald Brenan, a writer on the outskirts of the Bloomsbury Group, who had come to visit Powys and with whom Gamel Woolsey fell in love, forsaking Llewelyn for him and going to live in Spain. There was also the complex situation of Sylvia Townsend Warner, Powys's close friend and neighbor, who underwent a sometimes stormy partnership with Valentine (née Mary or Molly) Ackland—with whom both of Powys's sons at one time or another fancied themselves in love—and who, in her turn, for a time was in love with a visiting American, Elizabeth Wade White. The one time Powys is known to have visited London was to see his elder son off to Africa where, in 1931, Dickie died violently, believed to have been attacked by lions. Almost concurrently, the young woman who was to become his younger son Francis's wife, Sally Upfield, became pregnant. Her lover, Count Potocki of Montalk, a colorful man of letters, had been put in jail on a trumped-up charge of obscene publication. At a meeting of his friends to raise money for an appeal against this sentence, Sally Upfield met Francis Powys and fell in love with him. At the same time, her pregnancy brought about dismissal from her job at the General Post Office. She went back to her father, a headmaster in Dorset, who placed her in a home for fallen women. She eventually left this institution, and was looked after by a friend until the child was born. Meanwhile, Francis had retired

to his parents' home in East Chaldon; he was suffering from what was suspected to be tuberculosis. This was a false alarm. He lived until 1988, when he died following a paralytic stroke. In any case, he rejected the child, who was adopted by the elder Powyses, presumably in the belief that Francis was her natural father. The truth seems to have come out some years later.

Theodora, as the child was named, wrote an affectionate memoir of her adopted father, published in the early 1980s in *The Powys Review* under her married name, Theodora Gay Scutt in an extended version, as *Cuckoo in the Powys Nest* (2000), and an unaffectionate memoir of her natural father, under the name Theodora Gay Potocka, as *Potocki: A Dorset Worthy?* (1983). Theodora never seems to have got on with her adopted mother, Violet, but summoned Count Potocki, then resident in Provence, to Dorset to help their finances in the aftermath of T. F. Powys's death. This event took place on the 26th of November 1953, by which time Powys had long since ceased writing. He had suffered a paralytic stroke in 1937 and another, more severe one, in 1940. Because of army activity around East Chaldon, in this latter year the family moved further inland to Mappowder. There Powys struck up a friendship with the local vicar, the Reverend Samuel Jackson. He often attended compline, the last of the seven canonical hours of divine service. He and the vicar were usually the only worshipers present. We may picture the two grizzled heads in the deserted church as the sun declines, giving the true bass note to the colors of the evening, expressing the loveliness of a final peace with God. Powys was separated by no more than a stone wall from the graveyard in which he frequently meditated, getting to know the names of the inhabitants therein. This echoes the positive that seems to underpin his work, that expressed by old John Toole in one of Powys's most memorable stories, "Mr Pim and the Holy Crumb." He says, "I be well content to bide where I be now. There baint no work to do here and all be ease and comfort, and many a merry story do we bones tell together" (*No Painted Plumage* p. 20). Toole is dead, and long dead, like several of Powys's more memorable characters—Aunt Crocker (*Innocent Birds*) and Auctioneer Pratt (*The Market Bell*)—or, like Old Barker, evoked as a constant with reference to cemeteries, as in "The Lonely Lady," "No Room," "The Stone and Mr. Thomas" (in *No Painted Plumage*), and "Godfather Dottery" (in *Captain Patch*). Mr. Weston himself longs to drink the dark wine of dissolution. It seems that only in the grave can T. F. Powys, hymnodist of bereavement, see no shadow of another parting.

SELECTED BIBLIOGRAPHY

I. COLLECTED WORKS. *The White Paternoster and Other Stories,* includes *Feed My Swine, The Bride, The Rival Pastors, What Lack I Yet?, Christ in the Cupboard,* and "The Two Horns" (London, 1930); *Bottle's Path and Other Stories,* includes *The Key of the Field, When Thou Wast Naked, The Only Penitent, The Dove and the Eagle, The Better Gift* (aka *Goat Green*), and *The Dewpond* (London and Toronto, 1946); Charles Prentice, ed., *God's Eyes a-Twinkle: An Anthology of the Stories of T. F. Powys,* comprising selections from *The Left Leg, The House with the Echo, No Painted Plumage, The White Paternoster, Captain Patch,* and *Bottle's Path* (London and Toronto, 1947).

II. NOVELS. *Black Bryony* (London and New York, 1923); *Mark Only* (London and New York, 1924); *Mr. Tasker's Gods* (London and New York, 1925); *Mockery Gap* (London and New York, 1925); *Innocent Birds* (London and New York, 1926); *Mr. Weston's Good Wine* (London and New York, 1927); *Kindness in a Corner* (London and New York, 1930). *Unclay* (London and New York, 1931); Ian Robinson and Elaine Mencher, eds., *The Market Bell,* written 1924 (Gringley-on-the-Hill, Yorkshire, 1991; afterword by J. Lawrence Mitchell).

III. SHORT STORIES AND NOVELLAS. *The Left Leg,* includes title novella and short stories "Hester Dominy" and "Abraham Men" (London and New York, 1923); *A Strong Girl and The Bride: Two Stories* (London, 1926; *The Bride* collected in *The White Paternoster*); *Feed My Swine* (London, 1926; collected in *The White Paternoster*); *A Stubborn Tree,* sequel to "The Two Horns" in *The House with the Echo* (London, 1926); *What Lack I Yet?* (London and San Francisco, 1927; collected in *The White Paternoster*); *The Rival Pastors* (London, 1927; collected in *The White Paternoster*); *The House with the Echo* (London and New York, 1928); *The Dewpond: A Story* (London, 1928; collected in *Bottle's Path*); *Fables* (London and New York, 1929; repub. as *No Painted Plumage,* London, 1934); *Christ in the Cupboard* (London, 1930; collected in *The White Paternoster*); *The Key of the Field,* foreword by Sylvia Townsend Warner (London, 1930; collected in *Bottle's Path*); *Uncle Dottery: A Christmas Story* (Bristol, England, 1930); *Uriah on the Hill* (Cambridge, 1930); *The Only Penitent* (London, 1931; collected in *Bottle's Path*); *When Thou Wast Naked* (Waltham St. Lawrence, Reading, Berks, 1931; collected in *Bottle's Path*); *The Tithe Barn and The Dove and

the Eagle* (London. 1932; "The Dove and the Eagle" collected in *Bottle's Path*); *The Two Thieves,* includes title story, "God," and "In Good Earth" (London and New York, 1932; stories reprinted in *The Sixpenny Strumpet*); *Captain Patch: Twenty-one Stories* (London, 1935); *Make Thyself Many* (London, 1935); *Goat Green; or, The Better Gift* (London, 1937; collected under title *The Better Gift* in *Bottle's Path*); *Rosie Plum and Other Stories,* probably written c. 1923–1924, ed. by Francis Powys (London, 1966); *Two Stories: "Come and Dine" and "Tadnol,"* "Come and Dine" written 1931, "Tadnol," a reworking of an unpublished novel, "Sheep's Clothing," written 1915, ed. by Peter Riley (Hastings: R. A. Brimmell, 1967); *Three Short Stories,* includes "The Midnight Hour," first published in *Everyman,* 23 February 1934, "Emily Vine," and "The Atheist" (Loughton, 1971); *Father Adam,* written 1919, ed. by Ian Robinson (Gringley-on-the-Hill, Yorkshire, 1990); *Mock's Curse: Nineteen Stories,* mostly perhaps written c. 1924–1928, ed. by Elaine and Barrie Mencher (Denton, Norfolk, 1995); *The Sixpenny Strumpet,* title story written 1930, also includes "In Good Earth," "God," and "The Two Thieves," ed. by Ian Robinson and Elaine Mencher, textual history by J. Lawrence Mitchell (Denton, Norfolk, 1997).

IV. OTHER WORKS. *An Interpretation of Genesis* (privately printed 1908; rep. London and New York, 1929); *The Soliloquy of a Hermit* (New York, 1916), repub. as *Soliloquies of a Hermit* (London, 1918; rep. London, 1929); "This is Thyself," intoduced and annotated by J. Lawrence Mitchell, *The Powys Review* 20 (1987).

V. BIBLIOGRAPHIES P. H. Muir and B. van Thal, eds., *Bibliographies of the First Editions of Books by Aldous Huxley and by T. F. Powys* (London, 1927); Peter Riley, *A Bibliography of T. F. Powys* (Hastings, 1967); Francis Feather, "From Type Design to T. F. Powys: Metamorphosis of a Book Collector," *Powys Journal* 3 (1993); "The Bissell Collection," with an introduction by Peter J. Foss, *Powys Journal* 4 (1994).

VI. BIOGRAPHICAL STUDIES. Llewelyn Powys, *Skin for Skin* (London, 1926); John Cowper Powys, *Autobiography* (London and New York, 1934); Louis Marlow (pseud.), *Welsh Ambassadors: Powys Lives and Letters* (London, 1936); Louis Marlow (pseud.), *Seven Friends: Oscar Wilde, Frank Harris, Aleister Crowley, John Cowper Powys, T. F. Powys, Llewelyn Powys, William Somerset Maugham* (London, 1953); R. C. Churchill, *The Powys Brothers* (London, 1962); David Garnett, *The Familiar Faces: Being Volume Three of The Golden Echo* (London, 1962); Kenneth Hopkins, *The Powys Brothers: A Biographical Appreciation* (London and Rutherford, N.J., 1967); Count Potocki of Montalk, *Dogs' Eggs: A Study in Powysology,* Part One (Draguignan, 1972); Count Potocki of Montalk, *Dogs' Eggs: A Study in Powysology,* Part Two (Draguignan, 1971); Peter Riley, "T. F. Powys at Mappowder: A Consideration of His Fiction in the Light of the Final Twenty Years of Nonwriting," *Powys Review* 3 (summer 1978); Llewelyn Powys, "Conversations with Theodore Powys, Summer 1931," *Powys Review* 4 (winter/spring 1978–1979); Belinda Humfrey, ed., *Recollections of the Powys Brothers: Llewelyn, Theodore, and John Cowper* (London, 1980); R. T. Risk, *Why Potocki?* (Francestown, N.H., 1981); Theodora Scutt, "Theodore Powys, 1934–1953," *Powys Review* 9 (1981–1982); Theodora Scutt, "Theodore Powys, 1934–1953: A Continuation," *Powys Review*

10 (spring 1982); Richard Percival Graves, *The Brothers Powys* (London and New York, 1983); Theodora Gay Potocka (aka Scutt), *Potocki: A Dorset Worthy?* (Francestown, N H , 1983); J Lawrence Mitchell, "The Education of T. F. Powys," *Powys Review* 19 (1986); Wendy Mulford, *This Narrow Place: Sylvia Townsend Warner and Valentine Ackland: Life, Letters and Politics, 1930–1951* (London, 1988); Judith Stinton, *Chaldon Herring: The Powys Circle in a Dorset Village* (Woodbridge, Suffolk, 1988); Robert Gibbings, "Llewelyn and Theodore," *Powys Journal* 3 (1993); Patrick Wright, *The Village That Died for England: The Strange Story of Tyneham* (London, 1995); J. Lawrence Mitchell, "Getting into Print: From *Mr. Tasker* to *Mr. Weston*," *Powys Journal* 9 (1999). Theodora Gay Scutt, *Cuckoo in the Powys Nest* (Denton, Norfolk, 2000); Richard Garnett, "Theodore Powys and the Garnetts: A Record of Friendship," *Powys Journal* 11 (2001).

VII. CRITICAL STUDIES Louis Wilkinson, *Blasphemy and Religion: A Dialogue About John Cowper Powys's "Wood and Stone" and Theodore Powys's "The Soliloquy of a Hermit"* (New York, 1916); William Hunter, *The Novels and Stories of T. F. Powys* (Cambridge, 1930; rep. Beckerton, Kent, 1977); F. R. Leavis, "T. F. Powys," *Cambridge Review* (9 May 1930); Richard H. Ward, *The Powys Brothers* (London, 1935); Dylan Thomas, "How to Begin a Story," in his *Quite Early One Morning* (London, 1954; rep. 1974); H. Coombes, "T. F. Powys's Good Wine," *Delta* (Cambridge) 14 (spring 1958); W. I. Carr, "Reflections on T. F. Powys," *Delta* (Cambridge) 19 (October 1959); H. Coombes, *T. F. Powys* (London, 1960); David Holbrook, "Two Welsh Writers: T. F. Powys and Dylan Thomas," in Boris Ford, ed., *The Pelican Guide to English Literature,* vol. 7 (Harmondsworth, Middlesex, 1961, rev. 1970); Geoffrey Strickland, "T. F. Powys," *Delta* (Cambridge) 23 (February 1961); Father Brocard Sewell, ed., *Theodore: Essays on T. F. Powys* (Aylesford, Kent, 1964); David Holbrook, introduction to *Mr. Weston's Good Wine* (London, 1967, rep. 1974); Richard Luckett, "T. F. Powys: Aspects of His Language," *Powys Review* 2 (winter 1977); J. Lawrence Mitchell, *T. F. Powys 1875–1953* (Minneapolis, Minnesota, 1982); John Williams, "Theodore Powys: 'All Good Books Tell the Same Tale,'" *Powys Review* 10 (spring 1982); Ronald Blythe, introduction to *Mr. Weston's Good Wine* (London, 1984); Laurence Coupe, "The Comic Vision of T. F. Powys," *Powys Review* 14 (1984); Marius Buning, *T. F. Powys: A Modern Allegorist* (Amsterdam, 1986); William Empson, "Death and Its Desires," in his *Argufying: Essays on Literature and Culture* (London and Iowa City, Iowa, 1987); John Williams, "Theodore Powys and the Devil," *Powys Journal* 2 (1992); J. Lawrence Mitchell, "'Lift Up Thine Eyes to the Hills': The Visionary World of T. F. Powys," *Powys Journal* 4 (1994); John Williams, "T. F. Powys: A Strengthening Antidote," *Powys Journal* 6 (1996); Charles Lock, "T. F. Powys: Fables and the Silence of the Person," *Powys Journal* 8 (1998); Judith Stinton, "Theodore: A Rondeau," *Powys Journal* 8 (1998); David Gervais, "Religious Comedy in T. F. Powys," *Powys Journal* 9 (1999).

VIII. MANUSCRIPT COLLECTIONS. The Bissell Collection, Harry Ransom Humanities Research Center, University of Texas at Austin; The Powys Society Collection and Archive, Dorset County Museum, Dorchester, England.

PETER READING

(1946–)

Robert Potts

PETER READING HAS been one of England's most original poets since 1970, though his work has roots in a traditional line—leading from Wordsworth, via Thomas Hardy and A. E. Housman, to Philip Larkin—notable for its elegiac sadness, pessimism, and nostalgia. Indeed, his is one of the most experimental voices in the mainstream of English poetry since World War II, radical poetry having been effectively marginalized over this period. Many of his techniques might be regarded as postmodern—the mingling of different registers; the admission of "found" material, documents, and eavesdropped dialogue; the self-conscious blurring of fiction and fact; and the use of personae who bear an unstable relation to the poet himself. To these he has added novelistic devices; books often have plots and subplots elliptically developed across a volume, and characters and events occur in more than one book.

Despite frequently suggesting that poetry is at best impotent and at worst futile and without a future (a view he sometimes seems to hold of the human species), he has written over twenty volumes of poetry, which have explored almost every verse technique and established meter available to a modern poet, as well as inventing a few along the way. He is a poet who wrestles with some irresolvable paradoxes, and has written about some of the darkest subjects imaginable: disease, madness, war, torture, tragedy, environmental catastrophe, destitution. Despite this, and his rigorously unsentimental, sometimes ludic, approach to these subjects, his work is comical, energetic, and often deeply moving.

LIFE

Peter Reading was born on 27 July 1946 in Liverpool to Gray and Mary Reading. His father, an electrical engineer, was a Japanese prisoner of war during World War II who returned home with permanent scars, a fact alluded to in Reading's collection *Stet* (1986), where he remembers his childhood perspective:

'54: old Miss Clio was teaching us
all about *Frontiers* (Asia and everywhere);
my mate's big brother, so he told me
"died in Career for one of those things" ...

when he was in the bath, you could see scars on both
 of Dad's shoulders
(carrying rails for Japan) — I hated flipping Frontiers.
(*Collected, Vol. 2*, p. 111)

The family lived on the outskirts of Liverpool, in a once-rural area; from an early age, Reading was a keen birdwatcher, and his ornithological passion and expertise informs many of his poems. This passion also gave him an early understanding of environmental issues, as he saw the rivers and canals near his home becoming steadily more polluted, and as he witnessed the damage done to the habitats of the birds he cared so much for.

Literature was an early passion, as was art. Reading had started writing poetry at the age of fourteen, and was reading W. H. Auden, Robert Frost, Gerard Manley Hopkins, and Samuel Beckett, as well as H. B. Cotterill's translation of Homer's *Odyssey*, which had a profound effect on him. From the state grammar school, he went on, at the age of sixteen, to Liverpool College of Art, graduating with a first in 1967. For various reasons, he decided that writing would be his career, although he had artwork exhibited shortly after graduating and taught art and art history for a few years. Nearly all of the poems in *Water and Waste* (1970), a small chapbook published at the instigation of the editor of *Outposts* magazine,

261

to whom Reading had submitted his work, found their way into his first full-length book, *For the Municipality's Elderly* (1974), issued by Secker and Warburg, a major publisher. From that point on, Reading published a new volume every one or two years, an unusually consistent and unusually fast rate of production. Still more strikingly, the work demonstrates a remarkable integrity of vision; each volume offers a coherent body of poems, many having been clearly conceived as volumes; and the volumes together also form a coherent corpus. Later volumes refer to the very earliest, quite self-consciously (there are poems and pamphlets with titles like *Reiterative*).

In 1970, when *Water and Waste* was published, Reading moved to Shropshire, a deliberate escape from academia, city life, commerce, and what he called in an interview "the end of England." He took work in a feed mill, which was sufficiently undemanding (if poorly paid), to allow himself to write. He performed most jobs during the twenty-two years he worked there, hauling sacks, blending feed for the farm animals, and acting as a weighbridge operator (weighing the raw materials and finished products). The characters, the rural landscape, the routine, and the peace and quiet were all conducive to his writing, from which he made relatively little money. His only break from farming was a writer's residency at Sunderland Polytechnic (now Sunderland University), between 1981 and 1983.

In 1992 a new firm took over the local farm and, among other innovations, insisted that the employees all wear green uniforms. Reading refused and was fired. During this period his first marriage, to Diana Reading, ended, and he traveled briefly to Australia with Deborah Shuttleworth, who would become his second wife. In 1990 he had won a Lannan Literary Award (an award established to aid "the careers of emerging and under-recognized artists"). As well as providing Reading with enough money to live, it set up reading tours in the United States and a literary residency in Marfa, a small town in Texas (which gave rise to the volume *Marfan*). The award was renewed for two years in 2000. For an artist who always detested commerce, and for whom a small agriculture job in Shropshire was for years his best compromise with that loathing, the receipt of philanthropic patronage was perhaps the only effective means of survival, and it came at just the right moment for the poet.

EXPERIMENTS WITH FORM

For the Municipality's Elderly gathered up all but three of the poems from *Water and Waste* and added seventeen new ones. It was a strikingly mature debut; and if influences can be detected in terms of style and tone (Frost, late Auden, Larkin, among others), Reading was already establishing many of the themes and perspectives he would pursue throughout the rest of his work, and had already firmly rejected certain poetic routes. Indeed, "Juvenilia" (which had been the first poem in *Water and Waste*) has him throwing all his youthful poems into the river:

Juvenilia, scattered now in the slack,
coil to the weir and are sucked under oil.
Traces of rainbow remain of loves
more turbid than ever before or since,
though far too desperately set down
—my being, believe it or not, at the time
involved and willing to commentate,
incredible now though it seems.
Politics too, less than half understood,
and a half baked kind of philosophy.

But having found love I am left with nothing to say,
And I find, in the place of Socialist leanings,
a ninety per cent misanthropy,
which once expressed gains nothing by repetition.
                    (*Collected, Vol. 1,* pp.42–43)

There are some ironies here—a poem in which a new writer declares himself will not often confess that he has nothing to say, nor compare poems to "waste" washed away in a polluted river—and the line "once expressed gains nothing by repetition" establishes a Beckettian approach in which nihilistic repetitions become themselves a tacit resistance to nihilism. It is, however, true that, like Philip Larkin, Reading's work shows little interest in overt political statements; pessimism and nihilism tend to subsume any thoughts of social action or progress.

For the Municipality's Elderly is also a distinctively, even self-consciously, English volume in the landscapes and seasonal changes it describes and in the landmarks, both topographical and poetic. One of its preoccupations is a sense of anonymity and decline (common to much post-Imperial English poetry), which, in Reading's hands, modulates subtly into a sense of gathering apocalypse. While some of the poems worry at the idea of monuments—the idea of leaving something behind after death, of achieving some form of posterity—other poems take a darker view of whether there will be any posterity at all. In "Raspberrying," Reading begins with a self-consciously lyrical description of rotting blackberries before criticizing the lines immediately for their anachronistic pastoralism and suggesting that Nature itself (if environmental collapse continues) will soon be "as anachronistic . . . as a poem about it" (*Collected, Vol. 1*, p. 37).

Perversely for a first book, we seem to be saying goodbye to poetry (and much else besides) from the beginning. In "St James," it is not just physical landmarks that are seen to fade but poetic ones, too; in a clear and pointed riposte to Philip Larkin's famous "Church Going," it also manages references to John Betjeman and Geoffrey Hill, English poets with a care for, respectively, church architecture and religious history. Reading cannot even stir himself to the skeptical atheistic consolations of Larkin's poem, writing instead:

and I descended into the chancel,
observing, not from interest, but a sense
of having to have a sense of history,
the aimless woodworms' doodles in the roof.

> (*Collected, Vol. 1*, p. 58)

Against these positions—nihilism, the absence of posterity and imminent apocalyptic catastrophe—people are seen as leading ordinary, pointless, and anonymous lives that are, at best, an end in themselves, and not even, perhaps, evince an almost heroic stoicism ("Perhaps continuing will be no worse / than struggling across a busy street / giving assistance to an ageing wife . . . If so then we must owe a debt to life, / and I suppose our payment is to live" [*Collected, Vol. 1*, pp. 33–34]).

Reading's subsequent books adjust his sense of scale. Although *For the Municipality's Elderly* contained precise descriptions of landscapes, cities, and villages, and evoked domestic relationships and personal reflections, there was in many of the poems a tendency, having established the local and the particular, to generalize out to an overarching philosophical position. However much an individual place or person might have been precisely and carefully rendered, they were then rendered negligible and obsolescent by the shuttling out of the vision to a more cosmic viewpoint. While this tactic recurs throughout the later work (especially by his adoption of personae such as paleontologists and physicists, whose objects of study—epochs, galaxies—dwarf the individual human subject), Reading's books throughout the 1970s and 1980s contained individual characters, and interconnecting tragicomic dramas, establishing a Dickensian social commentary (often satirical) that could nest within his other perspectives, and work in tension with them.

The volumes also blend the traditional and the experimental. While Reading shows a facility for meter, whether traditional iambic pentameter, regularly stressed lines, or other inherited forms, he also demonstrates skepticism about such arrangements. "Early Stuff," which begins *The Prison Cell and Barrel Mystery* (1976), offers snippets of juvenilia between commentary by the ex-girlfriend for whom it was written; the tension between the fashioned verses (by turns cruel or grandiose or stylish or seductive) and the cool, retrospective, almost prosaic assessment of them establishes a distancing effect from the declining relationship they chronicle, until the final deadpan lines offer a truth beyond the grasp of the ostensibly clever poet, and one that requires no poeticizing: "He seems not to have known I loved him then / (he married someone else) but found out later" (*Collected, Vol. 1*, p. 70).

In "10 x 10 x 10," which foreshadows the later and more adventurous book-length technical experiments in *5x5x5x5x5* and *C*, Reading tells an apparently aimless though amusing anecdote in ten stanzas of ten lines of ten syllables each, ending with the protagonist falling and losing consciousness, represented by asterisks, which arbitrarily fill out the form.

* * * * * * When he regained
consciousness, he was considering the
arbitrary nature of the Sonnet –
"One might as well invent any kind of
structure (ten stanzas each of ten lines each
of ten syllables might be a good one),
the subject matter could be anything."

(Collected, Vol. 1, p. 131)

Missed chances and mistakes in relationships and marriages are woven through the books, some incidents related as if by the protagonists, others through eavesdropped conversations or pastiched scraps of manuscripts, with thematically related stories counterpointing the main narratives. It becomes impossible to attribute any of the specific details to the poet's own life, and by the time he has finished "Fiction," Reading manages to eliminate himself as a distinctive authorial or confessional voice, offering instead characters called "Peter Reading," or fictitious characters through whom he could refract his various concerns and perspectives.

Pseudonymous characters—"Don," "Donald Donaldson," "Peter Reading"—are established, and some are described as pseudonyms or fictions of each other. Found materials (old texts, overheard conversations, signs, crossword puzzles) are presented, but many of them are altered or invented; when foreign poets are invoked, and when mock-translation of their work is displayed, their names often turn out to be the names of foreign wines. In the anecdotes and poems of these collections, it is made almost impossible for the reader to determine where fiction stops and where a genuine authorial confession or position is stated. In "Diptych" (from *Nothing for Anyone*), two parallel panels of imagined conversation about Reading refer to his procedures in art and literature, to amusing effect; in "Opinions of the Press" (from *Fiction*), Reading offers a collage of reviewers' comments (negative and positive) on his work to date, using the word "I" instead of "my work" ("I am drab rhythmless demotic") and ending with the provocative question *"but am I Art?"* (*Collected,*

Vol. 1, p. 167). Both are comic poems, but they also serve to warn readers that a conflation of art and artist—especially for readers used to a confessional stance in which the author simply mediates his confessional self through his poems—cannot be made.

Although these postmodern techniques are no longer novel (and Reading himself dismisses them as "literary techniques for tiny tots"), they do serve to establish the starting points for his later, complex and symphonic, work. We know, from Reading's facility with meter and diction, his easy execution of certain traditional forms, and his knowing and self-conscious references to tropes, that he has the ability to write conventionally; however, many poems in these early volumes can be seen as anti-poetic, not least in choice of subject matter. Reading was determined from the outset to tackle "difficult" subjects, including dark and unhappy ones; and by finding appropriate (or grotesquely inappropriate) literary forms for them, he both honors the standard poetic dictum that form should match content and subverts it.

DARK SUBJECTS

In *Tom O'Bedlam's Beauties* (1981), Reading produced the first of a number of volumes unified around subject matter, in this case madness. The book bears the hallmarks of his previous work—an epigraph that immediately unsettles the reader's position, the employment of different poetic forms, a cross-referencing of characters and stories between different poems, a deliberate blurring of factual and fictional material, and a clinical distance in the descriptive and analytical passages, reliant on technical terms and a certain scientific callousness.

It is that tone—lofty, dismissive, scornful in places—that emerges most often in Reading's poetry; and that has led to charges that his poetry, in its insistent focus on pain, has a sadistic, relishing, or voyeuristic element. One reviewer famously compared Reading to the fat boy in Dickens, who likes to make people's flesh creep. Reading proceeded to incorporate the charge into his poems: the image of the poet as a vulture recurs. *Tom O'Bedlam's Beauties* begins with an epigraph:

> *(I once considered nursing them*
> *—even went for an interview*
> *—magnanimous of me, eh?*
>
> *Backed out—like them, eschewing*
> *the risky Real for Illusion.)*

In all of the accounts of madness that follow, this teasing division needs to be kept in mind. The "pity" a writer or reader might feel for the mad is undercut by an inability to cope with the mad, to be willing to "deal" with them. And a comparison is made, between the mad who live in an "unreal" world and the sane who—in T. S. Eliot's phrase—"cannot bear much reality," least of all that of the lives of mad people. This is as much to say that readers who find the material in *Tom O'Bedlam's Beauties* (and in *C, Ukulele Music,* and *Perduta Gente*) unbearable and "unpoetic" are desperate for illusion themselves; the illusion that life is better and happier than it is.

The poems that follow exemplify Reading's talent for disturbing black comedy and oddly affecting pathos. Cruelties, vulnerabilities, and a sense of powerlessness abound, but many of the poems are narrated in a darkly humorous fashion. In the title poem, Reading and his childhood friends cruelly throw apples at the inmates of an asylum, and "we resolved to repeat the prank / discreetly dubbed *Sanes and Loonies.*" There is a pun on "discreet"; it evokes "discrete," the setting apart of the mad, the exercise of a cruel discrimination. The rest of the book suggests that the walls between the two camps are not secure, and forces the reader to examine his or her own attitudes to the mentally ill.

In *Diplopic* (1983), Reading tackled head-on the issue that had disturbed readers from his earliest volumes (though the charges did not go away). The epigraphs to the volume, as ever, are fictitious but instructive. The first is a pastiche of a badly translated phrase-book: "*Optician, I am having Double Visions to see one thing from two sides. Only give me a Spectacle and I am de-*lighted." The second offers two verses by a fictitious Japanese poet, Kokur Niznegorsky, comparing poetic activity with the unfeeling rapaciousness of a vulture; the last, ostensibly an eavesdropped comment in a Greek restaurant, is "*Is that Thalia* and *Melpomene or am I seein double?*"—Thalia and Melpomene being the Greek muses of comedy and tragedy, respectively.

These epigraphs give more than enough assistance to the reader in terms of what follows. Reading takes a number of incidents, many grisly, and renders them from two or more perspectives (hence "*I am having Double Vision to see one thing from two sides*"), calling attention frequently to the procedures by which he does so. These perspectives are not, however, balanced ideological positions, but different registers and rhetoric; diary entries, monologues, journalism, headlines, textbooks, translations, scientific descriptions are played off against each other. In each pair of related poems, the second is always some form of sonnet; it is as if Reading is playing up to the accusation of his critics, as expressed in the epigraph, that the ordering of tragic or horrific material by an artist is necessarily a cruel and callous activity: the self-conscious artistry, and the dispassionate use of a traditionally romantic lyric form for his distressing subject matter, do make Reading seem coldly exploitative of his material. One monologue, "Ex Lab," is in the voice of Reading's paleontologist persona, whose nihilism and atheism, combined with his interest in broad sweeps of geological time and his concomitant lack of interest in individual human lives, make him a heartless observer of contemporary events.

It would be too easy to infer that this self-conscious presentation of callousness in fact represented Reading's own views; while fearful of sentimentality, Reading leaves enough indications in the text to unsettle the easy view that the poet (or any artist) exploits suffering for ornamental ends, arranging his subjects heartlessly for the voyeuristic and sadistic relish of author and reader alike ("*only give me a Spectacle and I am delighted*"). The pairing of "P.S." and "Hints" (*Collected, Vol. 1,* pp. 219–220) is perhaps the most telling example of what Reading can achieve without spelling emotion out for the reader. "P.S." is in the form of an address to a bereaved friend, and manages, by invoking an embarrassed reticence—"I mailed you my useless sympathy but . . . withheld admiration and love for you (old-fashioned words) / who, having a grim chore to finish, get on with the job"—to convey all the appropriate emotions precisely through such restraint. In "Hints," Reading, in the guise of giving advice to young writers, offers a commentary on the strengths and weaknesses of his own poetic procedures:

Find ways to make the narrative compel,
I advise students; as, in retailing this,
you might lend the issue added poignancy
by being distanced—

before rounding on himself: "Compelling, maybe, but mere narrative / —no moral or intellectual envoy." He then advocates the accentuation of the braveness and dignity of the bereaved that we have just seen in "NB," before bringing both poems to their point: the walking toward an electrified railway of a daughter, who "being blind, observed no warning." It is breathtakingly done, and extraordinarily poised between its different approaches and its own commentaries on those approaches; and its triumph is that its emotional resonance not only survives but in many ways springs from the self-conscious devices enclosing the narrative.

Throughout, the emotional work is left, as with Reading's earlier work, for the reader; but the structure within which appropriate responses can be formed is established with some care. The dominant voice of the paleontologist, for instance, with its scorn for the human beings around him, cannot be regarded (despite its overlap with Reading's own evident atheism and skepticism) as privileged; another poem in the collection sees that character meet a grotesquely comic demise when a lorry carrying Portaloos (portable toilets) sheds its load and buries the scientist under a pile of lavatories. With its skewed visions, and its constant interrogations of poetic authority and motivation, not to mention the challenges to readers who want to be spoonfed their responses, *Diplopic* shows Reading in assured and uncompromising form.

Between *Diplopic* and *C* (1984), Reading published *5x5x5x5x5*, in collaboration with the artist David Butler. Composed of five sections of five pages of five verses of five lines of five syllables each, it forms, through the interwoven monologues of its characters, a strange and unhappy series of tales revolving around pubs. *5x5x5x5x5* was followed by the more ambitiously structured *C*.

C stands for cancer; it is also the Roman numeral for 100. In his treatment of this untreatable (in more than one sense) subject, Reading produces 100 units of 100 words each. The number 100, it is suggested, might be the number of days of life left to someone with a terminal diagnosis of three to four months. From this premise, Reading produces a text, composed of prose and poetry (in many different verse forms and meters), in which the terminally ill, the caregivers, the families and the bereaved, friends, colleagues, and strangers all have their perspective on the illness. Throughout, Reading is concerned with the uselessness of poetry in facing the business of dying.

In earlier books, he had been critical of poets (including such revered figures as Ted Hughes) writing about nature, in particular those who sentimentalized or anthropomorphized their subjects. In *Diplopic,* he had written

Phoney rustic bards,
spare us your thoughts about birds,
butterflies, fish, snakes
and mammals (including us)
—biologists write more sense.
                    ("Nips," *Collected, Vol. 1*, p. 230)

In *C*, he turns again on what he calls "The Plashy Fen school" of poetry:

Poetical mawkish duff gen
where a buzzard is "noble" and lands
in a tree (surprise, surprise!) . . . .
Bullshit, bullshit, bullshit
of the Plashy Fen school.
Peterson, Mountfort and Hollom
write more sense than you
bloody carpetbaggers.
                    (*Collected, Vol. 1*, p. 289)

Peterson, Mountfort, and Hollom are ornithologists; by employing scientific and technical names and descriptive terms, Reading aims to avoid poetic sentimentality and trite anthropomorphism. He remains insistent that much of the horror he describes stems from superstition (and he includes religious belief in that word) and an arrogant disregard by man for his environment, based on the "duff" belief that *Homo sapiens* remains uniquely outside the evolutionary cycles and periodic species extinctions that it has discovered and analyzed. Reading's own view on this subject can be found in "The Con Men," from *Nothing for Anyone*, skeptically observing that attempting now to conserve species (including the human species) may well be both arrogant and pointless, and offering a chilling final line, "the only thing it matters to is us" (*Collected*, *Vol. 1*, p. 133); this can be usefully compared with the paleontologist's line in *Diplopic*: "It is a fucking good job / that it all does not matter" (*Collected*, *Vol. 1*, p. 235). What Reading is suggesting is that significance—things mattering—is created by human beings, and is a more fragile thing than we tend to realize: placed in a vast perspective of billions of years, in a universe of millions of stars, human concerns, however passionate, can look trivial. However, it would be wrong to imagine that Reading himself is indifferent to human life: he offers too many alternative perspectives.

While *C* takes both skepticism and an insistence on the superiority of scientific terminology even further ("verse is for healthy / arty-farties. The dying / and surgeon use prose," Reading writes in a sly haiku), it also finds ways to dignify its failing, terrified subjects. Partly, it achieves this by its honesty; one section contrasts surveys in which the majority of doctors do not want to tell their patients that they have a terminal condition and those in which the majority of patients would prefer to be told. Although the indignities of bodily infirmity are unflinchingly expressed, the bravery (as well as the grief and fear) of the dying and their caregivers emerges equally strongly. What Reading refuses to do is sentimentalize his subject.

Among the characters in the book (some, like the paleontologist, familiar from Reading's earlier work) is the self-styled "Master of the 100 100-word units," sometimes discussing his choices of poetic form, sometimes referred to by other figures. He refers to himself as "C"; the book *C* becomes his legacy. Throughout it, he is obsessed with the fact that "treating" his cancer in verse does not translate into "treating" it medically; and that this most unpoetic subject can have no appropriate poetic form:

> I used to pepper my poetics with sophisticated allusions to dear Opera and divine Art (one was constantly reminded of A. du C. Dubreuil's libretto for Piccini's Iphegenia in Tauris; one was constantly reminded of Niccolo di Bartolomeo da Foggia's bust of a crowned woman, doubtless an allegory of the Church, from the pulpit of Ravello Cathedral ca. 1272) but suddenly these are hopelessly inadequate. Where is the European cultural significance of tubes stuck up the nose, into the veins, up the arse? A tube is stuck up my prick, and a bladder carcinoma diagnosed. One does not recall Piccini.
> (*Collected*, *Vol. 1*, p. 280)

Elsewhere, he tries and discards a wide range of poetic devices: limericks, acrostics, sonnets, including the "13-line sonnet for unlucky people (100 words including title)," choriambs, elegiac couplets, blank pentameters, Spenserian stanzas. All are seen ultimately as useless:

> Even though sometimes I talk about this abdominal cancer,
> my mental ease demands lies, comfort of make believe games—
>
> such as this one that I play now in distich, almost pretending
> verse has validity. No. Verse is fuck-all use here, now.
> (*Collected*, *Vol. 1*, p. 305)

There is no question that *C* is a grueling read. The games it plays, with increasing mania, balance a form of heroism—continued activity in the face of extinction—against futility and insignificance. Through the figure of the paleontologist, Reading periodically compares and contrasts individual deaths with the larger prospect of the entire human species at some point being extinct. Near the end, when the "dying" poet decides to commit suicide in a favorite valley, but is attempting to finish a last verse for the sequence, Reading delivers a supremely nihilistic verdict: "suddenly, alas, the subtle grafting of a cdcdee Spenserian sestet onto an ab-baabba Petrarchan octave does not matter. . . . Nor does the Precambrian subdivision Longmyndian, ca. 600 million yrs. old, nor Holocene H. sap with terminal & c., nor the conception of its not mattering, nor" (*Collected, Vol. 1*, p. 317).

But Reading's achievement, in a formidably well-researched and truthful set of fictionalized accounts, is that the lives he presents, without false hope and without especially heroic qualities, become significant nonetheless, testifying to a spirit of humanity all the more powerful for its being dwarfed by mortality, pain, fear, and anonymity. The final stanza confesses that the planned suicide is another consoling fiction— "Bodily weakness prevents my moving from the bed. The dismay to my wife and child which suicide would occasion renders such a course untenable"—but ends on a peculiar and affirming anti-poetic note: "My wife patiently washes my faece-besmirched pyjamas, for prosaic love" (*Collected, Vol. 1*, p. 317). The word "love" is always hard-earned in Reading, only admitted when all cant and self-serving deception have been stripped away; when it does arrive, triumphantly closing the volume, its triumph is the greater for being "prosaic." Reading's admiration for those who can face life and pain honestly and still carry on is a persistent motif in a poetry that might otherwise be merely despairing and hopeless.

If the subject matter of *C* had seemed grim, there was to be no respite in Reading's next volume, *Ukulele Music* (1994). Having been chided in reviews for the bleakness of his vision, Reading turned savagely on his critics, offering a bleak vision of 1980s Britain. *Ukulele Music* recounts numerous assaults and acts of violence from the newspapers whose reviewers had taken Reading to task:

"Life is too dark as he paints it" and "Reading's nasti-
 ness sometimes
seems a bit over the top" thinks a review—so does he.

Too black & over the top, though, is what the Actual
 often
happens to be I'm afraid. He don't invent it, you know.
(*Collected, Vol. 2*, p. 19)

Part of the book was subject to controversy before it was published; an excerpt, under the title "Cub," appeared in the *Times Literary Supplement*. The poem was written in the persona of a novice reporter (or "cub") remembering an incident in Lebanon, which he describes in disgusted (and dehumanizing) detail: a "soldier/homunculus" opens fire on a "fat juicy jeep of Israelis"; they return fire, killing their attacker, who turns out to be only twelve years old. Although the incident is reported by a callow persona (whose colleague is called "Dickie Pratt"—"pratt" is a British word for a fool) and is indiscriminate in its contempt for Arab and Israeli alike, the lines "Well, / nobody looks for a motive from these Old testament shitters— / thick hate is still in the genes" was interpreted by many as anti-Semitic.

The controversy played itself out in the national press, mostly in the letters pages of the *Times Literary Supplement* and the *Times*. At one point, feces were sent in an envelope to the offices of the *Times Literary Supplement*. Reading's intention had been to offer an ironic account of atrocity, war, and insensitivity; his opponents interpreted the poem otherwise. He incorporated the controversy, and his own position, into *Going On*, the companion poem to *Ukulele Music*:

I am traduced in the press (for a
poem weary of war-rent
mad bloody Lebanon) as
Antisemitic, Bad Hat.

No, no, not antisemitic, dears,
antibutchery only . . .
(*Collected, Vol. 2*, p. 50)

Ukulele Music is written mostly in elegiac couplets, with reported outrages from the newspapers interwoven with notes from the poet's cleaning lady, Viv (a stoical malapropistic working-class voice, whose subliteracy is not patronized but affectionately milked of its unintentional comedy), the reminiscences of an old sea captain

Viv also cleans for, and the instructions for a teach-yourself ukulele kit. It is as skeptical as *C* as to the redemptive properties of poetry, what is offered is a complicated negotiation between the mayhem and bloodletting purveyed by the press, the inadequacies of poetry either to mediate such subjects or to change the society that gives rise to them, and the stoicism of ordinary people under pressure.

It is also, oddly, the closest that Reading comes to offering any kind of explanation for his continued writing of a poetry that is so concerned with its own impotence, obsolescence, and irrelevance. In one of Viv's notes she says,

> but well what can you do only get on with it. as you cant' sort it all out can you? we are like the man in music Hall song that goes he play his Uka uke Youkalaylee while the ship went down. only we all have problems like my sister and Goverments so can only carry on best we can
>
> (*Collected, Vol. 2,* p. 14)

The image of ships going down recurs throughout; and when Viv offers the English cliché "worse things happen at sea" (a platitude intended to cheer people up), Reading offers a series of narratives of terrible disasters at sea, all of them concluding with the survivors, in whatever state, fashioning instruments to play upon; music becomes

ye dignified defiance
in us towards our fateful
merciless element . . .

(*Collected, Vol. 2,* p. 33)

However, the "ship of state," as metaphor, is also clearly heading toward disaster; the terrible urban violence Reading writes about is overshadowed by the threat of nuclear conflict (or accident). And, throughout, Reading's own music—the dactylic rhythms of the elegiac couplets—is counterpointed by the "plinka plinka plunk" of an out-of-tune ukulele, and the ironic excerpts from its instruction manual: "Now you are ready for those oldies we know and love! Yes, Sir! Sing, hum or whistle the tune as you play! Play each chord as indicated until a new chord is shown. Do not change until you see another chord indicated! Everyone's just *got to*

join in and **sing right along there!**" (*Collected, Vol. 2,* p. 41).

By the end of the poem, these strands are blended together, the sea captain's final voyage, the ghastly cheerfulness of the uke manual, Reading's own sardonic recounting of atrocities, and Viv's splendid, brave chirpiness. Despite the unnerving subject matter, it is this voice of resilience, and the music (or meter) of "dignified defiance," that emerge most strongly, though the final couplet is simply the plinka-plonk of the ukulele, rendered into the rhythmic pattern of the elegiac couplet. Reading balances impotence against defiance; as he writes, "to recognize is not to acquiesce."

Going On, a book-length work published in the same volume as *Ukulele Music,* picks up where the previous poem left off (there is another note from Viv, and more appalling newspaper material) but also contains some pastoral celebrations, and a new voice: a nineteenth-century clergyman who, worried by the "madness" of his own century, finds solace in writing metrical English translations of classical verses. (This figure is so clearly an alter ego of the poet's that we are perhaps meant to be reminded that narratives of decline and hopelessness are not specific to the contemporary period.) Reading still dextrously balances his callousness of delivery with his anger and his impotence.

Bit of a habit, the feigned indignation,
various metres, Alcmanic and so forth,
ludic responses to global debacles.
Just Going On remains possible through the
      slick prestidigital art of Not Caring/
      Hopelessly Caring.

(*Collected, Vol. 2,* p. 76)

The volume finds a pathetic nobility in "just going on," and in using secular humanism and harmless versification as bulwarks against the cruelties and lunacies the poet sees everywhere.

ELEGIES

Stet (1986) blends the Alcmanic stanzas Reading had introduced in *Going On* with the elegiac couplets of *Ukulele Music.* The whole volume is elegiac: for a dead friend, a lost Empire, the end of a species. Reading had established, with the grim social observations of *Ukulele Music* and *Going On*, a reputation as a poet offering a left-wing critique of Thatcherite Britain; the degree of nostalgia for Britain's Imperial past came as a surprise to some readers. The fact is that Reading does not have a politics as such, beyond a basic humanism. As he said in an interview with Isabel Martin:

> The sort of thing I write about . . . can't really exist without being, in some broader sense, political in that anything that concerns humanity and is treated in literature and any of the arts is ipso facto political in that it is about the way that humanity conducts itself. So that's the only kind of political sway that holds there, I think . . . . I wouldn't want to be thought of as a sort of radical or a left or a right . . .
>
> (*Reading Peter Reading*, p. 129)

Even so, the elegiac tone of *Stet* is not uncomplicated; few of its voices can be taken as unequivocal statements of Reading's own position, except his Lucretian loathing of religious violence (he has often quoted the line *Tantum religio potuit suadere malorum* from *De Rerum Natura*) and his contempt for any brutality, whether political or domestic. The poet's memories of childhood, and events such as the death of King George VI and the coronation of Queen Elizabeth, develop into one account of national decline—Britain's humiliation over the Suez Canal crisis, religious and racial sectarian violence—offset by periodic reminders that Britain's cosy imperial belief that "cruelty and mess, one assumed, reigned elsewhere" was a myth; but that, on the other hand, "cruelty and mess, I suppose, may be worse elsewhere than here."

Stet uses different metrical forms for the different stances and voices of the poem: a combination of an Alcaic stanza and an elegiac couplet for his portrayals of his childhood in the 1950s and 1960s; prose for the hyper-rational voice of an astronomer whose interest in stars renders the planet Earth negligible ("Yes, well, I've no interest whatsoever in our local system, in isolation");

a dactylic meter for the sane and stoic, if subliterate, chatter of a man in a bar (whose favorite drink is "bitter and mild mixed," a self-referential pun); various combinations of these for the poet's own tetchy humanist voice, attacking violence and stupidity but also attacking himself for the futility of his poetry, and particularly his elegies.

One of these elegies is for a childhood friend of Reading's, with whom he went bird watching and remained friends until the man's death in a car crash. Reading's loathing of sentimentality (or "mawkishness," as he most often calls it in the poems and in interviews) makes the writing of heartfelt elegy a difficult business for him. His tactic is to keep his words as descriptive and emotionally level as possible, to simply state the situation; and to interrupt himself with heckling interjections to offset the sentiment that comes with deep grief.

> [Batty / unhealthy—verse at the best of times
> chunters to insubstantial minorities,
>> as for addressing lines to *dead men!*
>> arrogant therapy / piffle, claptrap.]
>> (*Collected, Vol. 2,* p. 104)

A further ironic counterpoint throughout the collection is examples of the doggerel printed in a local newspaper by amateur poets (though, in Reading's fiction, they are actually written by the editors of those pages, in order to take the prize money for himself!). These dreadful examples of moral censure or cheerful platitudes ("Our land is no as bad as all that!") further complicate the texture of a book that does seem unfashionably elegiac about the decline of England, but is uncompromising about the perils of nationalism and false nostalgia, as in this aggressive late stanza, uneasily combining the determination to remain sane and survive with a snarling patriotism:

> . . . for some shite god,
> possession, border, tenet, goons blast cack
> out of each others chitterlings . . . I don't care
> two fucks for any other pratt. UK's
> OK. I'm lucky and intend to stay so.
> What do you want, me to go batty too?
>> (*Collected, Vol. 2,* p. 114)

Stet was awarded the Whitbread Prize for poetry. Its publication alongside *Essential Read-*

ing (a selection of his earlier poems) and *3 in 1* (the reprinting in one volume of *Diplopic*, *C*, and *Ukulele Music*) marked a transition in Reading's reputation as a poet. He became more widely known and recognized, and more readers were able to get past his apparently unpoetic and unappealing subject matter and appreciate the technical agility with which he treated it.

Reading's pessimism—national and environmental—is often accompanied by the symbolic decline (or death) of his characters and personae. *C* is the most striking example, though there are many others. In *Final Demands* (1988), the hypochondria seems more real. It is hard to know quite what to make of the book's intense and occasionally maudlin anxieties as to personal mortality:

[*What's 40 years here or there on the chrono-
    stratigraph?*, you wrote.
Striking a stance you were, then; really believe it
    though, now.]

(*Collected*, Vol. 2, p. 135)

As well as the familiar device of cross-referenced subplotting, in which surviving letters of families from several previous generations add tone and texture to the portraits of cruelty, tragic loss, and national decline, Reading here further develops some favorite personal images. One is his pastiche of a scene from the *Odyssey*, in which storm-tossed Laertides crawls beneath leaves and makes himself a comfortable bed; throughout Reading's oeuvre, he imagines similarly bedding down, but with a fine wine (the wine indeed seems to get better with each reference) and a bottle of pills, in order to commit suicide.

Final Demands also invokes the "democratic" catastrophes of AIDS and radiation (the Chernobyl disaster is alluded to throughout); viruses and irradiated winds are no respecters of national borders or social status. Reading's apocalyptic vision, in which even the papers and inscriptions he alludes to will eventually become dust, is offset by some apposite allusions, especially to the "Out, brief candle" speech in Shakespeare's *Macbeth*. His counterpointing stoicism, represented through impotent music and poetry, is also present in this book, although what shines through is the lyricism with which he transforms the "rot" and squalor of pollution and decay. A discarded page of newspaper is caught in a gust of wind, and its flight upward described with zesty lyricism; Coke cans rolling along an iced-over pond, or the wind in the wires of a supermarket cart are described as musical ("zither," "tintinnabulant").

The book has a gentleness, in terms of its ability to represent affection for human frailty, and its decision to celebrate what is left of life. Its main tone, though, is indeed morbid and hypochondriacal, and raises again the question of diminishing returns in a poetry that, having stated from the outset its own pointlessness, and further expressed its value solely in a certain dignity of resilience, has almost nowhere else to go.

HOMELESSNESS AND DEPARTURE

Without departing from his established themes—human tragedy and cruelty, environmental catastrophe, the absence of posterity, the futility of art, and the peculiar urge, despite all that, to produce art—in *Perduta Gente* (1989) Reading did return to the specific, the local, and the human. *Perduta gente* means "the lost people"; it is a phrase from Dante. The volume treats the homeless and dispossessed (mostly of London and England, but by extension of everywhere) and is, like *C*, exceptionally well researched. It is a volume that, taken with some of the grim social realism of *Ukulele Music,* led left-wing commentators to praise Reading, though some also noted that the vastness of his perspectives, and his pessimism and despair, never lead him to advocate a political program for change, but simply and impotently render misery; indeed, the pessimism—the belief that nothing can be done and that most activity is pointless—has even led some critics to discern a conservativism in Reading.

"But what does Peter Reading want?" one reviewer wrote, in some despair. It is a question to which Reading unusually gave a specific reply, in an interview with the author:

It presupposes that poetry is some sort of tool to engineer something. It can be, but it doesn't need to be so calculating as that. Paintings don't do that; when you look at a Rothko or Giotto, you're not assailed by the question "What does he want?" There are certain allegiances, but you don't ask that question . . . you see the thing, and a kind of vision. . . . "What—to be crassly naive about it— what I want in *Perduta Gente* is an end to the unpleasant circumstances which its heroes and heroines have to put up with.

(*Oxford Poetry*, p. 95)

The book is a tour de force of compassion, unflinching vision, and technique. Through the use of elegiac meter, with its heavy, falling cadences, the inexorable doom of the protagonists is brought home. There are allusions to Dante, as if we are offered an *Inferno* or *Purgatorio*, and to biblical lament ("woe vnto woe vnto woe") and Anglo-Saxon elegy ("gone are the youthfully beautiful whom I / loved in my nonage; / strength and vitality, gone; / roof-tree and cooking-hearth, gone"; *Collected, Vol. 2*, p. 171).

Grotesque (and real) ironies are starkly offered in the documentation of the lives of the homeless. At night, they insulate themselves with newspapers, excerpts of which show rising house prices or letters from retired military men suggesting cruel solutions to the "vagrancy problem." The book demonstrates an unsentimental sympathy for the vagrants; their own acts of violence, cruelty, boorishness, and cupidity are not brushed aside, and the degradations they sink into are unsparingly described. At the same time, in keeping with Reading's interest in catastrophe as "democratic," which he earlier related to the impartial workings of illness or radiation poisoning, here he points out that bankruptcy and homelessness can affect people from vastly different backgrounds: "Bankrupted, batty, bereft— / don't think it couldn't be you" (*Collected, Vol. 2*, p. 173).

A further leveling device is produced by Reading's insertion of fictional characters, revealed through pastiched diaries, monologues, and an imaginary biographical work on the author. One fictional character is a university graduate who had worked for an atomic power station but was fired for giving papers to the press (this section uses genuine papers in Reading's possession, revealing plans to cover up the radiation risks to the employees of a damaged nuclear plant). With no work, and having lost his wife to cancer, this character joins all the other drunks, drug addicts, and bankrupts who live under railway arches and even, as an initial juxtaposition makes clear, London's Royal Festival Hall. (Reading was writing about a phenomenon that increased greatly throughout the 1980s and 1990s: homelessness on a very large scale, leading to the establishment of entire communities of dispossessed figures huddled among the garbage not far from cultural centers, luxury accommodations, and thriving businesses.) The fictional "Peter Reading," as snippets of a fictionalized biography make clear, has slipped into this terrible world himself.

Hanging over these Stygian scenes of loss and calamity—alcoholism, madness, destitution, filth—is the prospect of a nuclear accident that would render everyone "bankrupted, batty, bereft"; Reading implicitly compares some of the drunks' symptoms (vomiting, diarrhea) to those of radiation poisoning. One haunting question, in a book that makes much of the savage disparities between rich and poor in Britain, is the fragility of the barriers between them. In a pastiche biblical accusation, Reading asks:

What will you do with yr wealth
in the day of the storme which shall come
from afarre, when all that remaines
is to crouch with those ye haue oppressed?

(*Collected, Vol. 2*, p. 185)

After this extraordinary blend of prophetic sadness and social commentary, Reading returned to his more global or universal anxieties, producing the abstract and slightly incoherent uber-elegy of *Evagatory* (1992). As he admitted in an interview with the author at the time, his work exhibits "a Beckettesque tension that becomes increasingly difficult to play along with. The logical thing would be to pack up. . . . It's an alarming prospect. I keep hoping I may try something different. But of course I don't know what that is" (*Guardian*, 1992, p. 30).

Evagatory was to be the last volume in this particular phase of Reading's poetry. The characters that populate his earlier works are absent; the grandiloquent tone of the elegiac meters has become a reiteration of decline and catastrophe. Written in the form of a miniature travelogue, combining Odyssean wanderings with pastiched Anglo-Saxon statements of impermanence and oblivion, it constantly trails off, diminuendo, into evocations of eternal silence—"all that remains, the stench of their excrement," "guideless, directionless, lightless, silence"—and a vision of his "collected works," blowing around in a post-apocalyptic storm, where only mutated cockroaches have survived. The final image is of a space probe drifting further from earth, the lines printed in smaller and smaller typeface, until finally "drifting, 290 000 / years beyond launch-pad, in towards Sirius" (*Collected, Vol. 2,* p. 244). (Sirius is the Dog Star; and the phrase for decline, "going to the dogs," is tacitly suggested.)

REITERATIONS

The three books that follow *Evagatory* hone and round off an integrated and comprehensive poetic corpus. *Last Poems* (1994) adopts a device to kill off "Peter Reading," a figure we had already seen dispatched in *Fiction* (as a fiction), *C* (as a cancer victim), *Final Demands* (as a hypochondriac who "really believes it" this time), *Perduta Gente* (as a terminal alcoholic), *Evagatory* (seen lapsing into silence, "soused in weisswein" [drunk], and slithering in "shweinschmalz," [pigshit]). The suicidal nature of Reading's persona and his poetry, with each volume pitched as if it might be his last, was, by *Last Poems* (1994), wearing a little thin, and may explain the rather flat final poem in *Work in Regress* (1997):

All that remained was to tidy the desk and
    type out the distich,
        then end the myth that they don't
        do it who *threaten* they will.

                    (p. 61)

Reading, of course, continued to live, and to write.

Last Poems, introduced as if they were indeed the found papers of a dead author, contains a number of translations and versions; of Ovid, of part of the *Odyssey*, and of some famous Anglo-Saxon laments. All are thematically in keeping with Reading's now-familiar concerns, but the advantage of the distancing effect created by the elimination of the contemporary authorial voice, and the rendering of different eras and nations, is to universalize Reading's philosophy, rescuing his stoic nihilism from those critics who saw him primarily as a social critic in the mold of Dickens rather than a faintly misanthropic pessimist and satirist in the mold of Swift.

Ob. (1999) also contains versions and translations, particularly in the section "Chinoiserie," which, though ostensibly versions of poems by the Chinese poet Li Po, are mostly made-up. These celebrate drink and love, while mourning exile or absence. The delight Reading takes in alcohol, throughout all his work, as a source of amnesia or celebration, is notable; as is the fact that he is as knowledgeable about wine as he is about ornithology. In "[untitled]" and "Faunal," many of the poems combine the two pleasures; the spotting of a rare or beautiful species is accompanied by the drinking of beer or wine. At one point Reading singles out "three consolations at least: / verse; viticulture; love."

Notable among these later works is *Work in Regress*, the most personally elegiac of Reading's works, celebrating and mourning dead friends and idols in an affecting and humorous way, particularly the late poet George Macbeth, who had encouraged Reading early on in his career, and given him several breaks. In "*I.M.* G.MacB.," Reading recalls a conversation with his late friend, in which Reading reiterated his belief (stated, as we have seen, in *Stet*) that writing or talking to the dead is absurd. The poem ends gently:

"Just a convention, of course,
just a convention," you said.

               (*Work in Regress*, p. 32)

Reading concedes the point simply by using the pronoun "you" for his dead friend; this, in itself, is a significant and loving tribute, carrying an extraordinary emotional charge.

Admirable or funny or assured as many of the poems in these volumes are, they are a return to the format of individual poems in loose groupings, rather than the ferociously unified and cross-referenced volumes of the 1980s. The quality is uneven, and there is a sense of exhaustion throughout. Reading had carefully interlinked characters and phrases throughout his work, but in these books the returns add little to what had already been achieved. "Reiterative" recycles the title poem of *Nothing for Anyone*, which had attacked the complacency with which people were watching the environment being destroyed, and points out that needing to "reiterate" such material is precisely the problem; the earlier poem was a wake-up call that went unheeded:

[That was in '76
the hackneyed text is eroded,
somebody ain't been listening –
you, at the back, sit up
and fucking well pay attention.]

(*Collected, Vol. 2*, p. 264)

A TEXAN EXILE

The money and opportunities afforded Reading by the award from the Lannan Foundation included a year's residency in the small town of Marfa, Texas. It gave rise to one of Reading's best books since 1990. He returns to the anecdote, characterization, and reportage that comprised much of his earlier work, and also the use of cross-referenced sections and stanzas, rather than individually titled poems.

In various meters and registers, Reading describes the inhabitants of Marfa, its history, its politics, its superstitions, its geology and fauna though verbatim conversation, snippets from the local paper, caricatures, collages, and Catullan satires, along with epiphanies and darker moods. Reading sardonically calls attention to his peculiar place as an English poet in Texan Hicksville:

For I am catapulted to the grandeur
of Marfan Literary Resident
(sinecure recently inaugurated

by the beneficence of Patrick Lannan
blessandpreservehimandhiswholefoundation).

(p. 22)

The tradition of literary gratitude to patrons is parodied here, though the sentiment is genuine; and later he writes, deadpan and self-deprecatingly, "Twas then they sent in Lannan's secret weapon." More realistically, he also notes "When this gets published I shall have to be / beyond the City Limits in a Greyhound" (p. 21).

Marfa houses the work of another artist who enjoyed patronage, Donald Judd, who built, in Reading's words, "one hundred waist-high milled aluminium boxes . . . billion-dollar, minimalist, / factory-finish, self-indulgent art games" (pp. 23–24), but who whined about the noise from the mill near his apartment: "Seems to me carpetbaggers shouldn't complain" (p. 24). But Reading has other "carpetbaggers" in his sights: the Americans who kicked out the "injuns" ("the indigenous can fuck off outa here") and who kick out the "Spiks" from Mexico; and the "arties, architects, carpetbaggers, entrepreneurs / 'gallery owners,' leather coat boutiquers" (p. 51) snapping up real estate in Marfa; indeed, the human species itself, replacing the pterosaurs who "in the late Cretaceous . . . darkly traversed the Big Bend floodplain" (p. 57).

These various perspectives, constantly overriding or undercutting each other, demonstrate Reading's continual compassion for the dispossessed as well as a delicate blend of contempt and respect for the lunacies of the townspeople he encounters. His vicious and emetic response to the "How y'all" greeting of the inhabitants of Marfan locals is offset by a quotation from Nathaniel Hawthorne on his trip to Liverpool in 1953: "The British / sodden in strong beer, have a conversation / like a plum pudding—stodgy, bilious." An incongruous *Wisden* (an annual reference book charting the year's cricket matches in England and around the world) in the public library "charts the achievement of that English summer / before climacteric and post-bellum slump." Reading is not, that is, an Anglophile xenophobe; and a gnomic one-liner—"we term it Marfa, but we mean the lot" (p. 18)—suggests that drawing a clear line between the specific and the general is not part of the plan.

Amid a wealth of detail—personal stories, local history and folklore, politics, paranoia, art, religion—Reading situates himself as a small and transitory speck in the bigger picture (his cherished "Rothko sunset") while treating the reader to his witty spleneticisms, brief sentimentalities, precise descriptions, and not ungenerous amusement. As ever, despair is never absent; but this is an appreciative, defiantly humane, volume, and a remarkable poetic evocation of a real place. It is a sign that, although much of his late work might be seen as variations on exhausted themes, a poetry moving in ever decreasing circles, there are still vivid surprises and pleasures possible.

SELECTED BIBLIOGRAPHY

I. INDIVIDUAL WORKS. *Water and Waste* (Surrey, 1970); *For the Municipality's Elderly* (London, 1974); *The Prison Cell and Barrel Mystery* (London, 1976); *Nothing for Anyone* (London, 1977); *Fiction* (London, 1979); *Tom O'Bedlam's Beauties* (London, 1981); *Diplopic* (London, 1983); *5x5x5x5x5* (Tyne & Wear, 1983); *C* (London, 1984); *Ukulele Music* (London, 1994); *Stet* (London, 1986); *Final Demands* (London, 1988); *Perduta Gente* (London, 1989); *Shitheads* (London, 1989); *Evagatory* (London, 1992); *Last Poems* (London, 1994); *Work in Regress* (Newcastle upon Tyne, 1997); *Ob.* (Newcastle upon Tyne, 1999); *Marfan* (Newcastle upon Tyne, 2000); *[untitled]* (Newcastle upon Tyne, 2001); *Faunal* (Newcastle upon Tyne, 2002).

II. SELECTED AND COLLECTED WORKS. *Essential Reading* (London, 1986); *3 in 1* (London, 1992); *Ukulele Music & Perduta Gente* (Chicago, 1994); *Collected 1: Poems 1970–1984* (Newcastle upon Tyne, 1996); *Collected 1: Poems 1985–1996* (Newcastle upon Tyne, 1996).

III. BIOGRAPHICAL AND CRITICAL STUDIES. Tom Paulin, "Junk Britain: Peter Reading" in *Minotaur: Poetry and the Nation State* (London, 1992); David Kennedy, "Elegies for the Living: The Poetry of Peter Reading," in *New Relations: The Refashioning of British Poetry 1980–94* (Bridgend, 1996); Sean O'Brien, "The Poet as Thatcherite?" in *The Deregulated Muse: Essays on Contemporary British and Irish Poetry* (Newcastle upon Tyne, 1998); Isabel Martin, *Reading Peter Reading* (Newcastle upon Tyne, 2000).

IV. INTERVIEWS. Ian Hamilton, *Bookmark*, BBC2 television (1 November 1986); Alan Jenkins, "Making Nothing Matter," *Poetry Review*, Vol. 75, No. 1 (April 1985); Robert Potts, "An Interview with Peter Reading," *Oxford Poetry* (December 1990), pp. 94–98; and "Poet Pete Ponders His Last Protest," *Guardian* (6 February 1992), p. 30; and "Through a Glass Darkly," *Guardian* (9 September 1997), p. 9.

GEORGE WILLIAM RUSSELL (AE)

(1867–1935)

Joseph A. Lennon

THE IRISH WRITER, painter, mystic, and agrarian organizer George William Russell, widely known by the pseudonym AE, once wrote that he had a quarrel with historians: "they seem to assume that the birth of great imaginations is not subject matter for history as much as great wars, or treaties or political or economic systems! Is only history to deal with effects, and not with causes?" ("The Antecedents of History," *The Living Torch*, p. 134). AE might have been reproving future literary historians for neglecting his own career. To examine Russell's life and works is to study one of the catalytic imaginations of the early twentieth century, such was his influence in literature, politics, culture, mysticism, agricultural reform, and Irish nationalism. Although he produced no major works in the literary canon, he was one of Ireland's great personalities in the decades surrounding the turbulent years when it won independence from Great Britain (1916–1921). Russell inspired writers, politicians, cultural figures, and Irish culture in general for generations. Since his death, scholars, understandably, have tended to regard his life and influence, more than his writings, as his significant contribution to the world of letters.

Literary historians tend to be more concerned with the major authors, works, and events of a literary period than with minor writers and cultural figures. The most intriguing figures, however, are often not the most anthologized. AE is such an example. Beside his mystical interests, he was primarily concerned with Ireland's birth as a cosmopolitan culture and modern nation following centuries of English domination. His far-reaching criticism, commentaries, essays, poems, novels, and drama help illuminate the varied motifs of Ireland's literary and cultural renaissance, the Celtic Revival. Through his advice and support, he aided an emerging generation of writers, including James Joyce, Padraic Colum, Liam O'Flaherty, Frank O'Connor, and Patrick Kavanagh and moved in diverse circles. He was in contact with nearly every prominent person in early twentieth-century Ireland and with writers, thinkers, and heads of state in Great Britain and America.

After moving to Dublin as a boy and spending years training as a painter and writer and working as a clerk, Russell found employment with the Irish Agricultural Organization Society (I.A.O.S.), first as a cooperative organizer in rural Ireland and later as an editor of its influential journal, the *Irish Homestead*. Alongside this work, he began his long study of Theosophy and practice as a mystic. Later, he edited and wrote for Ireland's main cultural journal of the 1920s, the *Irish Statesman*. During these years, he continued painting, produced his own writing, and began lecturing abroad. Over his lifetime, he published seventeen books and pamphlets of poetry, seven books of prose, and countless commentaries, essays, letters, pamphlets, and reviews, also selling and donating many paintings. His most prominent works illustrate the range of his writing: *Collected Poems* (1913), *The Candle of Vision* (mystical essays, 1918), *Imaginations and Reveries* (essays, 1915), *The National Being* (cultural and political critique, 1916), *The Avatars* (mystical novel, 1933), *The House of Titans and Other Poems* (1934), and his posthumous collection of essays from the *Irish Statesman*, *The Living Torch* (1937). While much of his work has not been reprinted, his collected works are emerging, and his key writings have remained significant to critics and readers, primarily those concerning mysticism, the Celtic Revival, early-twentieth century poetry, agricultural co-operatives, Irish modernity, and cultural imperialism.

He received wide recognition for his service to Ireland and his writings, in the form of honorary doctorates from Trinity College, Dublin, and Yale University and Ireland's Gregory Medal, awarded by the Irish Academy of Letters. British, American, and Irish government officials sought Russell's opinions on politics and agriculture. He served as a delegate to the Anglo-Irish Treaty Convention during the Irish War for Independence (1919–1921) and as a consultant to the United States Department of Agriculture during the 1930s. When he died, on 17 July 1935, his funeral was attended by the Ireland's foremost leaders, writers, and dignitaries; the procession extended for a mile through Dublin.

THE FORMATIVE YEARS: 1867–1898

George William Russell was born on 10 April 1867 in Lurgan, a small Ulster market town in County Armagh, which is now in Northern Ireland. His parents belonged to the Protestant minority in Ireland, attending the state-sponsored Church of Ireland, but his father had more evangelical leanings and also attended Primitive Methodist services. No particular family member, however, seems to have inspired AE's mystical and visionary interests, except to guide him away from sectarian conflict. Russell's father, Thomas Elias Russell, was a book-keeper for a Quaker firm, and, for a time in his twenties, George followed him into the world of business. His mother, Marianne Armstrong Russell, came from the Armagh countryside and bore three children: Mary Elizabeth, the eldest who died at age eighteen, Thomas, who died a few years before AE, and George, the youngest. For the first ten years of his life, the family remained in Lurgan, surrounded by fertile farm and pasture lands. The town had a thriving linen industry and a number of houses of worship: Church of Ireland, Quaker, Catholic, and Presbyterian.

AE's biographer, Henry Summerfield, reports that "Lurgan had an unenviable reputation for religious fanaticism. All his life Russell remembered how 'at any time a chance word might provoke a battle, and a whole horde of wild fanatics lying in ambush might rush out of the doors at a signal given, and in the name of God try to obliterate His image on each other's faces'" (*That Myriad-Minded Man*, p. 3). Critics have often suggested that such violent sectarianism partly motivated AE's later attraction to the mystical philosophy of Theosophy. The Theosophical Society, founded by Helen Petrovna Blavatsky, grounds its ideas in a set of somewhat bizarre mystical beliefs based upon Blavatsky's own visions and writings, Hindu mysticism, and, to a lesser extent, the mystical traditions of Buddhism, Christianity, and Islam. Theosophists, however, have argued that all of their beliefs become self-evident truths to the mystical seeker, while acknowledging its debt to a synthesis of religions, myth, and science. Critics have seen it as a movement of charlatans and self-righteous visionaries.

At age four George joined his siblings in attending the Model School. He enjoyed writing, drawing, and listening to fairy stories. In 1877 the family left religiously charged Lurgan and moved to Dublin, where his father worked at an accounting firm, probably as a book-keeper. George excelled in school, receiving a number of scholastic prizes, and attended the Metropolitan School of Art in the evenings in 1880; he returned, after finishing school, in the years 1883–1884. The family's move from Lurgan to urban Dublin, and later suburban Rathmines, did not inhibit Russell from developing a strong attraction to the natural world that bordered on romanticism. Russell's poetry and prose is often filled with natural imagery, echoing Keats, Blake, and Shelley, and, for many years as an adult, he spent summer vacations in Donegal, painting natural and supernatural scenes:

> I had not always this intimacy with nature. [. . .] I was not conscious in my boyhood of any heaven lying about me. I lived in the city, and the hills from which aid was to come to me were only a far flush of blue on the horizon. Yet I was drawn to

them, and as years passed and [my] legs grew longer I came nearer and nearer until at last one day I found myself on the green hillside.

(*The Candle of Vision*, collected in *The Descent of the Gods*, p. 84)

The physical distance from the countryside seems only to have increased his later ardent romantic interest in nature and rural living. After school, having already embraced temperance and a firm standard of ethics, Russell rejected a job at the Guinness factory, which his brother and father had secured for him, and began to work in other Dublin offices, all the while pursuing his ambition to become an artist.

AE'S MYSTICISM: THE BIRTH OF AEON

During the mid-1880s, his apprentice years, Russell's passion for painting, literature, and spiritual exploration contrasted vividly with his numbing daily routine behind various desks. In 1884, at the Metropolitan Art School, he met the young poet and aesthete William Butler Yeats (1865–1939), who encouraged his mystical interests and introduced him to the works of Madame Blavatsky and Theosophy, which immediately fired Russell's imagination. Russell continued to paint, enrolling at the more rigorous Royal Hibernian Academy in 1885. That same year he had a chance meeting with Charles Johnston, with whom, until Johnston left for India three years later, he became a close friend. Johnston founded the Hermetic Society in 1884 and, in 1885, the Dublin chapter of the Theosophical Society. Russell did not join either for a number of years, but he was intimate with their members. Johnston also introduced Russell to the esoteric works of Edwin Arnold, Mabel Collins, and A. P. Sinnett and arranged the 1885 Dublin visit of a traveling Bengali mystic, Mohini Chatterjee, who spoke across Europe as a sort of Asian representative of Theosophy. This single event sparked the interest of many young Irish artists, mystics, and writers in Orientalism and Indian mysticism and mythology, opening them to criticism and mockery from those less interested in spiritualism.

AE gradually rejected the materialism of Darwinism and the strict interpretations of the divine in Christianity in favor of Theosophical principles of spiritual evolution and reincarnation. Theosophy also included, among its more rarefied ideas, explanations of telepathy, astral travel, and the lost mythical city of Atlantis. Not all of Theosophy is so unconventional. Throughout his life, Russell adhered to the tenets of Theosophy but not of the Theosophical Society, from which he distanced himself later in the 1890s after Madame Blavatsky's death and the revelation of many of its leaders as charlatans. During the decade 1884–1894, however, Russell, who had then adopted the name AE (short for Aeon), increasingly favored mystical training and visionary experiences over his artistic ambitions.

The story of how Russell took the name AE illustrates a central tenet of his early mystical and poetic philosophy. As he lay in bed on vacation in Armagh, seeking a name for a series of paintings that portrayed humanity's mystical birth from the "Divine Mind," he heard, he later wrote, a voice whisper to him:

Something beyond reason held me, and I felt like one who is in a dark room and hears the breathing of another creature, and himself waits breathless for its utterance, and . . . while I was preternaturally dilated and intent, something whispered to me, "Call it the Birth of Aeon."

(*The Candle of Vision*, pp. 72–73)

Russell continues his explanation of the myth of Aeon, combining the traditional Christian creation myth with the fall of Milton's rebellious Lucifer:

The word "Aeon" thrilled me . . . and I think it was the following day that, still meditative and clinging to the word as a lover clings to the name of the beloved, a myth incarnated in me, the story of an Aeon, one of the first starry emanations of Deity, one pre-eminent [. . .] and so high in pride that he would be not less than a god himself and would endure no dominion over him save the law of his own will. This Aeon of my imagination revolted against heaven and left its courts, descending into the depths where it mirrored itself in chaos, weaving out of the wild elements a mansion for its spirit.

That mansion was our earth and that Aeon was the God of our world.

(p. 73)

This story somehow spoke to Russell, but it only became a lasting key to his identity through a serendipitous event. Weeks later in the National Library, he came across a book opened to the page defining "Aeon" as the name given by Gnostics to the original beings who first separated from God. Convinced that his identity would be bound somehow to this myth, he signed one of his first publications "Aeon," implying, either boldly or humbly, that his words had divine inspiration. The word did not stand, because the printer could not read the handwriting and wrote in the proofs, "AE—?" When Russell saw the letters, he delightedly let AE stand as his pseudonym, accepting it as a manifestation of deep mystical meaning.

In *The Candle of Vision* (1918) he further ruminates on the word "aeon," concluding its sounds contain an inherent meaning when pronounced and contemplated, signifying the movement of the "Deity" into existence and its return to the divine. "The roots of human speech are the sound correspondences of powers which in their combination and interaction make up the universe" (p. 138). He later abandoned his pseudo-linguistic formulations on the correspondence between sound and spirit, which have no etymological or philological support. These ideas, however, inspired much of his early and mid-career poetry. Russell also came to believe strongly in the sort of mystical serendipity he experienced, what he and other Theosophists call "spiritual gravity"—that spiritually akin people and ideas are drawn together and that seemingly random events happen for mystical reasons.

In 1890, Russell took a position with more responsibility as a clerk in Pim's, a large drapery shop in Dublin. The same year, he officially joined the Theosophical Society, and the two activities, one practical and the other visionary, typify the foundational impulses of AE's life. He moved out of his parents' house in 1891 to live with a group of Theosophists, helping establish a community, known as "the Household," which would become well known in Dublin artistic circles over the next six years. Some commentators have considered these six studious years as AE's experiential equivalent of university years. But AE was not studying and discussing a traditional curriculum; his study focused on the texts of Theosophy, Hindu spiritual texts, and mystical literature as he learned meditation and investigated other, more esoteric, practices. Meanwhile, the work at Pim's gave him financial independence and some security, but his workdays consisted of much drudgery. He later wrote to his younger friend C. C. Coates about his time there:

> What was worst to me in this overwork is what happens now and then in the hot room, the sudden flashes of recollection in looking out for a moment at the sunlight over the houses, golden white, the blue ether, the distance, the haze. Then it all comes over one, the sense of some Divine thing missed, swift like a lightning flash, incapable of analysis, only leaving a blurred impression on the mind, as the lightning does on the eye.
>
> (Coates, *Some Less Known Chapters in the Life of A.E. (George Russell)*, p. 5)

Such elusive flashes increasingly drew Russell's curiosity, and these became the subject matter of much of his writing and painting, along with representations of mystical beings. In 1894 he published his highly influential, first volume of poems, *Homeward: Songs by the Way* and began writing for the *Irish Theosophist*, which he co-founded. The next year he met two of the most significant people in his life: his future wife, an Englishwoman, Violet North, and the American mystic J. M. Pryse, who mentored AE's mystical studies in the 1890s. When they came to stay at the Household, they brought Madame Blavatsky's press with them and began to publish the *Irish Theosophist*, which Violet North edited after Pryse left Dublin.

Russell wrestled with his attraction for this independent, cigarette-smoking woman, feeling conflicted, in part, because of the general disapproval with which Theosophists view sexuality and romantic love. Many of his poems from this period reflect his wrestling with desire, the speaker often oscillating between physical and divine love. In "The Message," the speaker in the opening and closing stanzas asks the beloved to be satisfied with platonic love.

Do you feel the white glow in your breast, my bird?
    That is the flame of love I send to you from
      afar:
Not a wafted kiss, hardly a whispered word
    But love itself that flies as a white-winged
      star.

...

Do not ask for the hands of love or love's soft eyes:
    They give less than love who give all, giving
      what wanes.
I give you the star-fire, the heart-way to Paradise,
    With no death after, no arrow with stinging
      pains.

(Collected Poems, p. 100)

Despite these poetic appeals to abstinence, George Russell and Violet North married in 1898 and raised a family. They remained devoted for the duration of their marriage (North died in 1932), although both were exceedingly independent, and AE was increasingly drawn away from their family by political and national issues.

IRISH IDEALS: ESSAYS AND POEMS OF THE 1890S

Russell remained at Pim's and in the Household until 1897. The same year he was recruited as an organizer for the Irish Agricultural Organization Society (I.A.O.S.), which Sir Horace Plunkett had begun in 1894. W. B. Yeats had recommended him to Plunkett, who was seeking an energetic individual to help organize agricultural cooperatives. At first, he found the work trying, in part because he had never spoken in public and had never been outgoing. Early friends and acquaintances repeatedly described him as solitary, reflective, and dreamy. He was doubtful that he would continue the work, or be much of a success, but, after organizing a few meetings and studying the problems of farmers and rural workers, he became a persuasive orator and eventually helped organize thousands of rural cooperatives. The primary problem the I.A.O.S.

confronted concerned the fact that middlemen and merchants took the bulk of the farmers' profits, leaving the rural population in frequent economic peril, if not dire poverty.

AE traveled the countryside for eight years, sometimes for weeks at a stretch, organizing community banks, dairies, and stores; he would later boast in the *Irish Homestead* that he had personal experience in every county of Ireland. This increased familiarity opened his writings to a powerful growing force in Ireland in the 1890s, eventually uniting his mystical and practical activities. Irish cultural nationalism, focusing on the revival of Irish cultural and artistic forms, imbued his work and writings with a sense of duty and hope for the future. References to Irish myth began to crop up in his writings and speeches as cultural renewal became a primary ideal.

Two volumes of a *History of Ireland* (1878 and 1880) by Standish James O'Grady, an Irish barrister, cultural nationalist, and political Unionist, particularly influenced AE, Yeats, and others in the newly formed Irish Literary Society (1895). These volumes retold many of Ireland's major myths, particularly those in the Ulster Cycle concerning Cuchulain; they shaped a national mood perhaps more so than any other text at the time. The volumes only became widely read in the late 1880s and the 1890s, ten years after publication, following the praise bestowed on them by AE, Yeats, and other enthusiasts. AE fanned the flames of the reading public's interest, as we see in his essay on O'Grady.

> We praise the man who rushes into a burning mansion and brings out its greatest treasure. So ought we to praise this man who rescued from the perishing Gaelic tradition its darling hero and restored him to us, and I think now that Cuchulain will not perish . . . and he will be the courtesy which shall overcome the enemy that nothing else may overcome.
>
> *(Imaginations and Reveries, pp. 19–20)*

O'Grady translated Irish myth and folklore into a heroic nineteenth-century language, also AE's poetic style. Today, these retellings seem dated and sanitized Victorian stories, especially compared with more recent and exacting translations, such as Thomas Kinsella's *The Táin* (1969). But while O'Grady somewhat purified the texts to conform with late nineteenth-century British standards of decency, reading heroic feats of ancient Ireland gave Irish artists new material and pride. The myths hit AE with the force of revelation; for centuries much of this material had been dismissed as barbaric and uncivilized tales. Now AE boldly claimed for Ireland a lost mythic and literary heritage comparable to those of Britain, Greece, and India.

He read the myths at first through the lens of the Theosophy and eastern mysticism and mythology, suggesting fantastic interpretations. In an 1895 essay, "The Legends of Ancient Eire" printed in the *Irish Theosophist*, he argues for recovering the wisdom of the druids, asserting that the prehistoric giants of Celtic legend, the Firbolgs, or Fomorians, probably hailed from Atlantis; that Tír na n'Óg (the mythical Land of Youth), where the Irish hero Oisin mysteriously spent hundreds of years without aging, could be better understood in Tibetan terms as "Devachan," or the "Abode of the Gods," where beings exist between incarnations. He further argues that St. Patrick's banishing of the snakes from Ireland really had to do with the Christian banning of ancient "Serpentine Power" from Europe; this common Theosophical argument identifies this "Power," symbolized by the snake, with the practice of kundalini yoga in India. While readers today, over a century later, may find Russell's revelations strange, we should understand that he was by no means alone in drawing such conclusions. Irish intellectuals and artists were suspicious of both the modernity and the moral righteousness heralded by the British Empire. In the 1890s these Irish circles sought such ideas to recover cultural autonomy for Ireland and lend validity to their culture, independent of British tradition. AE's enthusiasm points not only to his Theosophical fervor but to the seeds of the Celtic Revival.

In 1897 AE published his second volume of poems, *The Earth Breath and Other Poems*. The title poem treats Irish rural life as the manifestation of a Celtic spiritual aesthetic:

Aureoles of joy encircle
    Every blade of grass
Where the dew-fed creatures silent
    And enraptured pass.
And the restless ploughman pauses,
    Turns and, wondering,
Deep beneath his rustic habit
    Finds himself a king;
For a fiery moment looking
    With the eyes of God
Over fields.

                (*Collected Poems*, p. 39)

As in most of his poems, the meter and rhyme are conventional and differ greatly from the emerging modernist aesthetic of England, France, and America. Many poems are in blank verse, but the majority rely upon rhyme to unify the sentiment, pushing the verse toward incantation, AE's preferred method of reciting. Complementing these nativistic and mystical poems, he also printed two pamphlets in 1897, vigorously arguing for the ancient pedigree of Irish culture and its immanent rebirth. Both *The Future of Ireland and the Awakening of the Fires* and *Ideals in Ireland: Priest or Hero?* argue for an appreciation of the vigor of pre-Christian Ireland, seeking a cultural form that predated all outside influences:

The genius of the Gael is awakening after a night of troubled dreams. It returns instinctively to the beliefs of its former day and finds again the old inspiration. It seeks the gods on the mountains still enfolded by their mantle of multitudinous traditions, or sees them flash by in the sunlit diamond airs. How strange, but how natural is all this!
    (*Ideals in Ireland: Priest of Hero?* collected in
    The Descent of the Gods, p. 367)

The pamphlets brought some notoriety to AE, who had been known chiefly around Dublin as the poet of *Homeward: Songs by the Way*. As far away as Belfast he was admired, and a young Northerner, James Cousins, reports in his autobiography *We Two Together* (1950) that *Homeward* transformed his sense of Irish poetry: "I read the little book through in an interval, and went on fire with the realization that immortal poetry had been given to Ireland" (p. 33).

GEORGE WILLIAM RUSSELL (AE)

The last years of the 1890s brought tumultuous changes for Russell. His mother died in 1897, the same year the Household broke. His and North's first son was born and died in 1899; the following year Russell's father died and their second son, Brian, was born. In 1901, a daughter was born but lived only a month, and in 1902 their last son, Diarmuid, was born. Amid all of these family births and deaths, in 1898 he was appointed assistant secretary of the I.A.O.S. and began serving as the Dublin editor of the Theosophical publication, *The Internationalist*. That same year, AE resigned from the Theosophical Society, disillusioned by the charges of charlatanism increasingly leveled at the organization and by the years of political infighting over leadership in the wake of the death of Blavatsky in 1891. While AE adhered to many of Blavatsky's and Theosophy's doctrines throughout his life, he distanced himself from the organization that continued after her death. Instead, he resurrected the Hermetic Society, originally founded by Charles Johnston. He hosted its initial meetings and served as president until 1933.

AE's living room became a meeting place for artists, mystics, writers, intellectuals, Celtophiles, and cultural nationalists, particularly once he moved, in 1906, to 17 Rathgar Street, where he remained until his wife's death. His weekly salons resonated with conversation, monologue, and debate, and hundreds of prominent visitors from Ireland and abroad attended over the next several decades. At the dawn of the new century, along with Irish culture, AE was coming into his own. He had lost the shyness and detached dreaminess that had marked his early years, and he was becoming a multifaceted public figure: a poet, a mystic, an organizer, and, soon, an editor and commentator for a major Irish periodical.

THE NATIONAL STAGE: 1899–1922

Anti-imperial and nationalist movements swelled during the early years of the century in English and French colonies around the globe. Later, in a remarkable forty-year period of decolonization, most of these colonies broke from their imperial centers. The first nation to break from the British Empire was Ireland. For the first decade of the century, Irish physical force nationalists had little support; most people in Ireland favored peace over independence. The activities of cultural nationalists gradually became prominent as they touted a distinct Irish "National Being" (to borrow AE's term) separate from England. They developed ideas and moods that all Irish nationalists would later build upon. In 1913, labor tensions turned violent in Dublin during a bitter labor strike, and resentment grew toward Britain over a suspended Irish Home Rule bill. In 1916 a small armed insurrection, the Easter Rising, surprised everyone in Dublin. British forces put down the rebellion with great force and executed its leaders in a drawn-out fashion. A few years later, Ireland was openly at war with England, seeking immediate independence. In 1921, after two years of bloody guerrilla war, the provisional government of Ireland signed a treaty with Great Britain that granted independence to a twenty-six-county Irish Free State. The remaining six counties of Northern Ireland remained part of Great Britain. The treaty and partition, however, was not well received by hard-line nationalists, and civil war raged for ten months.

During these troubled years, AE continued his commentary on the new Irish nation and recommended nonviolent solutions to the conflicts. He enthusiastically encouraged cultural, economic, and social reforms that diverged from British ideals, particularly if they were seen as native to Ireland. Along with mystical essays, poetry, and agricultural reports, AE also wrote drama, literary criticism, journalism, and political and economic essays. Indeed, he soon became one of the most read and renowned figures of his day, consulted on matters ranging from Celtic spiritualism to the fixing of import levies. He established his national prominence as an editor, and he is still known in Ireland as a practical man who conversed with the fairies, and as a poet-philosopher-statesman.

AE AND THE CELTIC REVIVAL: DRAMA AND POETRY

The rise of public interest in Irish myth and folklore led to the emergence of a strong theater tradition in Ireland. In 1899 W. B. Yeats, Lady

Gregory, and Edwyn Martin formed the Irish Literary Theatre, with AE as a guarantor who assisted the productions, in part through his painting. These plays set off an unexpected controversy in the *Daily Express* about the staging of Irish mythological heroes—later reprinted as a collection of essays, *Ideals in Ireland,* by W. B. Yeats, John Eglinton (William Magee), AE, and William Larminie. Characteristically, AE sought to reconcile the two perspectives of Yeats and Eglinton. Yeats advocated staging Irish myths in order to bring them to public, whereas Eglinton believed putting the myths on the stage (usually associated at the time with music hall comedies and melodramas) would make them base and common. AE argued that the ideals of the writers were not incompatible, that Irish myth could be presented to modern audiences, if handled respectfully. To ground his argument, AE offered the first act of what became his only play, *Deirdre*—a tragic myth of love, betrayal, and suicide. With AE playing a druid character, the verse drama was performed in 1902 along with Lady Gregory and Yeats's famous co-written play, *Cathleen ni Houlihan*, to enthusiastic, packed houses.

While the play was immensely popular, today its elevated dialogue, once intended to resound like mythical pronouncements, now sounds only antiquated and ponderous, and the performance models upon which he relied, such as tableaux and poetry recitation, make the play seem more a blend of painting, philosophy, and verse than a compelling drama. Deirdre's last speech becomes, in AE's hands, a vehicle for neo-Celtic philosophy rather than one of the most passionate laments in Irish myth:

> My spirit is sinking away from the world. I could not stay after Naisi. After the Lights of Valour had vanished, how could I remain? The earth has grown dim and old, fostermother. The gods have gone far away, and the lights from the mountains and the Lions of the Flaming Heart are still. O fostermother, when they heap the cairn over him, let me be beside him in the narrow grave.
>
> (*Imaginations and Reveries,* p. 314)

Audiences adored the play's heroism and grandeur. The following year AE became vice-president (after declining the presidency in favor of Yeats) of the newly formed Irish National Theatre Society. The officers also included important figures of the Revival: Lady Augusta Gregory, William Fay, Maud Gonne, and Douglas Hyde (founder of the Gaelic League and Ireland's first president). But AE did not remain active in the theater company, later reconfigured as the Abbey Theatre. Following debates with Yeats over plays (particularly those of the young Belfast playwright and poet James Cousins) and various policies, AE affably resigned, not wanting to undermine the unity of the company.

In the end of 1903 and the beginning of 1904, with the publication of his third and fourth volume of poems, AE was increasingly regarded as an important new poet of the aesthetic school eventually referred to as the "Celtic Twilight," a disparaging reference to Yeats's collection of the same name. AE's poems often focus on Ireland's mythical Celtic past, accessible to the poet through mystical vision and imagination. In December, the new Dun Emer press (later Cuala Press), founded by the two artistic sisters of W. B. Yeats, Lily and Lolly, released a selection of AE's old and new poems in a limited edition, *The Nuts of Knowledge*. In 1904 Macmillan signed him, signifying his international stature as a poet, and after 1904, his poems found a wider audience in Europe and America. The poems continued their focus on mystical and visionary experience, filling a desire for Irish poetry and Celticism in Ireland, England, and America.

The poems are generally celebratory but occasionally lament the poet's attachment to the world. As in his earlier poems, AE explores, and often breaches, the chasm between the spiritual and physical. "A Return," at first a lament for a lost idealized rural culture, turns into a celebration of the imagination. It begins, "We turned back mad from the mystic mountains"—a place redolent with "elfin gold" and "fires enchanted" (*Collected Poems,* p. 222). Although the narrators regret returning to "The iron clang" of the town, in the end vision overrides despondency: "We could not weep in our bitter sorrow, / But joy as an Arctic sun went down." The poems in his fourth volume, *The Divine Vision and Other*

Poems, were even more accomplished, but today the language seems somewhat overwrought in tone and idiom, relying upon alchemically charged words, such as amethyst, gold, twilight, and emerald, and archaic phrasings like "the ancient fount sublime" ("Our Thrones Decay," p. 194). The verse was popular, however, and in these years AE also edited a prominent anthology of emerging Irish poets, entitled *New Songs*.

AE gained a reputation for helping writers hone their craft, offering critiques, avenues for publication, and encouragement. New poets and writers as well as established men and women of letters often made their way to his Sunday evenings to talk about literature, art, and mysticism amid his paintings of mystical beings. Yeats, who hosted more select salons, was known to support only a few writers, such as the playwright J. M. Synge (1871–1909). AE and Yeats grew more distant, only occasionally attending one another's "at homes." Although Yeats scornfully dubbed AE's protégés his "canaries," these writers did not ape AE's style. Rather, they developed new approaches to representing Irish culture, setting stories and novels in stark urban environments and brutal small towns. A brief list of these writers includes James Cousins, Padraic Colum, Alice Milligan, James Stephens, Eva Gore-Booth, Liam O'Flaherty, Frank O'Connor, and Sean O'Faolain.

IRISH COMMENTARIES: PROSE, POETRY, CONVERSATION, JOURNALISM

In the early years of the century, Russell continued to travel the Irish countryside organizing cooperatives, often staying with priests, farmers, and storytellers and learning local legends and fairy lore. In 1905, Horace Plunkett offered Russell the opportunity to succeed H. F. Norman as the Dublin editor of the *Irish Homestead*, a position that would eventually make AE the leading journalistic figure in Dublin. The I.A.O.S. had grown substantially in the last decade, and its publication was read for more than prices and yield indexes. The *Irish Homestead* voiced nonsectarian and religiously neutral perspectives on social and political issues and cooperative

news; technical information; and stories and poems related to the countryside and Irish tradition. AE had regularly contributed commentary with his organizing reports and soon began writing popular editorials. Issues such as Irish emigration, the revival of Gaelic culture, and Unionist and Nationalist unified support for agricultural cooperation continued to be its main issues under Russell's editorship. Moreover, AE continued to run new short stories and poems by emerging Irish writers, including poems from the Irish language (with translations), a feature that Norman had begun in 1901.

In 1905 AE published his first collection of fiction, *The Mask of Apollo and Other Stories*, gathered from stories and short pieces he had printed in the *Irish Theosophist* and elsewhere. As the preface makes clear, these were AE's first attempts at fiction. He intended them to represent not only his own mind but the mystical backdrop of the age in Ireland. The pieces reveal an internationalism that is rarely acknowledged as an aspect of the Celtic Revival, borrowing from Greek, Indian, and Jewish sources, focusing on mystical traditions that countered the practical materialism, realism, and naturalism of English literature. He treated these other traditions as precursors to the rebirth of Irish culture and mysticism. AE prophesied that this new Celtic culture, based on ideals of art and beauty, would be brought about by a new leader, a divine incarnation of a god, or an avatar. While Russell never found this avatar, he later imagined two in his novel *The Avatars* (1933).

During this extraordinarily productive time, Russell also returned to painting, with some financial success. He had not painted regularly since 1890, when he had dropped out of art school and begun his serious mystical studies (Summerfield, p. 119). In 1904, however, the flamboyant Count and Countess Markievicz, who were involved in the Celtic Revival and nationalist politics, pressed AE to contribute some of his paintings to a public exhibition of Celtic art that they were organizing. He spent much of the spring and summer painting. To his surprise, forty pieces sold to enthusiastic buyers. The following year, both to continue painting and to keep in contact with the countryside, AE began an annual summer trip to Donegal, where he became somewhat of a local celebrity. He continued these trips regularly for the next decade, sometimes with his wife but more often with a close friend such as James Stephens.

From the time that the Russells moved in 1906 to 17 Rathgar Avenue up until the Dublin Strike of 1913, AE's life became more routine, as he spent his days editing, painting, and writing about Irish and Celtic themes. In 1906, he published his fourth volume of poems, *By Still Waters*, many of which had appeared in various Dublin periodicals, including the nationalist periodical *Sinn Fein* ("we ourselves" or "ourselves alone" in the Irish language). Another collection of his essays appeared the same year, culled from the *Homestead* and elsewhere and aptly titled *Some Irish Essays*. These years mark the beginning of AE's prominence as a journalist and writer in Irish periodicals and demonstrate perhaps his most lasting contribution to Irish literature. Under AE's editorship, the *Irish Homestead* expanded far beyond the cooperative movement, and playwright George Bernard Shaw likened it to the great eighteenth-century English periodicals the *Tatler* and the *Spectator* (Summerfield, p. 134). An incident illustrating AE's growing sphere of influence as an editor occurred in 1912 when, from comments in his weekly column, he inspired a new women's organization, the United Irishwomen. It was an important force in Irish culture until the mid-1930s, when the conservative Catholic state dominated Irish culture.

AE developed his thought in his wide-ranging discussions with visitors to his Sunday evening sessions, growing famous for his talk in Dublin, a city where conversation skills have long been greatly esteemed. His reputation was rivaled only by his close friends Stephen MacKenna, a classical scholar and translator of Plotinus, and James Stephens, a writer and poet who later became a BBC radio host. In 1937 a younger friend of AE's, Monk Gibbon, recorded Stephens on AE: "He awakened as a conversationalist and he conversed mightily until he slept again" (*The Living Torch*, Gibbon, p. 37). We get a glimpse of that ability in Monk Gibbon's account of AE, who after showing paintings to a visitor would return:

> [He] would soon be caught into the current of one or other of the discussions in progress then and, drawing the threads together, he would begin to discover some principle or unity in the debate, which before seemed absent. . . . There is no doubt that his conversation had an astonishing range and that he had the gift of evoking whatever was most interesting in others simply by the prodigality with which he gave himself.
>
> (*The Living Torch*, pp. 36–37)

Many of his writings, especially his prose pieces and editorials, developed out of these conversations.

Over the next few years, he would publish three more prose books of essays and lectures, many from the pages of the *Irish Homestead*. The most significant of these collections is *Co-operation and Nationality* (1912), which was disseminated as a guide for nationalist organizers and the cooperative movement, which by 1909 had grown to include over one hundred thousand farmers out of the roughly half a million in Ireland (Summerfield, p. 147). Although AE later felt the book to be a piece of rushed journalism, it was eventually translated into a number of languages and read by Mahatma Gandhi and Rabindranath Tagore in India as well as in Bulgaria by its Prime Minister, Alexander Stamboliski (1879–1923), who established mandatory agrarian volunteer corps on AE's model (Bolger, "Foreword" to reprint of *Co-operation and Nationality*).

In 1913 AE boldly commented on the Dublin strikes, supporting the strikers in the pages of the *Homestead* and the *Irish Times*. He also rebuked the Catholic Church (and drew fire) when it organized mass demonstrations preventing the children of strikers from being temporarily sent to non-Catholic union families in England. He also joined the Industrial Peace Committee, which formed to protect the strikers and later became the Irish Citizen Army. But as it grew militant in the hostile streets of Dublin, AE backed away, holding to his lifelong view (which wavered only during Ireland's war with Britain) that all war is unethical.

In these years the unease surrounding the issue of Irish national independence increased as a private Protestant and Unionist militia was raised in Ulster by Sir Edward Carson. The militia, reputedly numbering over 200,000, was intended to fend off a possible nationalist takeover of Ireland. Added to this pressure, a version of the Home Rule Bill had finally passed the British Parliament but was immediately suspended until after the war. In 1914, during the mounting tensions, AE was invited to England to meet with British Prime Minister Herbert Henry, First Earl of Oxford and Asquith (Prime Minister Asquith, for short) and Chief Secretary for Ireland, Augustine Birrell. They discussed the "Irish Question" and how best to implement Home Rule. They reached no definite conclusion, but for the rest of his life, AE would be consulted on political, economic, and agricultural matters by Irish, British, and the United States governments.

One of AE's more pointed pleas for nonviolence came in response to Rudyard Kipling's 1912 poem "Ulster," which promotes religious bigotry and sectarian hatred. AE wrote an open letter to the London *Daily News*, referencing himself as an Ulsterman who, like Kipling, had come out of the Protestant tradition. He whittles down Kipling's argument, treating his inspiration as petty opportunism. He closes by scolding the British jingoist as a "brother poet" aiming to profit from such hateful verse, which Kipling had copyrighted and sold in the United States.

Although the years between 1912 and 1914 were troubled for Ireland and Europe, AE referred to them as "Dublin's Golden Age" (Summerfield, p. 152). We might properly understand these years to be AE's best ones, a time when his considered opinions most mattered in Ireland and England, just as the dams of peace broke across Europe in 1914. In 1913, Macmillan released his *Collected Poems*, and his opinion was again sought in England, this time on agricultural matters. In 1914 he privately printed a pamphlet entitled *Oxford University and the Co-operative Movement*. The following year, collecting his poems about European militarism and the outbreak of World War I, he privately printed his volume of poems *Gods of War, with Other Poems* (1915). If the tone in these poems is slightly moralistic, it also brings political concerns into relation with mystical ones. Another collection of essays, *Imaginations and Reveries*, came out in 1915. This volume, more than any others he edited, reflects the wide contribution that AE made to Ireland and Irish culture. It contains mystical essays; his play *Deirdre*; some short fiction; essays on rural, national, and cosmopolitan ideals; and commentary on cultural figures such as W. B. Yeats and Standish O'Grady. Such myriad topics made the volume interesting to a wide readership and distinguished AE's multifaceted approach.

AE AND THE "TROUBLES"

In 1916, the year of the Easter Uprising, AE published his extended, provocative, and still important critical essay *The National Being: Some Thoughts on Irish Polity*. Some of what he argues here prefigures criticism that developed years later in former European colonies about nationhood and colonialism. The work repeats some theories for a cooperative commonwealth put forward in *Co-operative and Nationality*, but what is added is an increased awareness of the struggle between labor and capital (following his experience with the Dublin strikes of 1913). Also, AE added a discussion on the metaphysical characteristics of nations, which encompass both an ancient past and the promise of a unified future. He differentiates the "National Being," however, from the nation state—both of which he sees as essential. He asks: "[Is it] that a State—even a bad State—must be preserved by its citizens, because it is at least an attempt at organic unity? It is a simulacrum of the ideal; it contains the germ or possibility of that to which the spirit of man is travelling" (p. 160). As Robert Davis, a Russell scholar, has suggested, AE treated a colony's move toward nationality as a spiritual journey, "a fulfillment of the divine purpose" (*George William Russell*, p. 103). AE's text shares the epochal tone of the writings of the leaders of the Rising, and particularly their

Proclamation, which announced a new Irish nation. Indeed, the text presages the 1916 Rising itself, commenting that rebellion was often an unavoidable expression of the National Being:

> We are here for the purposes of soul, and there can be no purpose in individualizing the soul if essential freedom is denied to it and there is only a destiny. Wherever essential freedom, the right of the spirit to choose its own heroes and its own ideals is denied, nations rise in rebellion.
>
> (*The National Being*, p. 163)

But this is not a blindly nationalist text; AE also critiques the passion, bigotry, and sectarianism in Ireland, advocating for a more just and careful consideration of Irish ideals: "What too many people in Ireland mistake for thoughts are feelings. It is enough to them to vent like or dislike, inherited prejudices or passions, and they think when they have expressed feeling they have given utterance to thought" (p. 6). The text also outlines an ideal government, composed of two legislative bodies, one elected and the other consisting of a body of appointed experts in various fields. The work closes by asking Ireland's spiritual leaders to promote a cooperative, not competitive, model for the emerging nation.

When the Irish Volunteers and the Irish Citizen's Army temporarily took control of Dublin during the Easter Rising of 1916, AE, like most people, was surprised by the dramatic turn of events, especially because a Home Rule bill had been passed. As a pacifist, he saw little to admire in the violent and doomed insurrection, feeling that the distraught urban poor had continued to follow the leaders of the 1913 strikes into battle in order to vent labor frustrations (Summerfield, p. 178). But he grew increasingly sympathetic as the British authorities, wanting to make a firm show of strength, jailed his old friend Lady Constance Markievicz and executed the leaders of the Rising, three of whom AE knew closely. Over the next few months, newspaper accounts carried the details of the shootings, and the tide of public sympathy turned. AE soon was at work on a long memorial poem, *Salutation*, commemorating those who had died in the insurrection, which he printed later in the year. He wrote his most accomplished poem on the topic, an elegy for a single fictional soldier, "Michael," three years later in 1919.

During 1917 and 1918, AE devoted much of his nonjournalistic writing to an account of his mystical experiences from boyhood to the present, *The Candle of Vision*. This work lays out a great deal of his principles and practices and includes chapters on meditation, imagination, dreams, power, and Celtic myth. His overall argument concerns the importance of imagination and, by extension, mystical insight. He critiques modern science and psychology as being dismissive of the imagination:

> I think few of our psychologists have had imagination themselves. They have busy brains, and, as an Eastern proverb says, 'The broken water surface reflects only broken images.' . . . They discuss the mode of imagination as people might discuss art, who had never seen painting or sculpture.
>
> (*The Candle of Vision*, collected in *The Descent of the Gods*, p. 102)

Believing that imagination was integral for the wholeness of individuals and nations, AE argued that it and vision joined individuals to their nation and the divine. His mysticism, while often anti-modern, never led him away from practical matters such as agricultural reform and political mediation.

Until 1918 he remained involved in the efforts to find acceptable terms for Irish independence, serving as a member of the Irish Home Rule Convention in London and printing his ideas in the pamphlet *Thoughts for a Convention*. The Convention became bogged down in trying to find a solution acceptable to the Ulster Unionists, the Irish Nationalists, and Great Britain, and he eventually resigned, not wanting to sabotage future efforts. Drawing again from his editorials, AE put out another pamphlet in 1918, *Conscription for Ireland: A Warning to England*. As Davis notes, this pamphlet, when added to his other political writings, firmly established AE as "the conscience of his country. He was that greatly needed but inadequately respected figure in every nation, the philosophical statesman" (*George William Russell*, p. 145). During both the Irish War for Independence and Ireland's Civil War (1919–1923), he continued to assert the need for agricultural cooperatives in the new nation and wrote a number of tightly argued essays. British "Black and Tan" soldiers had repeatedly targeted Irish cooperatives for retribution after rebel attacks on British barracks, pouring out milk and burning buildings. His *A Plea for Justice* (1920) emerged from his angry columns in the *Irish Homestead*; in it, Russell demanded an independent inquiry into the destruction of specific cooperatives. His "Open Letter to the Irish Republicans" in the *Irish Times* in 1922 sought to mediate conflict over the Anglo-Irish Treaty, which divided the sides in the Irish Civil War. Other pamphlets concerned England-Ireland economic and political issues: *The Economics of Ireland, and the Policy of the British Government* came out in 1920 at the height of the Anglo-Irish war and echoes his ideas for a cooperative commonwealth. Both *The Inner and Outer Ireland* and *Ireland and the Empire at the Court of Conscience* appeared in 1921, when the war was reaching its conclusion and the treaty was accepted. *Ireland, Past and Future* came out during the Civil War in 1922.

Often these pamphlets did not argue polemical positions. Instead, AE reframed the discussion into terms that were more acceptable to all parties involved. At times his arguments did not reveal a readily identifiable position, as in the case of *Ireland and the Empire at the Court of Conscience*, which puts forth multiple arguments, in multiple voices, for and against Ireland's remaining a part of Great Britain. By recasting the arguments, he moved the locus of debate away from retribution, race, religion, and the inflammatory rhetoric that often invades sectarian politics. As Summerfield notes, AE was "one of the very few in whose presence and home men passionately committed to opposite sides could meet in social harmony" (p. 186). In synthesis alone, AE argued, could a new Ireland emerge.

His first novel, *The Interpreters*, published by Macmillan in 1922, employs a similar approach. The book is an ideological novel, more a series of disquisitions on philosophic, mystical, cultural, and political matters than a narrative. It delimits a number of social and philosophical perspectives, demonstrating their strengths and weaknesses through characters (an historian, an artist, a socialist, an imperialist, a mystic) who both espouse and embody in their persons various positions. AE sets the novel in the future, in a fictional nation undergoing a revolution. Questions about humanity and its prospects dominate everyone's thinking.

> Every one in this age sought for the source and justification of their own activities in that divine element in which matter, energy, and consciousness when analysed disappeared. It was an era of arcane speculation, for science and philosophy had become esoteric after the visible universe had been ransacked and the secret of its being had eluded the thinkers.

("The Interpreters," *The Descent of the Gods,* p. 274)

As we have seen, the device of multiple perspectives had been used earlier, in *The Court of Conscience*. Here, all of the characters have been put in the same jail room by a twist of fate, and throughout the novel they debate issues of state, nation, spirituality, economics, art, and literature, the ultimate question being Plato's: what is the good life? Their fate will be decided by the outcome of the turmoil raging outside the prison. The situation in Ireland had repeatedly verged on anarchy in these years, and much about its future remained uncertain. In exploring the problem from many angles, AE looked to resolve the entrenched conflict.

AN INTERNATIONAL IRISHMAN: JOURNALISM, POETRY, PROSE, 1923–1935

The years 1922–1923 proved to be a time of transition for AE and for Ireland. With the formation of the Irish Free State, Sir Horace Plunkett, an Irish statesman, political economist and founder of the I.A.O.S., and Irish and American backers sought the creation of a newspaper that would air the issues the new Irish nation faced. The *Irish Homestead* merged with the new paper and AE's office became the headquarters of the *Irish Statesman,* with AE as editor-in-chief and Susan Mitchell as his assistant. For the next seven years, every major debate in Ireland would find space in these pages. AE's editorials and columns became even more prolific, and his best pieces were collected by Monk Gibbon in *The Living Torch*, two years after his death in 1937. Some critics have concluded that this volume is AE's true literary masterpiece.

AE visited Paris in 1926 and made three trips to America between 1928 and 1930, where he read and spoke. Over the next decade five more volumes of poems were published: *Voices of the Stones* (1925), *Midsummer Eve* (1928), *Enchantment and Other Poems* (1930), *Vale and Other Poems* (1931), and *The House of Titans and Other Poems* (1934). While the poems advance familiar themes, they rely less upon stock alchemical phrases and standard forms. Indeed, his most accomplished poems—"Germinal," "Dark Rapture," "The Dark Lady," "To One Who Wanted a Philosophy from Me," "An Idle Reverie," and "The House of Titans"—are to be found in *Vale and Other Poems* and *The House of Titans*. Although repetitive in theme, these volumes move beyond mystical meditations into dramatic monologues and picturesque verse.

"The Dark Lady" gives voice to a famous, elusive figure, the woman of Shakespeare's sonnets in order to explore the nature of his inspiration:

> O, No, I was not wanton with that man.
> But to his imaginations, yes. I made
> Myself a hundred natures. It is writ,
> My myriad girlhood, in that printed page.
> Or was it I? Did I but play the part
> His magic plotted for me? Did he know
> That his imaginations lived in me
> And swayed me to be one of their own kind,
> To act the bawd for whom an emperor
> Might cast his world away
>
> (*The House of Titans*, p. 46)

The speaker describes various characters she embodied, being the model for Shakespeare's art, and falling in love with him. Seeking intimacy through imagination, she has given her abilities to him, but, in return, she has not been given devotion, love or understanding:

> When I liked myself to him, the myriad minded
> Who gathered knaves and heroes with like love
> to snatch the inmost secret of them

> . . . And I had not yet won
> Spirits enough to be mate for him
> learned in so many hearts.

The speaker, as the playwright's model, has imagined a myriad of characters for him. But, this has not satisfied her—she has only "masked her soul." Soon she realizes that her abilities are more significant than as tools of his art; she realizes that as a mystic, she is the greater imaginative artist. As her admiration of the playwright's literary skills lessens, she also becomes disillusioned with the playwright himself.

> For he, who painted me
> In many scarlet dyes, came ere the end
> To breathe forgiveness. I had once imagined
> For his delight myself to be a maid
> Bred on a fairy isle who knew not man.
> . . . but when I saw his face
> It was not the face I loved, but was the face
> Beautiful, mad, hopeless, of that boy.
>
> (pp. 53–55)

The dramatic monologue privileges the power of imagination over the power of literature, and, in some ways, this is one of AE's lasting thoughts on the place of literature in relation to the spiritual—that is, that poetry should serve the mystical and not vice versa. This poem has little in common with the experimental techniques of AE's high modernist contemporaries, who often valued art and literature over all. But this, and other of his poems, can be better appreciated as accomplishments if we see them in the vein of Robert Browning and other late-nineteenth-century and Victorian poets.

In 1932, AE published his second work expressly devoted to exploring mystical experiences, *Song and Its Foundations*. This slim book sought to explain some of the roots of mystical poetry and provides a key to understanding much that is arcane in his verse. Also, his long-planned mystical novel, *The Avatars*, finally appeared in 1933; its initial inspiration came from a vision he had in his younger years about an avatar, an incarnation of a powerful mystical being, who would reshape Ireland. Unlike *The Interpreters*, this novel has a successful narrative. The characters live in the same fictional land as in the earlier work, a heavily industrialized, futuristic Ireland. A group of artistic and mystical characters are drawn together in a rural cottage. Throughout the book they witness the arrival, influence, disappearance, and remembrance of two Irish avatars, who catalyze the gestalt of the time and become the founding heroes of a nation based on artistic and romantic principles.

Amid the turmoil and violence of Ireland's break from England, AE's personal life also had its share of difficulties. In 1920, Violet Russell developed cancer, and she remained an invalid, often in considerable pain, for twelve years until her death. AE's longtime friend and assistant, Susan Mitchell, died in 1926. These difficulties, however, brought AE closer to his son Diarmuid, who had known his father only as a distant figure. In 1926 Diarmuid began to help his father at the *Irish Statesman*, working in the crowded office for three years before he immigrated to Chicago.

Perhaps the most stressful trials of these years occurred at the height of AE's success as an editor and commentator in Ireland. Russell had great difficulty with the growing nativistic and conservative religious state. From 1927 to 1928, conservative Catholic forces nearly forced the *Irish Statesman* into bankruptcy through costs associated with a bogus libel suit. The action stemmed from a book review by Dr. Donal O'Sullivan criticizing a work of inexact translations from the Irish by an amateur translator and his wife, Seamus and T. K. Clandillon L.A.G. Strong's account of AE's court testimony reveals the poet's wit in difficult circumstances; asked by the judge if parts of the book did not contain some merit, he replied:

"Certainly, my Lord. . . . Parts of it were good."

"In that case, Mr. Russell, why did your paper describe it as a bad book?"

"My Lord, if you had an egg at your breakfast this morning, and parts of it were bad, and parts of it were good, I think you would have described it as a bad egg."

(Summerfield, p. 247)

While the suit was eventually dismissed from court, the legal costs nearly destroyed the paper. A committee of intellectuals and liberal Catholics, however, gathered sufficient subscriptions to keep the paper afloat.

The Russell family, never well-off, also began to suffer financial difficulties. Amid the libel suit, medical costs arising from treatments for Violet Russell required AE to travel to America on a lecture tour in early 1928. He spoke at dozens of venues, including Harvard and Yale universities, traveling as far west as Chicago, meeting with leaders of business, academic, and social organizations, giving agricultural advice, and lecturing on Irish, mystical, literary, and artistic topics. He returned after four months, considerably impressed with the United States, commenting in the *Statesman* in his usual optimistic tone that in America he saw the possibility of a global consciousness and universal brotherhood. His trip had been a great success; he had even been offered a six-month appointment at Yale. He refused it but agreed to make another cross-Atlantic journey to receive an honorary doctorate from Yale.

The following summer, 1929, he received an honorary doctorate from Trinity College, Dublin. In 1930 the *Irish Statesman* was finally discontinued due to a lack of funds; its American supporters were rumored to have pulled out because they lost too much money in the stock market crash of 1929. The same year, however, AE was feted and presented with eight hundred Irish pounds by the governor general of the Irish Free State as a token of esteem for Russell's years of devoted work to the nation. In 1931 Russell returned to the United States for an extended lecture tour and as a consultant to the U.S. Department of Agriculture. He also visited his son in Chicago and journeyed as far as California before returning home. Poems from these years reflect his experiences abroad, especially the series in *Vale* consisting of "Atlantic," "New York," "The Cities," "In a Strange City," "The Forge," and "Fugitive." The question in this last poem, which also ends the volume, "Did it seem shuttlecock / That soul, now hear, now there, / That seemed to have no goal / In intellectual air?" demonstrates both a new ease in tone and the continued prominence of spiritual issues. Indeed, spiritual musings are the unifying characteristic of all of his poetry.

When Violet died, he moved out of Rathgar Street permanently, put his possessions in storage, and moved to England to be with friends and avoid loneliness. He returned to Ireland for a visit and made a last trip to the United States in 1934 but was forced to return to England early due to failing health, in particular cancer. After receiving the Royal Irish Academy's Gregory Medal, for distinction as a writer, he grew progressively ill. He died a quiet death in London in 1935, going over proofs of his *Selected Poems* and corresponding with friends.

CONCLUSION

AE's vision of an ideal rural society coincided with some ideals of conservative isolationism of the Irish government in the 1930s through the 1960s. His works, like those of many writers in the early century, were later treated as promoting the same official nationalist image of a wholesome Irish population: Catholic, traditional, rural, and satisfied with frugal comforts. This misreading of his works, combined with the often inaccessible mysticism and nineteenth-century tone, has kept many of today's readers from his writings. But his rural idealism differed considerably from that of the Catholic state, and AE vigorously critiqued the stances of the new conservative politicians, particularly on the issues of emigration, restrictions on women, censorship of the arts, and the dominance of the Catholic Church in Irish government and society. Moreover, although AE's poems, drama, essays, and novels are rarely read today for literary merit, they contain much that is notable and worthy, especially his later poetry. His less "literary" essays and collected journalism remain significant and may be his best works.

AE's diverse works shed light on the Celtic Revival, the emerging Irish nation, and Theosophical mysticism, and they reveal a wide-ranging talent and vision. His contributions to the Irish cultural revival cannot be overstated. Criticism of AE's work varies in tone from the hagiographic, venerating his mystical visions and arcane speculations, to the harshly critical, attacking his lack of literary innovation and strange spiritualism as a form of neo-Celtic posturing (as in the representation of AE by playwright Sean O'Casey). A fairer assessment probably falls somewhere between these two poles. His best works—*Imaginations and Reveries*, *The National Being*, *The Avatars*, *Vale and Other Poems*, *The House of Titans*, *The Living Torch*—offer valuable insights on culture, humanity, colonialism, and metaphysics. His most experimental work, *The Interpreters*, falls short of being readable, but his similarly structured pamphlet, *Ireland and the Empire at the Court of Conscience* is compelling. It is his mystical prose, however, particularly *The Candle of Vision* and *Song and Its Fountains*, that have achieved a lasting audience, and he is probably read for pleasure most often in mystical circles.

SELECTED BIBLIOGRAPHY

I. POETRY. *Homeward Songs by the Way* (Dublin, 1894); *The Earth Breath and other Poems* (New York and London, 1897); *The Nuts of Knowledge* (Dublin, 1903); *The Divine Vision and other Poems* (New York and London, 1904); *By Still Waters* (Dublin, 1906); *Collected Poems* (London, 1913); *Gods of War and Other Poems* (Dublin, 1915); *Salutation, A Poem on the Irish Rebellion of 1916* (London, 1917); *Michael* (Dublin, 1919); *Voices of the Stones* (London, 1925); *Midsummer Eve* (New York, 1928); *Dark Weeping* (London, 1929); *Enchantment and other Poems* (London, 1930); *Vale and other Poems* (London, 1931); *Verses for Friends* (London, 1932); *The House of the Titans and other Poems* (London, 1934); *Selected Poems* (London, 1935).

II. FICTION. *The Mask of Apollo* (London, 1905); *The Interpreters* (London, 1922); *The Avatars* (London, 1933).

III. DRAMA. *Deirdre* (London, 1903).

IV. ESSAY COLLECTIONS. *Some Irish Essays* (London, 1906); *Co-operation and Nationality* (Dublin, 1912); *Imaginations and Reveries* (Dublin and London, 1915); *The National Being* (Dublin and London, 1916); *The Candle of Vision* (1918); *Song and Its Fountains* (London, 1932).

V. PAMPHLETS. *To the Fellows of the Theosophical Society* (Dublin, 1894); *The Future of Ireland and the Awakening of the Fires* (Dublin, 1897); *Ideals in Ireland: Priest or Hero?* (Dublin, 1897); *Co-operative Credit* (Dublin, 1898); *An Artist of Gaelic Ireland* (Dublin, 1901); *Controversy in Ireland* (Dublin, 1904); *The Hero in Man* (London, 1909); *The Building Up of a Rural Civilisation* (Dublin, 1910); *The Renewal of Youth* (Dublin, 1911); *The Rural Community* (Dublin, 1913); *To the Masters of Dublin* (Dublin, 1913); *The Tragedy of Labour in Dublin* (London, 1913); *The Dublin Strike* (Dublin, 1913); *Oxford University and the Co-operative Movement* (Oxford, 1914); *Ireland,*

Agriculture and the War (Dublin, 1915); *Talks with an Irish Farmer* (Dublin, 1916); *Templecrone. A Record of Cooperative Effort* (Dublin, 1917); *Thoughts for a Convention* (Dublin and London, 1917), *Conscription for Ireland: A Warning for England* (Dublin, 1918); *Literary Imagination* (Dublin and London, 1918); *A Plea for Justice* (Dublin, 1920); *The Economics of Ireland, and the Policy of the British Government* (New York, 1920); *Thoughts for British Co-operators* (Dublin, 1921); *The Inner and Outer Ireland* (Dublin, 1921); *Ireland and the Empire at the Court of Conscience* (Dublin, 1921); *Ireland, Past and Future* (Dublin, 1922).

VI. POSTHUMOUS COLLECTED WORKS. *The Living Torch* (ed. Monk Gibbon, London, 1937); *Selections from Contributions to the Irish Homestead, by AE* (ed. Henry Summerfield, 2 vols., Bucks, England, 1978); *The Descent of the Gods: Comprising the Mystical Writings of G. W. Russell—A.E.* (eds. Raghavan Iyer and Nandini Iyer, Buckinghamshire, 1988).

VI. LETTERS. *Some Passages from the Letters of AE to W. B. Yeats* (Dublin, 1936); *AE's Letters to Mínanlábáin* (ed. Lucy Porter, New York, 1937); *Letters from AE* (ed. Alan Denson, London, New York, and Toronto 1961).

VIII. EDITED COLLECTIONS AND SYMPOSIA. *New Songs* (ed. AE, Dublin, 1904); *Literary Ideals in Ireland* (Dublin, 1899); *Ideals in Ireland* (ed. Lady Augusta Gregory, London, 1901).

IX. MODERN EDITIONS. *A Candle of Vision* (Wheaton, Illinois, 1974); *Co-operation and Nationality* (foreword by Patrick Bolger, Dublin, 1982); *Song and Its Fountains* (New York, 1991).

X. PRINCIPAL BIOGRAPHICAL AND CRITICAL STUDIES. Darrell Figgis, *A.E. George W. Russell: A Study of a Man and a Nation* (Dublin, 1915, New York, 1970); St. John Ervine, *Some Impressions of My Elders* (New York, 1922); William Magee (John Eglington), *A Memoir of George William Russell* (London, 1937); C. C. Coates, *Some Less Known Chapters in the Life of A.E. (George Russell)* (Dublin, 1939); Abinash Candra Bose, *Three Mystic Poets: A Study of W. B. Yeats, A.E. and Rabindranath Tagore* (Kolhapur, India, 1945, Folcroft, Pennsylvania, 1970); Sean O'Casey, *Inishfallen Fare Thee Well* (New York, 1949); Francis Merchant, *A.E.: An Irish Promethean: A Study of the Contribution of George William Russell to World Culture* (Columbia, South Carolina, 1954); Alan Denson, *Printed Writings by George William Russell (A.E.)* (London and Evanston, Illinois, 1961); Henry Summerfield, *That Myriad-Minded Man: A Biography of George William Russell "A.E." 1867–1935* (Bucks, England, 1975); Robert Bernard Davis, *George William Russell* (Boston, 1977).

W. G. SEBALD

(1944–2001)

Judith Kitchen

On 14 December 2001, W. G. Sebald was tragically killed in an automobile accident near his home in Norwich in East Anglia, ending a career that had only just begun to reach prominence. Only a month earlier, Edmund White had proclaimed him "the greatest living novelist," and his most recent publication, *Austerlitz*, had topped the *New York Times* Editor's Choice for the year. In the brief five years since his work first appeared in English, W. G. Sebald's reputation had grown exponentially among serious readers of literature, and his obituary noted that his "four books firmly established Mr. Sebald in the literary pantheon, where he was regarded as a future candidate for the Nobel Prize in Literature." But that was speculation. Now those four books are all we have by which to evaluate the scope of his vision, to assess the importance of his truncated career, and to measure the enormity of his loss.

A notoriously private man, Sebald was seen as an enigma throughout the time his reputation was blossoming in England and the United States. Contacted for biographical information, his British publisher responded via e-mail: "The biographical information on the book jacket is all we have. He isn't exactly a recluse, but he doesn't share information too freely." His own agent claimed never to have met him. And his Home Page at Britain's University of East Anglia was only marginally more forthcoming—the photograph of a kindly-looking man, gray-haired, blue button-down shirt open at the collar, navy sweater vest, droopy white mustache, wire-rimmed glasses, plus the following text:

Max Sebald, Professor of European Literature.

Areas of interest mainly in the field of 19th and 20th century German literature.

Teaches German Prose Fiction, Post-war European Prose Fiction, 20th c. European Autobiographical Writing, Kafka's Shorter Prose Fiction, Weimar Cinema, Creative Writing.

If you clicked *contact*, where other professors give an e-mail address, it said "by pigeon-hole only."

Born Winfried Georg Maximilian Sebald (pronounced Say-bald) on 18 May 1944 in Wertach im Allgäu, Bavaria, Germany, the writer (as opposed to the professor, Max) published under the name of W. G. Sebald. Although this may remind some readers of H. G. Wells, E. M. Forster, or C. S. Lewis, suggesting a strong identification with British literary tradition, in many ways Sebald's use of his initials was just another manner in which he reserved for himself a separate identity as the author of his many nameless narrators. Sebald did not begin publishing until his mid-forties; he wrote only in German, and his books were then translated (with his collaboration) into English.

The first to appear in English was *The Emigrants*, translated by the poet Michael Hulse, in 1996. It was immediately praised as a masterpiece by such critics as A. S. Byatt, Susan Sontag, Eva Hoffman, and Anita Brookner. Then came *The Rings of Saturn* in 1998, *Vertigo* (his first book, written in 1990) in 1999, and, most recently, *Austerlitz*, in 2001. Now translated into sixteen languages in nineteen countries, *The Emigrants* was awarded the Berlin Literature Prize, the Heinrich Böll prize, the Heinrich Heine prize, the Literatur Nord Prize, the Johannes Bobrowski medal; *The Rings of Saturn* was chosen as the *Los Angeles Times* Best Fiction Book of 1998 and the *Irish Times* pronounced it the "Book of the Decade." Only recently have lengthier critical assessments begun to appear. Sebald himself said little about his writing, and scarcely more about

295

the issues that concerned him most. He gave few readings, fewer interviews.

The details of Sebald's life are sketchy. His parents were from conventional, Catholic, anti-communist, working-class backgrounds; his mother, Rosa, was the daughter of a country policeman and his father, Georg, from a family of glassmakers in the Bavarian forest. At the age of eighteen, his father joined the army, and when the National Socialist party came to power in 1933, he continued to serve. During the 1930s, the family prospered. Max was born in 1944, near the end of the war, the younger brother to three older sisters. His father, however, was by then absent—first fighting the war on the Polish front, then held in France as a prisoner of war. He returned to the family in 1947, when Sebald was three years old, taking a job in another town and returning to the family only on Sundays. Young Max's grandfather served as a substitute father, and his death when Sebald was twelve was a loss from which he never quite recovered.

The education of Max Sebald might make an interesting story in itself. Although his formal education seems fairly "normal" (primary school in the village, then grammar school at Oberst-dorf, Freiburg University, postgraduate studies in Switzerland and Manchester University), Sebald also grew up in what he called the "seas of silence" of postwar Germany, ignorant of much of what had happened during the Nazi regime. In an interview with Maya Jaggi of *The Manchester Guardian* (22 September 2001), he stated, "it was an idyllic environment, and only at 17 or 18 did you get inklings." At grammar school, they were once shown a film of the liberation of Belsen, but there was no discussion afterwards: "You didn't know what to do with it." When Sebald was at Freiburg University in 1965, the Frankfurt trial of Auschwitz personnel began:

> It gave me an understanding of the real dimensions for the first time: the defendants were the kinds of people I'd known as neighbors—postmasters or railway workers—whereas the witnesses were people I'd never come across—Jewish people from Brooklyn or Sydney. They were a myth of the past. You found out they too had lived in Nuremberg and

Stuttgart. So it gradually pieced itself together, along with the horrific details.

In 1966, Sebald came to Manchester, England, as an assistant lecturer in European literature. After a year, he returned to Switzerland, and then in 1970 he took a position at the University of East Anglia, where he remained, serving as a professor of European literature and, in 1989, founding the British Center for Literary Translation. He and his Austrian wife, Ute, lived in a Victorian brick rectory on the outskirts of Norwich. They had one daughter, Anna. Although Sebald had lived in England for thirty years, he claimed that he felt "chronically unsettled." Talking to Jaggi about his own experience as an emigrant, he remarked, "The longer I stay here the less I feel at home. In Germany I feel as distant. My ideal station is probably a Swiss hotel."

"Pigeon-hole only," said Sebald's Web page, but it is difficult to pigeonhole W. G. Sebald, and that is at least part of what has intrigued readers and critics alike. "Who is W. G. Sebald?" asked reviewer Nicole Krauss in *The Partisan Review*. "Scattered throughout all three books are grainy photographs, and occasionally we glimpse Sebald peering out from behind his weeping-willow mustache. But these snapshots have the odd effect of making him seem not more familiar but more otherworldly, as elusive as the eccentric figures from history who haunt his pages. Sebald guides us through time across Europe. But he is always moving, always just ahead of us, already speaking to us from the shadowy realm of the beyond."

"THE SEBALD ZONE": METHOD AND MADNESS

In an article in *The New York Times*, W. S. Di Piero recounts a time when he was traveling in Italy. Someone showed him a collection of vintage postcards, one of which, from the town of Limone sul Garda, was a photograph of a set of square pillars used to protect lemon trees from the cold. Later, reading *Vertigo*, on page 85 he discovered a photo very like the one he had just seen. "I had unknowingly entered the Sebald

Zone, where events and encounters align themselves into an ominously smooth tissue of coincidence." (The "Sebald Zone" creates its own bizarre dimensions. There are no photographs on page 85 of the New Directions edition and no photo of the pillars of Limone sul Garda on any other page. Could the English editions contain a different set of photos? However, on page 93, there is a detailed description of the pillars as seen from a boat on the lake.) This anomaly might have amused Sebald, who would have turned it over in his mind, looking for connections:

> What connection could there be, I then wondered and now wonder again, between those two beautiful female readers and this immense railway terminus which, when it was built in 1932, outdid all other train stations in Europe; and what relation was there between the so-called monuments of the past and the vague longing, propagated through our bodies, to people the dust-blown expanses and tidal plains of the future.
>
> (*Vertigo*, p. 107)

Coincidence haunted Sebald: co-incidence, as opposed to chance. Speaking of his birth in May 1944, he realized that that was the same month Kafka's sister was deported to Auschwitz. "It's bizarre; you're pushed in a pram through the flowering meadows, and a few hundred miles to the east these horrendous things are happening. It's the chronological contiguity that makes you think it is something to do with you" (Jaggi, *Guardian*). Chronology fueled his imagination, but so too did a deep historical sense in which a specific place can hold layers of event, a palimpsest of sorts.

So it hardly seems like coincidence in *Vertigo*, when, traveling through Italy in 1987, the narrator sees an adolescent boy who resembles the young Kafka who had traveled this exact route on his way to Riva in 1913. Improbably, the boy has an identical twin brother. Refused permission to take a photograph, the narrator is "consumed with an impotent rage at the fact that I would now have no evidence whatsoever to document this most improbable coincidence" (p. 90). This is underscored when he steps off the train in Mi-

lan: "I walked through the colonnades to the eastern side, the wrong side of the station. Under the archway that gives onto the Piazza Savoia was a Hertz advertisement bearing the words LA PROSSIMA COINCIDENZA" (p. 108).

All of W. G. Sebald's "novels" adopted a similar stance. In them, a narrator, a loner whose life closely resembles what is known of the life of Sebald himself, provides a first-hand account of his own travels. Almost always, this narrator acts like a "displaced person," moving into strange new landscapes or returning to old haunts that appear at once familiar and remote. Each scene unfolds with such documentary detail—the hushed sounds of early morning in Venice; a steady, assiduous rain in the Tyrol; the architectural design of a railroad station; the smell of camphor in an abandoned attic; the green metal table and old atlas from childhood—that they lay claim to a Proustian dusting of things recalled. The speaker is haunted by the past, sometimes to the point of paralysis. In addition, this narrator often recounts, secondhand, the stories of others—stories of people and places lost to history.

Sometimes the stories belong to historical figures (often writers: Stendhal, Kafka, Conrad, Edward Fitzgerald, Thomas Browne). Sometimes they belong to lesser-known—but real—people: family members, a former teacher, a landlord. Sometimes the character is a composite; sometimes completely fictional, a fellow traveler whose path, coincidentally, crosses the narrator's. Real characters impossibly appear at improbable times (Dante walking down the streets of Vienna, or the figure of Nabokov flitting through four separate narratives). Usually, Sebald's characters are a blend of the real and the imagined, and, because all are presented in such precise detail, it becomes increasingly difficult for the reader to discern which is which. Malcolm Jones of *Newsweek* describes this phenomenon: "Reading a Sebald book is like nothing else. Confronted with his strange, intoxicating brew of fact and fiction and digressions on everything from European train stations to the lives and times of certain moths, you wind up not knowing what to believe, or who."

In a profile for *The Paris Review*, James Atlas stated, "Sebald's books elude easy classification. Are they fiction or nonfiction? History or a Borgesian fabrication built upon fact?" Critics almost universally described Sebald as defying genre (the British edition of *Vertigo* called it "Fiction/Travel/History" on the cover jacket). Sebald himself was unconcerned with definitions, but he did make distinctions. In his interview in *Newsweek*, he elucidated:

> I don't really call them anything in terms of genre, and I don't consider them to be novels, not in the strict sense. They are some form of prose fiction. The form is indeterminate, I would say. It's hybridized in all sorts of ways. . . . If you keep the form open, you have a much greater liberty to do things. . . . And the only thing that you have that's really different from the standard novel is greater freedom. You can still have characters. You can also have historical figures.

Sebald not only blurred and disrupted the separation between memoir and fiction, he also added to the mix travelogue, historical research, scholarly essays, documentary, his own brand of magical realism, and fantasy. The books contain an interweaving of the verbal and the visual; throughout the text, photographs (portraits, informal snapshots, old postcards, ticket stubs, other memorabilia) play a role in how the story is read. In fact, sometimes (especially in photographs of newspaper articles) they serve as primary text. The effect is one of confirmation. The book jacket declares "novel" while its text and photos almost insist "nonfiction." However, as time goes on, the reader sometimes has the unsettling feeling that, rather than confirming events, the photographs may give rise to imagined ones. Thus it is possible to interrogate the "facts" as they are presented.

Although Sebald's books all employ similar techniques, they are characterized most by their tone—a tone that contains both the weight of his content and the lightness of his style, which was described by Michiko Kakutani as prose "so lively and tactile, his descriptions so luminous with pointillist detail, that his narratives actually make for quicksilver reading." Many reviewers refer to Sebald's particular brand of melancholy, but very few mention his humor, which takes the form of subtle irony, dark comedy, a strong sense of play. "Melancholy" is a word that best describes his characters. The narrator himself, while clearly somber, is more detached, noted less for sadness than for the pensive, introspective quality of his inner voice. And this voice is governed by the long, convoluted sentences that serve to question, qualify, or modulate. The comma is everywhere, creating a sentence that can only be called "majestic."

In each successive book, the density increased; sentences became longer (some lasting for more than a page), and the paragraphs began to extend over several pages until, in *Austerlitz*, Sebald dispensed with paragraphs altogether. It is very difficult to describe the way these books hold the reader captive, suspended in their hypnotic, measured pace. An oppressive silence, as much as the slow unfolding of the facts, dominates Sebald's fiction. The events are so meticulously reconstructed, the details so precise that, through the evocation of an irredeemable past, the unrealized future of Europe makes itself felt. Time barely matters in the Sebald Zone, where the past catches up with the present, insinuates itself, infusing it with alternative possibilities. Loss is his subject, but the tone of the books is not so much nostalgic as elegiac.

VERTIGO

In 1990, *Vertigo* was published in German under the title *Schwindel. Gefühle* (in German, the word "*Schwindelgefühle*" means dizziness, but by breaking the title into two words, Sebald was able to emphasize the first, which means "lie" or "fraud"). The book did not appear in English translation until 1999, the third of his books to be translated. To read *Vertigo* is to enter the disorienting swirl of memory, where reader and writer are "both very much present and altogether elsewhere" (p. 104). As in Hitchcock's film of the same name, plots and fates intersect in ways that send the protagonist spiraling down into despair. But who, one wonders, is the true protagonist of Sebald's book? *Vertigo* is divided into four sections and has as its focus four separate people: Stendhal (using his given name of Marie Henri Beyle); Casanova (imprisoned in an attic cell in Venice); Kafka, especially the Kafka of his letters and notebooks; and an elusive narrator who dominates the second and fourth sections—a German native who lives in England but criss-crosses Europe, ending up in a Bavarian village called "W" where he had lived for his first nine years.

Vertigo is a tale of journeys within journeys, stories within stories, memories pulled from within memory itself. At one point, the narrator meets a man who, in telling someone else's story, describes it as "more like an essay in form" (p. 128). The first section is an account of Beyle's crossing the St. Bernard pass with Napoleon's army, derived from Stendhal's own memoir thirty-six years after the event (and then presented under the thinly veiled title *The Life of Henry Brulard*). In this version, Beyle recalls the disparity between the memory of the battle itself and the scene one year later, a vast plain littered with bones bleaching in the sun. Even as the skulls confirm the memory, they obliterate it. His description of Beyle (as told by the narrator) actually summarizes Sebald's own style: "A curious lightness such as he had never known took hold of him, and it is the recollection of that lightness which informs the account he wrote seven years later of a journey that may have been wholly imaginary, made with a companion who may likewise have been a mere figment of his own mind" (p. 23).

In 1987, seven years after a debilitating journey through the Italian Alps, the narrator of the second section finds himself retracing his earlier steps: Vienna to Venice to Verona, and finally to Desenzano and Lake Garda, following the footsteps of Kafka and Stendhal (with an imaginative digression as he contemplates Casanova in his cell in Venice). Each element connects tangentially with another, yet the connections feel somewhat contrived, as though history itself were being manipulated.

The third section reveals Dr. K. in a precarious mental state as he arrives at the baths of Riva to recuperate. The narrator here is less visible, but he has become a necessary device. He is most present as a source of information—referring to Kafka's tortured letters to Felice, he captures Kafka's blend of romantic intensity and existential pessimism. In fact, this section fleshes out the "story" that can only be read between the lines of Kafka's diaries. Sebald is marvelously adept at creating the state that Kafka calls "the terrible uncertainty of my inner existence." When Kafka admits his attraction to the son of a bookshop owner, the narration takes on the speculative tone of an essay: "At this point Dr. K. surely came within an inch of admitting to a desire which we must assume remained unstilled" (p. 167). Through the narrator's more distanced commentary, we become witness to Dr. K.'s crippling loneliness.

The fourth section reintroduces the "I" of the narrative and gives the speaker a more central role. As he travels into his childhood, the voice becomes increasingly intimate. Memories become almost casual, and many of them conform to what has been written about Sebald's own origins. In an offhand reference to some gypsies, the war is first mentioned: "Where they came from, how they had managed to survive the war, and why of all places they had chosen that cheerless spot by the Ach bridge for their summer camp, are questions that occur to me only now . . ." (p. 184). Pandora's box has been opened; the Second World War creeps into the story, seen from a child's perspective—a father suddenly returned to force him to go to the barber's; a teacher who adds to the list of disasters that had befallen the village's 125 men who died for the fatherland between 1941 and 1945; newsreels that, along with other current events, showed "the mountains of rubble in places like Berlin or Hamburg, which for a long time I did not associate with the destruction wrought in the closing years of the war, knowing nothing of it, but considered them a natural condition of all larger cities" (p. 187).

At this point, the autobiographical voice produces more lucid prose, but Sebald still keeps himself at one remove from his material. Memory provides a simple lens, and then it clouds again, fraught with the symbolic (for example, the ancient Austrian tunic in the attic that, at a touch, disintegrates into dust). The story takes on its most fictive aspects as the net of connections tightens. Images and events recur, giving them random significance. For example, the year 1913 takes on dramatic proportions. Kafka arrived at Lake Garda at the height of modernism, the world on the brink of war. On his own journey, the narrator discovers a novel about a murder case entitled *1912 + 1*; when he returns to his hometown, he sees "1913" inscribed over a door; and on his return to London, he buys the 1913 edition of Pepys's diary. Coincidence has been both uncovered and fabricated. The child's memory of seeing a dead huntsman is almost an exact replica of Kafka's fable of a barque continually ferrying the body of a huntsman from shore to shore. Literature and life become inextricably entwined—and who is to say whether Kafka's story caught Sebald's young narrator's attention because it touched on his experience, or whether, in memory, the experience has taken on the hues of another writer's voice?

lthough *Vertigo* interrogates the very nature of memory, the "fraud" of the title may be memory itself. The photographs meant to replicate experience may, in fact, have been a source of dream. The more the details accumulate, the less certain the picture becomes. As the narrator leaves Germany, he looks out through adult eyes at the bleak, winter-bound landscape. There are no people in sight. The reader is reminded that, throughout the book, the sense of loneliness and isolation has been acute. The figure of the writer is best represented by Kafka sitting alone at dinner, the deliberately nameless woman to his left now departed from the spa, the old general to his right dead the previous afternoon of suicide.

To the extent that the book is autobiographical, *Vertigo* chronicles the writer's obsessions with writing. Remembering, traveling, and writing become the same act:

> On one occasion she asked if I was a journalist or a writer. When I said that neither the one nor the other was quite right, she asked what it was that I

was working on, to which I replied that I did not know for certain myself . . .

> (p. 95)

> The more images I gathered from the past, I said, the more unlikely it seemed to me that the past had actually happened in this or that way, for nothing about it could be called normal: most of it was absurd, and if not absurd, then appalling.

> (p. 212)

In the face of the appalling, Sebald honors the imagination. Halfway through the book, he recounts seeing a troupe of artistes in a train station, a group he says "seemed to me to belong to an era that ended at least half a century ago" (p. 112). Father, mother (dressed in a tailor-made suit straight out of the 1930s)—Giorgio and Rosa Santini—and their three young daughters. You can sense his writerly pleasure as he gives them the names of his own parents and imagines them balanced on the tightrope—the very antithesis of vertigo—their true home "the freedom of the air."

THE EMIGRANTS

The first of Sebald's books to be translated into English was *The Emigrants*. Having already received critical acclaim in Germany, the book was instantly perceived as an important literary landmark. *The Emigrants* remains Sebald's most important work, but it is interesting to note that it takes on added significance when read in conjunction with both his earlier and his later work. Its themes are reinforced, its methods established, and its vision authenticated.

As in *Vertigo*, the book is divided into four sections, each with a focus on an individual life—and all told (or discovered) by the same narrator, whose own life (as an "emigrant" to the United Kingdom) provides the connective tissue for the tales. The narrator, born, like Sebald, in May 1944, grew up in the shadow of the war, with its unspoken implications for his generation. *The Emigrants* has been described—in almost every instance—as being about the Holocaust, and it is often found listed under a term that Sebald despised: "Holocaust literature." Although references to the Holocaust are oblique (the events of Kristallnacht, the deportations and narrow escapes, are mentioned as background only), knowledge of the Holocaust informs each and every page. Its absence is the largest presence in the book, and the reader's internal dialogue with that absence is the dynamic on which the book operates. We are forced to see these characters not only as they lived but as they might have lived.

Contrary to statements by all too many critics, the four characters are not all German Jews forced to flee the rising Nazi regime. In fact, they represent the many forces at work in Europe in the late nineteenth and early twentieth centuries. Thus they (along with other peripheral characters) represent not only the wandering, exiled Jew or the newly middle-class German but also those who were inadvertently caught in the miasma of the Holocaust and those who, by chance or by calculation, escaped it. The emphasis is on the aftereffects, not the causes, which appear like forces of nature, as inevitable as an earthquake or a flood. The Holocaust haunts the book, but the tone is posthumous—already turned to mourning—a retrospective look at a Europe that has dismantled its life force.

The first of the book's four main characters, an eccentric misfit named Henry Selwyn, born Hersh Seweryn, came as a child to England from Lithuania in 1899. When the narrator meets him, he is living in a hermitage on his wife's estate and spends most of his time in the garden. It is only now, with some prodding, that he has begun to feel "homesick," and the stories of his boyhood seem to surface as if from some deep underground cave. The details of his story are presented as a remote and distant past, a little like looking through the wrong end of a telescope. The family had planned to go to New York but their ship docked in London instead, so young Henry grew up British by default. He succeeded in school, and later became a relatively successful surgeon, concealing his background as he rose in status.

The one clear memory dominating Selwyn's thoughts is that of Johannes Naegeli, an Alpine guide he met in Switzerland in the summer of 1913. They became friends as they climbed together. After war broke out, Henry returned to England and was conscripted. He later heard that Naegeli had fallen into a crevasse and died. Years later, after the death of Selwyn by suicide, the narrator reads (a photograph of the newspaper attests to factual accuracy) that, seventy-two years after his fall, the remains of the guide had been released from the Oberaar glacier.

Is this the story of Selwyn, Naegeli, the narrator's connection with them, or some combination of all three? "And so they are ever returning to us, the dead. At times they come back from the ice more than seven decades later and are found at the edge of the moraine, a few polished bones and a pair of hobnailed boots" (p. 23). So memories surface, fragment by fragment, while the glacial movement of history leaves the larger picture blurred and indistinct.

In 1984, the narrator is informed of another suicide—that of his former primary-school teacher. Remembering him as open-minded and inventive, the narrator feels compelled to uncover his story: "Such endeavors to imagine his life and death did not, as I had to admit, bring me any closer to Paul, except at best for brief emotional moments of the kind that seemed presumptuous to me. It is in order to avoid this sort of wrongful trespass that I have written down what I know of Paul Bereyter" (p. 29). Unlike Selwyn, Bereyter had been an unwilling emigrant, forced to give up teaching because he was one-quarter Jewish. He spent the prewar years as a tutor in France, but returned to Germany to fight in the army ("those who were only three-quarters Aryans were apparently included in the muster") and then resumed teaching at the end of the war. In the end, his was a life that defied understanding. He was so profoundly attached to his country that he simply could not live in exile. And yet, though he returned to the town, his past had been eradicated.

Much of Bereyter's story is told secondhand by Mme Landau, a female friend from his later years. Through her, some anger is expressed: "I do not find it surprising, said Mme Landau, not in the slightest, that you were unaware of the meanness and treachery that a family like the Bereyters were exposed to in a miserable hole such as S then was, and such as it still is despite all the so-called progress; it does not surprise me at all, since that is inherent in the logic of the whole wretched sequence of events" (p. 50). Her voice rings loud and clear. Even though Sebald was two steps removed from this anger, it might be safe to say that it represented his own growing sense of a Germany to which he, too, was unable to return. His narrator later expresses this feeling: "I felt increasingly that the mental impoverishment and lack of memory that marked the Germans, that the efficiency with which they had cleaned everything up, were beginning to affect my head and my nerves" (p. 225).

Lack of memory becomes a refrain. Each of the characters exhibits this condition in one form or another, but none is more interesting than Uncle Ambros Adelwarth. Because he is part of the narrator's family history, his section seems by far the most intimate. It is filled with photographs, many seemingly from a family album. The son of a large Bavarian Catholic family, Adelwarth was the first of an extended family migration to the United States. He took a job as a manservant to a wealthy Jewish family on Long Island, spent years as the companion to their unstable son Cosmo, and after Cosmo's death in a sanatorium remained with the family in increasing isolation as the head butler.

In the family photos, Adelwarth is only one among many, but his story takes on importance as the narrator traces his uncle's movements in search of a frame in which to put his own displaced memories. The reader is treated to a two-pronged journey—the narrator's into the past, and Adelwarth's into what was to be his future. Luckily, Adelwarth provided a diary that chronicles his days with Cosmo at the gaming tables and spas of Europe and documents their trip through Greece, Turkey, and the Holy Land. The writing in the diary is pellucid, filled with a lightness of being. In contrast to the Victorian interiors of the album, the accompanying photographs are exotic. They, along with the tone of the diary, give rise to the narrator's fanciful dreams in which he sees the impeccably dressed, perfectly mannered pair as the talk of the town, always fading just as he is about to approach them.

Just what the relationship between Adelwarth and Cosmo was remains unclear, though one relative refers to Ambros as being "of the other persuasion." It is clearly a measure of his devotion that, as an old man, Adelwarth committed himself to the same sanatorium in Ithaca, New York, where Cosmo had faded away. Adelwarth spent his last days as the victim of psychological experimentation, receiving shock therapy every few days. The narrator discovers one of his doctors, now fiercely opposed to such treatment, waiting for the ruined building to collapse.

As a child, the narrator had heard his great-uncle giving a speech: "I gradually became convinced that Uncle Adelwarth had an infallible memory, but that, at the same time, he scarcely allowed himself access to it" (p. 100). And when Adelwarth could no longer ward off his past, he allowed his memories to be erased entirely. This sounds very like Sebald's descriptions of Germany itself. The diary has the last word: "Memory, he added in a postscript, often strikes me as a kind of dumbness. It makes one's head heavy and giddy, as if one were not looking back down the receding perspectives of time but rather down on the earth from a great height . . ." (p. 145).

So it is not surprising that the final section concentrates on a man who has deliberately suppressed his past. The painter Max Ferber, a composite character drawn from Sebald's landlord in Manchester and the painter Frank Auerbach in London, reveals a past so dark that he cannot look it in the face. Even his paintings are dark; Ferber's method is to scrape away paint, erasing his subject over and over. He has consigned himself to paint in a murky, dust-filled warehouse in a crumbling section of Manchester. Once the booming city of the Industrial Revolution, the Manchester of 1966 is pictured as the mirror image of the bombed cities of Germany.

Ferber's story comes to light years after the narrator made his acquaintance. Ferber, a German Jew, was sent as an adolescent to England in 1939. His parents were to follow, but it became clear that they were unable to save themselves and, in 1941, they were deported and "murdered" (the word is intentionally uncompromising). Ferber's life has been truncated: ". . . time, he went on, is an unreliable way of gauging these things, indeed it is nothing but a disquiet of the soul. There is neither a past nor a future. At least not for me" (p. 181). He is locked in his solitude; the fragmentary scenes of his memories are of a Germany "frozen in the past, destroyed, a curiously extraterritorial place, inhabited by people whose faces are both lovely and dreadful" (p. 181).

One of those faces is that of Ferber's mother, whose story animates the entire book. Sensing her fate, she had written a memoir which she sent to her son. He, in turn, passed this on to the narrator. In it, she reveals the singular nature of life—a childhood filled with innocent wonders in a village where Jews had been living since the seventeenth century. Her days are filled with the ordinary (corned beef, Hannukah candles, the schoolmaster's birthday, a green velvet armchair), and the memoir is told with a freshness that brings it to life: "If I think back nowadays to our childhood in Steinach (Luisa's memoirs continue at another point), it often seems as if it had been open-ended in time, in every direction—indeed, as if it were still going on, right into these lines I am now writing" (207). With parenthetical insertions, the narrator keeps reminding us that this, also, is an indirect account, and that the act of writing is an act of recovery. *The Emigrants* is an elegy, a stone placed carefully on the gravestone of European culture.

The book contains some moments of sheer fantasy—especially the fleeting figure of "the butterfly man" who graces all four sections. He is not merely a likeness of Nabokov but a whimsical transformation of the famous Russian emigré. The butterfly man is spotted in the Alps in the early part of the century, and then sighted again in Ithaca, where Nabokov taught until the end of his life. His most magical appearance is as a somewhat willful child, coming to an Alpine resort with his Russian father. Just what he represents is unclear, but certainly he is a testament to the powers of the imagination, to the writerly impulse to speak to, and through, memory.

On the other hand, Sebald seems to doubt even the act of writing. In the final pages, the narrator duplicates Ferber's method of painting:

> Not infrequently I unravelled what I had done, continuously tormented by scruples that were taking tighter hold and steadily paralyzing me. These scruples concerned not only the subject of the narrative, which I felt I could not do justice to, no matter what approach I tried, but also the entire questionable act of writing. . . . By far the greater part had been crossed out, discarded, or obliterated by additions.
>
> (p. 230)

The reader looks down, as from some high vantage point, to see that, for all its density, *The Emigrants* is riddled with holes that memory cannot fill. The individual stories, by and large, can be plotted; they are full of facts, which we get from many layers of text—written and oral—all filtered through an ambiguous narrator. The narrator, however, becomes actively caught up in those lives. Yet there is a gap between the lives as they are lived from inside and the way any external observer can know them. There is another, all-embracing gap between these lives, with their fullness and their silences, and the larger history of which they are almost unknowingly a part. We look to history for meaning, but history is unable to give the lives a sense of coherence. Indeed, they fade away without ever having achieved closure or clear delineation. And they are all we have. In that way, Sebald, like Kafka, combines specificity of detail with a nearly nihilistic absence of any larger frame of reference. Thus the book's ultimate subject is not the unspeakable, but the unspoken.

THE RINGS OF SATURN

The Rings of Saturn turns away from Sebald's native Germany to focus on the eastern coast of England. However, where *The Emigrants* revealed the powerful reach of history, *The Rings of Saturn* undermines that lesson. In the even longer view, nothing lasts. Again, the story is told through a narrator who, on a walking tour of the underpopulated coast of East Anglia, meets a variety of other characters, both present and past. The cast of characters here is more diffuse, containing numerous people met along the way, as well as people resuscitated through memory or research. They reach out from the obscurity to which history has relegated them in order to reinforce the interconnectedness of time and place. Once again, the narrative unfolds with the archival aid of photographs that, as relics of former times, add simultaneously to the book's factual authenticity and to its dreamlike quality.

Ten chapters—each meticulously described by key topics in the table of contents—chronicle the solitary walker's journey into England's past. One glance at the scope of Chapter IV and the reader can identify Sebald's obsessions with history and architecture, with mundane topics as well as philosophical questions:

> IV The Battle of Sole Bay—Nightfall—Station Road in The Hague–Mauritshuis—Scheveningen—The tomb of St. Sebolt—Schiphol airport—The invisibility of man—The Sailors' Reading Room—Pictures from the Great War—The concentration camp at Jasenovac on the Sava.

No matter where he goes, the circuitous roads of thought lead to the large historical event that casts its shadow over Sebald's own life. Here, too, we see Sebald's interest in coincidence: St. Sebolt's name is instantly equated with the author; the Great War becomes another, greater war.

To the extent that *The Rings of Saturn* is more meditative, the narrating "I" (what James Atlas refers to as his "shadowy pronoun") seems close to representing Sebald himself. The reader accompanies him through a number of digressive excursions as though moving into the unconscious. But the reader must beware: once again the narrator is, if not unreliable, at least uncanny. The "state of almost total immobility" in which the narrator is taken into the hospital on the first page was not a nervous breakdown (as is clearly implied) but, in actuality, a shattered disc that necessitated an operation and a long period of recovery. Sebald was willing to bend the facts of his life for the sake of his fiction.

The Rings of Saturn follows the routes of associative thought rather than the coincidental couplings of random events. The narrator, as if through the rhythm of his own walking, allows his thoughts to be governed by what he sees, what he hears, and what he can discover through a variety of sources (libraries, residents, and, of course, photographs). The physical geography is the desolate Suffolk coast, but the emotional territory is one of spiritual malaise.

The Rings of Saturn is a reverie on death and decay. What is at stake is what is gone, and what is not gone is in decline. The tour begins at the crumbling mansion of Somerleyton, where the gardener describes watching World War II bombers take off at night for their raids: ". . . I pictured in my mind's eye the German cities going up in flames . . ." (p. 38). The tour takes us through more deteriorating estates (with their curious owners), towns empty of people, a sandstorm in a forest completely felled by a freak hurricane in 1987, the abandoned harbor at Lowestoft, where Conrad first set foot in England, the lost city of Dunwich, which has been slowly toppling into the sea, abandoned railroad bridges, and vast deserted dunes and beaches. Erosion, war, economics—everything seems to be in flux. Yet each of these places carries with it a history, preserved in museums, libraries, mausoleums, and the stories of those who have witnessed their transformations.

The narrator burrows beneath the surface to learn of battles in both world wars, the eighteenth-century silk trade in Norwich, the heyday of Britain's empire, slave trade in the Belgian Congo, the plight of the herring fisheries. Along the way, he finds himself in the company (sometimes physically, sometimes mentally) of those who made the history, or those who chronicled it: the seventeenth-century naturalist and physician Thomas Browne, Joseph Conrad, Chateaubriand, Rembrandt, the translator Edward Fitzgerald, his own compatriot exile, the German-English writer Michael Hamburger. The walk has become a quest. And yet its goal remains elusive. Mystery, Sebald seems to be saying, is part of the natural history. Even as we uncover more and more of the past, by extension, it reveals to us how much more there is yet to know.

In what might be called an extended interior monologue, the narrator becomes almost obsessive in his search for meaning. He speculates on the nature of burial rituals and finds himself on the trail of Thomas Browne's skull. This, in turn, takes him into Rembrandt's painting *The Anatomy Lesson*, watching the dissection with the dispassionate eye of the observer and with the subjective eye of the body itself. He goes so far as to place Browne at the lesson, as though he could take us into inception of modern scientific thought. Sebald's method mirrors life, not literature. He moves quickly from one subject to another in the arbitrary manner of thought or event. Nothing feels contrived; that is, there are no structural moves toward meaning. Yet there is a deeper level on which meanings strive to make themselves known. So Sebald returns to the silk trade, weaving its threads from China to Norwich, from the Imperial past to the diminished present, from dream to reality and back again to dream.

The figure of Thomas Abrams of Orford, who has been building a model of the Temple of Jerusalem for the past twenty years, may be emblematic. With every new finding, alterations need to be made. And the project takes time:

> I would more than likely never have started building the Temple if I had had any notion of how my work would get out of hand, and of the demands it would make on me as it became ever more complex. . . . Now, as the edges of my field of vision are beginning to darken, I sometimes wonder if I will ever finish the Temple and whether all I have done so far has not been a wretched waste of time.
>
> (p. 245)

It is impossible not to wonder whether Sebald felt a similar futility in the act of writing. As he contemplates the isolate figure of Edward Fitzgerald, describing the long hours he spent translating *The Rubaiyat of Omar Kayyam*, he answers his own questions with a statement that reads as a kind of *ars poetica*:

The English verses he devised for the purpose, which radiate with a pure, seemingly unselfconscious beauty, feign an anonymity that disdains even the least claim to authorship and draw us, word by word, to an indivisible point where the mediaeval orient and the fading occident can come together in a way never allowed them by the calamitous course of history.

> (p. 200)

In the story of St. Sebolt lighting a fire with icicles, Sebald discovers the writer's urge to create new life: "This story of the burning of the frozen substance of life has, of late, meant much to me, and I wonder now whether inner coldness and desolation may not be the pre-condition for making the world believe, by a kind of fraudulent showmanship, that one's own wretched heart is still aglow" (p. 86). In *The Rings of Saturn*, the distance between the author and the narrator narrows to the point of becoming nearly imperceptible, and when the narrator speaks about writing itself, then it is almost safe to say we hear Sebald's voice:

> But the fact is that writing is the only way in which I am able to cope with the memories which overwhelm me so frequently and so unexpectedly. If they remained locked away, they would become heavier and heavier as time went on, so that in the end I would succumb under their mounting weight. Memories lie slumbering within us for months and years, quietly proliferating, until they are woken by some trifle and in some strange way blind us to life. How often this has caused me to feel that my memories, and the labours expended in writing them down are all part of the same humiliating and, at bottom, contemptible business! And yet, what would we be without memory? We would not be capable of ordering even the simplest thoughts, the most sensitive heart would lose the ability to show affection, our existence would be a mere neverending chain of meaningless moments, and there would not be the faintest trace of a past.
>
> (p. 255)

AUSTERLITZ

With the publication of *Austerlitz* in 2001, Sebald reinforced his claim to be writing "prose fiction." The book exhibits many more of the characteristics we associate with a novel: it has a plot; it has only one main character (two, if you count the narrator, who, in this novel, acts more like a cipher than a protagonist); its characters seem to "develop" over time; it even has a kind of oddly recollected and reconstructed dialogue. It also hinges on mystery, and the gradual unearthing of facts that contain partial answers. Still, the inclusion of photographs raises some of the same issues of genre that troubled readers of the other books. At least three separate reviewers went so far as to state that the photograph on the front cover is that of Sebald as a boy (it is ostensibly of Jacques Austerlitz, a fictional character, and in reality is a childhood photograph of one of Sebald's good friends). But enough was known about Sebald for most critics to realize that, despite the photographic evidence, this book is heavily imaginative, more clearly novelistic in its intentions.

Sebald admitted that the story was loosely based on a "true-life" story of a woman who had been abused as a child. In later life, she began to remember details, and ended up tracing her arrival on a *kindertransport*, trainloads of unaccompanied children shipped to safety in England in 1938 and early 1939. Seeing the woman on television, Sebald noted that her birthday—18 May—compellingly was his own. And thus began his entry into the life of a man named Jacques Austerlitz.

To complicate matters, though, Austerlitz was not always Austerlitz. He grew up as Dafydd Elias in the Welsh town of Bala, and the story is one long, paragraphless search for his origins. It begins with repression. The narrator, somewhat disoriented by the overwhelming architecture of the railway station in Antwerp, meets a fellow traveler who, it turns out, is an architectural historian. They strike up the first of what will be many conversations as their paths keep crossing in a variety of circumstances. Early in the book, Austerlitz's lecture on the concentric fortifications at Breendonk foreshadows what will follow. Eventually, the abandoned fort was taken over by the Nazis and used as a detention center. This pattern is repeated throughout until the mes-

sage is clear: "outsized buildings cast the shadow of their own destruction before them." The architecture of the nineteenth century points the way toward twentieth-century history. In the grand scale of such edifices, the human is lost. The system itself becomes oppressive.

The narrator is fascinated by Austerlitz's ability to see connections, describing his method as one that is very like Sebald's own working method: "I was astonished by the way Austerlitz put his ideas together as he talked, forming perfectly balanced sentences out of whatever occurred to him, so to speak, and the way in which, in his mind, the passing on of his knowledge seemed to become a gradual approach to a kind of historical metaphysic, bringing remembered events back to life" (p. 13). But Austerlitz himself senses the danger in this metaphysic. In studying the past, he has denied himself the present:

> A clock has always struck me as something ridiculous, a thoroughly mendacious object, perhaps because I have always resisted the power of time out of some internal compulsion which I myself have never understood, keeping myself apart from so-called current events in the hope, as I now think, said Austerlitz, that time will not pass away, has not passed away, that I can turn back and go behind it, and there I shall find everything as it once was, or more precisely I shall find that all moments of time have co-existed simultaneously, in which case none of what history tells us would be true, past events have not yet occurred but are waiting to do so at the moment when we think of them, although that, of course, opens up the bleak prospect of everlasting misery and neverending anguish.
>
> (p. 101)

It becomes clear that Austerlitz has made no real use of his extensive knowledge. He is constantly making notes for what could be a definitive study of European architecture, but the task will never be completed. In fact, he is crippled by his inability to make real sense of it. At a point of deep depression, he actually burns his voluminous notes.

In *Austerlitz*, Sebald confronts the events of the Holocaust, though even here it is secondhand, and oblique. Almost thirty years after first meeting the narrator, Austerlitz begins to experience brief flashbacks, sensations that lead him to believe he might once have lived in Prague. Although he had discovered his real name as a schoolboy, it had remained his only link to a past to which he had no access. Going to Prague in search of his identity, he has a relatively easy time discovering the building in which his mother had lived. There he meets an old woman, Vera, who had known his mother and father before the war. Indeed, as a young woman she had lived in their building and often cared for the young Jacques. Austerlitz begins to recover some fitful memories.

The rest of the story is predictable. Austerlitz learns of the fate of his mother, Agáta, who, as she sensed the tightening restrictions on Jews, had sent him off on the *kindertransport* at the age of four with hopes of reuniting at a later time. Instead, she had been rounded up and sent to Terezín (Theresienstadt), and presumably then on to a death camp. Austerlitz learns even less of his father, Maximilian. A leftist sympathizer, he had been forced to flee to Paris, possibly to work in the underground. His letters had stopped and nothing else is known. There is nothing more terrifying than the photographs of the library in which Austerlitz continues his futile search for his father. This is a building designed to stymie the very discoveries it houses. Austerlitz cannot uncover the past, and so is forced to live in it endlessly.

To all intents and purposes, Austerlitz takes over from the narrator, who remains as a listener only. The device becomes less a meeting of two congruent minds and more a vehicle for Austerlitz's unfolding tale. As the narrator recedes, Sebald needs to make the reader aware of his continued presence. This involves some convoluted constructions, demonstrating, if nothing else, the layers of distance as the story passes from person to person. This is nowhere more true than in the search for the father. For example, not only is Austerlitz telling the narrator, but Vera is telling Austerlitz: "Nonetheless, said Vera, Austerlitz continued, Maximilian did not in any way believe . . ." and "From time to time, so Vera recollected, said Austerlitz, Maximilian would tell . . ." (p. 167).

Austerlitz suffers from this recessive narrator. It does not have the tension of the other books as they hover between genres, demanding that the reader suspend not disbelief, but belief. The coincidences have the ring of "plot." They occur logically to advance the "story." The mystery of living is given over to uncovering the answers to a single mystery.

Despite the photographs that give the book its haunting sense of inevitability, the reader has the feeling that, as often as not, they give rise to the plot. Sebald almost admitted this in an interview with Kenneth Baker of the *San Francisco Chronicle*: "If there's an image you want to use, you often write toward it or away from it."

In a sense, the photographs function as a second plot. From the images of the odd, owlish eyes of the nocturnal animals in the Antwerp zoo to the stilled eyes in the movie images of those incarcerated in Theresienstadt, from the ground plans of the fort near Antwerp to the architectural drawing of a concentration camp, from the huge ceilings of the train stations to the curiously deserted facades of present-day Terezín, the photos stop time and cause the viewer to address what went before, what came after. They give rise to our reflections. When Vera shows Jacques two photographs—one of the stage set for an opera, the other of him dressed in costume about six months before he left for England—she speaks, in some ways, for all survivors who must live in the post-Holocaust world:

> I heard Vera again, speaking of the mysterious quality peculiar to such photographs when they surface from oblivion. One has the impression, she said, of something stirring in them, as if one caught small sighs of despair, *gémissements de désespoir* was her expression, said Austerlitz, as if the pictures had a memory of their own and remembered us, remembered the roles that we, the survivors, and those no longer among us had played in our former lives.
>
> (p. 182)

"THE SEBALD ZONE": GENRE REVISITED

It is fast becoming possible to brand a book "Sebaldian"—a distinctive mix of tone, style, and method. Sebald's books do not "conclude" in a way that allows us to discuss them definitively. Instead, as in essays, they interrogate the material—personal, imagined, and historical—in order to confront the reader with the very real and enduring nature of twentieth-century horrors. He makes little or no effort to wrest narrative meaning from these horrors. In "Dead Man Writing" (written while Sebald was still very much alive), Pico Iyer describes the effect: "There is no explicit context to his inquiries, and there is nothing in them that seems susceptible to reason. The reader is left in precisely the state that Sebald has made his own—unmoored, at a loss, in the dark."

The lack of a definitive controlling vision in Sebald's work makes it especially vulnerable to the dominant concerns of others. Thus Cynthia Ozick sees his work as obsessed with the Holocaust; her reading of *The Emigrants* is generous in its scope, but at the same time unnecessarily limits the possibilities of interpretation. The Holocaust has been, in a sense, the darkest blip on the radar screen of history. Sebald peels back history to reveal not only the root cause, but the root cause of root cause, the way violence has begotten violence. His books have become a litmus test of just what German literature should be burdened with.

This is not without controversy. The German novelist Georg Klein disliked what he called Sebald's "sweet melancholic masochism towards the past" and his "false intimacy with the dead." At the time of his death, Sebald left a collection of poems and a nonfiction book about the Allied bombings in which 600,000 German civilians perished, soon to be translated into English. It will be interesting to note just how British and American critics, who admired Sebald for his hard look at German culture, will respond when his somewhat caustic eye is cast in their direction.

For his part, Sebald dismissed many postwar German writers as writing from a compromised position. He preferred such writers as Peter Weiss, Jean Amery, and Walter Benjamin. In an interview with Thea Abbott, he said, "It was that sort of company I knew I could never find in Germany, because the people don't exist any more. And it's one of the reasons why I feel ill at ease there, because I always sense that absence."

The past, memory, and the abstract nature of history—the way it determines individual lives by its absence as well as its presence—these form the identifiable themes of Sebald's work. But "theme" is associated with fiction. The nonfictional aspects of his work ask us to differentiate between "theme" and "issue." Sebald was more concerned with questions than with answers. There may be an autobiographical basis for this. In one interview for *The Los Angeles Times*, he discussed the fact that he had a friend whose father, a member of the Resistance, was killed in Tulle, France, in the final months of 1944. Sebald commented, "My own father was stationed an hour's drive away from Tulle." And then he asked the unanswerable question: "Who murdered my friend's father in 1944?"

There has been a tendency to read the narrator as Sebald himself—an error common to most reviews and articles. (Sebald courted this confusion, but as his friend Michael Hoffman said, "He has obvious affinities with Max, but it's playing on our naiveté, because the reader is always tempted to identify the narrator with the writer. He's taunting us.") The problem becomes significant when critics, such as Vivian Gornick, make claims—and arguments—for genre. In *The Situation and the Story*, she directly contradicts Sebald's claim to "prose fiction" by labeling his books nonfiction: "For me, Sebald is transparently a memoirist in that his work takes its life from a speaking voice that is clearly his own and belongs to a narrator writing to puzzle out if not exactly himself, then certainly a position that will include himself in what for the sake of brevity we will call the world" (p. 149). There is nothing tentative in Gornick's declaration:

It is, I think, a measure of the bankruptcy of fiction that *The Rings of Saturn* is repeatedly called a novel. Sebald is doing an old-fashioned thing here, entering into the narrating self in a way that ignores modernism and postmodernism alike and is as far from the gargantuan, language-besotted, mythical abstractions of contemporary fiction writers like Pynchon, Powers, and DeLillo as literature will allow itself to go. Yet the critics cannot believe that the power to make us feel this, our one and only life, as very few novels actually do these days, is coming from a memoirist—a nonfiction truth speaker—who has entered our common situation and is telling the story we now want told. But it is.

(pp. 155–156)

The elusive author of the elusive "I" might smile and say, as he said to Kenneth Baker, "The similarities between myself and the narrator are by no means one-to-one." Or, as he said with slightly different emphasis to James Atlas, "I prefer to look at the trajectories of other lives that cross one's own trajectory—do it by proxy rather than expose oneself in public." Or, as he said in yet another way to Malcolm Jones, ". . . if ever I were to write something that was autobiographical, I would attempt to make a virtue of the recognized problem that autobiographers never tell the truth."

Gornick narrows her field of vision for the sake of polemic, but she is wrong to think that novels cannot do what his have clearly done—or to imply that the narrative position, as such, defines genre. She is right, however, to address the issues of modernism and postmodernism since Sebald seems to fit neither "category." He was actively critical of at least one form of postmodern "play" with reality: "I consider the gratuitous invention of horror one of the major faults of our present culture" (Jones, *Newsweek*).

It is possible that W. G. Sebald will be seen as the precursor of yet a new movement in literature. Truth, for Sebald, extended beyond the confines of the known. By playing one genre off the other, Sebald generated a space, called the Sebald Zone—a realm where truth is indeterminate, the narrator is indirect, the characters are enigmatic, the story is inconclusive, and history is uncertain.

Those who would abolish genre would abolish many of the subtleties—and much of the significance—of Sebald's achievement. They would deny imaginative entry to a place that implicates us all.

SELECTED BIBLIOGRAPHY

I. FICTION. *Vertigo,* trans. by Michael Hulse (London, 1999; New York, 2000); *The Emigrants,* trans. by Michael Hulse (London, 1996; New York, 1997); *The Rings of Saturn,* trans. by Michael Hulse (London and New York, 1998); *Austerlitz,* trans. by Anthea Bell (London and New York, 2001).

II. POETRY. *After Nature,* trans. by Michael Hamburger (London, 2002); *For Years Now* (New York, 2002).

III. NONFICTION. *Air War and Literature* (London, 2002).

IV. MONOGRAPHS AND COLLECTED ESSAYS. *Carl Sternheim* (Stuttgart, 1969); *Der Mythus der Zerstörung in Werk Alfred Döblins* (Stuttgart, 1980); *Die Beschreibung des Unglücks* (Salzburg, 1985); *Unheimlich Heimot* (Salzburg, 1991); *Logis in einem Landhaus* (Munich, 1998).

V. CRITICAL STUDIES. James Atlas, "W. G. Sebald: A Profile," in *The Paris Review* (summer 1999); Vivian Gornick, *The Situation and the Story: The Art of Personal Narrative* (New York, 2001); Pico Iyer, "Dead Man Writing," in *Harper's* (October 2000); Cynthia Ozick, "The Posthumous Sublime," in *Quarrel & Quandary* (New York, 2001).

VI. FEATURE ARTICLES. Mel Gussow, Obituary, in *The New York Times* (15 December 2001); Maya Jaggi, "Recovered Memories—*The Guardian* Profile: W. G. Sebald," in *The Manchester Guardian* (22 September 2001); Susan Salter Reynolds, in *The Los Angeles Times* (November 2001).

VII. REVIEWS. Thea Abbott, "Where no friends are buried nor Pathways stopt up," in appleonline.net (2001); W. S. Di Piero, "Another Country," in *The New York Times* (11 June 2000); Michiko Kakutani, "In a No Man's Land of Memories and Loss," in *The New York Times* (26 October 2001); Nicole Krauss, "Arabesques of Journeys," in *Partisan Review*, 32, no. 4 (2001).

VIII. INTERVIEWS. Kenneth Baker, "Up Against Historical Amnesia," in *San Francisco Chronicle* (October 2001); Malcolm Jones, "Outside the Box," in *Newsweek* (October 2001).

CHRISTOPHER WALLACE-CRABBE

(1934–)

Andrew Zawacki

CHRISTOPHER WALLACE-CRABBE CHARACTERIZES his earliest poems, published between 1959 and 1967, as "Four-square and syllogistic" and "written by a Lockean rationalist who had for reasons of culture and influence formed an attachment to the Church of England" (*Selected Poems,* p. vii). His first book, *The Music of Division* (1959), is replete with poems composed in strict rhyme that investigate religious matters, as though bearing out his observation in the neatly ordered octave "In Summer" that, "As the long afternoon went drifting on / Words took their pattern in an ordered dance / Until, at last, the low red sun had gone / And all things by some quiet ordinance / Shared the one shade" (*Selected Poems*, p. 20). Yet these poems are also attuned to the banalities of everyday life, the corruption endemic to politics and society, and an insistence on edenic, if ephemeral, sexual love. In "Citizen," Wallace-Crabbe examines the "sacred ritual of work," treating with vitriol the modern culture of commuting, from its "hasty breakfasts" to how "traffic ran one way" (*Selected Poems*, p. 18). The poem figures this frenzy to be latent complacency, implying that the rites of rush hour and their economic impetus have replaced authentic living. "It was at times like this," the poem proceeds, "That decent violence beset his brain."

Broadening his scope in "Ancient Historian," Wallace-Crabbe demonstrates that the seeds of contemporary disarray may be linked to the ambitions of antiquity. The poem posits a scholar telling himself that "vitality" is a "virtue proper to both man and state" which allows individuals and societies to become great (*Selected Poems*, p. 17). He halts, however, when he has a vision of a "town once founded on vitality, / Rome, sprawling and gone rotten at the core, / And the lean Goths encroaching silently." By introducing political and moral dissolution Wallace-Crabbe renders fatal what, on first glance, seemed vital. Where true life can certainly be located, though, is expressed in "Paolo to Francesca." The couple is beset by "lean despair," Paolo remarks, as "Guilt and folly wait until / We should move apart again" (*Selected Poems*, p. 21). In being together, however, they find safety, with "the circuit of my arms / For your present certainty." Even if "rapture cannot make / Gods of us, who fail and fall," still the lovers feel sure that love will not dissolve: "And if God yields a time of grace / To us now, lie close," Paolo urges Francesca, "and say / We know perfection till the coming day."

The poems subsequent to Wallace-Crabbe's debut are, according to their author, "marked increasingly by a political interest in Australian culture and a lyrical interest in psychomachia," as well as being "largely concerned with the foundations of belief and the principles of growth" (*Selected Poems*, p. vii). Psychomachia can be defined as the play of internal conflicts and contraditions, especially when externally dramatized. The poems of *In Light and Darkness* (1963) are explicit about faith, fallenness, figures of capable imagination, and a world that, though beautiful, is a place to beware. "The Swing," a prose poem credo, offers that progress does not occur in merely one direction: "From lighter to darker I go, from dark to light; but only, as ever, to return" (*Selected Poems*, p. 28). The poem addresses a problem that becomes increasingly urgent throughout Wallace-Crabbe's poetry, the relative obscurity of the universe and the extent to which the self seeks—and generally fails to achieve—clarity:

> Here we live in the imperfect syntax of light and darkness; wanting to write a sentence as perfect as the letter o in praise of things. For things exist supremely; all our values cohere in things.
>
> The austere prose which could outline the world with a physicist's clarity never arrives. We move through the fugal elaboration of leaves, through centuries of drowning flowers. Unsatisfied, uncertain, I am swinging again in the park.
>
> *(Selected Poems*, p. 28)

Wallace-Crabbe's poems make a method out of vacillation, swinging between moods, modes, forms, conceptions of the self, and systems of belief, aligned with the principle "Equilibrium is death" (*Selected Poems*, p. 13). What holds constant, however, is his conviction that "We will neither be simple nor clear till the end of our days" (*Selected Poems*, p. 6).

EARLY LIFE

Wallace-Crabbe was born on 6 May 1934, in Richmond, Victoria, a suburb of Melbourne, where he grew up in a number of rented houses. His father, Kenneth Eyre d'Inverell Wallace-Crabbe, was a journalist, illustrator, and "jack of all conceivable trades" who "took on the inconceivable ones as well" ("My First Love," p. 6). While his father, who spent four years in Asia during the Second World War, "worked like a Stakhanovite," as Wallace-Crabbe recollects in the essay "My 1930s," his mother, née Phyllis Cock Passmore, "played the piano and she played it well" (*Melbourne,* p. 63). Part of Wallace-Crabbe's youth was spent during the great economic depression, but he recollects that, "We knew plenty of people who resented the Depression, plenty who bellyached about it, but we knew none who had, so far as a child could see, been visibly damaged" (*Melbourne*, p. 62). Art took an early hold in the youthful Wallace-Crabbe, who recalls that he saw *The Wizard of Oz* four times before the end of his childhood, and that, as a kid, he read lots of picture books and books about travel, including *The Voyage of the Beagle, Letters to Channy, Little Men, Blinky Bill*, and *Snugglepot and Cuddlepie* (*Melbourne,* p. 61). In fact, Wallace-Crabbe reports that he could read even before he started school, thanks to his mother, "a secret writer of verse," to his father, who used to tell him, "Your friends will betray you in the end, but a book will never desert you," and to his aunt Violante ("My First Love," p. 3). Soon after, he discovered Rudyard Kipling's tales of Roman Britain and India, while *Puck of Pook's Hill* had the "long-term effect"— nearly fifty years later—of "tak[ing] me and my family along Hadrian's Wall, across the miles of drizzling fells." At age eleven, he gave his mother Palgrave's *Golden Treasury* anthology for her birthday, and remembers that "it was in this modest little navy-blue book that I was later to encounter some of the seductive obscurities of modern poetry" ("My First Love," p. 6).

Upon leaving school, Wallace-Crabbe undertook to become a cadet metallurgist, an ambition he calls "oddly concurrent" with his immersion in Mark Twain and Sir Arthur Conan Doyle ("My First Love," p. 6). Eventually giving up his aspirations in metallurgy, he worked at various jobs while studying part-time at the University of Melbourne, his literary attention then straying to Keats, Auden, Iris Murdoch, and Stendahl. He received his bachelor's degree in 1956, became a Lockie Fellow in Australian Literature and Creative Writing in 1961, and earned his master's degree in 1964. Wallace-Crabbe became part of the so-called Melbourne University poets emerging in the late 1950s, along with Vincent Buckley, Evan Jones, and R. A. Simpson. Yet he stood between the mainstream poetics of the previous decade and the "New Poetry" of the succeeding twenty years (Wilde, *Australian Poets*, p. 280). In 1965, he went to Yale on a two-year Harkness Fellowship, and since then he has lived intermittently in Exeter, Venice, Florence, and Oxford, while many connections have linked him with India. In 1984, he was elected a Fellow of the Australian Academy of the Humanities. Five years later he became inaugural director of the Australian Centre at the University of Melbourne, a position he held for half a decade. He has won numerous awards for his poetry, including the

Grace Leven Prize for Poetry in 1986, the Dublin Prize for Arts and Sciences in 1987, the Human Rights Award for Poetry in 1992, the D. J. O'Hearn Prize for Poetry in 1995, *The Age* Book of the Year Award in 1995, and, most recently, the Philip Hodgins Medal. In addition to writing, he enjoys drawing, in an abstract idiom, a minor obsession he links to his father's forays outside journalism: "In my infancy," Wallace-Crabbe relates, " the back room was filled with the diversified implements—and smells—required for photography, etching, wood and linocutting, drawing and the Lord knows what. My brother and I grew up eating paper and India ink" ("My First Love," p. 6).

His early poem, "A Wintry Manifesto" proffers an apology for the restless imagination, in language that, while forceful, hedges its bets. Evoking *Paradise Lost* and Wallace Stevens' assertion that the death of Satan was a tragedy for the imagination, the poem begins with the devil's demise, claiming that it was the "knowledge that earth holds though kingdoms fall, / Inured us to a stoic resignation, / To making the most of a shrunken neighbourhood" (*Selected Poems*, pp. 35–36). In Milton's blank verse epic, Satan boasts that the mind is its own place, capable of making a heaven of hell. Wallace-Crabbe's poem gives the impression of following the Romantic avatar's lead, yet the power of "making the most" of a given locale is qualified by the reference to resignation. Nor does the poem clarify its precise stance toward Satan: it might be praising Lucifer as a courageous innovator, or else it could be condemning the fallen angel for hubris. "[W]e knew / That we had forged the world we stumbled through," the poem says, "as if celebrating the inventive faculties of humanity. Built our own refuge in a flush of pride // Knowing that all our gifts were for construction." It is hard, though, to miss that theologically loaded word "pride," and immediately there follows the reservation, "purged of the sense of evil, / These were the walls our folly would destroy." The poet seems trapped between valorizing the imagination for its limitless creative capacities and, on the other hand, recognizing that attempts to invent can, if treated without caution, become dangerous.

Despite the promise its title holds out of arguing a case, the poem abandons easy answers to a difficult question, relinquishing any notion of the perfect—or perfected—place, while maintaining a soft spot for the heroic: "Finding our heroism in rejection / Of bland Utopias and of thieves' affection: / Our greatest joy to mark an outline truly / And know the piece of earth on which we stand."

Something short of joy marks Wallace-Crabbe's early view of his native piece of earth. "Melbourne" is in five rhyming sestets, and it is the city's parallel regularity, among other things, that bothers the poet. "[L]ike the bay," he writes, "our blood flows easily, / Not warm, not cold (in all things moderate), / Following our familiar tides" (*Selected Poems*, p. 32). This temperament of idleness and conservatism is anything but laudable to the chameleonic Wallace-Crabbe, who prizes experiment, risk, difference. "Ideas are grown in other gardens," he laments, "while / This soil throws up its harvest of / Imported and deciduous platitudes, / None of them flowering boldly or for long." The constricted nature of the city is reflected in the poem's vaguely claustrophobic form, and the invective is unmistakable. The closing stanza bespeaks this sense of choking, which forces local artists to flee, or else to suffer: "Highway by highway the remorseless cars / Strangle the city, put it out of pain, / Its limbs still kicking feebly on the hills. / Nobody cares. The artists sail at dawn / For brisker ports, or rot in public bars. / Though much has died here, little has been born." The poem addresses the so-called "brain drain" that pocked the Australian intellectual landscape in the 1950s and 1960s. While Wallace-Crabbe was not himself among the writers who left the antipodes to live permanently in Europe or the United States, he was acutely aware that domestic conditions were making it necessary, or at least desirable, for many intellectuals to take their careers overseas. These departures, of course, further impoverished Australian culture.

In his essay "Melbourne in 1963," Wallace-Crabbe rails against Sydney's sister city with the frustrated condescension that is often the young poet's reaction to his stifling environs. The city is "not merely large," he asserts, "but to an extraordinary degree, sprawling and centreless" (*Melbourne or the Bush*, p. 66). He objects to a powerful Presbyterian influence that has instigated exceedingly restrictive alchohol laws and an "unrelievedly dreary Sabbath" (*Melbourne*, p. 76), and worries that the suburbs suffer a "double deprivation" by being alienated from the potentially active core of the city while offering no sense of community in exchange (*Melbourne*, p. 72). He argues that Melbourne "remains another anonymous market hooked up in world-wide networks of production, distribution and information" (*Melbourne*, p. 67), with few claims to its own singularity. Hence he sees Melbourne as the site of a larger, more distressing cultural malaise, whereby Australian society manifests a "continuing lack of maturity and clear-sightedness." Australians consider their own cities to be mere suburbs of London, Paris, and New York, he complains, a phenomenon of comparing Australia disparagingly to Europe that was known in intellectual circles as the "cultural cringe." Australians live in a detached country, and a major sign of their disconnection is that they consider their local city "big enough" (*Melbourne*, p. 68).

Having registered reservations about the "dullness of Melbourne life" and Australia's "lack of cultural autonomy," Wallace-Crabbe does find aspects of the city refreshing. The "ill-conceived" and "lamentably arbitrary" styles of late nineteenth-century architecture in the suburbs, for example, nevertheless possess "something attractive today": they are eclectic (*Melbourne*, p. 69). The influx of Italian, Greek, and Maltese migrants has enlivened an otherwise homogeneous Anglo-Celtic society, a dynamic made more productive by the fact that internationalization has aroused little resentment. Wallace-Crabbe also admires the "vigorous dissent" characteristic of Melbourne's political climate (*Melbourne*, p. 77). Finally, despite the flourishing of critical life at the expense of creativity, Melbourne had become, in the 1950s, the source of the most innovative, disruptive, and energizing artistic undertaking the literary scene had seen, around the journal *Angry Penguins*. Laudatory of noncomformity provided it is intelligent and well-intentioned, Wallace-Crabbe is pleasantly surprised at how "Surrealism, Dadaism, Marxism, Freudianism, and Imagism were blended in the one pot-pourri, and useful, though erratically aimed, blows were dealt to the dreary orthodoxies of Australian culture" (*Melbourne*, p. 80).

Asked about "Melbourne" over thirty years later, Wallace-Crabbe said he no longer felt such hostility, his poem having been the "dramatization of a historical moment" in which figures like poet Peter Porter, essayist Clive James, and theorist Germaine Greer left Australia to pursue their careers (*Verse*, p. 77). Now, he says, reputations can be made at home, and one can move back and forth easily and quickly between Australia and anywhere else. He has traveled extensively himself, participating in international literary festivals and academic symposia. He remains attached to Melbourne, while increasingly feted in the United States and in England: he held a visiting chair of Australian Studies at Harvard University (1987–1988), and with the publication of his *Selected Poems 1956–1994*, he joined the international Oxford Poets list (Wilde, *Australian Poets*, pp. 279–280).

A pair of poems in his third volume, *The Rebel General* (1967), picks up where "Melbourne" and "Melbourne in 1963" leave off, yet with more affection. In "Terra Australis," Wallace-Crabbe says the land down under is where "Paradise lingers like a tapestry; / The web has not been torn" (*Selected Poems*, p. 40), admitting the continent's innocence but blessing, rather then berating, this naivete. Imagining the land before the advent of the Enlightenment and even before Socrates, he names the inhabitants "the final children of the earth / Whom knowledge has not scarred, / Delighting still in sunlight and green grass / Back in our own backyard." Evoking the myth of Eden as well as the beatitude that promises that the meek shall inherit the earth, the poem makes a virtue of infancy and inexperience: "Gaping, we hear the tales of adulthood / Where life is dour and hard, / Far, far away, beyond some wicked wood." This refreshing take on Australia is corroborated by the closing remarks in his introduction to *Six Voices: Contemporary Australian Poets* (1963), an anthology of several midcentury Australian poets. "[I]t is probably true that poets in this country have been less markedly post-Symbolist, more discursively explicit and more good-humoured in the face of the world's pressures than their European and American counterparts," Wallace-Crabbe concedes. "If this is true, they may be presenting us with an image of how life is on this continent: the modes of desperation current in so much Western culture are not necessarily essential truth" (*Six Voices*, p. 4). Even if "Drab skyline, yellowing papers, a fat land" serve as synecdoche for Australia in "An Allegiance," still it happens, "To these I am drawn / Tightly and unreasonably because / I was born here." Wallace-Crabbe's native country has not been exhausted by history or burdened by tradition, as in Europe and America, but remains a "paper blankness / On which all writing is still to be done" (*Selected Poems*, p. 40).

Mistrust of historical grandeur and unchecked ambition impels myriad poems. The cutthroat subject of "The Rebel General" is "driven by the laws of history, / Straight as a die," as though he takes no responsibility for his actions, which stem from "a host of garbled impulses" (*Selected Poems*, pp. 49–50). His army having deserted him years ago, this dictator is beset by hesitation and sorrow, reduced to being a "custodian of failure" who now commands only "second-rate conspirators." Wallace-Crabbe displays equally ambivalent feelings toward that other grand ruler, God, in "The Secular," when he asserts that the durability of nature is ironically poised against the ephemerality of human life. "Look, I grant all that you say: / Whoever the creator / He brutally botched the job, / But how tough his furniture / Really is made, piece by piece!" the speaker replies to an unknown someone, resolving, "I jump on his solid stones / Or dance on these rustling fields / And hear the sap leap in the trees / Already marked out for death" (*Selected Poems*, p. 41).

The vivacity of the natural world, regardless of its inevitable death drive, nevertheless sustains Wallace-Crabbe. He is bolstered by a flower's "explosion of / Substantial pink" and inspired by its "energies," which "drive our crinkled flesh into this world" (*Selected Poems*, p. 39). Moreover, even if the "wonder" and "profusion" of nature are such that "nobody can claim it makes good sense / Or testifies to clarity," as stated in "Nature, Language, the Sea: An Essay," the poet's rage for order might yet make heads or tails of it all (*Selected Poems*, pp. 8–10). The poet's vocation is to name and number, to order what is disheveled and disorienting, to rectify the divine "mistakes of a creator" by "chisel[ing] // The small hard statues of his poetry" until they bear "the assurance of being right." An index of both passion and morality, "the formal," he declares, "is at last the good," so poetry rings of that ever-elusive clarity.

Finally, in a lyric that pursues an existential allegory in river rafting, Wallace-Crabbe determines that though "Our cries are lost in the clash of waters," still some benign, albeit mysterious, guidance is available, and helps us to "glide upon that nameless flood, / A twilit river at the core of things" (*Selected Poems*, pp. 44–45). What interests him, though, is why humans would disturb the "tranquillity" of gardens, "easy streams," and "mild wind" in the first place, to launch into turbulent rapids. Answer: "but we are most ourselves / Climbing beyond the known."

TAKING SHAPE

The varieties and verities of selfhood are among Wallace-Crabbe's preeminent concerns. "I am essential self," he writes in "The Centaur Within," from *Where the Wind Came* (1971), employing a declarative presence that is radically disrupted throughout his work, even if an intact, accountable self remains a dream or goal (*Where the Wind Came*, p. 22). "Self / is the springer, / the limber light evader shooting through / past all our fences," he says in "The Joker," en route to describing the problem of selfhood as frustrating (*Wind*, p. 23). Just when it seems one has gotten hold of one's self—fixed it inside its "heavy neighbour, / personality"—it transforms into something different or escapes definition. "Dear self," he addresses the agile runaway, "you flip out of anyone's grip / like a wet watermelon seed . . . / there you are . . . off again." In myriad corners of Wallace-Crabbe's work the transformative properties of the self are endearing, but he can also be overheard plaintively telling it, "You tear me apart."

In "The Mind Is Its Own Place," a title that again evokes the empowering—though perhaps misguided or deluded—rhetoric of Satan, the speaker "turned old laundry scraps of self / into a recognizable quilt, / surviving, working still" (*Wind*, p. 43). Yet if this patchwork self is functional, the price at which it has been achieved is high: melancholy, solitude, emptiness. "The mind is a dark / and most solitary place," the speaker states, "throw in a little stone and you hear it / rattling and echoing off steep sides / all the way down." Rarely does the self appear capable of stability, and the few occasions when it does, by dint of the mind's effort, it entails a sacrifice. "All changes," Wallace-Crabbe iterates sadly in "Quitting Bulleen," but he reminds himself that to seek to stop or reverse flux is akin to insanity: "The straight road to madness goes / in quest of permanence" (*Wind*, p. 49). It is unclear whether a self to call one's own is possible for more than a moment, without experiencing pain that might subvert the very desire for such a self. While Wallace-Crabbe has noted that "it is impossible to arrive at the essential self," he also points out that "poetry, like the other arts, is driven by the yearning to arrive at the essential self, to reach beyond the fragmentary, divided, psychologically-complex, repeatedly provisional self-moments and to move toward something that seems to be a permanent locus" (*Verse*, p. 81).

Minimal consolation resides in the fact that the self is not *constantly* inconstant. "[A]ll of us have access to perfectly solid selves *some* of the time," Wallace-Crabbe observes, poking fun at the nomenclature of academic debates surrounding the decentered self: "you can't be a Lacanian sceptic and be playing tennis simultaneously, and a discursive site really can't ride the waves at Bell's Beach" (*Verse*, p. 82). Yet if this is true, then what he says in his 1989 James McAuley Memorial Lecture is also true—and less reassuring: "On some mornings one wakes up as a lyric poet, on others as a loving father, that's the way of it" (*Poetry and Belief*, p. 8). One is never the

same self one was before, and one cannot be a single self in and across all contexts: life imposes that hard fact. His point is that because different situations engender a single person's different selves, no self-evident correspondence should be drawn between the poet as person and the self depicted in a poem. The beliefs that inform the one who writes do not necessarily announce themselves in what gets written, nor is poetry under contract to present a "transparent policy statement about what it might believe in"—let alone what the poet might believe (*Poetry and Belief*, p. 12).

It is worth asking, then, whether the often desired end of immobile selfhood justifies the means, whether success in finding an immutable self balances the cost. In a world lit by "a dying sun," however, a "ruined mansion of the world" where "Hitler made his contribution / To the wintry bonfire of aesthetics" (*Wind*, pp. 27, 24, 59), the pursuit of self-sufficient durability is certainly understandable, if not dignified. Such a desiccated world, imbued with threatening despotism, is Wallace-Crabbe's focus in "Blood Is the Water." A seven-part account of a Latin American military dictator's rise to power, the poem interrogates the extent to which "Irrational forces have a hand in action" (*Wind*, p. 12). Looked at one way, the politically hungry strong man, who reads Clausewitz and "got what he was after," is the culprit (*Wind*, p. 3), having decided he can conquer whatever is in his way: "Aggression like a madness he exalted / Quick to stake all on the one straight throw, / Not least the lives of men" (*Wind*, p. 12). From another vantage, however, history is to blame for the dictator's ascension: "For history, old friend, confederate, / Has got the young man firmly on its wheel" (*Wind*, p. 4). The terms of the debate are thus established: history versus personal responsibility. While Wallace-Crabbe is inclined to depict the outcome of this eternal question— "Blood is the water in a thousand streams, / Incredible patterning of ebb and flow / Through watersheds and deltas of the flesh, / Endless recirculation and returning" (*Wind*, p. 5)—he abstains from pointing his finger. Left to query the supreme power that reigns over everything,

CHRISTOPHER WALLACE-CRABBE

"Whose consciousness contains our history?" he asks, "What are the laws?" (*Wind*, p. 14).

It comes as no surprise that Wallace-Crabbe readily owns up to being as "fascinated by politics as drama" (*Verse*, p. 77). "I love watching, in a sort of Shakespearean way," he explains, "what makes and breaks leaders. I love watching how the votes are counted. I love watching how the numbers might work within a political party. It's one of the things I turn to first in the newspapers: struggles for leadership, plans of campaigns." In "Roman Thoughts in Autumn" the poet says Catiline was the "favourite classic figure of my childhood," elaborating on his general attraction to the rise and fall of empires and individuals: "That's something I always had as a boy," he recalls, "a yen for failures; / give me the defeated every time, / legions, battalions / that fail in the mist and flee through the hedges / in tatters" (*Wind*, pp. 55, 54). There is an element of the Australian pride in the underdog here, but Wallace-Crabbe tends to valorize unlikely heroes on account of their defeats, rather than for some imagined, rags-to-riches, against-the-odds victory. Such enthusiasm for the complex, occasionally melodramatic machinations of the political process and its minions is often accompanied in his poetry by cynicism about the genuine possibilities for improvement, since more often than not politics is dominated by those who change things for the worse—and find themselves immeasurably worsened.

"And yet there's another side of myself that remains idealist about politics," Wallace-Crabbe notes, "that is, I suppose in most matters, fairly fiercely of the left." This assertion of the half-full political glass might be intuited from "The Collective Invention," in which he imagines a silver-caped, plastic-winged Captain Melbourne "Doing the common good all day long, / A handful of thunderbolts in his shoulder holster" (*Selected Poems*, p. 110). The poet is the first to admit, however, that such a vision is little more than "myth," elsewhere observing that "as one gets older, there is no one party that corresponds to one's yearnings, needs and ideals" (*Verse*, p. 77). Wallace-Crabbe is a realist with radical impulses—or a radical with realist tendencies—

describing himself as "a perfect mixture of a rural conservative and a Marxist." Hence he is not always suspicious of ambition, though he usually celebrates it only when it drives spiritual development. Imagining his son climbing a tree in "The Tree," for instance, he follows the boy's movements "Wherever his limbs might go; // Wherever a boy might go / Spurred on by aspirations / That drive us all / Up into shattery branches," until, triumphantly, "Upward and outward he climbed" (*Wind,* p. 64). Less personally, Wallace-Crabbe offers a pilgrims' progress in "Meditations with Memories," paying homage to the travelers who enter "rough towns waiting for new selves, / Waiting to shape our ways, / The outlines of a future we prepare" (*Wind,* p. 39).

The extent to which humans can shape anything, not to mention the ethical dilemmas posed by acts of shaping, fascinates Wallace-Crabbe, foremost as an aesthetic issue, but eventually with reference to the colonization of Australia, as well. On the one hand, "form is perhaps the visible / counterpart of hope," he writes in "Familiar Endeavours" (*Selected Poems,* p. 106). In a statement also written in the early 1970s, however, he begins to work against this adage, positing, "After stoical-formalist beginnings, I seek a poetry of Romantic fullness and humanity. I want to see how far lyrical, Dionysian impulse can be released and expressed without a loss of intelligence" (quoted in Wilde, p. 280). "Meditation with Mountains" stages this impetus, while offering a cautionary tale about the inability to domesticate the world through art. "All—but the all is never to be caught," the poet realizes, having climbed to a solitary, snow-tipped peak:

The range is never to be civilized
In a green cramp of farms, plough, fallow, crop
And heavy hay constricted in its bales,
Emblems of order put upon the world:
The snowline and the ragged screes abide.
A lofty brightness holds
Where charity and wisdom have no place
And love is like a thin blue line of smoke,
Barely in evidence in all that air.

(*Wind*, p. 40)

The mountain range represents the unassimilable, that which cannot be tamed. Moreover, the "wild austerity" of the "naked rock" means human conceptions such as charity and love do not apply there, as "wisdom shatters on the rocks like glass," until only "awe remains."

In the face of this awesome, resistant peak—reminiscent of Mont Blanc, so crucial in the English Romantic poets' experience of the sublime—the poet is led to an even greater, more terrifying discovery, that humans "do not know what blue giant huffs, / What magus mutters in the mountain tops, / Nameless, not captured by the camera." The poem reminds us that the divine—whoever or whatever that principle of creation is—cannot be perceived or portrayed within the parameters of human understanding, not even enough to be named. Likewise, the mountain—despite its characterization as "sculpted" and the description of its materials as "Promethean"—cannot be brought under human control, either. The mind, Wallace-Crabbe reckons, may be its own place, but it definitively cannot fashion heaven out of hell or hell from heaven; it cannot even harness nature, let alone God.

Several poems in *The Foundations of Joy* (1976) are also preoccupied with questions about what can and cannot be given shape. "Real Estate" seems to suggest that the future, because it has no specific architecture or arc, needs to be endowed with contour by those who are always living through it: "The structure / of the future / has no pilaster, // vault or architrave. / Its prospects always strive / with what we have, // hammering our hopes / into queer shapes / and breakneck slopes" (*Selected Poems 1956–1994*, p. 26). If the line endings of each tercet are regular, the grammar of the argument remains ambiguous: Who exactly hammers our hopes "into queer shapes / and breakneck slopes"? Is it "we" who create our own destiny, patterning our pending days according to a structure we envision? Or is it the future itself, that takes our strivings and bends them along its own crooked avenues, foiling even our best-laid plans? The poem concludes without assurance either way: "Listen, mister, / the nightly planner / of your future / is death's well-known brother." Presumably Wallace-Crabbe is insinuating that dreams plot our futures—but is he speaking of noble aspirations, or of pipe dreams? Are we to value the sense of transcending our circumstances and ourselves that dreams inspire, or should we suspect their delusive power? The final allusion to the "brother" of death is sinister, to say the least, while a life lacking the vertigo of "breakneck slopes" does not seem worthwhile, either.

Often more troubling than the future, though, is the past. Nostalgia plays a significant role in Wallace-Crabbe's work, and, indeed, as early as *Where the Wind Came*, he writes sadly but wittily, "In memory's yellow eye it's always summer, / nobody ever worked, the grass grew thick, / coffee cups, unlike women, had no bottoms" (*Wind*, p. 35). Despite this yearning for childhood and purity, however, he becomes, in his later work, exceedingly uneasy about the dystopic aspects of the past, particularly regarding the settlement of Australia. The signs of that disapproval are intermittently visible early on. In "Traditions, Voyages," in *The Rebel General*, Wallace-Crabbe compares Australia to Jamaica, pondering the history of the former as a penal colony: "We had, perhaps, our Middle Passage too, / Irishman and felon stank in the holds / When frail barques ferried the Enlightenment, / Already dim and faint" (*Selected Poems 1956–1994*, p. 15). Even poems that ostensibly have nothing to do with the treatment of aboriginal culture, such as "The Wild Colonial Puzzler," are hard not to read as subtle commentaries on the issue, with lines such as "beware of Australians bearing gifts" assuming political significance in light of more recent debates about colonialism (*Selected Poems 1956–1994*, p. 28).

The malleability of shapes moves to the forefront of Wallace-Crabbe's mind in "The Shape-Changer," in his sixth volume, *The Emotions Are Not Skilled Workers* (1980). The poem charts the daily metempsychosis of Proteus, who refuses to reside contentedly in any particular incarnation or adhere to any but a seemingly arbitrary itinerary. "The first day he was travelling to Asia," the poem begins, "the next day he flew the flight of a wedge-tailed eagle, / the next day he was the gusting wind" (*Selected Poems 1956–1994*, p. 36). Proteus becomes a campfire, a seal, "the little cousin of Death," a snake, clock, tree, and a lion. At the end of the poem—which presumably is not the end of Proteus' physical and metaphysical peregrinations—the mythical figure is described as one who "never dreamed at all," signifying that when one can become literally anything, the inventive and associative prerogatives of dream are no longer necessary. Moreover, the poem itself acts as a sort of dream, that of a poet who wishes to maximize John Keats's notion of "negative capability," the Romantic capacity whereby an individual inhabits whatever body or object he decides. Hence Wallace-Crabbe, in a 1981 interview with David Carter, is forthcoming about his drive to "invent, if you like, new cartoon characters, new mythic characters, that dance out the many things that mind is, because I think that a mind or self is as amorphous and evasive as a concept of poetry is. Indeed more so" (Carter, "Shape Changing," p. 105). The outcome of Keats's idea is that the poet, by transforming into alternatives and ulteriors, becomes nothing and nobody himself—that is, his chameleonic incarnations mean he possesses no single, singular, proper "self" at all. Yet by sacrificing a solo self, he assumes infinite guises.

MID-CAREER

"Suppose I were to eat you," the speaker of the opening, title poem of *The Amorous Cannibal* (1985) wonders. In roving over the other's body, considering how to gobble her up "delicacy by tidbit," he resolves that she would finally return as a ghost to ravish him. The poem bespeaks sexual intensity, certainly, but it also illuminates Wallace-Crabbe's increasing, more general preoccupation with the primitive. His earliest books having been obsessed with the sorts of formal constraints indicative of high art, if not explicitly associated with Europe, the newer work becomes interested in more primal responses to the self, communities of selves, and the world at large, discovering an authenticity in the Australian landscape, lingo, and artistic lineage.

To begin with, "we are remarkably Frenchified in this country," he relates, thinking especially of

the influence of Mallarmé and Rimbaud (*Poetry and Belief*, p. 7). Elsewhere he notes, among "many writers of my own generation," such as Peter Porter and Peter Steele, there is a pronounced "postwar bias toward a British cultural frame" ("The Repeated Rediscovery of America," *Approaching Australia*, p. 92). Wallace-Crabbe has also documented the "continuous" presence of American electronic arts and "the exotic freedom American writers had to be anything they wanted to be" within Australian culture, with poets such as Robert Lowell, Elizabeth Bishop, and Marianne Moore having influenced a wide range of antipodean writers ("Repeated Rediscovery," pp. 93, 94). Wallace-Crabbe's own engagement with these traditions is vigorous, usually salutary, and occasionally antagonistic, under the aegis "I do not subscribe to the theory that no muse is good muse" (*Selected Poems*, p. vii). He values Randall Jarrell for his plain speech and John Berryman for his "potentially destructive emotions kicking against a tight verse form and a humorous quickness of mind," while proposing that an "Australian John Ashbery is inconceivable," that *A la Recherche du Temps Perdu* is a deeply Australian novel, and frequently inveighing against an experimentation for its own sake that he blames on faddish French and American aesthetic movements (*Toil*, pp. 120, 135).

However, Wallace-Crabbe has simultaneously conceded, in an essay on folk poet and author of "Waltzing Matilda," Banjo Paterson, a predilection toward "cheerful and easy simplicity," offering that "sub-rationally or unconsciously I have always believed the bushman to be our true alterego" (*Toil*, p. 28). Hence he has expressed an "urge to get back to the oral spontaneity of cultures in an earlier stage of development," to write against "high-octane critical terminology," and pairs his admiration for elegance with a love of the loud and unleashed: "The extraordinarily artifical modes of Beethoven, Wagner, Tolstoy, Joyce, Antonioni and all the rest are our classics," he stipulates, "but we find excitement and release when we are given access to something simpler" (*Melbourne*, pp. 85, 88). The poem "Bennelong," titled after the name of an Aborigine who was taken back to London soon after the First Settlement, articulates this desire to explode the hard shell of Europe, the landscapes of which are "pretty / follies," not genuine but only "colourful imitations / of the crazy landlord's personal set / of watercolours," tainted by history and gaudiness, "fatigue and kitsch" (*Selected Poems 1956–1994*, p. 37). The poet begins by withholding his forgiveness and prays, finally, to be realigned with antipodean climate and textures: "When I blew to Europe in the big white bird / or nibbled at lettucegreen England / I could never forgive the landscapes // for not being southern. . . . The big dry bones / are wedged under my flesh . . . leathery leaves are whispering in my guts; / slow brown waters churn through me. / O Jesus, Jesus, turn me inside out." Once despondent over the cultural inadequacy of his native Australia, Wallace-Crabbe is here asserting its utter importance to his "personal geology."

This reverence for his local identity informs his views on literary creation. Having previously disparaged Australians for not looking far enough afield, in the essay "The Solitary Shapers" he diagnoses an inverse malady: Australian writers' neglect of what is endemic to, and therefore significant about, their native land and literature. "The cultural problem is this," he asserts:

> However we may aspire towards an intelligent cosmopolitanism in our literature, however we exercise that process of borrowing which enriches the soil out of which a culture grows, there must remain some awareness of the historical uniqueness of our situation. And our situation is more than political and geographical, ecological and climatic: it includes what has been thought and said and written in Australia. The writer who chooses to ignore this part of his environment renders his task correspondingly harder, running the danger of eccentricity or of aggressive self-assertion.
>
> (*Melbourne*, p. 4)

Wallace-Crabbe's critical output evidences an extreme familiarity and intense involvement with Australian art. His essays of over four decades address the novelists Henry Lawson, Joseph Furphy, Martin Boyd, David Malouf, and others; the poets A. D. Hope, James McAuley, Gwen Harwood, Judith Wright, Bruce Dawe, and Kenneth Slessor; and the historical significance of literary

periodicals such as *The Bulletin*, *Boomerang*, *Meanjin Papers* (now *Meanjin*), and *Southerly*—to say nothing of his writings on multiculturalism, autobiography, and painting. His understanding of all modes of artistic production in Australia extends even to the critical essay itself, which, he explains in the introduction to *The Australian Nationalists: Modern Critical Essays* (1971), "would seem to have sprung from the appropriate muse's head some time in the mid-1940s," when academics shifted their attention to debates about Australian tradition and culture and published their views in journals devoted to exactly that (*The Australian Nationalists*, p. xi).

Equally at home writing criticism about non-Aussie literati W. H. Auden, Thomas Hardy, and Ezra Pound, Wallace-Crabbe has determined that, in crafting poems, "One way to escape from European ghosts that lean over one's shoulder and jog one's pen is by paying careful attention to the facts of immediate environment" (*Melbourne*, p. 8). *The Amorous Cannibal* is full of attention to local, natural detail: pigface, coprosma, samphire, "kikuyu, fescue, bent and oats" abound (*Amorous*, pp. 16, 51). At the same time, however, "Sacred Ridges above Diamond Creek" relays the cosmopolitan poet's "alien response" to echidna, dingo, platypus, magpie, possum, wagtail, kangaroo, and other indigenous wildlife, while "The Home Conveyancing Kit" and "River" wind past mortgages, veggie gardens, failed marriages, skirt-chasing, domestic ennui, and the city's physical sprawl of "medical ranches / to scrubby suburbs of mudbrick, Volvos / and odd literati / hoarding their dirt roads" (*Amorous*, pp. 53, 40, 42). Wallace-Crabbe claims that there is "an achievement in seeing one's environment and getting its names and relationships into verse" (*Melbourne*, p. 8), and for him that environment is both urban and rural. "I have been brought up all my life in cities and suburbs, and so the matrix into which I fit experience is an open matrix," he has noted (*Verse*, p. 76). Halfway between the countryside poetics exemplified by Australian poet Les Murray and the gentrified aesthetics of expatriate Australian poet Peter Porter, Wallace-Crabbe explains that "while

I have certain kinds of Freudian oceanic feeling that are released by and into nature, it's that oceanic feeling that is peculiar to *urban* people, who can romanticize nature."

In "The Fall of the West," then, he plays the part of a futuristic city dweller and wonders how "bushland scene" has been allowed to rampage a college, asking, "Why did they vamoose and let the bush take over?" (*Amorous*, p. 32). In "Puck Is Not Sure About Apollo," however, he dismisses the sun god as "Mister Smoothie with his sun-blades" and "Choric odes," deriding the classical and urbane in favor of "whatever is tousled, / windy, brownish, water-kissed, / lit by irregular streaks of glinting / and, above all, out of place" (*Amorous*, p. 31). He subordinates the ordered, mythical principle of nature to nature itself, in all its disorder. "Looking back from this point in time," he writes in 1971, "we are likely to be struck by how *little* the complex of attitudes which created the bushman image has found expression in the best literature of the twentieth century" (*Australian Nationalists*, p. x). Much of Wallace-Crabbe's poetry seeks to remedy how the bushman "ceased to be an image of possibility and became a static figure, either as a dreamily vague *alter ego* or as a rustic buffoon." In "Panoptics," he imagines a prehistoric race who honored the primacy of sexuality and "gave myth to the stars" by naming their constellations "The Kiss, The Groin, / The Phallus and The First Dream, / Climax and Dayspring, / The Hip, The Labia, / The Great Exploring Tongue / and Semen of the Gods" (*Amorous*, p. 17). He regrets their having been replaced by a less magical, "new taxonomy." The book's conclusion, "A Stone Age Decadent," begins with a grunt, "Uh. / Uh," and examines not so much civilization as its discontents, complaining that "laws and restrictive totems" are "Banal, sublime, bestial, that's how / My fellow tribespeople make out the world" (*Amorous*, pp. 58–59). Whether he is arguing that so-called civilization is actually barbaric, or else making a plea for modern society's return to a more humble, primal state, he proclaims that, despite everything, "Just to stare / With care at this or that makes the world seem good: . . . I like it here" (*Amorous*, p. 60).

Many of the poems in *I'm Deadly Serious* (1988) interrogate where, exactly, "here" is, and investigate how, if at all, language is able to account for presence. The aptly titled "There" speaks of a "clear lake" at "the bottom of consciousness," the source of "the slubbing barabble of language, / Gust and pith, cacophony, glossolalia, / Gift of the gab and purple rhetoric, / Moaning in rut, scream, snicker, and the rip / That is sheer pain" (*I'm Deadly Serious*, p. 6). Despite the clarity of this figurative lake, Wallace-Crabbe pronounces his uncertainty about the mechanisms of the subconscious, especially its relationship to the words supposedly formed therein, noting, "I'm afraid I don't know what paths / Lead up from the pool where I think and talk." In exploring the sounds and articulations that bubble up from below, he can confidently assert, "Yes, these are of language," but he must qualify that what is "of language" is, as he says, "not yet *it*." What he searches for is not linguistic offshoots or instances, not even their origin or ends, but rather language *per se*.

What he intuits is that language, to be discovered, must be constantly made anew. "The important thing is to build new sentences," he writes in "The Thing Itself," to "give them a smart shape, / to get acquainted with grammar like a new friend" (*Deadly*, p. 10). But to arrive at the new, he observes, one needs to "go right back, / devising a sentence / unlike any such creature in creation." Wallace-Crabbe's ideal is that in refusing to write poetry that "rubs down syntax / into a coarse familiarity," an original—perhaps ab-original—utterance will "glitter, articulate, / strum and diversify," until finally, "It would be the thing itself." This objective involves being "free of your fetters," as he puts it in "Objects, Odours," eschewing the stylistically cooked in favor of raw statement, while also rejecting too familiar language and the tyranny of canonical literature, which predetermine new poetry (*Deadly*, p. 9).

"Stuff Your Classical Heritage" inclines toward throwing out the baby of fatigued phrases with the bathwater of Western art. "Gull, grevillea, galvo, Gippsland, grit—," he starts, flexing an alliterative declension of Australian words, "just singing out the chorus, bit by bit / will get me some purchase on the primal scene" (*Deadly*, p. 8). In admonishing, "Keep Jehovah in his place," he calls for the imprisonment or excommunication of logocentrism, of dominant discourses, and advocates misprision as a way of writing with "ripe new words // or old ones triumphantly misapplied, / every solecism a seal of triumph." He celebrates his commitment to the "twiggy particular," under the assumption that, "By naming, I seem to crush the past / like a mattress, hard down in history's / rusty cabin-trunk: stick it in the cellar." With the past securely, violently buried, the poet is free to begin naming the world again, as if from scratch. Looked at from another angle, however, it may be, as critic David McCooey has argued, that, "Rather than *expelling* the 'classical heritage' from the Australian landscape the poem actually incorporates it: Jehovah is in his place, and Oedipus romps through the undergrowth. . . . The Father in his inevitable wilderness and the tragic son strongly imply (if comically) an oedipal relationship with European culture" (McCooey, "Leisure and Grief," p. 334).

The oppressive dominion of history and its arbiter cannot always be so easily dismissed or incorporated. If, as Wallace-Crabbe writes in "Sonnets to the Left," it is possible that "All our beyond is in this life" (*Deadly*, p. 28), he cannot help but entertain the antithetical notion that there exists some other, transcendent place, governed by something like a god, that will harbor us after death. "The answering bay of calm / is probably religious," he writes in "There is Another World but It is in This One," looking out over water and proposing its divine source, before recalling, "but you lost your way to all that salt coherence / two centuries ago" (*Deadly*, p. 16). Despite his alienation from received notions of the divine, Wallace-Crabbe declares that "not a bloody thing / can, yet, now, quite stop me feeling / we are connected to a coursing stream or tide / incomparably larger than ourselves." The staccato spondees of "can, yet, now, quite stop me" evidence a severity of statement, a *gravitas*, even a reluctant gratitude for the sensation that humanity is infinitely cared for. Again, "I'd like to believe in

something / Much larger than myself," he affirms in "Thermodynamics," probing the mysteries of biology and religious theories, "But all the designs are crook / Or disproportionate / Or just more bloody art" (*Deadly*, p. 20). The poem ends when the speaker receives a phone call informing him that his father has died; the anxiety and exigency of that interruption suddenly force the poet to surrender talk of "intellectual systems" and their practicalities. Instead he concentrates on "the deaths of us all," resolving—in the dual sense of arriving at an answer and assembling one's courage—that "Spirit finds queer lodging. / I am in the front line now" (*Deadly*, pp. 22, 23). What had been a merely mental exercise in pondering the meaning of life, as if, by seeming absent, death were only an object of contemplation, has now become a way of life, within death's ever-present horizon.

It is death, too, that presides over Wallace-Crabbe's ninth individual volume, *For Crying Out Loud* (1990). Published after the death of his adult son and adhering to the idea that "Damage is where we start from," the book also contains elegies in memory of the Freudian scholar A. F. Davies and fellow poet Vincent Buckley (*For Crying Out Loud*, p. 3). The opening poem, "They," claims the dead exist "like the square root of minus one," their appearance not only impossible but also a reminder, in Heidegger's lexicon, of the constant possibility of our own impossibility: "Lamenting them, we weep for ourselves" (*Crying*, p. 1). Moreover, the poem describes the dead as being "ahead of us / in a meadow," as if awaiting our arrival. However, many of Wallace-Crabbe's poems of this period, particularly "An Elegy," bear the inverse quality of waiting for the dead—for those who arrived at death too early. "I wish again / it were possible to pluck my son / out of dawn's moist air . . . before he ever hit the ground," the speaker intones, to "gather him gasping back into this life" (*Crying*, p. 19). That the speaker cannot bring the son back to life is, of course, a mark of his own mortality.

Other poems pitch their grief in less overtly elegiac tones. "The Evolution of Tears" is characterized by stoicism: "One slides into the ground / who had been a spirit, horsed round and laughed as we do / and now joins the majority . . . in a horizontal kingdom underfoot," and "We do not understand. / Together we rise, / feather, turn and fly away" (*Crying*, p. 11). Nor are anger and frustration ever far off. Addressing the question of faith in "Inversion Layer: Oxfordshire," the speaker whispers, "'I'm a non-believer,'" ordering the wind, "'Be off. Go stand in a fairy ring, / disturb the filthy starlings / and may dry rot powder your corky soul'" (*Crying*, p. 26). Lest the volume be overburdened with pain, though, Wallace-Crabbe brightens it with the "willy-wagtail's flirting pirouettes," "a wildly seductive idiom of flowers," and other signs of life and levity (*Crying*, pp. 43, 44). "Puck and Saturn" revels in the "pounce and jump" of the universe and the planets' manner of "spanking through gossamer revolutions," as if paying tribute to both the quixotic "buoyancy of the world" and its celestial regularity (*Crying*, p. 42). The "yes, oh yes" of the penultimate poem, "The Shining Gift," is finally affirming, as it ascertains "intimations of petalled grace, / the good moment flying / into your loaf of bread" (*Crying*, p. 59). In a volume fraught with images of falling, the poet finds consolation in transitory surges of ascension, surprise, awakening, opening up: "just when a light-shaft / leans in on the study carpet / you have felt warmth for a mo / come in on the short wave. . . . One lifespan is a gift / slowly being unwrapped / in the milky April morning. / The coloured paper crinkles" (*Crying*, pp. 59–60).

BY AND LARGE *AND OTHER WORKS*

"Coming not to bury but to praise," the elegy, Wallace-Crabbe says, "is tactically committed both to recalling past events and to stressing the fact of present annihilation of the past" (*Falling into Language*, p. 20). Both *Rungs of Time* (1993) and *Whirling* (1998) resound with elegies that evoke the past while reminding that the past is no longer. Most of these elegies are for Wallace-Crabbe's late son, but a few inventory the poet's own aches and pains, both physical and emotional, and anticipate his death. In "Trace Elements," Wallace-Crabbe refuses to think of the end as final: "but surely," the speaker pleads, "the dead must walk again," as he imagines his son shambling down a footpath (*Rungs*, p. 10). "Space-time is no longer their medium," he claims of the dead, revving up a mind at once scientific and theological; instead "they inhabit / antipodes of the radiant fair dinkum, / post-Heisenberg, transphysical, post-Planck, / taunting us all with quips of anti-matter." Similarly, "Will Ye No' Come Back Again?" pictures the dead as if come back to life, as part of our own lives: "and the dead are suddenly walking / through our pale bodies / like frost or influenza, // enabled all of a sudden" (*Whirling*, p. 30). "Years On" and "Erstwhile," on the other hand, seek to come to terms with the hard fact of death's irrevocability. In the former, the poet returns to his son's grave, claiming that "what his name betokens / is nothing more than bones" (*Whirling*, p. 31). The four rhyming quatrains conclude with a poignant admission of ignorance about how long it would take for water to soak down and cover his son's bones: "I do not know, merely recall / moments of pleasure and mirth. / As he trod lightly on you, / rest lightly on him, earth." As David McCooey points out, "The (slightly loosened) ballad stanza in this context seeks to contain an emotion too readily drawn to disorderliness" (McCooey, "Leisure and Grief," p. 340). By contrast, "Erstwhile" is emotionally, mentally, and formally staggered, doubling back on itself as if unable to make clear or coherent progress in the process of mourning. "Your girlfriend rang me up today," it begins, "your former girlfriend, / no, that isn't right, / the present friend of all that once was you, / your fetch or / what remains in the little photographs" (*Whirling*, p. 21). If, as Wallace-Crabbe says in another poem, "our dying / cannot find the words / for someone who shudders near the brink," then it is equally impossible to find words for one already dead, even if humanity entered the world "pollenated with naming" (*Rungs*, pp. 9, 26). Having lost himself in photographs of his erstwhile son, "Oh yes," he brings himself back to the present, "she rang today . . . and we were sad together / on the phone," he explains, "for a hard while / thinking of you, long gone now" (*Whirling*, p. 21). Unlike other elegies in which Wallace-Crabbe, in effect, resurrects the dead, here, "rather than attempting to invoke a presence," he "draws attention to an absence which cannot be understood" (McCooey, "Leisure and Grief," p. 341). "The loss remains behind / like never being well" (*Whirling*, p. 21). This loss as sickness recalls the fall from Eden, which resulted in the fracturing of language, while testifying to how integral a part of the father's very self was the son.

Never being well is manifested intermittently in these more recent volumes, but often with humor, since "Silliness," Wallace-Crabbe claims, "helps to ease the pain" (*Rungs*, p. 9), and because "we have to see ourselves in a comic light to have access to the only kind of earthly salvation" ("Self Portrait," p. 8). In the jaunty "Medico's Song," for instance, the speaker enumerates various discomforts via the names of their discoverers, with the refrain, "Tourette, Hodgkins, Graves, Down, / Parkinson, Ménière, old uncle Alzheimer and all" (*Rungs*, p. 35). The engagement with growing older, however, is often serious. "You're lucky to be alive," he states in "Summer's Breath," before realizing that the phrase "contains its personal shadow of disbelief" (*Whirling*, p. 3). So when, in "My Ghost," the poet imagines his ghost playing tennis, he is forced to ask, "Whom does he play against? / And by what power?" (*Rungs*, p. 33). Resistant to orthodox religious answers to such a question, Wallace-Crabbe claims in "A Barbarian Catechism" that grace "would make sense" even to "a perfectly heathen soul" (*Whirling*, p. 38). What makes sense, though, does not necessarily provide consolation or always even turn out to be true, and Wallace-Crabbe constantly tests the limits of rational responses to queries that demand irrational, unlikely solutions. "My own belief system is, of course, a mess," he admits in a 1987 issue of *Australian Book Review* ("Self Portrait," p. 9). "I am aware, on the one hand, of the passionate injunctions of the Life Force, but on the other I feel the wicked jokes of the Trickster God." More often than not, in Wallace-Crabbe's poetic universe, "A meaning of my life is far beyond my reach," if only because "things grow more complicated and eccentric / the more you peer at them" (*By and Large*, pp. 73, 65). The future, like the gods, is "what we cannot see," while "You can't get back to the laws of infancy," either, so it remains only to guess and go onward, as gracefully and graciously as possible.

Growing older frequently manifests itself humorously and generally sardonically in Wallace-Crabbe's poetry through his mistrust of postmodernity. "Postmodern Blues" laments postmodernism's indulgence in simulacra, deferral, high jinks, irony, the substitution of sterile text for throated song, and self-aggrandizing strategies of self-effacement. Postmodernism, according to Wallace-Crabbe, is where "raw life sprawls ripped," while "desire dwindles to description" (*Rungs*, p. 32). As "the life from life gets stripped / and we settle down as script," what passes too often as intelligence and sincerity is actually "dereliction," a point he reinforces by framing his poem in chiseled couplets showcasing traditional rhyme and slant rhyme. The backbone of his most recent collection, *By and Large* (2001), is a poem in forty parts called "Modern Times," a rant against the worst aspects of contemporary consumer culture. Its vitriol is redeemed by an *ars poetica* anatomizing Wallace-Crabbe's dual impulse for romancing language to its own seductive ends while being attentive to its content and substance, enjoying both the *how* and the *what* of a poem. The poet admits to "Teasing language to fill up the frame" and to "Following where my verbs have led." At the same time, however, "I respect / The way that Gaia might look at us," he states, reminding himself that the linguistic explosiveness of every utterance must never sacrifice its necessity or ethical importance (p. 53). As early as 1979, in the essay "Simplicities," he had noted the tug between the solipsistic desire to run away with the language of one's own experience and the opposing need to engage in the larger world:

Perhaps the major creative conflict for twentieth-century poets has been that between the "high and aloof" lyricism of the romantic sensibility which feels itself alone, testifying against the dark fibres of a coarsening world, and the wish to escape from

CHRISTOPHER WALLACE-CRABBE

privateness, to come down into the democratic marketplace, to speak with the common tongue and draw strength from such popular traditions as may still be available

(*Toil*, p. 29)

Wallace-Crabbe has endeavored to honor both artistic avenues. "Life involves maintaining oneself / between the shoulders of contradiction," he says in "Tongues of Fire," and though poetry is sometimes no less committed to this balancing act, writing often means, in Whitman's spirit, acquiescing to such contradictions (*Rungs*, p. 61).

Wallace-Crabbe's facility for shifting shapes; adopting different and opposed views; blending registers of diction, form, and style, what he calls "mixing modes or breaking up decorum" ("Self Portrait," p. 8); reveling in joy and sadness; playing the Aussie bushman as well as the Anglo-European gentleman; honoring Old World tenets while remaining firmly rooted in the New World are only a few of his hallmarks. Wallace-Crabbe "has become the consummate mediator; his poems dwell comfortably in the middle ground they establish," writes the American poet and critic Brian Henry, "This gives his poetry its humanity, its ability to embrace contradiction" ("Review of *Whirling*," p. 174).

SELECTED BIBLIOGRAPHY

I. POETRY. *The Music of Division* (Sydney, 1959); *Eight Metropolitan Poems* (Adelaide, 1962); *In Light and Darkness* (Sydney, 1963); *The Rebel General* (Sydney, 1967); *Where the Wind Came* (Sydney and London, 1971); *The Foundations of Joy* (Sydney, 1976); *Selected Poems* (Sydney and London, 1973); *The Emotions are Not Skilled Workers* (Sydney, 1979); *The Amorous Cannibal* (Oxford and New York, 1985); *I'm Deadly Serious* (Oxford and New York, 1988); *For Crying Out Loud* (Oxford and New York, 1990); *Rungs of Time* (Oxford and New York, 1993); *Selected Poems 1956–1994* (Oxford and New York, 1995); *Whirling* (Oxford and New York, 1998); *By and Large* (Manchester and Rose Bay, New South Wales, 2001).

II. CRITICISM. *Melbourne or the Bush: Essays on Australian Literature and Society* (Sydney and London, 1974); *Toil & Spin: Two Directions in Modern Poetry* (Melbourne and London, 1979); *Three Absences in Australian Writing* (Townsville, Australia, 1983); *Falling into Language* (Oxford and New York, 1990); *Poetry and Belief—1989 James McAuley Memorial Lecture* (Hobart, Tasmania, 1990).

III. EDITED VOLUMES. *Six Voices: Contemporary Australian Poets* (Sydney and London, 1963; rev. ed. 1974; Westport, Conn., 1979); *Australian Poetry 1971* (Sydney, 1971); *The Australian Nationalists: Modern Critical Essays* (Wellington and New York, 1971; Melbourne, 1981); *The Golden Apples of the Sun: Twentieth Century Australian Poetry* (Melbourne, 1980); *Clubbing the Gunfire: 101 Australian War Poems*, with Peter Pierce (Melbourne, 1984); *Multicultural Australia: The Challenges of Change*, with David Goodman and D. J. O'Hearn (Newham, Victoria, 1991, 1992); *From the Republic of Conscience*, with Kerry Flattley (Melbourne and New York, 1992); *Ur Riki Samviskunnar*, with Kerry Flattley and Sigurdur A. Magnusson (Reykjavik, 1994); *Author, Author! Tales of Australian Literary Life* (Melbourne, 1998); *Approaching Australia: Papers from the Harvard Australian Studies Symposium*, with Harold Bolitho (Cambridge, Mass., 1998).

IV. ASSOCIATE EDITOR. *The Oxford Literary History of Australia*, with Bruce Bennett and Jennifer Strauss (Melbourne, 1998).

V. INDIVIDUAL ESSAYS. "Self Portrait," in *Australian Book Review* 93 (August 1987); "Autobiography," in *The Penguin New Literary History of Australia*, ed. by Laurie Hergenhan (Ringwood, 1988); "Beyond the Cringe: Australian Cultural Overconfidence?" (London, 1990); "The Language of Poetry," in *The Languages of Australia*, ed. by Gerhard Schulz (Canberra, 1993); "My First Love," in *The Age* (29 July 1995); "Years On," in *Quadrant* 39, no. 11 (1995); "Poetry and the Common Tongue," in *The Space of Poetry: Australian Essays in Contemporary Poetics*, ed. by Lyn McCredden and Stephanie Trigg (Melbourne, 1996); "The Repeated Rediscovery of America," in *Approaching Australia: Papers from the Harvard Australian Studies Symposium*, with H. Bolitho (Cambridge, Mass., 1998).

VI. FICTION. *Splinters* (Adelaide, 1981).

VII. RECORDING. "Chris Wallace-Crabbe Reads from His Own Verse" (St. Lucia, Australia, 1973).

VIII. INTERVIEWS. David Carter, "Shape-Changing," in *Helix* 7/8 (1981); Barbara Williams, in *Ariel* 21, no. 2 (1990); Rosemary Sorensen, in *Australian Book Review* 155 (1993); Andrew Zawacki, in *Verse* 12, no. 3 (1995).

IX. CRITICAL STUDIES. Peter Steele, in *Meanjin Quarterly* 23, no. 4 (1964); Peter Porter, in *Overland* 113 (1988); Mark Wormald, in *Times Literary Supplement* (29 March 1991); David McCooey, "At Play in the Fields of Language," in *The Age* (10 June 1995); Geoff Page, "Writing Lightly about Serious Things," in *Canberra Times* (2 September 1995); Peter Porter, "Peter Porter Reviews the *Selected Poems* of Chris Wallace-Crabbe," in *Australian Book Review* (July 1995); David McCooey, "Leisure and Grief: The Recent Poetry of Chris Wallace-Crabbe," in *Australian Literary Studies* 17 (1996) and *Artful Histories: Modern Australian Autobiography* (Melbourne, 1996); William Wilde, *Australian Poets and Their Works: A Reader's Guide* (Melbourne and New York, 1996); Brian Henry, "Review of *Selected Poems 1956–1994*," in *Harvard Review* 12 (spring 1997); "Review of Whirling," in *Harvard Review* 17 (fall 1999); Kevin Hart, "The Courage of Poetic Reinvention," in *The Age* (1 September 2001).

MASTER INDEX

The following index covers the entire British Writers series through Supplement VIII. All references include volume numbers in boldface Roman numerals followed by page numbers within that volume. Subjects of articles are indicated by boldface type.

"Afternoon in Florence" (Jennings), **Supp. V:** 210

Afternoon Men (Powell), **VII:** 343–345

Afternoon Off (Bennett), **Supp. VIII.** 27

"Afternoons" (Larkin), **Supp. I:** 281

"Afterthought, An" (Rossetti), **V:** 258

"Afterwards" (Hardy), **VI:** 13, 19; **Retro. Supp. I:** 119

"Against Absence" (Suckling), **II:** 227

"Against Dryness" (Murdoch), **Supp. I:** 216, 218, 219, 221

Against Entropy (Frayn), see *Towards the End of Morning*

"Against Fruition" (Cowley), **II:** 197

"Against Fruition" (Suckling), **II:** 227

Against Hasty Credence (Henryson), **Supp. VII:** 146, 147

Against Religion (Wilson), **Supp. VI:** 297, **305–306,** 309

"Against Romanticism" (Amis), **Supp. II:** 3

Against Venomous Tongues (Skelton), **I:** 90

Agamemnon (Seneca), **II:** 71

Agamemnon (Thomson), **Supp. III:** 411, 424

Agamemnon, a Tragedy Taken from Aeschylus (FitzGerald), **IV:** 349, 353

Agamemnon of Aeschylus, The (tr. Browning), **IV:** 358–359, 374

Agamemnon of Aeschylus, The (tr. MacNeice), **VII:** 408–409

Agate, James, **Supp. II:** 143, 147

Age of Anxiety, The (Auden), **VII:** 379, 388, 389–390; **Supp. IV:** 100; **Retro. Supp. I:** 11

Age of Bronze, The (Byron), **IV:** xviii, 193

Age of Indiscretion, The (Davis), **V:** 394

Age of Iron (Coetzee), **Supp. VI:** 76, **85**

Age of Longing, The (Koestler), **Supp. I:** 25, 27, 28, 31–32, 35

Age of Reason, The (Hope), **Supp. VII:** 164

Age of Shakespeare, The (Swinburne), **V:** 333

Age of the Rainmakers, The (Harris), **Supp. V:** 132

Agents and Patients (Powell), **VII:** 345–346

Aglaura (Suckling), **II:** 226, 238

Agnes Grey (Brontë), **V:** xx, 129–130, 132, 134–135, 140–141, 153; **Supp. IV:** 239; **Retro. Supp. I:** 52, 54–55

"Agnes Lahens" (Moore), **VI:** 98

Agnostic's Apology, An (Stephen), **VI:** 289

"Agonies of Writing a Musical Comedy" (Wodehouse), **Supp. III:** 451

Ah, But Your Land Is Beautiful (Paton), **Supp. II:** 353–355

"Ah, what avails the sceptred race" (Landor), **IV:** 88

"Ahoy, Sailor Boy!" (Coppard), **Supp. VIII:** 97

Aids to Reflection (Coleridge), **IV:** 53, 56

Aiken, Conrad, **VII:** 149, 179; **Supp. III:** 270

Aimed at Nobody (Graham), **Supp. VII:** 106

Ainger, Alfred, **IV:** 254, 267

"Air and Angels" (MacCaig), **Supp. VI:** 185

Ainsworth, Harrison, **IV:** 311; **V:** 47

"Air Disaster, The" (Ballard), **Supp. V:** 33

"Aire and Angels" (Donne), **II:** 197

"Aisling" (Muldoon), **Supp. IV:** 418–419

"Aisling Hat, The" (McGuckian), **Supp. V:** 286, 288, 289

Aissa Saved (Cary), **VII:** 185

"Akbar's Bridge" (Kipling), **VI:** 201

Akerman, Rudolph, **V:** 111

Akhmatova, Anna, **Supp. IV:** 480, 494

"Al Som de l'Escalina" (Eliot), **VII:** 152

Alamanni, Luigi, **I:** 110–111

Alamein to Zem–Zem (Douglas), **VII:** xxii, 441

Alarcos (Disraeli), **IV:** 306, 308

Alaric at Rome (Arnold), **V:** 216

"Alas, Poor Bollington!" (Coppard), **Supp. VIII:** 94–95

"Alaska" (Armitage), **Supp. VIII:** 5

Alastair Reid Reader, An: Selected Poetry and Prose (Reid), **Supp. VII:** 333, 336

Alastor (Shelley), **III:** 330, 338; **IV:** xvii, 195, 198, 208, 217; **Retro. Supp. I:** 247

"Albergo Empedocle" (Forster), **VI:** 399, 412

Albert's Bridge (Stoppard), **Supp. I:** 439, 445

Albigenses, The (Maturin), **Supp. VIII:** 201, 207, 208

"Albinus and Rosemund" (Gower), **I:** 53–54

"Albion & Marina" (Brontë), **V:** 110

Albion and Albanius (Dryden), **II:** 305

Album Verses (Lamb), **IV:** 83, 85

Alcazar (Peele), see *Battle of Alcazar, The*

Alcestis (Euripides), **IV:** 358

Alchemist, The (Jonson), **I:** 304–341, 342; **II:** 4, 48; **Retro. Supp. I:** 163

"Alchemist in the City, The" (Hopkins), **V:** 362

Alcott, Louisa May, **Supp. IV:** 255

Aldington, Richard, **VI:** 416; **VII:** xvi, 36, 121

Aldiss, Brian, **III:** 341, 345; **Supp. V:** 22

Aldous Huxley (Brander), **VII:** 208

Alexander, Peter, **I:** 300n, 326

Alexander, William (earl of Stirling), **I:** 218; **II:** 80

"Alexander and Zenobia" (Brontë), **V:** 115

Alexander Pope (Sitwell), **VII:** 138–139

Alexander Pope (Stephen), **V:** 289

Alexander Pope as Critic and Humanist (Warren), **II:** 332n

Alexander's Feast; or, The Power of Musique (Dryden), **II:** 200, 300, 304

Alexanders saga, **Supp. VIII:** 237, 242

Alexandria: A History and Guide (Forster), **VI:** 408, 412

Alexandria Quartet (Durrell), **Supp. I:** 94, 96, 97, 98, 100, 101, **104–110,** 113, 122

"Alfieri and Salomon the Florentine Jew" (Landor), **IV:** 91

Alfred (Thomson and Mallet), **Supp. III:** 412, 424–425

Alfred Lord Tennyson: A Memoir (Tennyson), **IV:** 324, 338

Alfred the Great of Wessex, King, **Retro. Supp. II:** 293, 295–297

Algernon Charles Swinburne (Thomas), **VI:** 424

Alice in Wonderland (Carroll), see *Alice's Adventures in Wonderland*

Alice Sit–by–the–Fire (Barrie), **Supp. III:** 8, 9

Alice's Adventures in Wonderland (Carroll), **V:** xxiii, 261–265, **266–269,** 270–273

Alice's Adventures Under Ground (Carroll), **V:** 266, 273; see *Alice's Adventures in Wonderland*

"Alicia's Diary" (Hardy), **VI:** 22

Alien (Foster), **III:** 345

"Alien Corn, The" (Maugham), **VI:** 370, 374

Alien Sky, The (Scott), **Supp. I:** 261–263

"Alien Soil" (Kincaid), **Supp. VII:** 221, 229

All About Mr. Hatterr (Desani), **Supp. IV:** 445

"All blue and bright, in glorious light" (Brontë), **V:** 115

"All Day It Has Rained" (Lewis), **VII:** 445

All Day on the Sands (Bennett), **Supp. VIII:** 27

"All Flesh" (Thompson), **V:** 442

All Fools (Chapman), **I:** 235, 238, 244

All for Love (Dryden), **II:** 295–296, 305

All for Love (Southey), **IV:** 71

All My Eyes See: The Visual World of G. M. Hopkins (ed. Thornton), **V:** 377n, 379n, 382

All My Little Ones (Ewart), **Supp. VII:** 36

All Ovid's Elegies (Marlowe), **I:** 280, 291, 293

"All philosophers, who find" (Swift), **IV:** 160

All Quiet on the Western Front (Remarque), **VII:** xvi

All Religions Are One (Blake), **III:** 292, 307; **Retro. Supp. I:** 35

"All Saints: Martyrs" (Rossetti), **V:** 255

"All Souls' Night" (Cornford), **Supp. VIII:** 112

All That Fall (Beckett), **Supp. I:** 58, 62; **Retro. Supp. I:** 25

All the Conspirators (Isherwood), **VII:** 310

"All the hills and vales along" (Sorley), **VI:** 421–422

All the Usual Hours of Sleeping (Redgrove), **Supp. VI:** 230

All the Year Round (periodical), **V:** 42

All Trivia (Connolly), **Supp. III:** 98

All What Jazz: A Record Diary, 1961–1968 (Larkin), **Supp. I:** 286, 287–288

Allan Quatermain (Haggard), **Supp. III:** 213, 218

"Allegiance, An" (Wallace-Crabbe), **Supp. VIII:** 315

Appeal to England, An (Swinburne), **V:** 332

Appeal to Honour and Justice, An (Defoe), **III:** 4, 13; **Retro. Supp. I:** 66, 67

Appeal to the Clergy of the Church of Scotland, An (Stevenson), **V:** 395

"Appius and Virginia" (Gower), **I:** 55

Appius and Virginia (R. B.), **I:** 216

Appius and Virginia (Webster), **II:** 68, 83, 85

Apple Broadcast, The (Redgrove), **Supp. VI:** 235

Apple Cart, The: A Political Extravaganza (Shaw), **VI:** 118, 120, 125–126, 127, 129

"Apple Tragedy" (Hughes), **Supp. I:** 351, 353

"Apple Tree, The" (du Maurier), **Supp. III:** 138

"Apple Tree, The" (Galsworthy), **VI:** 276

"Apple Tree, The" (Mansfield), **VII:** 173

Applebee, John, **III:** 7

Appley Dapply's Nursery Rhymes (Potter), **Supp. III:** 291

Apollonius of Tyre, **Retro. Supp. II:** 298

Apology for Poetry, An (Sidney), **Retro. Supp. II:** 332–334, 339

"Appraisal, An" (Compton–Burnett), **VII:** 59

Appreciations (Pater), **V:** 338, 339, 341, 351–352, 353–356

"Apprentice" (Warner), **Supp. VII:** 380

"April" (Kavanagh), **Supp. VII:** 188

"April Epithalamium, An" (Stevenson), **Supp. VI:** 263

April Love (Hughes), **V:** 294

"Apron of Flowers, The" (Herrick), **II:** 110

Apropos of Dolores (Wells), **VI:** 240

"Aquae Sulis" (Hardy), **Retro. Supp. I:** 121

"Aquarius" (Armitage), **Supp. VIII:** 12

"Arab Love Song" (Thompson), **V:** 442, 445, 449

"Arabella" (Thackeray), **V:** 24

"Arabesque—The Mouse" (Coppard), **Supp. VIII:** 88

Arabian Nights, The, **III:** 327, 335, 336; **Supp. IV:** 434

"Araby" (Joyce), **Retro. Supp. I:** 172

Aragon, Louis, **Supp. IV:** 466

"Aramantha" (Lovelace), **II:** 230, 231

Aran Islands, The (Synge), **VI:** 308–309; **Retro. Supp. I:** 291–294

Ararat (Thomas), **Supp. IV:** 484

Aratra Pentelici (Ruskin), **V:** 184

Arbuthnot, John, **III:** 19, 34, 60

"Arcades" (Milton), **II:** 159

Arcadia (Sidney), **I:** 161, 163–169, 173, 317; **II:** 48, 53–54; **III:** 95; **Retro. Supp. II:** 330–332, 340

Arcadia (Stoppard), **Retro. Supp. II:** 355–356

Arcadian Rhetorike (Fraunce), **I:** 164

"Archdeacon Truggin" (Powys), **Supp. VIII:** 256

Archeology of Love, The (Murphy), **Supp. V:** 317

Archer, William, **II:** 79, 358, 363, 364; **V:** 103, 104, 113

Architectural Review (periodical), **VII:** 356, 358

Architecture in Britain: 1530–1830 (Reynolds), **II:** 336

Architecture, Industry and Wealth (Morris), **V:** 306

"Arctic Summer" (Forster), **VI:** 406

Arden of Feversham (Kyd), **I:** 212, 213, 218–219

Arden, John, **Supp. II:** 21–42

"Ardour and Memory" (Rossetti), **V:** 243

Ardours and Endurances (Nichols), **VI:** 423

"Are You Lonely in the Restaurant" (O'Nolan), **Supp. II:** 323

Area of Darkness, An (Naipaul), **Supp. I,** 383, 384, 387, 389, 390, 391–392, 394, 395, 399, 402

Arendt, Hannah, **Supp. IV:** 306

Areopagitica (Milton), **II:** 163, 164, 169, 174, 175; **IV:** 279; **Retro. Supp. II:** 277–279

Aretina (Mackenzie), **III:** 95

"Argonauts of the Air, The" (Wells), **VI:** 244

Argonauts of the Pacific (Malinowski), **Supp. III:** 186

Argufying (Empson), **Supp. II:** 180, 181

Argument ... that the Abolishing of Christianity ... May ... be Attended with some Inconveniences, An (Swift), **III:** 26, 35

"Argument of His Book, The" (Herrick), **II:** 110

Argument Shewing that a Standing Army ... Is Not Inconsistent with a Free Government, An (Defoe), **III,** 12

Ariadne Florentina (Ruskin), **V:** 184

Ariel Poems (Eliot), **VII:** 152

Arians of the Fourth Century, The (Newman), **Supp. VII:** 291

Aristocrats (Friel), **Supp. V:** 122

Aristophanes, **V:** 227

Aristophanes' Apology (Browning), **IV:** 358, 367, 370, 374; **Retro. Supp. II:** 30

Aristos, The: A Self–Portrait in Ideas (Fowles), **Supp. I:** 293–294, 295, 296

"Armada, The" (Macaulay), **IV:** 283, 291

Armadale (Collins), **Supp. VI:** 91, 93–94, **98–100,** 101, 103

Armitage, Simon, **Supp. VIII: 1–17**

Arms and the Covenant (Churchill), **VI:** 356

Arms and the Man (Shaw), **VI:** 104, 110, 120; **Retro. Supp. II:** 313

Armstrong, Isobel Mair, **V:** xi, xxvii, 339, 375

Armstrong, William, **V:** xviii, xxxvii

Armstrong's Last Goodnight (Arden), **Supp. II:** 29, 30

Arnold, Matthew, **IV:** 359; **V:** viii–xi, 14, 156–158, 160, **203–218,** 283, 285, 289, 342, 352–353; works, **III:** 23, 174, 277; **V:** 206–215; literary criticism, **I:** 423; **III:** 68, 277; **IV:** 220, 234, 323, 371; **V:** 160, 165–169, 352, 408; **Supp. II:** 44, 57; **Retro. Supp. I:** 59

Arnold, Thomas, **V:** 155–156, 157, 165, 207, 208, 277, 284, 349

Arnold Bennett (Lafourcade), **VI:** 268

Arnold Bennett (Pound), **VI:** 247, 268

Arnold Bennett (Swinnerton), **VI:** 268

Arnold Bennett: A Biography (Drabble), **VI:** 247, 253, 268; **Supp. IV:** 203

Arnold Bennett: A Last Word (Swinnerton), **VI:** 268

Arnold Bennett and H. G. Wells: A Record of a Personal and Literary Friendship (ed. Wilson), **VI:** 246, 267

Arnold Bennett in Love (ed. and tr. Beardmore and Beardmore), **VI:** 251, 268

Arnold Bennett: The AEvening Standard-"Years (ed. Mylett), **VI:** 265n, 266

Arouet, Françoise Marie, *see* Voltaire

Around Theatres (Beerbohm), **Supp. II:** 54, 55

"Aromatherapy" (Redgrove), **Supp. VI:** 236

Arraignment of London, The (Daborne and Tourneur), **II:** 37

Arraignment of Paris (Peele), **I:** 197–200

"Arrest of Oscar Wilde at the Cadogan Hotel, The" (Betjeman), **VII:** 356, 365–366

Arrival and Departure (Koestler), **Supp. I:** 27, 28, 30–31

Arrow in the Blue (Koestler), **Supp. I:** 22, 25, 31, 34, 36

Arrow of Gold, A (Conrad), **VI:** 134, 144, 147

Ars Longa, Vita Brevis (Arden and D'Arcy), **Supp. II:** 29

Ars Poetica (Horace), **Retro. Supp. I:** 166

"Arsonist" (Murphy), **Supp. V:** 326

"Art and Criticism" (Harris), **Supp. V:** 140

"Art and Extinction" (Harrison), **Supp. V:** 156

Art & Lies: A Piece for Three Voices and a Bawd (Winterson), **Supp. IV:** 542, 547, 552–553, 554–555, 556, 557

"Art and Morality" (Stephen), **V:** 286

Art and Reality (Cary), **VII:** 186

Art and Revolution: Ernst Neizvestny and the Role of the Artist in the U.S.S.R. (Berger), **Supp. IV:** 79, 88

"Art and Science" (Richards), **Supp. II:** 408–409

Art History and Class Consciousness (Hadjinicolaou), **Supp. IV:** 90

"Art McCooey" (Kavanagh), **Supp. VII:** 190

Art Objects: Essays on Ecstasy and Effrontery (Winterson), **Supp. IV:** 541, 542, 544, 557

Art of Angling, The (Barker), **II:** 131

Art of Being Ruled, The (Lewis), **VII:** 72, 75, 76

Art of English Poetry, The (Puttenham), **I:** 94, 146, 214

Art of Fiction, The (James), **VI:** 46, 67

Art of Fiction, The (Kipling), **VI:** 204

Bowen's Court (Bowen), **Supp. II:** 78, 84, 91

Bowers, Fredson, **II:** 44

Bowles, Caroline, **IV:** 62, 63

"Bowling Alley and the Sun, or, How I Learned to Stop Worrying and Love America, The" (Lodge), **Supp. IV:** 373

Bowra, C. M., **VI:** 153

Bowra, Maurice, **V:** 252–256, 260

Boy and the Magic, The (tr. Fry), **Supp. III:** 195

Boy Comes Home, The (Milne), **Supp. V:** 299

Boy Hairdresser, The (Orton), **Supp. V:** 363, 364, 367

Boy in the Bush, The (Lawrence), **VII:** 114; **Retro. Supp. II:** 230–231

Boy: Tales of Childhood (Dahl), **Supp. IV:** 204, 205, 206, 208, 225

Boy Who Followed Ripley, The (Highsmith), **Supp. V:** 171

"Boy Who Talked with Animals, The" (Dahl), **Supp. IV:** 223, 224

Boy with a Cart, The; Cuthman, Saint of Sussex (Fry), **Supp. III:** 191, 194, 195, 196

Boyd, H. S., **IV:** 312

Boyer, Abel, **II:** 352

Boyhood: Scenes from Provincial Life (Coetzee), **Supp. VI:** 77–78

Boyle, Robert, **III:** 23, 95

Boys Who Stole the Funeral, The: A Novel Sequence (Murray), **Supp. VII:** 270, 284–286

"Boys' Weeklies" (Orwell), **Supp. III:** 107

Bradbrook, M. C., **I:** xi, 292, 329; **II:** 42, 78; **VII:** xiii–xiv, xxxvii, 234

Bradbury, Ray, **III:** 341

Bradbury, Malcolm, **Supp. IV:** 303, 365

Braddon, Mary Elizabeth, **V:** 327; **Supp. VIII:** 35–52

Bradley, A. C., **IV:** 106, 123, 216, 235, 236

Bradley, F. H., **V:** xxi, 212, 217

Bradley, Henry, **VI:** 76

Brady, F., **III:** 249

Braine, John, **Supp. IV:** 238

Brand (Hill), **Supp. V:** 199, 200–201

Brander, Laurence, **IV:** xxiv; **VII:** xxii

Branwell Brontë (Gerin), **V:** 153

Branwell's Blackwood's (periodical), **V:** 109, 123

Branwell's Young Men's (periodical), *see Branwell's Blackwood's*

Brass Butterfly, The (Golding), **Supp. I:** 65, 75

"Brassneck" (Armitage), **Supp. VIII:** 5

Brassneck (Hare and Brenton), **Supp. IV:** 281, 282, 283, 284–285, 289

Brave New World (Huxley), **III:** 341; **VII:** xviii, 200, 204

Brave New World Revisited (Huxley), **VII:** 207

"Bravest Boat, The" (Lowry), **Supp. III:** 281

Brawne, Fanny, **IV:** 211, 216–220, 222, 226, 234

Bray, Charles, **V:** 188

Bray, William, **II:** 275, 276, 286

Brazil (Gilliam), **Supp. IV:** 442, 455

"Breach, The" (Murray), **Supp. VII:** 276

"Bréagh San Réilg, La" (Behan), **Supp. II:** 73

"Break My Heart" (Golding), **Supp. I:** 79

"Break of Day in the Trenches" (Rosenberg), **VI:** 433, 434

"Breake of day" (Donne), **Retro. Supp. II:** 88

"Breaking Ground" (Gunn), **Supp. IV:** 271

"Breaking the Blue" (McGuckian), **Supp. V:** 287

Breath (Beckett), **Supp. I:** 60; **Retro. Supp. I:** 26

Brecht, Bertolt, **II:** 359; **IV:** 183; **VI:** 109, 123; **Supp. II:** 23, 25, 28; **Supp. IV:** 82, 87, 180, 194, 198, 281, 298

"Bredon Hill" (Housman), **VI:** 158

Brendan (O'Connor), **Supp. II:** 63, 76

Brendan Behan's Island (Behan), **Supp. II:** 64, 66, 71, 73, 75

Brendan Behan's New York (Behan), **Supp. II:** 75

Brennoralt (Suckling), *see Discontented Colonel, The*

Brenton, Howard, **Supp. IV:** 281, 283, 284, 285

Brethren, The (Haggard), **Supp. III:** 214

"Breton Walks" (Mahon), **Supp. VI:** 168, 172

Brett, Raymond Laurence, **IV:** x, xi, xxiv, 57

Brickfield, The (Hartley), **Supp. VII:** 131–132

Bricks to Babel (Koestler), **Supp. I:** 37

Bridal of Triermain, The (Scott), **IV:** 38

"Bride and Groom" (Hughes), **Supp. I:** 356

"Bride in the 30's, A" (Auden), **Retro. Supp. I:** 8

Bride of Abydos, The (Byron), **IV:** xvii, 172, 174–175, 192

Bride of Frankenstein (film), **III:** 342

Bride of Lammermoor, The (Scott), **IV:** xviii, 30, 36, 39

Brides of Reason (Davie), **Supp. VI:** 106–107

"Brides, The" (Hope), **Supp. VII:** 154

"Bride's Prelude, The" (Rossetti), **V:** 239, 240

Brideshead Revisited (Waugh), **VII:** xx–xxi, 290, 299–300; **Supp. IV:** 285

"Bridge, The" (Thomas), **Supp. III:** 401

"Bridge for the Living" (Larkin), **Supp. I:** 284

"Bridge of Sighs, The" (Hood), **IV:** 252, 261, 264–265

Bridges, Robert, **II:** 160; **V:** xx, 205, 362–368, 370–372, 374, 376–381; **VI:** xv, **71–83**, 203

Brief History of Moscovia ... , A (Milton), **II:** 176

Brief Lives (Aubrey), **I:** 260

Brief Lives (Brookner), **Supp. IV:** 131–133

Brief Notes upon a Late Sermon ... (Milton), **II:** 176

Briefing for a Descent into Hell (Lessing), **Supp. I:** 248–249

Briggflatts (Bunting), **Supp. VII:** 1, 2, 5, 7, 9–13

Bright, A. H., **I:** 3

"Bright Building, The" (Graham), **Supp. VII:** 109, 110–111

"Bright–Cut Irish Silver" (Boland), **Supp. V:** 49–50

Bright Day (Priestley), **VII:** 209, 218–219

"Bright Star!" (Keats), **IV:** 221

Brighton Rock (Greene), **Supp. I:** 2, 3, **7–9,** 11, 19; **Retro. Supp. II:** 153–155

"Brigid's Girdle, A" (Heaney), **Retro. Supp. I:** 132

"Brilliance" (Davie), **Supp. VI:** 113

"Brilliant Career, A" (Joyce), **Retro. Supp. I:** 170

Bring Larks and Heroes (Keneally), **Supp. IV:** 345, 347, 348–350

"Bringing to Light" (Gunn), **Supp. IV:** 269–270

Brink, Andre, **Supp. VI:** **45–59**

Brinkmanship of Galahad Threepwood, The (Wodehouse), *see Galahad at Blandings*

Brissenden, R. F., **III:** 86n

Bristow Merchant, The (Dekker and Ford), **II:** 89, 100

Britain and West Africa (Cary), **VII:** 186

Britannia (periodical), **V:** 144

Britannia (Thomson), **Supp. III:** 409, 411, 420

Britannia Rediviva: A Poem on the Birth of the Prince (Dryden), **II:** 304

"Britannia Victrix" (Bridges), **VI:** 81

"British Church, The" (Herbert), **I:** 189

British Dramatists (Greene), **Supp. I:** 6, 11

"British Guiana" (Ewart), **Supp. VII:** 38

British History in the Nineteenth Century (Trevelyan), **VI:** 390

British Magazine (periodical), **III:** 149, 179, 188

British Museum Is Falling Down, The (Lodge), **Supp. IV:** 363, 365, 367, 369–370, 371

British Women Go to War (Priestley), **VII:** 212

Briton (Smollett), **III:** 149

Brittain, Vera, **II:** 246

Britten, Benjamin, **Supp. IV:** 424

"Broad Bean Sermon, The" (Murray), **Supp. VII:** 275

"Broad Church, The" (Stephen), **V:** 283

Broadbent, J. B., **II:** 102, 116

Broadcast Talks (Lewis), **Supp. III:** 248

"Broagh" (Heaney), **Retro. Supp. I:** 128

"Brodgar Poems" (Brown), **Supp. VI:** 71

Broken Chariot, The (Sillitoe), **Supp. V:** 411, 421

Broken Cistern, The (Dobrée), **V:** 221, 234

"Broken heart, The" (Donne), **Retro. Supp. II:** 90

"Distress of Plenty" (Connolly), **Supp. III:** 108

Distress'd Wife, The (Gay), **III:** 67

"Disturber of the Traffic, The" (Kipling), **VI:** 169, **170–172**

"Disused Shed in County Wexford, A" (Mahon) **Supp. VI:** 169–170, 173

Diversions of Purley and Other Poems, The (Ackroyd), **Supp. VI:** 3Diversions of Purley and Other Poems, The (Ackroyd), Supp. VI: 3

"Diversity and Depth" (Wilson), **Supp. I:** 167

"Divided Life Re–Lived, The" (Fuller), **Supp. VII:** 72

Divine and Moral Songs for Children (Watts), **III:** 299

Divine Comedy, The (Dante), **II:** 148; **III:** 306; **IV:** 93, 187, 229; **Supp. I:** 76; Supp. IV: 439

"Divine Judgments" (Blake), **III:** 300

"Divine Meditations" (Donne), **Retro. Supp. II:** 98

Divine Poems (Waller), **II:** 238

Divine Vision and Other Poems, The (Russell), **Supp. VIII:** 284–285

"Divine Wrath and Mercy" (Blake), **III:** 300

Diviner, The (Friel), **Supp. V:** 113

"Diviner, The" (Friel), **Supp. V:** 115

"Diviner, The" (Heaney), **Supp. II:** 269–270

"Division, The" (Hardy), **VI:** 17

Division of the Spoils, A (Scott), **Supp. I:** 268, 271

Dixon, Richard Watson, **V:** 362–365, 371, 372, 377, 379; **VI:** 76, 83, 167

Dixon Hunt, John, **VI:** 167

"Dizzy" (Strachey), **IV:** 292

"Do not go gentle into that good night" (Thomas), **Supp. I:** 178

"Do Take Muriel Out" (Smith), **Supp. II:** 471, 472

Do What You Will (Huxley), **VII:** 201

"Do you remember me? or are you proud?" (Landor), **IV:** 99

Dobell, Sydney, **IV:** 310; **V:** 144–145

Dobrée, Bonamy, **II:** 362, 364; **III:** 33, 51, 53; **V:** 221, 234; **VI:** xi, 200–203; **V:** xxii

"Dockery and Son" (Larkin), **Supp. I:** 281, 285

Doctor, The (Southey), **IV:** 67n, 71

Doctor Birch and His Young Friends (Thackeray), **V:** 38

Dr. Faust's Sea–Spiral Spirit (Redgrove), **Supp. VI:** 231, 233–234

Doctor Faustus (film), **III:** 344

Doctor Faustus (Marlowe), **I:** 212, 279–280, **287–290; Supp. IV:** 197

Doctor Fischer of Geneva; or, The Bomb Party (Greene), **Supp. I:** 1, 17–18

Doctor Is Sick, The (Burgess), **Supp. I:** 186, 189, 195

Doctor Therne (Haggard), **Supp. III:** 214

Doctor Thorne (Trollope), **V:** xxii, 93, 101

Doctors' Delusions, Crude Criminology, and Sham Education (Shaw), **VI:** 129

Doctor's Dilemma, The (Shaw), **VI:** xv 116, 129; **Retro. Supp. II:** 321–322

"Doctor's Legend, The" (Hardy), **VI:** 20

Doctors of Philosophy (Spark), **Supp. I:** 206

Doctor's Wife, The (Braddon), **Supp. VIII:** 44–46

Doctrine and Discipline of Divorce ... , The (Milton), **II:** 175; **Retro. Supp. II:** 271

"Doctrine of Scattered Occasions, The" (Bacon), **I:** 261

Doctrine of the Law and Grace Unfolded, The (Bunyan), **II:** 253

Documents in the Case, The (Sayers and Eustace), **Supp. III:** 335, 342–343

Documents Relating to the Sentimental Agents in the Volyen Empire (Lessing), **Supp. I:** 252–253

Dodge, Mabel, **VII:** 109

Dodgson, Charles Lutwidge, *see* Carroll, Lewis

"Does It Matter?" (Sassoon), **VI:** 430

"Does That Hurt?" (Motion), **Supp. VII:** 263–264

"Dog and the Lantern, The" (Powys), **Supp. VIII:** 255

"Dog and the Waterlily, The" (Cowper), **III:** 220

Dog Beneath the Skin, The (Auden and Isherwood), **VII:** 312, 380, 385; **Retro. Supp. I:** 7

Dog Fox Field (Murray), **Supp. VII:** 280–281, 282

"Dogged" (Saki), **Supp. VI:** 239

Dog's Ransom, A (Highsmith), **Supp. V:** 176–177

"Dogs" (Hughes), **Supp. I:** 346

"Doing Research for Historical Novels" (Keneally), **Supp. IV:** 344

Doktor Faustus (Mann), **III:** 344

Dolben, Digby Mackworth, **VI:** 72, 75

"Doldrums, The" (Kinsella), **Supp. V:** 261

"Doll, The" (O'Brien), **Supp. V:** 340

Doll's House, A (Ibsen), **IV:** xxiii, 118–119; **V:** xxiv; **VI:** ix, 111

"Doll's House, The" (Mansfield), **VII:** 175

"Doll's House on the Dal Lake, A" (Naipaul), **Supp. I:** 399

"Dollfuss Day, 1935" (Ewart), **Supp. VII:** 36

Dolly (Brookner), **Supp. IV:** 134–135, 136–137

Dolores (Compton–Burnett), **VII:** 59, 68

"Dolores" (Swinburne), **V:** 313, 320–321

"Dolorida" (Swinburne), **V:** 332

Dolphin, The (Lowell), **Supp. IV:** 423

Dombey and Son (Dickens), **IV:** 34; **V:** xxi, 42, 44, 47, 53, 57–59, 70, 71

"Domestic Interior" (Boland), **Supp. V:** 50

"Domicilium" (Hardy), **VI:** 14

Don Fernando (Maugham), **VI:** 371

Don Juan (Byron), **I:** 291; **II:** 102n; **IV:** xvii, 171, 172, 173, 178, 183, 184, 185, **187–191**, 192

Don Quixote (Cervantes), **II:** 49; **IV:** 190; **V:** 46; **Retro. Supp. I:** 84

Don Quixote in England (Fielding), **III:** 105

Don Sebastian, King of Portugal (Dryden), **II:** 305

"Dong with a Luminous Nose, The" (Lear), **V:** 85

"Donkey, The" (Smith), **Supp. II:** 468

Donkeys' Years (Frayn), **Supp. VII:** 60–61

Donne, John, **I: 352–369; II:** 102, 113, 114, 118, 121–124, 126–128, 132, 134–138, 140–143, 147, 185, 196, 197, 209, 215, 221, 222, 226; **IV:** 327; **Supp. II:** 181, 182; **Supp. III:** 51, 57; **Retro. Supp. II: 85–99**, 173, 175, 259, 260

Donne, William Bodham, **IV:** 340, 344, 351

Donnelly, M. C., **V:** 427, 438

Donohue, J. W., **III:** 268

Don't Look Now (du Maurier), **Supp. III:** 148

"Doodle Bugs" (Harrison), **Supp. V:** 151

"Doom of the Griffiths, The" (Gaskell), **V:** 15

Doom of Youth, The (Lewis), **VII:** 72

"Door in the Wall, The" (Wells), **VI:** 235, 244

Door Into the Dark (Heaney), **Supp. II:** 268, **271–272; Retro. Supp. I:** 127

Dorando, A Spanish Tale (Boswell), **III:** 247

Dorian Gray (Wilde), *see Picture of Dorian Gray, The*

"Dorinda's sparkling Wit, and Eyes" (Dorset), **II:** 262

Dorothy Wordsworth (Selincourt), **IV:** 143

Dorset, earl of (Charles Sackville), **II:** 255, **261–263**, 266, 268, 270–271

Dorset Farm Laborer Past and Present, The, (Hardy), **VI:** 20

Dostoyevsky, Fyodor, **Supp. IV:** 1, 139

Dostoevsky: The Making of a Novelist (Simmons), **V:** 46

Doting (Green), **Supp. II:** 263, 264

Double Falsehood, The (Theobald), **II:** 66, 87

"Double Life" (MacCaig), **Supp. VI:** 186

"Double Looking Glass, The" (Hope), **Supp. VII:** 159

Double Man, The (Auden), **Retro. Supp. I:** 10

Double Marriage, The (Fletcher and Massinger), **II:** 66

"Double Rock, The" (King), **Supp. VI:** 151

Double Tongue, The (Golding), **Retro. Supp. I:** 106–107

"Double Vision of Michael Robartes, The" (Yeats), **VI:** 217

Double–Dealer, The (Congreve), **II:** 338, 341–342, 350

Doublets: A Word–Puzzle (Carroll), **V:** 273

Doubtful Paradise (Friel), **Supp. V:** 115

Doughty, Charles, **Supp. II:** 294–295

Doughty, Oswald, **V:** xi, xxvii, 246, 297n, 307

Douglas, Gavin, **I:** 116–118; **III:** 311

Essays, Moral and Political (Southey), **IV:** 71

Essays of Elia (Lamb), **IV:** xviii, 73, 74, 75, 76, 82–83, 85

Essays of Five Decades (Priestley), **VII:** 212

Essays on Freethinking and Plainspeaking (Stephen), **V:** 283, 289

Essays on His Own Times (Coleridge), **IV:** 56

Essays on Literature and Society (Muir), **Supp. VI:** 202

Essays on Shakespeare (Empson), **Supp. II:** 180, 193

Essays, Theological and Literary (Hutton), **V:** 157, 170

Essence of Christianity, The (tr. Eliot), **V:** 200

Essence of the Douglas Cause, The (Boswell), **III:** 247

"Essential Beauty" (Larkin), **Supp. I:** 279

Essential Gesture (Gordimer), **Supp. II:** 226, 237, 239, 242, 243

"Essential Gesture, The" (Gordimer), **Supp. II:** 225

Essential Reading (Reading), **Supp. VIII:** 270–271

Essex Poems (Davie), **Supp. VI: 109–111**

Esslin, Martin, **Supp. IV:** 181; **Retro. Supp. I:** 218–219

Estate of Poetry, The (Muir), **Supp. VI:** 197–198, 202, **203,** 209

Esther Waters (Moore), **VI:** ix, xii, 87, 89, 91–92, 96, 98

"Et Dona Ferentes" (Wilson), **Supp. I:** 157

Et Nobis Puer Natus Est (Dunbar), **Supp. VIII:** 128

"Et Tu, Healy" (Joyce), **Retro. Supp. I:** 169

"Eternal Contemporaries" (Durrell), **Supp. I:** 124

Eternal Moment, The (Forster), **VI:** 399, 400

Eternity to Season: Poems of Separation and Reunion (Harris), **Supp. V:** 132, 136

Etherege, Sir George, **II:** 255, 256, **266–269, 271,** 305

Etherege and the Seventeenth–Century Comedy of Manners (Underwood), **II:** 256n

Ethical Characters (Theophrastus), **II:** 68

Ethics of the Dust, The (Ruskin), **V:** 180, 184

Ethnic Radio (Murray), **Supp. VII:** 270, 276–277

Etruscan Places (Lawrence), **VII:** 116, 117

Euclid and His Modern Rivals (Carroll), **V:** 264, 274

Eugene Aram (Bulwer–Lytton), **IV:** 256; **V:** 22, 46

"Eugene Aram" (Hood), *see* "Dream of Eugene Aram, The Murderer, The"

Eugene Onegin (Pushkin), **Supp. IV:** 485

"Eugene Pickering" (James), **VI:** 69

Eugenia (Chapman), **I:** 236, 240

Eugénie Grandet (Balzac), **Supp. IV:** 124

Eugenius Philalethes, pseud. of Thomas Vaughan

Euphranor: A Dialogue on Youth (FitzGerald), **IV:** 344, 353

Euphues and His England (Lyly), **I:** 194, 195–196

Euphues, The Anatomy of Wit (Lyly), **I:** 165, 193–196

Euripides, **IV:** 358; **V:** 321–324

"Europe" (James), **VI:** 69

Europe. A Prophecy (Blake), **III:** 302, 307; **Retro. Supp. I:** 39, 41–42

European Tribe, The (Phillips), **Supp. V:** 380, 384–385

European Witness (Spender), **Supp. II:** 489–490

Europeans, The (James), **VI:** 29–31

"Eurydice" (Sitwell), **VII:** 136–137

Eurydice, a Farce (Fielding), **III:** 105

"Eurydice to Orpheus" (Browning), **Retro. Supp. II:** 28

Eustace and Hilda: A Trilogy (Hartley), **Supp. VII:** 119, 120, 122, 123–124, 127, 131, 132

Eustace Diamonds, The (Fuller), **Supp. VII:** 72

Eustace Diamonds, The (Trollope), **V:** xxiv, 96, 98, 101, 102

Eustace, Robert, *see* Barton, Eustace

Eva Trout (Bowen), **Supp. II:** 82, 94

"Evacuees, The" (Nicholson), **Supp. VI:** 214

Evagatory (Reading), **Supp. VIII:** 272–273

Evan Harrington (Meredith), **V:** xxii, 227, 234

Evans, Abel, **II:** 335

Evans, G. Blakemore, **I:** 326

Evans, Marian, *see* Eliot, George

"Eve" (Rossetti), **V:** 258

"Eve of St. Agnes, The" (Keats), **III:** 338; **IV:** viii, xviii, 212, **216–219,** 231, 235; **V:** 352; **Retro. Supp. I:** 193

Eve of Saint John, The (Scott), **IV:** 38

"Eve of St. Mark, The" (Hill), **Supp. V:** 191

"Eve of St. Mark, The" (Keats), **IV:** 212, 216, 218, 220, 226

"Eveline" (Joyce), **Retro. Supp. I:** 172

"Evening Alone at Bunyah" (Murray), **Supp. VII:** 272

Eve's Ransom (Gissing), **V:** 437

Evelina (Burney), **III:** 90, 91; **IV:** 279; **Supp. III:** 64, 67, 68, 69, 70, 71–72, 75–76

"Eveline" (Joyce), **VII: 44**

Evelyn, John, **II:** 194, 196, **273–280, 286–287**

Evelyn Innes (Moore), **VI:** 87, 92

Evelyn Waugh (Lodge), **Supp. IV:** 365

"Even So" (Rossetti), **V:** 242

"Even Such Is Time" (Ralegh), **I:** 148–149

Evening (Macaulay), **IV:** 290

Evening Colonnade, The (Connolly), **Supp. III:** 98, 110, 111

Evening Standard (periodical), **VI:** 247, 252, 265

Evening Walk, An (Wordsworth), **IV:** xv 2, 4–5, 24

Evening's Love, An; or, The Mock Astrologer (Dryden), **II:** 305

Events and Wisdom (Davie), **Supp. VI:** 109

"Events at Drimaghleen" (Trevor), **Supp. IV:** 505

"Events in your life" (Kelman), **Supp. V:** 251

Ever After (Swift), **Supp. V:** 438–440

"Ever drifting down the stream" (Carroll), **V:** 270

"Ever Fixed Mark, An" (Amis), **Supp. II:** 3

"Ever mine hap is slack and slow in coming" (Wyatt), **I:** 110

"Everlasting Gospel" (Blake), **III:** 304

Everlasting Man, The (Chesterton), **VI:** 341–342

Everlasting Spell, The: A Study of Keats and His Friends (Richardson), **IV:** 236

"Evermore" (Barnes), **Supp. IV:** 75–76

Every Changing Shape (Jennings), **Supp. V:** 207, 213, 215

Every Day of the Week (Sillitoe), **Supp. V:** 423

Every Good Boy Deserves Favour (Stoppard), **Supp. I:** 450, 451, 453; **Retro. Supp. II:** 351

Every Man for Himself (Bainbridge), **Supp. VI: 25–26,** 27

Every Man out of His Humor (Jonson), **I:** 336–337, 338–340; **II:** 24, 27

Every–Body's Business, Is No–Body's Business (Defoe), **III:** 13–14

Everybody's Political What's What? (Shaw), **VI:** 125, 129

Everyman, **II:** 70

Everyman in His Humor (Jonson), **I:** 336–337; **Retro. Supp. I:** 154, 157–159, 166

"Everything that is born must die" (Rossetti), **V:** 254

Evidence for the Resurrection of Jesus Christ as Given by the Four Evangelists, Critically Examined (Butler), **Supp. II:** 99, 102

Evidences of Christianity (Paley), **IV:** 144

Evil Genius: A Domestic Story, The (Collins), **Supp. VI:** 103

Evolution and Poetic Belief (Roppen), **V:** 221n

"Evolution of Tears, The" (Wallace-Crabbe), **Supp. VIII:** 322–323

Evolution Old and New (Butler), **Supp. II:** 106, 107

Ewart, Gavin, **VII:** 422, 423–424, **Supp. VII: 33–49**

Ewart Quarto, The (Ewart), **Supp. VII:** 44

"Ex Lab" (Reading), **Supp. VIII:** 265

Ex Voto (Butler), **Supp. II:** 114

Examen Poeticum (ed. Dryden), **II:** 290, 291, 301, 305

Examination, The (Pinter), **Supp. I:** 371

"Examination at the Womb Door" (Hughes), **Supp. I:** 352; **Retro. Supp. II:** 207

Examination of Certain Abuses, An (Swift), **III:** 36

Ladies Triall, The (Ford), *see Lady's Trial, The*

Ladies Whose Bright Eyes (Ford), **VI:** 327

"Ladle" (Berger), **Supp. IV:** 93

Lady Anna (Trollope), **V:** 102

"Lady Appledore's Mesalliance" (Firbank), **Supp. II:** 207

Lady Athlyne (Stoker), **Supp. III:** 381

Lady Audley's Secret (Braddon), **Supp. VIII:** 35, 41–42, 43, 48, 50

"Lady Barbarina" (James), **VI:** 69

Lady Chatterley's Lover (Lawrence), **VII:** 87, 88, 91, **110–113; Supp. IV:** 149, 234, 369; **Retro. Supp. II:** 226, 231–232

"Lady Delavoy" (James), **VI:** 69

Lady Frederick (Maugham), **VI:** 367–368

"Lady Geraldine's Courtship" (Browning), **IV:** 311

Lady Gregory, **VI:** xiv

Lady Gregory: A Literary Portrait (Coxhead), **VI:** 318

"Lady Icenway, The" (Hardy), **VI:** 22

Lady in the Van, The (Bennett), **Supp. VIII:** 33

Lady Jane (Chettle, Dekker, Heywood, Webster), **II:** 68

Lady Lisa Lyon (Mapplethorpe photography collection), **Supp. IV:** 170

"Lady Louisa and the Wallflowers" (Powys), **Supp. VIII:** 249

Lady Maisie's Bairn and Other Poems (Swinburne), **V:** 333

"Lady Mottisfont" (Hardy), **VI:** 22

Lady of Launay, The (Trollope), **V:** 102

Lady of May, The (Sidney), **I:** 161; **Retro. Supp. II:** 330

"Lady of Quality, A" (Kinsella), **Supp. V:** 260

"Lady of Shalott, The" (Tennyson), **IV:** xix, 231, 313, 329, 331–332

Lady of the Lake, The (Scott), **IV:** xvii, 29, 38

"Lady of the Pool, The" (Jones), **Supp. VII:** 176, 177, 178

Lady of the Shroud, The (Stoker), **Supp. III:** 381

"Lady Penelope, The" (Hardy), **VI:** 22

"Lady Rogue Singleton" (Smith), **Supp. II:** 466–467, 470

Lady Susan (Austen), **IV:** 108, 109, 122; **Supp. IV:** 230

Lady Windermere's Fan (Wilde), **V:** xxvi, 412, 413–414, 419; **Retro. Supp. II:** 369

Lady with a Laptop (Thomas), **Supp. IV:** 489–490

"Lady with the Dog, The" (Chekhov), **V:** 241

"Ladybird, The" (Lawrence), **VII:** 115

"Lady's Dream, The" (Hood), **IV:** 261, 264

"Lady's Dressing Room, The" (Swift), **III:** 32

Lady's Magazine (periodical), **III:** 179

"Lady's Maid, The" (Mansfield), **VII:** 174–175

Lady's Not for Burning (Fry), **Supp. III:** 195, 202

Lady's Pictorial (periodical), **VI:** 87, 91

Lady's Trial, The (Ford), **II:** 89, 91, 99, 100

Lady's World, The (periodical), **Retro. Supp. II:** 364

Lafourcade, Georges, **VI:** 247, 256, 259, 260, 262, 263, 268

"Lagoon, The" (Conrad), **VI:** 136, 148

Lair of the White Worm, The (Stoker), **Supp. III:** 381–382

Laird of Abbotsford: A View of Sirt Walter Scott, The (Wilson), **Supp. VI:** 301

Lake, David J., **II:** 1, 2, 21

Lake, The (Moore), **VI:** xii, 88, 89, 92–93, 98

"Lake Isle of Innisfree, The" (Yeats), **VI:** 207, 211; **Retro. Supp. I:** 329

Lakers, The (Nicholson), **Supp. VI:** 223

"L'Allegro" (Milton), **II:** 158–159; **IV:** 199

Lamarck, Jean–Baptiste, **Supp. II:** 105–106, 107, 118, 119

Lamb, Charles, **II:** 80, 86, 119n, 143, 153, 256, 340, 361, 363, 364; **IV:** xi, xiv, xvi xviii, xix, 41, 42, **73–86,** 128, 135, 137, 148, 252–253, 255, 257, 259, 260, 320, 341, 349; **V:** 328

Lamb, John, **IV:** 74, 77, 84

Lamb, Mary, **IV:** xvi, 77–78, 80, 83–84, 128, 135

"Lamb to the Slaughter" (Dahl), **Supp. IV:** 215, 219

Lambert, Gavin, **Supp. IV:** 3, 8

"Lament" (Gunn), **Supp. IV:** 277–278

Lament for a Lover (Highsmith), **Supp. V:** 170

"Lament for the Makaris, The" (Dunbar), **Supp. VIII:** 118, 121, 127–128

Lament of Tasso, The (Byron), **IV:** 192

"Lament of the Images" (Okri), **Supp. V:** 359

Lamia (Keats), **III:** 338; **IV:** xviii, 216, 217, 219–220, 231, 235; **Retro. Supp. I:** 192–193

Lamia, Isabella, The Eve of St. Agnes, and Other Poems (Keats), **IV:** xviii, 211, 235; **Retro. Supp. I:** 184, 192–196

Lamming, George, **Supp. IV:** 445

"Lamp and the Jar, The" (Hope), **Supp. VII:** 158

Lamp and the Lute, The (Dobrée), **VI:** 204

Lampitt Papers, The (Wilson), **Supp. VI:** 297, 304, **306–307**

Lancelot and Guinevere (Malory), **I:** 70–71, 77

Lancelot du Laik, **I:** 73

Lancelot, The Death of Rudel, and Other Poems (Swinburne), **V:** 333

"Lancer" (Housman), **VI:** 160

"Land of Counterpane, The" (Stevenson), **Retro. Supp. I:** 260

Land of Heart's Desire, The (Yeats), **VI:** 221; **Retro. Supp. I:** 326

"Land of Loss, The" (Kinsella), **Supp. V:** 271

Land of Promise, The (Maugham), **VI:** 369

"Land under the Ice, The" (Nicholson), **Supp. VI:** 216

Landing on the Sun, A (Frayn), **Supp. VII:** 62 63

"Landlady, The" (Behan), **Supp. II:** 63–64

"Landlady, The" (Dahl), **Supp. IV:** 215–216, 217

Landleaguers, The (Trollope), **V:** 102

Landlocked (Lessing), **Supp. I:** 245, 248

Landmarks in French Literature (Strachey), **Supp. II:** 502–503

Landnámabók, Supp. VIII: 235, 238

Landon, Letitia, **IV:** 311

Landor, Walter Savage, **II:** 293; **III:** 139; **IV:** xiv, xvi, xviii, xix, xxii, **87–100,** 252, 254, 356; **V:** 320

Landscape (Pinter), **Supp. I:** 375–376

"Landscape Painter, A" (James), **VI:** 69

Landscapes Within, The (Okri), **Supp. V:** 347, 348, 350, 352, 353–354, 360

Landseer, Edwin, **V:** 175

Lane, Margaret, **V:** 13n, 16

Lang, Andrew, **V:** 392–393, 395; **VI:** 158; **Supp. II:** 115

Lang, C. Y., **V:** 334, 335

Langland, William, **I:** vii, **1–18**

"Language Ah Now You Have Me" (Graham), **Supp. VII:** 115

Language Made Plain (Burgess), **Supp. I:** 197

Language of Fiction: Essays in Criticism and Verbal Analysis of the English Novel (Lodge), **Supp. II:** 9; **Supp. IV:** 365, 366

Language, Truth and Logic (Ayer), **VII:** 240

Languages of Love, The (Brooke–Rose), **Supp. IV:** 99, 100–101

Lannering, Jan, **III:** 52

"Lantern Bearers, The" (Stevenson), **V:** 385

"Lantern out of Doors, The," (Hopkins), **V:** 380

Lantern Slides (O'Brien), **Supp. V:** 341

Laodicean, A; or, The Castle of the De Stancys (Hardy), **VI:** 4–5, 20

Laon and Cynthia (Shelley), **IV:** 195, 196, 198, 208; **Retro. Supp. I:** 249–250; *see also Revolt of Islam, The*

"Lapis Lazuli" (Yeats), **Retro. Supp. I:** 337

Lara (Byron), **IV:** xvii, 172, 173, 175, 192; *see also* Turkish tales

"Large Cool Store, The" (Larkin), **Supp. I:** 279

Lark, The (Fry), **Supp. III:** 195

"Lark Ascending, The" (Meredith), **V:** 221, 223

"Larkin Automatic Car Wash, The" (Ewart), **Supp. VII:** 41

Larkin, Philip, **Supp. I:** 275–290; **Supp. II:** 2, 3, 375; **Supp. IV:** 256, 431

"Lars Porsena of Clusium" (Macaulay), **IV:** 282

Lars Porsena; or, The Future of Swearing and Improper Language (Graves), **VII:** 259–260

"Last Address, The" (Lowry), **Supp. III:** 272

McElroy, Joseph, **Supp. IV:** 116
McEwan, Ian, **Supp. IV:** 65, 75, **389–408; Supp. V:** xxx
McGann, Jerome J., **V:** 314, 335
McGuckian, Medbh, **Supp. V: 277–293**
McHale, Brian, **Supp. IV:** 112
Machiavelli, Niccolò, **II:** 71, 72; **IV:** 279; **Retro. Supp. I:** 204
"Machine Stops, The" (Forster), **VI:** 399
McInherny, Frances, **Supp. IV:** 347, 353
Mack, Maynard, **Retro. Supp. I:** 229
Mackail, J. W., **V:** 294, 296, 297, 306
McKane, Richard, **Supp. IV:** 494–495
Mackay, M. E., **V:** 223, 234
Mackenzie, Compton, **VII:** 278
Mackenzie, Henry, **III:** 87; **IV:** 79
MacKenzie, Jean, **VI:** 227, 243
MacKenzie, Norman, **V:** 374n, 375n, 381, 382; **VI:** 227, 243
McKenney, Ruth, **Supp. IV:** 476
Mackenzie, Sir George, **III:** 95
"Mackery End, in Hertfordshire" (Lamb), **IV:** 83
MacLaren, Moray, **V:** 393, 398
McLeehan, Marshall, **IV:** 323n, 338, 339
Maclure, Millar, **I:** 291
Macmillan's (periodical), **VI:** 351
MacNeice, Louis, **VII:** 153, 382, 385, **401–418; Supp. III:** 119; **Supp. IV:** 423, 424
Macpherson, James, **III:** 336; **Supp. VIII: 179–195; Supp. II:** 523
Macready, William Charles, **I:** 327
McTaggart, J. M. E., **Supp. II:** 406
Mad Forest: A Play from Romania (Churchill), **Supp. IV:** 179, 188, 195–196, 198, 199
Mad Islands, The (MacNeice), **VII:** 405, 407
Mad Lover, The (Fletcher), **II:** 45, 55, 65
"Mad Maids Song, The" (Herrick), **II:** 112
"Mad Mullinix and Timothy" (Swift), **III:** 31
Mad Soldier's Song (Hardy), **VI:** 11
Mad World, My Masters, A (Middleton), **II:** 3, 4, 21
Madagascar; or, Robert Drury's Journal (Defoe), **III:** 14
Madame Bovary (Flaubert), **V:** xxii, 429; **Supp. IV:** 68, 69
"Madame de Mauves" (James), **VI:** 69; **Supp. IV:** 133
"Madame Rosette" (Dahl), **Supp. IV:** 209–210
Madan, Falconer, **V:** 264, 274
Maddox, Brenda, **Retro. Supp. I:** 327, 328
"Mademoiselle" (Stevenson), **Supp. VI:** 255
Mademoiselle de Maupin (Gautier), **V:** 320n
Madge, Charles, **VII:** xix
"Madman and the Child, The" (Cornford), **Supp. VIII:** 107
Madness of George III, The (Bennett), **Supp. VIII:** 31–33
Madoc (Muldoon), **Supp. IV:** 420, 424–427, 428

"Madoc" (Muldoon), **Supp. IV:** 422, 425–427, 430
Madoc (Southey), **IV:** 63, 64–65, 71
"Madoc" (Southey), **Supp. IV:** 425
"Madonna" (Kinsella), **Supp. V:** 273
Madonna and Other Poems (Kinsella), **Supp. V:** 272–273
Madonna of the Future and Other Tales, The (James), **VI:** 67, 69
"Madonna of the Trenches, A" (Kipling), **VI:** 193, **194–196**
Madras House, The (Shaw), **VI:** 118
Madwoman in the Attic, The (Gilbert/Gubar), **Retro. Supp. I:** 59–60
Maggot, A (Fowles), **Supp. I:** 309–310
"Magi" (Brown), **Supp. VI:** 71
Magic (Chesterton), **VI:** 340
Magic Box, The (Ambler), **Supp. IV:** 3
Magic Finger, The (Dahl), **Supp. IV:** 201
"Magic Finger, The" (Dahl), **Supp. IV:** 223–224
Magic Toyshop, The (Carter), **III:** 345; **Supp. III:** 80, 81, 82
Magic Wheel, The (eds. Swift and Profumo), **Supp. V:** 427
Magician, The (Maugham), **VI:** 374
Magician's Nephew, The (Lewis), **Supp. III:** 248
Maginn, William, **V:** 19
"Magna Est Veritas" (Smith), **Supp. II:** 471, 472
"Magnanimity" (Kinsella), **Supp. V:** 263
Magnetic Mountain, The (Day Lewis), **Supp. III:** 117, 122, 124–126
Magnetick Lady, The (Jonson), **Retro. Supp. I:** 165
Magnificence (Skelton), **I:** 90
"Magnolia" (Fuller), **Supp. VII:** 78
Magnus (Brown), **Supp. VI: 66–67**
"Magnus" (Macpherson), **Supp. VIII:** 186
Magnusson, Erika, **V:** 299, 300, 306
Magus, The (Fowles), **Supp. I:** 291, 292, 293, **295–299,** 310
Mahafty, John Pentland, **V:** 400, 401
Mahon, Derek, **Supp. IV:** 412; **Supp. VI: 165–180**
"Mahratta Ghats, The" (Lewis), **VII:** 446–447
Maid in the Mill, The (Fletcher and Rowley), **II:** 66
Maid in Waiting (Galsworthy), **VI:** 275
Maid Marian (Peacock), **IV:** xviii, 167–168, 170
Maid of Bath, The (Foote), **III:** 253
"Maid of Craca, The" (Macpherson), **Supp. VIII:** 186, 187
"Maiden Name" (Larkin), **Supp. I:** 277
Maiden's Dream, A (Greene), **Supp. VIII:** 142
Maid's Tragedy, The (Beaumont and Fletcher), **II:** 44, 45, **54–57,** 58, 60, 65
Maid's Tragedy, Alter'd, The (Waller), **II:** 238
Mailer, Norman, **Supp. IV:** 17–18
"Maim'd Debauchee, The" (Rochester), **II:** 259–260
"Main Road" (Pritchett), **Supp. III:** 316–317

Mainly on the Air (Beerbohm), **Supp. II:** 52
Maitland, F. W., **V:** 277, 290; **VI:** 385
Maitland, Thomas, pseud. of Algernon Charles Swinburne
Maitū njugīra (Ngūgī wa Thiong'o/Ngūgī wa Mīriī), **Supp. VIII:** 216, 224, 225
Maiwa's Revenge (Haggard), **Supp. III:** 213
Majeske, Penelope, **Supp. IV:** 330
Major, John, **Supp. IV:** 437–438
Major Barbara (Shaw), **VII:** xv, 102, 108, **113–115,** 124; **Retro. Supp. II:** 321
Major Political Essays (Shaw), **VI:** 129
Major Victorian Poets, The: Reconsiderations (Armstrong), **IV:** 339
Make Thyself Many (Powys), **Supp. VIII:** 255
Makin, Bathsua, **Supp. III:** 21
Making Cocoa for Kingsley Amis (Cope), **Supp. VIII:** 67, 69, 70–74, 81
Making History (Friel), **Supp. V:** 125
Making of a Poem, The (Spender), **Supp. II:** 481, 492
Making of an Immortal, The (Moore), **VI:** 96, 99
"Making of an Irish Goddess, The" (Boland), **Supp. V:** 44–45
Making of the English Working Class, The (Thompson), **Supp. IV:** 473
Making of the Representative for Planet 8, The (Lessing), **Supp. I:** 252, 254
"Making Poetry" (Stevenson), **Supp. VI:** 262
Mal vu, mal dit (Beckett), **Supp. I:** 62
Malayan trilogy (Burgess), **Supp. I:** 187
Malcolm Lowry: Psalms and Songs (Lowry), **Supp. III:** 285
Malcolm Mooney's Land (Graham), **Supp. VII:** 104, 106, 109, 113–115, 116
Malcontent, The (Marston), **II:** 27, 30, **31–33,** 36, 40, 68
Malcontents, The (Snow), **VII:** 336–337
Male Child, A (Scott), **Supp. I:** 263
Malign Fiesta (Lewis), **VII:** 72, 80
Malinowski, Bronislaw, **Supp. III:** 186
Mallet, David, **Supp. III:** 412, 424–425
Malone, Edmond, **I:** 326
Malone Dies (Beckett), **Supp. I:** 50, 51, 52–53, 63; **Supp. IV:** 106; **Retro. Supp. I:** 18, 22–23
Malory, Sir Thomas, **I: 67–80; IV:** 336, 337; **Retro. Supp. II: 237–252**
Malraux, André, **VI:** 240
"Maltese Cat, The" (Kipling), **VI:** 200
Malthus, Thomas, **IV:** xvi, 127, 133
Mamillia: A Mirror, or Looking-Glasse for the Ladies of England (Greene), **Supp. VIII:** 135, 140
"Man" (Herbert), **Retro. Supp. II:** 176–177
"Man" (Vaughan), **II:** 186, 188
Man, The (Stoker), **Supp. III:** 381
Man Above Men (Hare), **Supp. IV:** 282, 289
"Man and Bird" (Mahon), **Supp. VI:** 168
"Man and Boy" (Heaney), **Retro. Supp. I:** 132

"Mr. Crabbe—Mr. Campbell" (Hazlitt), **III:** 276

"Mr. Dottery's Trousers" (Powys), **Supp. VIII:** 248, 249

"Mr. Eliot's Sunday Morning Service" (Eliot), **VII:** 145

"Mr. Feasey" (Dahl), **Supp. IV:** 214

Mr. Foot (Frayn), **VII:** 57

Mr. Fortune's Maggot (Warner), **Supp. VII:** 370, 374–375, 379

Mr Fox (Comyns), **Supp. VIII:** 53, 56, 64–65

"Mr. Gilfil's Love Story" (Eliot), **V:** 190; **Retro. Supp. II:** 103–104

"Mr. Gladstone Goes to Heaven" (Beerbohm), **Supp. II:** 51

"Mr. Graham" (Hood), **IV:** 267

Mr. H (Lamb), **IV:** 80–81, 85

"Mr. Harrison's Confessions" (Gaskell), **V:** 14, 15

Mister Heracles (Armitage), **Supp. VIII:** 1

Mr. John Milton's Character of the Long Parliament and Assembly of Divines ... (Milton), **II:** 176

Mister Johnson (Cary), **VII:** 186, 187, 189, 190–191

"Mr. Know–All" (Maugham), **VI:** 370

Mr. Macaulay's Character of the Clergy in the Latter Part of the Seventeenth Century Considered (Babington), **IV:** 291

"Mr. McNamara" (Trevor), **Supp. IV:** 501

Mr. Meeson's Will (Haggard), **Supp. III:** 213

Mr. Noon (Lawrence), **Retro. Supp. II:** 229–230

"Mr. Norris and I" (Isherwood), **VII:** 311–312

Mr. Norris Changes Trains (Isherwood), **VII:** xx, 311–312

"Mr. Pim and the Holy Crumb" (Powys), **Supp. VIII:** 255, 257

Mr. Polly (Wells), *see History of Mr. Polly, The*

Mr. Pope's Welcome from Greece (Gay), **II:** 348

Mr. Prohack (Bennett), **VI:** 260, 267

"Mr. Reginald Peacock's Day" (Mansfield), **VII:** 174

"Mr. Robert Herricke His Farewell unto Poetrie" (Herrick), **II:** 112

"Mr. Robert Montgomery's Poems" (Macaulay), **IV:** 280

Mr Sampath (Naipaul), **Supp. I:** 400

Mr. Scarborough's Family (Trollope), **V:** 98, 102

"Mr. Sludge 'the Medium' " (Browning), **IV:** 358, 368; **Retro. Supp. II:**26–27

Mr. Smirke; or, The Divine in Mode (Marvell), **II:** 219

Mr. Stone and the Knights Companion (Naipaul), **Supp. I:** 383, 389

"Mr. Strugnell" (Cope), **Supp. VIII:** 73

Mr. Tasker's Gods (Powys), **Supp. VIII:** 2 **Supp. VIII:** 51, 249–250

"Mr. Tennyson" (Trevor), **Supp. IV:** 502

Mr. Waller's Speech in the Painted Chamber (Waller), **II:** 238

"Mr. Waterman" (Redgrove), **Supp. VI:** 228–229, 231, 235, 237

Mr. Weston's Good Wine (Powys), **VII:** 21; **Supp. VIII:** 245, 248, 252–254, 255, 256

Mr. Whatnot (Ayckbourn), **Supp. V:** 2, 13

"Mr. Whistler's Ten O'Clock" (Wilde), **V:** 407

"Mrs. Acland's Ghosts" (Trevor), **Supp. IV:** 503

"Mrs. Bathurst" (Kipling), **VI:** 193–194

Mrs. Browning: A Poet's Work and Its Setting (Hayter), **IV:** 322

Mrs. Craddock (Maugham), **VI:** 367

Mrs. Dalloway (Woolf), **VI:** 275, 279; **VII:** xv, 18, 21, 24, 28–29; **Supp. IV:** 234, 246; **Retro. Supp. I:** 316–317

Mrs. Dot (Maugham), **VI:** 368

Mrs. Eckdorf in O'Neill's Hotel (Trevor), **Supp. IV:** 501, 508

Mrs. Fisher; or, The Future of Humour (Graves), **VII:** 259–260

Mrs. Harris's Petition (Swift), **Retro. Supp. I:** 283

"Mrs. Jaypher found a wafer" (Lear), **V:** 86

Mrs. Leicester's School (Lamb and Lamb), **IV:** 80, 85

Mrs. McGinty's Dead (Christie; U.S. title, *Blood Will Tell*), **Supp. II:** 135

"Mrs. Medwin" (James), **VI:** 69

"Mrs. Nelly's Complaint," **II:** 268

"Mrs. Packletide's Tiger" (Saki), **Supp. VI:** 242

Mrs. Perkins's Ball (Thackeray), **V:** 24, 38

"Mrs. Silly" (Trevor), **Supp. IV:** 502

"Mrs. Simpkins" (Smith), **Supp. II:** 470

"Mrs. Temperley" (James), **VI:** 69

Mrs. Warren's Profession (Shaw), **V:** 413; **VI:** 108, 109; **Retro. Supp. II:** 312–313

Mistral, Frederic, **V:** 219

Mistras, The (Cowley), **II:** 194, 198, 202, 236

"Mistress of Vision, The" (Thompson), **V:** 447–448

"Mists" (Redgrove), **Supp. VI:** 228

Mist's Weekly Journal (newspaper), **III:** 4

Mitford, Mary Russell, **IV:** 311, 312

Mitford, Nancy, **VII:** 290

Mithridates (Lee), **II:** 305

Mixed Essays (Arnold), **V:** 213n, 216

"Mixed Marriage" (Muldoon), **Supp. IV:** 415

Mo, Timothy, **Supp. IV:** 390

Mob, The (Galsworthy), **VI:** 280, 288

Moby–Dick (Melville), **VI:** 363

Mock Doctor, The (Fielding), **III** 105

Mock Speech from the Throne (Marvell), **II:** 207

Mock–Mourners, The: ... Elegy on King William (Defoe), **III:** 12

Mockery Gap (Powys), **Supp. VIII:** 251, 256

"Model Prisons" (Carlyle), **IV:** 247

Mock's Curse: Nineteen Stories (Powys), **Supp. VIII:** 251, 252, 256

Modern Comedy, A (Galsworthy), **VI:** 270, 275

Modern Fiction (Woolf), **VII:** xiv; **Retro. Supp. I:** 308–309

Modern Husband, The (Fielding), **III:** 105

"Modern Love" (Meredith), **V:** 220, 234, 244

Modern Love, and Poems of the English Roadside ... (Meredith), **V:** xxii, 220, 234

Modern Lover, A (Moore), **VI:** 86, 89, 98

Modern Movement: 100 Key Books from England, France, and America, 1880–1950, The (Connolly), **VI:** 371

Modern Painters (Ruskin), **V:** xx, 175–176, 180, 184, 282

Modern Painting (Moore), **VI:** 87

Modern Poetry: A Personal Essay (MacNeice), **VII:** 403, 404, 410

"Modern Times" (Wallace-Crabbe), **Supp. VIII:** 324

Modern Utopia, A (Wells), **VI:** 227, 234, 241, 244

"Modern Warning, The" (James), **VI:** 48, 69

Modernism and Romance (Scott–James), **VI:** 21

Modes of Modern Writing: Metaphor, Metonymy, and the Typology of Modern Literature, The (Lodge), **Supp. IV:** 365, 377

"Modest Proposal" (Ewart), **Supp. VII:** 46

Modest Proposal, A (Swift), **III:** 21, 28, 29, 35; **Supp. IV:** 482

"Moestitiae Encomium" (Thompson), **V:** 450

Moffatt, James, **I:** 382–383

Mohocks, The (Gay), **III:** 60, 67

Mohr, Jean, **Supp. IV:** 79

Moi, Toril, **Retro. Supp. I:** 312

"Moisture–Number, The" (Redgrove), **Supp. VI:** 235

Molière (Jean Baptiste Poquelin), **II:** 314, 318, 325, 336, 337, 350; **V:** 224

Moll Flanders (Defoe), **III:** 5, 6, 7, 8, 9, 13, 95; **Retro. Supp. I:** 72–73

Molloy (Beckett), **Supp. I:** 51–52; **Supp. IV:** 106; **Retro. Supp. I:** 18, 21–22

Molly Sweeney (Friel), **Supp. V:** 127

"Molly Gone" (Hardy), **Retro. Supp. I:** 118

Moly (Gunn), **Supp. IV:** 257, 266–268

"Moly" (Gunn), **Supp. IV:** 267

Molyneux, William, **III:** 27

"Moment, The: Summer's Night" (Woolf), **Retro. Supp. I:** 309

"Moment of Cubism, The" (Berger), **Supp. IV:** 79

Moments of Being (Woolf), **VII:** 33; **Retro. Supp. I:** 305, 315

Moments of Grace (Jennings), **Supp. V:** 217–218

Moments of Vision, and Miscellaneous Verses (Hardy), **VI:** 20

Monastery, The (Scott), **IV:** xviii, 39

Sixth Heaven, The (Hartley), **Supp. VII:** 124, 125, 127

"Sixth Journey, The" (Graham), **Supp. VII:** 109

Sizemore, Christine Wick, **Supp. IV:** 336

"Skating" (Motion), **Supp. VII:** 251, 256

Skeat, W. W., **I:** 17

"Skeleton, The" (Pritchett), **Supp. III:** 325

Skelton, John, **I: 81–96**

"Sketch, A" (Rossetti), **V:** 250

Sketch Book (Irving), **III:** 54

"Sketch from Private Life, A" (Byron), **IV:** 192

"Sketch of the Great Dejection, A" (Gunn), **Supp. IV:** 274

"Sketch of the Past, A" (Woolf), **Retro. Supp. I:** 314–315

Sketches and Essays (Hazlitt), **IV:** 140

Sketches and Reviews (Pater), **V:** 357

Sketches and Travels in London (Thackeray), **V:** 38

Sketches by Boz (Dickens), **V:** xix, 42, 43–46, 47, 52, 71

"Sketches for a Self–Portrait" (Day Lewis), **Supp. III:** 128

Sketches from Cambridge, by a Don (Stephen), **V:** 289

Sketches of the Principal Picture–Galleries in England (Hazlitt), **IV:** 132, 139

"Skin" (Dahl), **Supp. IV:** 216

Skin (Kane), **Supp. VIII:** 148, 149, 157–158

Skin Chairs, The (Comyns), **Supp. VIII:** 53, 55, 62–63

Skin Game, The (Galsworthy), **VI:** 275, 280, 288

Skírnismál, Supp. **VIII:** 230

Skotlands rímur, Supp. **VIII:** 243

Skriker, The (Churchill), **Supp. IV:** 179, 180, 197–198

Skull Beneath the Skin, The (James), **Supp. II:** 127; **Supp. IV:** 335–336, 337

"Sky Burning Up Above the Man, The" (Keneally), **Supp. IV:** 345

"Skylarks" (Hughes), **Retro. Supp. II:** 206

Skylight (Hare), **Supp. IV:** 282, 298–299

"Skylight, The" (Heaney), **Retro. Supp. I:** 132

Slag (Hare), **Supp. IV:** 281, 283

"Sleep" (Cowley), **II:** 196

"Sleep, The" (Browning), **IV:** 312

"Sleep and Poetry" (Keats), **IV:** 214–215, 217, 228, 231; **Retro. Supp. I:** 184, 188

Sleep Has His House (Kavan), see *House of Sleep, The*

Sleep It Off, Lady (Rhys), **Supp. II:** 389, 401, 402

Sleep of Prisoners, A (Fry), **Supp. III:** 194, 195, 199–200

Sleep of Reason, The (Snow), **VII:** 324, 331–332

Sleepers of Roraima (Harris), **Supp. V:** 132

Sleep of the Great Hypnotist, The (Redgrove), **Supp. VI:** 231

"Sleeping at Last" (Rossetti), **V:** 251–252, 259

Sleeping Beauty, The (Sitwell), **VII:** 132

Sleeping Fires (Gissing), **V:** 437

Sleeping Lord and Other Fragments, The (Jones), **Supp. VII:** 167, 170, 178–180

Sleeping Murder (Christie), **Supp. II:** 125, 134

Sleeping Prince, The (Rattigan), **Supp. VII:** 318–319

Sleepwalkers, The: A History of Man's Changing Vision of the Universe (Koestler), **Supp. I:** 37–38

Sleuths, Inc. (Eames), **Supp. IV:** 3

Slight Ache, A (Pinter), **Supp. I:** 369, 371; **Retro. Supp. I:** 222–223

"Slips" (McGuckian), **Supp. V:** 281–282

Slocum, Joshua, **Supp. IV:** 158

Slot Machine, The (Sillitoe), **Supp. V:** 411

"Slough" (Betjeman), **VII:** 366

"Slumber Did My Spirit Seal, A" (Wordsworth), **IV:** 18

"Small Boy" (MacCaig), **Supp. VI:** 194

Small Boy and Others, A (James), **VI:** 65

Small Family Business, A (Ayckbourn), **Supp. V:** 3, 12, 14

Small g: A Summer Idyll (Highsmith), **Supp. V:** 179

Small House at Allington, The (Trollope), **V:** xxiii, 101

"Small Personal Voice, The" (Lessing), **Supp. I:** 238

Small Place, A (Kincaid), **Supp. VII:** 217, 225–226, 230, 231

Small Town in Germany, A (le Carré), **Supp. II:** 300, **303–305,** 307

Small World: An Academic Romance (Lodge), **Supp. IV:** 363, 366, 371, 372, 374, 376–378, 384, 385

"*Small World: An Introduction*" (Lodge), **Supp. IV:** 377

Smeaton, O., **III:** 229n

"Smile" (Thomas), **Supp. IV:** 491–492

"Smile of Fortune, A" (Conrad), **VI:** 148

Smile Please (Rhys), **Supp. II:** 387, 388, 389, 394, 395, 396

Smiles, Samuel, **VI:** 264

Smiley's People (le Carré), **Supp. II:** 305, 311, **314–315**

Smith, Adam, **IV:** xiv, 144–145; **V:** viii

Smith, Alexander, **IV:** 320; **V:** 158

Smith, Edmund, **III:** 118

Smith, George, **V:** 13, 131, 132, 147, 149, 150, 279–280

Smith, Henry Nash, **VI:** 24

Smith, James, **IV:** 253

Smith, Janet Adam, **V:** 391, 393, 395–398

Smith, Logan Pearsall, **Supp. III:** 98, 111

Smith, Nichol, **III:** 21

Smith, Stevie, **Supp. II: 459–478**

Smith, Sydney, **IV:** 268, 272; **Supp. VII: 339–352**

Smith, William Robertson, **Supp. III:** 171

Smith (Maugham), **VI:** 368

Smith and the Pharaohs and Other Tales (Haggard), **Supp. III:** 214, 222

Smith, Elder & Co. (publishers), **V:** 131, 140, 145, 150; *see also* Smith, George

Smith of Wootton Major (Tolkien), **Supp. II:** 521

Smithers, Peter, **III:** 42, 53

"Smoke" (Mahon), **Supp. VI:** 177

Smollett, Tobias, **III: 146–159; V:** xiv 52

Smyer, Richard I., **Supp. IV:** 338

"Snail Watcher, The" (Highsmith), **Supp. V:** 180

Snail Watcher and Other Stories, The (Highsmith), **Supp. V:** 180

"Snake" (Lawrence), **VII:** 119; **Retro. Supp. II:** 233–234

Snake's Pass, The (Stoker), **Supp. III:** 381

"Snap–dragon" (Lawrence), **VII:** 118

Snapper, The (Doyle), **Supp. V:** 77, 82–85, 88

"Snayl, The" (Lovelace), **II:** 231

"Sneaker's A (Mahon), **Supp. VI:** 175–176

"Sniff, The" (Pritchett), **Supp. III:** 319, **320–321**

"Sniper, The" (Sillitoe), **Supp. V:** 414

Snobs of England, The (Thackeray), see *Book of Snobs, The*

Snodgrass, Chris, **V:** 314

Snooty Baronet (Lewis), **VII:** 77

Snorra Edda, Supp. **VIII:** 243

Snow, C. P., **VI:** 235; **VII:** xii, xxi, 235, **321–341**

"Snow" (Hughes), **Supp. I:** 348

"Snow" (MacNeice), **VII:** 412

"Snow Joke" (Armitage), **Supp. VIII:** 3

Snow on the North Side of Lucifer (Sillitoe), **Supp. V:** 424, 425

Snow Party, The (Mahon), **Supp. VI:** 169, **172–173**

"Snow Party, The" (Mahon), **Supp. VI:** 172

"Snowmanshit" (Redgrove), **Supp. VI:** 234

Snowstop (Sillitoe), **Supp. V:** 411

"Snow–White and the Seven Dwarfs" (Dahl), **Supp. IV:** 226

"So crewell prison howe could betyde, alas" (Surrey), **I:** 113

So Lovers Dream (Waugh), **Supp. VI:** 272

"So Much Depends" (Cope), **Supp. VIII:** 78

"So On He Fares" (Moore), **VI:** 93

"So sweet love seemed that April morn" (Bridges), **VI:** 77

"So to Fatness Come" (Smith), **Supp. II:** 472

"Soap–Pig, The" (Muldoon), **Supp. IV:** 423

"Social Life in Roman Britain" (Trevelyan), **VI:** 393

Social Rights and Duties (Stephen), **V:** 289

Socialism and the Family (Wells), **VI:** 244

Socialism: Its Growth and Outcome (Morris and Box), **V:** 306

"Socialism: Principles and Outlook" (Shaw), **VI:** 129

Society for Pure English Tracts, **VI:** 83